Proceedings of the Fourth International Conference on

Parallel and Distributed Information Systems

Proceedings of the Fourth International Conference on

Parallel and Distributed Information Systems

December 18–20, 1996   Miami Beach, Florida

Sponsored by

IEEE Computer Society
Technical Committee on Data Engineering

ACM SIGMOD

IEEE Computer Society Press
Los Alamitos, California

Washington • Brussels • Tokyo

IEEE Computer Society Press
10662 Los Vaqueros Circle
P.O.Box 3014
Los Alamitos, CA 90720-1264

IEEE Computer Society Press Order Number PR07475
IEEE Order Plan Catalog Number 96TB100085
ISBN 0-8186-7475-X
Microfiche ISBN 0-8186-7477-6

Additional copies may be ordered from:

IEEE Computer Society Press Customer Service Center 10662 Los Vaqueros Circle P.O. Box 3014 Los Alamitos, CA 90720-1314 Tel: +1-714-821-8380 Fax: +1-714-821-4641 Email: cs.books@computer.org	IEEE Service Center 445 Hoes Lane P.O. Box 1331 Piscataway, NJ 08855-1331 Tel: +1-908-981-1393 Fax: +1-908-981-9667 misc.custserv@computer.org	IEEE Computer Society 13, Avenue de l'Aquilon B-1200 Brussels BELGIUM Tel: +32-2-770-2198 Fax: +32-2-770-8505 euro.ofc@computr.org	IEEE Computer Society Ooshima Building 2-19-1 Minami-Aoyama Minato-ku, Tokyo 107 JAPAN Tel: +81-3-3408-3118 Fax: +81-3-3408-3553 tokyo.ofc@computer.org

Editorial production by Penny Storms
Cover by Joseph Daigle / Studio Productions
Printed in the United States of America by KNI, Inc.

The Institute of Electrical and Electronics Engineers, Inc.

Table of Contents

Foreword

These proceedings contain the papers selected for presentation at the 1996 PDIS Conference in Miami Beach, Florida, on December 18-20.

Parallel and distributed database technology is at the heart of many mission-critical applications such as online transaction processing, data warehousing, business workflow management, interoperable information systems, and information brokering in global networks. While commercial systems in this arena are gradually maturing, new challenges are posed by the growing demand for large-scale, enterprise-wide solutions and the proliferation of services on the "information superhighway." Future parallel and distributed information systems will have to support millions of clients and will face tremendous scalability challenges with regard to massive data volume, performance, availability, and also administration and long-term maintenance.

The program of the PDIS'96 conference reflects both the breadth of the relevant subjects and the rapid progress of this area. The 22 papers that were selected from 121 submissions cover the full spectrum ranging from Web-related issues and data mining to core technologies such as indexing and transactions. In addition to these research papers, the conference also includes 8 industrial contributions on the latest commercial developments and future trends. The conference is preceded by two tutorials on data warehousing and on parallel and distributed real-time systems.

We would like to express our sincere thanks to the people who have contributed to the success of PDIS'96: the program committee members for ensuring the quality of the scientific program; the authors who submitted papers to the conference; the tutorial chair, Hank Korth, for arranging two hot-topic tutorials; Beau Shekita and Honesty Young for putting together the industrial track program; David DeWitt, for giving the keynote address; Marek Rusinkiewicz, for organizing and moderating a panel discussion; and Maurice van Keulen, Jacek Skowronek, and Markus Sinnwell for their software and help to organize the program committee's work;

Heartfelt thanks also go to Weiyi Meng for his setting up and maintaining the homepage of PDIS'96 and preparing various publication; Cyril Orji for local arrangement; Chungmin Chen for financial arrangement; and Paul Attie for registration; Sushil Jajodia, Naphtali Rishe, and Amit Sheth and the Steering Committee for guidance and helpful advice. The support from IEEE Computer Society and its Technical Committee on Data Engineering has been essential for putting up PDIS'96 together. Kerry Bedford and Penny Storms of IEEE Computer Society Press have done a superb job in supervising the production of the proceedings and other publication. All of their volunteer efforts are highly appreciated.

We look forward to seeing you at Miami Beach for an exciting PDIS'96 Conference.

Wei Sun
General Chair
Florida International University, USA

Jeffrey Naughton	**Gerhard Weikum**
Program Co-Chair	*Program Co-Chair*
University of Wisconsin, USA	*University of the Saarland, Germany*

Organizing Committee

General Chair

Wei Sun
School of Computer Science
Florida International University
Miami, FL 33199, USA
Phone: (305) 348-3751
Fax: (305) 348-3549
weisun@fiu.edu

Program Co-Chairs

Jeffrey Naughton
Computer Science Department
University of Wisconsin
1210 West Dayton Street
Madison, WI 53706, USA
naughton@cs.wisc.edu

Gerhard Weikum
Computer Science Department
University of the Saarland
Im Stadtwald
D-66123 Saarbruecken, Germany
weikum@cs.uni-sb.de

Tutorials

Henry Korth
Bell Laboratories, Lucent Technologies Inc.

Finance

Chungmin Chen
Florida International University

Registration

Paul Attie
Florida International University

Publicity

Weiyi Meng
SUNY Binghamton

Local Arrangements

Cyril Orji
Florida International University

Industrial Program

Honesty Young *and* Eugene Shekita
IBM Almaden Research Center

Steering Committee

Sushil Jajodia (Chair), *George Mason University*
Susan Davidson, *University of Pennsylvania*
Hector Garcia-Molina, *Stanford University*
Masaru Kitsuregawa, *University of Tokyo*
Shamkant Navathe, *Georgia Institute of Technology*
Naphtali Rishe, *Florida International University*
Amit Sheth, *University of Georgia*

Program Committee

Divyakant Agrawal, *UC Santa Barbara*
Peter Apers, *University of Twente*
Chaitanya Baru, *San Diego Supercomputing Center*
Yuri Breitbart, *University of Kentucky*
Wolfgang Effelsberg, *University of Mannheim*
Christos Faloutsos, *University of Maryland*
Alan Fekete, *University of Sydney*
Mike Franklin, *University of Maryland*
Shahram Ghandeharizadeh, *University of Southern California*
Leana Golubchik, *Columbia University*
Theo Harder, *University of Kaiserslautern*
Jayant Haritsa, *Indian Institute of Science, Bangalore*
Kien Hua, *University of Central Florida*
Svein-Olaf Hvasshovd, *Telenor Trondheim*
Yannis Ioannidis, *University of Wisconsin*
H.V. Jagadish, *AT&T Research*
Anant Jhingran, *IBM T.J. Watson Research Center*
Martin Kersten, *CWI Amsterdam*
Masaru Kitsuregawa, *University of Tokyo*
David Kotz, *Dartmouth College*
David Lomet, *Microsoft*
Hongjun Lu, *National University of Singapore*
Tadeusz Morzy, *Technical University of Poznan*
Eliot Moss, *University of Massachussets*
Marie-Anne Neimat, *Hewlett-Packard Labs*
Hamid Pirahesh, *IBM Almaden Research Center*
Calton Pu, *Oregon Graduate Institute*
Erhard Rahm, *University of Leipzig*
Doron Rotem, *Lawrence Berkeley Labs*
Marek Rusinkiewicz, *MCC*
Hans Schek, *ETH Zurich*
Donovan Schneider, *Red Brick Systems*
Marc Scholl, *University of Konstanz*
Timos Sellis, *National Technical University of Athens*
Jaideep Srivastava, *University of Minnesota*
Patrick Valduriez, *INRIA Paris*
Ouri Wolfson, *University of Illinois*

Referees

Tutorial Abstracts

Tutorial 1

Data Warehousing and Parallel Data Systems

Instructor

Rick Stellwagen

CTO, Parallel Systems Division NCR Corporation,

Data warehousing has developed into a rapidly growing business. Today, there are hundreds of production-level data-warehouse installations. Parallel database systems and decision-support systems have provided the foundation for most of these production data warehouses.

Currently, thousands of data warehouses and data marts are being planned and installed. A substantial number of new products along with new methods and models have appeared on the market that claim to be data-warehousing "solutions." This has resulted in a wide variety of definitions of the data-warehousing problem.

This tutorial will review the current industry definitions of data warehousing. The various components of data warehouse systems will be outlined, including inflows (transformation), administration, user-information access and database processing. More in-depth discussions will center around data warehouse architectures, the types of user access that are most prevalent in commercial data warehouses, and data models and programming models for achieving performance objectives. Also to be discussed are special techniques that are used to address performance issues based on characteristics of the workload.

This tutorial will define a framework that allows the true potential for re-use and data sharing. This includes optimizations that are maximized with use of a scaleable parallel system as the hub and spokes in a two- and three- tier data warehouse implementation. Several different database and parallel database products will be studied to show how they fit into the various data-warehousing architectures. Finally, the tutorial will consider the role of the internet and multi-media data in this environment.

About the speaker: Rick Stellwagen received his B.S. in Computer Science from S.U.N.Y at Brockport in 1979. He has been active in both research and development of database and information products for the past 17 years.

He produced heterogeneous distributed information systems in early 1980s and was the architect and lead developer for DBSR, NCR's first relational DBMS in early and mid 1980s. He has built and designed query tools, message-oriented middleware for data and meta-data placement and integration, along with performance, simulation, and modeling tools.

Rick was an architect and director of the Data Navigator and Configurator project (later to be Sybase MPP) that NCR and Sybase pioneered as the first open parallel database system designed for deployment on commodity clusters of servers.

His experience includes being a member of the ANSI X3H2 and RDA committee on databases, and a founding member of the SQL Access committee. Today he is responsible for strategy and architecture of NCR's Data Warehouse Program.

2

Tutorial 2

Parallel and Distributed Real-Time Systems

Instructor

Albert M. K. Cheng

Associate Professor, Real-Time Systems Laboratory,
Department of Computer Science, University of Houston, University Park, Texas

Computer systems embedded in a real-time environment must satisfy stringent response-time constraints in addition to logical correctness constraints. Parallel and distributed computer systems research and development has produced systems capable of attaining very high performance in terms of speed and versatility at very attractive cost-to-speed ratio. Recently, parallel and distributed systems are emerging as a highly promising candidate for implementing the next generation of high-performance embedded real-time systems which are adaptive to the rapidly changing environment. However, "fast" does not necessarily mean "real-time." Therefore, parallel and distributed systems must be fine-tuned before they can be trusted to monitor and control critical real-time processes. The formal verification of real-time systems to ensure that they satisfy the specified integrity and timing requirements is thus essential if such systems are to be used in safety-critical environments. This tutorial introduces a formal framework and powerful techniques for the design and development of this class of systems, including the aspects of specification, design, analysis, implementation, verification, "and validation. Programming in real-time/rule-based languages is described. Specification and verification tools such as Statechart, Modechart, and Estella are used to help design experimental parallel and distributed real-time systems.

About the speaker: Albert Mo Kim Cheng received the B.A. with Highest Honors in Computer Science, graduating Phi Beta Kappa, the M.S. in Computer Science with a minor in Electrical Engineering, and the Ph.D. in Computer Science in 1990, all from The University of Texas at Austin, where he also held a GTE Foundation Doctoral Fellowship. Dr. Cheng is an Associate Professor in the Department of Computer Science at the University of Houston--University Park, where he directs the Real-Time Systems Laboratory. His research interests include real-time systems, multimedia tools, rule-based expert systems, reliable software systems, and fault-tolerant distributed and parallel systems.

He is the author/co-author of over forty refereed publications, and has served or is serving on the program committees of several conferences in his areas of research. Dr. Cheng has received numerous awards, including the National Science Foundation Research Initiation Award, the Texas Higher Education Coordinating Board Advanced Research Program Award, and the University of Houston Research Initiation Grant. He is a member of the honor societies of Phi Beta Kappa, Phi Kappa Phi, Upsilon Pi Epsilon, Beta Alpha Phi, and Golden Key. He has presented tutorials in several conferences, has given invited seminars at many universities, and has served as a technical consultant for several organizations, including IBM. Dr. Cheng is a senior member of the IEEE.

Session 1

Keynote Speech

Parallel Object / Relational DBMS: Challenges and Opportunities

David DeWitt
University of Wisconsin

Session 2A

Data Mining

An Efficient Approach to Discovering Knowledge from Large Databases*

Show-Jane Yen   and   Arbee L.P. Chen

Department of Computer Science
National Tsing Hua University
Hsinchu, Taiwan 300, R.O.C.
Email: alpchen@cs.nthu.edu.tw

Abstract

In this paper, we study two problems: mining association rules and mining sequential patterns in a large database of customer transactions. The problem of mining association rules focuses on discovering *large itemsets* where a large itemset is a group of items which appear together in a sufficient number of transactions; while the problem of mining sequential patterns focuses on discovering *large sequences* where a large sequence is an ordered list of sets of items which appear in a sufficient number of transactions. We present efficient graph-based algorithms to solve these problems. The algorithms construct an *association graph* to indicate the associations between items and then traverse the graph to generate large itemsets and large sequences, respectively. Our algorithms need to scan the database only once. Empirical evaluations show that our algorithms outperform other algorithms which need to make multiple passes over the database.

1   Introduction

From a large amount of data, potentially useful information may be discovered. Techniques have been proposed to find knowledge (or rules) from databases [1, 2, 3, 6, 9, 10, 15, 17, 21, 22, 24]. The knowledge discovered can be used to answer cooperative queries [7, 14], handle null values [20] and facilitate semantic query optimization [8, 12, 17, 18, 19, 23].

Data mining has also high applicability in retail industry. The effective management of business is significantly dependent on the quality of its decision making. It is therefore important to analyze past transaction data to discover customer purchasing behavior and improve the quality of business decision. In order to support this analysis, a sufficient amount of transaction items needs to be collected and stored in a database. A transaction in the database typically consists of customer identifier, transaction date (or transaction time) and the set of items (itemset) purchased in the transaction. Because the amount of these transaction data is very large, an efficient algorithm needs to be devised for discovering useful information embedded in the transaction data.

In this paper, we study two problems: mining association rules and mining sequential patterns in a large database of customer transactions. The problem of mining association rules over customer transactions was introduced in [2]. An association rule describes the association among items in which when some items are purchased in a transaction, others are purchased too.

In order to find association rules, we need to discover the itemsets which occur often enough within transactions. The first step to find association rules is therefore to identify all itemsets that are contained in a sufficient number of transactions above a certain minimum threshold. After discovering all such itemsets, the association rules can be generated as follows [2]: If the discovered itemset $Y = I_1 I_2 ... I_k, k \geq 2$, all rules that reference items from the set $\{I_1, I_2, ..., I_k\}$ can be generated. The antecedent of each of these rules is a subset X of Y, and the consequent is $Y - X$. The rule $X \implies Y - X$ holds in the database D of transactions with *confidence factor* c if at least $c\%$ of the transactions in D that contain X also contain $Y - X$. An example of such an association rule is "95% of transactions in which coffee and sugar are purchased, milk is purchased too." The form of this rule is "coffee, sugar $\implies$ milk." The antecedent of this rule consists of coffee and sugar and the consequent consists of milk alone. The percentage 95% is the confidence factor of the rule.

The following definitions are adopted from [2]. A transaction *supports* an itemset Z, if Z is contained in the transaction. The *support for an itemset* is defined as the ratio of the total number of transactions which support this itemset to the total number of transactions in D. Hence, the major work of mining association rules is to find all itemsets that satisfy a certain user-specified *minimum support*. Each such itemset is referred to as *large itemset*. An itemset of length k is called a k-itemset and a large itemset of length k a large k-itemset.

The problem of mining sequential patterns in a

---

*This work was partially supported by the Republic of China National Science Council under Contract No. NSC 86-2213-E-007-009.

large database of customer transactions was introduced in [5]. An example of such a pattern is that customers buy books about "basic computer concepts," and then about "programming language," and then about "system programming."

The problem is stated as follows [5]: A *sequence* is an ordered list of itemsets. A sequence s is denoted as $< s_1, s_2, ..., s_n >$, where s_j is an itemset. The items in s_j represent that these items were bought together. A sequence $< a_1, a_2, ..., a_n >$ is contained in another sequence $< b_1, b_2, ..., b_m >$ if there exist integers $i_1 < i_2 < ... < i_n$, $1 \leq i_k \leq m$, such that $a_1 \subseteq b_{i_1}, ..., a_n \subseteq b_{i_n}$. In a set of sequences, a sequence s is *maximal* if s is not contained in any other sequence. All the transactions of a customer, ordered by increasing transaction-time is a *customer-sequence*.

A customer *supports* a sequence s if s is contained in the customer-sequence for this customer. *The support for a sequence* is defined as the fraction of total customers who support this sequence. Each sequence satisfying a certain minimum support threshold is a *large sequence*. A sequence of length k is called a k-sequence and a large sequence of length k a large k-sequence. The problem of mining sequential patterns [5] is to find the maximal large sequences among all large sequences.

Various algorithms [2, 4, 5, 11, 13, 16] have been proposed to discover large itemsets or sequential patterns. These algorithms generate candidate k-itemsets (k-sequences) ($k \geq 1$) for large k-itemsets (lare k-sequences), scan each transaction in a database to count the supports of these candidate k-itemsets (k-sequences) and find all large k-itemsets (k-sequences) in the kth iteration based on a pre-determined minimum support. However, because the size of the database can be very large, it is very costly to scan the database to count supports for candidate itemsets in each iteration. Hence, the key issue to improve the performance of large itemset and large sequence discovery is to reduce the number of candidates and the amount of data that has to be scanned in each iteration.

In this paper, we propose two algorithms, DLG (Direct Large itemset Generation) and DSG (Direct Sequential pattern Generation), for efficient large itemset generation and efficient sequential pattern generation, respectively, which are significantly different from previous approaches [2, 4, 5, 11, 13, 16]. DLG and DSG are very efficient for finding large itemsets and sequential patterns, respectively, because they need not generate candidates and need to scan the database only once. The algorithms DLG and DSG construct an *association graph* to indicate the associations between items, and then traverse the graph to generate large itemsets and sequential patterns, respectively.

The rest of this paper is organized as follows: Section 2 describes the related work. The algorithm DLG proposed for generating large itemsets and the experimental results for the performance evaluation are presented in Section 3. Section 4 describes the algorithm DSG for sequential pattern generation and evalutes the performance of DSG. Finally, we conclude this paper and present directions for future research in Section 5.

2 Related Work

An algorithm for finding all association rules, called AIS algorithm, was presented in [2]. AIS generates candidate itemsets and counts their supports as the database is scaned in each iteration. After reading a transaction, it is determined which of the large itemsets found in the previous iteration are contained in this transaction. During a database scan, new candidate itemsets are generated by extending these large itemsets with other items in the transaction, and support information is collected to evaluate which of the candidates actually are large. However, it was found [4] that the problem with AIS is that it generates too many candidates that later turn out to be small. Hence, the AIS algorithm is rather inefficient.

The Apriori and AprioriTid algorithms [4] generate the candidate itemsets to be counted in an iteration by using only the itemsets found large in the previous iteration without considering the transactions in the database. This results in generation of a smaller number of candidate itemsets. However, for each candidate itemset, it needs to count its appearances in all transactions. In the Apriori algorithm, each iteration requires one pass over the database. In the AprioriTid algorithm, the database is not scanned after the first iteration. Rather, the transaction-id and candidate k-itemsets which were present in each transaction are generated in each iteration. This is used to count supports for candidate $k + 1$-itemsets during the next iteration. It was found that in the initial stages, Apriori is more efficient than AprioriTid, since there are too many candidate k-itemsets to be tracked during the early stages of the process. A hybrid algorithm of the two algorithms was also proposed in [4], and shown to lead to better performance in general.

Park, Chen and Yu [16] pointed out that the key issue to improve the performance of large itemsets discovery is the initial candidate set generation, especially for the candidate 2-itemsets, and the amount of data that has to be scanned during large itemset generation in each iteration. They utilized hash method to reduce the number of candidate 2-itemsets generation and employed pruning techniques to progressively trim the transaction database. The pruning techniques are described as follows: an item in a transaction can be trimmed if it does not appear in at least k of the candidate k-itemsets in the kth iteration. However, in order to reduce the number of candidate 2-itemsets, the overhead for building hash table is large. Moreover, in order to trim the database, it is necessary to scan each transaction in the database to determine which of the candidate itemsets are contained in the transaction.

Agrawal and Srikant [5] presented two algorithms called AprioriAll and AprioriSome for mining sequential patterns in a large database of customer transactions. These two algorithms make multiple passes over the data. In each pass, they use a seed set to generate candidate sequences, and count supports for each candidate sequence. At the end of the pass, it is determined which of the candidate sequences are actually large. These large candidates become the seed for the next pass. The two algorithms generate too many candidate sequences to be counted, and the database needs to be scaned repeatedly.

In [16], the DHP algorithm is shown to provide the best performance for large itemsets generation. Hence, DHP is used as the base algorithm to compare with our algorithm DLG. The analysis and experimental results are shown in Section 3.3. AprioriAll and AprioriSome have the similar performance, which is shown in [5]. We take AprioriAll algorithm to compare with our algorithm DSG. The analysis and the experimental results are shown in Section 4.3.

3 Association Rule Discovery

In this section, we present the algorithm DLG for efficient large itemset generation. There are three phases in the DLG algorithm: The first phase is the *large 1-itemset generation phase* which generates large items (large 1-itemsets) and records related information. The second phase is the *graph construction phase* which constructs an *association graph* to indicate the associations between large items. In this phase, large 2-itemset can also be generated. The last phase is the *large itemset generation phase* which generates large k-itemsets ($k > 2$) based on the constructed association graph.

In the previous approaches [2, 4, 11, 13, 16], they all need to sort the items in each transaction in their lexicographic order. However, our approach need not to sort the items in each transaction.

3.1 Association graph construction

Before performing the DLG algorithm, each item is assigned an integer number. Suppose item i represents the item whose item number is i. In the first phase, algorithm DLG scans the database once to count the support and build a bit vector for each item. The length of each bit vector is the number of transactions in the database. If an item appears in the ith transaction, the ith bit of the bit vector associated with this item is set to 1. Otherwise, the ith bit of the bit vector is set to 0. The bit vector associated with item i is denoted as BV_i. The number of 1's in BV_i is equal to the number of transactions which support the item i, that is, the support for the item i.

For example, consider the database in Table 1. Each record is a <TID, Itemset> pair, where TID is the identifier of the corresponding transaction, and Itemset records the items purchased in the transaction.

TID	Itemset
100	3 1 4
200	5 3 2
300	1 2 3 5
400	5 2

Table 1: A database of transactions

Assume that the minimum support is 2 transactions. In the large 1-itemset generation phase, the large items found in the database shown in Table 1 are items 1, 2, 3 and 5, and BV_1, BV_2, BV_3 and BV_5 are (1010), (0111), (1110) and (0111), respectively.

Property 1. The support for the itemset $\{i_1, i_2, ..., i_k\}$ is the number of 1's in $BV_{i_1} \wedge BV_{i_2} \wedge ... \wedge BV_{i_k}$, where the notation "$\wedge$" is a logical AND operation.

After the first phase, the database need not be scanned again. In the graph construction phase, DLG constructs an association graph to indicate the associations between items. For the association graph, if the number of 1's in $BV_i \wedge BV_j$ ($i < j$) is no less than the minimum support, a directed edge from item i to item j is constructed. Also, itemset $\{i,j\}$ is a large 2-itemset. The association graph for the above example is shown in Figure 1, and the large 2-itemsets are $\{1,3\}$, $\{2,3\}$, $\{2,5\}$ and $\{3,5\}$.

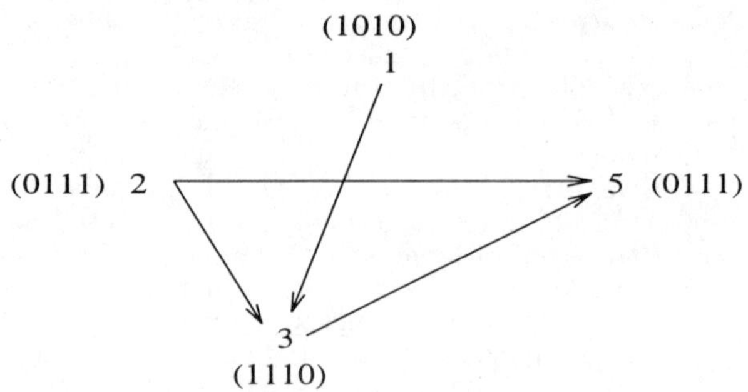

Figure 1: The association graph and the bit vector associated with each large item for Table 1

3.2 Large itemset generation

The large k-itemsets ($k > 2$) are generated based on the association graph constructed in the second phase. The data structure used to implement the association graph is a linked list.

The large 2-itemsets L_2 is found in the graph construction phase. In the large itemset generation phase, the DLG algorithm generates large k-itemsets L_k ($k > 2$). For each large k-itemset in L_k ($k \geq 2$), the last item of the k-itemset is used to extend the itemset into $k + 1$-itemsets. Suppose $\{i_1, i_2, ..., i_k\}$ is a large k-itemset. If there is a directed edge from item i_k to item u, then the itemset $\{i_1, i_2, ..., i_k\}$ is extended into $k + 1$-itemset $\{i_1, i_2, ..., i_k, u\}$. The itemset $\{i_1, i_2, ..., i_k, u\}$ is a large $k + 1$-itemset if the number of 1's in $BV_{i_1} \wedge BV_{i_2} \wedge ... \wedge BV_{i_k} \wedge BV_u$ is no less than the minimum support. If no large k-itemsets can be generated, the DLG algorithm terminates.

For example, consider the database in Table 1. In the second phase, the large 2-itemsets $L_2 = \{\{1,3\}, \{2,3\}, \{2,5\}, \{3,5\}\}$ is generated. For large 2-itemset $\{2,3\}$, there is a directed edge from the last item 3 of the itemset $\{2,3\}$ to item 5. Hence, the 2-itemset $\{2,3\}$ is extended into 3-itemset $\{2,3,5\}$. The number of 1's in $BV_2 \wedge BV_3 \wedge BV_5$ (i.e., (0110)) is 2. Hence, the

3-itemset $\{2,3,5\}$ is a large 3-itemset, since the number of 1's in its bit vector is no less than the minimum support. The DLG algorithm terminates because no large 4-itemsets can be further generated. After completing the DLG algorithm on Table 1, the large itemsets are $\{1,3\}$, $\{2,3\}$, $\{2,5\}$, $\{3,5\}$ and $\{2,3,5\}$. The DLG algorithm for each phase is shown as follows:

```
\* Large 1-itemset generation phase *\
forall items i do
    set all bits of BV_i to 0;
for (j = 1; j ≤ N; j + +) do begin
\* N is the number of transactions in database D *\
    forall items i in the jth transaction do begin
        i.count++;
        set the jth bit of BV_i to 1;
    end
end
L_1 = φ;
forall items i in database D do begin
    if i.count ≥ minsup then
    \* minsup is the minimum support threshold *\
        L_1 = L_1 ∪ {i};
end

\* Graph construction phase *\
if L_1 ≠ φ then begin
    forall large 1-itemsets l ∈ L_1 do
        allocate a node for Item[l] and
        Item[l].link=NULL;
    L_2 = φ
    for every two large items i, j (i < j) do begin
        if (the number of 1's in BV_i ∧ BV_j) ≥ minsup
        then begin
        \* create an directed edge
        from i to j in the association graph *\
            allocate a node p;
            p.link = Item[l_a].link;
            p.Item = l_b;
            Item[l_a].link = p;
            L_2 = L_2∪ {{i,j}};
            \* generate large 2-itemsets *\
        end
    end
end

\* Large itemset generation phase *\
k = 2;
while L_k ≠ φ do begin
    L_{k+1} = φ;
    forall itemsets (i_1 i_2 ... i_k) ∈ L_k do begin
        pointer = Item[i_k].link;
        while pointer ≠ NULL do begin
            u = pointer.Item;
            if (number of 1's in BV_{i_1} ∧ ... ∧ BV_{i_k}
            ∧BV_u) ≥ minsup then
                L_{k+1} = L_{k+1}∪ {{i_1,...,i_k,u}},
            pointer = pointer.link;
        end
    end
    k = k + 1
end
```

3.3 Experimental results

To assess the performance of the DLG algorithm for large itemset generation, we perform several experiments on Sun SPARC/10 workstation. The experiments show that the DLG algorithm is very efficient for large itemset generation, because it takes only one database scan to generate large itemsets. We first describe how the datasets are generated for the performance evaluation. We then compare the performance of DLG and DHP [16] by performing experiments on the generated datasets. Finally, we demonstrate the scale-up properties of the DLG algorithm.

3.3.1 generation of synthetic data

The synthetic database of sales transactions is generated to evaluate the performance of the algorithms. The method to generate synthetic transactions is similar to the one used in [4]. The parameters used in our experiments are shown in Table 2.

$|D|$	Number of transactions
$|I|$	Average size of the potentially large itemsets
$|MI|$	Maximum size of the potentially large itemsets
$|L|$	Number of large itemsets
$|T|$	Average size of the transactions
$|MT|$	Maximum size of the transactions
N	Number of items

Table 2: The parameters

We first generate a set L of the potentially large itemsets, and then assign a large itemset picked up from L to a transaction. The size of each potentially large itemset is between 1 and $|MI|$. The probabilities for sizes 1, 2, ... and $|MI|$ are obtained by a Possion distribution with mean equal to $|I|$. These probabilities are normalized such that the sum of these probabilities is 1. For example, suppose average size $|I|$ of the large itemsets is 3 and maximum size $|MI|$ of the large itemsets is 5. According to the Possion distribution with mean $|I|$, the probabilities for sizes 1, 2, 3, 4 and 5 are 0.17, 0.26, 0.26, 0.19 and 0.12, respectively, after the normalization process. These probabilities are then accumulated such that each size falls in a range, which is shown in Table 3. For each potentially large itemset, we generate a random real number which is between 0 and 1 to determine the size of the potentially large itemset.

Size	Range
1	$0 \sim 0.17$
2	$0.18 \sim 0.43$
3	$0.44 \sim 0.69$
4	$0.70 \sim 0.88$
5	$0.89 \sim 1$

Table 3: The probabilities for the sizes of itemsets

The number of the potentially large itemsets in L is set to $|L|$. Items in the first large itemset are chosen randomly. Some fraction of items in subsequent large itemsets are chosen from the previously generated large itemset. For each item in the previous large itemset, we flip a coin to decide whether the item will be retained in the current large itemset. The remaining items in the large itemset are picked at random. After generating the set L of large itemsets, we then generate transactions in the database. The size of each transaction is picked from a Poisson distribution with mean equal to $|T|$, and the size is between 1 and $|MT|$. The method to determine the size of a transaction is the same as the method to determine the size of a large itemset. For a transaction, we randomly choose a large itemset from L to fit in the transaction and assign it to the transaction. The remaining items of the first transaction are chosen randomly. The fraction of the remaining items of the subsequent transaction are chosen from the previously generated transaction. For each item in the previous transaction, we also flip a coin to decide whether the item is retained in the transaction. After choosing the items from a large itemset and from the previous transaction, the remaining items in the transaction are picked at random. The same as [4], we also use a corruption level during the transaction generation to model the phenomenon that all the items in a large itemset are not always bought together. Each transaction is stored in a file system with the form of <transaction identifier, the number of items, items>.

We generate datasets by setting $N = 1000$ and $|L| = 2000$. We choose three values for $|T|$: 5, 10 and 20, and the corresponding $|MT| = 10$, 20 and 40, respectively. We choose two values for $|I|$: 3 and 5, and the corresponding $|MI| = 5$ and 10, respectively. The number $|D|$ of transactions is set to 100,000. We use $Ta.MTx.Ib.MIy$ to mean that $a = |T|$, $x = |MT|$, $b = |I|$ and $y = |MI|$. We generate the following datasets for the experiments: $T5.MT10.I3.MI5$, $T10.MT20.I3.MI5$, $T10.MT20.I5.MI10$ and $T20.MT40.I3.MI5$.

3.3.2 comparison of DLG and DHP

Figure 2 shows the relative execution time for DHP [16] and DLG, using the four synthetic datasets described in Section 3.3.1. In these experiments, the hash table size $|H_2|$ used in DHP is set to $\frac{1}{4} \times C_2^N$, which was found to have better overall performance in [16], where N is the number of items. Suppose there are $|D|$ transactions in database DB and m items in each transaction on the average. In the kth pass, the large k-itemsets L_k is generated. For the first pass, DLG and DHP both need to scan each transaction in DB to count support for each item. By the way, DLG records the bit vectors for each item. However, DHP needs to take extra overhead to combine every two items to form a 2-itemset in each transaction. Totally, there are $|D| \times C_2^m$ combinations needed. For each combination, DHP uses the hash function to locate the 2-itemset in the hash table. Hence, DHP takes much more time than DLG in the first pass.

Suppose there are $|L_k|$ large itemsets generated in the kth pass. In the second pass, DLG performs $\frac{|L_1|(|L_1|-1)}{2}$ logical AND operations on bit vectors to construct association graph and generate large 2-itemsets. DHP needs to generate candidate 2-itemsets and prune these candidate 2-itemsets using the hash table created in the first pass. Besides, DHP needs to scan database to count support for candidate 2-itemsets and trim the database DB to generate a reduced database. These jobs needed by DHP are more costly than these logical operations performed by DLG in the second pass.

In the kth ($k > 2$) pass, DLG extends each large $k-1$-itemset into k-itemsets according to the association graph and performs logical AND operations. Suppose on the average, each node (item) has q outdegrees in the association graph. DLG performs $(k-1) \times |L_{k-1}| \times q$ logical AND operations to find all large k-itemsets. Hence, as the minimum support decreases, the number of logical AND operations performed increases because the two values $|L_{k-1}|$ and q increase. In the kth pass, DHP generates candidate k-itemsets C_k from large $k-1$-itemsets L_{k-1}. After generating C_k, DHP scans each transaction in the database DB_k to count supports for these candidate k-itemsets and trim the database DB_k to generate another reduced database DB_{k+1}. Hence, the execution time of DHP depends on the number of generated candidate itemsets and the amount of data that has to be scanned.

pass	DLG	DHP				
	$|L_k|$	$|L_k|$	$|C_k|$	$|DB_k|$	M_k	m_k
1	288	288	1000	4.265MB	100,000	9.76
2	687	687	974	4.265MB	100,000	9.76
3	497	497	2964	2.014MB	90,747	5.04
4	295	295	832	1.270MB	45,649	5.12
5	118	118	302	502KB	20,258	5.54
6	30	30	84	305KB	10,076	6.33
7	4	4	23	98KB	2,480	6.89

Table 4: Comparisons of DLG and DHP

We perform an experiment on dataset T10.MT20.I5.MI10 with minimum support 0.75%. The experimental results are shown in Table 4, where M_k denotes the number of transactions in DB_k, and m_k denotes the number of items in each transaction on the average.

In this experiment, there are 238 nodes and 687 edges in the association graph. Hence, on the average, the out-degrees of each node is 3. Table 4 shows that in each pass, the number of logical AND operations performed by DLG is much less than the size of database scanned and the number of candidate itemsets generated by DHP. Hence, DHP takes much more time than DLG for large itemset generation. Figure 2 shows that the DLG algorithm outperforms the DHP algorithm significantly, and the performance gap increases as the minimum support decreases because the number of candidate itemsets and the number of database scans increases for DHP.

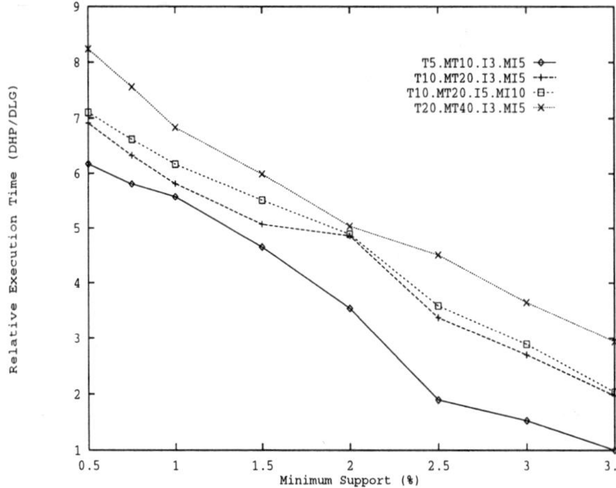

Figure 2: Relative Execution Time

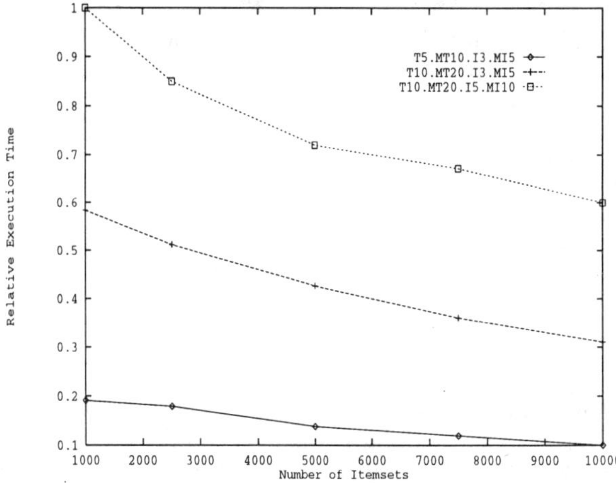

Figure 4: Scale-up: Number of Items

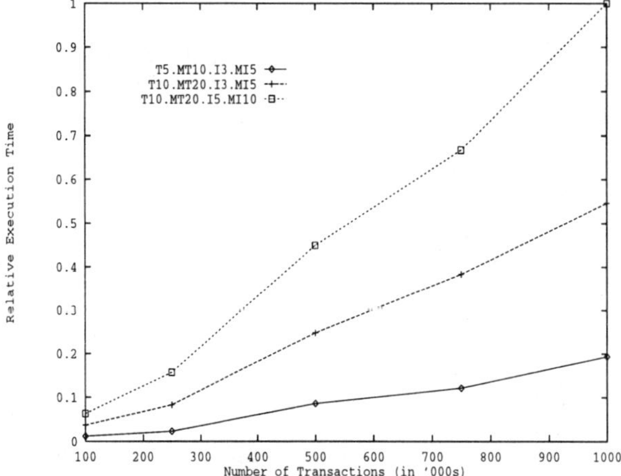

Figure 3: Scale-up: Number of Transactions

3.3.3 discussions for DLG

The memory space needed for performing DLG is dominated by the bit vectors. Since the length of each bit vector is the number of transactions $|D|$ in DB, there are $N \times |D|$ bits needed, where N is the number of items. In our experiments, $N = 10^3$ and $|D| = 10^5$. Hence, $10^3 \times 10^5$ bits (12.5MB) are needed to store all bit vectors.

Figure 3 shows how DLG scales up as the number of transactions is increased from 10,000 to 100,000 transactions. We use the three datasets $T5.MT10.I3.MI5$, $T10.MT20.I3.MI5$ and $T10.MT20.I5.MI10$, and set the minimum support to 1%. As shown, the execution times of DLG increase linearly as the database sizes increase, because the number of large itemsets increases.

Next, we examine how DLG scales up as the num-ber of items increases from 100,000 to 1,000,000 for the three datasets $T5.MT10.I3.MI5$, $T10.MT20.I3.MI5$ and $T10.MT20.I5.MI10$. The minimum support is set to 1% for this experiment, and the results are shown in Figure 4. The execution times decrease slightly, because the number of large itemsets de-creases as we increase the number of items.

4 Sequential Pattern Discovery

In this section, we present the algorithm DSG for ef-ficient sequential pattern generation. In [5], the prob-lem of mining sequential patterns is splitted into the following phases: 1. Sort phase, 2. Large itemset phase, 3. Transformation phase, 4. Sequence phase and 5. Maximal phase. The Sort phase is to con-vert the original transaction database into a database of customer-sequences. The customer-sequence is a list of itemsets which are ordered by increasing transaction-times. The Large itemset phase is to find all large itemsets (or large 1-sequences). The Transfor-mation phase is to transform each original customer-sequence into a transformed customer-sequence which is an ordered list of large itemsets.

The Sequence phase and the Maximal phase are the main portions for mining sequential patterns. In these two phases, we propose an algorithm DSG to generate sequential patterns, which needs only one database scan. The DSG algorithm is also splitted into two phases: The first phase is the *graph construction phase* which constructs an association graph to indi-cate the associations between large itemsets (or large 1-sequences) and records related information. In this phase, large 2-sequences can also be generated. The second phase is the *sequential pattern generation phase* which generates large k-sequences ($k > 2$) based on the constructed association graph and finds maximal large sequences (or sequential patterns).

4.1 Association graph construction

After completing the Transformation phase, we are given a database of transformed customer-sequences. In the graph construction phase, DSG algorithm scans each customer-sequence in the database to combine every two large itemsets to generate a 2-sequence and count support for the 2-sequence. For each 2-sequence, the set of identifiers of the customer-sequences where the 2-sequence appears is recorded. When the support for a 2-sequence achieves the minimum support threshold, the DSG algorithm creates a directed edge from the first itemset to the second itemset in the 2-sequence.

In the following, $\Im_s$ denotes the set of customer identifiers of the customer-sequences where sequence s appears. The cardinality of $\Im_s$ is equal to the number of customer-sequences which support the sequence s, that is, the support for the sequence s.

CID	Csequence
1	ABCD
2	CBE
3	ACB
4	AED
5	CBDE

Table 5: A database of customer-sequences

For example, Table 5 is a database of customer-sequences after completing the Transformation phase. Each record is a <CID, Csequence> pair, where CID is the customer identifier of the corresponding customer-sequence, and Csequence is the customer-sequence. Csequence is a list of large itemsets which are ordered by increasing transaction-times. A large itemset is denoted by an alphabet.

Assume the minimum support is 2 customer-sequences. After scanning the database of customer-sequences in Table 5, the association graph and the recorded information are shown in Figure 5, where the set of numbers on each edge $\overrightarrow{XY}$ is the set of customer identifiers of the customer-sequences where the large 2-sequence $< X, Y >$ appears. After completing the graph construction phase, the large 2-sequences are <A,B>, <A,C>, <A,D>, <B,D>, <B,E>, <C,B>, <C,D> and <C,E>, and the set $\Im_{<A,B>}$ of customer identifiers of the customer-sequences where the 2-sequence <A,B> appears is $\{1, 3\}$, and so on.

4.2 Sequential pattern generation

In this section, we describe how to generate large k-sequence ($k > 2$) based on the association graph and the recorded information, and further to find sequential patterns. The large 2-sequences LS_2 is found in the graph construction phase. In the sequential pattern generation phase, the DSG algorithm generates large k-sequences LS_k ($k > 2$). For each large k-sequence in LS_k ($k \geq 2$), the last itemset of the k-sequence is used to extend the sequence into $k + 1$-sequences.

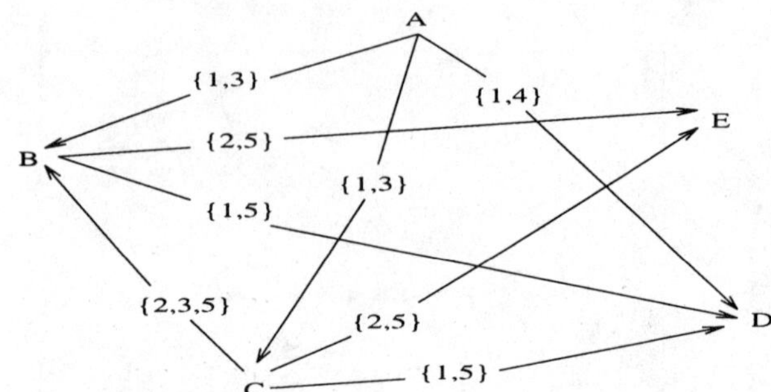

Figure 5: The association graph and the set of identifiers of the customer-sequences where each large 2-sequence appears for Table 5

Property 2. The support for the k-sequence $< s_1, s_2, ..., s_k >$ is the cardinality of the set $\Im_{<s_1,s_2>} \cap \Im_{<s_2,s_3>} \cap ... \cap \Im_{<s_{k-1},s_k>}$.

Suppose $< s_1, s_2, ..., s_k >$ is a large k-sequence. If there is a directed edge from itemset s_k to itemset v, the sequence $< s_1, s_2, ..., s_k >$ is extended into $k + 1$-sequence $< s_1, s_2, ..., s_k, v >$. The $k + 1$-sequence $< s_1, s_2, ..., s_k, v >$ is a large $k+1$-sequence if the support for the $k + 1$-sequence is no less than the minimum support. If no large k-sequence can be generated, the DSG algorithm terminates.

After finding all large sequences LS, the large sequences which are subsequences of the other large sequences are deleted from LS. The remaining large sequences are maximal large sequences, that is, sequential patterns.

For example, consider the database in Table 5 and the association graph in Figure 5. For large 2-sequence <C,B>, there is a directed edge from the last itemset B of the sequence <C,B> to itemset E. Hence, the 2-sequence <C,B> can be extended into 3-sequence <C,B,E>, and the set $\Im_{<C,B,E>}$ can be obtained by performing set intersection on sets $\Im_{<C,B>}$ and $\Im_{<B,E>}$. Because the set $\Im_{<C,B>}$ is $\{2,3,5\}$ and the set $\Im_{<B,E>}$ is $\{2,5\}$, the set $\Im_{<C,B,E>}$ is $\{2,5\}$. The 3-sequence <C,B,E> is a large 3-sequence, since the cardinality of set $\Im_{<C,B,E>}$ is no less than the minimum support. After completing the DSG algorithm on Table 5, the sequential patterns are <A,B>, <A,C>, <A,D>, <B,D>, <C,D> and <C,B,E>. The DSG algorithm for each phase is shown as follows:

```
\* Graph construction phase *\
LS_1 = { large 1-sequences }
\* result of the Large itemset phase *\
if LS_1 ≠ φ then begin
    forall large 1-sequences l ∈ LS_1 do
        allocate a node for Itemset[l] and
        Itemset[l].link=NULL
    forall permutation l_x l_y where l_x and l_y are
    selected from LS_1 do
        ℑ_<l_x,l_y> = φ
        \* ℑ_<l_x,l_y> records the set of identifiers of
        the customer-sequences where l_x l_y appears *\
```

$LS_2 = \phi$
for $(i = 1; i \leq N; i++)$ **do begin** $\backslash * \ N$ is the number of customer-sequences in database $D \ *\backslash$
    scan the ith customer-sequence c
    I_c = the set of all itemsets in c
    forall combination $l_a l_b$ **do begin**
    $\backslash * \ l_a$ and l_b are selected from $I_c \ *\backslash$
        $\Im_{<l_a,l_b>} = Im_{<l_a,l_b>} \cup \{i\}$
        $\backslash *$ record related information $*\backslash$
        if $< l_a, l_b > .count \leq minsup$ **then**
            $< l_a, l_b > .count++$
        if $< l_a, l_b > .count = minsup$ **then begin**
            $LS_2 = LS_2 \cup \{< l_a, l_b >\}$
            $\backslash *$ generate large 2-sequences $*\backslash$
            CreateEdge(l_a, l_b)
            $\backslash *$ create an edge from l_a to l_b
            in the association graph $*\backslash$
        end
    end
    end
end
CreateEdge(l_a, l_b)
    allocate a node p
    $p.link = Item[l_a].link$
    $p.Item = l_b$
    $Item[l_a].link = p$

$\backslash *$ Sequential pattern generation phase $*\backslash$
$k = 2$
while $LS_k \neq \phi$ **do begin**
    $LS_{k+1} = \phi$
    forall sequences $< s_1, s_2, ..., s_k >\in LS_k$ **do begin**
        $pointer = Itemset[s_k].link$
        while $pointer \neq$ NULL **do begin**
            $v = pointer.Itemset$
            if (the cardinality of set $\Im_{<s_1,s_2>} \cap$
        $\Im_{<s_2,s_3>} \cap ... \cap \Im_{<s_k,s_v>}) \geq minsup$ **then**
            $LS_{k+1} = LS_{k+1} \cup \{< s_1, s_2, ..., s_k, v >\}$
            $pointer = pointer.link$
        end
    end
    $k = k + 1$
end
Answer = Maximal sequences in $\cup_k LS_k$

4.3 Experimental results

To evaluate the performance of the DSG algorithm for sequential pattern generation, we also perform several experiments on Sun SPARC/10 workstation. The experiments show that the DSG algorithm is very efficient for sequential pattern generation, because it takes one database scan to construct an association graph and the large sequences are generated based on the association graph directly. We first generate datasets for the experiments, and then compare the performance between DSG and AprioriAll by performing experiments on the generated datasets. The scale-up properties of the DSG algorithm are also demonstrated.

4.3.1 generation of synthetic data

The method to generate synthetic datasets is similar to the one used in DLG algorithm. The difference between the two methods is described below. For the generated dataset used in DLG algorithm, the items in each transaction are generated in their lexicographic order. However, for the generated dataset used in DSG algorithm, the itemsets in each customer-sequence are generated in an arbitrary order. Each transaction is stored in a file system with the form of <customer-sequence identifier, the number of itemsets, itemsets>. The parameters used in the experiments are as shown in Table 2 with some modifications. In Table 2, the term "transactions" is changed to "customer-sequences," the term "itemsets" is changed to "sequences," the term "items" is changed to "itemsets," and the notation "L","T" and "MT" are changed to "LS," "C" and "MC," respectively. The number $|D|$ of customer-sequences is set to 100,000. We also set N =1000 and $|LS|$ =2000 for the generated datasets, and generate the four datasets: $C5.MC10.I3.MI5$, $C10.MC20.I3.MI5$, $C10.MC20.I5.MI10$ and $C20.MC40.I3.MI5$ in the experiments.

4.3.2 comparison of AprioriAll and DSG

Figure 6 shows the relative execution time for AprioriAll algorithm [5] and DSG algorithm over various minimum supports, ranging from 0.5% to 3.5%.

Suppose there are M customer-sequences in the database and m itemsets in each customer-sequence on the average. In the kth pass, the set of large k-sequences LS_k is generated.

In the second pass, AprioriAll uses LS_1 to generate $2 \times C_2^{|LS_1|}$ candidate 2-sequences CS_2. Moreover, AprioriAll scans the database to combine every two sequences to form a 2-sequence in each customer-sequence. Totally, there are $M \times C_2^m$ combinations needed. For each combination, AprioriAll searches for the candidate 2-sequences in CS_2 to determine whether the combination is in CS_2 for large 2-sequence generation. However, when $|LS_1|$ is large, $2 \times C_2^{|LS_1|}$ becomes an extremely large number. It is very costly to determine large 2-sequences from a large number of candidate 2-sequences. In this pass, DSG scans each customer-sequence in the database to combine every two sequences to form a 2-sequence and count support for the 2-sequence to determine whether the 2-sequence is large. Because AprioriAll needs to search for a large amount of candidate 2-sequences, DSG outperforms AprioriAll in this pass.

In the kth pass ($k > 2$), AprioriAll generates candidate k-sequences based on large $k-1$-sequences LS_{k-1} and scans the database to count supports for the candidate k-sequences for large k-sequence generation. AprioriAll needs to combine every k sequences to form a k-sequence in each customer-sequence, and totally, $M \times C_k^m$ combinations are needed. For each combination, AprioriAll searches for candidate k-sequences in CS_k to determine whether the k-sequence is in CS_k for

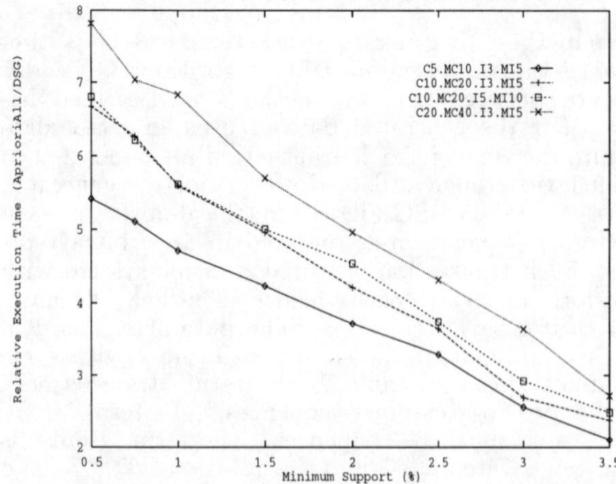

Figure 6: Relative Execution Times

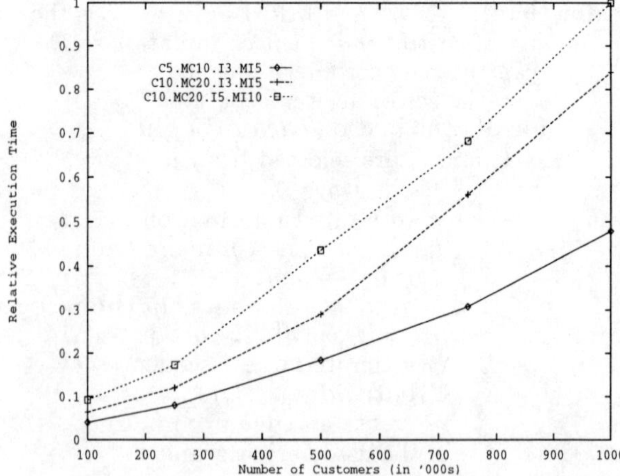

Figure 7: Scale-up: Number of Customers

large k-sequence generation. Hence, as the minimum support decreases, the execution time of AprioriAll increases because the candidate sequence generated increases and the number of database scans increases.

For DSG algorithm, the large k-sequences ($k > 2$) can be generated by extending large $k-1$-sequences into k-sequences based on the association graph and performing set intersections on the related information. Suppose on the average, the number of out-degrees of each node (itemset) in the association graph is q. In the kth ($k > 2$) pass, DSG performs $(k-1) \times q \times |LS_{k-1}|$ set intersections to find all large k-sequences. Hence, as the minimum support decreases, the number of set intersections performed increases, because the values q and $|LS_{k-1}|$ increases. However, DSG need not generate candidate k-sequences ($k \geq 1$) nor scan the database for large k-sequence generation ($k \geq 2$).

Since the number of set intersections performed for DSG is much less than the size of database scanned and the number of candidate itemsets generated for AprioriAll, DSG outperforms the AprioriAll for various minimum supports. Figure 6 shows that the performance gap increases as the minimum support decreases because the number of candidate itemsets generated by AprioriAll increases and the number of database scans also increases.

4.3.3 discussions for DSG

The main memory space needed for performing DSG is to store customer identifiers on each edge in the association graph. Suppose there are l edges in the association graph and on the average, the cardinality of the set of customer identifiers on each edge is k. $l \times k$ customer identifiers need to be stored.

Figure 7 shows how DSG scales up as the number of customer-sequences increases from 10,000 to 100,000 customer-sequences. We use the three datasets $C5.MC10.I3.MI5$, $C10.MC20.I3.MI5$ and

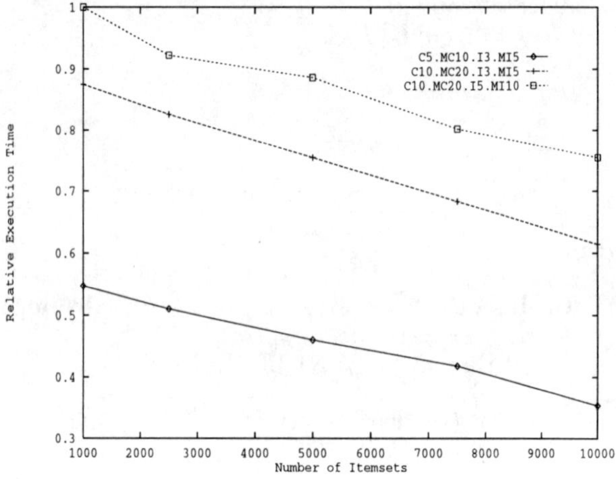

Figure 8: Scale-up: Number of Itemsets

$C10.MC20.I5.MI10$, and set the minimum support to 1.5%. As shown, the execution time of DSG increases linearly as the database size increases, because the number of large sequences increases.

Next, we investigate the scale up as we increase the number of itemsets from 1,000 to 10,000 for the three datasets $C5.MC10.I3.MI5$, $C10.MC20.I3.MI5$ and $C10.MC20.I5.MI10$. The minimum support is set to 1.5% for this experiment. Figure 8 shows the results. When the number of itemsets increases, the execution time decreases slightly, because the number of large sequences decreases.

5 Conclusion and Future Work

We study two problems: mining association rules and mining sequential patterns in a large database of customer transactions. The problems of mining association rules and mining sequential patterns focuses on discovering large itemsets and discovering large sequences, respectively.

We present two algorithms, DLG and DSG which need only one database scan, for efficient large itemset generation and efficient sequential pattern generation, respectively. These two algorithms construct an association graph to indicate the associations between items and then traverse the graph to generate large itemsets and large sequences, respectively.

We compare DLG and DSG algorithms to the previously known algorithms, DHP [16] and AprioriAll [5], respectively. The experimental results show that DLG and DSG outperform DHP and AprioriAll, respectively. When the minimum support decreases, the performance gap increases because the number of candidate itemsets (candidate sequences) generated by DHP (AprioriAll) increases and the number of database scans also increases.

We demonstrate that the execution time of these two algorithms increases linearly as the database size increases, and the execution time decreases slightly as the number of items (itemsets) increases.

For our graph-based approach, the related information may not fit in the main memory when the size of the database is very large. In the future, we shall develop a mining algorithm based on our graph-based approach, such that in a very large database environment, the mining algorithm can also be run in the main memory. We shall consider mining various different relationships among data in a large database of customer transactions, such as is-a relationships and part-of relationships. We shall also apply our graph-based approach on different applications, such as document retrieval and resource discovery.

References

[1] R. Agrawal and et al. Database Mining: A Performance Perspective. In *IEEE Transactions on Knowledge and Data Engineering*, pages 914–925, 1993.

[2] R. Agrawal and et al. Mining Association Rules Between Sets of Items in Large Databases. In *Proceedings of ACM SIGMOD*, pages 207–216, 1993.

[3] R. Agrawal and et al. An Interval Classifier for Database Mining Applications. In *Proceedings of International Conference on Very Large Data Bases*, pages 560–573, Vancouver, British Columbia, 1992.

[4] R. Agrawal and R. Srikant. Fast Algorithm for Mining Association Rules. In *Proceedings of International Conference on Very Large Data Bases*, pages 487–499, 1994.

[5] R. Agrawal and R. Srikant. Mining Sequential Patterns. In *Proceedings of International Conference on Data Engineering*, pages 3–14, 1995.

[6] Y. Cai, N. Cercone, and J. Han. An Attribute-Oriented Approach for Learning Classification Rules from Relational Databases. In *Proceedings of International Conference on Data Engineering, Los Angeles*, pages 281–288, Feb 1990.

[7] W. Chu and et al. Using Type Inference and Induced Rules to Provide Intensional Answers. In *Proceedings of International Conference on Data Engineering*, pages 396–403, 1991.

[8] M. Hammer and S.B. Zdondik. Knowledge-based query processing. In *Proceedings of International Conference on Very Large Data Bases*, pages 137–146, 1980.

[9] J. Han and et al. Knowledge Discovery in Databases: An Attribute-Oriented Approach. In *Proceedings of International Conference on Very Large Data Bases*, pages 547–559, 1992.

[10] J. Han and et al. Data-Driven Discovery of Quantitative Rules in Relational Databases. In *IEEE Transactions on Knowledge and Data Engineering*, pages 29–40, 1993.

[11] M. Houtsma and A. Swami. Set-Oriented Mining for Association Rules in Relational Databases. In *Proceedings of International Conference on Data Engineering*, pages 25–33, 1995.

[12] C. Malley and S. Zdonik. A Knowledge-Based Approach to Query Optimization. In *Proceedings of the First Expert Database System Conference*, pages 243–257, 1986.

[13] H. Mannila, H. Toivonen, and A.I. Verkamo. Efficient Algorithm for Discovering Association Rules. In *Proceedings of AAAI Workshop on Knowledge Discovery in Databases*, pages 181–192, 1994.

[14] A. Motro. Using Integrity Contraints to Provide Intensional Answers to Relational Queries. In *Proceedings of International Conference on Very Large Data Bases*, 1989.

[15] G. Oosthuizen. Lattice-Based Knowledge Discovery. In *Proceedings of AAAI Workshop on Knowledge Discovery in Databases*, pages 221–235, 1991.

[16] J.S. Park, M.S. Chen, and P.S. Yu. An Effective Hash-Based Algorithm for Mining Association Rules. In *Proceedings of ACM SIGMOD*, 24(2):175–186, 1995.

[17] M.S.E. Sciore and et al. A Method for Automatic Rule Derivation to Support Semantic Query Optimization. In *ACM Transactions on Database Systems*, pages 563–600, 1992.

[18] M. Siegel. Automatic Rule Derivation for Semantic Query Optimization. In *Proceedings of the Second International Conference on Expert Database Systems*, pages 371–385, 1988.

[19] U.Chakravarthy, D. Fishman, and J. Minker. Semantic Query Optimization in Expert Systems and Database Systems. In *Proceedings of the First International Conference on Expert Database Systems*, pages 326–340, 1984.

[20] S.J. Yen and A.L.P. Chen. Neighborhood/Conceptual Query Answering with Imprecise/Incomplete Data. In *Proceedings of International Conference on Entity-Relationship Approach*, pages 151–162, 1993.

[21] S.J. Yen and A.L.P. Chen. The Analysis of Relationships in Databases for Rule Derivation. In *Journal of Intelligent Information Systems*, Vol. 7, pages 1–24, 1996.

[22] S.J. Yen and A.L.P. Chen. An Efficient Algorithm for Deriving Compact Rules from Databases. In *Proceedings of International Conference on Database Systems for Advanced Applications*, pages 364–371, 1995.

[23] C. Yu and W. Sun. Automatic Knowledge Acquisition and Maintenance for Semantic Query Optimization. In *IEEE Transactions on Knowledge and Data Engineering*, pages 362–375, 1989.

[24] W. Ziarko. The Discovery, Analysis, and Representation of Data Dependencies in Databases. In *Proceedings of AAAI Workshop on Knowledge Discovery in Databases*, pages 195–209, 1991.

Hash Based Parallel Algorithms for Mining Association Rules

Takahiko SHINTANI   Masaru KITSUREGAWA

The University of Tokyo, Institute of Industrial Science
3rd Dept., 7-22-1, Roppongi, Minato, Tokyo 106, Japan
Email : {shintani, kitsure}@tkl.iis.u-tokyo.ac.jp

Abstract

In this paper, we propose four parallel algorithms (NPA, SPA, HPA and HPA-ELD) for mining association rules on shared-nothing parallel machines to improve its performance.

In NPA, candidate itemsets are just copied amongst all the processors, which can lead to memory overflow for large transaction databases. The remaining three algorithms partition the candidate itemsets over the processors. If it is partitioned simply (SPA), transaction data has to be broadcast to all processors. HPA partitions the candidate itemsets using a hash function to eliminate broadcasting, which also reduces the comparison workload significantly. HPA-ELD fully utilizes the available memory space by detecting the extremely large itemsets and copying them, which is also very effective at flattering the load over the processors.

We implemented these algorithms in a shared-nothing environment. Performance evaluations show that the best algorithm, HPA-ELD, attains good linearity on speedup ratio and is effective for handling skew.

1 Introduction

Recently, "Database Mining" has begun to attract strong attention. Because of the progress of bar-code technology, point-of-sales systems in retail company become to generate large amount of transaction data, but such data being archived and not being used efficiently. The advance of microprocessor and secondary storage technologies allows us to analyze this vast amount of transaction log data to extract interesting customer behaviors. Database mining is the method of efficient discovery of useful information such as rules and previously unknown patterns existing between data items embedded in large databases, which allows more effective utilization of existing data.

One of the most important problems in database mining is mining association rules within a database [1], so called the " basket data analysis" problem. Basket data type typically consist of a transaction identifier and the bought items par-transaction. By analyz-

ing transaction data, we can extract the association rule such as "90% of the customers who buy both A and B also buy C".

Several algorithms have been proposed to solve the above problem[1][2][3][4][5][6][7]. However most of these are sequential algorithms. Finding association rules requires scanning the transaction database repeatedly. In order to improve the quality of the rule, we have to handle very large amounts of transaction data, which requires incredibly long computation time. In general, it is difficult for a single processor to provide reasonable response time. In [7], we examined the feasibility of parallelization of association rule mining[1]. In [6], a parallel algorithm called PDM, for mining association rules was proposed. PDM copies the candidate itemsets among all the processors. As we will explain later, in the second pass of the Apriori algorithm, introduced by R.Agrawal and R.Srikant[2], the candidate itemset becomes too large to fit in the local memory of a single processor. Thus it requires reading the transaction dataset repeatedly from disk, which results in significant performance degradation.

In this paper, we propose four different parallel algorithms (NPA, SPA, HPA and HPA-ELD) for mining association rules based on the Apriori algorithm. In NPA (Non Partitioned Apriori), the candidate itemsets are just copied among all the processors. PDM mentioned above corresponds to NPA. The remaining three algorithms partition the candidate itemsets over the processors. Thus exploiting the aggregate memory of the system effectively. If it is partitioned simply (SPA : Simply Partitioned Apriori), transaction data has to be broadcast to all the processors. HPA (Hash Partitioned Apriori) partitions the candidate itemsets using a hash function as in the hash join, which eliminates transaction data broadcasting and can reduce the comparison workload significantly. In case the size of candidate itemset is smaller than

---

[1]The paper was presented at a local workshop in Japan.

19

the available system memory, HPA does not use the remaining free space. However HPA-ELD (HPA with Extremely Large itemset Duplication) does utilize the memory by copying some of the itemsets. The itemsets are sorted based on their frequency of appearance. HPA-ELD chooses the most frequently occurring itemsets and copies them over the processors so that all the memory space is used, which contributes to further reduce the communication among the processor. HPA-ELD, an extension of HPA, treats the frequently occurring itemsets in a special way, which can reduce the influence of the transaction data skew.

The implementation on a shared-nothing 64-node parallel computer, the Fujitsu AP1000DDV, shows that the best algorithm, HPA-ELD, attains satisfactory linearity on speedup and is also effective at skew handling.

This paper is organized as follows. In next section, we describe the problem of mining association rules. In section 3, we propose four parallel algorithms. Performance evaluations and detail cost analysis are given in section 4. Section 5 concludes the paper.

2 Mining Association Rules

First we introduce some basic concepts of association rules, using the formalism presented in [1]. Let $\mathcal{I} = \{i_1, i_2, \ldots, i_m\}$ be a set of literals, called items. Let $\mathcal{D} = \{t_1, t_2, \ldots, t_n\}$ be a set of transactions, where each transaction t is a sets of items such that $t \subseteq \mathcal{I}$. A transaction has an associated unique identifier called TID. We say each transaction *contains* a set of items X if $X \subseteq \mathcal{I}$. The itemset X has *support s* in the transaction set $\mathcal{D}$ if $s\%$ of transactions in $\mathcal{D}$ contain X, here we denote $s = support(X)$. An *association rule* is an implication of the form $X \Rightarrow Y$, where $X, Y \subset \mathcal{I}$, and $X \cap Y = \emptyset$. Each rule has two measures of value, *support* and *confidence*. The *support* of the rule $X \Rightarrow Y$ is $support(X \cup Y)$. The *confidence c* of the rule $X \Rightarrow Y$ in the transaction set $\mathcal{D}$ means $c\%$ of transactions in $\mathcal{D}$ that contain X also contain Y, which is can be written as the ratio $support(X \cup Y)/support(X)$. The problem of mining association rules is to find all the rules that satisfy a user-specified minimum support and minimum confidence, which can be decomposed into two subproblems:

1. Find all itemsets that have support above the user-specified minimum support. These itemset are called the *large itemsets*.

2. For each large itemset, derive all rules that have more than user-specified minimum confi-

dence as follows: for a large itemset X and any Y $(Y \subset X)$, if $support(X)/support(X - Y) \geq minimum\_confidence$, then the rule $X - Y \Rightarrow Y$ is derived.

For example, let $T_1 = \{1, 3, 4\}$, $T_2 = \{1, 2\}$, $T_3 = \{2, 4\}$, $T_4 = \{1, 2, 3, 5\}$, $T_5 = \{1, 3, 5\}$ be the transaction database. Let *minimum_support* and *minimum_confidence* be 60% and 70% respectively. Then, the first step generates the large itemsets $\{1\}, \{2\}, \{3\}, \{1, 3\}$. In the second step, an association rule $1 \Rightarrow 3$ ($support = 60\%, confidence = 75\%$) and $3 \Rightarrow 1$ ($support = 60\%, confidence = 100\%$) is derived.

After finding all large itemsets, association rules are derived in a straightforward manner. This second subproblem is not a big issue. However because of the large scale of transaction data sets used in database mining, the first subproblem is a nontrivial problem. Much of the research to date has focused on the first subproblem.

Here we briefly explain the Apriori algorithm for finding all large itemsets, proposed in [2], since the parallel algorithms to be proposed by us in section 3 are based on this algorithm. Figure 1 gives an overview of the algorithm, using the notation given in Table 1.

k-itemset	An itemset having k items.
L_k	Set of large k-itemsets, whose support is larger than user-specified minimum support.
C_k	Set of candidate k-itemsets, which is potentially large itemset

Table 1: Notation

In the first pass (pass 1), support_count for each item is counted by scanning the transaction database. Hereafter we prepare a field named support_count for each itemset, which is used to measure how many times the itemset appeared in transactions. Since itemset here contains just single item, each item has a support_count field. All the items which satisfy the minimum support are picked out. These items are called large 1-itemset (L_1). Here k-itemset is defines a set of k items. The second pass (pass 2), the 2-itemsets are generated using the large 1-itemset which is called the candidate 2-itemsets (C_2). Then the support_count of the candidate 2-itemsets is counted by scanning the transaction database. Here support_count of the itemset means the number of transactions which contain the itemset. At the end of scan-

$L_1 :=$ large 1-itemsets
$k := 2$
while $(L_{k-1} \neq \emptyset)$ **do**
  $C_k :=$ The candidates of size k generated from L_{k-1}
  forall transactions $t \in \mathcal{D}$
    Increment the support_count of all candidates in
    C_k that are contained in t
  $L_k :=$ All candidates in C_k which satisfy minimum
    support
  $k := k+1$
end
Answer $:= \bigcup_k L_k$

Figure 1: Apriori algorithm

ning the transaction data, the large 2-itemsets (L_2) which satisfy minimum support are determined. The following denotes the k-th iteration, pass k.

1. Generate candidate itemset:
   The candidate k-itemsets (C_k) are generated using large $(k-1)$-itemsets (L_{k-1}) which were determined in the previous pass (see Section 2.1).

2. Count support :
   The support_count for the candidate k-itemsets are counted by scanning the transaction database.

3. Determine large itemset:
   The candidate k-itemsets are checked for whether they satisfy the minimum support or not, the large k-itemsets (L_k) which satisfy the minimum support are determined.

4. The procedure terminates when the large itemset becomes empty. Otherwise $k := k + 1$ and goto "1".

2.1 Apriori Candidate Generation

The procedure for generating candidate k-itemsets using $(k-1)$-itemsets is as follows: Given a large $(k-1)$-itemset, we want to generate a superset of the set of all large k-itemsets. Candidate generation occurs in two steps. First, in the join step, join large $(k-1)$-itemset with $(k-1)$-itemset. Next, in the prune step, delete all of the itemsets in the candidate k-itemset where some of the $(k-1)$-subset of candidate itemsets are not in the large $(k-1)$-itemset.

3 Parallel Algorithms

In this section, we describe four parallel algorithms (NPA, SPA, HPA and HPA-ELD) for the first sub-problem, which we call count support processing here-

after, finding all large itemsets for shared-nothing parallel machines.

3.1 Algorithm Design

In the sequential algorithm, the count support processing requires the largest computation time, where the transaction database is scanned repeatedly and a large number of candidate itemsets are examined. We designed a parallel algorithm for count support processing.

If each processor can hold all of the candidate itemsets, parallelization is straightforward [2]. However for large scale transaction data sets, this assumption does not hold. Figure 2 shows the number of candidate itemsets and the large itemsets in each pass. These statistics were taken from the real point-of-sales data. In figure 2, the vertical axis is a log scale. The candi-

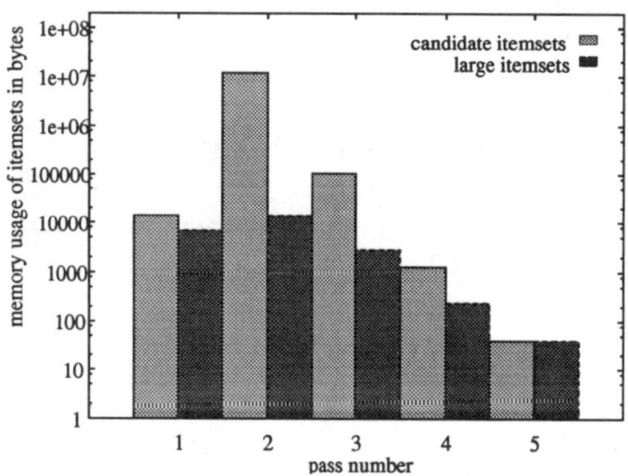

Figure 2: real point-of-sales data

date itemset of pass 2 is too large to fit within the local memory of a single processor. In NPA, the candidate itemsets are just copied amongst all the processors. In the case where all of the candidate itemsets do not fit within the local memory of a single processor, the candidate itemsets are partitioned into fragments, each of which fits in the memory size of a processor. Support count processing requires repetitive scanning transaction database. The remaining three algorithms, SPA, HPA and HPA-ELD, partition the candidate itemsets over the memory space of all the processors. Thus SPA, HPA and HPA-ELD can exploit the total system's memory effectively as the number of processors increases. For simplicity, we assume that the size of the candidate itemsets is larger than the size of local memory of single processor but is smaller than the sum of the memory of all the processors. It is easy

---

[2] We will later introduce an algorithm named NPA, where the reason why the parallelization is so easy will be clarified.

to extend this algorithm to handle candidate itemsets whose size exceeds the sum of all the processors memories.

3.2 Non Partitioned Apriori : NPA

In NPA, the candidate itemsets are copied over all the processors, each processor can work independently and the final statistics are gathered into a coordinator processor where minimum support conditions are examined. Figure 3 gives the behavior of pass k of the p-th processor in NPA, using the notation given in Table 2.

$C_1 :=$ All items
$\{C_1^d\} :=$ Partition C_1 into fragments each of which fits in a processor's local memory
for$(d = 1;\ d \le \lceil |C_1|/M \rceil;\ d++)$ **do**
  forall $t \in \mathcal{D}^p$ **do**
    Increment the support_count of all candidates in C_1^d that are contained in t
  end
end
Send the support_count of C_1^d to the coordinator
  /* Coordinator determine L_1^d which satisfy user-specified minimum support in C_1^d and broadcast L_1^d to all processors   */
Receive L_1^d from the coordinator
end
$\mathcal{L}_1 := \bigcup_d L_1^d$
$k := 2$
while $(L_{k-1} \ne \emptyset)$ **do**
  $C_k :=$ The candidates of size k generated from L_{k-1}
  $\{C_k^d\}(d = 1, \ldots, \lceil |C_k|/M \rceil)$
  $:=$ Partition C_k into fragments each of which fits in a processor's local memory
  for$(d = 1;\ d \le \lceil |C_k|/M \rceil;\ d++)$ **do**
    forall $t \in \mathcal{D}^p$ **do**
      Increment the support_count of all candidates in C_k^d that are contained in t
    end
    Send the support_count of C_k^d for to the coordinator
    /* Coordinator determine L_k^d which satisfy user-specified minimum support in C_k^d and broadcast L_1^d to all processors   */
    Receive L_k^d from the coordinator
  end
  $\mathcal{L}_k := \bigcup_d L_k^d$
  $k := k + 1$
end

Figure 3: NPA algorithm

Each processor works as follows:

1. Generate the candidate itemsets:

$\mathcal{L}_k$	Set of all the large k-itemsets.
$\mathcal{C}_k$	Set of all the candidate k-itemsets.
$|\mathcal{C}_k|$	The size of $\mathcal{C}_k$ in bytes.
M	The size of main memory in bytes.
$\mathcal{D}^p$	Transactions stored in the local disk of the p-th processor
C_k^d $(d = 1, \ldots, \lceil \frac{|C_k|}{M} \rceil)$ $(c_k = \bigcup_{d=1}^{\lceil \frac{|C_k|}{M} \rceil} c_k^d)$	Sets of fragment of candidate k-itemsets. Each fragment fits in the local memory of a processor.
$|C_k^d|$	The size of C_k^d in bytes.
L_k^d	Sets of large k-itemsets derived from C_k^d.

Table 2: Notation

  Each processor generates the candidate k-itemsets using the large $(k-1)$-itemsets, and insert it into the hash table.

2. Scan the transaction database and count the support_count value:
   Each processor reads the transaction database from its local disk, generates k-itemsets from the transaction and searches the hash table. If a hit occurs, increment its support_count value.

3. Determine the large itemsets:
   After reading all the transaction data, all processor's support_count are gathered into the coordinator and checked to determine whether the minimum support condition is satisfied or not.

4. If large k-itemset is empty, the algorithm terminates. Otherwise $k := k + 1$ and the coordinator broadcasts large k-itemsets to all the processors and goto "1".

If the size of all the candidate itemsets exceeds the local memory of a single processor, the candidate itemsets are partitioned into fragments, each of which can fits within the processor's local memory and the above process is repeated for each fragment. Figure 3, beginning at the while loop, shows the method by which each of the candidate itemsets are divided into fragments with each fragment being processed sequentially.

  Although this algorithm is simple and no transaction data are exchanged among processors in the second phase, the disk I/O cost becomes very large, since this algorithm reads the transaction database repeatedly if the candidate itemsets are too large to fit within the processor's local memory.

3.3 Simply Partitioned Apriori : SPA

In NPA, the candidate itemsets are not partitioned but just copied among the processors. However the candidate itemsets usually becomes too large to fit within the local memory of single processor, which generally occurs during the second pass ($k = 2$). SPA partitions the candidate itemsets equally over the memory space of all the processors. Thus it can exploit the aggregate memory of the systems, while memory efficiency is very low in copy based NPA.

Since the candidate itemsets are partitioned among the processors, each processor has to be broadcast its own transaction data to all the processors at second phase, while no such broadcast is required in NPA. Figure 4 gives the behavior of pass k by the p-th processor in SPA, using the notation in Table 3. Here we assume the size of candidate itemset is smaller than the size of sum of all the processor's memory. Extension of the algorithm to handle much larger candidate itemset is easy. We can divide the candidate itemsets into fragments like in NPA.

$\mathcal{L}_k$	Set of all the large k-itemsets.
C_k	Set of all the candidate k-itemsets.
$\mathcal{D}^p$	Transactions stored in the local disk of the p-th processor
C_k^p $(c_k = \bigcup_{p=1}^{N} c_k^p)$	Sets of candidate k-itemsets assigned the p-th processor (N means the number of processors)
L_k^p	Sets of large k-itemsets derived from C_k^p

Table 3: Notation

Each processor works as follows:

1. Generate the candidate itemsets:
   Each processor generates the candidate k-itemsets using the large $(k-1)$-itemsets and inserts a part of the candidate itemsets into its own hash table. The candidate k-itemsets are assigned to processors in a round-robin manner [3].

2. Scan the transaction database and count the support_count value:

---

[3] The k-itemsets are assigned equally to all of the processors in a round-robin manner. By round-robin we mean that the candidates are assigned to the processors in a cyclical manner with the i-th candidate assigned to processor i mod n, where n is the number of processors in the system.

$\{C_1^p\} :=$ All items assigned to the p-th processor
forall $t \in \mathcal{D}^p$ **do**
   Broadcast t to all the other processors
   Receive the transaction sent from the other processors and increment the support_count of all candidates that are contained in received transaction
end
$\{L_1^p\} :=$ All the candidates in C_1^p which satisfy user-specified minimum support
  /* Each processor can determine individually whether assigned candidate k-itemset satisfy user-specified minimum */ support or not
Send L_1^p to the coordinator
  /* Coordinator make up $\mathcal{L}_1 := \bigcup_p L_1^p$ and broadcast it to all the other processors */
Receive $\mathcal{L}_1$ from the coordinator
while $(\mathcal{L}_{k-1} \neq \emptyset)$ **do**
   $\{C_k^p\} :=$ The candidates of size k, assigned to the p-th processor, which is generated from L_{k-1}
  forall $t \in \mathcal{D}^p$ **do**
     Broadcast t to all the processors
     Receive the transaction sent from the other processors and increment the support_count of all candidates that are contained in the received transaction
  end
  $\{L_k^p\} :=$ All the candidates in C_k^p which satisfy the user-specified minimum support
  Send L_k^p to the coordinator
  /* Coordinator make up $\mathcal{L}_k := \bigcup_p L_k^p$ and broadcast it to all the processors */
  Receive $\mathcal{L}_k$ from the coordinator
  $k := k + 1$
end

Figure 4: SPA algorithm

Each processor reads the transaction database from its local disk and also broadcasts it to all the other processors. For each transaction entry, when read from its own disk or received from another processors, the support_count is incremented in the same way as in NPA.

3. Determine the large itemsets:
   After reading all the transaction data, each processor can determine individually whether each candidate k-itemset satisfy user-specified minimum support or not. Each processor send L_k^p to the coordinator, where $\mathcal{L}_k := \bigcup_p L_k^p$ are derived.

4. If large k-itemset is empty, the algorithm terminates. Otherwise $k := k + 1$ and the coordinator broadcasts large k-itemsets to all the processors and goto "1".

Although this algorithm is simple and easy to implement, the communication cost becomes very large, since this algorithm broadcasts all the transaction data at second phase.

3.4 Hash Partitioned Apriori : HPA

HPA partitions the candidate itemsets among the processors using the hash function like in the hash join, which eliminates broadcasting of all the transaction data and can reduce the comparison workload significantly. Figure 5 gives the behavior of pass k by the p-th processor in HPA, using the notation in Table 3.

Each processor works as follows:

1. Generate the candidate itemsets:
   Each processor generates the candidate k-itemset using the large $(k-1)$-itemsets, applies the hash function and determines the destination processor ID. If the ID is its own, insert it into the hash table. If not, it is discarded.

2. Scan the transaction database and count the support_count:
   Each processor reads the transaction database from its local disk. Generates k-itemsets from that transaction and applies the same hash function used in phase 1. Derives the destination processor ID and sends the k-itemset to it. For the itemsets received from the other processors and those locally generated whose ID equals the processor's own ID, search the hash table. If hit, increment its support_count value.

3. Determine the large itemset:
   Same as in SPA.

$\{C_1^p\} :=$ All items assigned to the p-th processor based on hashed value
forall $t \in \mathcal{D}^p$ **do**
  forall items $x \in t$ **do**
    Determine the destination processor ID by applying the same hash function which is used in item partitioning, and send that item to it. If it is its own ID, increment the support_count for the item. Receive the item from the other processors and increment the support_count for that item
  end
end
$\{L_1^p\} :=$ All the candidates in C_1^p with minimum support
  /* Each processor can determine individually whether assigned candidate k-itemset satisfy user-specified minimum support or not   */
Send L_1^p to the coordinator
  /* Coordinator make up $\mathcal{L}_1 := \bigcup_p L_1^p$ and broadcast to all the processors   */
Receive $\mathcal{L}_1$ from the coordinator
while $(\mathcal{L}_{k-1} \neq \emptyset)$ **do**
  $\{C_k^p\} :=$ All the candidate k-itemsets, whose hashed value corresponding to the p-th processor
  forall $t \in \mathcal{D}^p$ **do**
    forall k-itemset $x \in t$ **do**
      Determine the destination processor ID by applying the same hash function which is used in item partitioning, and send that k-itemset to it. If it is its own ID, increment the support_count for the itemset.
      Receive k-itemset from the other processors and increment the support_count for that itemset
    end
  end
  $\{L_k^p\} :=$ All the candidates in C_k^p with minimum support
  Send L_k^p to the coordinator
  /* Coordinator make up $\mathcal{L}_k := \bigcup_p L_k^p$ and broadcast to all the processors   */
  Receive $\mathcal{L}_k$ from the coordinator
  $k := k + 1$
end

Figure 5: HPA algorithm

4. If large k-itemset is empty, the algorithm terminates. Otherwise $k := k + 1$ and the coordinator broadcasts large k-itemsets to all the processors and goto "1".

3.5 HPA with Extremely Large Itemset Duplication : HPA-ELD

In case the size of candidate itemset is smaller than the available system memory, HPA does not use the remaining free space. However HPA-ELD does utilize the memory by copying some of the itemsets. The itemsets are sorted based on their frequency of appearance. HPA-ELD chooses the most frequently occurring itemsets and copies them over the processors so that all the memory space is used, which contributes to further reduce the communication among the processor. In HPA, it is generally difficult to achieve a flat workload distribution. If the transaction data is highly skewed, that is, some of the itemsets appear very frequently in the transaction data, the processor which has such itemsets will receive a much larger amount of data than the others. This might become a system bottleneck. In real situations, the skew of items is easily discovered. In retail applications certain items such as milk and eggs appear more frequently than others. HPA-ELD can handle this problem effectively since it treats the frequently occurring itemset entries in a special way.

HPA-ELD copies such frequently occurring itemsets among the processors and counts the support_count locally like in NPA. In the first phase, when the processors generate the candidate k-itemset using the large $(k-1)$-itemsets, if the sum of the support values for each large itemset exceeds the given threshold, it is inserted in all the processor's hash table. The remaining candidate itemsets are partitioned as in HPA. The threshold is determined so that all of the available memory can be fully utilized using sort. After reading all the transaction data, all processor's support_count are gathered and checked whether it satisfies the minimum support condition or not. Since most of the algorithm steps are equal to HPA, we omit a detailed description of HPA-ELD.

4 Performance Evaluation

Figure 6 shows the architecture of Fujitsu AP1000DDV system, on which we have measured the performance of the proposed parallel algorithms for mining association rules, NPA, SPA, HPA and HPA-ELD. AP1000DDV employs a shared-nothing architecture. A 64 processor system was used, where each processor, called cell, is a 25MHz SPARC with 16MB local memory and a 1GB local disk drive. Each pro-

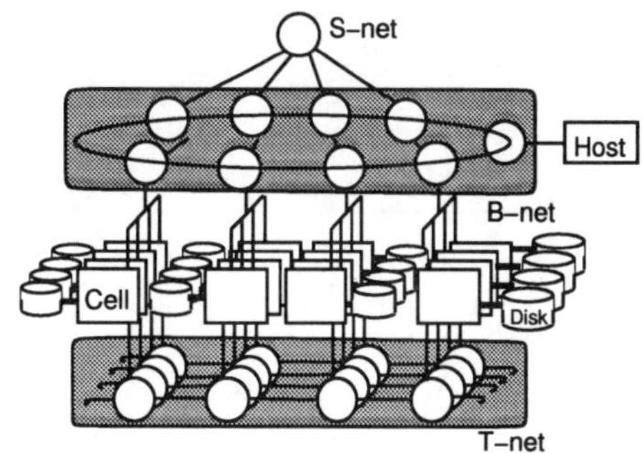

Figure 6: Organization of the AP1000DDV system

$	\mathcal{D}	$	the number of transactions
$	t	$	the average number of items in par-transactions
$	I	$	the average number of items in maximal potentially large itemsets

Name	$|t|$	$|I|$	$|\mathcal{D}|$	Size
t10.I4	10	4	2048K	100MB
t15.I4	15	4	2048K	145MB
t20.I4	20	4	2048K	187MB

Table 4: Parameters of data sets

cessor is connected to three independent networks (T-net, B-net and S-net). The communication between processors is done via a torus mesh network called the T-net, and broadcast communication is done via the B-net. In addition, a special network for barrier synchronization, called the S-net is provided.

To evaluate the performance of the four algorithms, synthetic data emulating retail transactions is used, where the generation procedure is based on the method described in [2]. Table 4 shows the meaning of the various parameters and the characteristics of the data set used in the experiments.

4.1 Measurement of Execution Time

Figure 7 shows the execution time of the four proposed algorithms using three different data sets with varying minimum support values. $16(4 \times 4)$ processors are used in these experiments. Transaction data is evenly spread over the processor's local disks. In these experiments, each parallel algorithm is adopted only for pass 2, the remaining passes are performed using NPA, since the single processor's memory cannot hold the entire candidate itemsets only for pass 2 and if it fits NPA is most efficient.

HPA and HPA-ELD significantly outperforms SPA.

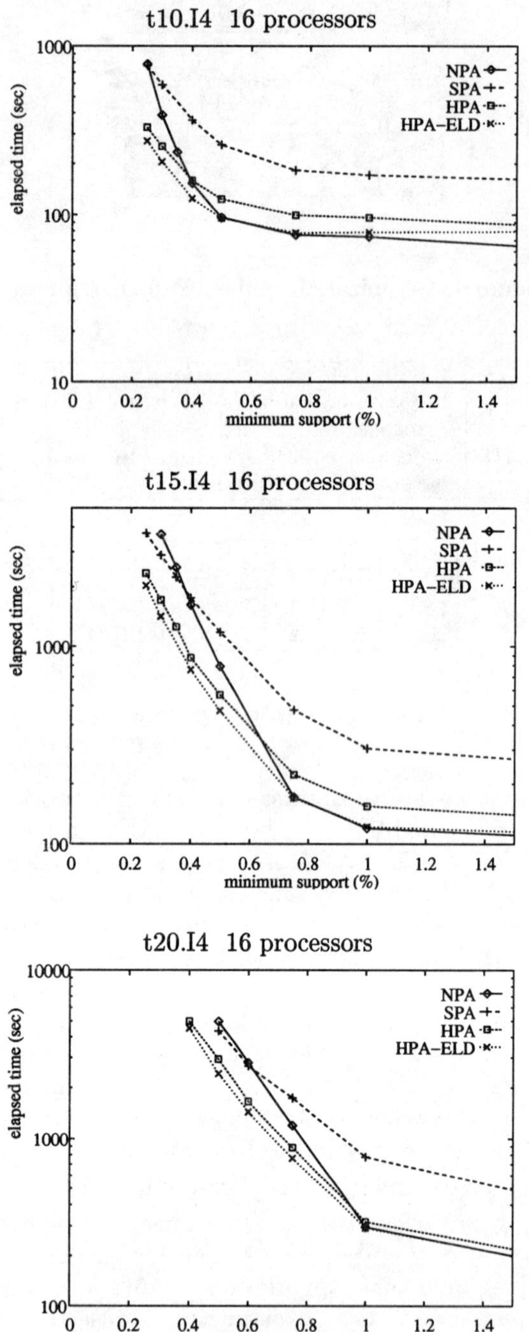

Figure 7: Execution time varying minimum support value

Since all transaction data is broadcast to all of the processors in SPA, its communication costs are much larger in SPA than in HPA and HPA-ELD where the data is not broadcasted but transfered to just one processor determined by a hash function. In addition SPA transmits the transaction data, while HPA and HPA-ELD transmit the itemsets, which further reduces the communication costs.

In NPA, the execution time increases sharply when the minimum support becomes small. Since the candidate itemsets becomes large for small minimum support, the single processor's memory cannot hold the entire candidate itemsets. NPA has to divide the candidate itemsets into fragments. Processors have to scan the transaction data repetitively for each fragment, which significantly increases the execution time.

4.2 Communication Cost Analysis

Here we analyze the communication costs of each algorithm. Since the size of the transaction data is usually much larger than that of the candidate itemset, we focus on the transaction data transfer. In NPA, the candidate itemsets are initially copied over all the processors, which incurs processor communication. In addition during the last phase of the processing, each processor sends the support count statistics to the coordinator where the minimum support condition is examined. This also incurs communications overhead. But here we ignore such overhead and concentrate on the transaction data transfer for SPA and HPA in second phase.

In SPA, each processor broadcasts all transaction data to all the other processors. The total amount of communication data of SPA at pass k can be expressed as follows.

$$M_k^{SPA} = \sum_{p=1}^{N} \sum_{i=1}^{T_p} t_{ip} \times (N-1)$$
$$\simeq |t| \times (N-1) \times |\mathcal{D}| \qquad (1)$$

where

p	processor ID ($p = 1, 2, \ldots, N$)
N	the number of processors
t_{ip}	the number of items in i-th transaction of p-th processor
T_p	the number of p-th processor's transactions
$\mid\mathcal{D}\mid$	the number of all the transactions ($\mid\mathcal{D}\mid = \sum_p T_p$)

In HPA, the itemsets of the transaction are transmitted to the limited number of processors instead of broadcasting. The number of candidates is dependent on the data synthesized by the generator. The total amount of communication for HPA at pass k can be expressed as follows.

$$M_k^{HPA} = \sum_{p=1}^{N} \sum_{i=1}^{T_p} t_{ip} C_k \times k \times \alpha_{ip}^k$$
$$\simeq |t| C_k \times k \times |\alpha^k| \times |\mathcal{D}| \qquad (2)$$

One transaction potentially generate $t_{ip} C_k$ candidates. However in practice most of them are filtered out, as is denoted by the parameter α_{ip}^k. Since α is usually small[4], $M_k^{SPA} \gg M_k^{HPA}$. Since it is difficult to derive α, we measured the amount of data received by each processor. Figure 8 shows the total amounts of received messages of SPA, HPA and HPA-ELD where t15.I4 transaction data was used with 0.4% minimum support. As you can see in Figure 8, the amount of messages received of HPA is much smaller then that of SPA. In HPA-ELD, the amount of messages received is further reduced, since a part of the candidate itemset is handled separately and the itemsets which correspond to them are not transmitted but just locally processed.

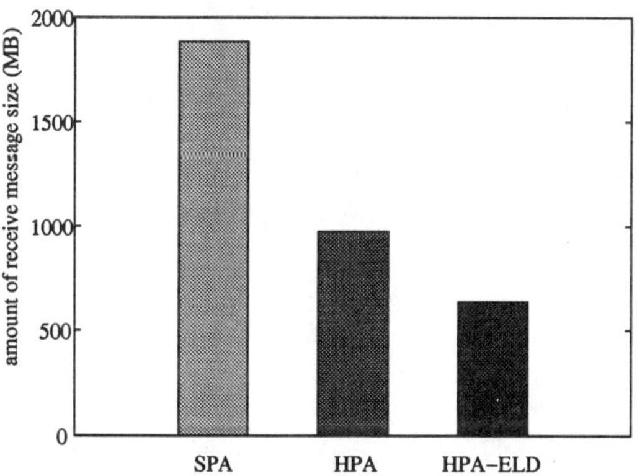

Figure 8: the amount of messages received (pass 2)

4.3 Search Cost Analysis

In the second phase, the hash table which consists of the candidate itemsets are probed for each transaction itemset.

---

[4]If the number of processors is very small and the number of items in transaction is large, then M_k^{HPA} could be larger than M_k^{SPA}. With reasonable number of processors, this does not happen as you can see in Figure 8. We are currently doing experiments on mining association rules with item's classification hierarchy, where combination of items becomes much larger than the ordinary mining association rules.

When α_k increases, M_k^{HPA} tends to increase as well. We will report on this case in a future paper.

In NPA, the number of probes at pass k can be expressed as follows.

$$S_k^{NPA} = \left\lceil \frac{CAN}{M} \right\rceil \sum_{p=1}^{N} \sum_{i=1}^{T_p} t_{ip} C_k \times \alpha_{ip}^k$$
$$\simeq |t| C_k \times |\alpha^k| \times |\mathcal{D}| \times \left\lceil \frac{CAN}{M} \right\rceil \qquad (3)$$

where

CAN	the amount of the candidate itemset in bytes
M	the size of main memory of a single processor in bytes

In NPA, if the candidate itemsets are too large to fit in a single processor's memory, the candidate itemsets are divided and the supports are counted by scanning the transaction database repeatedly.

In SPA, every processor must process all the transaction data. The number of searches at pass k can be expressed as follows.

$$S_k^{SPA} = N \times \sum_{p=1}^{N} \sum_{i=1}^{T_p} t_{ip} C_k \times \alpha_{ip}^k$$
$$\simeq |t| C_k \times |\alpha^k| \times |\mathcal{D}| \times N \qquad (4)$$

In HPA and HPA-ELD, the number of searches at pass k can be expressed as follows.

$$S_k^{HPA} = \sum_{p=1}^{N} \sum_{i=1}^{T_p} t_{ip} C_k \times \alpha_{ip}^k$$
$$\simeq |t| C_k \times |\alpha^k| \times |\mathcal{D}| \qquad (5)$$

The search cost of HPA and HPA-ELD is always smaller than SPA. It is apparent that $S_k^{HPA} < S_k^{SPA}$. Not only the communication cost but also search cost also can be reduced significantly by employing hash based algorithms, which is quite similar to the way in which the hash join algorithm works much better than nested loop algorithms. In NPA, the search cost depends on the size of the candidate itemsets. If the candidate itemset becomes too large, S_k^{NPA} could be larger than S_k^{SPA}. But if it fits, $S_k^{NPA} \simeq S_k^{HPA} < S_k^{SPA}$, that is, the search cost is much smaller than SPA and almost equal to HPA. Figure 9 shows the search cost of the three algorithms for each pass, where the t15.I4 data set is used under 16 processors with the minimum support 0.4%. In the experimental results we have so far shown, all passes except pass 2 adopts NPA algorithm. We applied different algorithms only for pass 2, which is computationally heaviest part of the total processing. However, here in order to focus on the search cost of individual algorithm more clearly, each algorithm is applied for all passes. The cost of

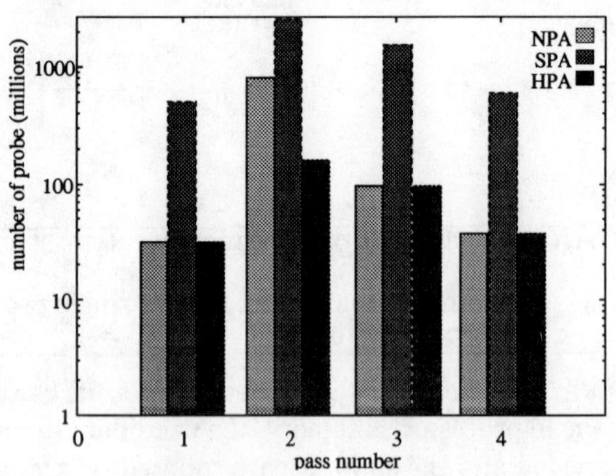

Figure 9: the search cost of SPA, NPA and HPA

NPA changes drastically for pass 2. The search cost of NPA is highly dependent on the size of available main memory. If memory is insufficient, NPA's performance deteriorates significantly due to the cost increase at pass 2. In Figure 9, the search cost of NPA is less than SPA. However as we explained before, it incurred a lot of additional I/O cost. Therefore the total execution time of NPA is much longer than that of SPA.

4.4 Comparison of HPA and HPA-ELD

In this section, the performance comparison between HPA and HPA-ELD is described. In HPA-ELD, we treat the most frequently appearing itemsets separately. In order to determine which itemset we should pick up, we use the statistics accumulated during pass 1. As the number of pass increases, the size of the candidate itemsets decreases. Thus we focused on pass 2. The number of the candidate itemsets to be separated is adjusted so that sum of non-duplicated itemsets and duplicated itemsets would just fit in the available memory.

Figure 10 shows the execution time of HPA and HPA-ELD for t15.I4 varying the minimum support value on a 16 processors system. HPA-ELD is always faster than HPA. The smaller the minimum support, the larger the ratio of the difference between the execution times of the two algorithms becomes. As the minimum support value decreases, the number of candidate itemsets and the count of support increases. The candidate itemsets which are frequently found cause large amounts of communication. The performance of HPA is degraded by this high communications traffic.

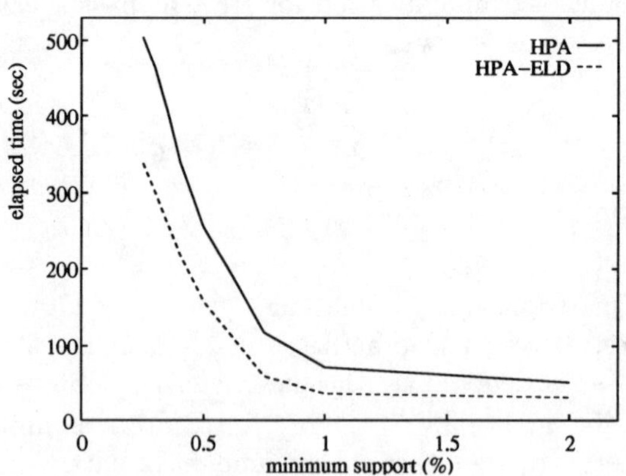

Figure 10: Execution time of HPA and HPA-ELD at pass 2

Figure 11 shows the number of probes in each processor for HPA and HPA-ELD for t15.I4 using a 16 processor system for pass 2. We picked up an example which is highly skewed. Horizontal axis denotes processor ID. In HPA, the distribution of the number

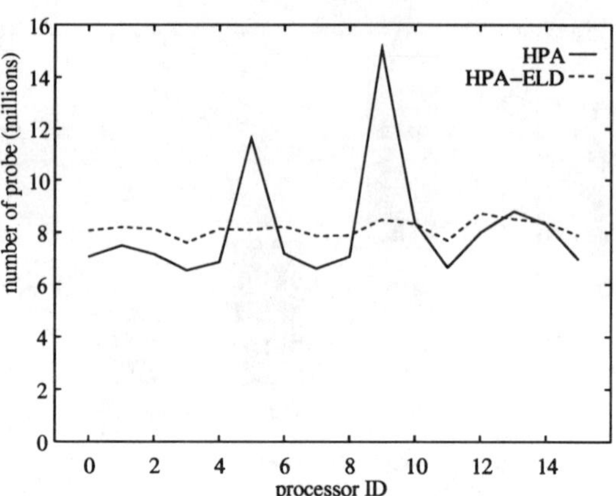

Figure 11: The number of search of HPA and HPA-ELD at pass 2

of probes is not flat. Since each candidate itemset is allocated to just one processor, the large amount of messages concentrate at a certain processor which has many candidate itemsets occurring frequently.

In HPA-ELD, the number of probes is comparatively flat. HPA-ELD handle certain candidate itemsets separately, thus reducing the influence of the data skew. However, as you can see in Figure 11, there still remain the deviation of the load amongst processors. If we parallelize the mining over more than 64 processors, we have to introduces more sophisticated load balancing mechanism, which requires further investigation.

4.5 Speedup

Figure 12 shows the speedup ratio for pass 2 varying the number of processors used, 16, 32, 48 and 64, where the curve is normalized with the 16 processor execution time. The minimum support value was set to 0.4%.

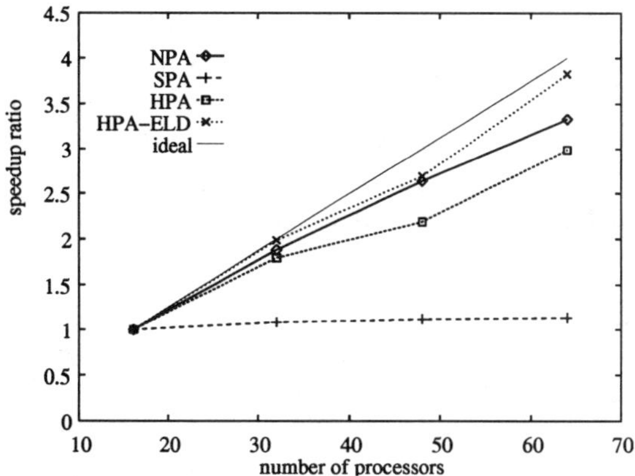

Figure 12: Speedup curve

NPA, HPA and HPA-ELD attain much higher linearity than SPA. HPA-ELD, an extension of HPA for extremely large itemset decomposition further increases the linearity.

HPA-ELD attains satisfactory speed up ratio. This algorithm just focuses on the item distribution of the transaction file and picks up the extremely frequently occurring items. Transferring such items could result in network hot spots. HPA-ELD tries not to send such items but to process them locally. Such a small modification to the original HPA algorithm could improve the linearity substantially.

4.6 Effect of increasing transaction database size (Sizeup)

Figure 13 shows the effect of increasing transaction database size as the number of transactions is increased from 256,000 to 2 million transactions. We used the data set t15.I4. The behavior of the results does not change with increased database size. The minimum support value was set to 0.4%. The number of processors is kept at 16. As shown, each of the parallel algorithms attains linearity.

5 Summary and related work

In this paper, we proposed four parallel algorithms for mining association rules. A summary of the four

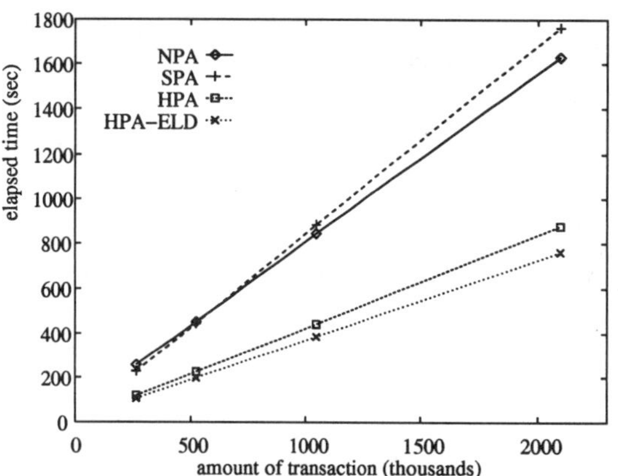

Figure 13: Sizeup curve

algorithms is shown in Table 5. In NPA, the candidate itemsets are just copied amongst all the processors. Each processor works on the entire candidate itemsets. NPA requires no data transfer when the supports are counted. However in the case where the entire candidate itemsets do not fit within the memory of a single processor, the candidate itemsets are divided and the supports are counted by scanning the transaction database repeatedly. Thus Disk I/O cost of NPA is high. PDM, proposed in [6] is the same as NPA, which copies the candidate itemsets among all the processors. Disk I/O for PDM should be also high.

The remaining three algorithms, SPA, HPA and HPA-ELD, partition the candidate itemsets over the memory space of all the processors. Because it better exploits the total system's memory, disk I/O cost is low. SPA arbitrarily partitions the candidate itemsets equally among the processors. Since each processor broadcasts its local transaction data to all other processors, the communication cost is high. HPA and HPA-ELD partition the candidate itemsets using a hash function, which eliminates the need for transaction data broadcasting and can reduce the comparison workload significantly. HPA-ELD detects frequently occurring itemsets and handles them separately, which can reduce the influence of the workload skew.

6 Conclusions

Since mining association rules requires several scans of the transaction file, its computational requirements are too large for a single processor to have a reasonable response time. This motivates our research.

In this paper, we proposed four different parallel algorithms for mining association rules on a shared-nothing parallel machine, and examined their viabil-

	NPA	SPA	HPA	HPA-ELD
Candidate itemset	copy	partition		partition (partially copy)
I/O cost	high	low		
Communication cost	–	high		low
Skew handling		×		○

Table 5: characteristics of algorithms

ity through implementation on a 64 node parallel machine, the Fujitsu AP1000DDV.

If a single processor can hold all the candidate itemsets, parallelization is straightforward. It is just sufficient to partition the transaction over the processors and for each processor to process the allocated transaction data in parallel. We named this algorithm NPA. However when we try to do large scale data mining against a very large transaction file, the candidate itemsets become too large to fit within the main memory of a single processor. In addition to the size of a transaction file, a small minimum support also increases the size of the candidate itemsets. As we decrease the minimum support, computation time grows rapidly, but in many cases we can discover more interesting association rules.

SPA, HPA and HPA-ELD not only partition the transaction file but partition the candidate itemsets among all the processors. We implemented these algorithms on a shard-nothing parallel machine. Performance evaluations show that the best algorithm, HPA-ELD, attains good linearity on speedup by fully utilizing all the available memory space, which is also effective for skew handling. At present, we are doing the parallelization of mining generalized association rules described in [9], which includes the taxonomy (is-a hierarchy). Each item belongs to its own class hierarchy. In such mining, associations between the higher class and the lower class are also examined. Thus the candidate itemset space becomes much larger and its computation time also takes even longer than the naive single level association mining. Parallel processing is essential for such heavy mining processing.

Acknowledgments

This research is partially supported as a priority research program by ministry of education. We would like to thank the Fujitsu Parallel Computing Research Center for allowing us to use their AP1000DDV systems.

References

[1] R.Agrawal, T.Imielinski, and A.Swami: "Mining Association Rules between Sets of Items in Large Databases", In *Proc. of the 1993 ACM SIGMOD International Conference on Management of Data*, pp207-216, May 1993.

[2] R.Agrawal, and R.Srikant: "Fast Algorithms for Mining Association Rules", In *Proc. of the 20th International Conference on Very Large Data Bases*, pp.487-499, September 1994.

[3] J.S.Park, M.-S.Chen, and P.S.Yu: "An Effective Hash-Based Algorithm for Mining Association Rules", In *Proc. of the 1995 ACM SIGMOD International Conference on the Management of Data*, SIGMOD Record Vol.24, pp.175-186, June 1995.

[4] H.Mannila, H.Toivonen, and A.I.Verkamo: "Efficient Algorithms for Discovering Association Rules", In *KDD-94:AAAI Workshop on Knowledge Discovery in Databases*, pp.181-192, July 1994.

[5] A.Savasere, E.Omiecinski, and S.Navathe: "An Effective Algorithm for Mining Association Rules in Large Databases", In *Proc. of the 21th International Conference on Very Large Data Bases*, pp.432-444, September 1995.

[6] J.S.Park, M.-S.Chen, and P.S.Yu: "Efficient Parallel Data Mining for Association Rules", In *Proc. of the 4th International Conference on Information and Knowledge Management*, pp.31-36, November 1995.

[7] T.Shintani, and M.Kitsuregawa: "Consideration on Parallelization of Database Mining", In *Institute of Electronics, Information and Communication Engineering Japan (SIG-CPSY95-88)*, Technical Report, Vol.95, No.47, pp.57-62, December 1995.

[8] T.Shimizu, T.Horie, and H.Ishihata: "Performance Evaluation of the AP1000 -Effects of message handling, broadcast, and barrier synchronization on benchmark performance-", In *SWoPP'92(92-ARC-95) Information Processing Society of Japan*, Vol.92, No.64, 1992.

[9] R.Srikant and R.Agrawal: "Mining Generalized Association Rules", In *Proc. of the 21th International Conference on Very Large Data Bases*, pp.407-419, September 1995.

A Fast Distributed Algorithm for Mining Association Rules *

David W. Cheung[†]   Jiawei Han[‡]   Vincent T. Ng[††]   Ada W. Fu[‡‡]   Yongjian Fu[‡]

[†] Department of Computer Science, The University of Hong Kong, Hong Kong. Email: dcheung@cs.hku.hk.

[‡] School of Computing Science, Simon Fraser University, Canada. Email: han@cs.sfu.ca.

[††] Department of Computing, Hong Kong Polytechnic University, Hong Kong. Email: cstyng@comp.polyu.edu.hk.

[‡‡] Department of Computer Science and Engineering, The Chinese University of Hong Kong, Hong Kong. Email: adafu@cs.cuhk.hk.

Abstract

With the existence of many large transaction databases, the huge amounts of data, the high scalability of distributed systems, and the easy partition and distribution of a centralized database, it is important to investigate efficient methods for distributed mining of association rules. This study discloses some interesting relationships between locally large and globally large itemsets and proposes an interesting distributed association rule mining algorithm, FDM (Fast Distributed Mining of association rules), which generates a small number of candidate sets and substantially reduces the number of messages to be passed at mining association rules. Our performance study shows that FDM has a superior performance over the direct application of a typical sequential algorithm. Further performance enhancement leads to a few variations of the algorithm.

1 Introduction

An association rule is a rule which implies certain association relationships among a set of objects (such as "occur together" or "one implies the other") in a database. Since finding interesting association rules in databases may disclose some useful patterns for decision support, selective marketing, financial forecast, medical diagnosis, and many other applications, it has attracted a lot of attention in recent data mining research [5]. Mining association rules may require iterative scanning of large transaction or relational databases which is quite costly in processing. Therefore, efficient mining of association rules in transaction and/or relational databases has been studied substantially [1, 2, 4, 8, 10, 11, 12, 14, 15].

Previous studies examined efficient mining of association rules from many different angles. An influential association rule mining algorithm, Apriori [2], has been developed for rule mining in large transaction databases. A DHP algorithm [10] is an extension of Apriori using a hashing technique. The scope of the study has also been extended to efficient mining of sequential patterns [3], generalized association rules [14], multiple-level association rules [8], quantitative association rules [15], etc. Maintenance of discovered association rules by incremental updating has been studied in [4]. Although these studies are on sequential data mining techniques, algorithms for parallel mining of association rules have been proposed recently [11, 1].

We feel that the development of distributed algorithms for efficient mining of association rules has its unique importance, based on the following reasoning. (1) Databases or data warehouses [13] may store a huge amount of data. Mining association rules in such databases may require substantial processing power, and distributed system is a possible solution. (2) Many large databases are distributed in nature. For example, the huge number of transaction records of hundreds of Sears department stores are likely to be stored at different sites. This observation motivates us to study efficient distributed algorithms for mining association rules in databases. This study may also shed new light on parallel data mining. Furthermore, a distributed mining algorithm can also be used to mine association rules in a single large database by partitioning the database among a set of sites and processing the task in a distributed manner. The high flexibility, scalability, low cost performance ratio, and easy connectivity of a distributed system makes it an ideal platform for mining association rules.

In this study, we assume that the database to be studied is a transaction database although the method can be easily extended to relational databases as well. The database consists of a huge number of transaction records, each with a transaction identifier (TID) and a set of data items. Further, we assume that the

---

*The research of the first author was supported in part by RGC (the Hong Kong Research Grants Council) grant 338/065/0026. The research of the second author was supported in part by the research grant NSERC-A3723 from the Natural Sciences and Engineering Research Council of Canada, the research grant NCE:IRIS/PRECARN-HMI5 from the Networks of Centres of Excellence of Canada, and a research grant from Hughes Research Laboratories.

database is "horizontally" partitioned (i.e., grouped by transactions) and allocated to the sites in a distributed system which communicate by message passing. Based on these assumptions, we examine distributed mining of association rules. It has been well known that the major cost of mining association rules is the computation of the set of *large itemsets* (i.e., *frequently occurring sets of items*, see Section 2.1) in the database [2]. Distributed computing of large itemsets encounters some new problems. One may compute *locally large* itemsets easily, but a locally large itemset may not be *globally large*. Since it is very expensive to broadcast the whole data set to other sites, one option is to broadcast all the counts of all the itemsets, no matter locally large or small, to other sites. However, a database may contain enormous combinations of itemsets, and it will involve passing a huge number of messages.

Based on our observation, there exist some interesting properties between locally large and globally large itemsets. One should maximally take advantages of such properties to reduce the number of messages to be passed and confine the substantial amount of processing to local sites. As mentioned before, two algorithms for parallel mining of association rules have been proposed. The two proposed algorithms PDM and Count Distribution (CD) are designed for share-nothing parallel systems [11, 1]. However, they can also be adapted to distributed environment. We have proposed an efficient distributed data mining algorithm FDM (Fast Distributed Mining of association rules), which has the following distinct feature in comparison with these two proposed parallel mining algorithms.

1. The generation of candidate sets is in the same spirit of Apriori. However, some interesting relationships between locally large sets and globally large ones are explored to generate a smaller set of candidate sets at each iteration and thus reduce the number of messages to be passed.

2. After the candidate sets have been generated, two pruning techniques, *local pruning* and *global pruning*, are developed to prune away some candidate sets at each individual sites.

3. In order to determine whether a candidate set is large, our algorithm requires only $O(n)$ messages for support count exchange, where n is the number of sites in the network. This is much less than a straight adaptation of Apriori, which requires $O(n^2)$ messages.

Notice that several different combinations of the local and global prunings can be adopted in FDM. We studied three versions of FDM: *FDM-LP, FDM-LUP,* and *FDM-LPP* (see Section 4), with similar

framework but different combinations of pruning techniques. FDM-LP only explores the *local pruning*; FDM-LUP does both local pruning and the *upper-bound-pruning*; and FDM-LPP does both local pruning and the *polling-site-pruning*.

Extensive experiments have been conducted to study the performance of FDM and compare it against the Count Distribution algorithm. The study demonstrates the efficiency of the distributed mining algorithm.

The remaining of the paper is organized as follows. The tasks of mining association rules in sequential as well as distributed environments are defined in Section 2. In Section 3, techniques for distributed mining of association rules and some important results are discussed. The algorithms for different versions of FDM are presented in Section 4. A performance study is reported in Section 5. Our discussions and conclusions are presented respectively in Sections 6 and 7.

2 Problem Definition

2.1 Sequential Algorithm for Mining Association Rules

Let $I = \{i_1, i_2, \ldots, i_m\}$ be a set of *items*. Let DB be a database of transactions, where each transaction T consists of a set of items such that $T \subseteq I$. Given an *itemset* $X \subseteq I$, a transaction T *contains* X if and only if $X \subseteq T$. An *association rule* is an implication of the form $X \Rightarrow Y$, where $X \subseteq I$, $Y \subseteq I$ and $X \cap Y = \emptyset$. The association rule $X \Rightarrow Y$ holds in DB with *confidence c* if the probability of a transaction in DB which contains X also contains Y is c. The association rule $X \Rightarrow Y$ has *support s* in DB if the probability of a transaction in DB contains both X and Y is s. The task of mining association rules is to find all the association rules whose support is larger than a *minimum support threshold* and whose confidence is larger than a *minimum confidence threshold*.

For an itemset X, its *support* is the percentage of transactions in DB which contains X, and its *support count*, denoted by $X.sup$, is the number of transactions in DB containing X. An itemset X is *large* (or more precisely, *frequently occurring*) if its support is no less than the minimum support threshold. An itemset of size k is called a *k-itemset*. It has been shown that the problem of mining association rules can be reduced to two subproblems [2]: (1) *find all large itemsets for a given minimum support threshold*, and (2) *generate the association rules from the large itemsets found*. Since (1) dominates the overall cost of mining association rules, the research has been focused on how to develop efficient methods to solve the first subproblem [2].

An interesting algorithm, *Apriori* [2], has been proposed for computing large itemsets at mining association rules in a transaction database. There have been many studies on mining association rules using sequential algorithms in centralized databases (e.g.,

[10, 14, 8, 12, 4, 15]), which can be viewed as variations or extensions to Apriori. For example, as an extension to Apriori, the DHP algorithm [10] uses a direct hashing technique to eliminate some size-2 candidate sets in the Apriori algorithm.

2.2 Distributed Algorithm for Mining Association Rules

We examine the mining of association rules in a distributed environment. Let DB be a database with D transactions. Assume that there are n sites $S_1, S_2, \ldots, S_n$ in a distributed system and the database DB is partitioned over the n sites into $\{DB_1, DB_2, \ldots, DB_n\}$, respectively.

Let the size of the partitions DB_i be D_i, for $i = 1, \ldots, n$. Let $X.sup$ and $X.sup_i$ be the support counts of an itemset X in DB and DB_i, respectively. $X.sup$ is called the *global support count*, and $X.sup_i$ the *local support count* of X at site S_i. For a given minimum support threshold s, X is *globally large* if $X.sup \geq s \times D$; correspondingly, X is *locally large* at site S_i, if $X.sup_i \geq s \times D_i$. In the following, L denotes the globally large itemsets in DB, and $L_{(k)}$ the globally large k-itemsets in L. The essential task of a distributed association rule mining algorithm is to find the globally large itemsets L.

For comparison, we outline the Count Distribution (CD) algorithm as the follows [1]. The algorithm is an adaptation of the Apriori algorithm in the distributed case. At each iteration, CD generates the candidate sets at every site by applying the Apriori_gen function on the set of large itemsets found at the previous iteration. Every site then computes the local support counts of all these candidate sets and broadcasts them to all the other sites. Subsequently, all the sites can find the globally large itemsets for that iteration, and then proceed to the next iteration.

3 Techniques for Distributed Data Mining

3.1 Generation of Candidate Sets

It is important to observe some interesting properties related to large itemsets in distributed environments since such properties may substantially reduce the number of messages to be passed across network at mining association rules.

There is an important relationship between large itemsets and the sites in a distributed database: *every globally large itemsets must be locally large at* some *site(s)*. If an itemset X is *both globally large and locally large* at a site S_i, X is called **gl-large** at site S_i. The set of gl-large itemsets at a site will form a basis for the site to generate its own candidate sets.

Two monotonic properties can be easily observed from the locally large and gl-large itemsets. First, if an itemset X is locally large at a site S_i, then all of its subsets are also locally large at site S_i. Secondly, if an itemset X is gl-large at a site S_i, then all of its subsets are also gl-large at site S_i. Notice that a similar relationship exists among the large itemsets in the centralized case. Following is an important result based on which an effective technique for candidate sets generation in the distributed case is developed.

Lemma 1 *If an itemset X is globally large, there exists a site S_i, $(1 \leq i \leq n)$, such that X and all its subsets are gl-large at site S_i.*
Proof. If X is not locally large at any site, then $X.sup_i < s \times D_i$ for all $i = 1, \ldots, n$. Therefore, $X.sup < s \times D$, and X cannot be globally large. By contradiction, X must be locally large at some site S_i, and hence X is gl-large at S_i. Consequently, all the subsets of X must also be gl-large at S_i. $\square$

We use GL_i to denote the set of gl-large itemsets at site S_i, and $GL_{i(k)}$ to denote the set of gl-large k-itemsets at site S_i. It follows from Lemma 1 that if $X \in L_{(k)}$, then there exists a site S_i, such that all its size-$(k-1)$ subsets are gl-large at site S_i, i.e., they belong to $GL_{i(k-1)}$.

In a straightforward adaptation of Apriori, the set of candidate sets at the k-th iteration, denoted by $CA_{(k)}$, which stands for size-k candidate sets from Apriori, would be generated by applying the Apriori_gen function on $L_{(k-1)}$. That is,

$$CA_{(k)} = \text{Apriori\_gen}(L_{(k-1)}).$$

At each site S_i, let $CG_{i(k)}$ be the set of candidates sets generated by applying Apriori_gen on $GL_{i(k-1)}$, i.e.,

$$CG_{i(k)} = \text{Apriori\_gen}(GL_{i(k-1)}),$$

where CG stands for candidate sets generated from gl-large itemsets. Hence $CG_{i(k)}$ is generated from $GL_{i(k-1)}$. Since $GL_{i(k-1)} \subseteq L_{(k-1)}$, $CG_{i(k)}$ is a subset of $CA_{(k)}$. In the following, we use $CG_{(k)}$ to denote the set $\cup_{i=1}^{n} CG_{i(k)}$.

Theorem 1 *For every $k > 1$, the set of all large k-itemsets $L_{(k)}$ is a subset of $CG_{(k)} = \bigcup_{i=1}^{n} CG_{i(k)}$, where $CG_{i(k)} = \text{Apriori\_gen}(GL_{i(k-1)})$.*
Proof. Let $X \in L_{(k)}$. It follows from Lemma 1 that there exists a site S_i, $(1 \leq i \leq n)$, such that all the size-$(k-1)$ subsets of X are gl-large at site S_i. Hence $X \in CG_{i(k)}$. Therefore,

$$L_{(k)} \subseteq CG_{(k)} = \bigcup_{i=1}^{n} CG_{i(k)} = \bigcup_{i=1}^{n} \text{Apriori\_gen}(GL_{i(k-1)}).$$

$\square$

Theorem 1 indicates that $CG_{(k)}$, which is a subset of $CA_{(k)}$ and could be much smaller than $CA_{(k)}$, can be taken as the set of candidate sets for the size-k large itemsets. The difference between the two sets, $CA_{(k)}$

and $CG_{(k)}$, depends on the distribution of the itemsets. This theorem forms a basis for the generation of the set of candidate sets in the algorithm FDM. First the set of candidate sets $CG_{i(k)}$ can be generated locally at each site S_i at the k-th iteration. After the exchange of support counts, the gl-large itemsets $GL_{i(k)}$ in $CG_{i(k)}$ can be found at the end of that iteration. Based on $GL_{i(k)}$, the candidate sets at S_i for the $(k+1)$-st iteration can then be generated. According to the performance study in Section 5, by using this approach, the number of candidate sets generated can be substantially reduced to about $10 - 25\%$ of that generated in CD.

Example 1 illustrates the effectiveness of the reduction of candidate sets using Theorem 1.

Example 1 Assuming there are 3 sites in a system which partitions the DB into DB_1, DB_2 and DB_3. Suppose the set of large 1-itemsets (computed at the first iteration) $L_{(1)} = \{A, B, C, D, E, F, G, H\}$, in which $A, B,$ and C are locally large at site S_1, $B, C,$ and D are locally large at site S_2, and $E, F, G,$ and H are locally large at site S_3. Therefore, $GL_{1(1)} = \{A, B, C\}$, $GL_{2(1)} = \{B, C, D\}$, and $GL_{3(1)} = \{E, F, G, H\}$. Based on Theorem 1, the set of size-2 candidate sets at site S_1 is $CG_{1(2)}$, where $CG_{1(2)} = $ Apriori_gen $(GL_{1(1)}) = \{AB, BC, AC\}$. Similarly, $CG_{2(2)} = \{BC, CD, BD\}$, and $CG_{3(2)} = \{EF, EG, EH, FG, FH, GH\}$. Hence, the set of candidate sets for large 2-itemsets is $CG_{(2)} = CG_{1(2)} \cup CG_{2(2)} \cup CG_{3(2)}$, total 11 candidates. However, if Apriori_gen is applied to $L_{(1)}$, the set of candidate sets $CA_{(2)} = $ Apriori_gen$(L_{(1)})$ would have 28 candidates. This shows that it is very effective to apply Theorem 1 to reduce the candidate sets. $\square$

3.2 Local Pruning of Candidate Sets

The previous subsection shows that based on Theorem 1, one can usually generate in a distributed environment a much smaller set of candidate sets than the direct application of the Apriori algorithm.

When the set of candidate set $CG_{(k)}$ is generated, to find the globally large itemsets, the support counts of the candidate sets must be exchanged among all the sites. Notice that some candidate sets in $CG_{(k)}$ can be pruned by a *local pruning* technique before count exchange starts. The general idea is that at each site S_i, if a candidate set $X \in CG_{i(k)}$ is not locally large at site S_i, there is no need for S_i to find out its global support count to determine whether it is globally large. This is because in this case, either X is small (not globally large), or it will be locally large at some other site, and hence only the site(s) at which X is locally large need to be responsible to find the global support count of X. Therefore, in order to compute all the large k-itemsets, at each site S_i, the candidate sets can be confined to only the sets $X \in CG_{i(k)}$ which are

locally large at site S_i. For convenience, we use $LL_{i(k)}$ to denote those candidate sets in $CG_{i(k)}$ which are locally large at site S_i. Based on the above discussion, at every iteration (the k-th iteration), the gl-large k-itemsets can be computed at each site S_i according to the following procedure.

1. **Candidate sets generation**: Generate the candidate sets $CG_{i(k)}$ based on the gl-large itemsets found at site S_i at the $(k-1)$-st iteration using the formula, $CG_{i(k)} = $ Apriori_gen $(GL_{i(k-1)})$.

2. **Local pruning**: For each $X \in CG_{i(k)}$, scan the partition DB_i to compute the local support count $X.sup_i$. If X is not locally large at site S_i, it is excluded from the candidate sets $LL_{i(k)}$. (Note: This pruning only removes X from the candidate set at site S_i. X could still be a candidate set at some other site.)

3. **Support count exchange**: Broadcast the candidate sets in $LL_{i(k)}$ to other sites to collect support counts. Compute their global support counts and find all the gl-large k-itemsets in site S_i.

4. **Broadcast mining results**: Broadcast the computed gl-large k-itemsets to all the other sites.

For clarity, the notations used so far are listed in Table 1.

D	number of transactions in DB
s	support threshold *minsup*
$L_{(k)}$	globally large k-itemsets
$CA_{(k)}$	candidate sets generated from $L_{(k)}$
$X.sup$	global support count of X
D_i	number of transactions in DB_i
$GL_{i(k)}$	gl-large k-itemsets at S_i
$CG_{i(k)}$	candidate sets generated from $GL_{i(k-1)}$
$LL_{i(k)}$	locally large k-itemsets in $CG_{i(k)}$
$X.sup_i$	local support count of X at S_i

Table 1: Notation Table.

To illustrate the above procedure, we continue working on Example 1 as follows.

Example 2 Assume the database in Example 1 contains 150 transactions and each one of the 3 partitions has 50 transactions. Also assume that the support threshold $s = 10\%$. Moreover, according to Example 1, at the second iteration, the candidate sets generated at site S_1 are $CG_{1(2)} = \{AB, BC, AC\}$; at site S_2, $CG_{2(2)} = \{BC, BD, CD\}$; and at site S_3, $CG_{3(2)} = \{EF, EG, EH, FG, FH, GH\}$. In order to compute the large 2-itemsets, the local support counts

$X.sup_1$		$X.sup_2$		$X.sup_3$	
AB	5	BC	10	EF	8
BC	10	CD	8	EG	3
AC	2	BD	4	EH	4
–	–	–	–	FG	3
–	–	–	–	FH	4
–	–	–	–	GH	6

Table 2: Locally Large Itemsets.

at each site is computed first. The result is recorded in Table 2.

From Table 2, it can be seen that $AC.sup_1 = 2 < s \times D_1 = 5$. AC is not locally large. Hence, the candidate set AC is pruned away at site S_1. On the other hand, both AB and BC have enough local support counts and they survive the local pruning. Hence $LL_{1(2)} = \{AB, BC\}$. Similarly, $LL_{2(2)} = \{BC, CD\}$, and $LL_{3(2)} = \{EF, GH\}$. After the local pruning, the number of size-2 candidate sets has been reduced to five which is less than half of the original size. Once the local pruning is completed, each site broadcasts messages containing all the remaining candidate sets to the other sites to collect their support counts. The result of this count support exchange is recorded in Table 3.

locally large candidates	broadcast request from	$X.sup_1$	$X.sup_2$	$X.sup_3$
AB	S_1	5	4	4
BC	S_1, S_2	10	10	2
CD	S_2	4	8	4
EF	S_3	4	3	8
GH	S_3	4	4	6

Table 3: Globally Large Itemsets.

The request for support count for AB is broadcasted from S_1 to site S_2 and S_3, and the counts sent back are recorded at site S_1 as in the second row of Table 3. The other rows record similar count exchange activities at the other sites. At the end of the iteration, site S_1 finds out that only BC is gl-large, because $BC.sup = 22 > s \times D = 15$, and $AB.sup = 13 < s \times D = 15$. Hence the gl-large 2-itemset at site S_1 is $GL_{1(2)} = \{BC\}$. Similarly, $GL_{2(2)} = \{BC, CD\}$ and $GL_{3(2)} = \{EF\}$. After the broadcast of the gl-large itemsets, all sites return the large 2-itemsets $L_{(2)} = \{BC, CD, EF\}$.

Notice that some candidate set, such as BC in this example, could be locally large at more than one site. In this case, the messages are broadcasted from all the sites at which BC is found to be locally large. This is unnecessary because for each of candidate itemset, only one broadcast is needed. In Section 3.4, an optimization technique to eliminate such redundancy will be discussed. $\square$

There is a subtlety in the implementation of the four steps outlined above for finding globally large itemsets. In order to support both step 2, "local pruning", and step 3, "support count exchange", each site S_i must have two sets of support counts. For local pruning, S_i has to find the local support counts of its candidate sets $CG_{i(k)}$. For support count exchange, S_i has to find the local support counts of some possibly different candidate sets from other sites in order to answer the count requests from these sites. A simple approach would be to scan DB_i twice, once for collection of the counts for the local $CG_{i(k)}$, and once for responding to the count requests from other sites. However, this would substantially degrade the performance.

In fact, there is no need of two scans. At S_i, not only is $CG_{i(k)}$ available at the beginning of the k-th iteration, but also are other sets, i.e., $CG_{j(k)}$ ($j = 1, \ldots, n$, $j \neq i$), because all the $GL_{i(k-1)}$, ($i = 1, \ldots, n$), are broadcasted to every site at the end of the $(k-1)$-st iteration, and the sets of candidate sets $CG_{i(k)}$, ($i = 1, \ldots, n$), are computed from the corresponding $GL_{i(k-1)}$. That is, at the beginning of each iteration, since all the gl-large itemsets found at the previous iteration have been broadcasted to all the sites, every site can compute the candidate sets of every other site. Therefore, the local support counts of all these candidate sets can be found in one scan and stored in a data structure like the hash-tree used in Apriori [2]. Using this technique, the data structure can be built in one scan, and the two different sets of support counts required in the local pruning and support count exchange can be retrieved from this data structure.

3.3 Global Pruning of Candidate Sets

The local pruning at a site S_i uses only the local support counts found in DB_i to prune a candidate set. In fact, the local support counts from other sites can also be used for pruning. A *global pruning* technique is developed to facilitate such pruning and is outlined as follows. At the end of each iteration, all the local support and global support counts of a candidate set X are available. These local support counts can be broadcasted together with the global support counts after a candidate set is found to be globally large. Using this information, some global pruning can be performed on the candidate sets at the subsequent iteration.

Assume that the local support count of every candidate itemset is broadcasted to all the sites after it is found to be globally large at the end of an iteration. Suppose X is a size-k candidate itemset at the k-th iteration. Therefore, the local support counts of all the size-$(k-1)$ subsets of X are available at every site. With respect to a partition DB_i, $(1 \leq i \leq n)$, we use $maxsup_i(X)$ to denote the minimum value of the local support counts of all the size-$(k-1)$ subsets of X, i.e, $maxsup_i(X) = min\{Y.sup_i \mid Y \subset X \text{ and } |Y| = k - 1\}$. It follows from the subset relationship that $maxsup_i(X)$ is an upper bound of the local support count $X.sup_i$. Hence, the sum of these upper bounds over all partitions, denoted by $maxsup(X)$, is an upper bound of $X.sup$. In other words, $X.sup \leq maxsup(X) = \sum_{i=1}^{n} maxsup_i(X)$. Note that $maxsup(X)$ can be computed at every site at the beginning of the k-th iteration. Since $maxsup(X)$ is an upper bound of its global support count, it can be used for pruning, i.e., if $maxsup(X) < s \times D$, then X cannot be a candidate itemset. This technique is called *global pruning*.

Global pruning can be combined with local pruning to form different pruning strategies. Two particular variations of this strategy will be adopted when we introduce several versions of FDM in Section 4. The first method is called *upper-bound-pruning* and the second one is called *polling-site-pruning*. We will discuss the upper-bound-pruning method here in detail. The polling-site-pruning method will be explained in Subsection 4.3. In the upper-bound-pruning, a site S_i first uses the techniques in Subsections 3.1 and 3.2 to generate and perform local pruning on the candidate sets. Before count exchange starts, the site S_i applies global pruning to the remaining candidate sets. A possible upper bound of the global support count of a candidate set X is the sum

$$X.sup_i + \sum_{j=1, j \neq i}^{n} maxsup_j(X).$$

where $X.sup_i$ is found already in the local pruning. Therefore, this upper bound can be computed to prune the candidate set X at site S_i.

Example 3 We examine the global pruning at S_1 after the local pruning done in Example 2. According to Table 2, the survived candidate sets in the local pruning are AB and BC. Their local support counts at S_1 can be found in Table 2. Furthermore, the local support counts of their subsets from all the sites are also available at S_1 and are listed in Table 4.

From Tables 2 and 4, an upper bound of the support count of AB, (denoted by $AB.\overline{sup}$), is given by

$$AB.\overline{sup} = AB.sup_1 + min(A.sup_2, B.sup_2) + min(A.sup_3, B.sup_3) = 5 + 4 + 4 = 13 < s \times D.$$

Since this upper bound is less than the support threshold, AB is removed from the set of candidate itemsets.

large 1-itemset	local support count at S_1		
	$X.sup_1$	$X.sup_2$	$X.sup_3$
A	6	4	4
B	10	10	5
C	4	12	5

Table 4: Local Support Counts.

On the other hand, an upper bound of the support count of BC, (denoted by $BC.\overline{sup}$), is given by

$$BC.\overline{sup} = BC.sup_1 + min(B.sup_2, B.sup_2) + min(B.sup_3, C.sup_3) = 10 + 10 + 5 = 25 > s \times D.$$

Since it is larger than the threshold, BC is not pruned away and remains as a candidate itemset at S_1. $\quad\square$

Global pruning is a useful technique for reducing the number of candidate sets. Its effectiveness depends on the distribution of the local support counts.

3.4 Count Polling

In the CD algorithm, the local support count of every candidate itemset is broadcasted from every site to every other site. Therefore, the number of messages required for count exchange for each candidate itemset is $O(n^2)$, where n is the number of partitions.

In our method, if a candidate itemset X is locally large at a site S_i, S_i needs $O(n)$ messages to collect all the support counts for X. In general, few candidate itemsets are locally large at all the sites. Therefore, the FDM algorithm will usually require much less than $O(n^2)$ messages for computing each candidate itemset. To ensure that FDM requires only $O(n)$ messages for every candidate itemset in all the cases, a count polling technique is introduced.

For each candidate itemset X, the technique uses an assignment function, which could be a hash function on X, to assign X a *polling site* (assuming that the assignment function is known to every site.) The polling site assigned to X is independent of the sites in which X is founded to be locally large. Therefore, even if X is found to be locally large at more than one site, it will still be sent to the same polling site. For each candidate itemset X, its polling site is responsible to find out whether X is globally large. To achieve that purpose, the polling site of X has to broadcast the polling request for X, collect the local support counts, and compute the global support count. Since there is only one polling site for each candidate itemset X, the number of messages required for count exchange for X is reduced to $O(n)$.

At the k-th iteration, after the pruning phase, (both local and global pruning), has been completed, FDM uses the following procedure at each site S_i to do the count polling.

1. Send candidate sets to polling sites: At site S_i, for every polling site S_j, find all the candidate itemsets in $LL_{i(k)}$ whose polling site is S_j and store them in $LL_{i,j(k)}$ (i.e., candidates are being put into groups by their polling sites). The local support counts of the candidate itemsets are also stored in the corresponding set $LL_{i,j(k)}$. Send each $LL_{i,j(k)}$ to the corresponding polling site S_j.

2. Poll and collect support counts: If S_i is a polling site, S_i receives all $LL_{j,i(k)}$ sent to it from the other sites. For every candidate itemset X received, S_i finds the list of originating sites from which X is being sent. S_i then broadcasts the polling requests to the other sites not on the list to collect the support counts.

3. Compute gl-large itemsets: S_i receives the support counts from the other sites, computes the global support counts for its candidates, and finds the gl-large itemsets. Eventually, S_i broadcasts the gl-large itemsets together with their global support counts to all the sites.

Example 4 In Example 2, assuming that S_1 is assigned as the polling site of AB and BC, S_2 is assigned as the polling site of CD, and S_3 is assigned as the polling site of EF and GH.

Following from the assignment, site S_1 is responsible for the polling of AB and BC. In the simple case of AB, S_1 sends polling requests to S_2 and S_3 to collect the support counts. As for BC, it is locally large at both S_1 and S_2, the pair $\langle BC, BC.sup_2 \rangle = \langle BC, 10 \rangle$ is sent to S_1 by S_2. After S_1 receives the message, it sends a polling request to the remaining site S_3. Once the support count $BC.sup_3 = 2$ is received from S_3, S_1 finds out that $BC.sup = 10 + 10 + 2 = 22 > 15$. Hence BC is a gl-large itemset at S_1. In this example, with a polling site, the double polling messages for BC has been eliminated. □

4 Algorithm for Distributed Mining of Association Rules

In this section, the basic version of FDM, i.e., the FDM-LP (FDM with Local Pruning) algorithm, is first presented, which adopts two techniques: *candidate set reduction* and *local pruning*, discussed in Section 3. According to our performance study in Section 5, FDM-LP is much more efficient than CD.

4.1 The FDM-LP algorithm
Algorithm 1 FDM LP: FDM with Local Pruning

Input: DB_i $(i = 1, \ldots, n)$: the database partition at each site S_i.

Output: L: the set of all globally large itemsets.

Method: Iteratively execute the following program fragment (for the k-th iteration) distributively at each site S_i. The algorithm terminates when either $L_{(k)} = \emptyset$, or the set of candidate sets $CG_{(k)} = \emptyset$.

(1)   if $k = 1$ then
(2) $T_{i(1)} = get\_local\_count(DB_i, \emptyset, 1)$
(3)   else {
(4) $CG_{(k)} = \cup_{i=1}^n CG_{i(k)}$
            $= \cup_{i=1}^n Apriori\_gen(GL_{i(k-1)})$;
(5) $T_{i(k)} = get\_local\_count(DB_i, CG_{(k)}, i)$; }
(6)   for_all $X \in T_{i(k)}$ do
(7)   if $X.sup_i \geq s \times D_i$ then
(8)   for $j = 1$ to n do
(9)   if $polling\_site(X) = S_j$ then
                insert $\langle X, X.sup_i \rangle$ into $LL_{i,j(k)}$;
(10) for $j = 1, \ldots, n$ do send $LL_{i,j(k)}$ to site S_j;
(11) for $j = 1, \ldots, n$ do {
(12)   receive $LL_{j,i(k)}$;
(13)   for_all $X \in LL_{j,i(k)}$ do {
(14)   if $X \notin LP_{i(k)}$ then
            insert X into $LP_{i(k)}$;
(15)   update $X.large\_sites$; } }
(16) for_all $X \in LP_{i(k)}$ do
(17) $send\_polling\_request(X)$;
(18) $reply\_polling\_request(T_{i(k)})$;
(19) for_all $X \in LP_{i(k)}$ do {
(20)   receive $X.sup_j$ from the sites S_j,
        where $S_j \notin X.large\_sites$;
(21) $X.sup = \sum_{i=1}^n X.sup_i$;
(22)   if $X.sup \geq s \times D$ then
        insert X into $G_{i(k)}$; }
(23) broadcast $G_{i(k)}$;
(24) receive $G_{j(k)}$ from all other sites S_j, $(j \neq i)$;
(25) $L_{(k)} = \cup_{i=1}^n G_{i(k)}$.
(26) divide $L_{(k)}$ into $GL_{i(k)}$, $(i = 1, \ldots, n)$;
(27) return $L_{(k)}$.

Explanation of Algorithm 1
In Algorithm 1, every site S_i is initially a "home site" of a set of candidate sets that it generates. Later, it becomes a polling site to serve the requests from other sites. Subsequently, it changes its status to a remote site to supply local support counts to other polling sites. The corresponding steps in Algorithm 1 for these different roles and activities are grouped and explained as the follows.

1. Home site: generate candidate sets and submit them to polling sites (lines 1 - 10).

At the first iteration, the site S_i calls get_local_count to scan the partition DB_i once and store the local support counts of all the 1-itemsets found in the array $T_{i(1)}$. At the k-th (for

$k > 1$) iteration, S_i first computes the set of candidate set $CG_{(k)}$, and then scans DB_i to build the hash tree $T_{i(k)}$ containing the locally support counts of all the sets in $CG_{(k)}$. By traversing $T_{i(k)}$, S_i finds out all locally large k-itemsets and group them according to their polling sites. Finally, it sends the candidate sets with their local support counts to their polling sites.

2. Polling site: receive candidate sets and send polling requests (lines 11 - 17).

   As a polling site, site S_i receives candidate sets from the other sites and insert them in $LP_{i(k)}$. For each candidate set $X \in LP_{i(k)}$, S_i stores all its "home" sites in $X.large\_sites$, which contains all those sites from which X is sent to S_i for polling. In order to perform count exchange for X, S_i calls $send\_polling\_request$ to send X to those sites not in the list $X.large\_sites$ to collect the remaining support counts.

3. Remote site: return support counts to polling site (line 18).

   When S_i receives polling requests from the other sites, it acts as a remote site. For each candidate set Y it receives from a polling site, it retrieves $Y.sup_i$ from the hash tree $T_{i(k)}$ and returns it to the polling site.

4. Polling site: receive support counts and find large itemsets (lines 19 - 23).

   As a polling site, S_i receives the local support counts for the candidate sets in $LP_{i(k)}$. Following that, it computes the global support counts of all these candidate sets and find out the globally large itemsets among them. These globally large k-itemsets are stored in the set $G_{i(k)}$. Finally, S_i broadcasts the set $G_{i(k)}$ to all the other sites.

5. Home site: receive large itemsets (lines 24 - 27).

   As a "home" site, S_i receives the sets of globally large k-itemsets $G_{i(k)}$ from all the polling sites. By taking the union of $G_{i(k)}$, $(i = 1, \ldots, n)$, S_i finds out the set L_k of all the size-k large itemsets. Further, S_i finds out from L_k the set $GL_{i(k)}$ of gl-large itemsets for each site by using the site list in $X.large\_sites$. The sets $GL_{i(k)}$ will be used for candidate set generation at the next iteration. □

The FDM-LP described above has utilized the techniques described in Subsections 3.1, 3.2, and 3.4. An illustration of FDM-LP by example can be found in Examples 1, 2 and 3 together.

In the following, two refinements of FDM-LP, by adoption of different global pruning techniques, are presented.

4.2　The FDM-LUP algorithm
Algorithm 2 FDM-LUP: FDM with Local and Upper-Bound-Pruning

Method: The program fragment of FDM-LUP is obtained from FDM-LP by inserting the following condition (line 7.1) after line 7 of Algorithm 1.

(7.1)　　if $g\_upper\_bound(X) \geq s \times D$ then

Explanation of Algorithm 2
The only new step in FDM-LUP is the one for upper-bound-pruning (line 7.1). The function g_upper_bound computes an upper bound for a candidate set X according to the formula suggested in Subsection 3.3. In other words, g_upper_bound returns an upper bound of X as the sum

$$X.sup_i + \sum_{j=1, j \neq i}^{n} maxsup_j(X).$$

As explained in Subsection 3.3, $X.sup_i$ is computed already in the local pruning step, and the values of $maxsup_j(X)$, $(j = 1, \ldots, n, \ j \neq i)$, can be computed from the local support counts from the $(k-1)$-st iteration. If this upper bound is smaller than the global support threshold, it is used to prune away X. FDM-LUP should usually have a smaller number of candidate sets for count exchange in comparison with FDM-LP. □

4.3　The FDM-LPP algorithm
Algorithm 3 FDM-LPP: FDM with Local Pruning and Polling-Site-Pruning

Method: The program fragment of FDM-LPP is obtained from Algorithm 1 by replacing its line 17 with the following two lines.

(16.1)　　if $p\_upper\_bound(X) \geq s \times D$ then
(17)　　　　$send\_polling\_request(X)$;

Explanation of Algorithm 3
The new step in FDM-LPP is the one for polling-site-pruning (line 16.1). At that stage, S_i is a polling site and has received requests from the other sites to perform polling. Each request contains a locally large itemset X and its local support count $X.sup_j$, where S_j is a site from which X is sent to S_i. Note that $X.large\_sites$ is the set of all the originating sites from which the requests for polling X are being sent to the polling site (line 15). For every site $S_j \in X.large\_sites$, the local support count $X.sup_j$ has been sent to S_i already. For a site $S_q \notin X.large\_sites$, since X is not locally large at S_q, its

local support count $X.sup_q$ must be smaller than the local threshold $s \times D_q$. Following from the discussion in Subsection 3.3, $X.sup_q$ is bounded by the value $min(maxsup_q(X), s \times D_q - 1)$. Hence an upper bound of $X.sup$ can be computed by the sum

$$\sum_{j \in X.large\_sites} X.sup_j +$$

$$\sum_{q=1, q \notin X.large\_sites}^{n} min(maxsup_q(X), s \times D_q - 1).$$

In FDM-LPP, S_i calls p_upper_bound to compute an upper bound for $X.sup$ according to the above formula. This upper bound can be used to prune away X if it is smaller than the global support threshold. $\square$

As discussed before, both FDM-LUP and FDM-LPP may have less candidate sets than FDM-LP. However, they require more storage and communication messages for the local support counts. Their efficiency comparing with FDM-LP will depend largely on the data distribution.

5 Performance Study of FDM

An in-depth performance study has been performed to compare FDM with CD. We have chosen to implement the representative version of FDM, FDM-LP, and compare it against CD. Both algorithms are implemented on a distributed system by using PVM (Parallel Virtual Machine) [6]. A series of three to six RS/6000 workstations, running the AIX system, are connected by a 10Mb LAN to perform the experiment. The databases in the experiment are composed of synthetic data.

In the experiment result, the number of candidate sets found in FDM at each site is between $10-25\%$ of that in CD. The total message size in FDM is between $10-15\%$ of that in CD. The execution time of FDM is between $65-75\%$ of that in CD. The reduction in the number of candidate sets and message size in FDM is very significant. The reduction in execution time is also substantial. However, it is not directly proportional to the reduction in candidate sets and message size. This is mainly due to the overhead of running FDM and CD on PVM. What we have observed is that the overhead of PVM in FDM is very close to that in CD, even though the amount of message communication is significantly smaller in FDM. From the results of our experiments, it is also clear that the performance gain of FDM over CD will be higher in distributed systems in which the communication bandwidth is an important performance factor. For example, if the mining is being done on a distributed database over wide area or long haul network. The performance of FDM-LP against Apriori in a large database is also compared. In that case, the response time of FDM-LP is only about 20% longer

Parameter	Interpretation	Value
| T |	transaction mean size	10
| I |	mean size of maximal potentially large itemsets	4
| L |	number of potentially large itemsets	2000
N	Number of items	1000
S_q	Clustering size	5 - 6
P_s	Pool size	50 - 70
c_r	Correlation level	0.5
M_f	Multiplying factor	1260 - 2400

Table 5: Parameter Table.

than $1/n$ of the response time of Apriori, where n is the number of sites. This is a very ideal speed-up. In terms of total execution time, FDM-LP is very close to Apriori.

The test bed that we use has six workstations. Each one of them has its own local disk, and its partition is loaded on its local disk before the experiment starts. The databases used in our experiment are synthetic data generated using the same techniques introduced in [2, 10]. The parameters used are similar to those in [10]. Table 5 is a list of the parameters and their values used in our synthetic databases. Readers not familiar with these parameters can refer to [2, 10]. In the following, we use the notation Tx.Iy.Dm to denote a database in which $D = m$ (in thousands), $|T| = x$, and $|I| = y$.

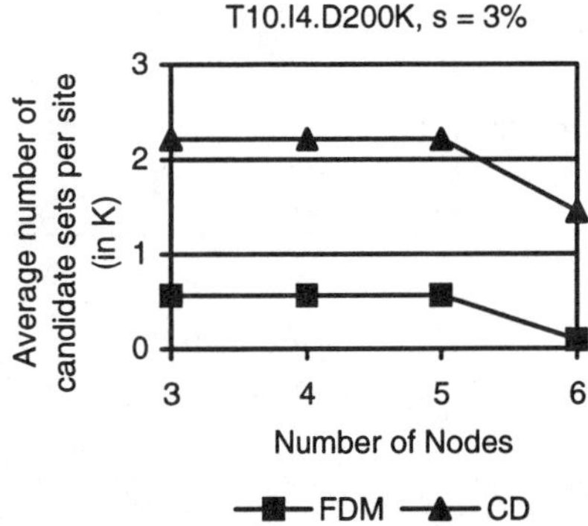

Figure 1: Candidate Sets Reduction (n = 3, 4, 5, 6)

5.1 Candidate Sets and Message Size Reduction

The sizes of the databases in our study range from 200K to 600K transactions, and the minimum support threshold ranges from 3% to 3.75%. Note that the number of candidate sets at each site are the same in CD and different in FDM. In our experiment, we witnessed a reduction of $75-90\%$ of candidate sets on

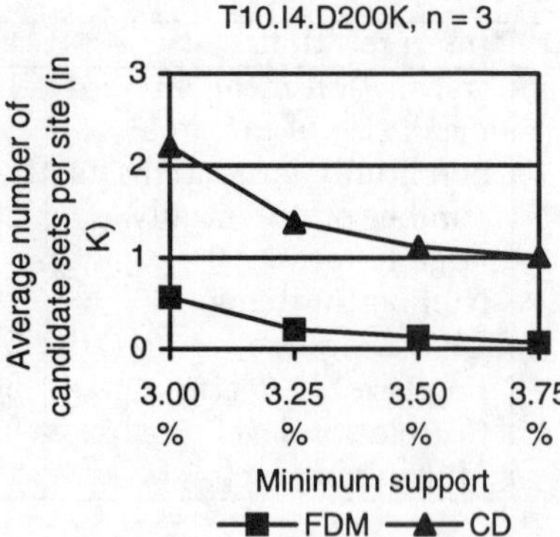

Figure 2: Candidate Sets Reduction

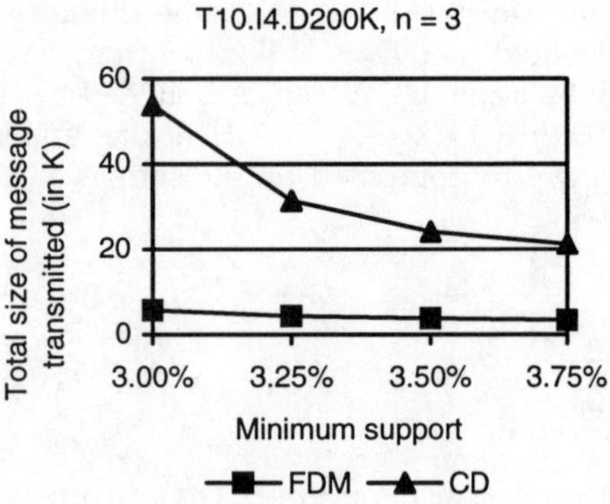

Figure 4: Message Size Reduction

average at each site when FDM-LP is compared with CD. In Figure 1, the average number of candidate sets generated by FDM-LP and CD for a 200K transaction database are plotted against the number of partitions. FDM-LP has a $75 - 90\%$ reduction in the candidate sets. The percentage of reduction increases when the number of partitions increases. This shows that FDM becomes more effective when the system is scaled up. In Figure 2, the same comparison between FDM-LP and CD is presented for the same database with three partitions on different thresholds. In this case, FDM-LP experienced a similar amount of reduction.

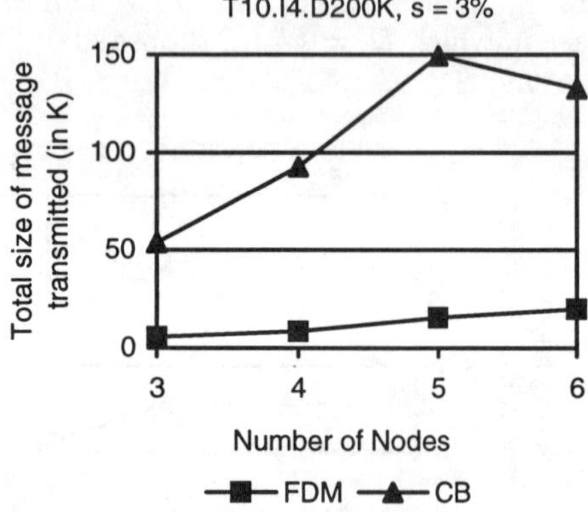

Figure 3: Message Size Reduction (n = 3, 4, 5, 6)

The reduction in candidate sets should have a proportional impact on the reduction of messages in the comparison. Moreover, as discussed before, the polling site technique guarantees that FDM only requires $O(n)$ messages for each candidate set, which is much smaller than the $O(n^2)$ messages required in CD. In our experiment, FDM has about 90% reduction in the total message size in all cases when it is compared with CD. In Figure 3, the total message size in FDM and CD for the same 200K database are plotted against the number of partitions. In Figure 4, the same comparison on the same database of three partitions with different support thresholds are presented. Both results confirm our analysis that FDM-LP is very effective in cutting down the number of messages required.

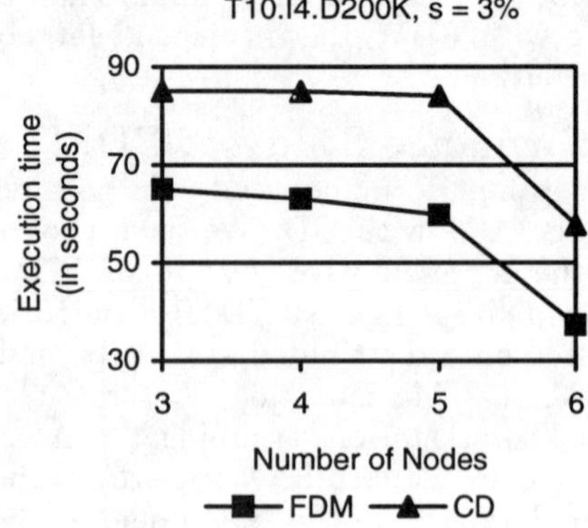

Figure 5: Execution Time (n = 3, 4, 5, 6)

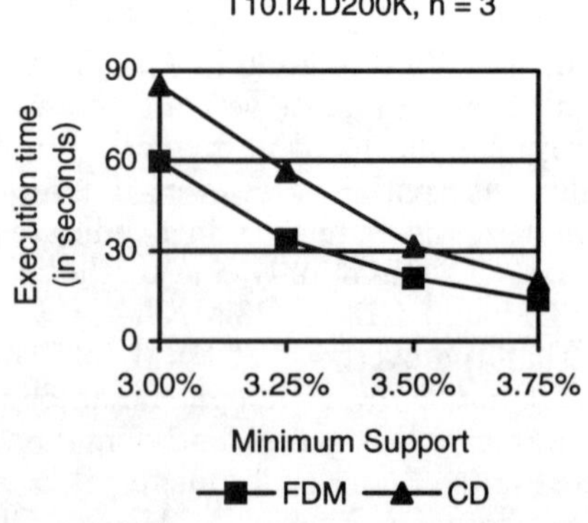

Figure 6: Execution Time

5.2 Execution Time Reduction

We have also compared the execution time between FDM-LP and CD. The execution time of FDM-LP and CD on a 200K database are plotted against the number of partitions in Figure 5. FDM-LP is about

$25 - 35\%$ faster than CD in all cases. In Figure 6, the comparison is plotted against different thresholds for the same database on three partitions. Again, FDM-LP is shown to have similar amount of speed-up as in Figure 5.

$n = 3, D = 600K, s = 2\%$	Apriori	FDM-LP
response time (sec)	1474	387
total execution time (sec)	844.7	842.9

Table 6: Efficiency of FDM-LP.

We have also compared FDM-LP on three sites against Apriori with respect to a 600K transactions database in order to find out its efficiency in large database. The result is shown in Table 6. The response time of FDM-LP is only slightly (20%) larger than 1/3 of that of Apriori. In terms of the total execution time, FDM-LP is very close to Apriori. For a large database, FDM-LP may have a bigger portion of the database residing in the distributed memory than Apriori. Therefore, it will be much faster than running Apriori on the same database in a single machine. This shows that FDM-LP on a scalable distributed system is an efficient and effective technique for mining association rules in large databases.

The performance study has demonstrated that FDM generates a much smaller set of candidate sets and requires a significantly smaller amount of messages when comparing with CD. The improvement in execution time is also substantial even though the overhead incurred from PVM prevents FDM from achieving a speed-up proportional to the reduction in candidate sets and message size. Even though, we have only compared CD with FDM-LP, there is enough evidence to show that FDM is more efficient than CD in a distributed environment. In the following sections, we will discuss our future plan of implementing the other versions of FDM.

6 Discussions

In this discussion, we will first discuss the issue of possible extension of FDM for fast parallel mining of association rules. Following that, we will discuss two other related issues: (1) the relationship between the effectiveness of FDM and the distribution of data, and (2) support threshold relaxation for possible reduction of message overhead.

The CD and PDM algorithms are designed for share-nothing parallel environment. In particular, CD has been implemented and tested on the IBM SP2 machine. In designing algorithm for parallel mining of association rules, not only the number and size of messages required should be minimized, but also the number of synchronizations, which is the number of rounds of message communication. CD has a simple synchronization scheme. It requires only one round of message communication in every iteration. Besides the second iteration, PDM also has the same synchronization scheme as CD. If FDM was used in the parallel environment, it has a shortcoming: even though it requires much less message passings then CD, it needs more synchronizations. However, FDM can be modified to overcome this problem. In fact, in each iteration, the candidate set reduction and global pruning techniques can be used to eliminate many candidates and then a broadcast can be used to exchange the local support counts of the remaining candidates. This approach will generate less candidate sets than CD and has the same number of synchronization. Therefore, it will perform better than CD in all cases. Performance studies has been carried out in a 32-nodes IBM SP2 to study several variations of this approach, and the result is very promising.

Another interesting issue is the relationship between the performance of FDM and the distribution of the itemsets among the partitions. From both Theorem 1 and Example 1, it is clear that the number of candidate sets decreases dramatically if the distribution of itemsets is quite skewed among the partitions. If most of the globally large itemsets were locally large at most of the sites, the reduction of candidate sets in FDM would not have been as significant. In the worst case, if every globally large itemset is locally large at all the sites, the candidate sets in FDM and CD will be the same. Therefore, data skewness may improve the performance of FDM in general. Special partitioning technique can be used to increase the data skewness to optimize the performance of FDM. Some further study is required to explore this issue.

The last issue that we want to discuss is the possible usage of the relaxation factor proposed in [11]. In FDM, if a site sends not only those candidate sets which are locally large but also those that are almost locally large to the polling sites, the polling sites may have local support counts from more sites to perform the *global pruning of candidate sets*. For example, if the support threshold is 10%, every site can send the candidate sets whose local support counts exceed 5% to their polling sites. In this case, for some candidate sets, their polling sites may receive local support counts from more sites than the no relaxation case. Hence, the global pruning may be more effective. However, there is a trade-off between sending more candidate sets to the polling sites and the pruning of candidate sets at the polling sites. More study is necessary on the detailed relationship between the relaxation factor and the performance of the pruning.

7 Conclusions

In this paper, we proposed and studied an efficient and effective distributed algorithm FDM for mining association rules. Some interesting properties between locally and globally large itemsets are observed, which leads to an effective technique for the reduction of candidate sets in the discovery of large itemsets. Two powerful pruning techniques, local and global prunings, are proposed. Furthermore, the optimization of the communications among the participating sites is performed in FDM using the polling sites. Several variations of FDM using different combination of pruning techniques are described. A representative version, FDM-LP, is implemented and whose performance is compared with the CD algorithm in a distributed system. The result shows the high performance of FDM at mining association rules.

Several issues related to the extensions of the method are also discussed. The techniques of candidate set reduction and global pruning can be integrated with CD to perform mining in a parallel environment which will be better than CD when considering both message communication and synchronization. Further improvement of the performance of the FDM algorithm using the skewness of data distribution and the relaxation of support thresholds is also discussed.

Recently, there have been interesting studies on the mining of generalized association rules [14], multiple-level association rules [8], quantitative association rules [15], etc. Extension of our method to the mining of these kinds of rules in a distributed or parallel system are interesting issues for future research. Also, parallel and distributed data mining of other kinds of rules, such as characteristic rules [7], classification rules, clustering [9], etc. is an important direction for future studies. For our performance studies, an implementation of the different versions of FDM on an IBM SP2 system with 32 nodes has been carried out and the result is very promising.

References

[1] R. Agrawal and J. C. Shafer. Parallel mining of association rules: Design, implementation, and experience. In *IBM Research Report*, 1996.

[2] R. Agrawal and R. Srikant. Fast algorithms for mining association rules. In *Proc. 1994 Int. Conf. Very Large Data Bases*, pages 487–499, Santiago, Chile, September 1994.

[3] R. Agrawal and R. Srikant. Mining sequential patterns. In *Proc. 1995 Int. Conf. Data Engineering*, pages 3–14, Taipei, Taiwan, March 1995.

[4] D.W. Cheung, J. Han, V. Ng, and C.Y. Wong. Maintenance of discovered association rules in large databases: An incremental updating technique. In *Proc. 1996 Int'l Conf. on Data Engineering*, New Orleans, Louisiana, Feb. 1996.

[5] U. M. Fayyad, G. Piatetsky-Shapiro, P. Smyth, and R. Uthurusamy. *Advances in Knowledge Discovery and Data Mining*. AAAI/MIT Press, 1996.

[6] A. Geist, A. Beguelin, J. Dongarra, W. Jiang, R. Manchek, and V. Sunderam. *PVM: Parallel Virtual Machine, A Users' Guide and Tutorial for Networked Parallel Computing*. MIT Press, 1994.

[7] J. Han, Y. Cai, and N. Cercone. Data-driven discovery of quantitative rules in relational databases. *IEEE Trans. Knowledge and Data Engineering*, 5:29–40, 1993.

[8] J. Han and Y. Fu. Discovery of multiple-level association rules from large databases. In *Proc. 1995 Int. Conf. Very Large Data Bases*, pages 420–431, Zurich, Switzerland, Sept. 1995.

[9] R. Ng and J. Han. Efficient and effective clustering method for spatial data mining. In *Proc. 1994 Int. Conf. Very Large Data Bases*, pages 144–155, Santiago, Chile, September 1994.

[10] J.S. Park, M.S. Chen, and P.S. Yu. An effective hash-based algorithm for mining association rules. In *Proc. 1995 ACM-SIGMOD Int. Conf. Management of Data*, pages 175–186, San Jose, CA, May 1995.

[11] J.S. Park, M.S. Chen, and P.S. Yu. Efficient parallel mining for association rules. In *Proc. 4th Int. Conf. on Information and Knowledge Management*, pages 31–36, Baltimore, Maryland, Nov. 1995.

[12] A. Savasere, E. Omiecinski, and S. Navathe. An efficient algorithm for mining association rules in large databases. In *Proc. 1995 Int. Conf. Very Large Data Bases*, pages 432–443, Zurich, Switzerland, Sept. 1995.

[13] A. Silberschatz, M. Stonebraker, and J. D. Ullman. Database research: Achievements and opportunities into the 21st century. In *Report of an NSF Workshop on the Future of Database Systems Research*, May 1995.

[14] R. Srikant and R. Agrawal. Mining generalized association rules. In *Proc. 1995 Int. Conf. Very Large Data Bases*, pages 407–419, Zurich, Switzerland, Sept. 1995.

[15] R. Srikant and R. Agrawal. Mining quantitative association rules in large relational tables. In *Proc. 1996 ACM-SIGMOD Int. Conf. Management of Data*, Montreal, Canada, June 1996.

Session 2B

Recovery

Distributed Multi-Level Recovery in Main-Memory Databases

Philip Bohannon[*]

James Parker[*]

Rajeev Rastogi[*]

S. Seshadri[†]

Avi Silberschatz[*]

S. Sudarshan[†]

[*] Bell Laboratories, Murray Hill, NJ

{plbohannon,rastogi,avi}@bell-labs.com

parker@lucent.com

[†] Indian Institute of Technology, Bombay, India

{seshadri,sudarsha}@cse.iitb.ernet.in

Abstract

In this paper, we present two schemes for concurrency control and recovery in distributed main-memory databases. In the client-server scheme, clients ship log records to the server, which applies the updates to its database copy. In the shared disk scheme, each site broadcasts its updates to other sites. The above enable our schemes to support concurrent updates to the same page at different sites.

Both schemes support an explicit multi-level recovery abstraction for high concurrency, reduced disk I/O by writing only redo log records to disk during normal processing, and use of per-transaction redo and undo logs to reduce contention. Further, we use a fuzzy checkpointing scheme that writes only dirty pages to disk, yet minimally interferes with normal processing, not requiring updaters to even acquire a latch before updating a page.

1   Introduction

A large number of applications (e.g., call routing and switching in telecommunications, financial applications, automation control) require high performance access to data with response time requirements of the order of a few milliseconds to tens of milliseconds. Traditional disk-based database systems are incapable of meeting the high performance needs of such applications due to the latency of accessing data that is disk-resident. An attractive approach to providing applications with low (and predictable) response times is to load the entire database into main-memory. Databases for such applications are often of the order of tens or hundreds of megabytes, which can easily be supported in main-memory. Further, machines with main memories of 8 gigabytes or more are already available, and with the falling price of RAM,

machines with such large main memories will become cheaper and more common.

One approach for implementing such high performance databases is to provide a large buffer-cache to a traditional disk-based system. In contrast, in a *main-memory database system* (MMDB) (see, e.g., [GMS92, LSC92, JLR+94, DKO+84]), the entire database can be directly mapped into the virtual address space of the process and locked in memory. Data can be accessed either directly by virtual memory pointers, or indirectly via location independent database offsets that can be quickly translated to memory addresses. During data access, there is no need to interact with a buffer manager, either for locating data, or for fetching/pinning buffer pages. Also, objects larger than the system's page size can be stored contiguously, thereby simplifying retrieval or in-place use. Thus, data access using a main-memory database is very fast compared to using disk-based storage managers, even when the disk-based manager has sufficient memory to cache all data pages.

Further performance improvements can be obtained for a number of applications by employing a distributed architecture in which several machines connected by a fast network perform database accesses and updates in parallel. This is especially the case in applications in which transactions are predominantly read-only and update rates are low (e.g., number translation and call routing in telecommunications). As a result, each machine can locally access data cached in memory, thus avoiding network communication which could be fairly expensive. A very different example is CAD processing, in which locality of reference is very high, update transactions are long, and interactive response time is very important. Finally, distribution also enhances fault tolerance, which is required in many mission-critical applications even if data fits easily in main-memory. In this case, especially with low update rates, a distributed database

---

[†]The work of these authors was performed in part while they were at Bell Labs.

44

is preferable to a hot-spare since load can be distributed in the non-failure case leading to improved performance.

The goal of the work described here was to extend the main-memory recovery scheme presented in [JSS93, BPR$^+$96] to the distributed case, maintaining the efficiencies of the single-site scheme, and supporting the applications described above. For example, we can make use of the MMDB optimization called *transient undo logging*, originally proposed in [JSS93], in which undo log records are kept in memory and only written to disk as required for checkpointing. This reduces the size of the log written to disk, and perhaps more importantly, the size of the log sent across network links in distributed protocols.

We present two distinct but related distributed recovery schemes, the first for *client-server* architectures and the second for *shared disk* architectures. These are both "data-shipping" schemes (e.g., [FZT$^+$92]) in which a transaction executes at a single site, fetching data (pages) as required from other sites. Distributed commit protocols are not needed as in "function-shipping" environments. While shared disk architectures have traditionally been closely tied to hardware platforms (e.g., VAXCluster), UNIX-based shared disk platforms and network of workstation architectures with similar performance characteristics are becoming more common.

A key property of our schemes is that concurrent updates are possible at granularities smaller than a page-size, minimizing false-sharing (and thus needless network accesses). In addition to the *transient redo logging* optimization described above, our algorithms provide advanced features such as explicit multi-level recovery (e.g., [WHBM90, MN94, Lom92]), and *fuzzy checkpointing* [SGM90a, Hag86]. Site or global recovery requires only a single pass over the system log, starting from the end of the system log recorded during the most recent checkpoint. As mentioned earlier, objects in the system can span one or more page boundaries.

The remainder of the paper is organized as follows. We present background on multi-level recovery and the single-site algorithm on which the present work is based in Section 2. We present our client-server recovery algorithm in Section 3, and the shared disk algorithm in Section 4. Related work and our conclusions are presented in Sections 5 and 6, respectively.

2 Overview of Main-Memory Recovery

In this section we present a review of multi-level recovery concepts and an overview of our single-site main-memory recovery scheme. Our centralized scheme extends the scheme presented in [JSS93] with multi-level recovery, and a fuzzy checkpointing scheme that only writes dirty pages. Low-level details of our scheme are described in [BPR$^+$96].

In our scheme, data is logically organized into *regions*. A region can be a tuple, an object, or an arbitrary data structure like a list or a tree. Each region has a single associated lock with exclusive (X) and

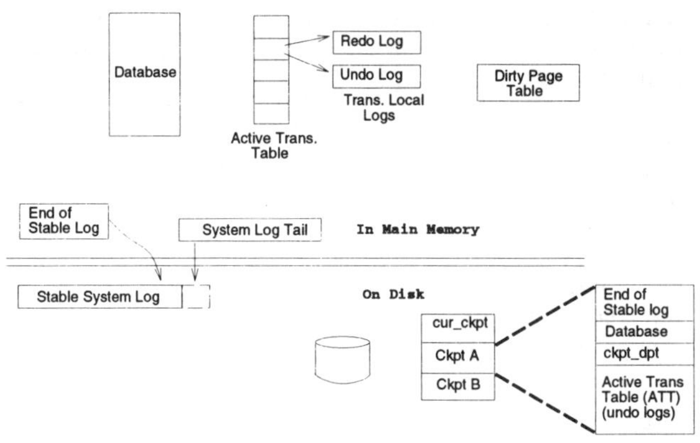

Figure 1: Overview of Recovery Structures

shared (S) modes, referred to as the *region lock*, that guards accesses and updates to the region.

2.1 Multi-Level Recovery

Multi-level recovery [WHBM90, MHL$^+$92, Lom92] provides recovery support for enhanced concurrency based on the semantics of operations. Specifically, it permits the use of weaker *operation* locks in place of stronger shared/exclusive region locks.

A common example is index management, where holding physical locks until transaction commit leads to unacceptably low levels of concurrency. If undo logging has been done physically (e.g. recording exactly which bytes were modified to insert a key into the index) then the transaction management system must ensure that these physical undo descriptions are valid until transaction commit. Since the descriptions refer to specific updates at specific positions, this typically implies that the region locks on the updated index nodes be held to ensure correct *recovery*, in addition to considerations for concurrent access to the index.

The multi-level recovery approach is to replace these low-level physical undo log records with higher level logical undo log records containing undo descriptions at the operation level. Thus, for an insert operation, physical undo records would be replaced by a logical undo record indicating that the inserted key must be deleted. Once this replacement is made, the region locks may be released and only (less restrictive) operation locks are retained. For example, region locks on the particular nodes involved in an insert can be released, while an operation lock on the newly inserted key that prevents the key from being accessed or deleted is held.

2.2 System Overview

Figure 1 gives an overview of the structures used for recovery. The database (a sequence of fixed size pages) is mapped into the address space of each process and is in main memory, with (two) checkpoint images Ckpt_A and Ckpt_B on disk. Also stored on disk are 1) cur_ckpt, an "anchor" pointing to the most recent valid checkpoint image for the database, and 2) a single system log containing redo information, with its tail in memory. The variable **end_of_stable_log** stores a

45

pointer into the system log such that all records prior to the pointer are known to have been flushed to the stable system log.

There is a single *active transaction table* (ATT) that stores separate redo and undo logs for active transactions. A dirty page table, dpt, is maintained in memory which records the pages that have been updated since the last checkpoint. The ATT (with undo logs) and the dirty page table are also stored with each checkpoint. The dirty page table in a checkpoint is referred to as ckpt_dpt.

2.3 Transactions and Operations

Transactions, in our model, consist of a sequence of operations. Similar to [Lom92], we assume that each operation has a level L_i associated with it. An operation at level L_i can consist of a sequence of operations at level L_{i-1}. Transactions, assumed to be at level L_n, call operations at level L_{n-1}. Physical updates to regions are level L_0 operations. For transactions, we distinguish between *pre-commit*, when the commit record enters the system log in memory establishing a point in the serialization order, and *commit* when the commit record hits the stable log. We use the same terminology for operations, where only the pre-commit point is meaningful, though this is sometimes referred to as "operation commit" in the paper.

Each transaction obtains an *operation* lock before an operation executes (the lock is granted to the operation if it commutes with other operation locks held by active transactions), and L_0 operations must obtain region locks. The locks on the region are released once the L_1 operation pre-commits; however, an operation lock at level L_i is held until the transaction or the containing operation (at level L_{i+1}) pre-commits. Thus, all the locks acquired by a transaction are released once it pre-commits.

2.4 Logging Model

The recovery algorithm maintains separate undo and redo logs in memory for each transaction. These are stored as a linked list off an entry for the transaction in the ATT. Each update (to a part of a region) generates physical undo and redo log records that are appended to the transaction's undo and redo logs respectively. When a transaction/operation pre-commits, all the redo log records for the transaction in its redo log are appended to the system log, and the logical undo description for the operation is included in the operation commit log record in the system log. Thus, with the exception of logical undo descriptors, only redo records are written to the system log during normal processing.

Also, when an operation pre-commits, the undo log records for its suboperations/updates are deleted from the transaction's undo log and a logical undo log record containing the undo description for the operation is appended. In-memory undo logs of transactions that have pre-committed are deleted since they are not required again. Locks acquired by an operation/transaction are released once they pre-commit.

The system log is flushed to disk when a transaction decides to commit. Pages updated by every redo log record written to disk are marked dirty in the dirty page table, dpt, by the flushing procedure. In our recovery scheme, update actions do not obtain latches on pages – instead region locks ensure that updates do not interfere with each other[1]. In addition, actions that are normally taken on page latching, such as setting of dirty bits for the page, are now performed based on log records written to the redo log. The redo log is used as a single unifying resource to coordinate the applications interaction with the recovery system, and this approach has proven very useful.

2.5 Ping-pong Checkpointing

Consistent with the terminology in main-memory databases, we use the term *checkpoint* to mean a copy of main-memory, stored on disk, and *checkpointing* refers to the action of creating a checkpoint. This terminology differs slightly from the terminology used, for example, in ARIES [MHL+92].

Traditional recovery schemes implement write-ahead logging (WAL), whereby all undo logs for updates on a page are flushed to disk before the page is flushed to disk. To guarantee the WAL property, a latch on the page (or possibly on the system log) is held while copying the page to disk. In our recovery scheme, we eliminate latches on pages during updates, since latching can significantly increase access costs in main-memory. It can also interfere with normal processing, as well as increase programming complexity. However, as a result it is not possible to enforce the write-ahead logging policy, since pages may be updated even as they are being written out.

For correctness, in the absence of write-ahead logging, two copies of the database image are stored on disk, and alternate checkpoints write dirty pages to alternate copies. This strategy, called *ping-pong checkpointing* (see, e.g., [SGM90b]), permits a checkpoint that is being created to be temporarily inconsistent; i.e., updates may have been written out without corresponding undo records having been written. However, after writing out dirty pages, sufficient redo and undo log information is written out to bring the checkpoint to a consistent state. Even if a failure occurs while creating one checkpoint, the other checkpoint is still consistent and can be used for recovery.

Keeping two copies of a main-memory database on disk for ping-pong checkpointing does not have a very high space penalty, since disk space is much cheaper than main-memory. As we shall see later, there is an I/O penalty in that dirty pages have to be written out to both checkpoints even if there was only one update on the page. However, this penalty is small for hot pages, and the benefits outweigh the I/O cost for typical main-memory database applications.

Before writing any dirty data to disk, the checkpoint notes the current end of the stable log in the variable end_of_stable_log, which will be stored with the checkpoint. This is the start point for scanning

---

[1] In cases when region sizes change, certain additional region locks on storage allocation structures may need to be obtained. For example, in a page based system, if an update causes the size of a tuple to change, then in addition to a region lock on the tuple, an X mode region lock on the storage allocation structures on the page must be obtained.

the system log when recovering from a crash using this checkpoint. Next, the contents of the (in-memory) ckpt_dpt are set to those of the dpt and the dpt is zeroed (noting of end_of_stable_log and zeroing of dpt are done atomically with respect to flushing). The pages written out are the pages that were either dirty in the ckpt_dpt of the last completed checkpoint, or dirty in the current (in-memory) ckpt_dpt, or in both. In other words, all pages that were modified since the current checkpoint image was last written, namely, pages that were dirtied since the last-but-one checkpoint, are written out. This is necessary to ensure that updates described by log records preceding the current checkpoint's end_of_stable_log have made it in the database image in the current checkpoint.

Checkpoints write out dirty pages without obtaining any latches and thus without interfering with normal operations. This *fuzzy* checkpointing is possible since physical redo log records are generated by all updates; these are used during restart recovery and their effects are idempotent. For any uncommitted update whose effects have made it to the checkpoint image, undo log records would be written out to disk after the database image has been written. This is performed by checkpointing the ATT after checkpointing the data; the checkpoint of the ATT writes out undo log records, as well as some other status information.

At the end of checkpointing, a log flush must be done before declaring the checkpoint completed (and consistent) by toggling cur_ckpt to point to the new checkpoint, for the following reason. Undo logs are deleted on transaction/operation pre-commit, which may happen before the checkpoint of the ATT. If the checkpoint completes, and the system then fails before a log flush, then the checkpoint may contain uncommitted updates for which there is no undo information. The log flush ensures that the transaction/operation has committed, and so the updates will not have to be undone (except perhaps by a compensating operation, for which undo information will be present in the log).

2.6 Abort Processing

When a transaction aborts, that is, does not successfully complete execution, updates/operations described by log records in the transaction's undo log are undone by traversing the undo log sequentially from the end. Transaction abort is carried out by executing, in reverse order, every undo record just as if the execution were part of the transaction.

Following the philosophy of *repeating history* [MHL+92], new physical redo log records are created for each physical undo record encountered during the abort. Similarly, for each logical undo record encountered, a new "compensation" or "proxy" operation is executed based on the undo description. Log records for updates performed by the operation are generated as during normal processing. Furthermore, when the proxy operation commits, all its undo log records are deleted along with the logical undo record for the operation that was undone. The commit record for the proxy operation serves a purpose similar to that served by *compensation log records* (CLRs) in ARIES – during restart recovery, when it is encountered, the logical undo log record for the operation that was undone is deleted from the transaction's undo log, thus preventing it from being undone again.

2.7 Recovery

Restart recovery, after initializing the ATT and transaction undo logs with the ATT and undo logs stored in the most recent checkpoint, loads the database image and sets dpt to zero. As part of the checkpoint operation, the end of the system log on disk is noted before the database image is checkpointed, and becomes the "begin-recovery-point" for this checkpoint once the checkpoint has completed. All updates described by log records preceding this point are guaranteed to be reflected in the checkpointed database image. Thus, during restart recovery, only redo log records following the begin-recovery-point for the last completed checkpoint of the database are applied (appropriate pages in dpt are set to dirty for each log record). During the application of redo log records, necessary actions are taken to keep the checkpointed image of the ATT consistent with the log as it is applied. These actions mirror the actions taken during normal processing. For example, when an operation commit log record is encountered, lower level log records in the transaction's undo log for the operation are replaced by a higher level undo description.

Once all the redo log records have been applied, the active transactions are rolled back. To do this, all completed operations that have been invoked directly by the transaction, or have been directly invoked by an incomplete operation have to be rolled back. However, the order in which operations of different transactions are rolled back is very important, so that an undo at level L_i sees data structures that are consistent [Lom92]. First, all operations (across all transactions) at L_0 that must be rolled back are rolled back, followed by all operations at level L_1, then L_2 and so on.

Note that for certain uncommitted updates present in the redo log, undo log records may not have been recorded during the checkpoint – this could happen for instance when an operation executes and commits after the checkpoint, and the containing transaction has not committed. However, this is not a problem since the undo description for the operation would have been found in operation commit log records during the forward pass over the system log earlier during recovery. Any redo log records for updates performed by an operation whose commit log record is not found in the system log are ignored (since these must be due to a crash during flush and are at the tail of the system log).

3 Client-Server Recovery Scheme

Other than integration with our multi-level recovery scheme, a key feature of the client-server scheme is fine-grained concurrency control for regions. Our algorithms hinge on the simple assumption that a region is controlled by a lock, thus may easily be adapted to record-oriented or object-oriented database models. The support of fine-grained concurrency, present in our Invalidate-on-Lock scheme for cache coherency, is particularly important for distributed main-memory applications where the cost of network access due to false sharing will be proportionally higher (i.e. as compared to a few memory accesses).

In this approach, we assume a single server with access to stable storage that is responsible for coordinating all the logging, and for performing checkpoints and recovery. Multiple clients (with or without disks) are connected to the server. For simplicity of presentation, the network is assumed to be FIFO and reliable, but all our schemes can be easily modified if this is not the case. Each client and the server has its own copy of the database in main memory. A transaction executes at a single client and updates/accesses the copy of the database at the client. As a result, database pages updated by a client may not be *current* at some other client. Our scheme maintains state information at each client about each database page. A page at a client is in one of two states – *valid* or *invalid*. Invalid pages contain stale versions of certain data, and are refreshed on access by obtaining the latest copy of the page from the server.

In our client-server scheme, log records for updates generated by a transaction at a client site are stored in that site's ATT as in the centralized case. Client sites do not maintain a system log on disk, but keep a system log tail in memory and append log records from the local redo logs to this tail when operations commit/abort. Furthermore, on the occurrence of certain events (e.g., transaction commit, lock release from a site), log records in the system log are shipped by the client to the server (note that pages are shipped only from the server to clients). The shipped redo log records are used to update the server's copy of the affected pages, ensuring that pages shipped to clients from the server are current. This enables our scheme to support concurrent updates to a single page at multiple clients since re-applying the updates at the server causes them to be merged (this approach is also adopted in [CDF⁺94]). Shipping the log records will usually be cheaper than shipping pages, and the cost of applying the log records themselves is small since, in our main-memory database context, the server will not have to read the affected pages from disk. The server maintains all the data structures described for the centralized case.[2] Checkpointing is performed solely at the server, and follows the same procedure as the centralized case.

Transactions follow the *callback locking* scheme [LLOW91, CFZ94] when obtaining and releasing locks. Each site has a *local lock manager* (LLM) which caches locks and a *global lock manager* (GLM) at the server keeps track of locks cached at the various clients. Transaction requests for locks cached locally are handled at the client itself. However, requests for locks not cached locally are forwarded to the global lock manager which *calls back* the lock from other clients that may have cached the lock in a conflicting mode (before granting the lock request). A client

relinquishes a lock in response to a callback if no transaction executing at the client is currently holding the lock.

In addition, the LLM at a client provides support for associating a point in the system log at the client with each lock; the purpose of this support will become clear later.

3.1 Basic Operations

We now describe the features which distinguish the client-server scheme from the centralized case, in terms of actions performed at the client and the server at specific points in processing. We present two variations for maintaining page state information, corresponding to "eager" versus "lazy" refresh. In both techniques, we allow two sites to concurrently update the *same page* when different locks cover different regions on the page. We begin with actions common to both methods.

- **Page Access:** In case a client accesses a page that is valid, it simply goes ahead without communicating with the server. Else, if the page is *invalid* (certain data on the page may be stale), then the client refreshes the page by 1) obtaining the most recent version of the page from the server, and 2) applying to the newly received page any local updates which have not been sent to the server (this step merges local updates with updates from other sites). It then marks the page as valid. The server keeps track of clients that have the page in a valid state.

- **Operation/Transaction Commit:** At the client, redo log records are moved to the system log, a commit record is appended, and appropriate actions are performed on the transaction's undo log in the ATT as described for the centralized case. In case of a transaction commit, however, the log records in the system log are shipped to the server, and further actions are delayed until the server has acknowledged that the log records have been flushed to disk.

  Finally, all the locks acquired by the operation/transaction are released locally.

- **Lock Release:** For each X mode region lock and operation lock that is released by a transaction, the end of the client system log is noted and stored with the lock. Thus, for any region lock, all redo log records in the system log affecting that region precede the point in the log stored with the lock. Similarly, for an operation lock, all log records relating to the operation (including operation commit) precede the point in the system log stored with the lock. This location in the log is client-site-specific.

  Before a client site relinquishes an X mode region lock or operation lock to the server due to the call-back described above, it ships to the server at least the portion of the system log which precedes the log pointer stored with the lock. This ensures that the next lock will not be acquired on

---

[2] We assume there is a one-to-one mapping between ATT entries at the client sites and the server.

the region until the server's copy is up to date, and the history of the update is in place in the server's logs. For X region locks, this flush ensures repeating of history on regions, while for operation locks this flush ensures that the server receives the logical undo descriptors in the operation commit log records for the operation which released the locks. Thus, if the server aborts a transaction after a site failure, the abort of this operation will take place at the logical level of the locks still held for it at the server.

- **Log Record Processing:** At the server, for each physical redo log record (received from a client), the undo log record is generated by reading the current contents of the page at the server. The new log record is then appended to the undo log for this transaction in the server's ATT. Next the update described by the redo log record is applied, following which the log record is appended to the redo log for the transaction in the server's ATT. Operation/transaction commit and abort log records received from the client are processed by performing the same actions as in the centralized case when the log records were generated. The exceptions are lock release, which is driven by the client, operation commit, where the logical undo descriptor is extracted from the commit log record, and transaction commit, where the client whose transaction committed is notified after the log flush to disk succeeds.

  By applying all the physical updates described in the physical log records to its pages, the server ensures that it always contains the latest updates on regions for locks which have been released to it from the clients. The effect of the logging scheme, as far as data updates are concerned, is just as if the client transaction actually ran at the server site.

- **Transaction Abort/Site Failures:** If a client site decides to abort a transaction, it processes the abort (as in the centralized case) using the undo logs for the transaction in the client's ATT. If the client site itself fails, the server will abort transactions that were active at the client using undo logs for the transaction in it's ATT. (Since the client cannot commit without communicating with the server, in case of partition, a decision to abort is is enforceable by the server.) If the server fails, then the complete system is brought down, and restart recovery is performed at the server as described in Section 2.7.

We now complete our client-server scheme by presenting two methods, invalidate-on-update, and invalidate-on-lock, for ensuring that data accessed by a client is up-to-date. All actions described so far are used in common by both schemes, and both schemes follow the rule that all log records are flushed to the server before the lock which covered these updates is released from the site. Since the server would have applied the log records to its copy of the data, this ensures that when the server grants a lock, it has the current version of all pages containing data covered by that lock. However, it is possible that the copy of one or more pages involved in the region for which the lock was obtained are not up-to-date at the client. Each scheme, by invalidating pages at the client, ensures that clients do not access stale data. The schemes permit regions to span multiple pages and do not require the pages spanned by a region to be known.

3.2   Invalidate-On-Update

The first invalidation scheme, based on updates, is simple, and is similar to the invalidation protocols followed in multi-processor machines in order to keep caches coherent. It is an eager protocol since a page at a client is invalidated whenever any update is made to the page at the server. The second scheme, in the next subsection, reduces these invalidation messages by tracking per-lock information at the server.

When the server receives log records from a client, it does the following. For each page that it updates, it sends *invalidate* messages to clients (other than the client that updated the page) that may have the page marked as valid. For all clients other than the client that updated the page, the server notes that the client does not have the page marked valid. Clients, on receiving the invalidate message, mark their page as invalid.

For example, consider two sites updating the same page concurrently under two different region locks. Whichever site flushes its updates to the server first will cause the server to send an invalidate message to the other site, which will then re-read the page from the server. However, if this site accesses the same page again *under the same lock*, then the invalidate was not necessary, since the data in the region it has locked has not changed. The following scheme takes advantage of this observation.

3.3   Invalidate-On-Lock

The invalidate-on-lock scheme attempts to decrease unnecessary invalidations and the overhead of sending invalidation messages by associating with the lock for a region information about updates to that region. Furthermore, pages containing updated portions of a region are invalidated only when the lock on the region is obtained by a client. As a result, if two clients are updating different regions on the same page, no invalidation messages are sent to either client. Additionally, by piggybacking invalidation messages for updated pages on lock grant messages from the server, the overhead of sending separate invalidation messages in the previous scheme is eliminated.

In the scheme, when updates described by a physical redo record are applied to pages at the server, the updated pages are associated with the lock for the updated region. Thus, the scheme requires that it be possible to determine the region lock from the redo record. This could be achieved by requiring that the lock for a region be specified by the user when the region is updated, which should be trivial since all updates must be made holding a region lock. The lock name can then be included in the redo log record.

This scheme also requires that the server associate a *Log Sequence Number* (LSN), with each log record, which reflects both the order in which the record was applied to the server's copy of the page and the order in which it was added to the system log. For each page, the server stores the LSN of the most recent log record that updated the page, and the identity of the client which issued it. In addition, for each client, the server maintains in a *client page table* (cpt), the state of the page at the client (valid/invalid), along with the LSN for the page when it was last shipped to the client.

The server also maintains for each region lock a list of pages that are dirty due to updates to the region. For each page in the list, we store the LSN of the most recent log record received by the server that recorded an update to the part of the region on this page, and the client which performed the update. Thus, when a client is granted a region lock, if, for a page in the lock list, the LSN is greater than the LSN for the page when it was last shipped to the client, then the client page contains stale data for the region and must be invalidated.

The additional actions for this scheme are as follows:

- **Log apply:** When the server applies to a page P a redo log record, LR, generated at client C under region lock L, it takes the following actions. First, the LSN for P is set to the LSN for LR. Second, the entry for P in the list of dirty pages for L is updated (or created), setting the client to C, and the LSN to the LSN for LR.

- **Lock grant:** A set of invalidate messages is passed back to the client with the lock acquisition. The invalidate messages are for pages in the list associated with the lock being acquired that meet three criteria: 1) the page is cached at the client in the valid state, 2) the LSN of the page in the cpt for the client is smaller than the LSN of the page in the lock list, and 3) the client acquiring the lock was not the last to update the page under this lock. The invalidated pages are marked invalid in the cpt for the client and at the client site.

- **Page refresh:** When the server sends a page to a client (page refresh), at the server, the page is marked valid in the cpt for the client and the LSN for the page in the cpt is updated to be the LSN for the page at the server.

- **Lock list cleanup:** We are interested in keeping the list of pages with every lock as small as possible. This can be achieved by periodically deleting pages P from the list of lock L such that the following condition holds, where C is the client noted in the list of pages for L as the last client to update P:

  > Every client other than C has the page cached either in an invalid state or with LSN greater than or equal to the LSN for the page in the list for lock L.

The rationale for this rule is that the purpose of region locks lists is to determine pages that must be invalidated. However, if for a page in a client's cpt, the LSN is greater than the LSN for the page in the lock list, then the client has the most recent update to the region on the page, and thus the page will not need to be sent in any invalidate list.

4 Shared Disk Recovery Scheme

In the shared disk approach, there is no server; every site has direct access to disks over a fast network. The shared disk environment is used in many systems, such as the DEC VAXclusters, and provides benefits over a shared nothing architecture, such as fast communication and fault tolerance. As in our client-server scheme, in addition to careful consideration of the interaction with multi-level recovery, our main concern is minimizing false sharing through fine-grained concurrency control. This allows, for example, read-only transactions with a fully cached working set to proceed at main-memory speeds, an important property for our intended applications.

In our shared disk model, each site maintains its own copy of the database and its own system log on disk. Sites obtain locks from a GLM; the function of the lock manager could be distributed for speed and reliability, but this is orthogonal to our discussion. Sites cache locks, and relinquish locks based on the *call back* locking mechanism described in Section 3. For simplicity of presentation, we assume the network is FIFO and reliable; however, the schemes can be extended if this were not the case.

We are interested in allowing multiple concurrent readers *and* writers of the same page at different sites, as long as the same region lock is not required by two sites in conflicting mode. A result of this is that copies of a page at different sites may contain a different set of updates, which must be merged before the page is written to disk. Unlike the client-server case, there is no server to carry out the task of merging updates.

To solve the above problems, in our scheme, log records generated at a site are broadcast to all other sites, so the updates can be carried out there. Since log records are shipped, there is no need to ship pages. The scheme ensures that every time a site obtains a region lock, the most recent version of the region is guaranteed to be accessed at the site. More precisely, it guarantees that every time a site obtains any lock (whether an operation lock or a region lock), all log records generated by all operations which held the same lock in a conflicting mode have been applied to the local page images.

The idea of broadcasting log records leads to an architecture that essentially implements distributed shared memory, without the overhead of shipping pages. Note that the overhead of broadcasting log records to all the sites may not be too severe if update rates are not too high. Also, in some network architectures (e.g., ethernet), the cost of sending a message to a single site may not be very different from the cost of a broadcast to all sites.

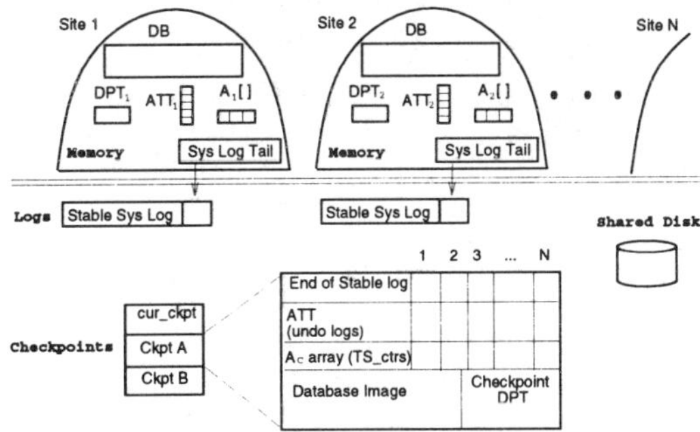

Figure 2: The Shared Disk Architecture

Finally, we note that although we have presented different schemes for the client-server and shared disk architectures (based on page invalidation for client-server, and based on log broadcasting for shared-disk), both schemes should be applicable to either architecture (perhaps with different performance tradeoffs, and with different requirements on concurrent updaters). For lack of space, we have not explored these alternatives here.

4.1 Data Structures

An overview of data structures used for our shared disk scheme is given in Figure 2. At each site, a global timestamp counter TS_ctr is maintained, and a timestamp obtained from this counter is stored in each physical redo log record for an update. At every site j, an array of TS_ctrs (one TS_ctr per site), A_j is maintained in memory. $A_j[i]$ stores the timestamp of the latest update from site i that has been applied to the database at site j.

Separate undo and redo logs are maintained for every transaction as described in the earlier schemes. Each site maintains its own version of the *dirty page table* dpt, system log, and an ATT which stores information relating to transactions that execute at that site.

A single pair of checkpointed images is maintained on disk for the database. A checkpoint image consists of an image of the database, the dirty page table ckpt_dpt, and for every site:

1. end_of_stable_log – the point in the site's system log from which the system log must be scanned during recovery.

2. the TS_ctr following which redo log records from the site must be applied to the database. Collectively these counters are referred to as A_C.

3. a copy of the ATT at the site (containing undo logs).

The LLM at a site stores a point in the system log with each lock as in the client-server scheme. Both the LLM and GLM also store a timestamp with each region lock, and the GLM notes which site most recently held the lock in X mode.

4.2 Normal Processing

We describe below the actions taken during normal processing to support distributed concurrency control and recovery. Recovery from system and site failure is described in subsequent sections.

- **Log Records:** Every time a physical redo log record is moved from a transaction's local redo log to the system log, TS_ctr is incremented by 1 and stored in the log record. The timestamps are used to order log records that describe conflicting updates.

- **System Log Flush:** When the system log at site i is flushed to stable storage, each redo log record which has hit the disk is also broadcast to the other sites. The sending site i, also sets $A_i[i]$ to the timestamp in the log record. Flushing of a sequence of log records is completed once every log record has been written to disk as well as sent to the remaining sites.

- **Log Record Receipt:** A site j processes an update broadcast to it from site i as follows (updates are processed in the order in which they are received). On receiving a broadcast log record, the site applies the update to its local copy of the affected page(s), and sets the appropriate bits in its dpt. After updating the appropriate pages, the site sets $A_j[i]$ to the timestamp contained in the update (redo log record).

- **Lock Release:** The lock managers aid correctness in two ways. First, similar to the client-server case, the current local end-of-log is noted when an operation or a region lock is released, and the LLM ensures that the log is flushed to this point before releasing the lock from the site. This aids in recovery by ensuring that history is repeated, and when lower level locks are released, the logical undo actions which accompany the higher level locks have made it to disk. Since logs are broadcast on flush, it helps ensure that another site will receive the necessary log records before getting the same lock in a conflicting mode. Note that this could require no log flushes if the log records have already been flushed earlier due to another lock release or some other transaction's commit.

  Second, when a transaction releases an X mode region lock, the timestamp for the lock is set to the current value of TS_ctr at the site. When this lock is called back by the GLM, this value is also sent and is associated with the lock by the GLM. When received by another site, the timestamp is used to ensure that log records for conflicting actions covered by this lock have increasing timestamp values. As an optimization, the site identifier can also be sent with the lock to the GLM; the purpose will become clear in the next point.

- **Lock Acquisition:** When a site receives an X mode region lock from the GLM, it bumps up

51

its own TS_ctr to be the maximum of its current TS_ctr and the timestamp associated with the lock (received for the GLM). Further, the lock is granted to a local transaction only after all outstanding (unapplied) updates at the time of acquiring the lock have been applied to the page. This is to ensure that data accessed at a site is always the most recent version of the data.

As an optimization, if a site identifier is provided with the lock by the GLM, it suffices to process log records up to (and including) the log record from the site with the timestamp provided.

4.3 Checkpointing

Checkpointing is initiated by a site, which coordinates the operation. The checkpointing operation consists, as for the centralized case, of three steps — 1) writing the database image by the co-ordinator, 2) writing the ATT at each site and 3) finally committing the checkpoint. The main difference from the centralized case lies in how each step is carried out. We describe each step below:

1. The coordinator announces the beginning of the checkpoint, at which time all other sites zero their dpts, and report their current end_of_stable_log values. Note that zeroing dpt and recording end_of_stable_log is done atomically with respect to flushes. The coordinator applies all outstanding updates, then atomically (with respect to processing further log records and flushing) records its end_of_stable_log, notes A_C from it's own A_j, and ckpt_dpt from its dpt, and then zeroes its own dpt. The coordinator then writes to the checkpoint image the ckpt_dpt, the end_of_stable_logs for each site, and the timestamp array A_C.

Applying outstanding updates at the coordinator before noting ckpt_dpt and A_C ensures that 1) updates preceding end_of_stable_log reported by other sites have been applied to the database pages, and 2) the pages are marked dirty in ckpt_dpt and thus, it is safe to zero dpts at sites when end_of_stable_log is noted. Also, since each site notes end_of_stable_log independently, it is possible that for a redo log record after end_of_stable_log at one site, a conflicting redo log record generated after it may be before end_of_stable_log noted at a different site. As a result, during restart recovery, applying every update after end_of_stable_log in the system log for a site could result in the latter update being lost. Storing A_C in the checkpoint and during restart recovery, applying only redo records at site i whose timestamps are greater than $A_C[i]$ eliminates the above problem since timestamps for both updates would be smaller than the corresponding TS_ctr values for the sites in A_C.

2. Next, the database image is written out by the coordinator in the same fashion as in the centralized case, writing out not only pages dirty in this checkpoint interval (in ckpt_dpt), but also pages dirtied in the previous checkpoint interval (in the ckpt_dpt stored in the previous checkpoint).

3. Once the coordinator has written out the database image, it instructs each site to write out its ATT. Note that, as in the single site algorithm, writing the ATT at a site causes the system log at the site to be flushed. Multiple sites can be concurrently writing out their ATTs.

4. Once every site has reported to the coordinator that its ATT has been written out, the database checkpoint is committed by toggling cur_ckpt as in the centralized case.

4.4 Recovery

Restart recovery in case of a system wide failure (where all sites have to be recovered) can be performed as follows by an arbitrary site j in the system. The database image and the checkpointed timestamp array A_C are read, and for each site, the ATT and the end_of_stable_log recorded in the checkpoint are read. Redo log records in the system logs for the various sites are then applied to the database image by concurrently scanning the various system logs. Each site's system log is scanned in parallel, starting from the end_of_stable_log recorded for the site in the checkpoint. At each point, if the next log record to be considered in any of the system logs is not a redo log record, then it is processed and the ATT for its site is modified as described for the centralized case in Section 2.7. On the other hand, if the next record to be considered in all the system logs is a redo log record, then the log record considered next is the one (among all the system logs on disk being considered) with the lowest timestamp value. For every redo log record encountered in the system log for a site, i, with a timestamp greater than $A_C[i]$, the update is applied and the affected pages are marked as dirty in j's dpt.

Once all the system logs have been scanned, TS_ctr at site j is set to the largest timestamp contained in a redo log record. In-progress and post-commit operations in the ATTs for the various sites are then rolled back and executed, respectively, at site j against the database at site j, beginning with level L_0 and then considering successive levels L_1, L_2 and so on (as described in Section 2.7). When an operation in an ATT entry for a site is being processed, actions are performed on the undo and redo logs for the entry. Furthermore, when an operation pre-commits/aborts, log records from the redo log are appended to the system log for the site and the timestamp for each redo log record appended is obtained by incrementing TS_ctr at site j.

Finally, every site's system logs are flushed causing appropriate pages in j's dpt to be marked dirty (updates are not broadcast, however), and the TS_ctr at every site and $A_k[i]$ for all sites k and i are set to the TS_ctr value at site j. The database image at every site is set equal to the database image at site j, the dpt for each site is copied from the dpt at site j, and recovery is completed.

For lack of space we omit a proof of correctness, but a sketch of the proof is provided in the appendix.

4.5   Recovery from Site Failure

Our recovery algorithm can also be extended to deal with a site failure *without* performing a complete system restart, so long as the GLM data has not been lost, or can be regenerated from the other sites. If this is not the case, a full system recovery is performed instead. Recovery from site failure, as with regular system recovery, has a redo pass, followed by rollback of in-progress operations.

Before beginning the redo recovery pass, the recovering site, say j, retrieves from the most recent checkpoint the database image, the ATT for site j, the timestamp array A_C and the end_of_stable_log for each site. It then informs other sites that it is up, and requests from each site i, that site's end_of_stable_log value, and the value of $A_i[j]$. At this point, other sites start sending log records to j; these are buffered and processed later. The redo pass is then performed by scanning all the system logs as described in the previous subsection except that 1) only the pages in the dpt for site j are marked dirty, 2) only actions on the ATT for site j are performed, and 3) the system log for a site is scanned until the end_of_stable_log returned by that site at the beginning of this recovery.

Also, log records in the tail end of the log of the recovering site may not have made it to other sites – since a log record is broadcast after it is flushed. For each site i (other than the recovering site, j) all log records in site i's system log that have timestamps greater than $A_i[j]$ are broadcast to site i as they are processed. Once the redo pass is completed, $A_j[i]$ is set to the maximum timestamp in a redo log record encountered during the redo pass in the system log for site i. Also, TS_ctr at site j is set to the maximum of $A_j[i]$ for all sites i. At this point, site j can begin applying updates described by log records received from other sites, as during normal processing, in the order received, and checkpoints can again be taken as normal.

Before rolling back in-progress operations, the locks that were cached at site j at the time it crashed are re-obtained by the lock manager at site j by consulting the GLM. These locks are all specially marked — none of these locks will be returned on call back until unmarked since they may have been held by some transactions at the local site at the time of the failure. As described in Section 2.7, rollback is performed level by level, with additional locks requested as is done during normal processing (see Section 4.2). Thus, TS_ctr at site j is bumped up and outstanding updates are applied when a new lock is obtained, TS_ctr is incremented when a redo log record is appended to the system log, and log flushes are performed when operation/X mode region locks are released by site j. Also, level L_i operation locks at site j are unmarked once all active operations at level L_{i+1} have been rolled back. The special treatment of marked locks, along with level-by-level rollback, ensures that an in-progress operation which held a lock will in fact be protected by the lock held on behalf of the site.

5   Connection to Related Work

Multi-level recovery and variants thereof, primarily for disk-based systems, have been proposed in the literature [WHBM90, Lom92, MHL+92]. Like these schemes, our schemes repeat history, generate log records during undo processing and log operation commits when undo operations complete (similar to CLRs described in [MHL+92]). Also, as in [Lom92], transaction rollback at crash recovery is performed level by level. Some of the main-memory features of our scheme which impact the distributed schemes are

1. No physical undo logs are written out to the global log except during checkpoints.

2. Separate undo logs are maintained in memory for active transactions. A result is that transaction rollback does not need to access the global log, part of which could be on disk.

3. Our scheme does not require latching of pages during updates, which is inconvenient and expensive in either a main-memory DB or an OODB setting. Actions that are normally taken on page latching, such as setting of dirty bits for the page, are efficiently performed based on physical redo log records written to the global log.

4. Our scheme uses transient undo logging which reduces the disk I/O.

In the ARIES-SD [MN91] family of schemes for recovery in the shared disk environment, each site maintains a separate log, and pages are shipped between sites. Our scheme does not ship pages, but instead broadcasts log records, taking advantage of cheap application of these log records in main-memory, and permitting *concurrent updates* at a smaller than page granularity. In our scheme, log flushes are driven by the release of a lock from a site, in order to support repeating of history and correct rollback of multi-level actions during crash recovery. The "super fast" method of ARIES-SD [MN91] does not describe flushes to protect the early release of locks, making it unclear how that scheme supports logical undo and high-concurrency index operations.

In [Rah91], the authors propose recovery schemes for the shared disk environment which assume page-level concurrency control and the NO-STEAL page write policy – neither of which are assumptions made in our schemes.

In [MN94], the authors show how the ARIES recovery algorithm described in [MHL+92] can be extended to a client-server environment. In contrast to our scheme, the scheme described here involves the clients as well as the server in the checkpointing process. We also support concurrent updates to a page by different clients, which is not supported in [MN94].

In [CFZ94], object-level as well as adaptive locking and replica management are discussed, but recovery considerations are not extensively addressed. In [FZT+92], the client-server recovery scheme for the Exodus storage manager (ESM-CS) is described. This recovery scheme, based on ARIES [MHL$^+$92], requires page-level locking until end of transaction (for example, the Commit Dirty Page List).

6   Concluding Remarks

In this paper, we showed how our multi-level recovery algorithm [BPR$^+$96] can be extended to a distributed data-shipping system while maintaining many of the original benefits of the single-site algorithm. The first scheme presented supports client-server processing in which a central system controls logs and checkpoints. In the second scheme, suitable for a cluster of computers with a shared disk, sites participate symmetrically in transaction processing activities. We described the details of recovery after the failure of clients or the server in the client-server case and from single site and system-wide failure in the shared disk case. Our scheme allows concurrent updates at multiple clients in a client-server environment or multiple sites of the shared disk environment. By allowing fine-grained and flexible concurrency control, our schemes are applicable to a range of distributed, main-memory applications which need transactional access to data.

Our distributed schemes are based on a multi-level scheme for recovery in main-memory databases which has been implemented in the Dali Main Memory Storage Manager [JLR$^+$94]. Thus, the benefits of this algorithm are extended to the distributed schemes, including fuzzy, dirty-page only checkpointing, reliance on the log for functions which are typically page based, low overhead logging with undo records written only due to a checkpoint, and per-transaction logs for low contention.

We plan to explore the performance of these schemes through experimentation, and then build a distributed, data-shipping version of Dali based on these algorithms.

References

[BPR$^+$96]   P. Bohannon, J. Parker, R. Rastogi, S. Seshadri, and S. Sudarshan. Distributed multi-level recovery in main-memory databases. Technical Report 112530-96-02-27-01TM, Lucent Technologies, Bell Laboratories, February 1996.

[CDF$^+$94]   M. J. Carey, D. J. Devitt, M. J. Franklin, N. E. Hall, M. L. McAuliffe, J. F. Naughton, D. T. Schuh, M. H. Solomon, C. K. Tan, O. G. Tsatalos, S. J. White, and M. J. Zwilling. Shoring up persistent applications. In *Proceedings of ACM-SIGMOD 1994 International Conference on Management of Data, Minneapolis, Minnesota*, pages 383–394, May 1994.

[CFZ94]   M. J. Carey, M. J. Franklin, and M. Zaharioudakis. Fine-grained sharing in a page server OODBMS. In *Proceedings of ACM-SIGMOD 1994 International Conference on Management of Data, Minneapolis, Minnesota*, pages 359–370, May 1994.

[DKO$^+$84]   D. J. DeWitt, R. Katz, F. Olken, D. Shapiro, M. Stonebraker, and D. Wood. Implementation techniques for main memory database systems. *Proc. ACM-SIGMOD 1984 Int'l Conf. on Management of Data*, pages 1–8, June 1984.

[FZT$^+$92]   M. J. Franklin, M. J. Zwilling, C. K. Tan, M. J. Carey, and D. J. DeWitt. Crash recovery in client-server EXODUS. In *Proceedings of ACM-SIGMOD 1992 International Conference on Management of Data, San Diego, California*, pages 165–174, June 1992.

[GMS92]   H. Garcia-Molina and K. Salem. Main memory database systems: An overview. *IEEE Transactions on Knowledge and Data Engineering*, 4(6):509–516, December 1992.

[Hag86]   Robert B. Hagmann. A crash recovery scheme for a memory-resident database system. *IEEE Transactions on Computers*, C-35(9):839–847, September 1986.

[JLR$^+$94]   H.V. Jagadish, Dan Lieuwen, Rajeev Rastogi, Avi Silberschatz, and S. Sudarshan. Dali: A high performance main-memory storage manager. In *Procs. of the International Conf. on Very Large Databases*, 1994.

[JSS93]   H.V. Jagadish, Avi Silberschatz, and S. Sudarshan. Recovering from main-memory lapses. In *Procs. of the International Conf. on Very Large Databases*, 1993.

[LLOW91]   C. Lamb, G. Landis, J. Orenstein, and D. Weinreb. The objectstore database system. *Communications of the ACM*, 34(10), October 1991.

[Lom92]   D. Lomet. MLR: A recovery method for multi-level systems. In *Proceedings of ACM-SIGMOD 1992 International Conference on Management of Data, San Diego, California*, pages 185–194, 1992.

[LSC92]   T. Lehman, E. J. Shekita, and L. Cabrera. An evaluation of Starburst's memory resident storage component. *IEEE Transactions on Knowledge and Data Engineering*, 4(6):555–566, December 1992.

[MHL$^+$92]   C. Mohan, D. Haderle, B. Lindsay, H. Pirahesh, and P. Schwarz. ARIES: A transaction recovery method supporting fine-granularity locking and partial rollbacks using write-ahead logging. *ACM Transactions on Database Systems*, 17(1):94–162, March 1992.

[MN91]   C. Mohan and I. Narang. Recovery and coherency-control protocols for fast inter-system page transfer and fine-granularity locking in a shared disks transaction environment. In *Proceedings of the Seventeenth International Conference on Very Large Databases, Barcelona*, pages 193–207, September 1991.

[MN94]   C. Mohan and I. Narang. ARIES/CSA: a method for database recovery in client-server architectures. In *Proceedings of ACM-SIGMOD 1994 International Conference on Management of Data, Minneapolis, Minnesota*, pages 55–66, May 1994.

[Rah91]   E. Rahm. Recovery concepts for data sharing systems. In *Proceedings of the Twenty first International Conference on Fault-Tolerant Computing (FTCS-21), Montreal*, pages 109–123, June 1991.

[SGM90a]   K. Salem and H. Garcia-Molina. System M: A transaction processing testbed for memory resident data. *IEEE Transactions on Knowledge and Data Engineering*, 2(1):161–172, March 1990.

[SGM90b]   K. Salem and H. Garcia-Molina. System M: A transaction processing testbed for memory resident data. *IEEE Transactions on Knowledge and Data Engineering*, 2(1):161–172, 1990.

[WHBM90] G. Weikum, C. Hasse, P. Broessler, and P. Muth. Multi-level recovery. In *Proceedings of the Nineth ACM SIGACT-SIGMOD-SIGART Symposium on Principles of Database Systems, Nashville*, pages 109–123, June 1990.

A Correctness of Shared Disk Algorithms

The basic idea behind the proof of correctness is to treat the combined system logs conceptually as a single log, merged according to the timestamps. The checkpointed timestamp array A_C is essentially a pointer into this logical log, and constitutes the logical log restart recovery point. We show correctness of the shared disk recovery and cache coherency algorithms by showing the following:

1. For every update written out during the checkpoint operation, and that had not committed before the end of checkpointing, the undo log record describing the update is also written out.

2. All updates described by log records before the logical log restart point (array A_C) noted in the checkpoint have made it to the database image.

3. History is repeated as a consequence of applying the redo log records during restart recovery.

Point 1 is ensured since the ATTs are checkpointed after an update completed, and every system log is flushed to disk before the checkpoint completes, so that all pre-committed updates get committed. Thus, the undo log for any uncommitted update is guaranteed to be written to disk.

Point 2 holds since when a page is written to disk during a checkpoint at site j, updates preceding $A_j[i]$ have made it to the image of the page at site j (due to the algorithm for application of incoming log records), and this page is dirty in j's dpt (because the dpt is noted atomically with A_C).

Point 3 is ensured due to the following reasons –

1. All physical log records are applied during recovery in timestamp order – immediate from the recovery algorithm.

2. For a given region, the order of log record timestamps reflects the order of updates which generated the log records. For every log record, L, (in the system log of a site) describing an update, the log record, L' for the preceding (conflicting) update is also in some site's stable log with timestamp less than the timestamp for this log record. The reason for this is that before a region lock is released by a site, updates covered by the region lock are appended to the system log, flushed to disk, and broadcast to the network. TS_ctr at the receiving site is bumped up and so must be larger than the timestamp contained in L' when log record L is moved to the system log and assigned a timestamp.

3. If a timestamp contained in a log record for site i is less than or equal to $A_j[i]$, then the log record's effects must have made it to the copy of the database at site j.

4. Finally, we show that if a log record, L1, from site i is applied to a page during recovery, then a conflicting log record, L2, from another site, j, with timestamp higher than the L1's timestamp, will also be applied. In other words, the timestamp of the second log record is greater than $A_C[j]$.

   Suppose log record L1 is applied during recovery, and it describes an update at site i. Suppose further that the update for L1 precedes another update at site j, described by L2. Then, at the coordinator site for the last completed checkpoint, L2's timestamp is larger than the timestamp array entry for j. The reason for this is that L1 is first broadcast before locks are released, and only later is L2 broadcast to all the sites. Since L1 is applied, its timestamp must be greater than $A_C[i]$, which means the broadcast of L1 did not reach the last site that did the checkpoint. But then neither could the broadcast of L2 – so the timestamp $A_C[j]$ must be less than the timestamp of L2, and L2 would be executed as well.

Performance of Recovery Time Improvement Algorithms for Software RAIDs

Jeff Riegel
IBM Almaden Research Center
650 Harry Rd.
San Jose, CA 95120
riegel@almaden.ibm.com

Jai Menon
IBM Almaden Research Center
650 Harry Rd.
San Jose, CA 95120
menonjm@almaden.ibm.com

Abstract

A software RAID is a RAID implemented purely in software running on a host computer. One problem with software RAIDs is that they do not have access to special hardware such as NVRAM. Thus, software RAIDs may need to check every parity group of an array for consistency following a host crash or power failure. This process of checking parity groups is called recovery, and results in long delays when the software RAID is restarted. In this paper, we review two algorithms to reduce this recovery time for software RAIDs: the PGS Bitmap algorithm we proposed in [5] and the List Algorithm proposed in [1]. We compare the performance of these two algorithms using trace-driven simulations. Our results show that the PGS Bitmap Algorithm can reduce recovery time by a factor of 12 with a response time penalty of less than 1%, or by a factor of 50 with a response time penalty of less than 2%, and a memory requirement of around 9 Kbytes. The List Algorithm can reduce recovery time by a factor of 50 but cannot achieve a response time penalty of less than 16%.

1. Introduction

RAID, as first described in [6], stands for Redundant Array of Inexpensive Disks. RAIDs, or disk arrays, allow improved performance through concurrent execution of requests on multiple disks. Due to the increased exposure to failures resulting from this arrangement, most RAIDs have some form of redundancy that allows one of the disks in the RAID to be recovered following a single failure.

There are six levels of RAID, RAID 0 through RAID 5. In this paper, we consider RAID Level 5 disk arrays. Such RAIDs are typically implemented in disk controllers, because such implementations can use hardware (e.g. Non-Volatile RAM) to improve RAID performance and reliability. We call such arrays *hardware RAIDs*. A *software*

RAID, on the other hand, is implemented purely in software running on a host computer. Such RAIDs usually do not have access to special hardware such as NVRAM often used by hardware RAIDs to aid recovery and performance.

This paper focuses on one of the main disadvantages of software RAIDs (and other RAIDs without NVRAM): the long time required to make data and parity blocks consistent after a system crash or power failure. We call this process *recovery* and the time required the recovery time. This process of recovery is not the same as the normal RAID *rebuild* process used to replace all the data on a disk after it has been replaced following a single disk failure.

First, we describe the traditional data first algorithm used by RAID 5 arrays to perform writes ([5]). This algorithm has the disadvantage of extremely long recovery time, since every parity group must be checked for consistency following a host crash or power failure. We then review two optimizations to the data first algorithm that can be used by software RAID 5 arrays to achieve adequate recovery time: the PGS Bitmap Algorithm we proposed in [5], and the List Algorithm proposed by Ed Lee et al. in [1].

Next, we describe the program we used to simulate these two algorithms, a trace-driven RAID 5 simulator written in C++ on an IBM RS/6000 running AIX. We also describe our method of collecting traces in the AIX operating system and the various traces we collected from database and file servers.

We then describe the results of our simulations.

2. The Data First Algorithm

The RAID 5 disk array uses a *parity* technique described in [6]. One parity disk block stores the parity information for a number of data blocks, one data block from each disk in the array. A *parity group* consists of these data blocks and their corresponding parity block. (A parity group is also known as a *parity stripe*, as described in

[4].) This parity information can be used to reconstruct any one of the data blocks in the parity group, provided that the other data blocks are still available.

Whenever the array receives a request to update a data block, it must also update the corresponding parity block for consistency.

If data D1 is altered, the new value of parity P1 is calculated as:

$$new\ P1 = (old\ D1\ XOR\ new\ D1\ XOR\ old\ P1)$$

So, these arrays require four disk accesses or disk I/O's [1] to update a data block: Read the old data; Read the old parity; Write the new data; and Write the new parity. (If an update request writes a full stripe of data, it is not necessary to read the old data or the old parity. The algorithms in this paper, skipping the appropriate steps, still apply to such requests.)

However, if a disk crash or power failure occurs in the middle of this process, either the data, the parity, or both may not have been fully written and may be inconsistent. In such a case, the controller must be able to determine whether the data or the parity is incorrect. The data first algorithm uses two key ideas: (1) write data before parity, so if a parity group is inconsistent, we know it's the parity that needs to be fixed; and (2) notify system of request completion before parity is written (after data is written).

Assume block B on disk i is to be updated from D to D'. Parity is block B on disk j. Its value must be changed from P to P', where P' is P xor D xor D'.

1. Lock the parity group consisting of block B from all disks in array. This prevents later host updates to data blocks in the same parity group from executing concurrently.

2. In parallel, issue requests to read block B from disk i (old data) and block B from disk j (old parity).

3. Write D' to block B on disk i.

4. Notify system that request is complete as soon as possible after D' written safely to disk.

5. XOR D' with D and P to produce P'. The XORing may begin before previous step.

6. Finally, write P' to disk j block B. This step must not be initiated until after D' has been written safely to disk i block B.

7. Unlock parity group.

---

[1] For the purposes of this paper, a high-level logical access to the RAID is referred to as a "request". The physical accesses that the the RAID controller makes to its component disks are referred to as "I/O's". E.g., a RAID 5 write request consists of 4 I/O's.

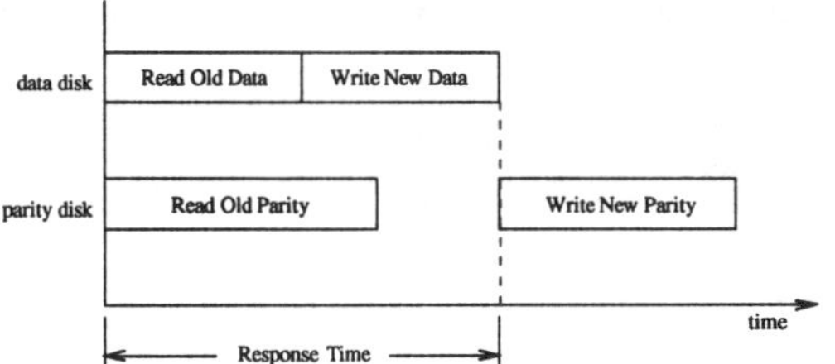

Figure 1. Data First Algorithm I/O timing for write request

Figure 1 shows the I/O timing for a typical write request with the Data First algorithm. Note that the response time of the request is the time until the write of new data completes.

On recovery from power failure, all parity groups must be scanned (assuming the software RAID does not have NVRAM available) to remember which parity groups are potentially inconsistent. For each parity group, all data blocks are read and XOR'd together to calculate parity, which is compared with the parity information stored in the parity block. If power failed before data was written, then data and parity will be consistent. If power failed after data was written, but before the write of parity could finish, then the parity calculated from the data blocks is written to the parity block. If power failed in the middle of writing data, the data field may contain garbage. However, in this case the host will never have been notified of completion of the write request, so presumably it will have some software means to recover this data, such as transaction rollback.

Note that this recovery process is not the same as the normal RAID rebuild process. The rebuild process is intended to restore the data on a single failed disk; the recovery process requires that all disks be available in order to compare the calculated parity with the stored parity. If both a disk and power have failed, this recovery process will not be possible. However, this is a dual failure which is a standard limitation of RAID's fault tolerance. For more information, see [5].

3. Algorithms for Faster Recovery

The main problem with the software implementation of the Data First algorithm is the long recovery time, as described above. In this section, we review two algorithms designed to reduce the recovery time: the PGS Bitmap Algorithm and the List Algorithm. The disadvantage of both algorithms is that in addition to the normal four disk accesses required for a RAID-5 update request, a fifth access is occasionally necessary, resulting in a longer response time.

3.1. The PGS Bitmap Algorithm

The PGS Bitmap Algorithm described in [5] is an enhancement to the Data First algorithm designed to reduce the recovery time described above. We review this algorithm below:

Group several parity groups to form a Parity Group Set (PGS). For example, assume 30,000 parity groups. Then, we could form 300 Parity Group Sets (PGS's). The first 100 parity groups would be in the first PGS, the second 100 parity groups would be in the second PGS, and so on. Figure 2 illustrates the physical disk layout of a RAID with a PGS size of p parity groups, or c cylinders per disk.

A bitmap is maintained, in memory and on disk, with 1 bit per PGS. The bit for a PGS is set if any parity group in the PGS may be inconsistent. Although the disk version will track the memory version closely, the two will not be identical at all times. At any given time, if a parity group in a PGS is inconsistent, the disk version of the bitmap will have its bit set; however, if all parity groups in a PGS are consistent, the disk version may still have the bit set. On a power failure, only the PGS's whose bits are set in the disk PGS bitmap will need to be scanned and possibly fixed.

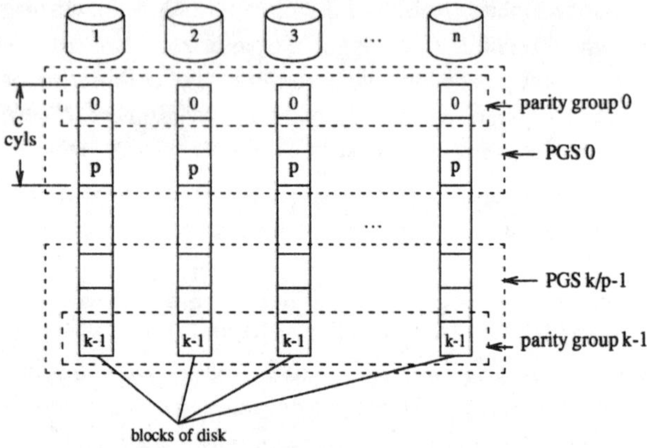

Figure 2. Parity Group Set layout on disk

Two copies of the PGS bitmap are kept on disk (2 PGS disk blocks) that are written to alternately. This avoids problems caused by power failures in the middle of writing the PGS disk block. Timestamps are used to detect partial writes of PGS blocks, and if one of the blocks is corrupt, the other is used. (See [5] for a more detailed description.)

For each PGS, a count (the PGS Count) of the number of concurrent updates in progress against that PGS is maintained in memory. The algorithm uses a global lock on the PGS bitmap before checking or changing the bitmap and/or the PGS count.

A data structure known as the PGS Pool is also maintained in memory. This pool stores PGS's which are consistent, but for which the resetting of the bits in the bitmap has been delayed in the expectation of these PGS's being referenced again. The pool acts as an LRU cache of PGS numbers. When the PGS Count reaches zero for a given PGS, indicating that there are no updates in progress against that PGS, the PGS number is added to the PGS Pool. When a PGS number is added to the pool, if the pool has reached its maximum size, the least recently referenced PGS number is removed and its bit is reset in the memory copy of the bitmap.

When an update request is enqueued to the array, the bitmap is checked to see if any of the PGS's being accessed do not have their bits set. If this is the case, the appropriate bits are set and the PGS Counts are incremented. The bitmap must then be written to disk before data or parity can be updated. It is not necessary to write the bitmap if all the appropriate bits are already set. The algorithm then proceeds with the steps of the Data First algorithm until parity has been updated. At this point the PGS Count is decremented for the appropriate PGS's. If it has reached zero, indicating no more concurrent accesses to these PGS's, the PGS's are added to the PGS Pool; the least recently referenced PGS's are removed from the pool and their bits are reset.

With this algorithm, a fifth disk I/O is sometimes needed to write the PGS bitmap after one or more bits have been set. In this way, we guarantee that the bit will be set in the disk copy of the bitmap as long as the PGS may be inconsistent. This fifth disk I/O is needed only if the appropriate bits in the bitmap were not already set; the bits will be set if the PGS's are already present in the PGS Pool or if an update is currently in progress against those PGS's. Figure 3 shows an example of the new write request I/O timing with a fifth I/O. It also shows the response time penalty caused by the write of the bitmap.

In fact, the fifth I/O is sometimes not needed even if the bits in the PGS were not already set. This is due to the fact that multiple update requests may share a bitmap write, amortizing the cost of the fifth write among the requests.

See [5] for a more detailed description of the PGS Bitmap algorithm.

3.2. The List Algorithm

An alternative to the PGS Bitmap Algorithm described above is an algorithm proposed by Ed Lee et al. in [1]. This

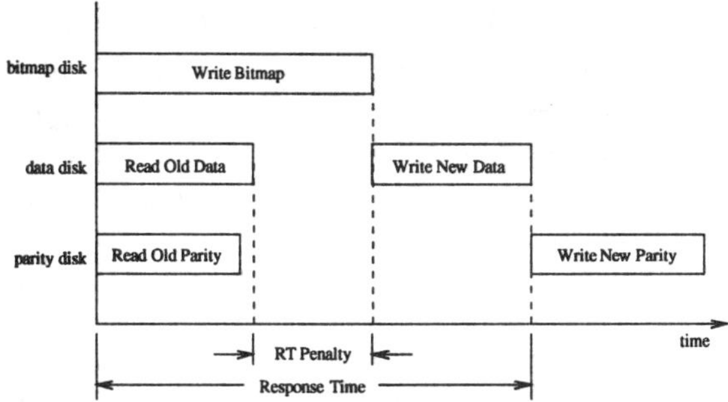

Figure 3. PGS Bitmap I/O timing for write request

algorithm was described extremely tersely, so we have had to make some assumptions of what they might have had in mind in order to make a complete description. We call this algorithm the "List Algorithm".

In this algorithm, instead of storing a bitmap of parity group sets that have been modified, a fixed-size list of the numbers of modified parity groups is maintained in memory and stored on disk. On a power failure, each of these parity groups will be scanned, and inconsistent ones will be fixed. We call this list of parity groups the "PG List".

The list acts like a LRU cache of parity group numbers. When an update request is enqueued to the array, the parity groups it accesses are added to the list, and some other member(s) of the list is removed if the list has become full. The list is then written to disk; the write must complete before the update of data or parity can begin. However, if all the parity groups being written are already stored in the list, no write of the list is necessary since the parity groups will already be checked at recovery time. The write of the list to disk only needs to proceed if one or more parity groups are not already present.

Once an update completes, the parity groups involved will be consistent, and a "consistent" flag is stored in the memory copy of the list for each of the groups. Parity group numbers are not removed from the list when they become consistent; instead, the list uses an LRU replacement policy and removes groups only when new groups are added. Only consistent groups may be safely removed, as inconsistent groups must remain in the list so they may be checked at recovery if there is a crash. If there are no consistent groups to remove, incoming update requests must be blocked until a previous update completes so its parity groups may be removed from the list. This means that there may be no more outstanding update requests than the maximum size of the list, significantly less if each update request writes more than one parity group.

The steps of the algorithm proceed as follows:

1. Follow the data first algorithm, until it is time to write data.

2. Check the PG List to see if any of the parity groups being written are stored in the list. If all are present and consistent, go to next step. If some are not consistent, the inconsistent parity groups must be currently being accessed by other requests, so block this request until the groups become consistent. If any are not present, check the number of consistent groups and free slots in the list. If the sum is less than the number of groups being written, block this request and place it on a list of blocked requests. Otherwise, add the group numbers to the list with an inconsistent status, replacing previous entries of the same group numbers if necessary. If the list becomes full, remove the least recently referenced consistent group(s). Awaken the list writing process to write the list to disk.

3. If all groups being written were not already present when we checked in Step 2, wait until the list writing process reports that the PG List with the entries added in Step 2 has been written to disk.

4. Continue with rest of data first algorithm.

5. Change status of appropriate parity groups to consistent.

6. Check the list of blocked requests. If there are now enough consistent groups or free space in the list for any to be started, return to Step 2 and resume the requests.

As in the PGS Bitmap Algorithm, one may amortize the cost of writing the list by combining several updates into a single disk I/O while waiting for a previous list write to complete.

4. Simulation Overview

The simulations were done using a trace-driven RAID 5 simulator written in C++. This simulator was originally designed to perform trace analysis and report I/O workload characteristics, but has been extended to perform full RAID simulation. Of the many statistics returned by the simulator, the ones relevant to this paper are: average response time for write requests, average response time for read requests, average recovery time, and the percentage of times an extra (fifth) I/O was needed for each update request to update data structures needed by the PGS Bitmap Algorithm or the List Algorithm.

4.1. Traces

Traces were collected using the AIX operating system's trace facility, which allows capturing of events dealing with a number of system facilities. We captured accesses to the SCSI disk device driver. Using the information contained in these traced events, we converted them to a more concise format. Each request contains the start time, end time, logical block address, size in bytes, and a flag indicating whether the request is a read or a write.

We collected a number of traces from various systems. The primary traces we used were 8-hour traces collected from an Andrew File System (AFS) file server at various times of the day. In addition, we collected a 10-hour trace from a system running an Oracle SQL database server and a 16-hour one from a server running the IBM Configuration Management Version Control system (CMVC). We averaged the results of the simulations using the various traces. The average overall workload contained around 80% writes with an average request size of 8KB, and mostly random, short seeks. The high percentage of writes in this workload was probably due to the fact that many reads were hits in the operating system cache, so they did not show up in a disk-level trace.

One problem we ran into was the small sizes of some of these traces. Each of the traces described above contained around 150,000 requests. In an attempt to provide fair testing, the simulator attempts to run in steady state, and does not include the results of trace requests into the final output until the PGS Pool or PG List fills up. This is due to the fact that when a real array implementing one of these algorithms starts up, it should still have the list or bitmap stored on disk, so it does not make sense for the simulator to start with an empty pool. Unfortunately, with a short trace, there are insufficient requests to fill up a large pool. We solved this problem by running the simulator on some extra AFS traces and saving the final contents of the pool/list to a file. The file is then read in at the beginning of subsequent runs to "pre-load" the pool/list.

4.2. The Simulator

For all the cases we tested for this paper, the disk array simulated was a 7+P RAID 5 array using eight 2GB IBM 0664 (Allicat) disks ([3]). The IBM 0664 drive is a 2GB SCSI drive with 512-byte blocks and about 2800 cylinders; each cylinder is 705K. We used one track as the stripe unit, where there are 15 tracks per cylinder, so each track is 47K (94 blocks) in size. Because these algorithms apply primarily to software RAIDs, we decided to assume no caching of data at the RAID controller level. For simplicity, only

the right-asymmetric parity placement is supported in this simulator (see [4] for a discussion of parity placements).

The simulator first reads a request from the trace file. The simulator sets the current simulated time to the start time of the request and checks to see if any previous requests have completed by this time. This involves checking each disk in the array to see if all of the appropriate component I/O's have completed by the current time. (For a read request, all of the I/O's must have completed; for a write request, only the write of new data needs to have completed before the request is considered done. See Figure 1.)

If all the I/O's associated with a particular request have completed, the request is complete, and the response time is factored into the overall average response time. Once it is known that no more requests have completed by the current time, the request read from the trace is enqueued to the array. This involves mapping the request to the appropriate disk numbers and disk blocks and enqueuing these I/O's to the appropriate disks.

Each disk is an object which is an instance of the C++ class that simulates a single disk. The disk object takes an I/O from its queue and determines the total response time for the I/O. The disk object accepts a number of parameters about the specific disk type, such as the rotation speed, average latency, and a table of seek times.

4.3. Simulation of the PGS Bitmap Algorithm

The Data First with PGS Bitmap Algorithm is implemented in the simulator as follows. The bitmap and PGS count are allocated in memory as contiguous memory arrays, while the PGS Pool is implemented using a hash table where the entries are also chained via a linked list. When a write request is enqueued to the RAID, the request's I/O's to read old data and old parity are enqueued to the appropriate disks. Then the appropriate PGS numbers for the request are calculated and the bitmap is checked to see if any of the bits associated with these PGS's are not set. If any are not set, the bits are set, the counts of the appropriate PGS's are incremented, and a disk I/O representing the write of the bitmap is enqueued to the appropriate disk.

The bitmap object contains a queue which consists of a maximum of two I/O's: the bitmap write currently in progress and a single queued write. There is no need for the queue to store more I/O's because the single queued write will be shared by any further update requests that need to perform a bitmap write. A bitmap write is assumed to be a one-block write to the first block of the first disk of the RAID. Optimizations such as replicating or striping the bitmap onto multiple disks or disk blocks are possible but were not implemented in this simulator.

Once the bitmap write associated with a request completes, the array may proceed to enqueue the data write I/O's to the disks. When these are complete, the parity write I/O's are enqueued and the request is considered done; the end time is calculated to be the time at which the last data write I/O finished. When the parity write completes, the PGS counts are decremented. Instead of immediately clearing the bits in the bitmap, however, the PGS's of the completed request are entered into the PGS pool. This pool is implemented using LRU replacement. PGS's that are evicted from the pool when the new ones are entered have their bits cleared (unless the PGS counts for those PGS's are greater than zero.)

When a write is in progress to a specific parity group, no other write request may access the parity group; locking is used to prevent this. This is done to prevent the parity and data disks from becoming inconsistent due to concurrent access, and is described more fully in [5]. Locking is simulated by using a bitmap of locks, one bit for each parity group, where the bit is set when the request is enqueued to the array. (This solution was specific to the simulator; a real implementation of the bitmap algorithm can use any mechanism it chooses to implement locking.) Other requests that need to access a locked parity group are instead placed on a separate "lock queue". Each time a write request completes, its lock bit is cleared and the lock queue is checked for any requests waiting on that lock; the first one is then enqueued. Note that an entire high-level request is suspended if any of the parity groups it accesses are locked, even if one or more of its component I/O's may not need to access the locked parity group. This was done for simplicity of bookkeeping. Potentially, this solution could lead to starvation of a large request, since small requests that bypass the suspended large request could continue to arrive and keep the locks set, but this situation should be extremely rare and did not occur during our simulation runs.

4.4. Simulation of the List Algorithm

The List Algorithm is implemented similarly to the bitmap algorithm. The PG List, like the PGS Pool, is implemented as a hash table with linked entries. The main difference from the bitmap implementation is that instead of checking a bitmap, the simulator checks the PG List for each of the parity groups in the request. If any of the parity groups are not on the list, the write of the list proceeds exactly like the write of the bitmap as described above. The other main difference is that the PG List is analogous to both the bitmap and the pool in the bitmap algorithm, so there is no need for a separate pool in this algorithm.

Locking for the List Algorithm was done as for the bitmap algorithm, except that the bitmap of locks was not needed because locked parity groups are the same groups that are marked inconsistent in the PG List. So instead of checking the lock bitmap, we check the list for inconsistent parity groups; any group found to be inconsistent must already have an access in progress to it, so the new write request is put on a lock queue as with the bitmap algorithm.

4.5. Recovery

In order to get an accurate idea of the amount of recovery time required after a disk crash, we simulated the process of recovery. After each hour of trace time, there was a simulated failure, and we then simulated the execution of I/O's that would be necessary for recovery given the contents of the memory copy of the bitmap or PG list that existed at the time of failure. (A real implementation would, of course, use the disk copy, but there should only be minor differences between the disk and memory copies since the memory copy is written to disk frequently. These minor differences should make minimal difference in recovery time.) Recovery consists of the following steps:

1. Coalesce contiguous parity group sets with bits set in the bitmap, or contiguous parity groups stored in the PG List, into multiple contiguous chunks.

2. For each chunk, do the following steps.

   (a) Calculate the physical block address and size of the chunk in physical disk blocks.

   (b) Enqueue a read I/O with the above physical block address and size to each of the disks in the RAID. (For simplicity, we assumed infinite buffer space; a real implementation would have a limit to the size of each chunk.)

   (c) After the reads complete, if any of the parity groups or parity group sets in the chunk is inconsistent, enqueue a write I/O with the above physical block address and size to the parity disk. Since we are only simulating the disks, we assume a PGS in the bitmap algorithm is inconsistent if its bit is set in the bitmap, but it is not present in the PGS Pool, and a parity group in the List Algorithm is inconsistent if it is present in the PG List but not marked consistent. A real implementation would XOR the data read from all the data disks and compare it to the data read from the parity disk; if they did not match, the result of the XOR would be written to the parity disk.

We assume that, during the recovery process, no other requests will be sent to the RAID (unlike the normal RAID rebuild procedure). Thus, the disks should be quite closely synchronized, which should make this algorithm reasonably efficient.

After the recovery, we resumed the trace-driven simulation where it left off, so the recovery-time simulation does not affect our other statistics.

Recovery time simulation was made simpler by the object-oriented nature of the simulator: an additional instance was made of the array and disk objects. This prevented the need to save and restore the current contents of the RAID and disk queues, since the recovery I/O's could be enqueued to the new instances of the disk objects, and the original instances could be used again once the normal trace-driven simulation was resumed.

5. Simulation Results

For the simulation runs, we varied the PGS size (for the bitmap algorithm) from .05 cylinders (70 parity groups) to 100 cylinders (around 14000 parity groups.) (See figure 2.) Each cylinder is 705K, or 1410 parity groups.

We also varied the PGS Pool/PG List size. In order to compare the results of different PGS sizes on the same graph, we show the pool/list size in units of parity groups on most of the following graphs. Thus, when we refer to a "larger pool size", we are referring to a pool containing more parity groups, even if the pool is actually storing a smaller number of PGS's. E.g., a pool containing two PGS's with a PGS size of 10 parity groups has a total size of 20 parity groups, and a pool containing 5 PGS's with a PGS size of 2 parity groups has a total size of 10 parity groups. The former pool is considered larger since more total parity groups are represented by its entries, even though it stores less actual entries in its PGS Pool.

Figure 4 shows the average percentage of update requests for which it was necessary to perform a fifth disk I/O for the PGS Bitmap and List algorithms. Since the PGS Pool and PG List are so similar in function, we relate their sizes directly on the same axis. Thus, the List Algorithm is effectively a special case of the PGS Bitmap Algorithm with a PGS size of 1 parity group.

The percentage of times a fifth I/O was necessary can be thought of as the "miss rate" of the bitmap and PGS pool. The results in figure 4 show that at smaller pool sizes, a smaller PGS size is better (requires a lower percentage of fifth writes) than a higher one. For example, at a total pool size of around 100,000 or less parity groups, a PGS size of .05 cyl is better than a PGS size of 1 cyl which is in turn

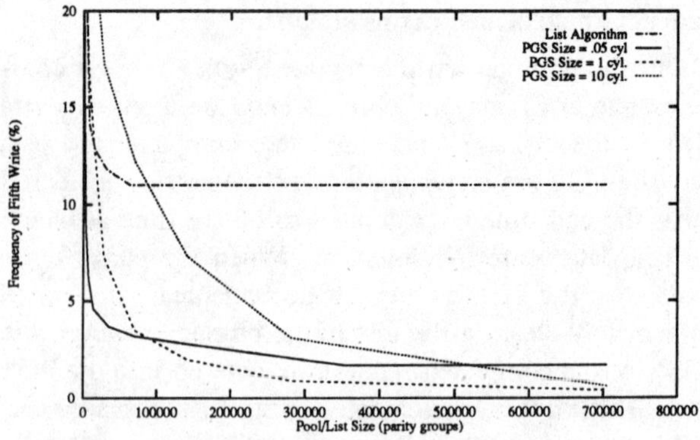

Figure 4. PGS Bitmap fifth write percentage vs pool size

better than a PGS size of 10 cyl. This is due to the fact that at small PGS sizes, the pool will contain more PGS's, and at small pool sizes it is more useful to hold many small PGS's rather than few large ones.

However, as the pool size increases, the percentage flattens out until it fails to gain any improvement from larger pool sizes. With larger PGS sizes, the percentage eventually achieves a lower value before it flattens out. For example, with a PGS size of .05 cyl, the percentage flattens out to 1.7% at a pool size of around 350,000 parity groups. In contrast, with a PGS size of 1 cyl, it flattens out to 0.4% at a pool size of around 700,000 parity groups. This appears to indicate that at very high pool sizes, the misses to the PGS pool become dominated by cold misses due to first-time access of a PGS. Increasing the PGS size reduces the miss rate in the same way that increasing block sizes reduces the effect of cold misses in caches, as described in [2].

This figure also shows results of the List Algorithm. Since this algorithm uses parity groups rather than parity group sets in its pool, it is very similar to using a very small PGS size in the bitmap algorithm, as mentioned above. Thus, its hit percentage flattens out very quickly to around 11%.

Figure 5 shows the average write response time for both algorithms at increasing pool sizes. The shapes of the curves in this figure are very similar to those in figure 4, as the write response time is directly affected by the need to perform a fifth disk I/O. Note that the PGS Bitmap Algorithm achieves considerably better write response times than the List Algorithm.

Figure 6 shows the recovery time related to the pool/list size. The approximately linear shapes of the curves show the direct relation between the size of the pool and the re-

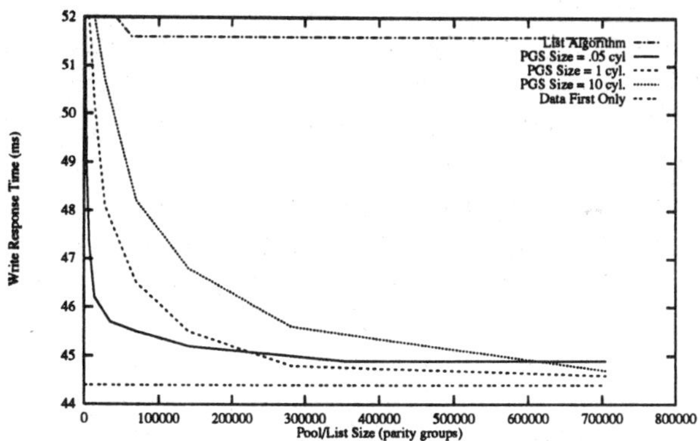

Figure 5. Write Response Time vs Pool/List Size

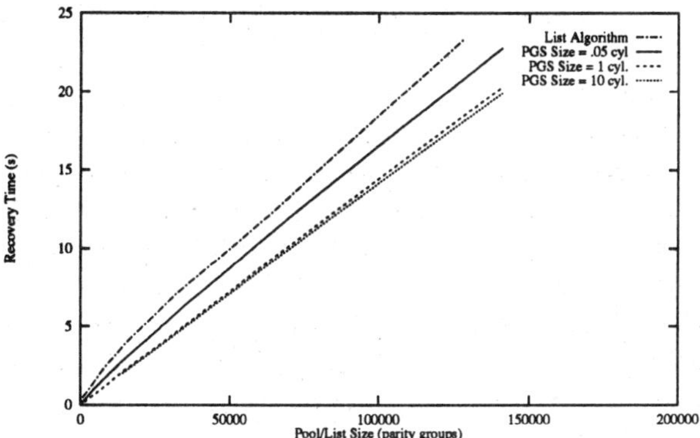

Figure 6. Recovery Time vs Pool/List Size

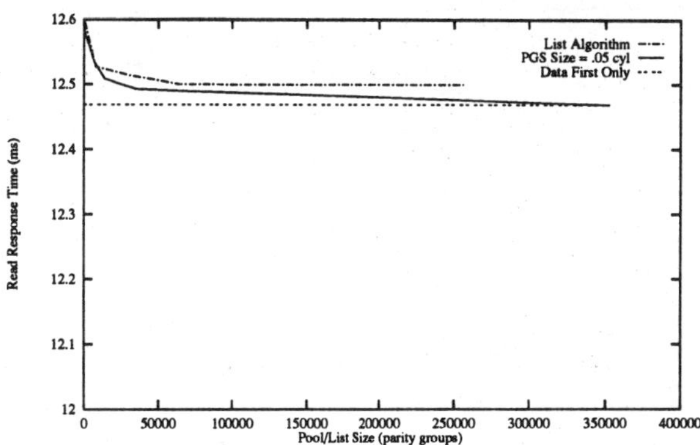

Figure 7. Read Response Time vs Pool/List Size

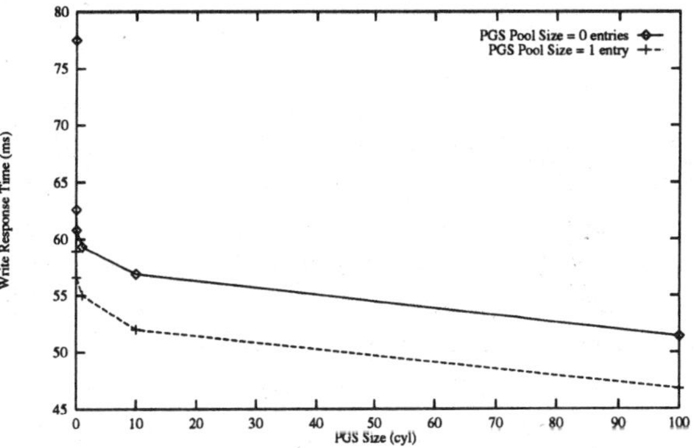

Figure 8. PGS Bitmap average write response times with and without pool

covery time. This is due to the fact that a larger pool size will mean that more bits are set in the bitmap at any given time (since the pool represents PGS's whose bits have been delayed from being reset.) At recovery, the controller must check each PGS whose bit is set, so it must check more PGS's with larger pool sizes. The varying slopes of the lines reflect the higher sequentiality of the recovery I/O's at higher PGS sizes; a smaller PGS size results in a higher slope since the parity groups to be recovered will be more scattered. The point where the Data First algorithm alone was used is not shown on this chart; it resulted in a recovery time of approximately 600 sec.

Figure 7 shows the average response time of read requests for increasing sizes of the pool/list with the PGS Bitmap Algorithm, List algorithm, and unenhanced Data First algorithm. From these results, it can be seen that the response time of the read requests is only negligibly worsened by the extra writes of the bitmap, with a maximum penalty in the worst case of around 0.2 ms or around 1.5%, which drops very quickly as the pool size is increased. For simplicity, PGS Bitmap results are only shown from one

PGS size, which is the worst case of all those tested. Similar results apply to the other PGS sizes.

Figure 8 shows the average write response time observed for the PGS Bitmap Algorithm at increasing PGS sizes for a PGS Pool of zero or one PGS entry. Note that the response time difference is kept relatively constant, at around 5 ms, as the PGS size increases. The one entry in the PGS pool allows one bit in the bitmap to be left set. Leaving this bit set is likely to save a large number of requests from needing to write the bitmap, particularly if the trace has a large amount of spatial locality.

The one-entry pool is especially valuable in workloads with high interarrival times. Without a pool, the fifth disk I/O will almost always need to be performed in such workloads because a previous request will finish before the next one arrives, so its bit will be reset. Thus, there is almost no benefit from having the bitmap even with large PGS sizes because the bit will be reset before it can be used. Adding

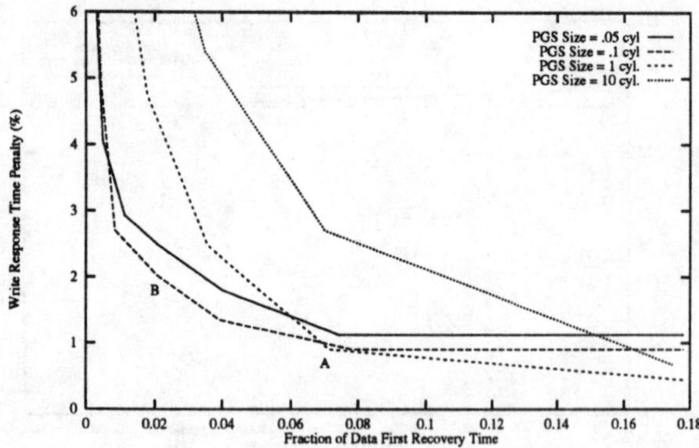

Figure 9. PGS Bitmap Write response time penalty vs recovery time

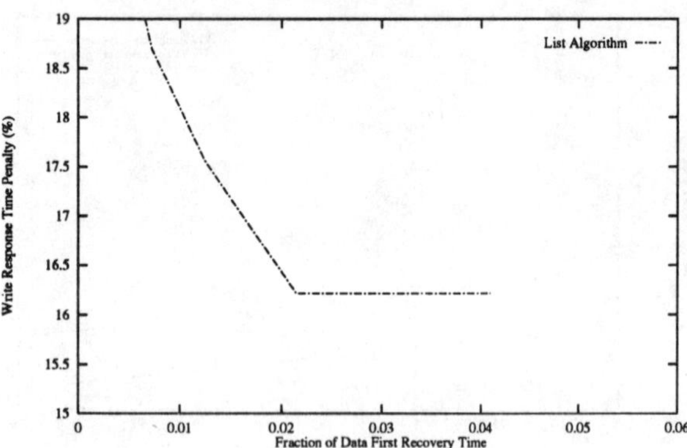

Figure 10. List Algorithm Write response time penalty vs recovery time

even a one-entry pool helps tremendously since leaving the bit set allows us to take advantage of the trace's spatial locality.

Figures 9 and 10 show the average write response time penalty vs. the fraction of the recovery time of the data first algorithm. These graphs directly show the tradeoff between recovery time and response time. It appears from these results that one optimal point to minimize both response time penalty and recovery time is at point "A" on figure 9 with a PGS size of 1 cylinder (1410 parity groups). At this point the write response time penalty is less than 1%, and the fraction of recovery time is 0.07, over 12 times faster than without the bitmap. Applications with specific requirements can choose other parameters to improve one of these measures at the expense of the other. The List Algorithm manages to reduce the recovery time to 1/50 of the time of a full scan recovery, but its response time penalty never gets lower than 16%. It is also possible to choose

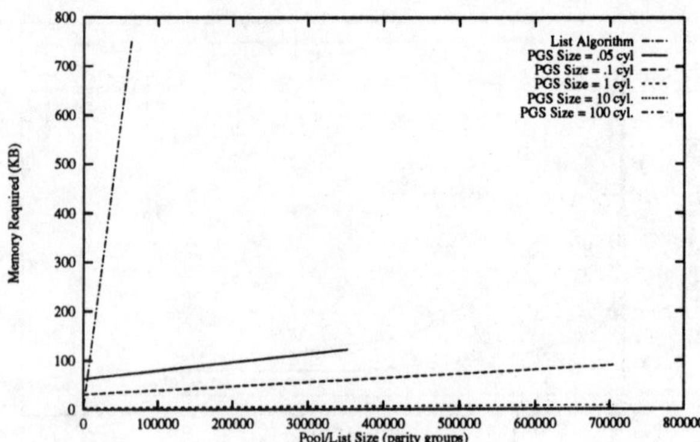

Figure 11. Memory usage

parameters for the PGS Bitmap Algorithm to achieve a recovery time reduction of 1/50, but with only a 2% response time penalty (see point "B" on Figure 9 with PGS size = .1 cyl).

Finally, figure 11 shows the memory usage of both algorithms vs the pool/list size. Because it uses a bitmap which is very memory efficient, and because of the larger granularity of PGS's, the bitmap algorithm is significantly cheaper than the List Algorithm. The optimal point (Point "A") described above (with response time penalty of around 1% and recovery time speedup of 12 times) has a pool size of 500 PGS's and a PGS size of 1 cylinder. A realistic implementation of the bitmap algorithm would probably use around 12 bytes per pool entry, 1 byte per PGS for the PGS count, and 1 bit per PGS for the bitmap. With a 1 cyl. PGS size, the array has around 2800 PGS's, so the total memory usage is $12 \times 500 + 1 \times 2800 + (1/8) \times 2800 \approx 9KB$. This is a completely trivial memory requirement.

The List Algorithm requires a list size of 32000 parity groups to achieve its best-case response time penalty of 16%. Assuming 12 bytes per list entry as in the PGS pool, total memory requirements are $12 \times 32000 \approx 375KB$, a somewhat higher but probably still insignificant memory requirement, considering today's memory densities and the fact that a software array can use the memory of the host system.

6. Conclusions

In this paper, we reviewed the PGS Bitmap Algorithm which was introduced in a previous paper as an optimization to the traditional data first algorithm. We also reviewed the List Algorithm, which is similar to the PGS Bitmap Algorithm, but uses only a list of parity groups and does no blocking of parity groups into parity group sets.

We then described the details of a simulator we implemented to test both algorithms, and described the results of our simulation runs. These runs showed that we could improve the recovery time of the data first algorithm to 12 times less than a full scan recovery at a response time penalty of 1%, and a memory cost of only 9KB. The List Algorithm, on the other hand, is able to achieve comparable recovery time improvement but cannot reduce the response time penalty below 16%, and the memory cost for this best case is 375KB.

The PGS Pool of the PGS Bitmap Algorithm can be seen to act much like a disk or memory cache, where the benefit of a hit is to avoid doing a write of the bitmap. Thus, the percentage of writes for which a fifth I/O was needed is effectively the "miss rate" of the pool. Increasing the pool size allows us to take greater advantage of the temporal locality of requests, but the price paid for this is higher recovery time.

Likewise, the PGS size is analogous to the cache block size. The effect of increasing the PGS size is to take greater advantage of the spatial locality of requests, since a write to one parity group will automatically bring its neighboring parity groups into the pool as part of the same PGS. The effect of decreasing the PGS size is to provide a finer unit of granularity. This allows more efficient use of a small overall pool size, but its performance flattens out as the pool gets larger due to becoming dominated by cold misses, which derive no benefit from a larger pool.

The List Algorithm can be seen to be largely a special case of the PGS Bitmap algorithm, using a PGS size of 1 parity group. The List Algorithm's PG List data structure serves the same function as the PGS Pool of the bitmap algorithm, and its consistent/inconsistent flags are analogous to the bitmap itself.

References

[1] P. M. Chen, E. Lee, G. Gibson, D. Patterson, and R. Katz. RAID: High-performance, reliable secondary storage. *ACM Computing Surveys*, 26(2):145–186, June 1994.

[2] J. L. Hennessy and D. A. Patterson. *Computer Architecture: A Quantitative Approach*, pages 422–423. Morgan Kaufmann Publishers, Inc., first edition, 1990.

[3] IBM Corporation, Havant, UK. *Allicat—SSA Functional Specification Level 1.6*, December 1993.

[4] E. K. Lee and R. H. Katz. The performance of parity placements in disk arrays. *IEEE Transactions on Computers*, 42(6):651–664, June 1993.

[5] J. Menon, J. Riegel, and J. Wyllie. Algorithms for software and low-cost hardware RAIDs. In *Proceedings of IEEE Compcon Conference*, San Francisco, 1995.

[6] D. Patterson, G. Gibson, and R. Katz. Reliable arrays of inexpensive disks (RAID). In *ACM Sigmod Conference 1988*, pages 109–116, Chicago, 1988.

Session 3A

Web-Based Information Systems

dSCAM: Finding Document Copies Across Multiple Databases [*]

Héctor García-Molina   Luis Gravano   Narayanan Shivakumar

Computer Science Department
Stanford University
Stanford, CA 94305-9040, USA

{hector,gravano,shiva}@cs.stanford.edu

Abstract

The advent of the Internet has made the illegal dissemination of copyrighted material easy. An important problem is how to automatically detect when a "new" digital document is "suspiciously close" to existing ones. The SCAM project at Stanford University has addressed this problem when there is a single registered-document database. However, in practice, text documents may appear in many autonomous databases, and one would like to discover copies without having to exhaustively search in all databases. Our approach, dSCAM, is a distributed version of SCAM that keeps succinct metainformation about the contents of the available document databases. Given a suspicious document S, dSCAM uses its information to prune all databases that cannot contain any document that is close enough to S, and hence the search can focus on the remaining sites. We also study how to query the remaining databases so as to minimize different querying costs. We empirically study the pruning and searching schemes, using a collection of 50 databases and two sets of test documents.

1   Introduction

In a renowned 1995 case [1], an author, who we will refer to as Mr. X for legal reasons, plagiarized several technical reports and conference papers, and resubmitted them under his own name to other conferences and journals. Unfortunately, most of these papers (nearly 18) passed undetected through the paper review process and were accepted to these conferences and journals. The topics of these papers ranged from Steiner routing in VLSI CAD, to massively parallel genetic algorithms, complexity theory, and network protocols. Mr. X also plagiarized papers from the database field, notably a paper in DAPD by Tal and Alonso [2] on three-phase locking, a paper in VLDB '92 by Ioannidis et al. [3] on parametric query optimization, and a paper in ICDE '90 by Leung and Muntz [4] on temporal query processing. The Stanford Copy Analysis Mechanism (SCAM) [5, 6] played an important role in identifying the papers that Mr. X had plagiarized. (See [7, 1] for further details.)

SCAM is a registration server mechanism that helps flag document-copyright violations in Digital Libraries. The target is not simply academic plagiarism, but any type of copying that can financially hurt authors and commercial publishers. SCAM is also useful for removing duplicates and near-duplicates in information retrieval systems [8]. Essentially, SCAM keeps a large database of documents along with indices to support efficient retrieval of stored documents that are "potential copies." SCAM attempts to find not just identical copies, but also cases of "substantial" overlap. For example, if a document contains several paragraphs or sections that were copied from a registered document, it should be flagged as a potential copy even if there are also significant portions where the documents differ. Documents flagged by SCAM have to be checked manually for actual violations since the copying may have been legal and since SCAM may produce some false positives.

The basic SCAM system requires a database of registered documents. In the future, publishers may indeed establish such "copyright registration servers" [9], and these servers can then automatically check public sources such as netnews articles and WWW/FTP sites for copies of the registered documents. However, if there are multiple registration servers, and one has a suspicious document to check, one has to decide what servers to check, since it may be impractical to go to all of them. Furthermore, we may also want to include in our search databases that may not be running a SCAM system. In this case, not only do we have to identify these databases, but we also need to pull out candidate documents so that SCAM can analyze them.

This is precisely what we had to do in Mr. X's case. Initially, we only had the abstracts of the papers that Mr. X had "written," i.e., we had the suspicious documents. Then we proceeded as follows:

---

[*]This material is based upon work supported by the National Science Foundation under Cooperative Agreement IRI-9411306. Funding for this cooperative agreement is also provided by DARPA, NASA, and the industrial partners of the Stanford Digital Libraries Project. Any opinions, finding, and conclusions or recommendations expressed in this material are those of the author(s) and do not necessarily reflect the views of the National Science Foundation or the other sponsors.

1. First we selected existing databases that we thought were likely to contain the matching registered documents. Based on the contents of the suspicious documents we decided that the Inspec and CS-TR databases were the most appropriate. (Inspec is a commercial database of electrical engineering and computer science abstracts; CS-TR is an emerging digital library of computer science technical reports, see http://elib.stanford.edu.)

2. We manually chose some keywords from Mr. X's abstracts, and issued queries such as "VLSI or Steiner or Routing" against the above databases.

3. We retrieved the abstracts (about 35,000 overall) that matched the above queries, registered them in SCAM, and then tested the suspicious documents against them. In this way we found a total of 14 cases of plagiarism, most of them previously unknown.

In this paper we develop *dSCAM*, a system that automates the entire copy search process. Automating this process is crucial as the number of document databases grows and as publishers rely more on digital publishing. As a matter of fact, appropriate safeguards for intellectual property rights are essential in a large scale public digital library, and an automated *dSCAM* can be one of the tools. In particular,

- *Discovery:* We present the *dSCAM* mechanism that, given many databases and a suspicious document, efficiently identifies the databases that may contain documents that SCAM would consider copies. This problem is fundamentally different from a conventional search problem: *dSCAM* has to flag a database even if it contains a single document that overlaps significantly with the suspicious document.

- *Extraction:* We present the *dSCAM* strategies for automatically generating a query that retrieves potential copies for subsequent analysis by SCAM.

For the discovery phase, we build on previous work in the resource-discovery area, more specifically, on the *GlOSS* approach [10, 11]. The idea is to collect in advance "metainformation" about the candidate databases. This can include, for example, information on how frequently terms appear in documents at a particular database. This metainformation is much smaller than a full index of the database or than what SCAM would actually need to detect copies. Then, based on this information, *dSCAM* can rule out databases that do not contain documents that SCAM would consider copies.

Notice that while *dSCAM* is structurally similar to *GlOSS*, there is a fundamental difference. *GlOSS* attempts to discover databases that satisfy a given query (Boolean or vector space). The *GlOSS* problem is a simpler one since all we need to know is that the candidate database contains the necessary terms. However, for *dSCAM*, finding documents that have similar terms to those of the suspicious document is not enough. For example, if the suspicious document only contains a subset that is a copy, then there are terms in the non-copy portion that are not relevant. Thus, simply treating the suspicious document as a *GlOSS* query will not lead us to the right databases.

Instead, *dSCAM* will need to keep more sophisticated statistics than *GlOSS* does, enough to let it identify sites that may have even a single copy, not just documents that are "similar" to the suspicious one in an information retrieval sense. The key challenge is to collect as little information as possible in *dSCAM* to be able to perform this difficult discovery task. Section 7 reports experiments that indeed show that our techniques are successful at isolating the databases with potential copies, with relatively few false positives.

In this paper we consider two types of discovery techniques: *conservative* and *liberal* ones. Conservative techniques only rule out a database if it is certain that SCAM would not consider *any* document there a potential copy. The clear advantage of conservative techniques is that they do not miss potential copies. In contrast, liberal techniques might in principle miss databases with potential copies. However, this is rarely the case, as we will see, and the liberal techniques search fewer unnecessary databases. In practice, the choice between conservative and liberal depends on how exhaustive the search must be and what resources are available.

For the extraction problem (i.e., the problem of generating a query to retrieve the potential copies from a database), a naive solution is to simply query each database (identified in the discovery phase) for all documents containing any of the terms in the suspicious document. That is, if the suspicious document contains words $w_1, \ldots w_N$, we could submit the query $w_1 \vee \ldots \vee w_N$ (or alternatively, request all the documents with w_1, then all the ones with w_2, and so on). Clearly, any potential copy would be extracted in this way. However, our goal here is to extract all the potential copies without having to perform such a massive query. Thus, to solve this problem we show how to find the minimal query, under two different cost metrics, that can extract all the desired documents. For example, one of our cost measures is the number of words in the submitted query. We will see that we can reduce such a number drastically by bounding the maximum "contribution" of every word to a potential copy.

We start in Section 2 by giving an overview of SCAM. In Section 3 we describe the data that *dSCAM* keeps about the databases. We use this data in Section 4 to define the conservative copy discovery schemes for *dSCAM*, while in Section 5 we relax these schemes to make them liberal. In Section 6 we present the extraction mechanisms. Finally, in Section 7 we discuss an experimental evaluation of our techniques, using a collection of 50 databases and two sets of suspicious documents.

2 Using SCAM for copy detection

Given a suspicious document S and a registered document D, SCAM detects whether D is a potential copy of S by deciding whether they overlap significantly. We have explored [5, 6] a variety of overlap measures. For example, we can say that S and D overlap if they contain at least some fraction of common sentences. A problem with this scheme is that it is often hard to detect sentence boundaries (e.g., periods in abbreviations get confused with the end of sentences). Also, it cannot detect partial-sentence overlaps.

A different measure we have studied uses *similarity*, in the information retrieval (IR) sense, as a starting point. Traditionally, two documents are said to be similar if the frequency with which words occur is correlated. If the distribution of word frequencies between S and D is identical, we say that the similarity is maximal at 1. As the distributions differ, the similarity decreases. This measure does not work for copy detection because the matching documents can have portions that are very different causing the word frequency distributions to differ significantly. However, this measure can be modified for copy detection as we will explain in this section. In this paper we will use this modified IR measure as the basis for *dSCAM* because our experimental results show it works best, at least for the relatively small documents found on the Internet.

To evaluate S and D using this modified IR measure, SCAM first focuses on the words that appear a similar number of times in S and D, and ignores the rest of the words. More precisely, given a fixed $\epsilon > 2$, the *closeness set* for S and D, $c(S, D)$, contains the words w_i with a similar number of occurrences in the two documents [5]:

$$w_i \in c(S, D) \Leftrightarrow \frac{F_i(S)}{F_i(D)} + \frac{F_i(D)}{F_i(S)} < \epsilon$$

where $F_i(d)$ is the frequency of word w_i in document d. If either $F_i(S)$ or $F_i(D)$ are zero, then w_i is not in the closeness set. Given ϵ, S determines a range of frequencies $Accept(w_i, F_i(S))$ such that w_i is in the closeness set for S and D if and only if $F_i(D) \in Accept(w_i, F_i(S))$.

The intuition behind this is as follows. If S and D share a substantial portion of identical text, then there ought to be a set of words unique to that text that will occur with similar frequencies. Focusing on words in the closeness set diminishes the effects of unrelated portions of text.[1]

Example 1 *Consider a suspicious document S and a database db with two documents, D_1 and D_2. There are four words in these documents, w_1, w_2, w_3, and w_4. The following table shows the frequency of the words in the documents.*

Document	F_1	F_2	F_3	F_4
S	1	3	3	9
D_1	1	3	0	0
D_2	0	8	5	0

For example, w_3 appears three times in S ($F_3(S) = 3$), five times in D_2 ($F_3(D_2) = 5$), and it does not appear in D_1 ($F_3(D_1) = 0$). Assuming $\epsilon = 2.5$ (a value that worked well in the experiments in [5]), $Accept(w_3, F_3(S)) = Accept(w_3, 3) = [2, 5]$. Thus, w_3 is in $c(S, D_2)$, the closeness set for S and D_2, because $F_3(D_2) = 5$ is in $Accept(w_3, F_3(S))$. Although $F_3(D_2)$ is higher than $F_3(S)$, these two values are sufficiently close for $\epsilon = 2.5$. In effect, $\frac{F_3(S)}{F_3(D_2)} + \frac{F_3(D_2)}{F_3(S)} = \frac{3}{5} + \frac{5}{3} = 2.27 < \epsilon = 2.5$. For the remaining cases, $Accept(w_1, F_1(S)) = [1, 1]$, $Accept(w_2, F_2(S)) = [2, 5]$, and $Accept(w_4, F_4(S)) = [5, 17]$. Then, $c(S, D_1) = \{w_1, w_2\}$, and $c(S, D_2) = \{w_3\}$.

After finding the closeness set for S and D, SCAM computes the similarity $sim(S, D)$ between the two documents. We would like to use traditional IR similarity measures (using only words in the closeness set), but this does not work because those measures give low values when S is a subset of D or vice versa. Instead we compute two measures, one for the case where S might be a subset of D and one for the reverse case, and take the maximum. In the former we ignore the norm (see below) of D since it could be a much larger document; in the latter we ignore the norm of S. That is, $sim(S, D) = \max\{subset(S, D), subset(D, S)\}$ where:

$$subset(D_1, D_2) = \sum_{w_i \in c(D_1, D_2)} \frac{F_i(D_1)}{|D_1|} \cdot F_i(D_2)$$

($|D| = \sum_{i=1}^{N} F_i^2(D)$ is the norm of document D and N is the number of terms.) If $sim(S, D) > T$, for some user-specified threshold T, then SCAM flags document D as a potential copy of the suspicious document S.

Example 1 (cont.) *Continuing with our example above,* $|S| = F_1^2(S) + F_2^2(S) + F_3^2(S) + F_4^2(S) = 1^2 + 3^2 + 3^2 + 9^2 = 100$. *Similarly,* $|D_1| = 10$ *and* $|D_2| = 89$. *To compute the similarity* $sim(S, D_2)$ *we just consider* w_3, *the only word in the closeness set for* S *and* D_2. *Then,*

$$sim(S, D_2) = \max\{F_3(D_2) \cdot \frac{F_3(S)}{|S|}, \frac{F_3(D_2)}{|D_2|} \cdot F_3(S)\}$$

$$= \max\{5 \cdot \frac{3}{100}, \frac{5}{89} \cdot 3\} = 0.17$$

Similarly, $sim(S, D_1) = 1$, *because SCAM regards* D_1 *as a strict "subdocument" of* S. *So, for* $T = 0.80$, *SCAM would not consider* D_2 *to be a potential copy of* S. *However, SCAM would find* D_1 *suspiciously close to* S.

Even though the SCAM similarity does not take into account word sequencing, the experiments in [5, 6] show that it detects potential copies relatively well. In these experiments, conducted with 50,000 netnews articles, false positives were very rare: the similarity measure flagged unrelated documents as copies (because they shared common vocabulary) in only 0.01% of the cases. False negatives were more common but still only 5% of the cases tested: in

---

[1] It also helps to ignore altogether words that occur frequently across documents [6]. Our experiments of Section 7 use the stop words in [6].

these cases, documents with relatively small overlap were not detected. Overall, the similarity measure performed better than the sentence overlap measure described earlier.

3 The *dSCAM* information about the databases

dSCAM needs information to decide whether a database db has potential copies of a suspicious document S. This information should be concise, but also sufficient to identify any such database. *dSCAM* keeps the following statistics (or a subset of them) for each database db and word w_i, where db_i is the set of documents in db that contain w_i:

- $f_i(db) = \min_{D \in db_i} F_i(D)$: $f_i(db)$ is the minimum frequency of word w_i in any document in db that contains w_i

- $F_i(db) = \max_{D \in db_i} F_i(D)$: $F_i(db)$ is the maximum frequency of word w_i in any document in db that contains w_i

- $n_i(db) = \min_{D \in db_i} |D|$: $n_i(db)$ is the minimum norm of any document in db that contains w_i

- $R_i(db) = \max_{D \in db_i} \frac{F_i(D)}{|D|}$: $R_i(db)$ is the maximum value of the ratio $\frac{F_i(D)}{|D|}$ for any document $D \in db$ that contains w_i

- $d_i(db)$ is the number of documents in db that contain word w_i

Example 1 (cont.) *The following table shows the dSCAM metadata for our sample database db. Note that there are no entries for w_4, since it does not appear in any document in db.*

Statistics	w_1	w_2	w_3
f_i	1	3	5
F_i	1	8	5
n_i	10	10	89
R_i	$\frac{1}{10}$	$\frac{3}{10}$	$\frac{5}{89}$
d_i	1	2	1

As mentioned earlier, db has two documents, D_1 and D_2. Document D_1 contains w_2 three times, and document D_2, eight times. Therefore, $f_2(db) = \min\{3, 8\} = 3$ and $F_2(db) = \max\{3, 8\} = 8$. Also, $|D_1| = 10$ and $|D_2| = 89$, so $n_2(db) = \min\{10, 89\} = 10$. Finally, $R_2(db) = \max\{\frac{3}{10}, \frac{8}{89}\} = \frac{3}{10}$, and $d_2(db) = 2$, since w_2 appears in both D_1 and D_2.

Notice that the table above is actually larger than our earlier table that gave the complete word frequencies. This is just because our sample database contains only two documents. In general, the information kept by *dSCAM* is proportional to the number of words or terms appearing in the database, while the information needed by SCAM is proportional to the number of words times the number of times the words appear in different documents. In a real database, many words appear in hundreds or thousands of documents, and hence the SCAM information can be much larger than the *dSCAM* information. We will return to this issue in Section 7. To obtain the necessary statistics, *dSCAM* periodically polls each potential source database, which then extracts the data from its index structures.

4 The conservative approach

Given a set of databases, a suspicious document S, and a threshold T, *dSCAM* selects all databases with potential copies of S, i.e., all the databases with at least one document D with $sim(S, D) > T$. To identify these databases, *dSCAM* uses the metadata of Section 3. In this section we focus on conservative techniques that never miss any database with potential copies. In other words, *dSCAM* cannot produce any *false negatives* with the techniques of this section. However, *dSCAM* might produce *false positives*, and consider that a database has potential copies when it actually does not. In Section 7 we report experimental results that study how often the latter takes place.

The information described in Section 3 can be used by *dSCAM* in a variety of ways. We present two alternatives, starting with the simplest. The more sophisticated technique will be less conservative: it will always identify the databases with potential copies of a document, but it will have fewer false positives than the simpler technique.

Given a database db, a suspicious document S, and a technique A, *dSCAM* computes an upper bound $Upper_A(db, S)$ on the similarity of any document in db and S. In other words, $Upper_A(db, S) \geq sim(S, D)$ for every document $D \in db$. Thus, if $Upper_A(db, S) \leq T$, then there are no documents in db close enough to S as determined by the threshold T, and we can safely conclude that database db has no potential copies of S. The two strategies below differ in how they compute this upper bound.

The *Range* strategy

Consider a word w_i in S. Suppose that w_i appears in some document D in db. We know that D contains w_i between $f_i(db)$ and $F_i(db)$ times. Also, w_i is in the closeness set for S and D if and only if $F_i(D) \in Accept(w_i, F_i(S))$. So, w_i is in the closeness set for S and D if and only if $F_i(D) \in [m_i, M_i] = [f_i(db), F_i(db)] \cap Accept(w_i, F_i(S))$. If this range is empty, then w_i is not in the closeness set for S and D, for any document $D \in db$, and therefore w_i does not contribute to $sim(S, D)$ for any D. If the range $[m_i, M_i]$ is not empty, then w_i can be in the closeness set for S and D, for some document D. For any such document D, $F_i(D) \leq M_i$. We then define the *maximum frequency* of word $w_i \in S$ in any document of db, $M_i(db, S)$, as:

$$M_i(db, S) = \begin{cases} M_i & \text{if } [m_i, M_i] \neq \emptyset \\ 0 & \text{otherwise} \end{cases}$$

Putting everything together, we define the upper bound on the similarity of any document D in db and S for technique *Range* as:

$$Upper_{Range}(db, S) =$$

$$\max\{Upper1_{Range}(db, S),\ Upper2_{Range}(db, S)\}$$

where:

$$Upper1_{Range}(db, S)\ =\ \sum_{i=1}^{N} M_i(db, S) \cdot \frac{F_i(S)}{|S|} \quad (1)$$

$$Upper2_{Range}(db, S)\ =\ \sum_{i=1}^{N} \frac{M_i(db, S)}{n_i(db)} \cdot F_i(S) \quad (2)$$

Note that since $n_i(db) \leq |D|$ for every $D \in db$ that contains w_i, then $Upper_{Range}(db, S) \geq sim(S, D)$ for every $D \in db$. Also note that the *Range* technique does not use the R_i statistics.

Example 1 (cont.) *Consider the db statistics and the suspicious document S. We have already computed $Accept(w_1, F_1(S)) = [1, 1]$, $Accept(w_2, F_2(S)) = [2, 5]$, $Accept(w_3, F_3(S)) = [2, 5]$, and $Accept(w_4, F_4(S)) = [5, 17]$. Also, dSCAM knows, for example, that word w_2 appears in db with in-document frequencies between $[f_2(db), F_2(db)] = [3, 8]$. Then, the interesting range of frequencies of w_2 in db is $[m_2, M_2] = [3, 8] \cap [2, 5] = [3, 5]$. The maximum such frequency is $M_2(db, S) = 5$. (Notice that there is no document D in db with $F_2(D) = 5$. $M_2(db, S)$ is in this case a strict upper bound for the frequencies of w_2 in db that are in $Accept(w_2, F_2(S))$.) Similarly, $M_1(db, S) = 1$, $M_3(db, S) = 5$, and $M_4(db, S) = 0$. Therefore,*

$$Upper1_{Range}(db, S)\ =\ 1 \cdot \frac{1}{100} + 5 \cdot \frac{3}{100} + 5 \cdot \frac{3}{100}$$
$$=\ 0.31$$
$$Upper2_{Range}(db, S)\ =\ \frac{1}{10} \cdot 1 + \frac{5}{10} \cdot 3 + \frac{5}{89} \cdot 3$$
$$=\ 1.77$$
$$Upper_{Range}(db, S)\ =\ 1.77$$

Therefore, if our threshold T is, say, 0.80, we would search db. This is of course the right decision since D_1 in db is indeed a potential copy.

The *Ratio* strategy

This technique is similar to the previous one, but uses the R_i statistics. Thus,

$$Upper_{Ratio}(db, S) =$$
$$\max\{Upper1_{Range}(db, S),\ Upper2_{Ratio}(db, S)\}$$

where:

$$Upper2_{Ratio}(db, S) =$$
$$\sum_{i \mid M_i(db, S) \neq 0} \min\{\frac{M_i(db, S)}{n_i(db)}, R_i(db)\} \cdot F_i(S) \quad (3)$$

It is immediate from the definition above that $Upper_{Ratio}(db, S) \leq Upper_{Range}(db, S)$ for every

database db and query document S. Therefore, *Ratio* is a less conservative technique than *Range*, and will tend to have fewer false positives than *Range*. Nevertheless, *Ratio* will always detect databases with potential copies of S, because $sim(S, D) \leq Upper_{Ratio}(db, S)$ for every $D \in db$.

Example 1 (cont.) *We have already computed $Upper1_{Range}(db, S) = 0.31$. Now,*

$$Upper2_{Ratio}(db, S)\ =\ \frac{1}{10} \cdot 1 + \frac{3}{10} \cdot 3 + \frac{5}{89} \cdot 3$$
$$=\ 1.17$$

which is lower than $Upper2_{Range}(db, S)$.

5   The liberal approach

The techniques of Section 4 are conservative: they never fail to identify a database with potential copies of a suspicious document (i.e., these techniques have no false negatives). A problem with these techniques is that they usually produce too many false positives. (See Section 7.) Consequently, we now introduce *liberal* versions of the *Range* and *Ratio* techniques. In principle, the new techniques might have false negatives. As we will see, false negatives occur rarely, while the number of false positives is much lower than that for the conservative techniques.

We modify the techniques of Section 4 in two different ways. First, we allow these techniques to focus only on the "rarest" words that occur in a suspicious document, instead of on all its words (or on all the words that SCAM uses). (See Section 5.1.) This way dSCAM can prune away databases where these rare words do not appear, thus reducing the search space. Second, we allow these techniques to use probabilities to estimate (under some assumptions) how many potential copies of a suspicious document each database is expected to have. (See Section 5.2.) Thus, the probabilistic techniques no longer compute upper bounds, again reducing the search space.

5.1   Counting only rare words

The techniques of Section 4 considered every word in a suspicious document S (i.e., every word that SCAM uses) to decide which databases to search for potential copies of S. Alternatively, dSCAM can just focus on the *rarest* words in S, i.e., on the words in S that appear in the fewest number of databases. dSCAM then decides to search a database only if at least a few of these rare words appear in it. If dSCAM uses enough of the rare words in S, any potential copy of S will tend to contain a few of these words. Furthermore, since these words appear in only a few databases, they will help dSCAM dismiss a significant fraction of the databases, thus reducing the number of false positives.

One specific way to implement these ideas is as follows. Given a suspicious document S, dSCAM just considers k percent of its words. These are the $k\%$ words in S that appear in the fewest available databases. dSCAM can tell which words these are from the metadata about the databases (Section 3). The remaining words in S are simply ignored.

Example 1 (cont.) *Consider suspicious document S, with words w_1, w_2, w_3, and w_4. Suppose that w_1 appears in 1 database, w_2 in 2, w_3 in 70, and w_4 in 20 databases. If dSCAM uses only 50% of the words in S ($k = 50$), it chooses w_1 and w_2, and ignores w_3 and w_4.*

As we mentioned before, $dSCAM$ now ignores words in S that SCAM uses for copy detection. Therefore, $dSCAM$ might in principle miss a database with potential copies of S. However, as we will see in Section 7, we can find values for k for which $dSCAM$ has very few false negatives, while producing much fewer false positives than with the conservative techniques of Section 4.

Given k, we adapt the $Upper_{Range}$ and $Upper_{Ratio}$ bounds of Section 4 (Equations 1, 2, and 3) to sum only over the $k\%$ rarest words in S. We refer to the new values as Sum_{Range} and Sum_{Ratio}, because they are no longer upper bounds on the similarities of the documents in the databases and S.

As we use fewer words in S (i.e., only $k\%$ of them), we need to adjust the threshold T (Section 2) for $dSCAM$ accordingly. We refer to the adjusted threshold as T^k. For example, if we are just considering 10% of the words in S, we could compensate by reducing the threshold $T^{10} = 0.10 * T$. We explore different values for T^k in Section 7. If $Sum_{Range}(db, S)$ (respectively, $Sum_{Ratio}(db, S)$) is higher than T^k, $dSCAM$ will search db for potential copies of S.

Example 1 (cont.) *In Section 4 we computed $Upper_{Range}(db, S) = 1.77$. Now, if dSCAM only considers the 50% rarest words in S (i.e., w_1 and w_2), only those words are counted, and we have:*

$$Sum1_{Range}(db, S) = 1 \cdot \frac{1}{100} + 5 \cdot \frac{3}{100} = 0.16$$

$$Sum2_{Range}(db, S) = \frac{1}{10} \cdot 1 + \frac{5}{10} \cdot 3 = 1.6$$

$$Sum_{Range}(db, S) = 1.6$$

The original SCAM threshold was $T = 0.80$. Since we are now considering only half of the words, we could scale down T to, say, $T^{50} = 0.5 \cdot T = 0.40$. At any rate, we would still search db, because $1.6 > 0.40$. This is the right decision, since D_1 in db is indeed a potential copy.

5.2 Using probabilities

So far, the techniques for $dSCAM$ compute the maximum possible contribution of each word considered, and add these contributions. However, it is unlikely that any document in a database will contain all of these words with this maximum contribution. In this section, we depart from this "deterministic" model, and, given a database db, try to bound the probability that db has potential copies of a suspicious document. If this probability is high enough, $dSCAM$ will search db.

Our goal is to bound the probability that a document in db has a similarity with S that exceeds the adjusted threshold T^k. For this, we define two random variables $XRange1$ and $XRange2$ (corresponding to $Sum1_{Range}$ and $Sum2_{Range}$, respectively). These variables model the similarity of the documents in db and S. Then,

$$Prob_{Range} = \max\{P(XRange1 > T^k), P(XRange2 > T^k)\}$$

If $Prob_{Range} \geq \frac{1}{|db|}$, $dSCAM$ will search db for potential copies of S, since there is at least one expected document that exceeds the adjusted threshold T^k.

Actually, instead of computing $P(XRange1 > T^k)$ and $P(XRange2 > T^k)$, we use an upper bound for these values as given by Chebyshev's inequality. This bound is based on the expected value and the variance of $XRange1$ and $XRange2$.

We now define random variable $XRange1$, following the definition of $Sum1_{Range}$. (Random variable $XRange2$ is analogous, using the definition of $Sum2_{Range}$.) The $XRange1$ is actually a sum of random variables: $XRange1 = XRange1_{i_1} + \ldots + XRange1_{i_s}$, where $w_{i_1}, \ldots, w_{i_s}$ are the $k\%$ rarest words in S. Random variable $XRange1_i$ corresponds to word w_i:

$$XRange1_i = \begin{cases} M_i(db, S) \cdot \frac{F_i(S)}{|S|} & \text{with prob. } \frac{d_i(db)}{|db|} \\ 0 & \text{with prob. } 1 - \frac{d_i(db)}{|db|} \end{cases}$$

This variable models the occurrence of word w_i in the documents of database db. Word w_i occurs in $d_i(db)$ documents in db, so the probability that it appears in a randomly chosen document from db is $\frac{d_i(db)}{|db|}$. To use Chebyshev's inequality and compute the variance of $XRange1$ and $XRange2$, we assume that words appear in documents following independent probability distributions. We define $Prob_{Ratio}$ in a completely analogous way.

6 Searching the databases with potential copies

Once $dSCAM$ has decided that a database db might have potential copies of a suspicious document S, it has to extract these potential copies from db. If database db happens to run a local SCAM server, $dSCAM$ can simply submit S to this server and get back exactly those documents that SCAM considers potential copies. However, if db does not run a SCAM server, we need an alternative mechanism to extract the potential copies automatically. For this, we will assume that db can answer boolean "or" queries, which most commercial search engines support. For example, we can retrieve from db all documents containing the words "copyright" or the word "SCAM" by issuing the query "copyright $\vee$ SCAM." (Alternatively, if some search engine does not support "or" queries, we could issue a sequence of queries, and then merge the sequence of results.)

Let $w_1, \ldots, w_N$ be the words in S. In principle, we could issue the query $w_1 \vee \ldots \vee w_N$ to db and obtain all documents that contain at least one of these words. However, such a query is bound to return too many documents that are not potential copies of S. In this section, we study how to choose a smaller set of words $\{w_{i_1}, \ldots, w_{i_n}\}$ that will not miss any potential copy from db. Furthermore, the resulting queries will tend not to extract documents that are not potential copies of S.

To choose a set of words to query, we define the *maximum contribution* $C_i(db, S)$ of word w_i in db as an upper bound on the amount that w_i can add to $sim(S, D)$, for any $D \in db$. We give two definitions of this maximum contribution, each corresponding to a technique of Section 4. The first of these is more conservative but uses less information. The other is less conservative but uses more information.

$$C_i(db, S) =$$
$$\begin{cases} \max\{M_i(db, S) \cdot \frac{F_i(S)}{|S|}, \ \frac{M_i(db,S)}{n_i(db)} \cdot F_i(S)\} \\ \qquad \text{for } Range \\ \max\{M_i(db, S) \cdot \frac{F_i(S)}{|S|}, \ \min\{\frac{M_i(db,S)}{n_i(db)}, R_i(db)\} \cdot F_i(S)\} \\ \qquad \text{for } Ratio \end{cases}$$

Now, let $C(db, S) = \sum_{i=1}^{N} C_i(db, S)$, and let T be the SCAM similarity threshold that the users specified. Then, any set of words $\{w_{i_1}, \ldots, w_{i_n}\}$ with the following property is sufficient to extract all the potential copies of S from db:

$$\sum_{j=1}^{n} C_{i_j}(db, S) \geq C(db, S) - T \qquad (4)$$

To see why it is enough to use the query $w_{i_1} \vee \ldots \vee w_{i_n}$, consider a document $D \in db$ that does not contain any of these n words. Then, $sim(S, D) \leq C(db, S) - \sum_{j=1}^{n} C_{i_j}(db, S) \leq T$. Therefore, the similarity of D and S can never exceed the required threshold T. This approach is conservative: we cannot miss any potential copy of a document by choosing the query words as above. Alternatively, we explored a liberal approach that would retrieve all potential copies most of the time, and has much fewer "false positives." For space limitations, we do not describe this liberal technique further, but we report some experimental results in Section 7.

To choose among all sets of words that satisfy Condition 4, we associate a cost p_i with each word w_i. We then choose a set of words $\{w_{i_1}, \ldots, w_{i_n}\}$ that satisfies Condition 4 and minimizes $\sum_{j=1}^{n} p_{i_j}$. We consider two different cost models for a query:

The *WordMin* cost model

In this case we minimize the number of words that will appear in the query. Thus, $p_i = 1$ for all i. Then, our problem reduces to finding the smallest set of words that satisfies Condition 4, which we can do optimally with a simple greedy algorithm.

The *SelMin* cost model

In this case we consider the selectivity of each word w_i that will appear in the query, i.e., the fraction of the documents in the database that contain word w_i. Thus, $p_i = Sel(w_i, db)$. By minimizing the added selectivity we will tend to minimize the number of documents that we retrieve from db.

We will find an optimal solution for this problem by reducing it to the *0-1 knapsack problem* [12]. The new formulation of the problem is as follows. A thief robbing a store finds N items (the words). The ith item is worth p_i dollars (the selectivity of word w_i) and weighs $C_i(db, S)$ pounds (the maximum contribution of w_i). The thief wants to maximize the value of the load, but can only carry up to T pounds. The problem is to find the right items (words) to steal. This formulation of the problem actually finds the words that will not appear in the final query, and maximizes the added selectivity of these words. The weight of the words is at most T. Therefore, the words that are not chosen weigh at least $C(db, S) - T$, satisfy Condition 4, and have the lowest added selectivity among the sets satisfying Condition 4. Assuming that T, the C_i's, and the p_i's have a fixed number of significant decimals, we can use dynamic programming to solve the problem in $O(T \cdot N)$ time, where N is the number of words in the suspicious document [12].

7   Experiments

This section presents experimental results for $dSCAM$. We focus on three sets of issues: How many false positives do the $dSCAM$ techniques report, how many false negatives do the liberal $dSCAM$ techniques produce, and how effective is the document extraction step?

For the registered-document databases, our experiments used a total of 63,350 ClariNet news articles. We split these articles evenly in 50 databases so that each database consists of 1,267 documents.

For the suspicious documents, our experiments used two different document sets. The first set, which we refer to as *Registered*, contains 100 documents from the 50 databases. Therefore, each suspicious document has at least one perfect copy in some database. (There could be more copies due to crosspostings of articles.) The second set, which we refer to as *Disjoint*, contains 100 later articles that do not appear in any of the 50 databases. This set models the common case when the suspicious documents are actually new documents that do not appear anywhere else.

Our first experiments are for the Sum_{Ratio} technique, which proved to work the best among the $dSCAM$ techniques, as we will see later. Figures 1 through 4 show different interesting metrics as a function of the adjusted threshold T^k, and for different values of k. In all of these plots, the SCAM threshold T is set to 1. For example, the curves for $k = 10$ correspond to considering only 10% of the words (the rarest ones) in the suspicious documents. Note that for $k = 100$ all of the words in the suspicious documents are used. In this case, Sum_{Ratio} coincides with the conservative technique $Upper_{Ratio}$.

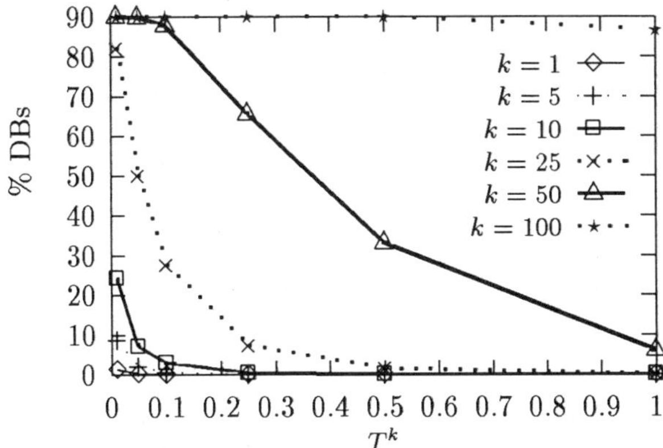

Figure 1: The percentage of the 50 databases that are searched as a function of the adjusted similarity threshold T^k (*Registered* suspicious documents; Sum_{Ratio} strategy; $T = 1$).

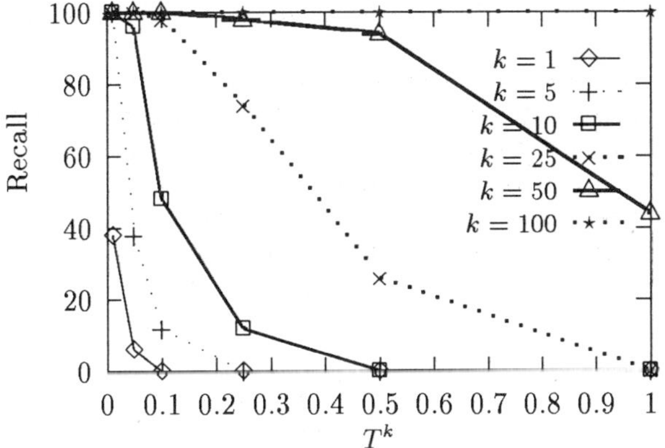

Figure 2: The average recall as a function of the adjusted similarity threshold T^k (*Registered* suspicious documents; Sum_{Ratio} strategy; $T = 1$).

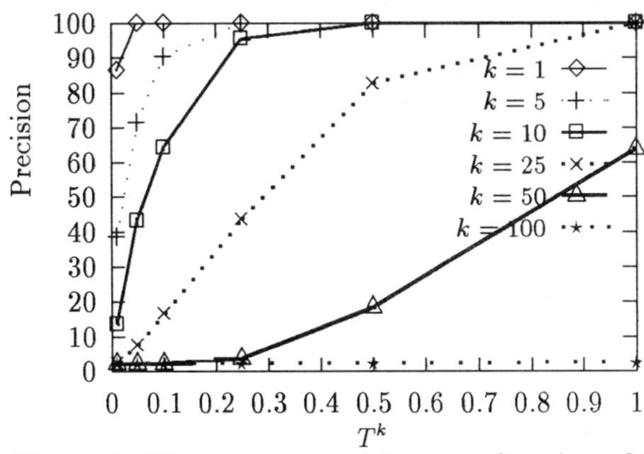

Figure 3: The average precision as a function of the adjusted similarity threshold T^k (*Registered* suspicious documents; Sum_{Ratio} strategy; $T = 1$).

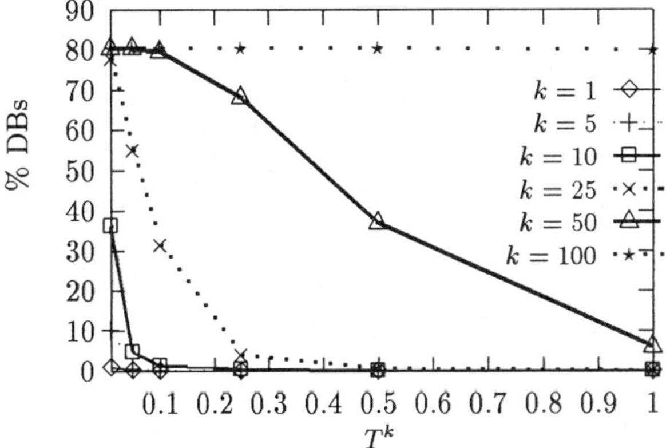

Figure 4: The percentage of the 50 databases that are searched as a function of the adjusted similarity threshold T^k (*Disjoint* suspicious documents; Sum_{Ratio} strategy; $T = 1$).

One way to evaluate the *dSCAM* strategies is to look at $d(S)$, the percentage of databases returned by *dSCAM* for a suspicious document S. Figure 1 shows the average $d(S)$ (averaged over all S in the *Registered* set), as a function of T^k. The more words *dSCAM* considers from the suspicious documents (i.e., the higher k), the more databases are searched: *dSCAM* considers the words as ordered by how rare they are. Therefore, when *dSCAM* starts considering "popular" words, more databases will tend to exceed the similarity threshold T^k. Also, for a fixed k, the higher T^k, the fewer databases that *dSCAM* searches, since only databases that exceed T^k are searched. For low values of k, *dSCAM* searches very few databases. For example, for $k = 10$ and $T^k = 0.05$, less than 10% of the databases are searched.

As we know, Sum_{Ratio} may produce false negatives for $k < 100$, i.e., it may tell us not to search databases where SCAM would find potential copies. It is interesting to study what percentage of the databases with potential copies *dSCAM* actually searches (or equivalently, what percentage of these databases are not false negatives). Let $s(S)$ be the number of databases with potential copies of S according to SCAM, and let $s'(S)$ be the number of databases with potential copies of S that *dSCAM* searches. Then, the *recall* of the technique used by *dSCAM* is the average value of $\frac{100 \cdot s'(S)}{s(S)}$ over our suspicious documents S.

Figure 2 shows the recall values for Sum_{Ratio} as a function of the adjusted threshold T^k. This figure is very similar to Figure 1: the more databases a technique searches, the higher its recall tends to be. Note, however, that some techniques have very few false negatives, while they search a low percentage of the databases. For example, for $k = 10$ and $T^k = 0.05$, recall is above 90%, meaning that for the average suspicious document, 90% of the databases with potential copies are chosen by *dSCAM*. As we have seen, just under 10% of the databases are searched for this value of k and T^k.

As we mentioned above, *dSCAM* produces false positives. We want to measure what percentage of the databases selected by $dSCAM$ actually contains potential copies. The *precision* of the technique used by $dSCAM$ is the average value of $\frac{100 \cdot s'(S)}{d(S)}$ over our suspicious documents S. Figure 3 shows the precision values for Sum_{Ratio} as a function of the adjusted threshold T^k. As expected, the more databases a technique searches, the lower its precision tends to be. For $k = 10$ and $T^k = 0.05$, precision is over 40%, meaning that for the average suspicious document, over 40% of the databases that $dSCAM$ searches have potential copies of the document. Actually, this choice of values for k and T^k is a good one: $dSCAM$ searches very few databases while achieving high precision and recall values.

We are evaluating $dSCAM$ in terms of how well it predicts the behavior of SCAM at each database. However, SCAM can sometimes be wrong. For example, SCAM can wrongly flag a document D in db as a copy of a suspicious document S. $dSCAM$ might then also flag db as having potential copies of S. However, we do not "penalize" $dSCAM$ for this "wrong" choice: the best $dSCAM$ can do is to predict the behavior of SCAM, and that is why we define precision and recall as above. It would be unreasonable to ask a system like $dSCAM$, with very limited information about the databases, to detect copies more accurately than a system like SCAM, which has complete information about the database contents.

To illustrate the storage space differences between $dSCAM$ and SCAM, let us consider the data that we used in our experiments. In this case, there are around 4 million word-document pairs, which is the level of information that a SCAM server needs, whereas there are only around 791,000 word-database pairs, which is the level of information that a $dSCAM$ server needs. As the databases grow in size, we expect this difference to widen too, since the $dSCAM$ savings in storage come from words appearing in multiple documents. For example, if we consider our 50 databases as a single, big database, $dSCAM$ needs only 138,086 word-database pairs, whereas the SCAM data remains the same. Therefore, $dSCAM$ has just around 3.36% as many entries as SCAM. We are considering alternatives to reduce the size of the $dSCAM$ data even further. As an interesting direction for future work, $dSCAM$ can store information on, say, only the 10% rarest words. Most of the time, the 10% rarest words that appear in a suspicious document will be among these 10% overall rarest words, so $dSCAM$ can proceed as usual. With this scheme, the $dSCAM$ space requirements would be cut further by an order of magnitude.

Figure 4 shows results for the *Disjoint* set of suspicious documents, again for the Sum_{Ratio} technique and $T = 1$. There are no potential copies of these documents in any of the 50 databases. Therefore, recall is always 100%, and precision is 0% if some database is selected. It then suffices to report the percentage of databases chosen for these documents (Figure 4). These values tend to be lower in general than those for the *Registered* suspicious documents of Figure 1, which is the right trend, since no database contains

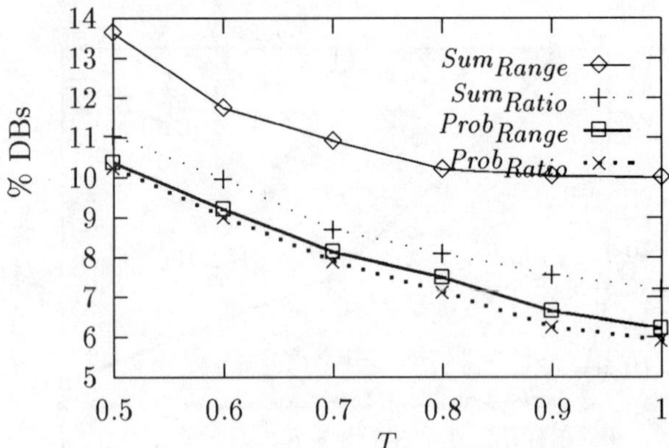

Figure 5: The percentage of the 50 databases that are searched as a function of the SCAM threshold T (*Registered* suspicious documents; $k = 10$; $T^k = 0.05 \cdot T$).

potential copies of the suspicious documents. For example, for $k = 10$ and $T^k = 0.05$, less than 5% of the databases are searched.

So far we have presented results just for the Sum_{Ratio} technique. Figures 5 through 7 show results also for Sum_{Range}, $Prob_{Range}$, and $Prob_{Ratio}$, as a function of the SCAM threshold T. In all of these plots, we have fixed $k = 10$ and $T^k = 0.05 \cdot T$, which worked well for both the *Registered* and the *Disjoint* suspicious documents when $T = 1$. In Figure 5, $Prob_{Range}$ and $Prob_{Ratio}$ search fewer databases than Sum_{Range} and Sum_{Ratio}, at the expense of significantly lower recall values (Figure 6). Sum_{Range} and Sum_{Ratio} have very high recall values (above 95% for all values of T). Precision is also relatively high, especially for the Sum_{Ratio} strategy (Figure 7). From all these plots, Sum_{Ratio} appears as the best choice for $dSCAM$, because of its high recall and precision, and low percentage of databases that it searches. Also, note that Sum_{Ratio} does not need the d_i statistics, resulting in lower storage requirements than those of $Prob_{Ratio}$, for example. However, if we want to be conservative, and be sure that we do not miss any potential copy of a document, then the best choice is also Sum_{Ratio}, but with $k = 100$ and $T^k = T$. (This technique coincides with the conservative $Upper_{Ratio}$ technique of Section 4.)

To determine whether the results above will still hold for larger databases, we performed the following experiment. Initially we have a single database with 1,267 documents (one of the databases that we used in this Section). $dSCAM$ decides whether this database should be searched or not for each of the *Disjoint* suspicious documents, with $T = 1$, the Sum_{Ratio} strategy, $k = 10$, and $T^k = 0.05$. The answer should be "no" for each of these documents, of course. Figure 8 shows that $dSCAM$ decides to search this database for less than 10% of the tested documents. This corresponds to a 0.10 probability of false positives. Then, we keep enlarging our only database by progres-

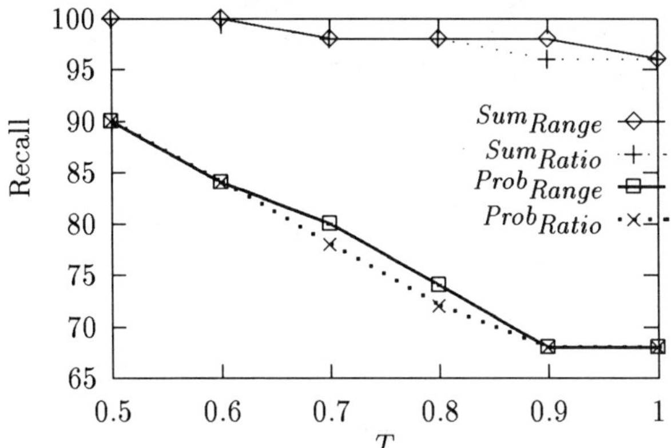

Figure 6: The average recall as a function of the SCAM threshold T (*Registered* suspicious documents; $k = 10$; $T^k = 0.05 \cdot T$).

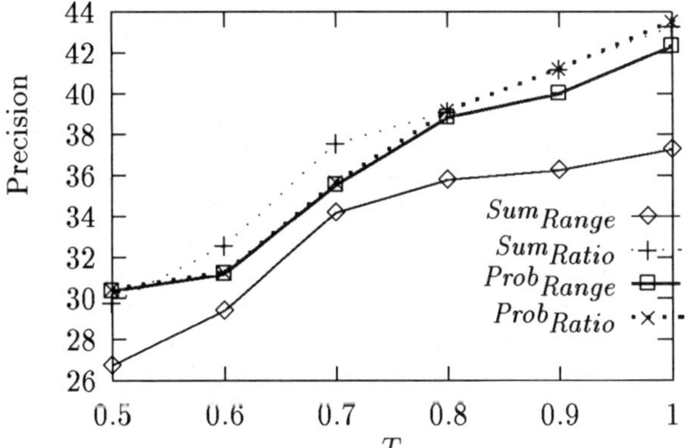

Figure 7: The average precision as a function of the SCAM threshold T (*Registered* suspicious documents; $k = 10$; $T^k = 0.05 \cdot T$).

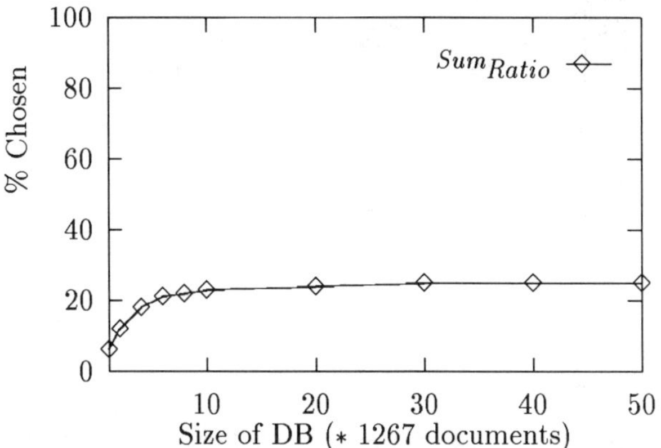

Figure 8: The average number of times that *dSCAM* (incorrectly) chooses to search the (growing) database, as a function of the size of the database (*Disjoint* suspicious documents; Sum_{Ratio} strategy).

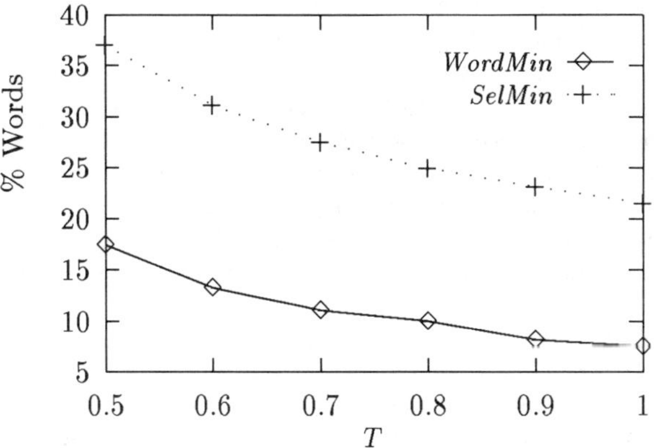

Figure 9: The percentage of words of the suspicious documents that are included in the query to extract the potential copies from the databases (*Registered* suspicious documents; *Ratio* strategy).

sively adding the documents from our original databases, until the database consists of all 63,350 documents. As we see from Figure 8, after an initial deterioration, *dSCAM* stabilizes and chooses to search the database around 25% of the time. These important results show that *dSCAM* scales relatively well to larger databases. That is, the probability of false positives is relatively insensitive (after an initial rise) to database size. Notice, incidentally, that the 25% false-positive probability can be made smaller by changing the T^k and k values (at a cost in false negatives). So the key observation from this figure is simply that the value is flat as the database size grows.

Our final set of experiments is for the results of Section 6. In that section we studied how to choose the query for each database that *dSCAM* selects. These queries retrieve all potential copies of the suspicious documents. There are many such queries, though. We presented two cost models, and showed algorithms to pick the cheapest query for each model.

Under our first cost model, *WordMin*, we minimize the number of words in the queries that we construct. Thus,

we choose a minimum set of words for our query from the given suspicious document. Figure 9 shows the percentage of words in the suspicious document that are chosen to query the databases, for the *Registered* documents and for different values of T. The number of words in the queries decreases as T increases. In effect, Condition 4 in Section 6 becomes easier to satisfy for larger values of T. For example, for $T = 0.80$ and *Ratio*, we need on average 9.99% of the suspicious-document words for our queries. If a particular database cannot handle so many words in a query, we should partition the query into smaller subqueries, and take the union of its results. As expected, the number of words chosen using the *SelMin* cost model is higher, because this cost model focuses on the selectivity of the words, and not on the number of words chosen.

While our second cost model, *SelMin*, uses the word selectivities, the *WordMin* cost model ignores these selectivities. Therefore, we analyze the selectivity for the queries to know what fraction of each database we will retrieve

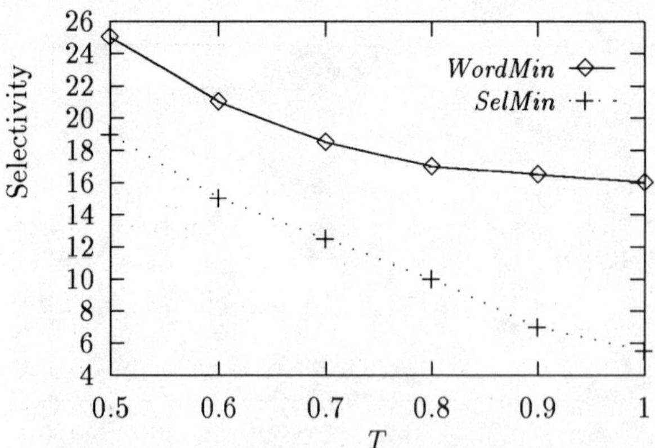

Figure 10: Average selectivity of the queries used to extract the potential copies from the databases, as a function of the SCAM threshold T (*Registered* suspicious documents; *Ratio* strategy).

with such queries. Figure 10 shows the average value of this selectivity for the *Registered* suspicious documents.

The number of query words and the added selectivity of the query words are relatively high. However, if all a database has is a Boolean-query interface, we have no choice but to ask the right queries to the database to extract all the potential copies of a suspicious document. (How to deal with a vector-space query interface [13] is part of our future work.) The results above show that we can do substantially better than the brute-force approach (i.e., when we use all the words in the suspicious document to build a big "or" query) by writing the queries as in Section 6.

We have also explored liberal techniques to extract the potential copies from a database. These liberal techniques might have false negatives (i.e., they might miss some potential copies) and they have much fewer false positives (i.e., they retrieve fewer documents that are not potential copies). Due to space limitations, we cannot describe these techniques here. However, we report some numbers for $T = 1$ to give an idea of the promising results that we obtained. For example, we queried the databases using only the 10% rarest words in the suspicious documents. These queries had an average selectivity of 0.49% (i.e., these "or" queries retrieved on average less than 1% of the database documents), and an average recall of 94% (i.e., these queries retrieved on average 94% of the potential copies). In contrast, the *WordMin* queries for $T = 1$ have fewer words on average (around 8% of the words), but their selectivity is much higher (around 16%). The *SelMin* queries for $T = 1$ have over 20% of the document words in them, and their average selectivity is still higher than that of the liberal technique (over 5%). Of course, recall is perfect for *WordMin* and *SelMin*, while this is not the case for the liberal techniques.

8   Related work

Protecting digital documents from illegal copying has received a lot of attention recently. Some systems favor the copy *prevention* approach, for example, by physically isolating information (e.g., by placing information on stand-alone CD-ROM systems), by using special-purpose hardware for authorization [14], or by using *active* documents (e.g., documents encapsulated by programs [15]). We believe such prevention schemes are cumbersome, and may make it difficult for honest users to share information. Furthermore, such prevention schemes can be broken by using software emulators [16] and recording documents. Instead of placing restrictions on the distribution of documents, another approach to protecting digital documents (one we subscribe to) is to *detect* illegal copies using registration server mechanisms such as SCAM [5, 6] or COPS [16]. Once we know a document to be an illegal copy, it is sometimes useful to know the originator of the illegal copy. There have been several proposals [17, 18] to add unique "watermarks" to documents (encoded in word spacing or in images) so that one can trace back to the original buyer of that illegal document.

A variety of mechanisms have been suggested for registration servers. In [19], a few words in a document are chosen as *anchors* and checksums of a following window of characters are computed. "Similar" files can then be found by comparing these checksums that are registered into a database. This tool is mainly intended for file management applications, and detection of files that are very similar, but not for detecting small text overlaps. The COPS [16] and SCAM registration servers however were developed to detect even small overlaps in text.

dSCAM builds on work in the resource-discovery area. (See [20, 21] for surveys.) This work usually focuses on finding the "best" sources for a query, where the best sources are usually those with the largest number of "relevant" documents for the query. (See for example [22], [10, 11], and [23].) These schemes are not tuned to choose databases with a potential copy of a suspicious document, in the sense of Section 2. Our problem requires that we identify databases even if they contain a single document that overlaps a suspicious document significantly.

9   Conclusion

Discovering a potential copy that might exist in one of many databases is a fundamentally difficult problem. One might say that it is harder than finding a "needle in a haystack:" the haystack is distributed across the Internet, we do not want *similar* items (e.g., a nail), and we also want to find any *piece* of the needle if it exists. It is a harder problem than simply finding similar items, as in traditional information retrieval. Given this difficulty it is somewhat surprising that *dSCAM* performs as well as we have found, especially when one considers the relatively small amount of index information it maintains. It is true that *dSCAM* can miss some potential copies or can lead us to sites without copies, but with the right algorithm and parameter settings, these errors can be made tolerable. For example, we found that *dSCAM* can miss fewer than 5% of the sites with potential copies, and for the sites it does lead us to, they actually have a potential copy roughly half the time.

dSCAM performs best when it only considers about 10% of the words in the suspicious document, those that are the "rarest." Intuitively, these rare words act as a "tell-tale signature" that makes it easier to pick out the target databases. We believe that this is the main reason that *dSCAM* performs better than one would expect, given the difficulty of the problem at hand. Some pirates may make it harder for *dSCAM* to detect these signatures by changing these rare words, but this is not a significant problem since our goal is to prevent widespread and direct copying of documents.

We believe that copy discovery will be an important service in distributed information systems. It will not prevent people from making illegal copies, but having effective discovery mechanisms (together with copy tracing schemes) may dissuade people from large scale duplication.

References

[1] P. J. Denning. Editorial: Plagiarism in the web. *Communications of the ACM*, 38(12), December 1995.

[2] A. Tal and R. Alonso. Commit protocols for externalized-commit heterogeneous database systems. *Distributed and Parallel Databases*, 2(2):209–34, April 1994.

[3] Y. E. Ioannidis, R. T. Ng, K. Shim, and T. K. Sellis. Parametric query optimization. In *Proceedings of the 18th International Conference on Very Large Data Bases*, pages 103–14, Vancouver, August 1992.

[4] T. Y. C. Leung and R. Muntz. Query processing for temporal databases. In *Proceedings of the 6th International Conference on Data Engineering*, pages 200–8, February 1990.

[5] Narayanan Shivakumar and Héctor García-Molina. SCAM: A copy detection mechanism for digital documents. In *Proceedings of the 2nd International Conference in Theory and Practice of Digital Libraries (DL'95)*, Austin, Texas, June 1995.

[6] Narayanan Shivakumar and Héctor García-Molina. Building a scalable and accurate copy detection mechanism. In *Proceedings of the 1st ACM Conference on Digital Libraries (DL'96)*, Bethesda, Maryland, March 1996.

[7] Narayanan Shivakumar and Héctor García-Molina. Information on SCAM. Available as `http://www-db.stanford.edu/~shiva/SCAM/scamInfo.html`.

[8] Tak W. Yan and Héctor García-Molina. Duplicate detection in information dissemination. In *Proceedings of the 1995 Very Large Databases Conference (VLDB'95)*, Zurich, Switzerland, September 1995.

[9] R. E. Kahn. Deposit, registration and recordation in an electronic copyright management system. Technical report, Corporation for National Research Initiatives, Reston, Virginia, August 1992.

[10] Luis Gravano, Héctor García-Molina, and Anthony Tomasic. The effectiveness of *GlOSS* for the text-database discovery problem. In *Proceedings of the 1994 ACM SIGMOD Conference*, May 1994.

[11] Luis Gravano and Héctor García-Molina. Generalizing *GlOSS* for vector-space databases and broker hierarchies. In *Proceedings of the 21st International Conference on Very Large Data Bases (VLDB'95)*, pages 78–89, September 1995.

[12] Thomas H. Cormen, Charles E. Leiserson, and Ronald L. Rivest. *Introduction to algorithms*. The MIT Press, 1991.

[13] Gerard Salton. *Automatic text processing: the transformation, analysis, and retrieval of information by computer*. Addison Wesley, 1989.

[14] G. J. Popek and C. S. Kline. Encryption and secure computer networks. *ACM Computing Surveys*, 11(4):331–356, December 1979.

[15] G. N. Griswold. A method for protecting copyright on networks. In *Joint Harvard MIT Workshop on Technology Strategies for Protecting Intellectual Property in the Networked Multimedia Environment*, April 1993.

[16] Sergey Brin, James Davis, and Héctor García-Molina. Copy detection mechanisms for digital documents. In *Proceedings of the ACM SIGMOD Annual Conference*, San José, May 1995.

[17] J. Brassil, S. Low, N. Maxemchuk, and L. O'Gorman. Document marking and identification using both line and word shifting. Technical report, AT&T Bell Laboratories, 1994.

[18] A. Choudhury, N. Maxemchuk, S. Paul, and H. Schulzrinne. Copyright protection for electronic publishing over computer networks. Technical report, AT&T Bell Laboratories, 1994.

[19] U. Manber and S. Wu. Glimpse: A tool to search through entire file systems. In *Proceedings of the Winter USENIX Conference*, January 1994.

[20] Michael F. Schwartz, Alan Emtage, Brewster Kahle, and B. Clifford Neuman. A comparison of Internet resource discovery approaches. *Computer Systems*, 5(4), 1992.

[21] Katia Obraczka, Peter B. Danzig, and Shih-Hao Li. Internet resource discovery services. *IEEE Computer*, September 1993.

[22] James P. Callan, Zhihong Lu, and W. Bruce Croft. Searching distributed collections with inference networks. In *Proceedings of the 18th Annual SIGIR Conference*, 1995.

[23] Mark A. Sheldon, Andrzej Duda, Ron Weiss, James W. O'Toole, and David K. Gifford. A content routing system for distributed information servers. In *Proceedings of the 4th International Conference on Extending Database Technology*, 1994.

Querying the World Wide Web

Alberto O. Mendelzon
Department of Computer Science
University of Toronto
mendel@db.toronto.edu

George A. Mihaila
Department of Computer Science
University of Toronto
georgem@db.toronto.edu

Tova Milo
Computer Science Department
Tel Aviv University
milo@math.tau.ac.il

Abstract

The World Wide Web is a large, heterogeneous, distributed collection of documents connected by hypertext links. The most common technology currently used for searching the Web depends on sending information retrieval requests to "index servers". One problem with this is that these queries cannot exploit the structure and topology of the document network.

In this paper we propose a query language, Web-SQL, that takes advantage of multiple index servers without requiring users to know about them, and that integrates textual retrieval with structure and topology-based queries. We give a formal semantics for Web-SQL using a calculus based on a novel "virtual graph" model of a document network. We propose a new theory of query cost based on the idea of "query locality," that is, how much of the network must be visited to answer a particular query. Finally, we describe a prototype implementation of WebSQL written in Java.

1   Introduction

The World Wide Web[BLCL+94] is a large, heterogeneous, distributed collection of documents connected by hypertext links. Current practice for finding documents of interest depends on *browsing* the network by following links and *searching* by sending information retrieval requests to "index servers" that index as many documents as they can find by navigating the network. The limitations of browsing as a search technique are well-known, as well as the disorientation resulting in the infamous "lost-in-hyperspace" syndrome. As far as keyword-based searching, one problem with it is that users must be aware of the various index servers (over a dozen of them are currently deployed on the Web), of their strengths and weaknesses, and of the peculiarities of their query interfaces. To some degree this can be remedied by front-ends that provide a uniform interface to multiple search engines, such as Multisurf[HGN+95], Savvysearch [Dre96], and Metacrawler [SE95].

A more serious problem is that these queries cannot exploit the structure and topology of the document network. In the hypertext literature, the need for such queries is well documented. For example, in an often-cited paper on the limitations of hypertext systems, Halasz says: [Hal88]

> Content search ignores the structure of a hypermedia network. In contrast, structure search specifically examines the hypermedia structure for subnetworks that match a given pattern.

and goes on to give examples where such queries are useful.

In the Web context, suppose for example that we are looking for an IBM catalog with prices for personal computers. A keyword search for the terms "IBM," "personal computer," and "price," using MetaCrawler, returns 92 references, including such things as an advertisement for an "I Bought Mac" T-shirt and the VLDB '96 home page. If we know the web address (called URL, or "uniform resource locator") of the IBM home page is `www.ibm.com`, we would like to be able to restrict the search to only sites located on the same server as the IBM home page and directly or indirectly reachable from this page. With currently available tools, this is not possible because navigation and query are distinct phases: navigation is used to construct the indexes, and query is used to search them once constructed. We propose instead a tool that can combine query with navigation. The emphasis must be however on *controlled* navigation.

There are currently tens of millions of documents on the Web, and growing; and network bandwidth is still a very limited resource. It becomes important therefore to be able to distinguish in queries between documents that are stored on the local server, whose access is relatively cheap, and those that are stored on remote serves, whose access is more expensive. It is also important to be able to analyze a query to determine its cost in terms of how many remote document accesses will be needed to answer it.

There are other reasons why queries that combine content and structure are important. We see a query language not primarily as an end-user tool, but as an aid in application development, just as SQL is used in combination with a programming language for building database applications. Many applications on the Web require accessing the structure defined by the links. For example, typical tasks in web site management include checking for dangling links, finding frequently used paths, finding unreachable documents, etc. In Section 6 we list other applications that would be facilitated by our language.

In this paper we propose a query language, *WebSQL*, that takes advantage of multiple index servers without requiring users to know about them, and that integrates textual retrieval with structure and topology-based queries. After introducing the language in Section 2, in Section 3 we give a formal semantics for WebSQL using a calculus based on a novel "virtual graph" model of a document network. In Section 4, we propose a new theory of query cost based on the idea of "query locality," that is, how much of the network must be visited to answer a particular query. We give an algorithm for characterizing WebSQL queries with respect to query locality. Finally, in Section 5 we describe a prototype implementation of WebSQL written in Java. We conclude in Section 6.

Related Work. There has been work in query languages for hypertext documents[BK90, CM89, MW93] as well as query languages for structured or semi-structured documents[GZC89, ACM93, CACS94, QRS+95]. Our work differs significantly from both these streams. None of these papers make a distinction between documents stored locally or remotely, or make an attempt to capitalize on existing index servers. As far as document structure, we only support the minimal attributes common to most HTML documents (URL, title, type, length, modification date). We do not assume the internal document structure is known or partially known, as does the work on structured and semi-structured documents.

As a consequence, our language does not exploit internal document structure when it is known; but we are planning to build this on top of the current framework.

Closer to our approach are the W3QL work by Shmueli and Konopnicki[KS95] and the WebLog language of Lakshmanan *et al.* [LSS96]. Neither one provides a clean semantics or methods for query analysis, which we consider two of the main contributions in our work.

Regarding the language design, our motivation is very similar to W3QL, but the approach is substantially different. They emphasize extensibility and interfacing to external user-written programs and Unix utilities. While extensibility is a highly desirable goal when the tool runs in a known environment, we aim for a tool that can be downloaded to an arbitrary client and run with minimal interaction with the local environment. For this reason, our query engine prototype is implemented in the Java programming language [SM]. and (part of it) can be downloaded as an applet by a Java-aware browser. Another difference is that we provide formal query semantics, and emphasize the distinction between local and remote documents. This makes a theory and analysis of query locality possible. On the other hand, they support filling out forms encountered during navigation, and discuss a view facility based on W3QL, while we do not currently support either. In this regard, it is not our intention to provide a fully functional tool, but a clean and minimal design with well-defined semantics that can be extended with bells and whistles later.

Another recent effort in this direction is the WebLog language of Lakshmanan *et al.* [LSS96]. Unlike WebSQL, WebLog emphasizes manipulating the internal structure of Web documents. Instead of regular expressions for specifying paths, they rely on Datalog-like recursive rules. Their paper does not describe an implementation or formal semantics.

Finally, Abiteboul and Vianu [AV97] propose formal models of general web queries and discuss various notions of computability.

2 The WebSQL Language

In this section we introduce our SQL-like language for the World Wide Web. We begin with a simple relational model of the WWW. Then we give a few examples of queries and present the syntax of the language. The formal semantics of queries is defined in the following section.

One of the difficulties in building an SQL-like query language for the Web is the absence of a database schema. Instead of trying to model document struc-

81

ture with some kind of object-oriented schema, as in [CACS94, QRS$^+$95], we take a minimalist relational approach. At the highest level of abstraction, every Web object is identified by its Uniform Resource Locator (URL) and has a binary content whose interpretation depends on its type (HTML, Postscript, image, audio, etc.). Also, Web servers provide some additional information such as the type, length, and the last modification date of an object. Moreover, an HTML document has a title and a text. So, for query purposes, we can associate a Web object with a tuple in a virtual relation:

$$Document[url, title, text, type, length, modif]$$

where all the attributes are character strings. The *url* is the key, and all other attributes can be null.

Once we define this virtual relation, we can express any *content query*, that is, a query that refers only to the content of documents, using an SQL-like notation.

Example 2.1 *Find all HTML documents about "hypertext".*

SELECT	*d.url, d.title, d.length, d.modif*
FROM	Document *d*
	SUCH THAT *d* MENTIONS "hypertext"
WHERE	*d.type* = "text/html";

Since we are not interested just in document content, but also in the hypertext structure of the Web, we make hypertext links first-class citizens in our model. In particular, we concentrate on HTML documents and on hypertext links originating from them. A *hypertext link* is specified inside an HTML document by a sequence, known as an *anchor*, of the form `<A HREF=`*href*`>`*label*`</A>` where *href* (standing for *hypertext reference*) is the URL of the referenced document, and *label* is a textual description of the link. Therefore, we can capture all the information present in a link into a tuple:

$$Anchor[base, href, label]$$

where *base* is the URL of the HTML document containing the link, *href* is the referred document and *label* is the link description [1]. All these attributes are character strings.

Now we can pose queries that refer to the links present in documents.

Example 2.2 *Find all links to applets from documents about "Java".*

---

[1]Note that *Anchor* is not, strictly speaking, a relation, but a multiset of tuples – a document may contain several links to the same destination, all having the same label.

SELECT	*y.label, y.href*
FROM	Document *x*
	SUCH THAT *x* MENTIONS "Java",
	Anchor *y* SUCH THAT *base = x*
WHERE	*y.label* CONTAINS "applet";

In order to study the topology of the Web we will want sometimes to make a distinction between links that point within the same document where they appear, to another document stored at the same site, or to a document on a remote server.

Definition 2.1 *A hypertext link is said to be:*

- interior *if the destination is within the source document;* [2]

- local *if the destination and source documents are different but located on the same server;*

- global *if the destination and the source documents are located on different servers.*

This distinction is important both from an expressive power point of view and from the point of view of the query cost analysis and the locality theory presented in Section 4.

We assign an arrow-like symbol to each of the three link types: let $\mapsto$ denote an *interior* link, $\rightarrow$ a *local* link and $\Rightarrow$ a *global* link. Also, let = denote the empty path. Path regular expressions are built from these symbols using concatenation, alternation ($|$) and repetition ($*$). For example, $= | \Rightarrow . \rightarrow^*$ is a regular expression that represents the set of paths containing the zero length path and all paths that start with a global link and continue with zero or more local links.

Now we can express queries referring explicitly to the hypertext structure of the Web.

Example 2.3 *Starting from the Department of Computer Science home page, find all documents that are linked through paths of length two or less containing only local links. Keep only the documents containing the string 'database' in their title.*

SELECT	*d.url, d.title*
FROM	Document *d* SUCH THAT
	"http://www.cs.toronto.edu" $= | \rightarrow | \rightarrow \rightarrow d$
WHERE	*d.title* CONTAINS "database";

---

[2]In HTML documents, links can point to specific named fragments within the destination document; the fragment name is incorporated into the URL. For example, `http://www.royalbank.com/fund.html#DP`; refers to the fragment named DP within the document with URL `http://www.royalbank.com/fund.html`. We will ignore this detail in the rest of the paper.

Of course, we can combine content and structure specifications in a query.

Example 2.4 *Find all documents mentioning 'Computer Science' and all documents that are linked to them through paths of length two or less containing only local links.*

```
SELECT    x.url, x.title, y.url, y.title
FROM      Document x SUCH THAT
              x MENTIONS "Computer Science",
          Document y
              SUCH THAT x = |→|→ . → y;
```

```
Query := SELECT AttrList FROM DomainSpec
           [ WHERE Condition ] ;
AttrList := Attribute {, Attribute}
Attribute := Field | TableVar.Field
Field := Id
TableVar := Id
DomainSpec := DomainTerm {, DomainTerm}
DomainTerm := Table TableVar
               SUCH THAT DomainCond
DomainCond := Node PathRegExp TableVar
          | TableVar MENTIONS StringConstant
          | Attribute = Node
Node := StringConstant
          | TableVar
Condition := BoolTerm {OR BoolTerm}
BoolTerm := BoolTerm {AND BoolTerm}
BoolTerm := Attribute = Attribute
          | Attribute = StringConstant
          | Attribute CONTAINS StringRegExp
          | (Condition)
PathRegExp := Link
          | PathRegExp *
          | PathRegExp PathRegExp
          | PathRegExp "|" PathRegExp
          | ( PathRegExp )
Link := = | #> | => | ->
```

Figure 1: A BNF Specification of WebSQL

Note we are using two different keywords, MENTIONS and CONTAINS, to do string matching in the FROM and WHERE clauses respectively. The reason is that they are used differently. MENTIONS is normally used with the first argument free and the second bound; that is, given a string, it returns the set of all documents that contain that string. CONTAINS is normally used with both arguments bound; it checks whether a given document contains a given string. This distinction is reflected both in the formal semantics of Section 3 and in the implementation. In fact, the implementation evaluates conditions in the FROM clause by sending them to index servers. The result of the FROM clause, obtained by navigation and index server query, is a set of candidate URL's, which are then further restricted by locally evaluating the conditions in the WHERE clause. This introduces opportunities for an optimization that moves local CONTAINS conditions to remotely evaluated MENTIONS conditions, avoiding unnecessary data movement across the network, but we do not discuss query optimization in this paper.

The BNF specification of the language syntax is given in Figure 1. The syntax follows the standard SQL SELECT statement. All queries are refer to the WWW database schema introduced above. That is, *Table* can only be **Document** or **Anchor** and *Field* can only be a valid attribute of the table it applies to.

3   Formal Semantics

In this section we introduce a formal foundation for WebSQL. Starting from the inherent graph structure of the WWW, we define the notion of *virtual graph* and construct a calculus-based query language in this abstract setting. Then we define the semantics of WebSQL queries in terms of this calculus.

3.1   Data Model

We assume an infinite set D of *data values*, and a finite set T of *simple Types* whose domains are subsets of D. Tuple types $[a1 : t1, ..., a_n : t_n]$ with attributes a_i of simple type t_i, $i = 1 \ldots n$ are defined in the standard way. The domain of a type t is denoted by $dom(t)$. For a tuple x, we denote by $x.a_i$ the value v_i associated with the attribute a_i.

We distinguish a simple type $Oid \in T$ of *object identifiers*, and two tuple types *Node* and *Link* with the following structure:

$$Node = [id : Oid, ..., a_i : t_i, ...]$$

$$Link = [from : Oid, to : Oid, ..., b_j : t_j, ...]$$

The attribute names in the two definitions are all distinct. We shall refer to tuples of the first type as *Node objects* and to tuples of the second type as *Link objects*. In our model of the World Wide Web, documents will be mapped to *Node* objects and the hypertext links between them to *Link* objects. In this context, the object identifiers (Oid) will be the URL's.

Virtual Graphs. The set of all the documents in the Web, although finite, is undetermined: no one can produce a complete list of all the documents available at a certain moment. There are only two ways one can find documents in the Web: navigation starting from known documents and querying of index servers.

Given any URL, an agent can either fetch the associated document or give an error message if the document does not exist. This behavior can be modeled by a *computable* partial function mapping Oid's to $Node$ objects. Once a document is fetched, one can determine a finite set of outgoing hypertext links from that document. This can also be modeled by a computable partial function mapping Oid's to sets of $Link$ objects. In practice, navigation is done selectively, by following only certain links, based on their properties. In order to capture this, we introduce a finite set of unary *link predicates* $\mathcal{P}_{Link} = \{\alpha, \beta, \gamma, ...\}$.

The second way to discover documents is by querying index servers. To model the lists of URL's returned by index servers we introduce a (possibly infinite) set of unary *node predicates* $\mathcal{P}_{Node} = \{P, Q, R, ...\}$ where for each predicate P we are interested in the set $\{x | x \in dom(Oid), \ P(x) = true\}$. For example, a particular node predicate may be associated with a keyword, and it will be true of all documents that contain that keyword in their text.

Definition 3.1 *A virtual graph is a 4-tuple* $\Gamma = (\rho_{Node}, \rho_{Link}, \mathcal{P}_{Node}, \mathcal{P}_{Link})$ *where* $\rho_{Node} : dom(Oid) \rightarrow dom(Node)$ *and* $\rho_{Link} : dom(Oid) \rightarrow 2^{dom(Link)}$ *are computable partial functions,* $\mathcal{P}_{Node}$ *is a set of unary predicates on* $dom(Oid)$, *and* $\mathcal{P}_{Link}$ *is a finite set of unary predicates on* $dom(Link)$.

- *The set* $\{\rho_{Node}(oid) | oid \in dom(Oid) \text{ and } \rho_{Node}$ *is defined on* $oid\}$ *is finite;*

- *if* $\rho_{Node}(oid) = v$ *then* $v.id = oid$;

- *for all* $oid \in dom(Oid)$: $\rho_{Node}(oid)$ *is defined* $\Leftrightarrow$ $\rho_{Link}(oid)$ *is defined;*

- *if* $\rho_{Link}(oid) = E$ *then* E *is finite and for all* $e \in E, e.from = oid$ *and* $\rho(e.to)$ *is defined (we say that* e *is an edge from* $v_1 = \rho_{Node}(e.from)$ *to* $v_2 = \rho_{Node}(e.to))$;

- *every predicate* $\alpha \in \mathcal{P}_{Link}$ *is a partial computable Boolean function on the set* $dom(Link)$, *and* α *is defined on all the links in* $\rho_{Link}(oid)$ *whenever* $\rho_{Link}(oid)$ *is defined.*

- *the function val* $: \mathcal{P}_{Node} \rightarrow 2^{dom(Oid)}$, *defined by* $val(P) = \{x | x \in dom(Oid), \ P(x) = true\}$ *is computable;*

Note that a virtual graph $\Gamma = (\rho_{Node}, \rho_{Link}, \mathcal{P}_{Node}, \mathcal{P}_{Link})$ induces an underlying directed graph $G(\Gamma) = (V, E)$ where $V = \rho_{Node}(dom(Oid))$ and $E = \bigcup_{oid \in dom(Oid)} \rho_{Link}(oid)$. However, a calculus cannot manipulate this graph directly because of the computability issues presented above.

3.2 The Calculus

Now we proceed to define our calculus for querying virtual graphs. We introduce path regular expressions to specify connectivity-based queries. We then present the notions of *range expressions* and *ground variables* to restrict queries so that their evaluation does not require enumerating every node of the virtual graph, and finally we define calculus queries.

Path regular expressions. Consider a virtual graph Γ and denote its underlying graph $G(\Gamma) = (V, E)$. A *path* in Γ is defined in the same way as in a directed graph: if $e_1, e_2, ..., e_k \in E$, we call $p = (e_1, e_2, ..., e_k)$ a path if and only if for every index $1 \leq i < k$, $e_{i+1}.from = e_i.to$. A path p is called *simple* if there are no different edges $e_i \neq e_j$ in p with the same starting or ending points.

In order to express queries based on connectivity, we need a way to define graph patterns. Recall $\mathcal{P}_{Link}$ is the set of link properties in a virtual graph. Let $\alpha \in \mathcal{P}_{Link}$ be some link property, and let e be a link object. If $\alpha(e) = true$ then we say that e has the property α. We define the *set of properties* of a link e by $\Lambda(e) = \{\alpha \in \mathcal{P}_{Link} | \alpha(e) = true\}$. We sometimes choose to view $\Lambda(e)$ as a formal language on the alphabet $\mathcal{P}_{Link}$. For each property α that is true of e, $\Lambda(e)$ contains the single-character string α. To study the properties of a path, we extend the definition of the set of properties of a link to paths as follows: if $p = (e_1, ..., e_k)$ is a path then we define

$$\Lambda(p) = \Lambda(e_1)...\Lambda(e_k)$$

where $LL' = \{xx' | x \in L, x' \in L'\}$ is the concatenation of the languages L and L'.

Example 3.1 *Suppose we want to require that a property* α *hold on all the links of a path* $p = (e_1, ..., e_k)$. *This can be expressed easily in terms of* Λ *by requiring that* $\alpha^k \in \Lambda(p)$.

In order to specify constraints like in the example above we introduce *path regular expressions*, which are nothing more than regular expressions over the alphabet $\mathcal{P}_{Link}$. With each regular expression R over the alphabet $\mathcal{P}_{Link}$ we associate a language $L(R) \subseteq \mathcal{P}_{Link}^*$ in the usual way.

Definition 3.2 *We say that the path p matches the path regular expression R if and only if:*

$$\Lambda(p) \cap L(R) \neq \emptyset$$

In other words, the path p matches the path regular expression R if and only if there is a word w in the set of properties $\Lambda(p)$ that matches the regular expression R.

Range expressions. The algebra for a traditional relational database is based on operators like select (σ), project (π) and Cartesian product ($\times$). Because all the contents of the database is assumed to be available to the query engine, all these operations can be executed, in the worst case by enumerating all the tuples. In the case of the World Wide Web, the result of a select operation cannot be computed in this way, simply because one cannot enumerate all the documents. Instead, navigation and querying of index servers must be used. We want our calculus to express only queries that can be evaluated without having to enumerate the whole Web. To enforce this restriction, we introduce *range conditions*, that will serve as restrictions for variables in the queries.

Definition 3.3 *Let $\Gamma = (\rho_{Node}, \rho_{Link}, \mathcal{P}_{Node}, \mathcal{P}_{Link})$ be a virtual graph. Let $G(\Gamma) = (V, E)$ be its underlying graph. A range atom is an expression of one of the following forms:*

- *$Path(u, R, x)$ where u, x are Oids or variable names, and R is a path regular expression;*

- *$P(x)$ where $P \in \mathcal{P}_{Node}$ and x is an Oid or a variable name;*

- *$From(u, x)$ where u, x are Oids or variable names;*

A range expression *is an expression of the form:* $\mathcal{E} = \{x_1 : T_1, x_2 : T_2, \ldots, x_n : T_n | A_1, A_2, \ldots, A_m\}$ *where $A_1, A_2, \ldots, A_m$ are range atoms, $x_1, x_2, \ldots, x_n$ are all the variables occurring in them and $T_i \in \{Node, Link\}$ specifies the type of the variable x_i, for $1 \leq i \leq n$.*

Consider a valuation $\nu : \{x, y, z, \ldots\} \rightarrow V \cup E$ that maps each variable into a node or an edge of the underlying graph. We extend ν to $dom(Oid)$ by

$\nu(oid) = \rho_{Node}(oid)$, that is, ν maps each Oid appearing in an atom to the corresponding node. The following definition assigns semantics to range atoms.

Definition 3.4 *Let $\Gamma = (\rho_{Node}, \rho_{Link}, \mathcal{P}_{Node}, \mathcal{P}_{Link})$ be a virtual graph. Let A be a range atom. We say that A is validated by the valuation ν if:*

- *for $A = Path(u, R, x)$, there exists a simple path from $\nu(u)$ to $\nu(x)$ matching the path regular expression R;*

- *for $A = P(x)$, $P(\nu(x).id) = true$.*

- *for $A = From(u, x)$, $\nu(x).from = \nu(u).id$*

Now we can give semantics to range expressions.

Definition 3.5 *Consider a range expression $\mathcal{E} = \{x_1, \ldots, x_n | A_1, \ldots, A_m\}$. Then the set of tuples*

$$\Psi(\mathcal{E}) = \{[\nu(x_1), \ldots, \nu(x_n)] | \nu \text{ is a valuation s.t. } A_1, \ldots, A_m \text{ are all validated by } \nu\}$$

is called the range of $\mathcal{E}$.

Example 3.2 *The set of all nodes satisfying a certain node predicate P together with all their outgoing links may be specified by the following range expression: $\{x : Node, y : Link | P(x), From(x, y)\}$*

Although Definition 3.5 gives a well-defined semantics for all range expressions, problems may arise when examining the evaluation of $\Psi(\mathcal{E})$ for certain expressions $\mathcal{E}$. For example, expressions like $\{x : Node, y : Node | Path(x, \alpha, y)\}$ (find all pairs of nodes connected by a link of type α) or $\{x : Node, y : Link | From(x, y)\}$ (find all nodes and all links outgoing from them) cannot be algorithmically evaluated on an arbitrary virtual graph, since their evaluation would involve the enumeration of all nodes. We impose syntactic restrictions to disallow such range expressions, in a manner similar to the definition of safe expressions in Datalog. We omit the details for lack of space and assume from now on that all range expressions are restricted in this way.

Queries. After restricting the domain from a large, non-computable set of nodes and links to a computable set, we may use the traditional relational selection and projection to impose further conditions on the result set of a query. This allows us to introduce the general format of queries in our calculus. We assume a given set $\mathcal{P}_s$ of binary predicates over simple types. Examples of predicates include equality (for any type), various inequalities (for numeric types), and substring containment (for alphanumeric types).

Definition 3.6 *A* virtual graph query *is an expression of the form:* $\pi_L\ \sigma_\phi\ \mathcal{E}$ *where:*

- $\mathcal{E} = \{x_1 : T_1, ..., x_n : T_n | A_1, ..., A_m\}$ *is a range expression;*

- *L is a comma separated list of expressions of the form $x_i.a_j$ where a_j is some attribute of the type T_i;*

- *ϕ is a Boolean expression constructed from binary predicates from $\mathcal{P}_s$ applied to expressions $x_i.a_j$ and constants using the standard operators $\wedge$, $\vee$, and $\neg$;*

The semantics of the select (σ) and project (π) operators is the standard one.

3.3 WebSQL Semantics

We are now ready to define the semantics of our WebSQL language in terms of the formal calculus introduced above. To do this, we need to model the Web as a virtual graph $W = (\rho_{Node}, \rho_{Link}, \mathcal{P}_{Node}, \mathcal{P}_{Link})$: $dom(Oid)$ is the infinite set of all syntactically correct URL's, and for every element $url \in dom(Oid)$, $\rho_{Node}(url)$ is either the document referred to by url, or is undefined, if the URL does not refer to an existing document. Note that $\rho_{Node}(url)$ is computable (its value can be computed by sending a request to the Web server specified in the URL). Moreover, $\rho_{Link}(url)$ is the set of all anchors in the document referred to by url, or is undefined, if the URL does not refer to an existing document. One can extract all the links appearing in an HTML document by scanning the contents in search of `<A>` and `</A>` tags. This means that the partial function $\rho_{Link}(url)$ is computable. In order to model content queries we consider the following set of $Node$ predicates: $\mathcal{P}_{Node} = \{C_w | w \in \Sigma^*\}$ where, for each $w \in \Sigma^*$, $C_w(n) = true$ if the document n contains the string w. Finally, we consider the following set of $Link$ predicates: $\mathcal{P}_{Link} = \{\rightarrow, \Rightarrow, \mapsto\}$ in accordance with the definition of path regular expressions in WebSQL.

The semantics of a WebSQL query is defined as usual in terms of selections and projections. Thus a query of the form:

$$\begin{array}{ll} \text{SELECT} & L \\ \text{FROM} & \mathcal{E} \\ \text{WHERE} & \phi \end{array}$$

translates to the following calculus query: $\pi_L\sigma_\phi\mathcal{E}'$ where $\mathcal{E}' = \{x_1, ..., x_n | A_1, ..., A_n\}$ is obtained from $\mathcal{E} = C_1, ..., C_n$ by using the following transformation rules:

- if $C_i =$ Document x SUCH THAT $u\ R\ x$
  then $A_i = Path(u, R, x)$

- if $C_i =$ Document x SUCH THAT
  x MENTIONS w
  then $A_i = C_w(x)$

- if $C_i =$ Anchor x SUCH THAT x.base $= u$.url
  then $A_i = From(u, x)$

We only allow as legal WebSQL queries those that translate into calculus queries that satisfy the syntactic restrictions of Section 3.2.

4 Query Locality

Cost is an important aspect of query evaluation. The conventional approach in database theory is to estimate query evaluation time as a function of the size of the database. In the web context, it is not realistic to try to evaluate queries whose complexity would be considered feasible in the usual theory, such as polynomial or even linear time.

For a query to be practical, it should not attempt to access too much of the network. Query analysis thus involves, in this context, two tasks: first, estimate what part of the network may be accessed by the query, and then the cost of the query can be analyzed in traditional ways as a function of the size of this sub-network. In this section, we concentrate on the first task. Note that this is analogous, in a conventional database context, to analyzing queries at the physical level to estimate the number of disk blocks that they may need to access.

For this first task, we need some way to measure the "locality" of a query, that is, how far from the originating site do we have to search in order to answer it. Having a bound on the size of the sub-network needed to evaluate a query means that the rest of the network can be ignored. In fact, a query that is sensitive only to a bounded sub-network should give the same result if evaluated in one network or in a different network containing this sub-network. This motivates our formal definition of query locality.

An important issue is the cost of accessing such a sub-network. In the current web architecture, access to remote documents is often done by fetching each document and analyzing it locally. The cost of an access is thus affected by document properties (e.g. size) and the by the cost of communication between the site where the query is being evaluated and the site where the document is stored. Recall that we model the web as a virtual graph. To model access costs, we extend the definition of virtual graphs, adding a function $\rho_c : dom(Oid) \times dom(Oid) \rightarrow \mathcal{N}$, where $\rho_c(i, j)$ is the the cost of accessing node j from node i.

4.1 Locality Cost

We now define the formal notion of locality. For that we first explain what it means for two networks to contain the same sub-network. We assume below that all the virtual graphs being discussed have the same sets of node and link predicate names.

Definition 4.1

Let $\Gamma = (\rho_{Node}, \rho_{Link}, \rho_c, \mathcal{P}_{Node}, \mathcal{P}_{Link})$, $\Gamma' = (\rho'_{Node}, \rho'_{Link}, \rho'_c, \mathcal{P}'_{Node}, \mathcal{P}'_{Link})$ be two (extended) virtual graphs. Let $W \subseteq dom(Oid)$. We say that Γ **agrees** with Γ' about W if for all $w, w' \in W$,

1. $\rho_{Node}(w) = \rho'_{Node}(w)$, $\rho_{Link}(w) = \rho'_{Link}(w)$, $\rho_c(w, w') = \rho'_c(w, w')$,

2. for all the node predicates P_{Node}, if $n = \rho_{Node}(w)$ is defined, then $P_{Node}(n)$ holds in Γ iff it holds in Γ',

3. for all the link predicates P_{Link} and for all links $l \in \rho_{Link}(w)$, $P_{Link}(l)$ holds in Γ iff it holds in Γ'.

Informally this means that the two graphs contain the sub-network induced by W, the nodes of W have the same properties in both graphs, and in both graphs this sub-network is linked to the rest of the world in the same way.

Definition 4.2 *Let Q be a query, let $\mathcal{G}$ be a class of virtual graphs, let $\Gamma \in \mathcal{G}$ be a graph, and let $W \subseteq dom(Oid)$. We say that query Q **depends** on W, (for Γ and $\mathcal{G}$), if for every graph $\Gamma' \in \mathcal{G}$ that agrees with Γ about W, $Q(\Gamma') = Q(\Gamma)$, and there is no subset of W satisfying this.*

W is a minimal set of documents needed for computing Q. Note that W may not be unique. This is reasonable since the same information may be stored in several places on the network.

Definition 4.3 *For a virtual graph Γ, a set of oid's W for nodes in Γ, and some oid i for a node in Γ, the **cost of** W **from** i is the sum of $\rho_c(i, w)$ over all documents w in W such that $\rho_{Node}(w)$ is defined*

Definition 4.4 *The **locality cost** of a query Q, when evaluated at node i of virtual graph Γ, is the maximum, over all sets W on which Q depends in Γ, of the cost of W from i.*

We are interested in bounding this cost with some function of the cost of accessing all the nodes of the network, that is, the sum of $\rho_c(i, j)$ over all j such that $\rho_{Node}(j)$ is defined. If this total cost is n, note that the locality cost of a query is at most linear in n.

Obviously, queries with $O(n)$ locality are impractical - the whole network needs to be accessed in order to answer them. We will be interested in constant bounds, where the constants may depend on network parameters such as number of documents in a site, maximal number of URL's in a single document, certain communication costs, etc.

In general, access to documents on the local server is considered cheap, while documents in remote servers need to be fetched and are thus relatively expensive. To simplify the discussion and highlight the points of interest we assume below a rather simple cost function. We assume that local accesses are free, while the access cost to remote documents is bounded by some given constant. (Similar results can be obtained for a more complex cost function). In the next few examples, suppose the queries are evaluated at the node "http://www.cs.toronto.edu". Consider first the query

Q_0: SELECT x
    FROM Document x SUCH THAT
      "http://www.cs.toronto.edu" $\rightarrow x$

where "http://www.cs.toronto.edu" is at the local server. The query accesses local documents pointed to by the home page of the Toronto CS department, and no remote ones. Thus the locality cost is $O(1)$. On the other hand, the query

Q_1: SELECT x
    FROM Document x SUCH THAT
      "http://www.cs.toronto.edu" $(\rightarrow | \Rightarrow)$ x

accesses both local and remote documents. The number of remote documents being accessed depends on the number of anchors in the home page that contain remote URL's. In the worst case, all the URL's in the page are remote. If k is a bound on the number of URL's in a single document, then the locality cost of this query is $O(k)$.

As another example, consider the queries

Q_2: SELECT x
    FROM Document x SUCH THAT
      "http://www.cs.toronto.edu" $\rightarrow^* x$

Q_3: SELECT x
    FROM Document x SUCH THAT
      "http://www.cs.toronto.edu" $\Rightarrow . \rightarrow^* x$

Q_4: SELECT x
    FROM Document x SUCH THAT
      "http://www.cs.toronto.edu" $(\rightarrow | \Rightarrow)^* x$

Query Q_2 accesses local documents reachable from the CS department home page, and is thus of locality $O(1)$. Query Q_3 accesses all documents reachable by one global link followed by an unbounded number of local links. If k is a bound on the number of URL's in a single document, and s is a bound on the number of documents in a single server, then the locality cost of the query is $O(ks)$. This is because in the worst case all the URL's in the CS department home page reference documents in distinct servers, and all the documents on those servers are reachable from the referenced documents. The last query accesses all reachable documents. In the worst case it may attempt to access the whole network, thus its cost is $O(n)$.

The locality analysis of various features of a query language can identify potentially expensive components of a query. The user can then be advised to rephrase those specific parts, or to give some cost bounds for them in terms of time, number of sites visited, CPU cycles consumed, etc., or, if enough information is available, dollars. The query evaluation would monitor resource usage and interrupt the query when the bound is reached.

If the query language is too complex, locality analysis may be very complex or even impossible. Nevertheless, in many cases it can be done effectively and efficiently. This in particular is the case for the WebSQL query language. In the next subsection, we show that locality of WebSQL queries can be determined in time polynomial in the size of the query.

4.2 Locality of WebSQL queries

We start by considering simple queries where the FROM clause consists of a single path atom starting from the local server, as in the examples above. We then analyze general queries.

Analyzing single path expressions. The analysis is based on examining the types of links (internal, local, or global) that can be traversed by paths described by the path expression. Particular attention is paid to "starred" sub-expressions since they can describe paths of arbitrary length. Assume that the query is evaluated at some node i, and let n denote the cost of accessing the whole network graph from i. Let k be some bound on the number of URL's appearing in a single document, [3] and s some bound on the number of documents in a single server.

1. Expressions with no global links can access only local documents and thus have locality O(1).

2. Expressions containing global links that appear in "starred" sub-expression, can potentially access all the documents in the network. Thus the locality is $O(n)$;

3. Expressions with global links, but where none of the "starred" sub-expressions contain a global link symbol, can access remote documents, but the number of those is limited. All the paths defined by such expressions are of the form $\rightarrow^{l_1} . \Rightarrow . \rightarrow^{l_2} . \Rightarrow \ldots \rightarrow^{l_m}$. Let $l = 1 + max(l_1, \ldots, l_m)$. The number of documents accessed by such path is bounded by

$$min(n, (m(l+1)(k \ min(s, k^l))^m))$$

where k and s are the bounds above. This is because the number of different documents reachable by a path $\rightarrow^{l_i}$ is at most $min(s, k^{l_i})$, and in the worst case all the $k \min(s, k^{l_i})$ URL's in those documents point to files on distinct servers. The number of documents reached at the end of the path is thus at most $(k \min(s, k^l))^m$. In order to reach those documents, all files along the path need to be fetched. To get a bound on this, we multiply the number by the length of the path. Bounds for m and l can be computed in polynomial time by analyzing the path expression. (Details omitted). [4]

The number m is bounded by the number of global links appearing in the given path expression. l can be computed by analyzing the regular expression. (details omitted). All this can be done in time polynomial in the size of the expression. [5]

Observe that if any of the starred sub-expressions contains a local link, then $l = s$. This is because, in the worst case, such sub-expressions will attempt to access all the documents in the server. In this case the bound becomes $min(n, (m(s + 1)(k \ s)^m))$. Since servers may contain many documents, the locality cost may be very high. This indicates that such queries are potentially expensive and that the user should be advised to provide the query evaluator certain bounds on resources.

---

[3] If no such bound exists, every path expression containing a global link is of locality cost $O(n)$ (because in the worst case a single document may point to all the nodes in the network).

[4] The expression above is a simple upper bound on the locality cost. A tight bound can also be computed in polynomial time. The exact expression is complex and does not add much insight to the analysis, so we omit it.

[5] The above expression is an upper bound on the locality cost. The exact cost can also be computed in polynomial time. We chose to present the above bound since the exact expression is very complex and does not add much insight to the analysis.

Analyzing queries. To analyze a WebSQL query it is not sufficient to look at individual path atoms. The whole FROM clause needs to be analyzed. For example, consider a query

Q_5: SELECT z, w
FROM Document x
  SUCH THAT x MENTIONS "PDIS96"
Anchor y SUCH THAT base $= x$
Document z SUCH THAT $y \to^* z$
Document w SUCH THAT $x \to w$

The path expressions in the query involve only local links. But since the links returned by the index server may point to remote documents, the paths traversed by the sub-condition

FROM Document x
  SUCH THAT x MENTIONS "PDIS96"
Document w SUCH THAT $x \to w$

are actually of the form $(\Rightarrow . \to)$. Similarly, since the links traversed in "Anchor y SUCH THAT base $= x$" can be global, the paths traversed by the sub-condition

FROM Document x
  SUCH THAT x MENTIONS "PDIS96"
Anchor y SUCH THAT base $= x$
Document z SUCH THAT $y \to^* z$

are of the form $(\Rightarrow . \Rightarrow . \to^*)$. Thus the regular expression describing the path accessed by the query is $((\Rightarrow . \to) \mid (\Rightarrow . \Rightarrow . \to^*))$. Assume that querying an index server can be done with locality c, and that the number of URL's returned by an index server on a single query is bounded by some number m. The locality cost of evaluating this query is therefore bounded by c plus m times the locality bound of $(\Rightarrow . \to) \mid (\Rightarrow . \Rightarrow . \to^*)$.

Interestingly, every FROM clause of a WebSQL query can be transformed into a regular expression describing the paths accessed in its evaluation. This, together with the locality cost of querying the index severs used in the query, and the bounds on the size of their answers, lets us determine the locality of queries in time polynomial on the size of the query. This, together with the locality cost of querying the index severs used in the query, and the bounds on the size of their answers, lets us determine the locality of the FROM clause in time polynomial on the size of the query. Bounding the locality of the FROM clause provides an upper bound on the locality of the whole query; a slightly better bound can be obtained by analyzing the SELECT and WHERE clauses.

We omit the details for lack of space.

5 Implementation

This section presents our prototype implementation of a WebSQL compiler, query engine, and user interface.

Both the WebSQL compiler and query engine are implemented entirely in Java [SM], the language introduced by Sun Microsystems with the specific purpose of adding executable content to Web documents.

A prototype user interface for the WebSQL system is accessible from the WebSQL home page (`http://www.cs.toronto.edu/~georgem/WebSQL.html`) as a CGI script.

The WebSQL system architecture is depicted in Figure 2.

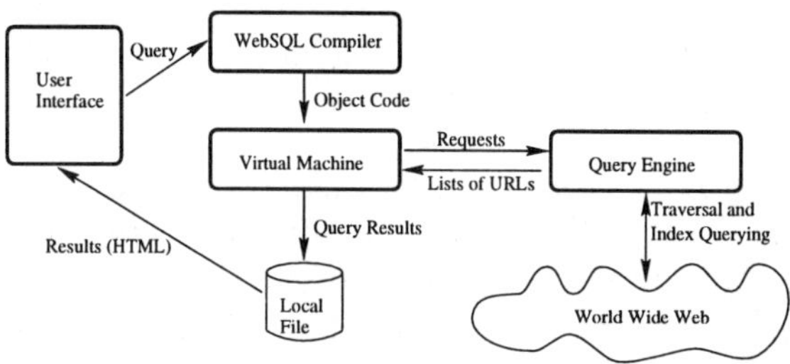

Figure 2: The Architecture of the WebSQL System

Figure 3: The WebSQL User Interface

The Compiler and Virtual Machine. The WebSQL compiler parses the query and translates it into a nested loop program in a custom-designed object language. The object program is executed by an interpreter that implements a stack machine. Its stack is heterogeneous, that is, it is able to store any type of object, from integers and strings to whole vectors of Node and Link objects. The evaluation of range atoms is done via specially designed operation codes whose results are vectors of Node or Link objects.

The Query Engine. Whenever the interpreter encounters an operation code corresponding to a range atom, the query engine is invoked to perform the actual evaluation. There are three types of atoms, according to Definition 3.3. Let us examine each of them in sequence:

- if $A = Path(u, R, x)$ the engine generates all simple paths starting at u that match R, thus determining the list of all qualifying values of x. Mendelzon and Wood give in [MW95] an algorithm for finding all the simple paths matching a regular expression R in a labeled graph. We adapted this algorithm for the virtual graph context. (For full details see [Mih96]).

- if $A = C_w$ the engine queries a customizable set of known index servers (currently Yahoo and Lycos) with the string w and builds a sorted list of URL's by merging the individual answer sets;

- if $A = From(u, x)$ the engine determines first if u is an HTML document and if it is, it parses it and builds a list of *Link* objects out of the set of all the anchor tags; if u is not an HTML document, the engine returns the empty list.

The User Interface. The appearance of the user interface is shown in Figure 3, a screen-shot of the HotJava browser.

The input form can be used as a template for the most common WebSQL queries making it easier for the user to submit a query. If the query is more complicated it can always be typed into an alternative text field. After the query is entered it may be submitted by pressing the appropriate button. At that point, the interface collects all the data from the input fields and assembles the WebSQL query. Then the query is sent to the Parser, which checks the syntax and produces the object code. The object code is then executed by the Interpreter and finally a query result set is computed. This set is formatted as an HTML document and displayed by the browser. All URL fields that appear in the result are formatted as anchors so that the user may jump easily to the associated documents.

Performance. The execution time of a WebSQL query is influenced by various factors related to the network accesses performed in the process of building the result set. Among these factors we can mention the number and size of the transferred documents, the available network bandwidth, and the performance and load of the accessed Web servers. Because our query processing system does not maintain any persistent local information between queries it has to access the Web for every new query. Therefore, care must be taken when formulating queries by estimating the number of documents that have to be retrieved. We executed a number of queries by running the Java implementation described in the previous section from within an instance of the HotJava browser running under Solaris 2.3 on a SUN Sparcserver 20/612 with 2 CPUs and 256 Mbytes of RAM.

The execution times for the queries we tested vary between under ten seconds, for simple content queries, to several minutes for structural queries involving the exploration of Web subgraphs with about 500 nodes.

6 Discussion

We have presented the WebSQL language for querying the World Wide Web, given its formal semantics in terms of a new virtual graph model, proposed a new notion of query cost appropriate for Web queries, and applied it to the analysis of WebSQL queries. Finally, we described the current prototype implementation of the language.

Looking at Figure 3, one is skeptical that this complex interface will replace simple keyword-based search engines. However, this is not its purpose. Just as SQL is by and large not used by end users, but by programmers who build applications, we see WebSQL as a tool for helping build Web-based applications more quickly and reliably. Some examples:

Selective indexing: As the Web grows larger, we will often want to build indexes on a selected portion of the network. WebSQL can be used to specify this portion declaratively.

View definition: This is a generalization of the previous point, as an index is a special kind of view. Views and virtual documents are likely to be an important facility, as discussed by Konopnicki and Shmueli [KS95], and a declarative language is needed to specify them.

Link maintenance: Keeping links current and checking whether documents that they point to have changed is a common task that can be automated with the help of a declarative query language.

Several directions for extending this work present themselves. First, instead of being limited to a fixed repertoire of link types (internal, local, and global), we would like to extend the language with the possibility of defining arbitrary link types in terms of their properties, and use the new types in regular expressions. For example, we might be interested in links pointing to nodes in Canada such that their labels do not contain the strings "Back" or "Home."

Second, we would like to make use of internal document structure when it is known, along the lines of [CACS94] and [QRS+95].

There is also a great deal of scope for query optimization. We do not currently attempt to be selective in the index servers that are used for each query, or to propagate conditions from the WHERE to the FROM clause to avoid fetching irrelevant documents. It would also be interesting to investigate a distributed architecture in which subqueries are sent to remote servers to be executed there, avoiding unnecessary data movement.

Acknowledgements

This work was supported by the Natural Sciences and Engineering Research Council of Canada, the Information Technology Research Centre of Ontario and by the Israeli Academy of Science.

References

[ACM93] Serge Abiteboul, Sophie Cluet, and Tova Milo. Querying and updating the file. In *Proceedings of the 19th VLDB Conference*, 1993.

[AV97] S. Abiteboul and V. Vianu. Queries and computation on the Web. In *Proc. ICDT '97*, 1997.

[BK90] C. Beeri and Y. Kornatzky. A logical query language for hypertext systems. In *Proc. of the European Conference on Hypertext*, pages 67–80. Cambridge University Press, 1990.

[BLCL+94] Tim Berners-Lee, Robert Cailliau, Ari Luotonen, Henrik Frystyk Nielsen, and Arthur Secret. The World-Wide Web. *Comm. of the ACM*, 37(8):76–82, 1994.

[CACS94] V. Christophides, S. Abiteboul, S. Cluet, and M. Scholl. From structured documents to novel query facilities. In *Proc. ACM SIGMOD'94*, pages 313–324, 1994.

[CM89] M. P. Consens and A. O. Mendelzon. Expressing structural hypertext queries in Graphlog. In *Hypertext'89*, pages 269–292, 1989.

[Dre96] Daniel Dreilinger. Savvysearch home page. 1996.
`http://guaraldi.cs.colostate.edu:2000/`.

[GZC89] Ralf Hartmut Güting, Roberto Zicari, and David M. Choy. An algebra for structured office documents. *ACM TOIS*, 7(2):123–157, 1989.

[Hal88] Frank G. Halasz. Reflections on Notecards: Seven issues for the next generation of hypermedia systems. *Comm. of the ACM*, 31(7):836–852, 1988.

[HGN+95] Masum Z. Hasan, Gene Golovchinsky, Emanuel G. Noik, Nipon Charoenkitkarn, Mark Chignell, Alberto O. Mendelzon, and David Modjeska. Visual Web surfing with Hy+. In *Proceedings CASCON '95*, Toronto, November 1995. IBM Canada. `ftp://db.toronto.edu/pub/papers/cascon95-multisurf.ps.Z`.

[KS95] D. Konopnicki and O. Shmueli. W3QS: A query system for the World Wide Web. In *Proc. of VLDB'95*, pages 54–65, 1995.

[LSS96] Laks V. S. Lakshmanan, Fereidoon Sadri, and Iyer N. Subramanian. A declarative language for querying and restructuring the Web. In *Proc. of 6th. International Workshop on Research Issues in Data Engineering, RIDE '96*, New Orleans, February 1996. In press.

[Mih96] G. A. Mihaila. WebSQL - An SQL-like query language for the World Wide Web. Master's thesis, University of Toronto, 1996.

[MW93] T. Minohara and R. Watanabe. Queries on structure in hypertext. In *Foundations of Data Organization and Algorithms, FODO '93*, pages 394–411. Springer, 1993.

[MW95] A. O. Mendelzon and P. T. Wood. Finding regular simple paths in graph databases. *SIAM J. Comp.*, 24(6), 1995.

[QRS+95] D. Quass, A. Rajaraman, Y. Sagiv, J. Ullman, and J. Widom. Querying semistructured heterogeneous information. In *Deductive and Object-Oriented Databases, Proceedings of the DOOD '95 Conference*, pages 319–344, Singapore, December 1995. Springer.

[SE95] Erik Selberg and Oren Etzioni. Multi-service search and comparison using the MetaCrawler. In *Proceedings of the Fourth Int'l WWW Conference*, Boston, December 1995. `http://www.w3.org/pub/Conferences/WWW4/Papers/169`.

[SM] Sun Microsystems. Java (tm): Programming for the internet. `http://java.sun.com`.

Characterizing Reference Locality in the WWW*

Virgílio Almeida[†§] Azer Bestavros[†] Mark Crovella[†] Adriana de Oliveira[‡]

(virgilio@bu.edu) (best@bu.edu) (crovella@bu.edu) (dri@dcc.ufmg.br)

Abstract

In this paper we propose models for both temporal and spatial locality of reference in streams of requests arriving at Web servers. We show that simple models based on document popularity alone are insufficient for capturing either temporal or spatial locality. Instead, we rely on an equivalent, but numerical, representation of a reference stream: a stack distance trace. We show that temporal locality can be characterized by the marginal distribution of the stack distance trace, and we propose models for typical distributions and compare their cache performance to our traces. We also show that spatial locality in a reference stream can be characterized using the notion of self-similarity. Self-similarity describes long-range correlations in the dataset, which is a property that previous researchers have found hard to incorporate into synthetic reference strings. We show that stack distance strings appear to be stongly self-similar, and we provide measurements of the degree of self-similarity in our traces. Finally, we discuss methods for generating synthetic Web traces that exhibit the properties of temporal and spatial locality that we measured in our data.

1 Introduction

The principle of locality of reference has very important consequences for computer systems design. Reference streams exhibiting *temporal* locality can benefit from caching; and reference streams exhibiting *spatial* locality can benefit from prefetching. The application of these principles (*e.g.*, in memory systems) is well understood [10, 23].

In order to apply these principles to the design of World Wide Web (Web) caching and prefetching systems, it's important to characterize the degree of locality present in typical Web reference streams. For Web accesses, temporal locality refers to the property that an item frequently accessed in the past is likely to be accessed in the future, whereas spatial locality refers to the property that items *neighboring* an item frequently accessed in the past are likely to be accessed in the future. For memory systems, such *neighborhoods* are easily defined in terms of address space proximity, giving rise to prefetching entities such as *cache lines* and *memory pages*. For the Web, we believe that the identification of similar prefetching entities is possible if spatial locality is characterized properly.

Previous research in the locality properties of symbolic reference streams have shown the benefits of transforming the reference stream into an equivalent, but numerical, representation: a *stack distance* stream [19]. This transformation preserves all of the information of the original trace except for the specific reference names, and so it is invertible, allowing reconstruction of the original trace (albeit with synthetic names). Two properties of the stack distance stream can be used to measure the notions of temporal and spatial locality: *marginal distribution*, and *correlation structure* [19, 22]. The marginal distribution measures the likelihood that two references to the same object are separated by some number of intervening references in the stream. The correlation structure of the stream measures the likelihood that we can predict future references based on the stream of past references.

In this paper we use quantitative methods based on stack distance to measure both the temporal and spatial locality properties for Web reference streams. We characterize reference streams collected at four Web servers, propose a model for marginal distribution of stack distance (and thus temporal locality) and show typical ranges of the relevant parameters. We also propose a model for spatial locality of our reference streams based on the correlation structure of stack distances. Using these measurements we show how to generate synthetic reference streams of arbitrary length whose performance properties mimic those of our empirically measured data.

A novel feature of our approach is the use of statistical *self-similarity* to capture the correlation structure of the reference stream. That is, we show evidence that Web stack distance streams are statistically self-similar and that this property can be used to explain aspects of the reference stream that are the result of spatial locality. The presence of self-similarity in the reference stream means that correlations between object references can occur at widely varying timescales (*long-range depen-*

---

*This work has been partially supported by NSF (grants CCR-9308344 and CCR-9501822) and by CNPq-Brazil.

†Computer Science Department, Boston University, Boston, MA 02215, USA.

‡Depto. de Ciencia da Computacão, Universidade Federal de Minas Gerais, Belo Horizonte, MG 30161, Brazil.

§On sabbatical at Boston University.

dence). A timeseries with long-range dependence appears much more "bursty" than series with only short-range or no dependence — which agrees with generally observed characterizations of reference locality. Long-range dependence in the stack distance series is also related to previously noted fractal properties of cache miss patterns [26], and we interpret prior work in fractal reference patterns in terms of our observations.

This method of measuring spatial locality also provides an interpretation for the notion of spatial locality when reference streams are composed of symbols rather than numbers. We consider object A to be close to object B if there is a high likelihood that a reference to A will immediately follow a reference to B. That is, the "distance" between objects is the inverse of the transition probability of object references considered as a first-order Markov chain. While this definition does not correspond to our usual notions of a norm (it is not symmetric), it does capture the important property of spatial locality for the purposes of prefetching: the likelihood that prefetching will be successful.

Our methods focus on the locality properties of reference streams without regard to document size. Thus in our simulations we consider caches to be sized to hold a fixed number of documents rather than a fixed amount of data. This assumption stems from the fact that we are interested in locality, which is a property of reference streams independent of any cache size.[2]

In the remainder of this section we describe the data on which our measurements and trace simulations are based. In section 2, we characterize the popularity of Web documents and show that a cache reference model based on popularity is not expressive enough to capture the temporal and spatial locality of reference properties exhibited in actual Web traces. Evidence of these locality of reference properties is presented in section 3. In sections 4 and 5, we characterize these properties and present statistical models that capture these characteristics. In section 6, we examine related work. We conclude in section 7 with a summary and directions for future work.

Data Collection: The Web is a large-scale distributed information system based on a client-server architecture. Thus, the workload viewed from a server standpoint consists of a number of requests originated at many different clients. In order to analyze reference locality, we examined the access logs for different Web servers, namely:

the NCSA Web server located at the National Center for Supercomputing Applications (NCSA), the SDSC Web server at the San Diego Supercomputer Center (SDSC), the EPA Web server located at Research Triangle Park, NC and the Web server at the Computer Science Department at Boston University (BU). In the case of the NCSA, the data refers only to one server (Costello). The SDSC and EPA logs are available at the Internet Traffic Archives [14], the NCSA log was obtained after contacting the staff at the site and the BU logs were collected at the departmental Web server.

The logs have one line of information per request processed by the server. Each line contains the name of the host making the request, the timestamp the request was made, the filename of the requested object and size in bytes of the reply. Table 1 summarizes the statistics about the logs of the four Web servers.

Log	NCSA	SDSC	EPA	BU
Duration	1 day	1 day	1 day	2 weeks
Start Date	Dec 19	Aug 22	Aug 29	Oct 08
Total requests	46,955	28,338	47,748	80,518
Unique requests	4,851	1,267	6,518	4,471

Table 1: Summary of Access Log Data

2 Characterizing Document Popularity

The highly uneven popularity of various Web documents is a well-documented phenomenon that has been exploited in previous caching, replication and dissemination studies. In these studies, it was shown that "Popular files are very popular" [4, 13]. In [9], Cunha, Bestavros, and Crovella characterized the popularity of *Web documents requested by clients* and confirmed the applicability of Zipf's law [27, discussed in [17]] to Web documents. Zipf's law was originally applied to the relationship between a word's popularity in terms of rank and its frequency of use. It states that if one ranks the popularity of words used in a given text[3] (denoted by ρ) by their frequency of use (denoted by P) then

$$P \sim 1/\rho.$$

Note that this distribution is a parameterless hyperbolic distribution. *i.e.*, ρ is raised to exactly -1, so that the nth most popular document is exactly twice as likely to be accessed as the $2n^{\text{th}}$ most popular document.

Our data shows that Zipf's law applies quite strongly to *Web documents serviced by Web servers*. This is demonstrated in Figure 1 for all 2135 documents accessed in the BU trace. The figure shows a log-log plot of

---

[2]Since we have shown in previous work [9] that document size is correlated with expected reference frequency, this assumption is somewhat limiting for direct use in cache performance analysis. For that reason we are currently extending this work to include document sizes in our analysis. Nonetheless we believe that the current methods provide a simple and effective way to capture both the spatial and temporal locality of Web reference streams.

[3]Zipf's law has subsequently been applied to other examples of popularity in the social sciences.

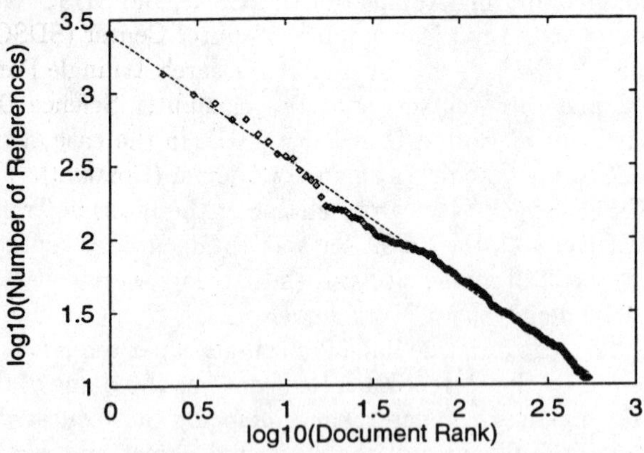

Figure 1: Zipf's Law Applied to Web Documents

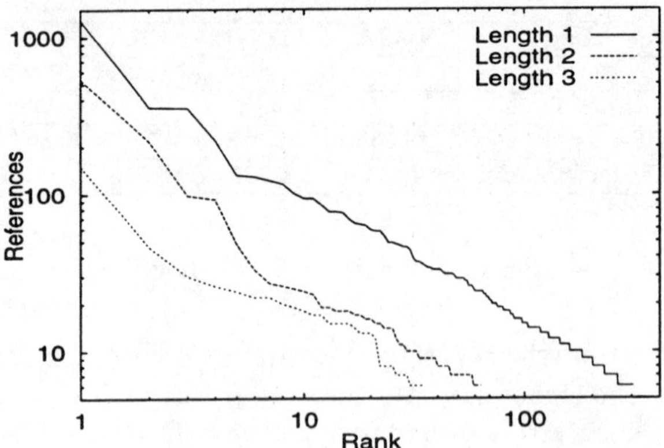

Figure 2: Zipf's Law for Web Document Sequences

the total number of references (Y axis) to each document as a function of the document's rank in overall popularity (X axis). The tightness of the fit to a straight line is strong ($R^2 = 0.99$), as is the slope of the line: -0.85 (shown in the figure). Thus the exponent relating popularity to rank for Web documents is very nearly -1, as predicted by Zipf's law.

Our measurements suggest that Zipf's law applies, not only to single requests for documents, but also to request *strides*. A request stride is a sequence of requests from the *same* client where the time between successive requests in that stride is not larger than a given *stride threshold*. Figure-2 shows a log-log plot of the total number of references (Y axis) to strides of length k (for $k = 1, 2, 3$) as a function of the stride's rank in overall popularity (X axis). The trace used for this plot is the BU trace and the stride threshold is set at 10 seconds. Again, the tightness of the fit for the family of curves in Figure-2 to straight lines slope close to -1 suggest that Zipf's law does apply to sequences of requests.

Given the above observations, one possible access model [12, 2] is to generate document requests according to the popularity profile of documents. We call this model the *Zipf-based model*. To test the validity of this model we measured the miss rate at the server when requests are generated synthetically, to satisfy the observed popularity profile of documents at BU, and compared these measurements with the measurements obtained when the actual BU trace is used to drive the simulation. The synthetic trace was generated by applying a random permutation to the actual trace for BU. The result of this comparison is shown in Figure 3.

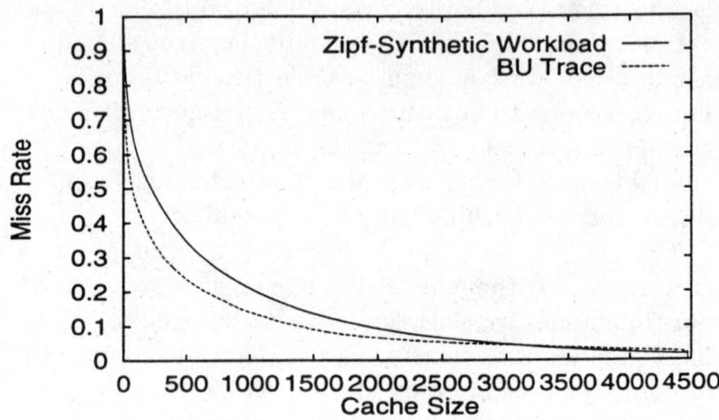

Figure 3: Miss rate for a Zipf-based synthetic workload and for an actual trace

Obviously, using popularity as the basis of a cache model for Web documents does not yield acceptable results. Figure 3 shows that for a cache size of 400 items, the miss rate that results from a Zipf-based cache model is nearly 33% less than the actual miss rate.

The main weakness of a Zipf-based model is that it does not capture the potential locality of reference properties that may be present in actual traces. In particular, while the Zipf-based synthetic trace preserves the general popularity profile of documents, it fails to capture the temporal and spatial locality of reference properties. In the next section we show evidence that these properties indeed exist in Web traces, and in sections 4 and 5, we provide simple, yet expressive statistical models thereof.

3 Evidence of Reference Locality

Temporal Locality: Temporal locality implies that recently accessed documents are more likely to be referenced in the near future. Based on the concepts proposed in [19, 24], we define a stack distance model that captures the temporal locality relationships present in a request stream. Let us consider a reference stream $R_t = r_1, r_2, ..., r_t$, where r_t denotes the name of the object requested at virtual time t. Our unit of time will be one request, so that virtual time t indicates that t requests have already arrived at a server. Let us also define the LRU stack S_t, which is an ordering of all objects of a server by recency of usage. Thus, at virtual time t, the LRU stack is given by:

$$S_t = \{o_1, o_2, \ldots, o_N\} \qquad (1)$$

where $o_1, o_2, \ldots, o_N$ are objects of the server and o_1 is the most recently accessed object, o_2 the next most recently referenced, etc. If o_1 is the most recently accessed document, then $r_t = o_1$. Whenever a reference is made to an object, the stack must be updated. Considering that $r_{t+1} = o_i$, then the stack becomes $S_{t+1} = \{o_i, o_1, o_2, ..., o_{i-1}, o_{i+1}, ..., o_N\}$. Suppose now that $S_{t-1} = \{o_1, o_2, ..., o_N\}$ and $r_t = o_i$. Then, we could say that request r_t is at distance i in stack S_{t-1}. Let d_t denote the stack distance of the document referenced at time t. We then have the following relation:

$$\text{if } r_t = o_i \text{ then } d_t = i \qquad (2)$$

Thus, for any request string $R_t = r_1, r_2, ..., r_t$ there is a corresponding distance string $\delta = d_1, d_2, ..., d_t$. We can then consider that the distance string and the request string are equivalent in terms of reference information. Since the distance string reflects the pattern in which Web users request documents from a server rather than the actual identity of the documents, it will be used as our model for object reference pattern.[4]

The marginal distribution of distance probabilities is an indication of temporal locality because it measures the number of intervening references between two references to the same object. Small stack distances result from frequent references to a document. In other words, the documents referenced most frequently tend to be those close to the top of the stack.

As a measure of the temporal locality present in our traces, we compare the average stack distance found in the BU trace with that of the scrambled BU trace. The results, shown in table 2, indicate that the average stack distance is apparently greater for the scrambled trace, meaning that temporal locality has been decreased.

Spatial Locality: The existence of spatial locality of reference could be established by comparing the total number of unique sequences observed in a trace and the total number of unique sequences that would be found in a random permutation of such a trace. Notice that

---

[4]The particular choice of LRU as the stack ordering algorithm does not restrict the applicability of our methods to use with any particular caching strategy; however it does allow direct evaluation of LRU caches as a means of testing the accuracy of our methods, which we will do in Section 4.

BU Trace	Original	Scrambled
Mean Stack Distance	479.798	645.586
Standard Deviation	941.430	968.840

Table 2: Evidence of Temporal Locality

a random permutation of a trace (henceforth called a *scrambled* trace) *preserves* the popularity profile of the various documents in that trace, but it *destroys* the spatial locality of reference that may exist in such a trace (by uncorrelating the sequence of references). If references are indeed correlated, then one would expect the total number of unique sequences observed in a trace to be much less than the total number of unique sequences observed in a scrambled trace.

Figure 4 shows the total number of unique sequences (Y axis) of length k (X axis) observed in the first week (the first 32,839 references) of the BU trace, which we call the BU1 server trace. Three cases are shown. The top curve shows the total number of unique k-long sequences observed in a scrambled BU1 trace. The middle curve shows the total number of unique k-long sequences observed in the BU1 trace. Since traces arriving at the server reflect an interleaving of a number of individual client traces, we plot in the bottom curve the total number of unique k-long sequences observed when separately considering individual clients in the BU1 trace.

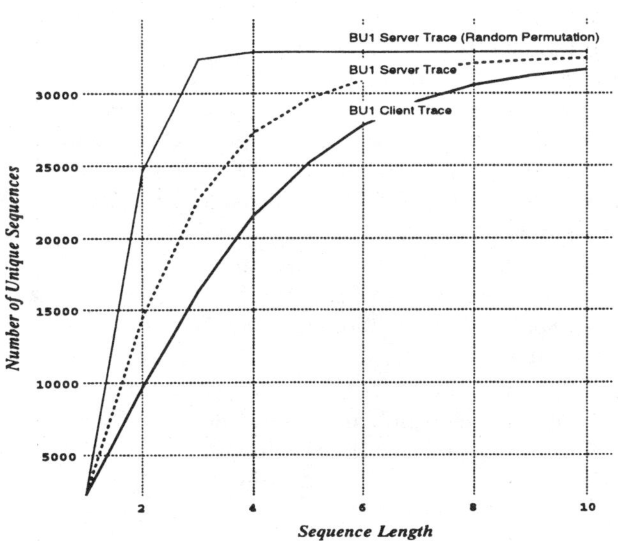

Figure 4: Unique sequences observed in the BU trace

All three curves show an increase in the total number of unique sequences as k increases,[5] with the random-

---

[5]The reason that all three curves level-off is related to the limited length of the trace. In particular, it is impossible to observe

ized trace showing the steepest increase and the client trace showing the slowest increase. These results confirm the existence of considerable spatial locality in client access patterns. For example, while up to 32,327 different sequences of length 3 are observed in the scrambled BU1 trace, only 16,114 (more than 50% less) different sequences of length 3 are observed in the BU1 client traces. This spatial locality is "diluted" to some extent (but still very much evident) in the BU1 server trace—22,680 (about 30% less) different sequences of length 3 are observed in the BU1 server trace.

4 Characterizing Temporal Locality

Since it is clear that real traces and scrambled traces differ significantly in the aggregate properties of their stack distance traces, we examine the marginal distributions of stack distances.

As discussed in Section 1, the marginal distribution of stack distance captures the temporal locality present in the trace. That is, if D is a random variable corresponding to stack distance (with distribution function F_D) and $M(C)$ is the miss rate of a cache that can hold C files (using the same replacement algorithm that was used to generate the stack distance trace), then:

$$P[D > C] = 1 - F_D(C) = M(C)$$

Thus, knowledge of the complementary distribution function $1 - F_D$ provides enough information to predict the performance of a cache of any size for the given trace.

To estimate distributions for the four traces we consider, histograms are shown in Figure 5. This figure shows that most of the stack distances are close to 1 (the traces show good temporal locality) and yet there are long tails to the distributions. We considered a number of long-tailed distributions to model this data. In particular we rejected the Pareto distribution ([8]) because although the tails are long, they do not seem to follow a power-law. The data were found to be best fit by a *lognormal* distribution. Data that follows a lognormal distribution has the property that its logarithm is normally distributed. The resulting distribution has a very long tail but is not *heavy-tailed* in the strict sense of following a power-law in the tails.

To illustrate the use of lognormal distributions to model stack distances, Figure 6 shows the empirically measured distributions and the fitted distributions. Each plot shows a histogram of the base 10 logs of the stack distance data; in addition the plot shows the shape of the corresponding fit of a lognormal distribution to the data. While the data sets may appear to vary from normal to some degree, in reality these differences have been

magnified by the log-transformation process. In fact the fit to the data is quite close as we will show below.

The parameters used to generate the fitted distributions shown in Figure 6 are given in Table 3. The $\hat{\mu}$ and $\hat{\sigma}$ columns show the mean and standard deviation *of the base 10 log* of the datasets. The table shows that for the traces we studied, the $\hat{\sigma}$ varies only slightly. Most of the variation between the datasets occurs in the $\hat{\mu}$ parameter.

	BU	NCSA	SDSC	EPA
$\hat{\mu}$	1.829	1.730	1.568	2.150
$\hat{\sigma}$	0.947	0.836	0.827	0.921

Table 3: Lognormal Distribution Parameters for Traces

The ability of lognormal distributions to predict actual miss rates in finite caches is shown in Figure 7. As discussed above we plot $P[D > C]$ since it is equivalent to miss rate. In each plot, we show the predicted miss rate using the lognormal stack distance model and the actual miss rate obtained from the data. The agreement between model and data in each case is good, except in the case of the EPA trace, which has very poor locality.

A comparison of the traces in terms of their fitted parameters is shown in Figure 8. This figure shows how temporal locality (measured by miss rate) varies across the traces, and the corresponding parameter values that capture that locality. The figure shows that as the temporal locality of a trace decreases, the mean of lognormal distribution increases (from about 1.6 up to 2.2) and the standard deviation of the lognormal distribution also tends to increase, although to a lesser degree (from 0.83 up to 0.95).

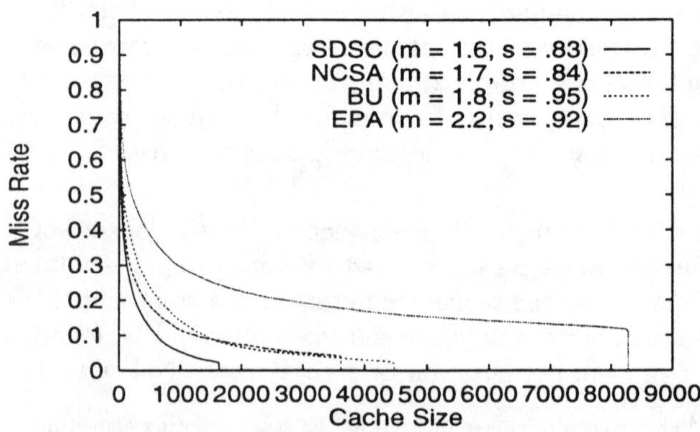

Figure 8: Temporal Locality Parameters

---

any more than $l - k$ unique k-long sequences in a trace of length l. For our experiments $l = 32,839$—hence the observed ceiling.

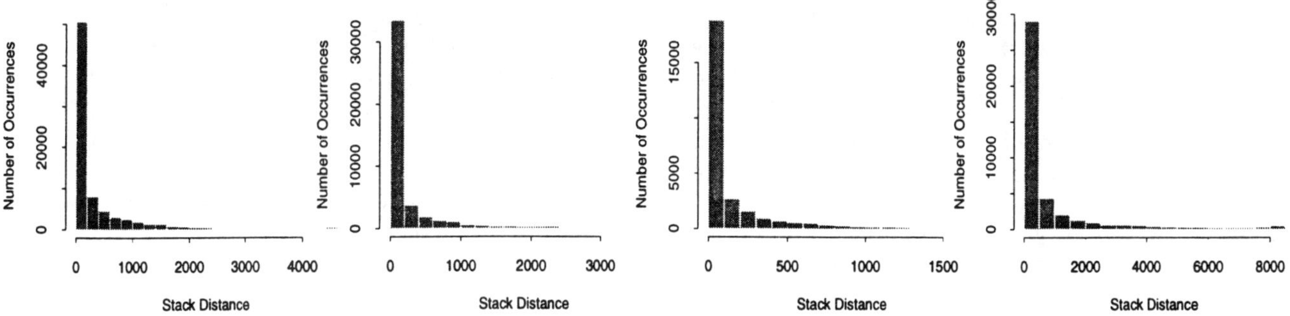

Figure 5: Empirical Stack Distance Distributions (Left to Right: BU, NCSA, SDSC, EPA)

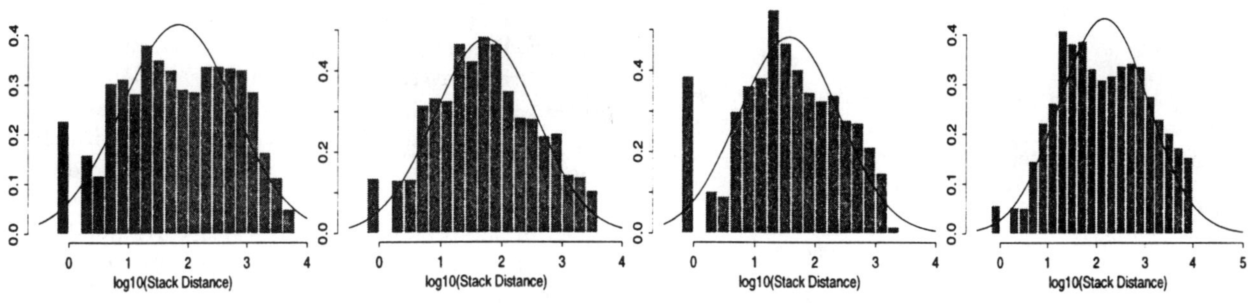

Figure 6: Lognormal Distributions of Stack Distance Traces (Left to Right: BU, NCSA, SDSC, EPA)

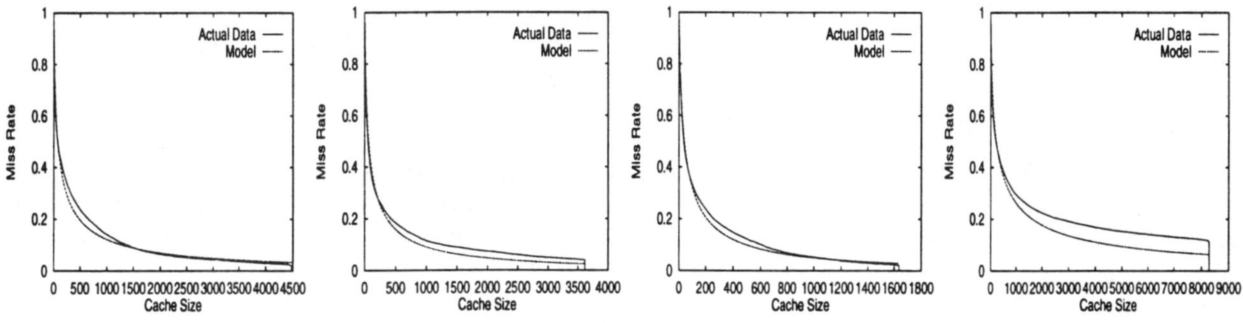

Figure 7: Actual and Predicted Miss Rates using Lognormal Models (Left to Right: BU, NCSA, SDSC, EPA)

5 Characterizing Spatial Locality

Having characterized the temporal locality present in our traces, we now present models for spatial locality. Previous work has shown that the correlation structure of the stack distance stream is useful for modeling spatial locality [22]; however previous attempts to model the correlation structure of reference strings have used models with only short-range dependence, such as finite first-order Markov chains. As pointed out in [24], such short-range dependent models are not capable of capturing the long-term structure of reference strings, which includes phase change behavior.

Measuring Stack Distance Self-Similarity: To capture the long-range dependence in stack distance strings we employ the statistics of self-similarity. We say that a series Y_t is H-self-similar if for any positive stretching factor c, the rescaled process with time scale ct, which is $c^{-H} Y_{ct}$, is equal in distribution to the original process Y_t. That is,

$$Y_t =_d c^{-H} Y_{ct} \quad \text{for all } c, t > 0. \tag{3}$$

This means that the series Y_t has fractal-like properties: detail is present at all scales. As a result, using only the single parameter H (related to the fractal dimension) we can capture variation at a wide range of scales.

Equation 3 applies to a motion process, such as Brownian motion (for which $H = 0.5$). For stationary processes like our stack distance traces, an equivalent definition is used, which relates the stationary process to its corresponding motion process (formed by taking successive sums of the stationary process):

Definition. Let $\{X_t\}$ be a stationary process with continuous time parameter t. Then we say that X_t is H-self-similar if for any positive aggregation factor m the series obtained by m-aggregating X_t is equal in distribution to X_t. That is:

$$X_t =_d m^{-H} \sum_{i=(t-1)m+1}^{tm} X_i \quad \text{for all } m \in N, t > 0 \tag{4}$$

Because of the correlations present on all scales that is implied by Equation 4, stationary self-similar processes also have the property of *long-range dependence*. A long-range dependent series typically has "bursts" (values above or below the mean) that occur on all time scales. That is, regardless of the scale at which the series is viewed, bursty patterns can be observed. This property is in strong contrast to short-range dependent models (such as Markovian processes or Poisson processes) which appear smooth at long timescales.

The property of burstiness at all timescales is noticeably present in stack distance series; it is this property that has been difficult to capture in the past using only short-range dependent models. An example of this effect is shown in Figure 9. The figure compares the BU stack distance trace with a trace formed by first randomly scrambling the BU dataset before calculating stack distances. Note that both traces consist of exactly the same set of file references; however in the case of the scrambled dataset the spatial locality has been destroyed.

The figure shows the two stack distance traces at varying levels of detail. In the bottom graphs each point in the series is formed by summing 5 consecutive points (in non-overlapping blocks) from the original traces. Moving up the next series is formed by summing 5 points from the lower series, and so on until at the top level each data point consists of the sum of 625 data points from the original stack distance series. In each plot we have only plotted 128 points so as to show equivalent levels of detail; at the top, this corresponds to the entire series, at lower levels, the plots are over ranges that are selected arbitrarily. When summing data in this way, short range dependences are averaged out; if the series is long-range dependent, bursts will still remain. This can be seen by comparing the scrambled trace (on the right) with the original trace (on the left). The bursts that are present in the original trace are evidence of very long-range correlations in the original dataset, which corresponds to long periods of very large stack distances – as would be caused by phase changes in file referencing behavior.

The degree of self-similarity in a series is captured by the parameter H, which takes values between 0.5 and 1.0. If $H = 0.5$, the series has no long-range dependence, and acts like Gaussian noise (whose motion process is Brownian motion). As $H \to 1$, the burstiness of the series becomes more pronounced at high levels of aggregation. To estimate the H parameter for our series, we use four methods. Three methods, the variance-time plot, the R/S plot, and the periodogram, are graphical. These methods are useful for assessing whether assumptions about the data are correct (such as stationarity) and for providing a single estimate of H. Each of the three graphical methods results in an X-Y plot; linearity in the plot is evidence of long-range dependence in the underlying series, and the slope of the line in each case can be used to estimate H. The fourth method is the maximum likelihood estimator for H, called the *Whittle* estimator, which provides confidence intervals as well. Interested readers are referred to [3, 16] for a discussion of these methods in more detail.

Plots of the graphical estimators for the BU trace are shown in Figure 10. On the left is the variance-time estimator; the plot appears strongly linear over most of its range, and the slope of the line yields an estimate

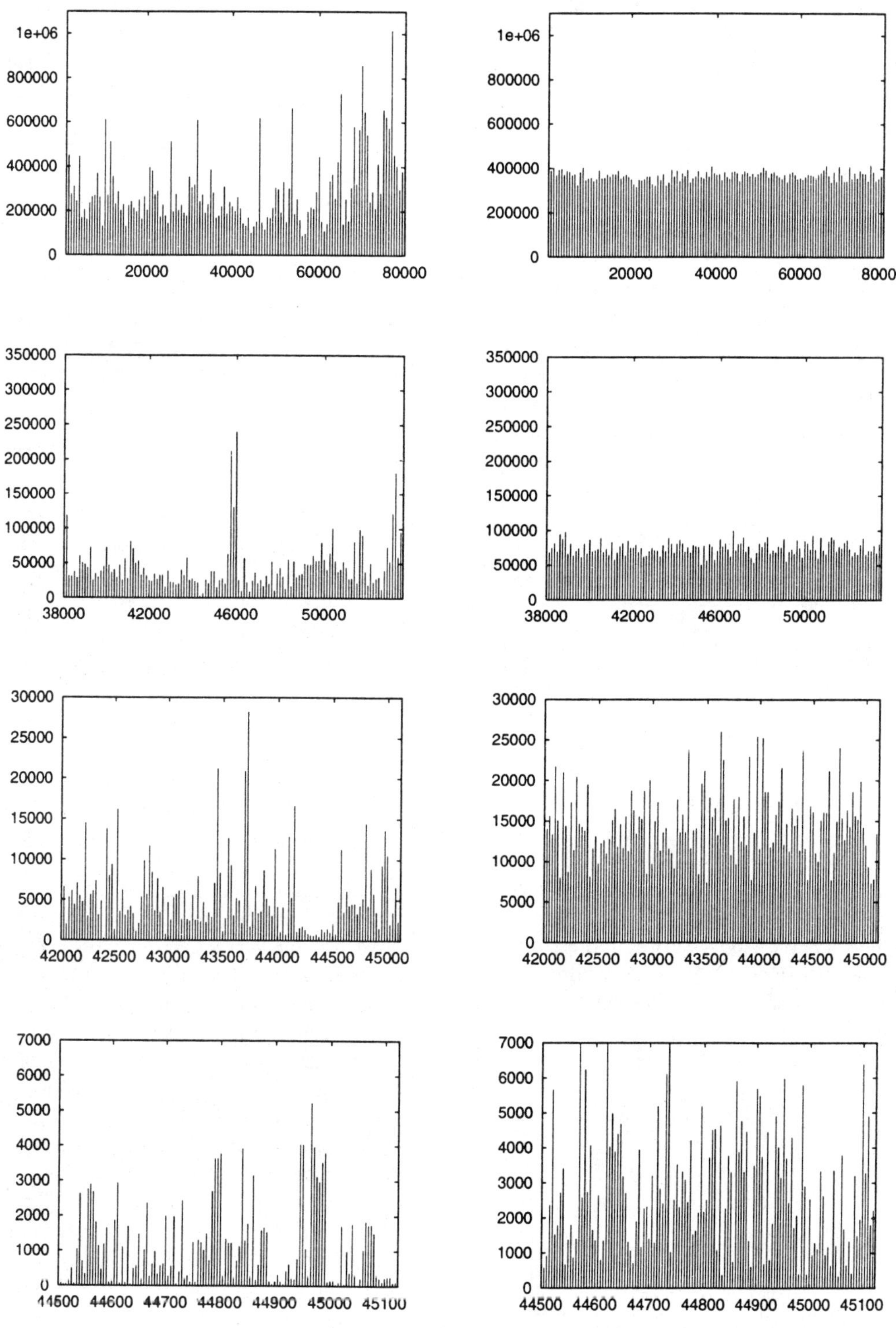

Figure 9: Stack Distance Scaling Behavior of Original (left) and Scrambled (right) BU Traces

of $\hat{H} = 0.82$ (the line corresponding to $H = 1/2$ is also plotted for reference). In the center is a plot of the R/S statistic; again, the evident linearity is evidence of long-range dependence, and the slope yields $\hat{H} = 0.78$. In this plot the lines corresponding to $H = 1/2$ and $H = 1$ are plotted for reference. On the right is the periodogram estimator; the significant scatter shown is typical in this plot, but a an underlying linear trend is present, and least-squares fit to the points yields $\hat{H} = 0.87$. Thus, each of these plots shows evidence of self-similarity. The graphical results for the other three stack distance traces are not shown, but they exhibit similar linearity.

In addition to the graphical estimators, we also used the Whittle MLE estimator to estimate H for our datasets. In all cases we found reasonable agreement between the estimators, and values of H significantly above $1/2$. The results for our four datasets are shown in Table 4. The values of H range from about 0.85 for the BU dataset to about 0.65 for the EPA dataset.

	V-T	R/S	Period.	Whittle MLE	(95% conf.)
BU	.82	.78	.87	.85	(0.84, 0.87)
NCSA	.71	.74	.74	.74	(0.73, 0.77)
SDSC	.71	.68	.69	.68	(0.66, 0.71)
EPA	.64	.66	.66	.65	(0.64, 0.67)

Table 4: Estimates of H for Datasets

We considered the possibility that the process of transforming the original traces into stack distance strings may have been responsible for introducing dependence into the data. To answer this question we randomly rearranged each dataset, calculated the corresponding new stack distance series, and estimated the H values of the resulting series. The results are shown in Table 5. These estimates are all very close to $1/2$, indicative of no long-range dependence in the series. As a result, we conclude that the presence of long-range dependence in these timeseries reflects actual correlations among the symbol pattern in the original reference traces.

	V-T	R/S	Period.	Whittle MLE
BU	.50	.55	.50	.50
NCSA	.50	.51	.51	.49
EPA	.52	.54	.50	.50
SDSC	.51	.55	.47	.50

Table 5: Estimates of H for *Scrambled* Datasets

Relationship to Fractal Cache Miss Patterns: Another way to look at Figure 9 is that, progressing from top to bottom, we are "zooming in" on the data. The fact that the plots on the left of the figure show roughly similar degrees of burstiness at all scales is evidence of fractal-like behavior of the stack distance trace.

In fact, fractal geometry has been noted in the past as a characteristic of reference locality in computer systems. In particular, Voldman *et. al.* [26] presented data on misses in cache memory systems for three different workloads (scientific, database, and general). The authors showed that each of these cache miss sequences shows fractal patterns: individual misses are clustered in time, clusters form clusters, and so on. One of their results is that if cache miss events are plotted on the number line using the sequence number of the reference as the coordinate, the result is a fractal pattern of dimension between 0 and 1.

To relate our results to those of Voldman *et. al.*, we first note that self-similarity of a stack distance trace implies that the stack distance trace is also a fractal. A statistically self-similar series X_t like the one shown on the left of Figure 9 has an almost sure fractal dimension (in the sense of either the Hausdorff $\dim_H$ or box-counting dimension $\dim_B$) of [11]

$$\dim(X_t) = 2 - H.$$

Thus the fractal dimension of such a series is $3/2$ for Gaussian noise ($H = 1/2$), and decreases to 1 as the correlation present in the series increases ($H \rightarrow 1$). This corresponds with the intuition that a series with more dependence is more "predictable" and fills space less completely.

The connection between our work and [26] then is that, if stack distances are self-similar, we expect cache misses to have fractal properties. The reason for this is as follows. Cache miss patterns can be seen to be the points of intersection between the stack distance trace and a line, parallel to the x axis, corresponding to some fixed cache size. The intersection of fractal X having $1 < \dim_H(X) < 2$ and a line L ($\dim_H(L) = 1$) is almost surely a new fractal X' with $\dim_H(X') = \dim_H(X) - 1$ [17]. This means that a cache miss fractal derived from a stack distance fractal such as our traces should have a dimension between 0 and 1. In fact we have observed this effect and have found that cache misses in our traces show fractal characteristics that are consistent with the patterns previously observed by Voldman *et. al.*

Thus our results can be seen as another perspective on the fractal nature of cache miss patterns; however, our work extends those results to the case of WWW reference patterns, and shows how to use fractal properties in generating synthetic traces, as discussed in the next section.

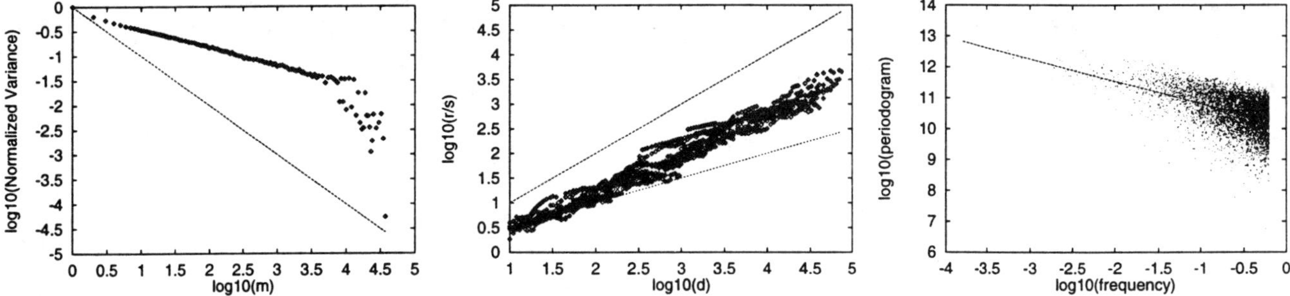

Figure 10: Graphical Estimators of H for BU Trace

Generating Synthetic Web Reference Traces: To generate synthetic Web reference traces it is important to mimic as closely as possible both the temporal and spatial locality present in real traces. The results in this paper suggest the following process:

1. Select parameters μ and σ reflecting temporal locality, and H reflecting spatial locality. These may be selected based on empirical measurement of traces that are to be imitated, or from the range of values measured in the traces reported here.

2. Generate a stack distance trace with marginal distribution determined by μ and σ and long-range dependence determined by H.

3. Invert the stack distance trace to form a sequence of file names.

On first glance, step 2 seems difficult. Fortunately recent results have shown that marginal distribution and long-range dependence can be considered as separate problems for trace generation [15]. That work shows that, given a long-range dependent series X_t with $H = H_X$ and marginal cumulative probability function $F_X(x)$, we can generate another long-range dependent series Y_t with $H = H_X$ and arbitrary marginal cumulative probability function $F_Y(x)$. This is achieved by individual transformation of the elements of X_t as follows:

$$Y_t = F_Y^{-1}(F_X(X_t)) \tag{5}$$

The authors in [15] show that this transformation preserves long-range dependence with the same value of H.

Thus, our approach to step 2 is as follows. First, generate a self-similar series with given H. This can be done in a number of ways; a fast approach is described in [20]. Then apply the transformation of Equation 5 to obtain a series with the proper lognormal marginal distribution.

We have begun to use the method for generating web reference traces and are currently evaluating the properties of the resulting traces. Initial experiments involving models of only temporal locality properties are encouraging.

6 Related Work

Modeling: Denning and Schwartz [10] established the fundamental properties that characterize the phenomenon of locality in hierarchical structures of memory. In [19], the authors studied stack algorithms and introduced stack distance as a means for analyzing behavior of demand-paged memory systems. They also discussed the significance of stack distance strings for evaluating performance of memory management schemes. Then, Spirn [24] proposes the use of distance string models to represent program behavior. Distance strings are equivalent in information content to the reference string, but are more easily handled by mathematical models. The distance string model and the LRU stack model are equivalent, since it is possible to determine the LRU stack at each time from the knowledge of the distance string. However, the proposed distance string model does not capture the long-range dependencies among references. As pointed out by the author, the model does not provide an accurate characterization of page faults, which tend in real programs to occur in clusters. When changes in locality occur gradually, page by page, it is relatively simple to model the reference locality. However, in a real program, the locality set of execution is completely disrupted by the execution of a new phase of the program. Usually, the abrupt changes in locality generate large distances in distance string model. Markov distance string models are capable of predicting bursts based on the most recent generated distances. Thus, the work in [24] argues that Markov models are not able to capture the behavior of real programs, which exhibit some form of long-range dependencies. The author also points out that those models, based on the distance probabilities, are not suitable for simulation studies of program behavior, because they lack the ability to mimic long-range effects.

Application of Fractals: As discussed in Section 5, the use of fractal geometry and self-similarity to analyze behavior of computer systems was pioneered by the work of Voldman *et. al.* [26]. The authors looked at memory reference traces of three software environments and found that the distributions of intermiss distances follow a power-law, indicative of fractal behavior. The cache misses are grouped over time in clusters, which are statistically self-similar. As a result of the analysis, they conjecture that the fractal dimension of a given cache miss distribution is a measure of the complexity of the underlying software.

Based on the work in [26], paper [25] models the patterns generated by a processor accessing memory as random walk with fractal dimension. The author proposes that in an asymptotic behavior the number of misses that a program encounters in an infinite cache is given by a hyperbolic function of the fractal dimension. The paper also presents an approximate analytical model for cache misses. The model has two distinct phases, one called forced mode, which represents the cold start process. The fractal mode phase models the stable phase of a cache. However, the model is not easily used because of the empirical process of obtaining and adjusting its parameters from plots of the traces. Also, the proposed model does not represent multiprogramming environments, where context switches occur frequently.

Our paper extends the work referenced in [26, 25, 24] to the context of large distributed systems and also adds parameters to fully describe locality aspects of a reference stream that arrives at a Web server.

Exploiting Web Reference Locality: Previous studies in caching, replication, dissemination, and prefetching protocols for large distributed information systems have recognized and exploited the various locality of reference properties examined in this paper. In the remainder of this section we present a brief review of these protocols. For space limitations, we limit ourselves to Web-related work.

Glassman [12] presents one of the earliest attempts for caching on the Web, whereby *"satellite relays"* (proxy caches) are organized into a tree-structured hierarchy with cache misses in lower relays percolating up through higher relays until the requested object is found. The performance of this caching system for a single relay with a rather small cache size indicated that it is possible to maintain a *"fairly stable"* 33% hit rate. Using a Zipf-based model, it was estimated that with an infinite-size cache, the maximum achievable hit rate is 40%. Another early attempt at characterizing Web access pat-

terns is the work of Recker and Pitkow [21], in which a model for Web information access is proposed based on two metrics borrowed from psychological research on human memory—namely the frequency and recency rates of past accesses.

The first comprehensive study of client-based caching for the Web was conducted by our Oceans group.[6] In that study [6], the effectiveness of session caching, host caching, and LAN proxy caching were established using a unique set of 5,700 client traces (almost 600,000 URL requests), which were obtained by intrumenting Mosaic [9]. This study concluded that LAN proxy caching—while effective in reducing response time by as much as a half—is ultimately limited by the low level of sharing of remote documents amongst clients of the same site. This finding agrees with Glassman's predictions [12] and was further confirmed for general proxy caching by Abrams *et al* [1].

In [18], Markatos examines the potential performance gains from using *Main Memory Web Caches*. He shows that a small amount of main memory could yield substantial improvement in performance if cache management methods that are sensitive to document popularity and to user preferences for small documents [9] are employed.

Exploiting the spatial locality of reference properties exhibited in Web access patterns was investigated in two recent prefetching studies of our Oceans group. In [7], Bestavros and Cunha propose a protocol that allows a client to prefetch Web documents based on Markov models built from the client's previous access patterns. In [5] Bestavros propose a protocol that allows prefetching to be initiated as a result of hints generated by servers based on a Markov model built by analyzing the server's access logs.

7 Conclusion

In this paper we have measured the locality present in reference traces arriving at four servers in the World Wide Web, and shown statistical models that capture the locality properties of our datasets. These models can be used to compare different reference streams, predict cache performance, and generate synthetic reference streams with realistic properties.

We first showed that simple methods for generating reference streams based only on document popularity capture neither the temporal nor the spatial locality present in a trace. We then measured the temporal locality properties of the reference traces, and showed that a reasonable model for stack distance distribution is the *lognormal* distribution. Finally, to model spatial locality, we argued that models incorporating long-range

---

[6]http://www.cs.bu.edu/groups/oceans

dependence were necessary in order to capture the long-term behavior of reference patterns.

Ongoing work is extending these models of locality to incorporate explicit modeling of document size. In addition, although our work is based on traces obtained from servers, we are also interested in the locality properties of client reference traces, and how those properties change when streams are captured close to the client, as compared to close to the server.

Acknowledgements: The authors thank John Dilley and PDIS anonymous referees for comments that improved the content and presentation of this paper.

References

[1] Marc Abrams, Charles R. Standridge, Ghaleb Abdulla, Stephen Williams, and Edward A. Fox. Caching proxies: Limitations and potentials. In *Proceedings of the Fourth Interntional Conference on the WWW*, Boston, MA, December 1995.

[2] S. Acharya, R. Alonso, M. Franklin, and S. Zdonik. Broadcast disks: Data management for asymmetric communications environments. In *Proceedings of ACM SIGMOD'95*, San Jose, CA, May 1995.

[3] Jan Beran. *Statistics for Long-Memory Processes*. Monographs on Statistics and Applied Probability. Chapman and Hall, New York, NY, 1994.

[4] Azer Bestavros. Demand-based document dissemination to reduce traffic and balance load in distributed information systems. In *Proceedings of SPDP'95: The 7th IEEE Symposium on Parallel and Distributed Processing*, San Anotonio, Texas, October 1995.

[5] Azer Bestavros. Using speculation to reduce server load and service time on the www. In *Proceedings of CIKM'95: The 4th ACM International Conference on Information and Knowledge Management*, Baltimore, Maryland, November 1995.

[6] Azer Bestavros, Robert Carter, Mark Crovella, Carlos Cunha, Abdelsalam Heddaya, and Sulaiman Mirdad. Application level document caching in the internet. In *IEEE SDNE'96: The Second International Workshop on Services in Distributed and Networked Environments*, Whistler, British Columbia, June 1995.

[7] Azer Bestavros and Carlos Cunha. A prefetching protocol using client speculation for the www. Technical Report TR-95-011, Boston University, CS Dept, Boston, MA 02215, April 1995.

[8] Mark E. Crovella and Azer Bestavros. Self-similarity in World Wide Web traffic: Evidence and possible causes. In *Proceedings of the ACM SIGMETRICS'96*, May 1996.

[9] Carlos A. Cunha, Azer Bestavros, and Mark E. Crovella. Characteristics of www client-based traces. Technical Report TR-95-010, Boston University Department of Computer Science, April 1995.

[10] P. Denning and S. Schwartz. Properties of the working set model. *Communications of the ACM*, 15(3):191–198, 1972.

[11] Kenneth Falconer. *Fractal Geometry*. John Wiley & Sons, Ltd., 1990.

[12] Steven Glassman. A caching relay for the world wide web. In *Proceedings of the First Interntional Conference on the WWW*, 1994.

[13] James Gwertzman and Margo Seltzer. The case for geographical push caching. In *In Proceedings of HotOS'95: The Fifth IEEE Workshop on Hot Topics in Operating Systems*, Washington, May 1995.

[14] The Internet Town Hall. The internet traffic archive. (http://www.town.hall.org/Archives/pub/ITA/), 1995.

[15] Changcheng Huang, Michael Devetsikiotis, Ioannis Lambadaris, and A. Roger Kaye. Modeling and simulation of self-similar variable bit rate compressed video: A unified approach. In *Proceedings of ACM SIGCOMM '95*, pages 114–125, 1995.

[16] W.E. Leland, M.S. Taqqu, W. Willinger, and D.V. Wilson. On the self-similar nature of Ethernet traffic (extended version). *IEEE/ACM Transactions on Networking*, 2:1–15, 1994.

[17] Benoit B. Mandelbrot. *The Fractal Geometry of Nature*. W. H. Freedman and Co., New York, 1983.

[18] Evangelos Markatos. Main memory caching of web documents. In *Proceedings of the Fifth International Conference on the WWW*, Paris, France, 1996.

[19] R. Mattson, J. Gecsei, D. Slutz, and I. Traiger. Evaluation techniques and storage hierarchies. *IBM Systems Journal*, 9:78–117, 1970.

[20] Vern Paxson. Fast approximation of self-similar network traffic. Technical Report LBL-36750, Lawrence Berkeley Lab, Berkeley, CA, 1995.

[21] Mimi M. Recker and James E. Pitkow. Predicting document access in large, multimedia repositories. Technical Report Technical Report VU-GIT-94-35, Georgia Tech—Graphics, Visualization, and Usability Center, August 1994.

[22] G. Shedlar and C. Tung. Locality in page reference strings. *SIAM Journal of Computing*, 1(3), Sept. 1972.

[23] Alan Jay Smith. Cache memories. *Computing Surveys*, 14(3):473–530, September 1982.

[24] Jeffrey Spirn. Distance string models for program behavior. *IEEE Computer*, 13(11), November 1976.

[25] Dominique Thiebaut. On the fractal dimension of computer programs and its application to the prediction of the cache miss ratio. *IEEE Transactions on Computers*, 38(7), July 1989.

[26] Jean Voldman, Benoit Mandelbrot, Lee W. Hoevel, Joshua Knight, and Philip L. Rosenfeld. Fractal nature of software-cache interaction. *IBM Journal of Research and Development*, 27(2):164–170, 1983.

[27] G. K. Zipf. *Human Behavior and the Principle of Least-Effort*. Addison-Wesley, Cambridge, MA, 1949.

Industrial Session 3B

Practical Issues in Large-Scale Systems

Production Data Warehouses with Teradata

R. Stellwagen

Practical Issues with Commercial Use of Federated Databases

J. Kleewein

Session 4A

Indexing and Storage Strategies

Replicated Indexes for Distributed Data

David Lomet
One Microsoft Way, Bldg. 9
Redmond, WA 98052
lomet@microsoft.com

Abstract

We describe a distributed index structure, in which data is distributed among multiple sites and indexes to the data are replicated over multiple sites. This permits good scalability as storage and accessing load are distributed over the sites and each site with an index replica has fast local access to the index structure, making remote requests at most for data at the leaves of the index tree. We call our method the dPi-tree because it is based on the Pi-tree. We replicate the index without the need for coherence messages. This works whether the index replica is persistent or a transient cached copy. We generalize a technique first used to provide recovery for Pi-tree indexes to independently and lazily maintain the index replicas. A further result is that each index replica is fully recoverable, an area not treated previously in replication schemes. We also show how the data in the leaves of the index can be distributed and re-distributed at very low cost.

1 Introduction
1.1 Scalability

Data mining, data warehousing, and the general escalation of the complexity of queries and the size of the underlying data put an increased premium on scaleable database systems. One aspect of that scalability is providing very efficient access to data as the size of the data explodes and the number of processors involved in accessing the data increases. This leads to an interest in distributed search structures in which the data is spread over multiple sites. This also leads to an interest in replicated search structures so that a substantial part of the computational cost of an access can be done locally, also reducing latency.

There are additional payoffs from data distribution and search structure replication. Data distribution enhances one's ability to access data in parallel, exploiting the set of processors at which the data resides. Index structure replication can, if done with real independence of index maintenance, greatly increase concurrency of access. Further, redundant index structures also enhance data read availability, as does replicated data in general. Availability of the distributed data does not become dependent on the availability of some single copy of the index stored on a possibly unavailable processor.

Consider two limited forms of distributed systems, client/server systems and cluster based systems.

Client/Server: Servers are typically very heavily used, and can easily become the bottleneck in system performance when accessing shared data. Replicated indexes permit all index traversal to be off-loaded to clients, with only the data leaf accesses remaining at the server. This improves response time and reduces network traffic as well.

Clusters: In clusters, any processor can play the role of both client and server. It then becomes possible to distribute the data over members of the cluster, while replicating the index at all members of the cluster. This improves upon client/server by spreading the data access load and permitting the accesses to proceed in parallel.

In both forms of distributed system above, caching has frequently been used to increase performance. We view cached index structures as transient replicas. Such transient replicas increase the desirability of our techniques for incrementally building replicas, as cached versions are continually being rebuilt.

The difficulty in exploiting distributed search structures is the update burden imposed. What search structure permits low cost maintenance when distributed over several processors? What search structure permits several replicas of its index to be easily and inexpensively maintained?

There has been recent interesting work on distributed and/or replicated search structures [2, 6, 7, 9, 10, 13]. This work attacks the cost of maintaining distributed and replicated search structures. The work of [9, 2, 13] is targeted at hashing structures. The DRT of [7] is a distributed (not replicated) binary tree.

1.2 Our Approach

Our system and communication models are similar to [6], and our search structure shares some structural and operation characteristics with their proposed dB-tree which is based on the B-link tree of [8]. Like the distributed DRT tree and RPs* of [10], we employ a form of "correction message". DRT, RPs*, and dB-tree all use lazy techniques to maintain distributed index trees over multiple processors.

We call our search structure the dPi-tree as it is a derivative of the Pi-tree of [11]. There, a correction mechanism was used to enable high concurrency and robust recovery for a centrally stored tree. When dealing with distributed and replicated trees, the correction mechanism requires messages, which we send lazily, and only when other information is requested. Correction is triggered in the same way as index recovery is triggered in [11], via detection of a misdirected search.

What distinguishes our techniques are their great simplicity and low cost, enabled by the *extremely* lazy way that we handle index structure maintenance. Unlike the dB-tree or an RP* tree, the dPi-tree does not require convergence of index replica node structure. No effort is made to keep the "replicated" index structures coherent- only the index content, i.e. the set of index terms, is important. All replica indexes must continue to effectively index and provide access to the underlying non-replicated data at the leaves of the index tree. Thus, the dPi-tree does not need to provide coherence messages in which one replica informs another of an index node split. The specific pagination of each index replica is managed solely by the replica itself, without reference to other replicas. Further, when data nodes of the index tree split, the posting of the index term for the new node in any of the index replicas can be very lazy since access to the data is always possible and the index term to be used can always be found via side traversals.

An additional bonus of our approach is that system failures can interrupt operation at arbitrary moments and the search correctness of the dPi-tree is not compromised. This is a natural consequence of the robustness of the Pi-tree, in which a system crash between the time a node split occurs and the time when its parent index node is updated does not effect search correctness, and the parent node is eventually updated during subsequent search operations. The dPi-tree inherits this robustness directly from the Pi-tree.

The fundamental insight that we exploit is that information about changes to the organization of data, its node splitting and its distribution, is propagated only on messages in which the exchange of data is required in any event. This is the same strategy as used with Pi-trees to ensure that interrupted splits eventually post an index term to the parent node. It is not unlike the correction messages of [7], but here such messages are always in response to explicit access requests. Each index replica can maintain itself based only on this information, and hence index replicas need not exchange messages to ensure structure convergence. Such convergence is not required. Our approach depends fundamentally on the unique structure provided by the Pi-tree, in particular, the presence of additional information on side links between sibling nodes.

The rest of the paper is organized as follows. In section 2, we describe the Pi-tree, emphasizing what it is that makes the Pi-tree unique, and sketching how that is exploited for concurrency control and recovery. Based on its very lazy concurrency and recovery technique, we describe in section 3 an index replication protocol that very lazily maintains dPi-tree replicas. How data can be distributed in a low cost way is described in section 4. The more complex re-balancing of data among processors of a cluster is also described there. It also exploits a very lazy approach to information propagation. We conclude in section 5 with a discussion of what has been accomplished and what might further be done.

2 Pi-Trees
2.1 Pi-tree Structure

The Pi-tree was introduced in [11] to provide a high concurrency index tree that also supported recovery. It was described then as a generalization of the B-link-tree [8] in that both search structures have side pointers connecting nodes at the same level on the search tree that are used to permit tree re-structuring that separate node splitting from the posting of the index term for the new node (see Figure 1.). The Pi-tree generalized B-link trees by permitting multi-dimensional index trees to exploit side pointers.

In one important sense, however, Pi-trees are not generalizations of B-link trees. It is that the links to sibling nodes of a Pi-tree are not purely pointers. Rather, they are the index terms that are to be posted to the parent node of the new sibling in directing the search to that node. This "indexed" side link is necessitated by the intent to support multi-dimensional searching. When traversing among the data nodes for data that is in some region of interest, a single dimensional search space trivially (by the nature of the search space) provides a search direction. With multi-dimensional index structures, the search direction of a

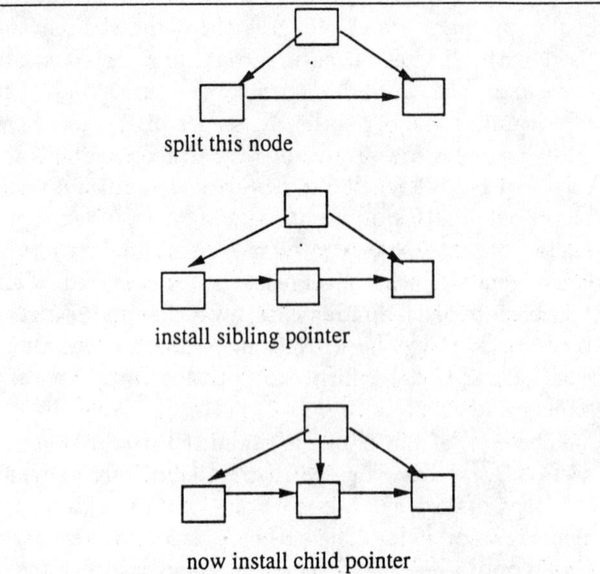

Figure 1: Side links permit node splits to be separated from index term postings because the new node is reachable via the side link without using the new index term. For Pi-trees, the side pointer comes with an index term describing the search space of the sibling.

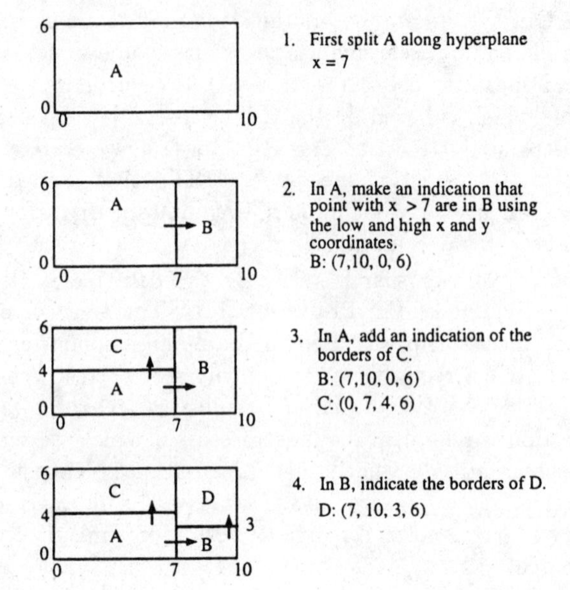

Figure 2: Space division and side pointers for a two dimensional search space are shown. Splits are by hyperplane with node space described via border coordinates. In a Pi-tree, nodes contain sibling terms for siblings split from them.

side link needs to be supplied explicitly by the index structure. One needs to know, e.g., that proceeding in the X direction exits a query range, but that additional items of the range exist in the Y direction. Hence, distinguishing X from Y in the links (i.e. having the links describe the space to which they refer) then becomes important. This division of the search space is illustrated in Figure 2.

More precisely, each node (within a single level of the Pi-tree) is given responsibility for a well defined part of the search space when it is created. The invariant that is preserved within the Pi-tree is that the entire space for which a node is responsible is reachable from that node. A node delegates responsibility for part of its search space to a new node during a node split. We call the original node the *container*, and the new node to which it has delegated responsibility for part of the search space the *extracted* node. To maintain the invariant that the search space for which it is responsible be reachable, the container must maintain an indexed side pointer that refers to the extracted node and identifies the space for which the extracted node is responsible.

An index node referencing a set of child nodes retains within its information the containment ordering among its children. This is trivial in the case of a one-dimensional B-link tree where simply ordering the

index terms by the single attribute is sufficient. With multi-dimensional searching, more complex containment can arise. With the hB-Pi-tree, such containment is reflected in the k-d tree that comprises the index node. Containment order is essential in managing node deletion.

2.2 Concurrency Control and Recovery

While side pointers are important for range searching, their intent in the B-link-tree is to provide high concurrency during tree structure modifications. The Pi-tree extends this to also ensure that recovery of the search tree is possible should the system crash at any arbitrary time. The foundation for this is that side pointers give you multiple paths to the data nodes at the leaves. In particular, during a node split, an updater can gain access to a new node via a side pointer, even before its index term is posted in its parent node. This means that, e.g. a Pi tree, does not need to lock (latch) an index node (so as to permit the immediate posting of the index term for a new child) while its children nodes are being split.

The same kind of reasoning that permits concurrency enables one to separate the structure modification into two atomic parts for recovery. Atomic action #1 splits a full node and provides an indexed side link to the new node in the original over-full node. Atomic action #2 posts the index term to the new node's parent. A system crash between the time a node has split and the time the index term for the new node is posted to its parent nonetheless leaves the tree well-formed, i.e., all data remains accessible and the structure continues to permit correct search by means of side index terms. The only thing that remains to be done is to ensure that this index term is eventually posted so that performance remains logarithmic in the size of the data. And this is exactly what the Pi-tree indexed side pointers permit.

For multi-dimensional search spaces, space decomposition can be quite complex. During a side traversal, one needs to know which of the possible directions a side pointer is taking the search. For "lazy" posting of an index term, one needs the exact description of the search space handled by the new node so that the index structure remains search correct. The Pi-tree provides this with indexed side pointers. When a side pointer is traversed, at any level of the Pi-tree, this occasion is used to post the missing index term. The sibling term's presence provides the information needed to update the parent. That is, the sibling term becomes the index (child) term posted to the parent node. Its posting is not an issue of search correctness, but solely of search performance.

Crashes may be quite frequent, index posting may be long delayed, and the Pi-tree index remains search correct because of the indexed side pointers. Indeed, the entire Pi-tree index between the root and the data leaves can be reconstructed via posting during side traversals. All the information needed to index the leaves is present in the leaves. This is not the case when the side pointers do not describe the search space of the new node. It is these indexed side pointers and this lazy index updating that we exploit in order to construct and maintain replicated and distributed indexes to the same data. And we do this with no need to keep the index replicas coherent, even eventually, and hence we can dispense with messages used to maintain coherent index structures [6].

3   Lazy Update of Replicated Indexes

This section describes how we deal with data node splitting which results, of course, from data being inserted into a leaf of the index structure. We begin with a primitive technique and proceed to a more effective but still very simple technique. We do not treat node consolidation (deletion) here, which we see as decidedly secondary. This is left to section 4.

We assume that the data that is being indexed is not itself replicated. We are only concerned, as was [6], with index replication, by which we mean "interior nodes", not leaf nodes. How data (leaf nodes) might be distributed among several processors of a distributed system is also discussed in section 4. Data distribution is orthogonal to the handling of the indexing structure and its replication. Replication of the index has an excellent cost/benefit ratio. The cost is low because the index is typically less than one percent of the file size. The performance benefit is large because the server is very effectively off-loaded. Only the data node search remains for the server, the client taking responsibility for the entire index portion of the search.

In the subsequent discussion, we are indifferent as to whether the replicated index is a persistent replica or simply represents a cached version of the interior nodes of the index.

3.1   The Primitive Technique

We describe initially a primitive technique that needs an absolute minimum of information from which to start and that maintains an index replica without knowledge of any other index. We describe this technique not because it is a practical method but to illustrates how little information is needed in order to maintain index replicas. Our pragmatic techniques exploit the existence of other indexes to more rapidly construct a replica with logarithmic search performance.

We assume that data has been entered into a collection of one or more data nodes and that these nodes are connected by indexed side pointers. We further assume that there is a pointer, which we call the *prime pointer(PP)* stored in a known location within our distributed system. The PP references the *prime node(PN)* which is responsible for the entire search space and which is connected to all other data nodes via side pointers, either directly or indirectly. There will usually be an existing index structure for accessing these data nodes as well, but our primitive index creation and maintenance method does not require or exploit it.

We pass the prime pointer to the site at which an index replica is desired. Search requests that arrive at that site trigger a traversal of the data nodes via side index pointers, starting with the data node referenced by the PP. Each traversal results in the posting of an additional index term to the index nodes maintained at the site. The first index term posted triggers the creation of an index root. Subsequent postings result in the index growing. Index nodes split at each site, completely independently of how they may be splitting at any other site. No coordination between the sites is required.

Replicated Pi-tree indexes need never be coherent. They can contain different nodes, with different index terms and even have different heights. The completeness of a Pi-tree index "replica" reflects how many side traversals have been done via the Pi-tree rooted at a site. These side traversals include the original sequence whose update necessitated the splitting of a data node. Importantly, here, even the splitting of a data node does not result in a broadcast to all index replicas. Only the replica whose traversal resulted in the update and data node split is notified, and even that notification may fail. Information about splits or index traversals is never broadcast to all replicas.

3.2 Index Sharing Technique

The primitive technique above stubbornly refuses to learn from others. It insists on discovering, in its entirety, all the index terms that it will need for each new index replica. We can do much better by permitting a new replica to learn from a prior replica. This is particularly important when we are dealing with a cached index, as we then will be starting from an "empty" replica. The idea is to gain access to the index terms that have already been discovered by another index replica that we call the *basis*. The basis could be located at a data server.

Our sharing technique is initiated as follows. Instead of passing to the new replica a copy of the prime pointer, we rather pass to it a copy of the root of the basis index. In this way, the new replica receives a batch of information about accessing the underlying data. The new replica is a partial one, sharing some of the index structure of the basis. This is similar to the technique used in Exodus [1] for creating a new version, but in this case, the intent is to optimize creation of the index replica. Thus, instead of cloning the path to an updated data node, as done in Exodus, we clone paths as we proceed through the tree doing searches. This incremental replica creation is is shown in Figure 3.

When the replica starts processing search requests, it traverses its own private nodes as it would were it a completely independent replica. When a search comes to an index term that references an *index node* of the basis (or some other replica, since sharing can be recursive), it requests the acquisition of that node of the shared index. When the node is received, it is replicated locally and the pointer that originally referred to the remote shared node is made to reference the local copy of the node. In this way, a new replica acquires index terms in node size batches, permitting it to provide efficient logarithmic access to the data

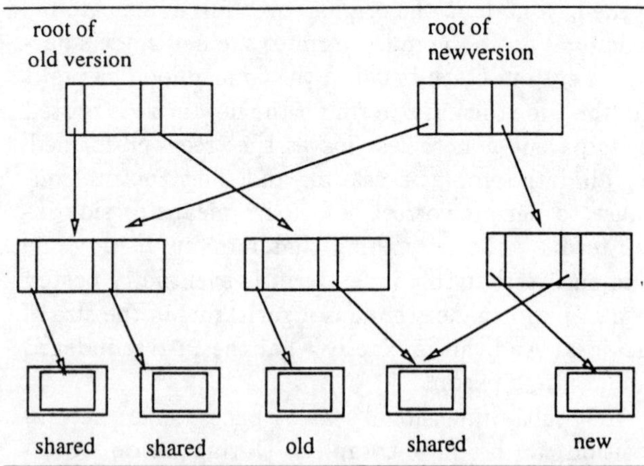

Figure 3: Exodus tree versioning has versions with unique roots but shared subtrees. For our distributed indexes, these versions are the local replicas. Each local replica starts with a copy of the root of a basis replica and initially shares the rest of the index with the basis.

immediately, assuming that its basis replica had such logarithmic access. This is a form of bulk correction message, i.e., where the index is grown a Pi-tree node at a time.

Within a cloned index node, the index terms carry with them a way of identifying the site at which the index nodes they reference are instantiated. A node that is returned to a requesting site and that will be replicated at that site will be in a form that is appropriate for the basis site. That is, all pointers to nodes in the basis site will be indicated as private pointers. But the replicated version of the node at the requesting site must treat these pointers as remote pointers to the basis site. Thus, our index pointers can no longer be simple local disk addresses. Note, however, that pointers to data nodes are unchanged by this optimization. These pointers, which are stored at the tree level immediately above the data level, constitute the vast majority of index terms, and they are unaffected by index replication. Only higher levels are impacted, which is much less than one per cent of the size of the replicated index.

Once again, there is no need for coherence messages. The index sharing technique is a performance enhancement that permits a more rapid construction of the replica. At any time after the replica has acquired a complete path to the prime node (PN), all index terms pointing to shared index nodes can be dropped without sacrificing search correctness or the ability to eventually complete the replica. However, shared index pointers continue to optimize the construction of every unfinished part of the new replica. So retention of the shared index is of great value.

What we are describing is an optimization: whenever index node sharing is not involved, our new technique can default to the primitive behavior. In particular, whenever a side index term is traversed, a new index term is posted in the parent node. This includes side index terms within an index replica as well as for the data nodes. In this case, in addition to doing the traversal, we also copy the node encountered. The index term posted is thus to the copied node.

3.3 Message Minimization

The protocol above requires request/response messages every time a single dPi-tree node is transferred. Essentially, nodes are transferred one by one as the Pi-tree node search path is traversed. There is leverage in terms of reduced message traffic if multiple nodes can be transferred in a single message. The procedure below returns all the nodes and their associated index terms for the search path that is traversed at a shared replica. Indeed, we accumulate the search path as we return from lower parts of the tree and pass it to sharing replicas that requested data indexed in the dPi-tree. Since we know the search request, we can in fact do this. We proceed as indicated in Figure 4.

Again, what we have described is a form of correction message. But now, the entire Pi-tree path from an initial local replicated node to the data is corrected in one large batch operation. Thus, it only requires modest access activity from an index site for the index maintained there to provide very effective access to the underlying data. Note also, that unlike [7], a tree merge is not required. Rather, the path returned is appended to the existing replica by replacing a remote reference to a reference to a local copy of the path. Also, we deal easily with the paths that are missing from the replica as the replica is built. The index information in such missing paths is reached via either child pointers or via side pointers to nodes in the basis or to nodes shared by the basis.

Requests from a client site to a site with a shared index do not require re-traversal of the shared index starting from the root. Rather, the search simply continues down the shared index from the node identified by the requesting replica. This avoids unnecessary work and reduces the access burden placed on shared sites. Thus, if a requesting replica has reached level n of the tree (as measured by distance from the leaves), the shared replica proceeds from level $n - 1$ onward. The search is not re-initiated at the root.

A shared replica, in trying to complete a search for a remote node, itself may become the remote node in

1. Replica A encounters a reference to a shared node N while processing a search request. Replica A sends a message to B (the owner of N) that identifies N and the search request itself.
2. Replica B receives the request from A and accesses N. It uses the search request from A to continue the search in N.
   - If the search leads to a data node reference, replica B returns node N's contents to replica A, where the node is replicated. In the replica at A, pointers in node N which had been to nodes local to B, become pointers to shared nodes that refer to replica B.
   - If the search leads to a node M at replica B, then the search is continued at B, adding the local nodes that it encounters in the search to the set of nodes that it will return to A. These include both child nodes and sibling nodes reached via side traversals.
   - If the search leads to a shared node M at yet another replica C, then B requests M from C and when C has returned the appropriate node or nodes that are further down the index tree, B concatenates those nodes with the nodes that it has traversed locally and returns the entire concatenated sequence to A. B also adds the nodes from C to its replica of the index.
3. Replica A replicates the returned sequence of index nodes in its local index replica, changing shared pointers to private pointers as appropriate. This conversion applies both to child pointers and to sibling pointers. It converts the remote pointer that triggered the remote request in step 1 to a local pointer to the first of the replicated nodes. It then continues the search to the data node P where one expects to find the data. This involves sending the search request and the address of P to the site where P resides.

4. Eventually (see the next section on data level organization), the data level responds with a list of side pointers traversed and the ultimate node Q that contains the data space specified in the request. Note that the data level does not send the contents of the traversed nodes, as these are not useful for maintaining the index replica.
5. Replica A adds the index terms returned to the appropriate node(s) of its index, performing structure modifications (i.e. node splits) as needed to store these new index terms.
6. Finally, the node returned (Q) is searched for the data requested in the search.

Figure 4: The procedure to build a replica index by adding to it all dPi-tree nodes in the path to the data as a correction message during an index search.

further processing of the search. This recursive process ensures that the shared replica has a complete path to the data prior to passing the path to its remote client replica. Note also that the data itself is not accessed by remote replicas holding the shared index nodes since the shared replica does not need the data itself. This saves a data access by the shared replica, putting that burden on the requesting replica.

3.4 "Seriously" Incomplete Replicas

A replica that is seriously incomplete will access multiple new nodes on the path to the data. This poses two problems.

- How do we keep the correction messages reasonable in size when multiple new nodes need to be returned?

  If the path traversed has too many nodes to comfortably fit into a single return message, this is not a large difficulty. Whenever results are returned that do not include the data requested, a pointer is returned to the node where the search may be continued. In the full optimization case, this will be to a data node. But should there be a large number of side traversals, this could be to a node at some remote index, either the basis replica returning the path, or to another. In all cases, the strategy is to include what is returned in one's own replica and to request a search continuation from the node referenced by this final pointer. Thus, how many nodes in the path to the data are returned to a requester can be very flexibly determined.

- How do we avoid long side traversal searches, which are a form of linear search, when a great deal of update activity may have moved the data of interest to a relatively remote node?

  We need a short circuiting mechanism that prevents such long side traversals if we make more than n side traversals in a search. A value of n that is approximately the height of the index tree should be reasonable. At that point, a particularly simple approach is to re-start the search at the root of the basis replica. Should we have the same problem with the basis, we re-apply the short-circuiting technique recursively. The result is to limit the number of node traversals to no more than $2 * height - of - tree * number - of - replicas$, though in practice, the number of node traversals should be very close to the height of the tree.

3.5 Shrinking the Replica

Not only can one grow the size of an index replica, but one can shrink it as well. This is the case for the same reason that we can be lazy in posting updates to the index. Data remains accessible via side pointers. Index size reduction is particularly important when dealing with transient (cached) replicas. This permits us to retain only the part of the tree that is active, and hence to maximize the effectiveness of the cache in reducing remote accesses. And this ensures that the prefix of the entire path to the data is always present at the replica.

It is almost always possible to delete an index term from a local replica, whether or not that index term points to a local node of the replica, a data (leaf) level node, or to a node that exists in the basis replica. Deletion of an index term must leave the containment structure of the index node well formed. The result is that the container for a node X whose index term we delete will appear to contain the space previously contained by X. Subsequent searches to the search space of X will be directed to X's container. Since the container has delegated responsibility for the space to X, sibling traversal from the container will lead to X. Such sibling traversals can be used to re-post the index term for X. Thus, deleting X's index term leaves the parent node of the dPi-tree in a state as if the container for X has been split with X being extracted, but before the index term for X has been posted.

We can delete an entire dPi-tree node N by dropping all its child index terms except for the index term to the child that serves as the containing node for the other children. At any point we can try to merge a node I with its container node. (And N will always contain at least this one child index term.) We insert the remaining contents of N into N's container node, including N's children as children of the container and N's siblings as siblings of the container. Sibling terms are never directly deleted. A sibling term is only removed when the node to which it refers is merged into the container. At this point the sibling index term referring to the node from the container is dropped.

Such deletion of index terms permits us to free space in a dPi-tree index node for more active parts of the tree. Dropping an entire index node permits us to reclaim space in the cache for other nodes. All information so dropped can be easily recovered should it be needed again. No coordination/coherence with other replicas is required for this. Subsequent reference to data in subtrees that are not represented in the index will result in the reconstruction in the local replica of the path to the data requested.

When we are dealing with transient replicas (cached copies of the dPi-tree index), a normal assumption is that no other replica is using it as a basis for replication. Thus, there are no other replicas with pointers to dPi-tree nodes of the transient replica. Hence, for these replicas, there is no need for coherence messages to cope with node deletion. Note here, however, that deleting nodes from an index replica is not simply a matter of dropping them and reaccessing them as needed, which is the way that caching is normally accomplished. Such simple node dropping is only possible if one were to retain an index term to a node in the basis. This is possible, but does not provide for the incremental construction of the replica and the complete independence among replicas that is so effective at reducing the search and update cost.

4 Data Level Organization

We have not yet addressed how the data itself might be managed by a data server, and how its updating and data node splitting is handled. That is the topic of this section. We describe two approaches for assigning data nodes to servers, one involving centralizing all data at a single server, the second involving distributing it among multiple sites.

4.1 Centrally Stored Data

The simplest way to manage the data, which is not replicated in our system model, is to assign all of it to a single data server. The data server itself should probably maintain an index to the data, from which future index replicas can be initialized. Our centralized data server maintains the data and the index for it very much as it would were there no index replicas involved. We describe here only the incremental difference that is made by the data server's need to cope with the index replicas and update requests that can come from multiple clients with replicas.

As with a search request, the data server receives an update request from a (index replica maintaining) client that identifies the data node at the server where the request activity is expected to occur. For a search or an update, this is the node that the client believes directly contains the portion of the search space desired. An update request is also accompanied by the new data and an indication of whether this is an update, insert, or delete.

The identified data node may contain the search space desired, or it may have delegated it to another node which can be accessed by side traversal from the originally identified node. Each side traversal results in a side index term being added to the message that will be sent back to the requester. These side pointers represent index terms that should be added to the

client's index replica to make its index more complete. A data node split in order to provide storage to accommodate the update is simply a particular instance of this process. (The only additional work is that the data server itself will probably want to update its own index to the data.)

Our central server needs to perform concurrency control and recovery on the data that it manages. This can most easily be handled by the Pi-tree technique itself [11] but other techniques are possible so long as side index terms are maintained [4, 11, 12]. There is no guarantee to the clients that any data node that it may have read will remain valid while the client caches it (in the traditional way). The client must take out explicit locks, on either some of the records of the data node, or on the node itself, at the server. An obvious optimization is to piggyback lock requests on the messages that request the data nodes themselves.

4.2 Distributing Data Among Sites
4.2.1 Distribution Strategy

Supporting index replicas to permit the index search to be off-loaded to clients permits a substantial scale-up in the number of clients that can be served with the indexed data. However, the single central data server remains a potential bottleneck. To scale further, the data itself needs to be distributed among multiple servers. A few of the several ways the distribution might be done are:

Opportunistic: Choose the updating site as the site for the new node that is created by the split. This reduces communication costs because the updating site is already a participant.

Randomized: Choose the site for the new node based on a randomization process that uniformly distributes the load, such as via a hash function applied to the key. While not precluding the need for re-balancing, it is much reduced.

Range: Assign particular sites ranges of key values to store. The new node goes to the site handling the key range involved. This localizes range searching to a smaller number of sites.

Where the new node in a node splitting index modification resides at the same site as the original node, the techniques used for centrally managed data suffice. However, redistribution of data among the sites will undoubtedly be required at times. System config urations change, update activity skews the load, too many keys fall into one range. Indeed, unbalanced load is possible with essentially all data placement policies without resorting to very substantial coordination message overhead. Re-balancing data between sites can be accomplished in terms of node deletion. To migrate a node, we perform a data node split", and move the entire contents of the old data node to the new node at a different site. This uses the node split protocol described below. Then we delete the old node. Clearly, the magic of this is in the handling of node deletes, the subject of section 4.3.

4.2.2 Distributed Node Splitting

For the tree restructuring resulting from a split to correctly survive a system crash, the action of splitting a node must be atomic. That is, within the same atomic action, two actions need to occur.

- The new node must be allocated and initialized with about half the contents of the old node.

- The old node must be updated so as to remove the contents now stored in the new node and have a sibling index term that now identifies the new node as the place where a search is to continue.

The new node and the old node may be co-located or at separate sites. In either event, we require atomicity. When co-located, such atomicity is easy to provide. When at separate sites, we require atomicity via a distributed commit protocol.

Two site atomicity can be achieved very inexpensively in this case. Site N writes the new node and prepares its part of the atomic action. N notifies site O that serves the old node that the old node has been split, the key value used in accomplishing the split, and the address of the new node. In the same message, N transfers commit coordination to O. O removes the data now in the new node from the old node, and inserts a side index link in the old node that refers to the new node at site N. O then commits the atomic action locally. N waits to receive a separate access request for the new node before committing its creation of the new node, thus using this access message as a lazy commit message. Should N wait too long, it asks O whether the action committed. It may need to do that in any event as commit messages may be lost. Site O remembers the commit status and can answer such inquiries by simply checking whether the old node has been updated with a side index link to the new node. This results in a normal case with only one message to both transfer information and to coordinate the distributed atomic action.

There is no commit processing overhead for site O. The overhead involves only site N's need for a durable "prepared" state which permits the new node to be deleted if site O does not commit. For index replica updating, a lazy message informs the updater of the node split trigged by its update. Other replicas will be notified during subsequent accesses. None of the index updating need be transactional as coherence is not required. The sibling index term will keep moved data accessible for search as well as providing the information needed for subsequent updating of the indexes.

4.3 Handling Deletes

4.3.1 The Deletion Structures

In order to keep the Pi-tree data level search correct when a data node N is deleted, we require the following actions to be atomically performed.

- Empty the deleted node N by updating N's "containing" node, i.e. the one with sibling index term referring to N, with the data and sibling terms of N so that all data for which the container is responsible remains accessible.

- Delete N and establish a tombstone for it containing a forwarding address to N's containing node. (We eventually garbage collect this tombstone.)

The strategy we pursue will preserve index correctness in a very lazy fashion. No index replica need be involved in a delete atomic action. A data node delete only requires an atomic action involving the site D with the node to be deleted and the site C with its container. These sites may have to handle accesses related to the deleted node for some time after the delete has been accomplished.

Site D keeps a tombstone for the deleted node N for as long as any index replica may have a pointer to N. The tombstone identifies the search space of N and contains a forwarding address to N's container, now responsible for the search space of N. This permits the system to distinguish invalid references to N from valid references to the same node when N is reused. All incoming accesses must check the tombstone table before accessing data nodes. This tombstone table must be persistent, but should be small enough to reside entirely in main memory while the index is being used. To keep it small, we garbage collect tombstones as described next.

4.3.2 Garbage Collecting the Tombstone

There is control information in each node describing every deleted node that the node has absorbed and that has an outstanding tombstone. This control information consists of a description of the search space of the deleted node together with a bit vector with a bit for each index replica. The bit is *on* if that index replica may have a dangling pointer to the deleted node, and *off* otherwise. When all the bits have been turned off, site C tells site D that the tombstone can be garbage collected.

There will usually be zero, sometimes one, rarely more than one such deleted node whose tombstone a container node needs cope with. Further, we assume that the number of index replicas is modest, say fewer than 64, perhaps fewer than 16. Thus the control information for a deleted node might be no more than a word per deleted node with tombstone, and a few words at most. Also, since deletes are optional and require that the container accept data as well as control information from the deleted node, the container node can refuse to participate in a delete to limit the number of such deleted nodes.

We distinguish two kinds of data access to the search space that had been handled by the deleted node.

Accesses by way of the tombstone When an access request comes to site D, the request is forwarded to C (as if it were a side traversal) together with an indication that this request comes via the tombstone. Site C satisfies the request, and includes in its response not only the data requested, but the container node address and an indication that the deleted node has in fact been deleted. The requester then removes its index term referring to the deleted node. This is analogous to the lazy way in which node splitting and index maintenance is handled. (Note: Since the index term is not removed within a coordinated atomic action with the request, we can only say that we expect it to be removed.)

Accesses directly to the container When an access specifying a search space handled by the deleted node comes directly to the container, it is clear that the requesting replica does not have a dangling pointer to the deleted node. The bit associated with that index replica in the container node is turned off (if not already off). The request is then answered in the normal fashion. [1]

When the bits representing the index replicas have all been turned off, site C notifies site D that the tombstone can be garbage collected. This does not require

---

[1] This assumes that once an index replica indicates that it knows about a node deletion, that no delayed request for the deleted node ever is made again from that replica. This requires some care by the replicas.

a two site atomic action. Rather, site D simply drops the tombstone in a local atomic action. It then notifies C that the tombstone is gone. Should either message be lost, C will eventually ask D to delete the tombstone again and D will comply or simply report that this has been done already. [This exploits tombstone existence as testable state for the atomic action.] Once the tombstone has been confirmed as garbage collected, the information in the container node for the tombstone can be discarded as well.

4.3.3 Additional Comments

The deleted node can serve as its own tombstone. The cost of this is that the node itself is not garbage collected until all replicas have referenced the container node directly. The benefit is that no separate tombstone table is needed, and there is no tombstone "lookaside" needed before accessing data nodes at a site. If deletion is sufficiently uncommon, this is a good strategy. If deletion becomes more common, then the need to reclaim space becomes more urgent, justifying a separate tombstone table.

Index node deletion for other than transient replicas(as opposed to data node deletion) does not appear to have much of a payoff. An index node will rarely become sufficiently empty because many data nodes must first be deleted. Further, each index is less than one percent of the size of the data so most of the gain from node deletion involves deleting data nodes. Index node deletion is a trivial task when no index sharing is involved (see section 3.4). However, supporting deletes with index sharing requires greater effort, which we do not describe, and complicates the sharing process itself.

5 Discussion

We have shown how to generalize an existing index structure, the Pi-tree, for index replication in a cluster-based or client/server system. The advantage of index replication is to off-load index traversals from the primary data server to the client or node performing the access. This also avoids the message overhead of a distributed search.

5.1 Very Lazy Replica Updating

The advantage of using dPi-trees over other index organizations is that dPi-trees enable a very lazy strategy for index maintenance. This exploits Pi-tree sibling index terms which were initially used to keep the Pi-tree recoverable while enabling high concurrency. No explicit (and separate) index coherence messages were required, and indeed, the node structure of the index replicas need not be coherent for the search to remain correct. It is the redundancy of paths through Pi-tree indexes (both child and sibling index terms) that makes this possible. Thus, our replication strategy has less overhead than any of its predecessors.

If other methods can refer to their update strategy as "lazy", then we can justifiably describe ours as "very lazy". Separate coherence messages are never used in index maintenance for node splitting. A "correction message" is always piggybacked on the response to an access request, and we describe how to return the entire shared path from the current point in the local index to the remote data. This permits a local replica to update its index with large batch operations. The result is that no tree is likely to be more than a few accesses away from providing excellent indexing performance. Even when dealing with deletes, we take a lazy approach of using tombstones and notifying an index replica that a delete has occurred as part of a response to an access request. Only data level restructuring involving splitting or deletion requires coordination via atomic actions. And these actions involve only sites that host data nodes. Index only sites need never be involved.

Messages to inform replicas of new data nodes are required in all approaches. However, with our approach, the messages needed to provide index replica coherence are never needed as replica coherence is itself unnecessary. Delays introduced by the need to synchronize for index coherence are thus completely avoided. Finally, the simplicity of the strategy makes its implementation cost modest compared with methods requiring more strenuous coherence measures.

We suggest that node deletion only occur within the index level of the dPi-tree for transient replicas. Such deletes are strictly local and have no impact on other replicas when we preclude cached (transient) replicas as the basis for other replicas. Hence, no coherence strategy of any sort is required for them.

5.2 Concurrency and Recovery

Each replica supports high concurrency and recovery at its site, an issue not addressed previously. Index concurrency and recovery can be handled at a single site by means of the Pi-tree algorithm [11]. Multisite coordination is not needed. Index node locking is needed only to provide synchronization among local updates to a replica. When a response to a remote requests needs to include a version of an index node, it is always acceptable to deliver a copy of an earlier version of the node since whether the node is out-of-date is not critical to our algorithms.

Data (as opposed to index) concurrency and recovery can be handled by a variant of the Pi-tree strategy.

Typically, this would exploit low level physical redo and high level logical undo. Because data nodes can be split between sites, recovery needs to cope with this distribution. But this is a standard part of distributed actions and poses no additional difficulties.

5.3 Range Searching

When a search request is for a range of values, a distributed search structure can execute the request in parallel. This is a very important aspect of index tree performance. During a range search, all children nodes of an index node that are within the range can be accessed in parallel. When the index is to distributed data, different nodes can return the data within the range while executing in parallel.

The search requesting node then needs to determine when the range search is complete. The existence of side pointers for dPi-trees makes this easy. We need compute twi sets as we perform the search.

nodes needed Addresses for data nodes within the range that are at other processes. This is initialized to the data nodes that are immediate children of the index nodes in the range.

nodes searched Addresses for all nodes that are within the range and that have been searched already.

Each process involved in the search returns (1) its data in the range, together with (2) the list of data node addresses in which the data was found, which is added to "nodes searched", and (3) the list of side pointers to nodes that are part of the range but that are located elsewhere, which are added to "nodes needed". When nodes searched equals nodes needed, the range search is complete.

5.4 Data Nodes

How to deal with the data at the leaf level of an index tree is largely orthogonal to index replication. We demonstrated lazy methods that are in the same spirit as our lazy index replication, to deal with distributing the leaves across multiple sites. We also showed how to lazily handle node deletes. These methods avoid the introduction of coherence messages. However, there is more complexity involved as splitting and deleting nodes requires atomicity, and distribution increases the cost and complexity of atomicity. We use a tombstone technique for coping with dangling references to deleted data nodes. Hence, lock coupling is not required when accessing the dPi-tree since its only function is to provide assurance that the reference found at one level of the tree is not dangling when used to access the next level.

5.5 Generality

The laziness of our method is enabled by the fact that Pi-trees maintain not only a side pointer to sibling nodes, but an entire side index term with both space description and pointer [11]. It is this index term that provides the source for lazy updating of index replicas as all replicas eventually store this index term. This is a very powerful paradigm for lazy distributed search structure maintenance that should find use in other distributed and/or replicated search structures, e.g. hashing or grid like structures. What we do require is that the search space for which a node is responsible not increase since we deal with node deletes in a rather special and less efficient fashion. This precludes the direct application of our techniques to spatial search using the R-tree [5]. We feel, however, that the hB-Pi-tree [3] is a more robust search structure in any event, and our techniques apply immediately to it.

Acknowledgments

Witold Litwin provided a valuable critical reading of an earlier version of this paper. In addition to correcting misunderstandings about existing distributed indexing methods, he raised two issues: bounding the worst case number of side traversals (see section 3.4) and parallel search for range queries, with its requirement to determine when such a query is complete (see section 5.3).

References

[1] Carey,M., DeWitt, D., Richardson, J., and Shekita, E. Object and File Management in the EXODUS Extensible Database System. *Proc. Very Large Databases Conf.*(Sept. 1986) 91-100.

[2] Devine, R. Design and Implementation of DDH: A Distributed Dynamic Hashing Algorithm. 4th Int'l Conf. on Foundations of Data Organization and Algorithms. (Oct. 1993) Evanston, IL

[3] Evangelidis, G., Lomet, D., and Salzberg, B. The hB-Pi-Tree: A Modified hB-tree Supporting Concurrency, Recovery, and Node Consolidation. *Proc. Very Large Databases Conf.*(Sept. 1995) Zurich, Switz. 551-561.

[4] Gray, J. and Reuter, A. *Transaction Processing: Concepts and Techniques* Morgan Kaufmann (1993) San Mateo, CA

[5] Guttman, A. R-trees: A Dynamic Index Structure for Spatial Searching. *Proc. ACM SIGMOD Conf.*(May 1984) Boston, MA 47-57.

[6] Johnson, T., and Krishna, P. Lazy Updates for Distributed Search Structure. *Proc. ACM SIGMOD Conf.*(May 1993) Washington, D.C. 337-346.

[7] Kroll, B. and Widmayer, P. Distributing a Search Tree Among a Growing Number of Processors. *Proc. ACM SIGMOD Conf.*(May, 1994) Minneapolis, MN 265-276.

[8] Lehman, P., and Yao, B. Efficient Locking for Concurrent Operations on B-trees. *ACM Trans. on Database Systems* 6,4 (Dec. 1981) 650-670.

[9] Litwin, W., Neimat, M-A, and Schneider, D. Linear Hashing for Distributed Files. *Proc. ACM SIGMOD Conf.*(May 1993) Washington, D.C. 327-336.

[10] Litwin, W., Neimat, M-A, and Schneider, D. RP*: A Family of Order-Preserving Scaleable Distributed Data Structures. *Proc. Very Large Databases Conf.*(Sept. 1994) Santiago, Chile

[11] Lomet, D. and Salzberg, B. Access Method Concurrency with Recovery. *Proc. ACM SIGMOD Conf.*(May 1992) San Diego, CA 351-360.

[12] Mohan, C. and Levine, F. ARIES/IM: An Efficient and High Concurrency Index Management Method Using Write-Ahead Logging. *Proc. ACM SIGMOD Conf.*(May 1992) San Diego, CA 371-380.

[13] Vingralek, R., Breitbart, Y., and Weikum, G. Distributed File Organization with Scaleable Cost/Performance. *Proc. ACM SIGMOD Conf.*(May, 1994) Minneapolis, MN 253-264.

k-RP*$_S$: A Scalable Distributed Data Structure for High-Performance Multi-Attribute Access

W. Litwin[1], M-A. Neimat[2]

Abstract

k-RP$_S$ is a new data structure for scalable multicomputer files with multi-attribute (k-d) keys. We discuss the k-RP*$_S$ file evolution and search algorithms. Performance analysis shows that a k-RP*$_S$ file can be much larger and orders of magnitude faster than a traditional k-d file. The speed-up is especially important for range and partial match searches that are often impractical with traditional k-d files. This opens up a new perspective for many applications.*

1. Introduction

Multicomputers, i.e., peer-to-peer networks of autonomous PCs and workstations (WSs) are becoming the favorite hardware configuration [C94], [T95], [ILP93], [G96]. They offer very attractive price/performance ratio, and combined processing power beyond the capabilities of traditional computers, including supercomputers [T95]. HP Laboratories in Palo Alto have, for instance, 1500 interconnected PCs and WSs with 50 GBytes of distributed RAM, and TBytes of disks. Much larger multicomputers can be anticipated. For example, [U94],expects a 10,000 node multicomputer over a Gbs (Gbit per sec.) net at Stanford in a few years, with 100 GBytes of disk and 1 GByte of RAM per WS.

To offer their full potential, multicomputers need new file structures that can scale to large sizes over a distributed storage of RAM and disks [JK93], [LNS93], [KW94], [T95]. One approach is Scalable Distributed Data Structures (SDDSs) [LNS93]. An SDDS file can expand from a single site to as many as needed, e.g., thousands. The LH* algorithms [LNS93], [LNS93a], [VBWY94], and the DDH algorithm [D93] were designed for scalable primary-key-hash files. The RP* family of SDDSs termed RP*$_N$, RP*$_C$, and RP*$_S$ [LNS93], and the distributed search trees of [KW94] were designed for primary-key-ordered files. An insert is completed in a single message, and a key search in two messages in most cases, or in a few messages in the worst case. A RAM file can reach dozens of GBytes, with a key search time of 1.2 ms over a 10 Mbs network such as Ethernet, and under 100 µs for a Gbs net such as ATM [LNS94]. Such access times are an order or two of magnitude faster than those of disk files, and are likely to remain impossible for mechanical devices.

Primary-key-based data structures are of great importance. Nevertheless modern applications, especially the database systems, need also efficient multi-attribute (multi-key or k-d) addressing schemes [K95]. A k-d structure may help a DBMS manage multi-attribute keys and queries through a more efficient clustering. Such structures are also useful for 2-d or 3-d spatial data. k-d structures are fundamental data structures, described in many text books, e.g., text books [S89], [K95]. Various schemes were proposed in the past 20 years, but none has entered a widespread use [ELS95]. One reason is that k-d structures were typically designed for disk files and have performance limitations inherent to such hardware. Range and partial match k-d searches are especially prohibitive, as the response time may easily run into many minutes requiring very many disk accesses. Proposals for k-d structures on supercomputers have been made to alleviate some of these problems, [MS91], and [HS94].

The new data structure presented below and termed k-RP*$_S$ is the first SDDS for k-d access. As other SDDSs, it is specifically aimed at taking advantage of a multicomputer, especially of its large RAM. A k-RP*$_S$ file supports k-d key search, through unicast (point-to-point) messaging, and range and partial match searches, through multicast or unicast messages. Queries may also be expressed over non-key attributes of a record. The key attributes can be alphabetic, or numerical. In the latter case, records can be seen, as usual, as k-d points in some geometrical space. A $2k$-d point may be the *representative point* of k-d spatial objects, i.e., it may represent the k-d rectangle bounding the object [S89].

---

[1] Université Paris 9, MIAGE, Place du Marechal de Lattre de Tassigny 75775 Paris Cedex 16 FRANCE litwin@dauphine.fr

[2] Hewlett-Packard Laboratories, PO Box 10490, Palo Alto CA 94303, USA, Mail Stop 1U-4 neimat@hpl.hp.com

The advantages of k-RP*$_S$ are the typical ones of SDDSs [LNS93]. A k-d file can reach dozens of GBytes while remaining in (a distributed) RAM for fast processing. Search times, especially for range or partial match search are in the range of milliseconds even for files on the order of tens of GBytes. This is orders of magnitude faster than the time of the same operations on a traditional k-d file. The k-d clustering typically also improves several times the search time of multi-attribute range and partial match queries over an RP* or an LH* file with the same records. All these features of k-RP*$_S$ open up a new perspective for applications, modern database systems especially.

Section 2 presents the k-RP*$_S$ file structure and its evolution under insertions. Section 3 discusses the file manipulation. Section 4 evaluates performance. Section 5 concludes the paper.

2. File structure and evolution

2.1 An overview

A k-RP*$_S$ file is an SDDS, hence it conforms to the general requirements on this type of data structures as defined in [LNS93]. Data reside on sites called *servers* that are accessed according to some scalable global addressing rule, e.g., linear hashing for LH* [LNS93]. To avoid a hot-spot, there is no centralized address calculus or directory. Servers are accessed through messages that are sent over the net from any number of autonomous sites called *clients*. A client is expected available for messaging from a server only when it accesses the server, otherwise it can be disconnected whenever and as long as it suits its needs. Changes to the addressing state of an SDDS while it scales up or shrinks, are therefore not posted synchronously to the clients. Every client has its own addressing schema called *image* (of the global rule) that can be partly outdated with respect to the actual addressing state. Images can differ among clients. A client may make an addressing error, sending a query to an incorrect server with respect to the global rule. The servers forward any such query among them to the correct address by the global rule. If inserts overload the servers, splits are generated and new servers are added. If a correct server is reached by a query through a forwarding, then it sends to the client a special message called Image Adjustment Message (IAM). The client adjusts its image to avoid repeating the error. A well designed SDDS should make addressing errors occasional, and forwards few. An LH* forward is done, for instance in at most two messages, regardless of the file size [LNS93].

A k-RP*$_S$ file consists of records stored at each server in a *bucket* of capacity $b \gg 1$ records. Buckets are indexed through a paged k-d (binary) tree called *kernel*.

Pages are distributed on different servers to avoid a hot-spot. A bucket that overflows splits and creates a new bucket at a new server node. Every split adds a new node to the kernel. A page that becomes full splits also, into two pages.

A client's *image* is also a k-d tree. Every image is a part of the current or past kernel. An IAM contains one or more pages of the kernel. These pages are merged with the existing image to produce a more accurate image.

2.2 Records

A record R of a k-RP*$_S$ file is a couple (c, n), where $c = (c_1, c_2 .., c_k)$ are the *key attributes* (also called addressing attributes) collectively constituting the *key* of R, and n are *non-addressing* attributes of R. The key attributes all together identify the *address* of R in the file, through some calculus. Although a file can have several R's with the same c called *duplicates*, one typically considers that c uniquely identifies R. This is also the case in what follows. A single attribute value typically has duplicates in the file. Often there is however a key attribute or a non-addressing one identifying each R, one calls it *candidate key*.

For instance, one can choose $c = $ (**Name, Age, SS#**), for records of people in a database with queries mostly on these attributes, hence requiring the corresponding clustering. **SS#** is then not only an addressing attribute, but usually also a candidate key. Perhaps a non-addressing attribute **Tel#** is a candidate key as well.

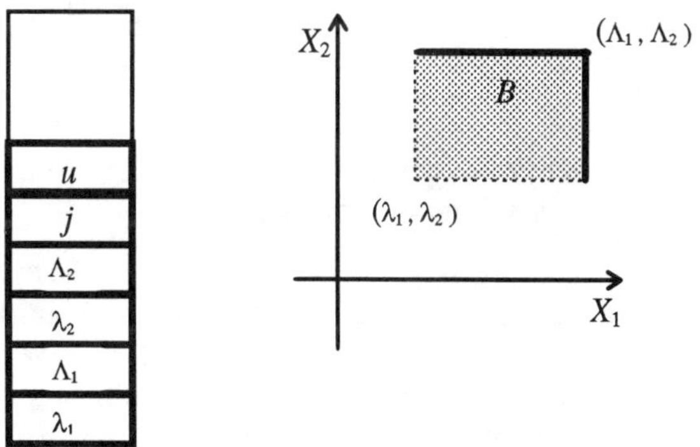

Fig. 1 A bucket of a 2-RP*$_s$ file with its header and its 2-d rectangle.

The values $j = 1,.., k$ are often called *dimensions*, especially for spatial applications of k-d files [S89]. The attribute c_j is then called j-th *coordinate* of the k-dimensional (k-d) key c. A k-d *record* which is a record with a k-d key c is often seen as a (hyper)point c in the k-d *key space*, let it be $X = X_1 \times X_2 .. \times X_k$. A $2k$-d record can represent a spatial object of a shape defined by n values enclosed within a bounding k-d rectangle $((c_i^1, c_i^2]..)$; $c_i^1 > c_i^2$ and $i = 1..k$. Below, we consider only k-

d records. See [LN94] for the discussion of spatial objects management using k-RP*$_S$.

2.3 Buckets

Buckets of a k-RP*$_S$ file are numbered $0,1,..,N$-1 in the order of their creation, regardless of their actual sites. Fig. 1 shows the structure of a 2-RP*$_S$ bucket. A k-RP*$_S$ bucket has the space for b records, and a *header* with the k-d range, noted $(\lambda_i , \Lambda_i)_{i=1..k}$; $-\infty \leq \lambda_i , < \Lambda_i \leq \infty$. The header values make every bucket a k-d rectangle in X, perhaps reaching $\pm\infty$ in some dimension. The header also contains a number called *split dimension*, noted j in the figure and discussed below. Finally, every header contains an *upward pointer* noted u above, and discussed later on.

Bucket 0 receives the first b inserts into the file. The initial ranges in bucket 0 will typically be, $\forall i$, $\lambda_i = -\infty$ and $\Lambda_i = \infty$, and $j = 1$. Other buckets are created when inserts overflow existing buckets. Every overflow triggers a split that appends bucket N to the file and moves to bucket N about half the overflowing bucket. A deletion can trigger an inverse process that is the merge of underloaded buckets. Deletes are typically infrequent, and merges are usually cumbersome for application-dependent reasons. We do not consider merges in what follows.

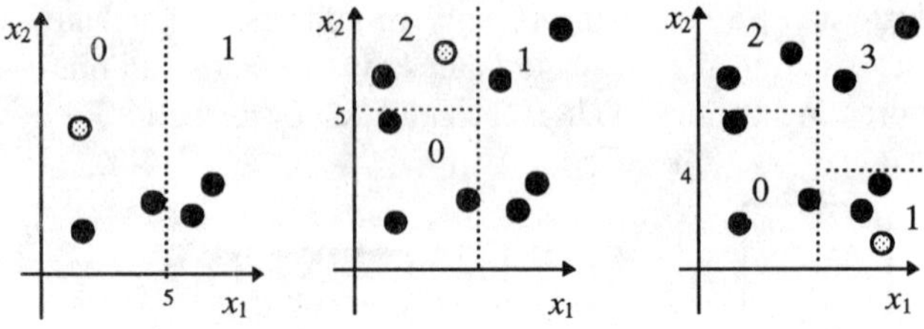

Fig. 2   A partitioning of k-RP*S file key space by successive splits (b = 4).

The global addressing rule of a k-RP*$_S$ file is that record R (c) resides in bucket B whose rectangle in X contains c. In other words, B is so that for every coordinate c_i of c,, one has $\lambda_i < c_i \leq \Lambda_i$. Splits in a k-RP*$_S$ are performed so that for every c there is always exactly one B.

2.3.1 Splits

A split is performed basically by choosing a record, let it be m, and the coordinate c^m_j , called *split value*, of key c^m. Record m should be such that c^m_j is, or is near, the middle of the ordered sequence of coordinates c_j of keys in the bucket. Λ_j is then set to $\Lambda_j \leftarrow c^m_j$. A new bucket is appended to the file. The range of the splitting bucket is copied to the new bucket, except that the new λ_j is set

to $\lambda_j \leftarrow c^m_j$. Every record with $c_j > c^m_j$ in the splitting bucket is moved to new bucket.

In Fig. 2, successive inserts lead to three splits when overflow records (dashed circles) present for storage. Buckets 1,2,3 result from. In geometrical terms, each split is performed using a hyperplane, parallel to one axis. Splits partition the key space. Every split partitions one bucket rectangle into two, and no rectangles overlap. Hence, every record has only one bucket address in a k-RP*$_S$ file.

Any splitting policy used for a traditional k-d tree (see [S87], and [S89]) applies to k-RP*$_S$ files. For instance, the *round-robin* policy, evenly chooses j values. In this case, a bucket is split first using j value in the split-dimension field, then j is set to $j \leftarrow (j + 1)$ mod k. The new bucket gets the new value of j in its header. Splits in Fig. 2 are performed according to this policy.

2.4 The kernel
2.4.1 Kernel structure

The kernel, as for instance in Fig. 3, and Fig. 5 is a paged and connected k-d tree T of order 2 describing the current partition of X and its successive refinements through bucket splits. T is initially empty. Then:

- Each bucket split generates a new node. A node contains j and c^m_j, and two downward pointers. An *internal* pointer points to a *child* node in the page. If n' is a child of n then n is the *parent* of n'. A child node can be also the root of another page in which case it is pointed to from the parent through the *page* pointer to that page. Finally, a *bucket* pointer can point to a bucket.

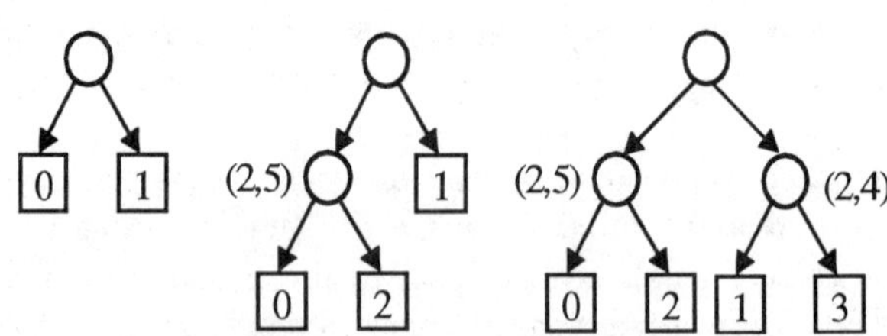

Fig. 3 Kernel trees corresponding to k-RP*$_S$ file evolution in Fig. 2

- The root node of a page contains also its k-d range. This range is that of the bucket whose split caused the creation of that root node, and it is this range right before the time at which the split occurred. Every other node also has a k-d range, but this range is not materialized in the kernel. It can be computed from that in the root. A *child* range is that of its parent, except that the split value is the upper bound for dimension j for the *left* child, and the lower bound for dimension j for the *right* child. The children ranges of a node n are called *left* and *right* (sub)range of n.

- A page has the capacity to contain b' nodes; $b' \gg 1$. A page P that overflows, as in Fig. 4 when new node o was just created, splits into two pages: P and some P'. The split cuts from the tree in P a (connected) subtree, as the tree rooted at node b in Fig. 4. This subtree moves to page P'. The internal pointer in P to the root of that subtree is replaced with the page pointer to P', Fig. 4.

- Every P' has an upward pointer initialized to point to P. Its goal is nevertheless to point to the page that has the parent of the root of P'. Initially this is P, but page splits can later move the parent to another page. The upward pointer is adjusted when an addressing error occurs, as presented in Section 3.1.2.

Fig. 5 presents three successive kernels of a k-RP*$_S$ file, corresponding to splits in Fig. 2. Nodes, buckets, and pages are numbered in the order of their creation. The page capacity is $b' = 4$.

2.4.2 Page splits

The k-RP*$_S$ page split algorithm is defined below. Fig. 4 illustrates the discussion. Page P has $b' = 16$, and it splits because the split of the bucket pointed through the left pointer of node n creates an overflowing node o. Observe in Fig. 4, that only nodes with bucket pointers can have new children. Such nodes are called *active*, and are shaded in gray in Fig. 4. The pointers to buckets are not shown explicitly, except for node j. All others are *inactive* nodes that do not change anymore for the lifetime of the file. An active node can point to one bucket, as node j in Fig. 4 or to two, as all other shaded nodes there. Hence active nodes may have different probability of having children. A child of an inactive node can be on the same or on a different page, P'' in Fig. 4. To balance the kernel length in pages, as well as page access activities, the page split algorithm should partition the active nodes between P and P' in a way to best equalize the probability that either page splits again. This depends on the way the inactive nodes are distributed by the page split. They occupy the space in a page, and the more there are, the less there is space for new children. The result of partitioning should be also two <u>connected</u> subtrees. The k-RP*$_S$ page split algorithm should examine all the potential cuts into two connected subtrees and choose the best one.

More precisely, let node n be the candidate root of the new page P', s be the size in nodes of the subtree in P', a' be the number of bucket pointers in the active nodes of P', and a be the total number of bucket pointers in the active nodes of P to split. Assuming that all the buckets pointed

to by the active nodes are equally likely to be accessed, one can show that the best cut minimizes the quantity:

$$D(n) = \left| \frac{b'-s}{a'} - \frac{s-1}{a-a'} \right|$$

The proof in [LN94] is omitted here because of the space limitations. The page split algorithm should traverse the tree in P and calculate D for every node except for the root of P. For example, for the graph in Fig. 4, node b should be chosen as the root of P'. After the cut, seven nodes will remain in P with three of them active, while P' will have six active nodes, and four inactive ones. Page P' is likely to split first, as more loaded with both active and inactive nodes, but there is no better cut for the graph in the figure.

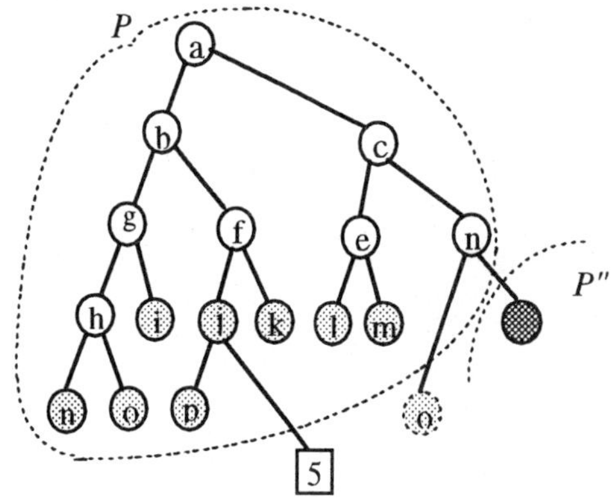

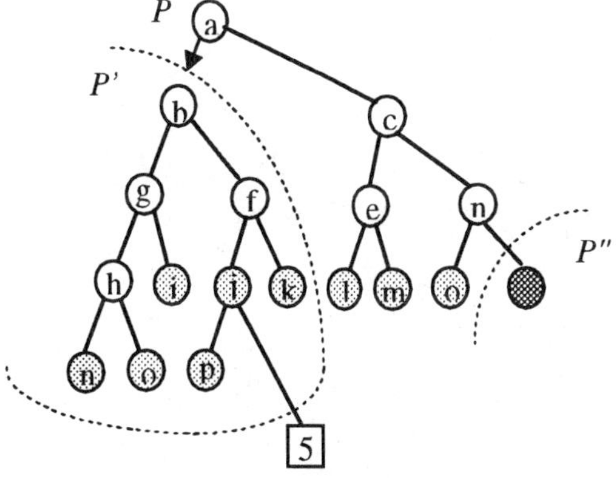

Fig. 4 k-RP*$_S$ page split

Observe that the length of a subtree in a page P grows with splits that affect nodes in P. The number of inactive nodes in P grows as well. The split algorithm should allow the inactive nodes to eventually fill P up to 100%, to maximize the average load factor of pages. After some splits, P is then filled up and has only one active node with one bucket pointer. When this bucket splits, the last active node becomes inactive, pointing to a new active node. There is only one active node then and the calculus of D would lead to $D = \infty$ for every n. To keep the active node in P while moving some inactive nodes to P' would be suboptimum, as P' would remain underloaded forever. The split algorithm should generate the partition of the resulting tree so that only the active node is moved to P'. This is always possible, as the tree in P has then the same arcs as before the split so remains connected, as well as the one node tree in P' which is a connected subtree by definition.

Algorithm A1 encodes all these ideas. It computes a' and s recursively for each visited node n. D' is computed whenever new candidate improves D. The last **else** recognizes the case of a single active node. Every node in P is considered as candidate for p'.

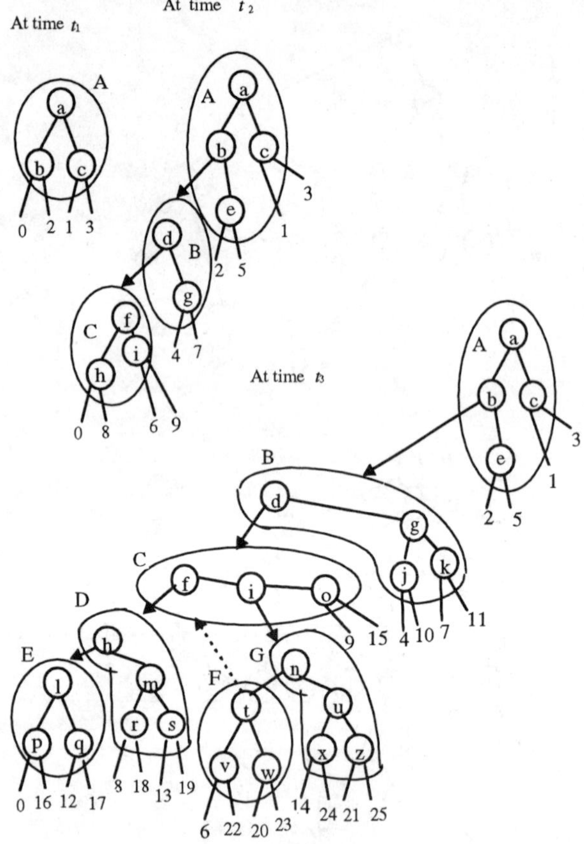

Fig. 5 k-RP*$_S$ **kernel evolution**

2.5 *The image*

k-RP*$_S$ image is a connected k-d tree of order 2 at most. It is called *incomplete* and denoted I below. Nodes and arcs in I are images of some of those in kernel T received by the client in pages of IAM messages. Incoming nodes are merged with an existing I as discussed in Section 3.1.3. Nodes and arcs in I have the same structure as in T, except for the following differences, illustrated in Fig. 6 and Fig. 7.

- A node $a \in I$ may point to a bucket while node $a' \in T$ with the same range, j and $c\,^m_j$ as a points to a node.

- A node n may be a child of a while a node n' with the same range, j and $c\,^m_j$, as n is a *descendant* (e.g. a grandchild) of a'. In this case, the range of n (of n') is strictly included in the left or right subrange of a (of a'). Dashed arcs in the figures correspond to these cases.

- Pointers in I other than to buckets are between nodes only, i.e., there are no page pointers. Every node in I is in contrast labeled with its page address in T.

- Node a can be *incomplete* in which case it does not have the values of j and $c\,^m_j$. It may have null pointers, e.g., the node labeled G in Fig. 6. It can alternatively have a single downward pointer, represented with fine dash lines, like the node labeled G in Fig. 7.

A1: k-RP*$_S$ page split algorithm

Pages maintain a values. P denotes the tree to split, p its root, p' is the result, i.e., the root of the subtree cut from P.

Set $D \leftarrow \infty$; and $p' \leftarrow$ nil.
Traverse P in post-order.
  While visiting node n do :
  let k be the number of bucket pointers of n.
  if n points to buckets or kernel pages:
  set $a'(n) \leftarrow k$; and $s(n) \leftarrow 1$;
  else if n points to a kernel page, and to node m in P:
  set $a'(n) \leftarrow a'(m)$; set $s(n) \leftarrow s(m) + 1$;
  else if n points to two nodes l and r in P,
  set $a'(n) \leftarrow a'(l) + a'(r)$; set $s(n) \leftarrow s(l) + s(r) + 1$;
  if $n \neq p$
  if $a'(n) \neq 0$ and $a'(n) \neq a$
    $D' \leftarrow |(b' - s(n)) / a'(n) - (s(n) - 1) / (a - a'(n))|$
    if ($D > D'$) set $D \leftarrow D'$; set $p' \leftarrow n$;
        else if $k > 0$ set $p' \leftarrow n$;
endtraversal.
endA1

---

3. Operations on a k-RP*S file

3.1 *Key search*

3.1.1 Address calculus

A key search is a query for a record with the key c sent within the query. A k-RP*$_S$ client sends a key search using a unicast message. The address for the message, i.e., that of the bucket that should contain c, is calculated from I. If I is empty, then the query is sent to bucket 0. Otherwise the root r of I is visited. It may happen that c is beyond the range of r. Then, c is sent to the page address labeling r in I, hence to the page containing r in the kernel, as one cannot do anything more efficient.

If c is in the range of r, then one sets $n \leftarrow r$ and attempts to visit the child n' of node n such that c is in the range of n'. There is at most one such n' since splits partition the key space X. There is no n' when c in the range of r is beyond the range of any of r's current children. The case may occur since I may have only some but not all pages of T. If there is an n', then one sets $n \leftarrow n'$ and recursively continues the visits. The query is finally sent to the bucket whose range contains c in I, or to the page whose address labels node n without n' for c.

Consider for instance the images in Fig. 6 assumed at the client named *client1*, using the file with the kernel in Fig. 5. Search through Image 1 always ends up with a message to a bucket. With Image 2, a searched key c could fit the range of node b but not that of node l. In this case, the search would be sent to page A. With Image 3, a key could also be sent to page G if it fits the range of the left pointer of node i. Finally, for Image 1 in Fig. 7, of another client *client2*, it could happen that c is even beyond the range of the root of I, node f in the figure. The message would be then sent to page C.

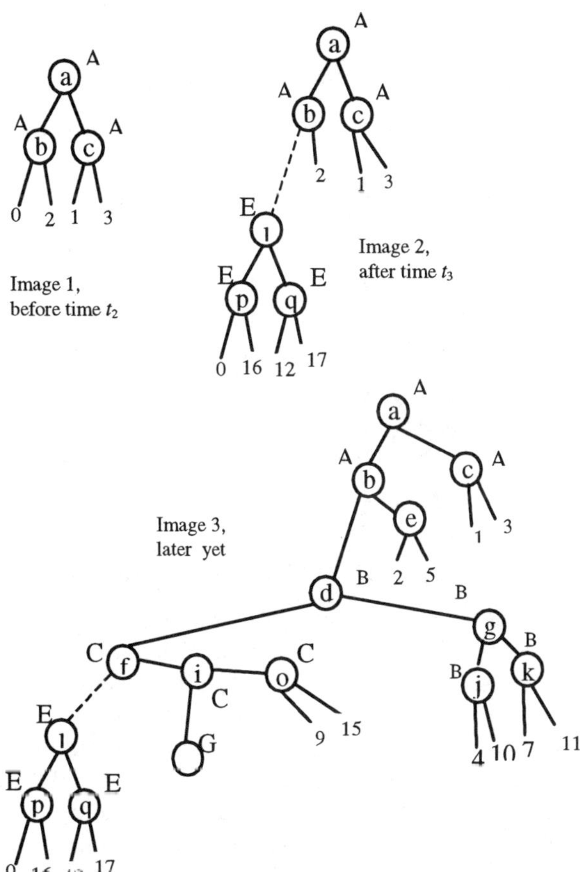

Fig. 6 *client1* image evolution

A server that receives a request for a search for a key c, at first tests whether c is in its bucket range. If so, it is the *correct* bucket for c, otherwise it is an *incorrect* bucket. A correct bucket getting c is searched, and the reply is sent, either with the record or with the information that there is no record with c. In contrast, an incorrect bucket simply forwards c to page P, the page pointed to by the bucket's upward pointer u. P examines whether c is in the range of its root. If so, a downward search through the subtree in P is initiated, similar to the one described above at the client, until an external pointer is reached. If this is a bucket pointer, the search is sent there. It is the correct bucket for sure. If the pointer is a page pointer, the search is sent to that page. This page is searched downward from the root in turn, etc. Several pages can be searched, but the correct bucket must be reached at one point.

Every page P that receives c not in the range of its root, from a server, or directly from a client, sends c to its parent page, let it be P'', pointed to through its upward pointer. P'' acts then recursively as P, either performing the downward search or sending the search upward again, etc. The upward search must stop at the latest at the root of T. Once the downward search starts, it can only continue downwards. The correct bucket is always located, regardless of I.

Fig. 5, Fig. 6, and Fig. 7 illustrate various cases that may happen. For instance, *client1* using Image 1 may search for c within bucket 0 in the image. The search would be sent to bucket 0. If c is within the actual range of bucket 0, the server replies. However, c may happen to be already in the range of bucket 6, as the file evolved since Image 1 was last updated to the state as at time t_2. Bucket 0 would forward c upward to C, which would forward it to bucket 6. With Image 2, consider a search for a key in the range of node b but not in that of node l, and in fact for bucket 25, unknown yet to the client. This search would be sent to page A, and forwarded down $A \rightarrow B \rightarrow C \rightarrow G \rightarrow 25$. In , a search using Image 2 of *client2*, and sent to bucket 6 although actually destined for bucket 21, would be forwarded up and down through the path $6 \rightarrow F \rightarrow C \rightarrow G \rightarrow 21$.

Anytime the client sends c to an incorrect bucket or to a page, an IAM message is built. The message consists of all the pages that c traverses, in the order they were visited. The correct bucket sends the IAM to the client, piggybacked on the reply.

3.1.2 Kernel adjustment algorithm

In forwarding path $6 \rightarrow F \rightarrow C \rightarrow G \rightarrow 21$ above, the forwarding is through the upward pointer $F \rightarrow C$. This situation occurred since page C split first creating page F as the child of node n which was in page C at that time.

Then C splits again creating page G and moving node n to it. At this point, the upward pointer in F needs an adjustment. In general, it would be cumbersome to visit perhaps several pages when a new page is created to find out whether there are upward pointers to adjust. In addition, a pointer could later require other adjustments, even if it remained unused in the meantime. Instead, in k-RP*$_S$, an upward pointer is adjusted only when a forwarding through it actually occurs.

Operationally, a page P'', which receives an upward search for c from some page P, tests whether its downward pointer is to P. If not, P'' flags P in the IAM, unless there is already a page $P^\wedge$ flagged so in the IAM. Page P''', which finally starts the downward search, sends then also the *kernel adjustment message* (KAM) to $P^\wedge$. The message contains the range of $P^\wedge$ and is sent through the downward traversal of the nodes whose ranges contain that range. A page that sends KAM to another page includes its address. A page that receives KAM compares this address to its upward pointer, and updates the pointer if needed. If its range is larger than that of $P^\wedge$ in the KAM, it must be a parent of $P^\wedge$ hence it forwards the KAM further down, with its own address. Eventually $P^\wedge$ must be reached and its upward pointer is updated. This would happen, in particular in the discussed example, ending up with the kernel where F points to G.

Note that it is enough to flag only $P^\wedge$, and to send only one KAM, since all pages traversed through upward pointers requiring adjustment must be ancestors of $P^\wedge$ in T.

3.1.3 Image adjustment

A client that receives an IAM adjusts its image I. This is done through the merge of I with the subtrees in the IAM not yet in I, or partly replacing those already in I. The latter case corresponds typically to the replacement of a bucket pointer, or of a null pointer, with a pointer to an internal node, with perhaps a tree under that node. Each page tree t in the IAM may end up connected to a current leaf of I. Alternatively, t may become a subgraph to be inserted between a parent and its child in I. Finally, t may be a supertree of I, i.e., where all of I becomes t's subtree. Every such change reflects a part of the evolution of T from the time the client received the last IAM.   and   illustrate all these cases, and the corresponding actions of the k-RP*$_S$ IA (image adjustment) algorithm.

Consider *client1*. Sometime after time t_1 and before t_2 it sends a search through its initially empty I to bucket 0 of the file with kernel as at t_1. The IAM that comes back has one page and Image 1 results from it. After time t_3, *client1* sends to bucket 0 key c which is in fact already in

the range of bucket 17. The IAM contains then page E. Comparing the range of node l with those of nodes already in I, it appears that the range of node l is strictly within the left subrange of node b. Hence node l in T is for sure a left descendant of node b although surely not its left child. It therefore becomes the left child of node b in I. The incoming subtree becomes also a new subtree of I. The corresponding arc is dashed, but only for didactic purpose. It shows that between the corresponding nodes in T there is in fact a subtree, that thus might arrive to the client later.

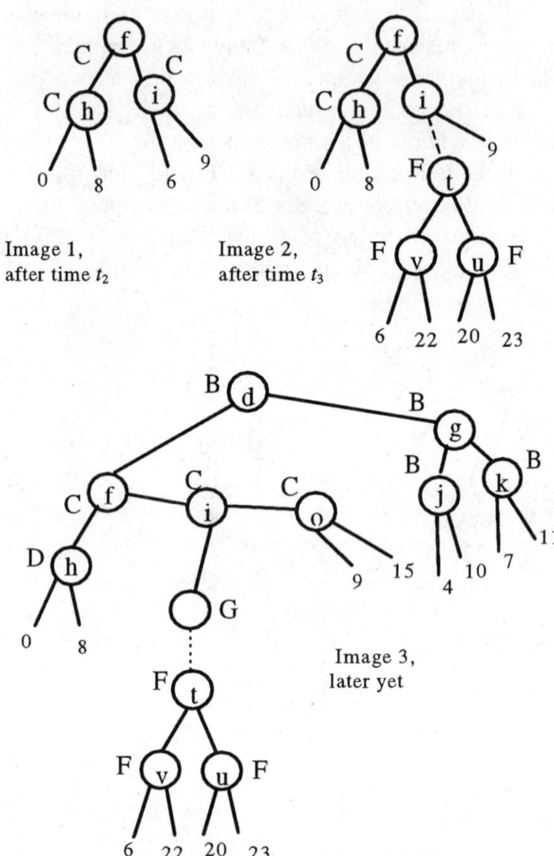

Fig. 7 *Client2* image evolution

Indeed, later on *client1* searches for a c whose correct address is 15. As such c is beyond the range of node l, the search is sent to page A. It is forwarded and the IAM that comes from bucket 15 contains pages A, B, C. The comparison of nodes already in I with those in the IAM shows first that node b in page A has a new child that is node e.   This node is added to I. Next, the comparison shows that the root d of B is the left child of node b in T, that root f is the left child of node d, and that in T, node l has to be a left descendant of node f, but it cannot be its left child. New nodes become a subtree to be inserted as in the figure, cutting the dashed arc between node b and node e. As the new arc (l, f) is dashed, I is still an incomplete image of T.

Node i has a page pointer to G, but since page G is neither in I nor in the IAM, nothing more than the range of the root of G is known to the client. In particular the split dimension, the split value, and pointers from this root are unknown. Hence, an incomplete node, only labeled with G in the figure, is created with null pointers, split dimension, and split value.

Consider now the case of *client2* in Fig. 7. First c was sent from an empty I to bucket 0, while intended for bucket 6, hence the IAM brought page C leading to Image 1. Later, another c was sent to bucket 6, but at that time its correct address should have been bucket 22. Hence the IAM arrived to *client2* with page F. The comparison of the range of its root t and of nodes already in I shows that the subtree in F should become left subtree of node i through a dashed arc. Finally, a key c intended for bucket 4 is searched. It is beyond the range of node f, but since it is at present the largest range known to the client, it is sent to page C anyway. Page C forwards it upward, and the IAM comes finally from bucket 4 with pages, C and B.

The comparison of I and of the IAM shows that nodes in B should become a supertree of node f in I. This time, the new arc (d, f) is plain, unlike in the case of *client1*. The comparison also shows that page C expanded in the meantime. New nodes have to be merged with the already existing ones in I. Finally, the examination of the IAM shows that the left pointer of node i in C points now to G. Hence, node t in T became a descendant of a node that must be in page G. However, *client2* has no nodes in page G yet. Hence, only the range of node n, the root of G, can be derived at present from node i at *client2*. An incomplete node is then created in I, in our case as the left child of node i, and labeled with G. Node t in I should become the child of the incomplete node. However, it is not known at *client2*, whether in T, node t is the left or right descendent of node n. Unlike the incomplete node in Fig. 6, the incomplete node here has then only one downward pointer, marked with fine dash in the figure.

The k-RP*$_S$ IA algorithm merges or inserts subtrees in the IAM with the current I, as discussed above. Its formulation is rather straightforward but lengthy, because of several cases to deal with, hence is omitted here. See [LN94] for its definition and further discussion.

3.2 Inserts

An insert is addressed as a key search, and sent through a point-to-point message. The bucket replies only when an IAM should be sent back. If many inserts

are to be performed, then *bulk inserts* of RP* are possible for k-RP*$_S$ as well [LNS94].

3.3 Range queries

A *range query* Q searches for all objects within range (rectangle, cube, ...) Q where $\forall j$, $-\infty < r_j \le R_j < \infty$ and $\exists j$, $r_j < R_j$. A *partial match* query Q is a search like a range query but with one or more open range i, i.e., $r_i = -\infty$ or $R_i = \infty$ and without the condition $\exists j$, $r_j < R_j$ (hence, the query rectangle is partly open, as in Fig. 8). The client is assumed to send Q out using a multicast message to all the N buckets of the file.

When Q is received at a bucket with range B, every and only buckets with $B' = B \cap Q$ and $B' \ne \varnothing$ sends back B, or B', and the records within B', if any were found. The search should terminate when the union of incoming rectangles covers Q. This is conceptually a simple termination. One may think therefore about computing the intermediate figures as if one played a puzzle. A new piece becomes a disconnected component (island), or is merged with an existing island to form a larger island. The search (puzzle) terminates when a single island covers Q completely. Unfortunately, for $k > 1$, to update the island definition expressions, and to find out whether one covers Q is a complicated computation [LN94].

One efficient approach is the *time-out termination* [LNS94]. It occurs simply some time after a reply, unless another reply comes before the time-out expires. Time-out terminations are however not deterministic. They can suffice for many applications, but sometimes are not suitable.

Algorithm A2 below provides the efficient deterministic termination for both range and partial match queries. The replying buckets are only those that may have the relevant keys, i.e., with $B' \ne \varnothing$. Every such bucket sends B' and all the records it has within B'. Algorithm A2 unions the B''s until Q is covered. To avoid the complexity of the naive approach, Algorithm A2 merges islands and incoming rectangles only in a <u>specific order</u>. The order is so that adjacent islands or bucket rectangles, merge iff they have every but one coordinate equal. This coordinate is one over which they must be adjacent. Otherwise, two rectangles can share a border, but remain distinct components. The major benefit is that every island is always a rectangle, perhaps half open. The islands are then easy to describe, as it suffices to store their ranges.

Fig. 8 illustrates the idea through three queries. Two B''s generated by the leftmost range query are siblings in both key space, and Q. They would be immediately merged by Algorithm A2 regardless of the order of arrival. The next query is a partial match. The incoming

127

B' rectangles from bucket 2 and 3 are siblings in *Q*, although the buckets are not siblings in the key space. Both bring records. They would be also immediately merged by Algorithm A2 regardless of the order of arrival. Finally the rightmost partial match query will lead to the merge of *B'*'s from buckets 0,1,3. The reply from bucket 1 can only merge with that from bucket 3, and their union (which is also a rectangle) can only merge with *B'* from bucket 0. If this reply comes first, it will become an island and an element *V*. The next arrival, whether it is from bucket 1 or from bucket 3, will result in two elements *V* and two components, although sharing a border. The third reply will finally trigger the merges in the discussed order.

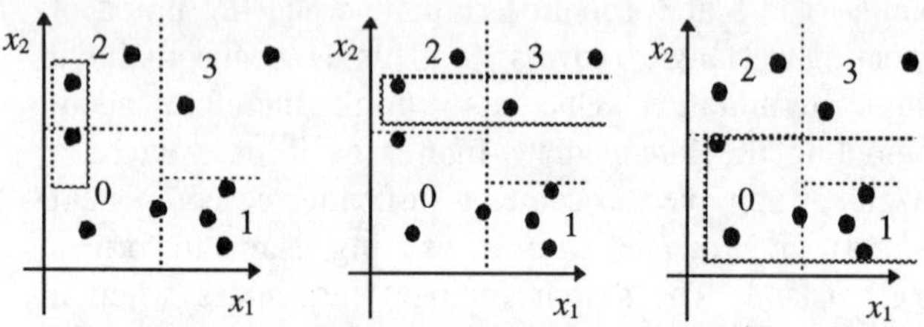

Fig. 8 Deterministic termination of range and partial match queries to k-RP*ₛ file

The behavior of Algorithm A2 will be similar if replies arrive in the orders (1,0,3) or (3,0,1). In contrast, if they arrive in the order (3,1,0) or (1,3,0), then every arrival will trigger a merge and there always will be only one *V*. Until the last arrival, some coordinate range of every *V* will however be strictly smaller than that of *Q* so the client will know that some replies are still outstanding. That is why the reply from bucket 3 is necessary, although in this case it does not bring any record.

A2 : k-RP*ₛ partial match search deterministic termination test

/* The list LIST, initially empty, contain entries *V* of the form < v_1, V_1,.., v_i, V_i,.., v_k, V_k >.

1. Wait for new *B'* = < l_1, L_1 ,..., l_k, L_k > ;
   Once *B'* is received, do :
   i. If LIST contains *V* with :
      ($v_j = L_j$ or $Vj = l_j$) and $v_i = l_i$ and $V_i = L_i$ for all $i \neq j$ then:
   for every *i* :
      if $v_j = L_j$ then set $L_j \leftarrow Vj$;
      if $V_j = l_j$ then set $l_j \leftarrow v_j$;
   endfor
      delete < v_1, V_1,.., v_i, V_i,.., v_k, V_k > ;
      go to step (i) ;
   ii. Insert < l_1, L_1 ,..., l_k, L_k > into LIST ;
2. If LIST contains a single *V = Q*, then terminate A2, otherwise goto Step 1.

The full proof of Algorithm A2 is [LN94]. We omit it here because of the space limitations. A simple deterministic termination algorithm for range queries on numerical fields is also in [LN94]. Yet another algorithm with performance somehow similar to Algorithm A2 is introduced in [N95].

3.4 General search

General search is an arbitrary selection, possibly including non-addressing attributes. The criteria for selection should be so that the computation is solely an intrabucket computation, e.g., interbucket joins are precluded. General search is basically done by function shipping, using multicast, to every bucket. Either every bucket sends a reply with its range and records found, or only buckets with selected records reply. In the former case, the client terminates when *M* buckets replied. In the latter case, a time-out is used.

3.5 Candidate key search

A candidate key search can be a particular case of a partial match search for all records with some $c_j = C$, or of a general query formulated similarly, when c_i is not among the *k* keys. The candidate key search can be more efficient for a successful search, in both cases. The query is sent, as usual, to all *N* buckets. The client can however terminate the search when the record is received. For the probabilistic strategy, only the bucket with the record will reply, somewhere within the first time-out period.

4. Performance analysis

4.1 Storage cost

In what follows, we consider the classical assumptions for the performance analysis of a *k*-d access method. These are (i) the uniform distribution of key values on each dimension, (ii) no correlation between values at different dimensions, (iii) even splitting of each bucket using the middle key, and (iv) a round-robin splitting policy, i.e., the same number of splits along each axis. Furthermore, storage on the servers should be basically used for the buckets, storage for the pages should be comparatively negligible. The average load factor of a *k*-RP*ₛ file, should therefore be as usual about 70 %.

On a client, the storage is needed for image *I*. Depending on the fraction of the file the client addresses, *I* contains between a few, and *O* [*N*] nodes where *N* is the number of buckets in the file. Each node requires storage for two pointers, the page label, the split dimension and the split value. A temporary storage is also required for the tables of Algorithm A2, which is executed at the client. A dozen of KBytes should suffice for storing *I*, in the worst case.

4.2 Messaging cost

Table 1 shows messaging costs of a k-RP*$_S$ file, defined in [LN94], and based on the classical assumptions in Section 4.1. The average cost s_{ave} of an insert or delete is in practice 1, and that of a key search is 2, as b, and b' >> 1. Recall that b is the capacity of a bucket, and b' is the capacity of an index page. The worst case s_{max} corresponds to the traversal of the whole index hierarchy from the bottom to the root and back. It should be very infrequent, and, in practice, should be at most $3 \div 4$ forwards for a 1000-site file. Bulk inserts and deletions are not shown, as they obviously cost one (multicast) message (assuming no limitation on a message length).

Formulae in the lower part of Table 1 assume the use of the multicast to send the query. Formulae for range and partial match deterministic termination search cost s_d closely correspond to the traditional disk access costs of a k-d file. Each value of n_i means that the query selects $1/n_i$ of the file range along the dimension i ; $1 \leq n_i \leq \sqrt[k]{N}$. The case of $n_i = 1$ corresponds to a partial match where all the values along dimension i are requested. The case of $n_i = \sqrt[k]{N}$ corresponds to a null range along the i-th dimension, i.e., $x_i = C_i$.

The formulae mean, for instance, that the average cost of a range search with $n_1 = n_2 = 6$, in a 2-d and large, $N = 900$, file is $s_d = 26$ messages. If $k = 3$, $N = 1000$, and $n_1 = n_2 = n_3 = 5$, then $s_d = 9$ messages only. For a partial match, for instance, for $k = 3$, $N = 1000$, $n_1 = 10$ and $n_2 = n_3 = 5$, one gets $s_d = 41$ messages. Note that if a single key SDDS was used to store the same records, the same searches could take up to N messages, i.e., up to 100 times more in our example, as one would need general queries.

For the candidate key, the upper value of s_d corresponds to searching for an addressing attribute. The lower value corresponds to searching for a non-addressing candidate key (hence all the buckets have to reply). For the search using a time-out T, we distinguish between a successful search, s_t, and an unsuccessful one, s'_t. We assume that if there is a reply, the first message arrives without any delay. The cost s_t for the general query can vary greatly depending on the number of sites found with the relevant records.

All together, the time-out termination appears useful only for the candidate key search and the general queries. In this case, it may lead to a substantial access performance improvement for a large file. If one expresses the time-out T in number of messages, the client could receive one after another, until T expires, then a practical value of T should be $3 \div 5$ messages. Hence, the cost of the probabilistic termination may be $s_t = 2$ or $s'_t = 5 \div 7$ messages, regardless of N. A deterministic candidate key search may, in contrast, require, for instance, 100 messages for $k = 3$, and $N = 1000$ bucket file, and a general query would even need 1000 messages. This is not exactly a great performance, and the phenomenon, expressed in disk access time, was often blamed as cause for a weak interest in k-d structures for database applications.

4.3 Search time

The values characterizing RP*$_S$ in [LNS94] apply to k-RP*$_S$ queries with the same messaging cost. For instance, assume that a typical message with a query is 100 bytes long, and a message with a record is 1000 bytes long [LNS94]. Then, a key search in a k-RP*$_S$ file with buckets in (distributed) RAM should take 1 ms on a 10 Mb/s network (e.g., Ethernet), termed *Mb-net* below, and under 100 µs on a 1 Gb/s network, called *Gb-net* in what follows. Similar performance is impossible to attain with the traditional k-d files. A disk typically requires at least $10 \div 15$ ms to access a record and to transfer it, hence it is an order or two of magnitude slower. Disk access times are likely to remain of this order in the predictable future.

	Insert & Deletes	Key search	Range query
s_{ave}	$1 + O(1/b,\ 1/b')$	$2 + O(1/b,\ 1/b')$	$1 + N / \prod_{i=1}^{k} n_i$
s_{max}	$1 + O(2\log_{b'} N)$	$2 + O(2\log_{b'} N)$	$1 + N / \prod_{i=1}^{k} n_i + T$

	Partial match	Candidate key	General query
s_d	$1 + N / \prod_{i=1}^{j-1} n_i$	$\dfrac{1 + (\sqrt[k]{N})^{k-1}}{1 + N}$	$1 + N$
s_t s'_t	$1 + N / \prod_{i=1}^{j-1} n_i + T$	$\dfrac{2}{1 + T}$	$\dfrac{1 \div 1 + N + T}{1 + T}$

Table 1. Messaging costs of k-RP*$_S$

Table 2 shows search times of three queries presented below, to a k-RP*$_S$ file on an Mb-net or an Gb-net, with 1000 byte long records in buckets of 40 MB of RAM, and with a load factor of 70 %. The file scales up to 1000 sites. The access times are calculated for file sizes of $F = 400$ MB, 4 GB and 40 GB, and with the file spanning over 10, 100 and 1,000 sites. The intra-bucket processing time is assumed negligible as compared to the OS time to access the network, and to the transfer data.

Table 2 also shows search times that would characterize the sample queries if they were posed to a traditional k-d file of the same size. This file is assumed to be structured into 4 KB, a commonly used page size in commercial products. We assume that the disk supporting the file has a 15 ms average access time, each access transferring one page. The search times are compared to the ones of k-RP*$_S$ and the corresponding speed up ratios are calculated. These ratios are noted S in Table 2. They illustrate the performance gains obtainable using k-RP*$_S$.

The specific values of S are not of primary importance. There are ways to ameliorate improve this or that query search time in a traditional k-d file, e.g., through a clever exploration of the sector or cylinder layout [O94]. Similarly, there are ways to speed-up the performance of a k-RP*$_S$ file that we neglect here as well. We evaluate the basic version of each method simply as a reference point. The outcome to note is the order of performance gains that appears from the comparison.

We consider the following queries, which are representative of many applications:

- Q_1 - A range query, which selects 1% of the file,
- Q_2 - A general query that is Q_1 and some additional predicate on non-key attributes selecting 0.5% of the records selected by Q_1 alone.
- Q_3 - A partial match $x_0 = c_0$ successful search in a 3-d file, where x_0 is a candidate key.

In Table 2, the Q_i's are indexed with the file type (t - traditional k-d file, e - k-RP*$_S$ on Mb-net, g - k-RP*$_S$ on Gb-net), and, for Q_3 for k-RP*$_S$, with the termination type (d - deterministic, and t - time-out). The search time unit of measure is in brackets. The formulae for the search times are easy, but tedious to present, [LN94], hence we omit their discussion. The factor S_i is equal to $Q_{i,t} / Q_{i,e}$ or $Q_{i,t} / Q_{i,g}$ for a given F. For the time-out termination S_3 is given only for $F = 40$ GB, i.e. the largest file.

With a load factor of 70%, query Q_1 retrieves the largest amount of data from the file, up to $0.7*400$ MB $= 280$ MB. The response time of a k-RP*$_S$ file ranges between 2.2 s and 224 s on an Mb-net, and between 20 ms and 2.24 s on a Gb-net, with the response time increasing as the file size increases. The response time of a traditional k-d file would range between 15 s and 1500 s. The latter value is clearly impractical. The speed-up S is between 7 times for the Mb-net, relatively slow on transfers, to 670 times for a Gb-net. S is relatively the smallest for range queries since Q_1 retrieves the largest amount of data. Nevertheless, k-RP*$_S$ still speeds up the search from 7 to 670 times, i.e., by one or two orders of magnitude.

For a Gb-net one naturally gains two more orders of magnitude, and the search time decreases under 10 ms for a 40 GB file. The speed up of the search time provided by k-RP*$_S$ is over three orders of magnitude for an Mb-net and over five orders of magnitude for a Gb-net, up to $S \cong 160,000$.

F [GB]	$Q_{1,t}$ [s]		$Q_{2,t}$ [s]
0.4	15		15
4	150		150
40	1,500		1,500

	$Q_{1,e}$ [s]	S_1	$Q_{2,e}$ [s]	S_2
0.4	2.24	7	0.01	1,674
4	22.40	7	0.09	1,674
40	224.00	7	0.90	1,674

	$Q_{1,g}$ [s]	S_1	$Q_{2,g}$ [ms]	S_2
0.4	0.02	669	0.11	136,861
4	0.22	670	0.92	163,755
40	2.24	670	8.98	163,755

F [GB]	$Q_{3,t}$ [s]
0.4	84
4	474
40	2667

	$Q_{3,e,d}$ [ms]	S_3
0.4	1.17	29,612
4	3.25	61,386
40	14.95	79,844
$Q_{3,e,t}$ [ms]	1	696,238

	$Q_{3,g,d}$ [μs]	S_3
0.4	31.70	1,045,393
4	52.50	3,375,681
40	169.46	6,494,760
$Q_{3,g,t}$ [μs]	31	22,459,301

Table 2. Access times to a k-RP*$_S$ file, and to a traditional file of the same size

The performance of k-RP*$_S$ predictably improves for Q_2. The reason is that most records in the query range are filtered in parallel at the servers, and less data are moved to clients. In contrast, the traditional file processing still has to bring from the disk all the corresponding pages, i.e., all the pages of Q_1. For Q_2, the search time on an Mb-net is between 100 ms and 1 s for the 40 GB file.

The speed up is naturally best for the partial match, where the traditional k-d files perform worse. One has to read indeed from the disk all the pages given by the formula for the partial match in Table 1. For k-RP*$_S$, in contrast, all but one searched record are filtered out in parallel, in RAM, at the servers. The resulting response time to Q_3 for the 40 GB file, is under 15 ms for an Mb-net, assuming deterministic termination, and decreasing to 0.2 ms for a Gb-net.

The time-out termination is independent of file size, reaching 1 ms for an Mb-net, and 31 µs for a Gb-net, and reaching a throughput of 32,000 operations/s. The traditional file offers at best a search time of 84 s for the 400 MB file, and slowing down to 2667 s, i.e., 45 min. for the 40 GB file. The speed-up provided by k-RP*$_S$ reaches this 6 orders of magnitude for the deterministic search and up to 22 orders of magnitude for the time-out termination.

Again, the specific values in Table 2 are to be used only as an illustration of the basic search performance of a k-RP*$_S$ file. They show nevertheless that the improvement over the traditional k-d file performance is very important. The difference appears also large enough to reasonably preclude hopes that an amelioration of the traditional design, or of the disk storage technology, bridges the gap in the foreseeable future.

5. Conclusion

SDDSs in general, and k-RP*$_S$ in particular, are aimed at taking full advantage of a multicomputer. We have shown that k-RP*$_S$ improves dramatically the access time of multi-attribute queries with respect to the traditional multi-attribute access methods. Future work should include deeper performance analysis. Several aspects of the method, novel to data structure theory, require more formal analysis. These include the range search termination algorithm, the kernel k-d tree paging algorithm, and the overall management of the incomplete k-d trees, constituting the partial images of the kernel at k-RP*$_S$ client sites.

One should furthermore experiment with actual applications. For inclusion within a database system, one should investigate query processing, concurrency control, and transaction management for k-RP*$_S$ files. As these files are inherently distributed, and have no centralized components, obvious extensions of the traditional principles will not work.

Finally, one should apply k-RP*$_S$ principles to design SDDSs on the basis of other popular multi-attribute access methods. These are multi-attribute hash schemes, quad-trees, R-trees... It should be interesting then to compare the relative performance.

Acknowledgments. *Discussions with Donovan Schneider, and Enrico Nardelli were very helpful to the progress of this work.*

REFERENCES

[C94] Culler, D. NOW: Towards Everyday Supercomputing on a Network of Workstations. *EECS Tech. Rep. UC Berkeley*, to app.

[D93] Devine, R. Design and Implementation of DDH: Distributed Dynamic Hashing. *Int. Conf. on Foundations of Data Organizations, FODO-93. Lecture Notes in Comp. Sc.,* Springer-Verlag (publ.), Oct. 1993.

[ELS95] Evangelis, G., Lomet, D., Salzberg, B. The hB^n-tree: A Modified hB-tree Supporting Concurrency, Recovery and Node Consolidation. VLDB95, 551-561.

[G96] Gray, J. Super-Servers: Commodity Computer Clusters Pose a Software Challemge. Microsoft, 1996. http:\\www.research microsoft..com\

[HS94] E.G. Hoel and H. Samet. Performance of Data-Parallel Spatial Operations. 20th Intl. Conf on Very Large Data Bases, (VLDB), Chile, Sep 1994.

[K95] Kim, W. *Modern Database Systems.* Addison-Wesley, 1995, 705.

[KW94] Kroll, B., Widmayer, P. Distributing a Search Tree Among a Growing Number of Processors. *ACM-SIGMOD Int. Conf. On Management of Data*, 1994.

[ILP93] Iftode, L., Li, K., Petersen, K. Memory Servers for Multicomputers. *IEEE-COMPSAC*, 1993, 538-547.

[JK93] Johnson, T. and P. Krishna. Lazy Updates for Distributed Search Structure. *ACM-SIGMOD Intl. Conf. On Management of Data*, 1993.

[LNS93] Litwin, W. Neimat, M-A., Schneider, D. LH* : Linear Hashing for Distributed Files. *ACM-SIGMOD Intl. Conf. On Management of Data*, 1993.

[LNS93a] Litwin, W., Neimat, M-A., Schneider, D. LH*: A Scalable Distributed Data Structure. (Nov. 1993). to app. ACM-TODS Dec. 1996.

[LNS94] Litwin, W., Neimat, M-A., Schneider, D. RP* : A Family of Order-Preserving Scalable Distributed Data Structures. *20th Intl. Conf on Very Large Data Bases (VLDB)*, 1994.

[LN94] Litwin, W., Neimat. k-RP*$_S$: a High Performance Multi-attribute Scalable Distributed Data Structure. HPL-DTD & Paris 9 Technical Report, 1994.

[MS91] Matsliach, G., Shmueli, O. An Efficient Method for Distributing Search Structures. *IEEE-PDIS Conf.*, 1991.

[N95] Nardelli, E. A Termination Algorithm for k-RP*$_S$ Partial Match and Range Queries. (unpublished HPL & UC Berkeley ICSI memo), 1995.

[S89] Samet, H. *The Design and Analysis of Spatial Data Structures.* Addison-Wesley, 1989.

[S87] Smith, H. *Data Structures. Forms and Function.* HBJ, 1987.

[T95] Tanenbaum, A., S. *Distributed Operating Systems.* Prentice Hall, 1995, 601.

[VBWY94] Vingralek, R., Breitbart, Y., Weikum, G. Distributed File Organization with Scalable Cost/Performance. *ACM-SIGMOD Int. Conf. On Management of Data*, 1994.

[U94] Ullman, J. New Frontiers in Database System Research. *Future Tendencies in Computer Science, Control, and Applied Mathematics.* Lecture Notes in Computer Science 653, Springer-Verlag, 1994. A. Bensoussan, J. P. Verjus, ed. 87-101.

A New Storage and Retrieval Method to Support Editing Operations in a Multi-Disk-based Video Server*

Chien-I Lee[†], Ye-In Chang[‡] and Wei-Pang Yang[†]

[†]Dept. of Computer and Information Science
National Chiao Tung University
Hsinchu, Taiwan, R. O. C.

[‡]Dept. of Applied Mathematics
National Sun Yat-Sen University
Kaohsiung, Taiwan, R. O. C.

Abstract

Since the storage ordering is assumed the same as the retrieval ordering in all the previous storage placement strategies, there is a requirement of a large amount of file copying or merging operations when users insert/delete some data into/from the media data. The observation is also important for video applications because features, like video editing, require the support of random access on individual video frames. In this paper, we propose a new strategy for the insert/delete operations on continuous media that are striped into multi- disks without reorganization of the whole data. From our performance analysis and simulation, the proposed algorithms for insertion/deletion may require only some additional movement cost.

1 Introduction

People frequently apply the term "multimedia" to almost any combination of text, graphics, animation, sound, and video. Text can be rich, typeset text, as in this article. In the context of multimedia, graphics include input devices such as pointers, touch screens, and mice. Animation explicitly introduces the notion of time, that is, graphics moving in real time. Thus, time joins the programming task as a new data type, and the synchronization of graphics and sound becomes a new problem as well as a new capability. Composite representation of data to be integrated in a multimedia application are based upon three types of data: *static*, *dynamic*, and *mixed*. Static types can be electronic documents consisting of text and images arranged in various spatial orientations. Dynamic types include voice annotations, video images, or general animations. Mixed types are formed by uniting both static and dynamic types in a single composite position.

Some media (such as audio and video) are classified as *continuous* because they consist of a separate of media *quanta* (such as audio samples or video frames), which convey meaning only when presented in time. Several multimedia types, in particular video, require high bandwidths and large storage space. For example, a one half hours of video based on the HDTV (High Definition Television) quality images has approximately 36 Gbits data and requires approximately a 100 Mbps bandwidth, while a current typical magnetic disk drive has only 80 Gbits capacity and serves approximately 20 Mbps bandwidth. In general, conventional file systems are unable to guarantee that clients can access continuous media in a way that permits delivery deadlines to be met under normal buffering conditions. Therefore, how to support a continuous retrieval of multimedia data at its required bandwidth and how to store the multimedia data are challenging tasks [2, 5, 4, 7, 13, 14, 20].

Previous approaches to support real-time applications of digital continuous media can be classified into three directions: *continuous retrieval*, *random access* and *interactive browsing*. To support *continuous retrieval*, some strategies clustered the data on a single disk to reduce the cost of disk head movement [6, 16, 17, 18, 21, 22], and some strategies tended to increase the bandwidth of disk device by using *parallelism*, which combines the bandwidths of multiple disks to provide a high data bandwidth requirement [1, 9, 12]. To support *random access*, like *editing operations*, since there is a trade-off between the flexible placement and the overhead of disk head movement in a disk drive, a straightforward idea is to find a compromise between them, which constrains a group of consecutive data to be stored consecutively in each cylinder on the disk. While a group of data can be randomly stored on any cylinder [11]. To support *interactive browsing* such as *fast forward* and *fast backward*, some strategies used the *scalable compression algorithms* to generate the multiresolution data [10], and some strategies supported browsing at any desired display speed by a predetermined *sampling* procedure [3].

In all of the previous proposed storage placement strategies [1, 6, 9, 12, 16, 17, 18, 21, 22], the storage ordering is assumed to be the same as the retrieval ordering; therefore, there is a requirement of a large amount of file copying or merging operations when users insert/delete some data into/from the media data. The observation is also important for video applications, since features, like video editing, require the support of random access on individual video frames. Although in [11], Liu et al. have proposed a strategy based

---

*This research was supported in part by the National Science Council of Republic of China under Grand No. NSC-86-2213-E-110-004.

on a single disk to support random access, they only consider the case when the the required bandwidth is lower than the bandwidth of a disk drive.

In this paper, we propose an efficient *conflict-resolution* approach to the insertion/deletion operations on continuous media. Since future demands for even high bandwidth are expected, we design the new strategy based on a multi-disk architecture which can increase the data transfer rate and the storage capacity in proportion to the number of disks. Basically, in our proposed strategy, the continuous media is split up into blocks and placed in various locations on the disks (called *simple striping* [1]). Under this situation, the striped subobjects are stored among the multi-disk drive in a predetermined sequence and must be read in this predetermined sequence to guarantee the continuous retrieval. An insertion or a deletion of subobjects may disturb the property of continuous retrieval because there may be a pair of two consecutive subobjects that are stored in the same disk and must be retrieved simultaneously. Therefore, an efficient *conflict-resolution* approach is proposed for the insertion/deletion operations on continuous media that are striped into a multi-disk drive without reorganization of the whole data. In the proposed approach, when a new subobject is inserted after subobject i, it will be assigned with an identification number $(i + 1)$ and be inserted to a disk that has minimum number of used blocks (for load balancing concerns) and in which the retrieval of the new subobject does not conflict with the retrieval of any other subobject, where a *conflict* means a pair of two consecutive subobjects that are stored in the same disk must be retrieved simultaneously. However, a new conflict on the same disk may occur since all the identification numbers of subobjects after subobject i are increased by one. Only when such a new conflict occurs, one movement operation is required, so does the case of a deletion operation. From our performance analysis and simulation results, we show that the average number of additional movements for any subobject insertion is no more than 5, when there is an object is divided into 120 subobjects, the object is striped on a multi-disk drive with 12 disks, and the required bandwidth is 2 times of the bandwidth of a single disk.

The rest of the paper is organized as follows. Section 2 surveys the related works on the data retrieval of digital continuous media. Section 3 briefly describes the *simple striping* strategy that is applied in our approach. Section 4 presents the algorithms for insertion and deletion operations on digital continuous media. Section 5 presents the performance analysis and simulation results of the algorithms. Section 6 contains a conclusion.

2 Related Works

In this section, we will survey several research directions in a video server that are classified into three areas, including *continuous retrieval*, *random access* and *interactive browsing*.

2.1 Continuous Retrieval

Since magnetic disks have large seek and rotational latencies that cause the display of a continuous media to starve, how to arrange and place the media data on disks in order to support real-time retrieval and flexible placement is an important task. Gemmell and Christodoulakis [6] were the first to develop a general theoretical framework for studying the performance of any display system with a dedicated storage device and discuss several strategies for placing audio data on a storage device in order to display multiple-channel audio synchronously. Yu et al. [22] proposed a storage placement strategy by using *gaps* between consecutive blocks to provide the necessary delays to match the consumption rate without requiring excessive buffering. Moreover, since blocks of a new data may be stored in the gaps of already existing data on the disk, there were several merging algorithms [16, 17, 18, 21, 22] proposed to utilize the disk space efficiently. However, these approaches are effective only when the maximum bandwidth of disk is higher than the required bandwidth.

Moreover, current studies in a multi-disk drive were proposed to increase the data transfer rate and the storage capacity in proportion to the number of disks. *Declustering* and *striping* are two popular techniques employed by both general purpose multi-disks I/O subsystems (e.g., disk arrays) and parallel database management systems (e.g., share-nothing architecture). In [9], they extended the concept of *declustering* to a parallel multimedia system based on the the shared-nothing architecture and proposed two alternative approaches to enable the system to support simultaneous display of multiple multimedia data. The first approach, termed *disk multitasking*, configures the system to support a fixed number of users (U_{max}) or simultaneous display The major disadvantage of *multitasking* is the limit on the number of requests and the waste of bandwidth when the total number of requests is less than U_{max}. The second approach replicates the fragments of a media data across several processors so that the system can use a fragment of a media data that resides on an idle processor to service a request. However, the replications have a high overhead of copying. In [1, 12], they used the concept of *striping* to support continuous retrieval of digital continuous media. Moreover, Berson et al. [1] further generalized the simple *striping* (called *staggered striping*) to support a database that consists of a mix of multimedia objects, each with a different bandwidth requirement.

2.2 Random Access

In previous described storage placement strategies, they require a large amount of file copying and merging operations in the editing on the continuous media. The observation is important for video applications since features, like video editing, require the support of random access on individual video frames. Liu et al. [11] were the first to investigate a solution based on a video-frame level, which offers more flexible storage placement and efficient buffering schemes. They proposed two buffering schemes which are the *two-buffer scheme* and the *k-buffer compensation scheme*. The *two-buffer scheme* requires only a small group of sequential video frames stored consecutively (i.e., clus-

tered) in each cylinder on the disk placement. The
k-buffer compensation scheme uses more than two
buffers and requires some blocks to be placed randomly in the same cylinder on disk placement. The
idea of *compensation* is motivated by the fact that the
disk data transfer rate varies; it is faster when video
frames are placed close together and slower when more
seek and latency time are required.

2.3 Interactive Browsing

One of most important challenges in a Video-On-
Demand system is to support *interactive browsing*
functions such as *fast forward with scan* and *fast
backward with scan*. There are several possible approaches to implementing these functions: (1) The
data is retrieved and transmitted at the desired rate
which times the normal display rate. Obviously, this
solution requires additional resources at the storage
system, the memory buffers, and the network. (2) The
storage system retrieves and transmits every desired
number of block to the end station. This solution also
requires significant additional system resources since
the multimedia file must be indexed to retrieve individual blocks. (3) The system switches over to a
separately coded "scan forward" data to scan. This
solution eliminates any additional read bandwidth or
network bandwidth. However, it is extremely expensive in terms of storage space and inflexible in which
it supports a fixed scan rate.

Chen et al. [3] proposed two new schemes for supporting interactive browsing for video display. The
first methods, called *segment-sampling* scheme, supports browsing at any desired speed while balancing the load on the disk array as well as minimizing the variation on the number of video segments skipped between samplings. Since *segment-
sampling* scheme makes the segments retrieved not
perfectly uniformly distributed, the second scheme,
called *segment-placement* scheme, uniformly retrieves
the segments in a predetermined fast-forward speed.

3 Simple Striping

Declustering and *striping* are two popular techniques employed by both general purpose multi-disks
I/O subsystems and parallel database management
systems. Since the *declustering* approach declusters
an object among a multi-disk drive into a sequence
of subobjects which are stored contiguously on disks,
there is a requirement of large overhead when data are
inserted or deleted. While in the *striping* approach,
data are split up into blocks and placed in various
locations on the disks. Consequently, the *striping*
approach allows more flexibility of editing operations
than the *declustering* approach. Therefore, in our
approach, we apply the *simple striping* strategy to
arrange the continuous media on a multi-disk drive.

For the rest of paper, for convenience, we will use
an object to denote an object of digital continuous media. Suppose the bandwidth of both the network and
the network device driver exceeds the bandwidth requirement of an object. Assume that there are N disks
which operate independently, called a *multi-disk* drive
and each disk has a fixed bandwidth d, a worst seek

time WS, and a worst latency time WL. The *simple
striping* strategy uses the aggregate bandwidth of several disk drives by striping an object across multiple
disks [1]. For example, an object X with bandwidth
requirement C at least requires the aggregate band-
width of $M = \lceil \frac{C}{d} \rceil$ disk drives to support the continuous display of X. (Note that the maximum aggregate
bandwidth of a multi-disk drive with N disks is ($N
\times d$) which must be not smaller than C.) Moreover,
object X is organized as a sequence of equi-sized subobjects ($X_0, X_1, X_2, ...$), where the size of a subobject
is s Mbits. Each subobject X_i represents a contiguous portion of X and is stored randomly in the disks.
For the load balance for each disk, the subobjects of
X are assigned to the N disks in a round-robin man-
ner and the N disks are divided into R ($= \lfloor \frac{N}{M} \rfloor$)
disk clusters, where each cluster is assigned to an ob-
ject for the retrieval of the M consecutive subobjects
to guarantee the real-time transfer. It is known that
concurrent pipelining of retrieval and displaying of an
object requires prefetching and at least two buffers
[16]. One buffer is for retrieval of the next M consecutive subobjects while the other one that stores the
previous retrieved M consecutive subobjects is being
displayed. The real-time retrieval can be achieved by
satisfying following equations:

$$M \geq \lceil \tfrac{C}{d} \rceil,$$

$$M \leq N,$$

$$R = \lfloor \tfrac{N}{M} \rfloor,$$

$$WS + WL + \tfrac{s}{d} \leq \frac{s}{\frac{C}{M}}, \text{ for each disk drive,}$$

where s denotes the block size.

Hence, the display of X employs only a single cluster at a time in a round-robin manner. In each cluster,
consecutive subobjects of object X are stored on those
M disks in a liner order. Figure 1 shows an example
of simple striping for an object X with bandwidth requirement 80 Mbps, where $N = 10$, $d = 20$ Mbps, $WS
= 30$ ms (ms $= 10^{-3}$ seconds), $WL = 10$ ms and the
value i denotes subobject X_i inside a disk. Suppose $M
= 5$ ($\geq \frac{80}{20}$), then s ($= \frac{(WS+WL) \times d \times \frac{C_i}{M}}{d - \frac{C_i}{M}}$) $= 3.2$ Mbits
(Mbits $= 10^6$ bits) and $R = 2$. Note that the display
of X first employs cluster 0 to read the subobjects X_0,
X_1, X_2, X_3 and X_4 from disks 0, 1, 2, 3 and 4, respectively, into a buffer. Second, subobjects X_5, X_6, X_7,
X_8 and X_9 are read into the other buffer from cluster
1. At the same time, the buffer (that stores subobjects
X_0, X_1, X_2, X_3 and X_4) is being displayed. Then, alternatively, the subsequent subobjects of X are read
from cluster 0 or cluster 1 into the two buffers that
are then being displayed.

4 The Conflict-Resolution Approach

Editing operations such as insertion, deletion and
modification are necessary for a general purpose file

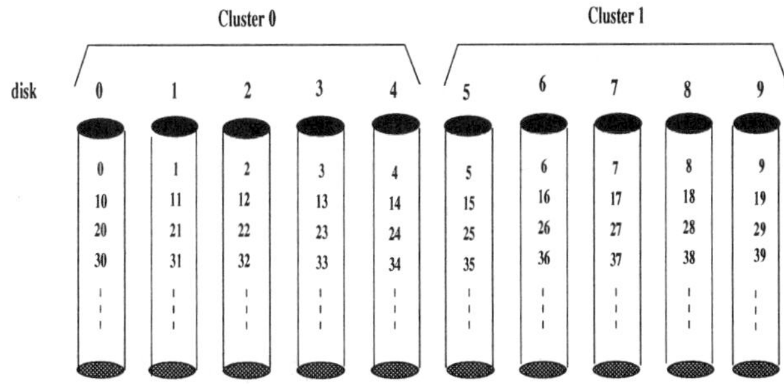

Figure 1: An example of object X striped on a multi-disk drive.

storage system. If an object is read only, then the object striped on a multi-disk drive is satisfied for the continuous display as described in Section 3. However, an insertion or a deletion of subobjects may disturb the property of continuous retrieval because there may be a pair of two consecutive subobjects that are stored in the same disk and must be retrieved simultaneously. Therefore, in the following subsections, we will present a *conflict-resolution* approach to support insertion and deletion operations to guarantee continuous display, respectively. (Note that a modification operation can be replaced with a deletion operation followed by an insertion operation.) In this approach, when a conflict is detected after an insertion or a deletion operation, a conflict-resolution operation is needed by moving one of the pair of conflicting subobjects to some other disks such that the conflict can be resolved. Since each subobject is organized as a block on the disks in terms of a sequence of continuously digital media, which sequence is immutable, we regards blocks as immutable objects. Therefore, we assume that a block (i.e., a subobject) is regarded as a unit for all editing operations.

4.1 Insertion

Assume that a new subobject is inserted into an object striped on a multi-disk drive. A straightforward approach to support an insertion operation will require substantial movements of subobjects after the inserted subobject to their corresponding disks depending on the simple striping placement strategy. Obviously, these movements will consume significant amount of time and space. Therefore, we propose an algorithm based on the conflict-resolution approach as shown in Figure 2 for inserting a new subobject x after the subobject with identification number $= i$ (i.e., subobject i) without reorganizing the whole data, which usually performs an insertion of subobject without requiring any additional movement cost of other subobjects.

First, when a new subobject is inserted after subobject i, all the identification numbers of subobjects after subobject i are increased by one. A *conflict* occurs when a pair of two consecutive subobjects that are stored in the same disk must read into the buffer simultaneously to guarantee the continuous display. Therefore, the new subobject with identification number $= (i + 1)$ should be inserted into a disk j in which the retrieval of the new subobject does not conflict

with the retrieval of any other subobject. Moreover, for load balancing concerns, disk j should be the one that has minimum number of used blocks. However, since all the identification numbers of subobjects after subobject i are increased by one, this may cause a new conflict to occur between a pair of subobjects with identification numbers $= k$ and v in the same disk, where $v > k > (i + 1)$. Therefore, one more movement operation to resolve such a conflict is needed if such a new conflict occurs. (Note that since an aggregation bandwidth of M disks is achieved by retrieving M subobjects from the M disks into a buffer at each round, simultaneously, a conflict can be detected by comparing the value of $\lfloor \frac{k}{M} \rfloor$ with the one of $\lfloor \frac{v}{M} \rfloor$. When these values are the same, a conflict occurs because that subobject k and subobject v will be retrieved from the same disk at the same time.) That is, these M subobjects must be stored in different disks to guarantee simultaneous retrieval. For load balancing concerns about the disks, this proposed algorithm requires the following two arrays: 1) an array of *counters* to record the number of used blocks for every disk; 2) an array of *flags* to record whether a conflict occurs when a subobject is moved into a disk.

For example, Figure 3-(a) shows the state of the multi-disk drive after the insertion of a new subobject X_{0a} after subobject X_0 of object X with bandwidth requirement $= 80$ Mbps, where $N = 5$, $d = 20$ Mbps, $WS = 30$ ms, $WL = 10$ ms, $M = 5$, $R = 1$, $s = 3.2$ Mbits and the number in "()" denotes the original identification number before any insertion operation occurs. First, all the identification numbers of subobjects after subobject 0 are increased by one. Then, the identification number of the new inserted object is assigned to 1. Figure 3-(b) shows the state of the multi-disk drive after X_{0b}, X_{0c} and X_{0d} are inserted. Moreover, Figure 3-(c) shows the state of the multi-disk drive after X_{0e} is inserted. (Note that at this moment, five subobjects are inserted in sequence after subobject 0; therefore, all the identification numbers after subobject 0 have been increased by 5.) At this moment, a new conflict occurs between subobject 5 (i.e., subobject 0a) and subobject 9. Therefore, subobject 5 is moved to disk 0 in which there is no subobject with an identification number $= g$ such that $\lfloor \frac{g}{M} \rfloor = \lfloor \frac{5}{M} \rfloor$.

Consequently, whenever a conflict between two subobjects k and v occurs on disk j, one of these two conflicting subobjects, say subobject k, must move to another disk f in which there will be no conflict after subobject k is moved. To prove that such a disk f exists at any time, that is, the repeat-until loop in algorithm *insertion* will always stop, the following theorem is used.

Theorem 1 *Given an object X striped on a multi-disk drive with N disks and a conflict between two subobjects with identification numbers k and v on disk l ($0 \leq l \leq N$ - 1), where $\lfloor \frac{k}{M} \rfloor = \lfloor \frac{v}{M} \rfloor$, there is a disk f ($0 \leq f \leq N$ - 1) in which there is no subobject with an identification number $= g$ such that $\lfloor \frac{k}{M} \rfloor = \lfloor \frac{g}{M} \rfloor$.*

procedure insertion(i, x);
var
  $Q[N]$: an array of counters;
  $CF[N]$: an array of flags;
  M : integer; /* the number of disks in a cluster */
  c, i, j, k, f, v, g, h : integer;
  x : BLOB; /* Binary Large OBject */
begin
  increase all the identification numbers of subobjects
  after subobject i by one;
  $CF[*] = 0$;   /* set all the values of CF to 0 */
  $c = 1$;
  repeat
   $j = \mathrm{cmin}(Q, c)$;
/* function cmin returns a disk identification number
   j that has the cth minimum used space
   (as recored in Q) among all the values in Q */
   for each subobject with an identification number
   g on disk j do
    if $\lfloor \frac{i+1}{M} \rfloor = \lfloor \frac{g}{M} \rfloor$ then $CF[j] = 1$;
   end for;
   $c = c + 1$;
  until $CF[j] = 0$;
  insert the new subobject x into disk j with an
  identification number $= (i + 1)$;
  $Q[j] = Q[j] +$ size of x;
   /* detect all the conflicts and resolve them */
  for $(j=0; j<N; j++)$ do
   while (there is a pair of subobjects in disk j
   with identification numbers k and v,
    where $\lfloor \frac{k}{M} \rfloor = \lfloor \frac{v}{M} \rfloor$, and $(i + 1) < k < v$) do
    /* a conflict is detected */
    $CF[*] = 0$;
    $c = 1$;
    repeat
     $f = \mathrm{cmin}(Q, c)$;
     for each subobject with an identification
     number g on disk f do
      if $\lfloor \frac{k}{M} \rfloor = \lfloor \frac{g}{M} \rfloor$ then $CF[f] = 1$;
     end for;
     $c = c + 1$;
    until $CF[f] = 0$;
    move the subobject with an identification
    number k to disk f;
    $Q[j] = Q[j] -$ size of subobject k;
    $Q[f] = Q[f] +$ size of subobject k;
   end while;
  end for;
end;

Figure 2: Algorithm insertion.

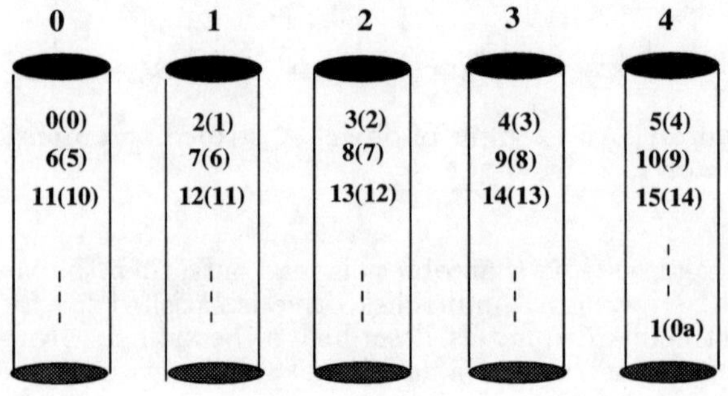

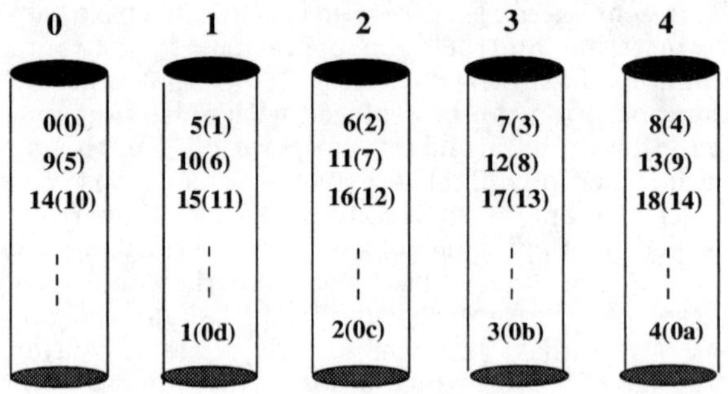

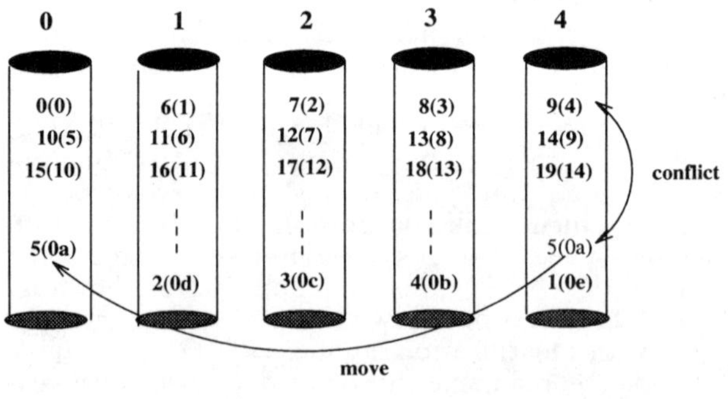

Figure 3: An example of a series of insertion operations: (a) after X_{0a} is inserted; (b) after X_{0b}, X_{0c} and X_{0d} are inserted; (c) after X_{0e} is inserted.

Proof. Assume that no such a disk f exists; that is, for every disk, there is a subobject with an identification number $= z$ such that $\lfloor \frac{k}{M} \rfloor = \lfloor \frac{z}{M} \rfloor = w$. Note that there are exact $(M - 1)$ different values of z (excluding k) which satisfy the equation. By using the *pigeonhole principle*, there is at least one empty pigeonhole if there are $(M - 1)$ pigeons that are put into N $(\geq M)$ pigeonholes. That is, there is at least one disk, say disk f, where there is no subobject with an identification number $= g$ on disk f such that $\lfloor \frac{k}{M} \rfloor = \lfloor \frac{g}{M} \rfloor = w$. Therefore, the previous assumption is wrong. Consequently, such a disk f exists at any time. $\qquad\Box$

4.2 Deletion

Similar to the case of an insertion, a deletion of subobject may disturb the property of continuous retrieval. The proposed algorithm for deleting a subobject with the identification number i without reorganizing the whole data is shown in Figure 4, which may need an additional movement cost for deleting a subobject. When a subobject i is deleted, all the identification numbers of subobjects after subobject i are decreased by one. Since the deletion of a subobject may result in a new conflict between two subobjects stored in the same disk, we must check the identification numbers k $(k \geq i)$ of subobjects in each disk. For load balancing concerns about the disks, this algorithm also requires those two arrays, *counters* and *flags*, as described before.

Consider an example shown in Figure 5-(a), where $N = 6$, $d = 20$ Mbps, $WS = 30$ ms, $WL = 10$ ms, an object X with bandwidth requirement $= 50$ Mbps, $M - 3$, $R = 2$, $s = 4$ Mbits and the number in $"()"$ denotes the original identification number before any deletion operation occurs. Figure 5-(a) shows the state of the multi-disk drive after subobjects X_1 is deleted. After subobject X_1 is deleted, all the identification numbers of subobjects after subobject 0 are decreased by one. In this case, since no conflict occurs, there is no additional movement. Next, after two more deletion operations on subobject 1 are executed, the state is shown in Figure 5-(b). Figure 5-(c) shows the state after one more deletion on subobject 1 is executed. At this time, a new conflict occurs between subobject 0 and subobject 2 in disk 0; therefore, subobject 0 must be moved to disk 1 (or disk 2 or disk 3 or disk 4), which has the minimum number of used blocks.

5 Performance Analysis and Simulation Results

In this section, we present the performance analysis and the simulation results of insertion/deletion operations for a striped object on a multi-disk drive by applying our proposed insertion/deletion algorithms. Since a deletion operation may cause the movement of the other subobjects as an insertion operation does, the performance analysis and the simulation results for a deletion operation is similar to those for an insertion operation. Therefore, we only discuss the performance of the insertion operations. In this analysis model, we assume that each disk in a multi-disk drive

```
procedure deletion(i);
var
    Q[N] : an array of counters;
    CF[N] : an array of flags;
    M : integer; /* the number of disks in a cluster */
    c, i, j, k, f, v, g, h : integer;
begin
    delete the subobject i from disk j;
    Q[j] = Q[j] - size of subobject i;
    decrease all the identification numbers of subobjects
    for the object after i by one;
    /* detect all the conflicts and resolve them */
    for (j=0;j<N;j++) do
      while (there is a pair of subobjects in disk j
      with identification numbers k and v,
        where ⌊ k/M ⌋ = ⌊ v/M ⌋, and (i + 1) < k < v) do
      /* a conflict is detected */
        CF[*] = 0;
        c = 1;
        repeat
            f = cmin(Q, c);
            for each subobject with an identification
            number g on disk f do
              if ⌊ k/M ⌋ = ⌊ g/M ⌋ then CF[f] = 1;
            end for;
            c = c +1;
        until CF[f] = 0;
        move the subobject with an identification
        number k to disk f;
        Q[j] = Q[j] - size of subobject k;
        Q[f] = Q[f] + size of subobject k;
      end while;
    end for;
end;
```

Figure 4: Algorithm *deletion*.

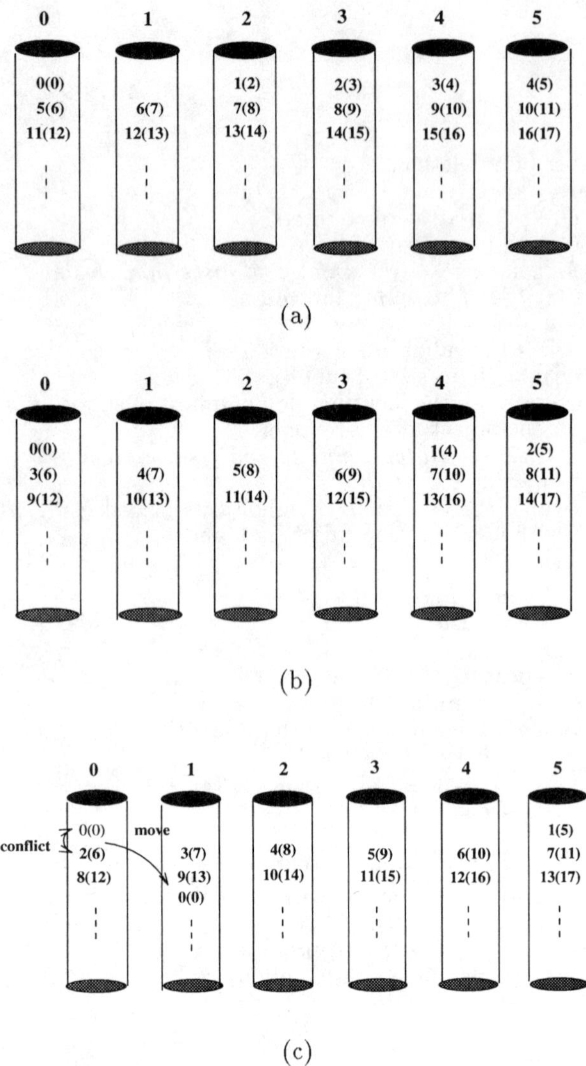

(a)

(b)

(c)

Figure 5: An example of a series of deletion operations: (a) after X_1 is deleted; (b) after two more X_1 are deleted; (c) after one more X_1 is deleted.

operates independently. When an I/O request arrives, it may be decomposed into subrequests, each of which will be serviced independently on a different disk. Objects are striped on the multi-disk drive by applying the *simple striping* strategy and all the subobjects of an object have the same size. Each disk has approximately the same number of subobjects, that is, load balancing. The performance measure is the number of read/write operations (including the write operation for the data insertion) in the multi-disk drive to guarantee the real-time retrieval after an insertion operation.

Suppose N is the number of disks in a multi-disk drive, in which each disk has a fixed bandwidth d, a worst seek time WS, and a worst latency time WL. An object X with a required bandwidth C is striped on the multi-disk drive. The values of R, M and s can be obtained by applying the equations as described in Section 3, where R denotes the number of clusters, M denotes the number of subobjects in a cluster, and s denotes the subobject size. Assume that the the size of object X is V_X and there are Num subobjects of object X with $Num = \lceil \frac{V_X}{s} \rceil$. Logically, we can view the current state of the object striped on the multi-disk drive as L $(= \lceil \frac{Num}{M} \rceil)$ groups numbered from 0 to $(L - 1)$, where the subobjects in each group must be retrieved, simultaneously. Each group has M subobjects except group $(L - 1)$. There are FS $(= Num - M \times (L - 1))$ subobjects in group $(L - 1)$. Figure 6-(a) shows a simple example of a logical view of an object X striped on a multi-disk drive with $N = 6$, where $Num = 10$, $M = 3$, $L = 4$ and $FS = 1$. (Note that, for those subobjects in the same logical group, we store them in different physical disks to guarantee the real-time retrieval.) In other words, the values of $\lfloor \frac{id}{M} \rfloor$ for these M consecutive subobjects are the same; i.e, they conflict with each other, where id denotes the identification number. In the above example, subobjects 0, 1 and 2 have the same value $\lfloor \frac{0}{M} \rfloor = \lfloor \frac{1}{M} \rfloor = \lfloor \frac{2}{M} \rfloor = 0$; therefore, they must be stored in different disks to avoid conflict, so do the other subobjects with the same value of $\lfloor \frac{id}{M} \rfloor$.

Whenever a new subobject is inserted after subobject i, this new subobject with identification number $(i + 1)$ is inserted into disk f, where no conflict occurs as described before. While the insertion may cause new conflicts between other subobjects behind the new inserted subobject to occur. The reason is that all the identification numbers greater than i must be increased by one. Logically, all the subobjects in those groups which are behind group t $(= \lfloor \frac{i}{M} \rfloor)$ that subobject i belongs to, must be re-clustered according to the order for displaying. Logically, the moved-out subobject in a group t will be the moved-in subobject in group $(t + 1)$. There are $(M - 1)$ subobjects that have not to be moved in each group. (Note that there is no conflict between any two subobjects of those $(M - 1)$ subobjects because, in the physical storage, these $(M - 1)$ subobjects are already stored in different disks.) Therefore, a conflict can occur only between the moved-in subobject and one of those $(M$

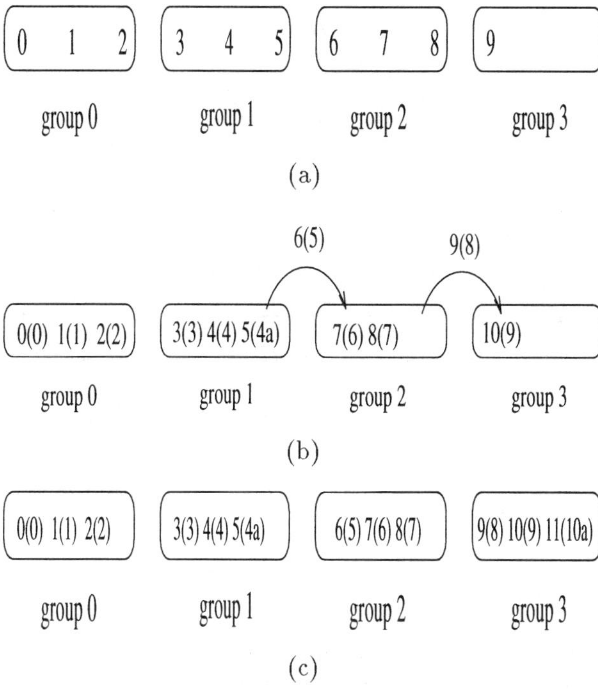

group 0   group 1   group 2   group 3

(a)

group 0   group 1   group 2   group 3

(b)

group 0   group 1   group 2   group 3

(c)

Figure 6: An example of a logical view of an object X striped on a multi-disk drive: (a) before any insertion occurs; (b) after a new subobject is inserted after subobject 4; (c) after a new subobject is inserted after subobject 10.

- 1) subobjects in the same disk. Consequently, after an insertion operation occurs, the probability of a conflict that occurs between a moved-in subobject and one of those (M - 1) subobjects in the same disk is $\frac{M-1}{N}$.

For example, Figure 6-(b) shows the state resulted from Figure 6-(a) after a new subobject 4a is inserted after subobject 4, where the number in "()" denotes the original identification number before any insertion operation occurs. In this example, all the identification numbers of subobjects after subobject 4 must be increased by one and the new subobject 4a is inserted into group 1 with an identification number 5. Since subobject 6(5) belongs to group 2 ($= \lfloor \frac{6}{M} \rfloor$), instead of group 1, subobject 6(5) must be moved from group 1 to group 2. Therefore, a conflict can occur in group 2 only between subobject 6(5) and subobjects 7(6), 8(7) since subobject 9(8) must be moved from group 2 to group 3 at the same time. Consequently, the probability of such a conflict is $\frac{2}{6}$. For the same reason, the probability of a conflict in group 3 between subobject 9(8) and subobject 10(9) is $\frac{1}{6}$. Moreover, Figure 6-(c) shows the state resulted from Figure 6-(b) after one more new subobject 10a is inserted after subobject 10(9). Since there are only 2 subobjects 10(9) and 11(10a) in group 3 after this new insertion operation is performed and no subobject must be moved out of group 3, the probability of a conflict is 0.

There are only two cases of inserting a new subobject in the last group (i.e., group (L - 1)). One case is that if the number of subobjects in group (L - 1) is smaller than M (i.e., $0 < FS < M$), the total number of subobjects in group (L - 1) will not be greater than M after the new subobject is inserted. Therefore, no subobject must be moved out from group (L - 1). In this case, the probability of a conflict of such a data insertion is 0 because no subobject must be moved out. The other case is that if the number of subobjects in group (L - 1) equals to M (i.e., $FS = 0$), the total number of subobjects in group (L - 1) is (M + 1) after the new subobject is inserted. Therefore, a subebject must be moved out from group (L - 1) to a new group, say group L. In this case, the probability of a conflict of such a data insertion is also 0 because the moved-out subobject from group (L - 1) to group L does not conflict with the others since no subobject is stored in group L before this data insertion. Therefore, the probability of a conflict of inserting a new subobject in the last group is always 0.

Since a conflict of each group occurs independently, the number of conflicts for an insertion after subobject i is obtained as

$$NC(i) = (\lfloor \tfrac{Num}{M} \rfloor - \lfloor \tfrac{i}{M} \rfloor - 1) \times \tfrac{M-1}{N} + \tfrac{FS}{N},$$
$$\text{when } \lfloor \tfrac{Num}{M} \rfloor > \lfloor \tfrac{i}{M} \rfloor$$

or $NC(i) = 0$, when $\lfloor \frac{Num}{M} \rfloor = \lfloor \frac{i}{M} \rfloor$,

and the total cost for an insertion after subobject i is given by

$$INS(i) = NC(i) \times 2 + 1.$$

Then, the average cost for an insertion can be obtained as

$$AV\_INS(Num) = \frac{\sum_{i=0}^{Num-1} INS(i)}{Num}.$$

Since $NC(u) = NC(v)$ when $\lfloor \frac{u}{M} \rfloor = \lfloor \frac{v}{M} \rfloor$, the cost for the insertion after subobject u is equal to the cost for the insertion after subobject v, that is, $INS(u) = INS(v)$. In other words, the cost for any insertion in a group has the same insertion cost. Therefore, the average cost for an insertion can also be given by

$$AV\_INS(Num) = \frac{\sum_{i=0}^{\lceil \frac{Num}{M} \rceil - 1} INS(i \times M)}{\lceil \frac{Num}{M} \rceil}$$

$$= \frac{((\lfloor \frac{Num}{M} \rfloor - 1) \times \frac{M-1}{N} + \frac{FS}{N}) \times 2 + 1}{\lceil \frac{Num}{M} \rceil}$$

$$+ \frac{((\lfloor \frac{Num}{M} \rfloor - 2) \times \frac{M-1}{N} + \frac{FS}{N}) \times 2 + 1}{\lceil \frac{Num}{M} \rceil} + \cdots$$

$$+ \frac{(0 \times \frac{M-1}{N} + \frac{FS}{N}) \times 2 + 1}{\lceil \frac{Num}{M} \rceil} + \frac{1}{\lceil \frac{Num}{M} \rceil}$$

$$= \frac{(\lfloor \frac{Num}{M} \rfloor - 1) \times \lfloor \frac{Num}{M} \rfloor \times \frac{M-1}{N} + \frac{FS}{N} \times \lfloor \frac{Num}{M} \rfloor \times 2}{\lceil \frac{Num}{M} \rceil} + 1,$$

when $FS > 0$, i.e., $\lfloor \frac{Num}{M} \rfloor < \lceil \frac{Num}{M} \rceil$, or

$$AV\_INS(Num) = (\lfloor \frac{Num}{M} \rfloor - 1) \times \frac{M-1}{N} + 1,$$
when $FS = 0$.

For a series of k insertion operations after subobjects $i_1, i_2, ..., i_k$, respectively, the total cost of these k insertion operations is obtained as the sum of the cost of an insertion after subobject i_j, $1 \le j \le k$. That is,

$$TOTINS(k) = \sum_{j=1}^{k} INS(k_j).$$

Note that the number Num of subobjects is increased by one after an insertion has been performed. The average cost for any series of k ($k > 0$) insertion operations can be obtained as

$$AV\_TOTINS(k) = \frac{\sum_{j=Num}^{Num+k-1} AV\_INS(j)}{k}.$$

Table 1 shows the results in terms of the number of read/write operations derived from the above formulas, where $N = 12$, $Num = 120$, $s = 1$ Mbits, $M = 2, 3, 4, 6$ and 12, respectively, and the number in "()" denotes the number of the additional movement operations. From this table, we observe that the additional movement cost is much smaller than the cost for reorganizing the whole object. (Note that the cost for the reorganization is $2 \times (Num - i - 1)$, when a new

N	M	Num	INS(1)	INS(60)	INS(118)	AV_INS(Num)	AV_TOTINS(120)/120
12	2	120	10.8(4.9)	5.8(2.4)	1(0)	5.9(2.5)	8.3(3.7)
12	3	120	14.0(6.5)	7.3(3.2)	1(0)	7.5(3.3)	10.7(4.9)
12	4	120	15.5(7.3)	8.0(3.5)	1(0)	8.2(3.6)	11.8(5.4)
12	6	120	16.8(7.9)	8.5(3.8)	1(0)	8.9(4.0)	12.8(5.9)
12	12	120	17.5(8.3)	8.3(3.7)	1(0)	9.2(4.1)	13.3(6.2)

Table 1: Analysis results

N	M	Num	INS(1)	INS(7)	INS(10)	AV_INS(Num)	AV_TOTINS(12)/12
4	2	12	2.0(0.5)	1.46(0.23)	1(0)	1.5(0.25)	1.76(0.38)
4	4	12	3.96(1.48)	2.52(0.76)	1(0)	2.49(0.745)	3.2(1.1)

(a)

N	M	Num	INS(1)	INS(7)	INS(10)	AV_INS(Num)	AV_TOTINS(12)/12
4	2	12	2.0(0.5)	1.5(0.25)	1(0)	1.5(0.25)	1.75(0.375)
4	4	12	4.0(1.5)	2.5(0.75)	1(0)	2.5(0.75)	3.25(1.125)

(b)

Table 2: Performance: (a) simulation results; (b) analysis results

subobject is inserted after subobject i.) Moreover, the cost for inserting a new subobject after subobject i is increased as i is decreased, because the probability of a conflict is increased. Since there are $(N!)^{\lceil \frac{Num}{N} \rceil}$ kinds of initial states of the multi-disk drive, it requires a lot of time to simulate all the cases if N or Num are too large. Therefore, in the simulation study, we consider a case with $N = 4$, $Num = 12$, $s = 1$ Mbits, $M = 2$ and 4, respectively. Table 2 shows the simulation results and analysis results under the same condition, where the number in "()" denotes the number of the additional movement operations. (Note that in this case, we simulate 5000 cases of all of the $(4!)^3$ ($= 13824$) initial states of the multi-disk drive and calculate the average results.) Compared with the analysis results shown in Table 2-(b), the simulation results shown in Table 2-(a) are very close to those shown in Table 2-(b). Note that the 12 new added subobjects are generated randomly.

6 Conclusion

In this paper, we have proposed an efficient *conflict-resolution* approach to the insertion/deletion operations on continuous media that are striped into a multi-disk drive without reorganization of the whole data. Only when a conflict occurs, one movement operation is required. From our performance analysis and simulation results, we have shown that the average number of additional movements for any subobject insertion with $M = (2 \times d)$ is no more than 5, when there is an object that is divided into 120 subobjects and is striped on a multi-disk drive with 12 disks. One of the most important challenges in a video server is to support *interactive browsing* functions such as *fast forward* and *fast backward*. How to support the continuous display of multiple objects at different display speed rates, simultaneously, without any additional resource, will be an important research direction.

References

[1] Berson, Steven, Ghandeharizadeh, Shahram, Muntz, Richard and Ju, Xiangyu, "Staggered Striping in Multimedia Information Systems," *ACM SIGMOD*, pp. 79-90, 1994.

[2] Buford, John F. K., "Multimedia File Systems and Information Models," in *Multimedia Systems*, Buford, John F. K., Editor, Addison-Wesley, 1994

[3] Chen, Ming-Syan, Kandlur, Dilip D. and Yu, Philip S., "Storage and Retrieval Methods to Support Fully Interactive Playout in a Disk-Array-Based Video Server," *ACM Multimedia Systems*, Vol. 3, pp. 126-135, 1995.

[4] Christodoulakis, S. and Koveos, L., "Multimedia Information Systems: Issues and Approaches," in *Modern Database Systems: the Object Model, Interoperability and Beyond*, Kim, W., Editor, Addison-Wesley, 1994

[5] Chaudhuri, S., Ghandeharizadeh, S. and Shahabi, S., "Avoiding Retrieval of Composite Multimedia Objects," *Proc. of VLDB*, pp. 287-298, 1995.

[6] Gemmell, Jim and Christodoulakis, Stavros, "Principles of Delay-Sensitive Multimedia Data Storage and Retrieval," *ACM Transactions on Information Systems*, Vol. 10, No. 1, pp 51-90, Jan. 1992.

[7] Gemmell, D. James, Vin, Harrick M., Kandlur, D. D., Rangan, P. Venkat and Rowe, L. A., "Multimedia Storage Servers: A Tutorial," *IEEE Computer*, pp. 40-49, May 1995.

[8] Ghandeharizadeh, Shahram and Dewitt, D., "A Multiuser Performance Analysis of Alternative Declustering Strategies," *Proc. of IEEE International Conference on Data Engineering*, pp. 466-475, 1990.

[9] Ghandeharizadeh, Shahram and Ramos, Luis, "Continuous Retrieval of Multimedia Data Using Parallelism," *IEEE Transactions on Knowledge and Data Engineering*, Vol. 5, No. 4, pp. 658-669, August 1993.

[10] Keeton, Kimberly, and Katz, Randy H., "Evaluating Video Layout Strategies for a High-Performance Storage Server," *ACM Multimedia Systems*, Vol. 3, pp. 43-52, 1995.

[11] Liu, Jonathan C L, Du, David H C and Schnepf James A, "Supporting Random Access on Real-Time Retrieval of Digital Continuous Media," *Computer Communications*, Vol. 18, No. 3, pp. 145-159, March 1995.

[12] Lougher, P. and Shepherd, D., "The Design of a Storage Server for Continuous Media," *The Computer Journal*, Vol. 36, No. 1, pp. 33-42, 1993.

[13] Ozden, Banu, Biliris, Alexandros, Rastogi, Rajeev, and Silberschatz, Avi, "A Low-Cost Storage Server for Movie on Demand Databases," *Proc. of VLDB*, pp. 594-605, 1994.

[14] Ozden, Banu, Rastogi, Rajeev, and Silberschatz, Avi, "On the Design of a Low-Cost Video-On-Demand Storage System," *ACM Multimedia Systems*, Vol. 4, pp. 40-54, 1996.

[15] Patterson, D., Gibson, G. and Katz, R., "A Case for Redundant Arrays of Inexpensive Disks (RAID)," *ACM SIGMOD*, pp. 109-116, 1988.

[16] Rangan, P. Venkat Rangan, and Vin, Harrick M., "Designing File Systems for Digital Video and Audio," *Proc. 13th ACM Symposium on Operating System Principles*, pp. 81-94, 1991.

[17] Rangan, P. Venkat Rangan, Vin, Harrick M. and Ramanathan, Srinivas, "Designing an On-Demand Multimedia Service," *IEEE Communications Magazine*, pp. 56-64, July 1992.

[18] Rangan, P. Venkat and Vin, Harrick M., "Efficient Storage Techniques for Digital Continuous Multimedia," *IEEE Transactions on Knowledge and Data Engineering*, Vol. 5, No. 4, pp. 564-573, August 1993.

[19] Salem, K. and Carcia-Molina, H., "Disk Striping," *Proc. of IEEE International Conference on Data Engineering*, pp. 336-342, 1986.

[20] Steinmetz, R., "Multimedia File Systems Survey: Approaches for Continuous Media Disk Scheduling," *Computer Communications*, Vol. 18, No. 3, pp. 133-144, March 1995.

[21] Vin, Harrick M. and Rangan, P. Venkat Rangan, "Designing a Multiuser HDTV Storage Server," *IEEE Journal on Selected Areas in Communications*, Vol. 11, No. 1, pp. 153-164, Jan. 1993.

[22] Yu, Clement, Sun, Wei, Bitton, Dina, Yang Qi, Bruno, Richard and Tullis, John, "Efficient Placement of Audio Data on Optimal Disks for Real-Time Applications," *Communications of ACM*, Vol. 32, No. 7, pp. 862-871, July 1989.

Industrial Session 4B

Parallelism in Commercial Systems

Parallel Data Warehouse Architecture

G. Hallmark

DB2 Common Server Parallelism

J. McPherson

Session 5A

Data Warehousing and Mediator Systems

The Strobe Algorithms for Multi-Source Warehouse Consistency[*]

Yue Zhuge, Hector Garcia-Molina, and Janet L. Wiener

Computer Science Department
Stanford University
Stanford, CA 94305-2140, USA
{zhuge,hector,wiener}@cs.stanford.edu
http://db.stanford.edu/warehouse

Abstract

A warehouse is a data repository containing integrated information for efficient querying and analysis. Maintaining the consistency of warehouse data is challenging, especially if the data sources are autonomous and views of the data at the warehouse span multiple sources. Transactions containing multiple updates at one or more sources, e.g., batch updates, complicate the consistency problem. In this paper we identify and discuss three fundamental transaction processing scenarios for data warehousing. We define four levels of consistency for warehouse data and present a new family of algorithms, the Strobe family, that maintain consistency as the warehouse is updated, under the various warehousing scenarios. All of the algorithms are incremental and can handle a continuous and overlapping stream of updates from the sources. Our implementation shows that the algorithms are practical and realistic choices for a wide variety of update scenarios.

1 Introduction

A *data warehouse* is a repository of integrated information from distributed, autonomous, and possibly heterogeneous, sources. Figure 1 illustrates the basic warehouse architecture. At each source, a monitor collects the data of interest and sends it to the warehouse. The monitors are responsible for identifying changes in the source data, and notifying the warehouse. At the warehouse, the integrator receives the source data, performs any necessary data integration or translation, adds any extra desired information, such as timestamps for historical analysis, and tells the warehouse to store the data. In effect, the warehouse caches a materialized view of the source data[13]. The data is then readily available to user applications for querying and analysis.

Most current commercial warehousing systems (e.g., Prism, Redbrick) focus on storing the data for efficient access, and on providing extensive querying facilities at the warehouse. They ignore the comple-

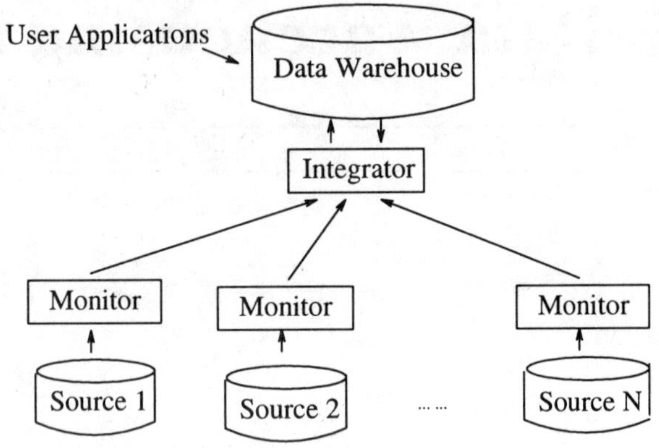

Figure 1: Data warehouse architecture

mentary problem of consistently integrating new data, assuming that this happens "off line" while queries are not being run. Of course, they are discovering that many customers have international operations in multiple time zones, so there is no convenient down time, a "night" or "weekend" when all of the recent updates can be batched and processed together, and materialized views can be recomputed. Furthermore, as more and more updates occur, the down time window may no longer be sufficient to process all of the updates [7].

Thus, there is substantial interest in warehouses that can absorb incoming updates and incrementally modify the materialized views at the warehouse, without halting query processing. In this paper we focus on this process and on how to ensure that queries see consistent data. The crux of the problem is that each arriving update may need to be integrated with data from other sources before being stored at the warehouse. During this processing, more updates may arrive at the warehouse, causing the warehouse to become inconsistent.

The following example illustrates some of the inconsistencies that may arise. For simplicity, we assume that both the warehouse and the sources use the relational model, and that the materialized view kept at the warehouse contains the key for each par-

---

[*]This work was partially supported by Rome Laboratories under Air Force Contract F30602-94-C-0237 and by an equipment grant from Digital Equipment Corporation.

146

ticipating relation. In this example, each update is a separate transaction at one of the sources. We also assume that the integrator is tightly coupled with the warehouse. Therefore, although the view maintenance computation is done by the integrator, and the actual view operation is done by the warehouse, we use the term *warehouse* (*WH*) to denote the combination of the integrator and the warehouse in Figure 1.

Example 1: View maintenance anomaly over multiple sources

Let view V be defined as $V = r_1 \bowtie r_2 \bowtie r_3$, where r_1, r_2, r_3 are three relations residing on sources x, y and z, respectively. Initially, the relations are

$$r_1 : \frac{A \quad B}{1 \quad 2} \qquad r_2 : \frac{B \quad C}{- \quad -} \qquad r_3 : \frac{C \quad D}{3 \quad 4}$$

The materialized view at the warehouse is $MV = \emptyset$. We consider two source updates: $U_1 = insert(r_2, [2, 3])$ and $U_2 = delete(r_1, [1, 2])$. Using a conventional incremental view maintenance algorithm [2], the following events may occur at the *WH*.

1. The *WH* receives $U_1 = insert(r_2, [2, 3])$ from source y. It generates query $Q_1 = r_1 \bowtie [2, 3] \bowtie r_3$. To evaluate Q_1, the *WH* first sends query $Q_1^1 = r_1 \bowtie [2, 3]$ to source x.

2. The *WH* receives $A_1^1 = [1, 2, 3]$ from source x. Query $Q_1^2 = [1, 2, 3] \bowtie r_3$ is sent to source z for evaluation.

3. The *WH* receives $U_2 = delete(r_1, [1, 2])$ from source x. Since the current view is empty, no action is taken for this deletion.

4. The *WH* receives $A_1^2 = [1, 2, 3, 4]$ from source z, which is the final answer for Q_1. Since there are no pending queries or updates, the answer is inserted into MV and $MV = [1, 2, 3, 4]$. This final view is incorrect. $\square$

In this example, the interleaving of query Q_1 with updates arriving from the sources causes the incorrect view. Note that even if the warehouse view is updated by completely recomputing the view — an approach taken by several commercial systems, such as Bull and Pyramid — the warehouse is subject to the same anomalies caused by the interleaving of updates with recomputation.

There are two straightforward ways to avoid this type of inconsistency, but we will argue that in general, neither one is desirable. The first way is to store copies of all relations at the warehouse. In our example, Q_1 could then be atomically evaluated at the warehouse, causing tuple $[1, 2, 3, 4]$ to be added to MV. When U_2 arrives, the tuple is deleted from MV, yielding a correct final warehouse state. While this solution may be adequate for some applications, we believe it has several disadvantages. First, the storage requirement at the warehouse may be very high. For instance, suppose that r_3 contains data on companies, e.g., their name, stock price, and profit history. If we copy all of r_3 at the warehouse, we need to keep tuples for *all* companies that exist anywhere in the world, not just

those we are currently interested in tracking. (If we do not keep data for all companies, in the future we may not be able to answer a query that refers to a new company, or a company we did not previously track, and be unable to atomically update the warehouse.) Second, the warehouse must integrate updates for all of the source data, not just the data of interest. In our company example, we would need to update the stock prices of all companies, as the prices change. This can represent a very high update load [4], much of it to data we may never need. Third, due to cost, copyright, or security, storing copies of all of the source data may not be feasible. For example, the source access charges may be proportional to the amount of data we track at the warehouse.

The second straightforward way to avoid inconsistencies is to run each update and all of the actions needed to incrementally integrate it into the warehouse as a distributed transaction spanning the warehouse and all the sources involved. In our example, if Q_1 runs as part of a distributed transaction, then it can read a consistent snapshot and properly update the warehouse. However, distributed transactions require a global concurrency control mechanism spanning all the sources, which may not exist. And even if it does, the sources may be unwilling to tolerate the delays that come with global concurrency control.

Instead, our approach is to make queries *appear* atomic by processing them intelligently at the warehouse (and without requiring warehouse copies of all relations). In our example, the warehouse notes that deletion U_2 arrived at the warehouse while it was processing query Q_1. Therefore, answer A_1 may contain some tuples that reflect the deleted r_1 tuple. Indeed, A_1 contains $[1, 2, 3, 4]$, which should not exist after $[1, 2]$ was deleted from r_1. Thus, the warehouse removes this tuple, leaving an empty answer. The materialized view is then left empty, which is the correct state after both updates take place. The above example gives the "flavor" of our solution; we will present more details as we explain our algorithms.

Note that the intelligent processing of updates at the warehouse depends on how and if sources run transactions. If some sources run transactions, then we need to treat their updates, whether they came from one source or multiple sources, as atomic units. Combining updates into atomic warehouse actions introduces additional complexities that will be handled by our algorithms. Since we do not wish to assume a particular transaction scenario, in this paper we cover the three main possibilities: sources run no transactions, some sources run local (but not global) transactions, and some sources run global transactions.

Although we are fairly broad in the transaction scenarios we consider, we do make two key simplifying assumptions: we assume that warehouse views are defined by relational project, select, join (PSJ) operations, and we assume that these views include the keys of all of the relations involved. We believe that PSJ views are the most common and therefore, it is a good subproblem on which to focus initially. We believe that requiring keys is a reasonable assumption, since keys make it easier for the applications to interpret and handle the warehouse data. Furthermore, if a user-specified view does not contain sufficient key information, the warehouse can simply add the key attributes to the view definition. (We have developed view maintenance algorithms for the case where some key data is not present, but they are not discussed here. They are substantially more complex than the ones presented here — another reason for including keys in the view.)

In our previous work [17] we considered a very restricted scenario: all warehouse data arrived from a single source. Even in that simple case, there are consistency problems, and we developed algorithms for solving them. However, in the more realistic multi-source scenario, it becomes *significantly* more complex to maintain consistent views. (For instance, the ECA and ECA-Key algorithms of [17] do not provide consistency in Example 1; they lead to the same incorrect execution shown.) In particular, the complexities not covered in our earlier work are as follows.

- An update from one source may need to be integrated with data from several other sources. However, gathering the data corresponding to one view update is not an atomic operation. No matter how fast the warehouse generates the appropriate query and sends it to the sources, receiving the answer is not atomic, because parts of it come from different, autonomous sources. Nonetheless, the view should be updated as if all of the sources were queried atomically.

- Individual sources may batch several updates into a single, source-local, transaction. For example, the warehouse may receive an entire day's updates in one transaction. These updates — after integration with data from other sources — should appear atomically at the warehouse. Furthermore, updates from several sources may together comprise one, global, transaction, which again must be handled atomically.

These complexities lead to substantially different solutions. In particular, the main contributions of this paper are:

1. We define and discuss all of the above update and transaction scenarios, which require increasingly complex algorithms.

2. We identify four levels of consistency for warehouse views defined on multiple sources, in increasing order of difficulty to guarantee. Note that as concurrent query and update processing at warehouses becomes more common, and as warehouse applications grow beyond "statistical analysis," there will be more concern from users about the consistency of the data they are accessing [7]. Thus, we believe it is important to offer customers a variety of consistency options and ways to enforce them.

3. We develop the Strobe family of algorithms to provide consistency for each of the transaction scenarios. We have implemented each of the Strobe algorithms in our warehouse prototype [16], demonstrating that the algorithms are practical and efficient.

4. We map out the space of warehouse maintenance algorithms (Figure 2). The algorithms we present in this paper provide a wide number of options for this consistency and distribution space.

The remainder of the paper is organized as follows. We discuss related work in Section 2. In Section 3, we define the three transaction scenarios and specify our assumptions about the order of messages and events in a warehouse environment. In Section 4 we define four levels of consistency and correctness, and discuss when each might be desirable. Then we describe our new algorithms in Section 5 and apply the algorithms to examples. We also demonstrate the levels of consistency that each algorithm achieves for the different transaction scenarios. In Section 6, we adapt the algorithms so that the warehouse can reflect every update individually, and show that the algorithms will terminate. We conclude in Section 7 by outlining optimizations to our algorithms and our future work.

2   Related research

The work we describe in this paper is closely related to research in three fields: data warehousing, data consistency and incremental maintenance of materialized views. We discuss each in turn.

Data warehouses are large repositories for analytical data, and have recently generated tremendous interest in industry. A general description of the data warehousing idea may be found in [11]. Companies such as Red Brick and Prism have built specialized data warehousing software, while almost all other database vendors, such as Sybase, Oracle and IBM, are targeting their existing products to data warehousing applications.

A warehouse holds a copy of the source data, so essentially we have a distributed database system with replicated data. However, because of the autonomy of the sources, traditional concurrency mechanisms are often not applicable [3]. A variety of concurrency control schemes have been suggested over the years for such environments. They either provide weaker notions of consistency, e.g., [6], or exploit the semantics of applications. The algorithms we present in this paper exploit the semantics of materialized view maintenance to obtain consistency without traditional distributed concurrency control. Furthermore, they offer a variety of consistency levels that are useful in the context of warehousing.

Many incremental view maintenance algorithms have been developed for centralized database systems, e.g., [2, 9, 5] and a good overview of materialized views and their maintenance can be found in [8]. Most of these solutions assume that a single system controls all of the base relations and understands the views and hence can intelligently monitor activities and compute all of the information that is needed for updating the views. As we showed in Example 1, when a centralized algorithm is applied to the warehouse, the warehouse user may see inconsistent views of the source data. These inconsistent views arise regardless of whether the centralized algorithm computes changes using the old base relations, as in [2], or using the new base relations, as in [5]. The crux of the warehouse problem is that the exact state of the base relations (old or new) when the incremental changes are computed at the sources is unknown, and our algorithms filter out or add in recent modifications dynamically.

Previous distributed algorithms for view maintenance, such as those in [14, 12], rely on timestamping the updated tuples. For a warehousing environment, sources can be legacy systems so we cannot assume that they will help by transmitting all necessary data or by attaching timestamps.

Hull and Zhou [10] provide a framework for supporting distributed data integration using materialized views. However, their approach first materializes each base relation (or relevant portion), then computes the view from the materialized copies; on the other hand, we propose algorithms to maintain joined views directly, without storing any auxiliary data. We compare our definition of consistency with theirs in Section 4. Another recent paper by Baralis, et al. [1] also uses timestamps to maintain materialized views at a warehouse. However, they assume that the warehouse never needs to query the sources for more data, hence circumventing all of the consistency problems that we address.

A warehouse often processes updates (from one or more transactions) in batch mode. Conventional algorithms have no way to ensure that an entire transaction is reflected in the view at the same time, or that a batch representing an entire day (or hour, or week, or minute) of updates is propagated to the view simultaneously. In this paper we present view maintenance algorithms that address these problems.

Finally, as we mentioned in Section 1, in [17] we showed how to provide consistency in a restricted single-source environment. Here we study the more general case of multiple sources and transactions that may span sources.

3 Warehouse transaction environment

The complexity of designing consistent warehouse algorithms is closely related to the scope of transactions at the sources. The larger the scope of a transaction, the more complex the algorithm becomes. In this section, we define three common transaction scenarios, in increasing order of complexity, and spell out our assumptions about the warehouse environment. In particular, we address the ordering of messages between sources and the warehouse, and define a source *event*. We use the relational model for simplicity; each update therefore consists of a single tuple action such as inserting or deleting a tuple.

3.1 Update transaction scenarios

The three transaction scenarios we consider in this paper are:

1. *Single update transactions.* Single update transactions are the simplest; each update comprises

its own transaction and is reported to the warehouse separately. Actions of legacy systems that do not have transactions fall in this category: as each change is detected by the source monitor, it is sent to the warehouse as a single update transaction.

2. *Source-local transactions.* A source-local transaction is a sequence of actions performed at the same source that together comprise one transaction. The goal is therefore to reflect all of these actions atomically at the warehouse. We assume that each source has a local serialization schedule of all of its source-local transactions. Single update transactions are special cases of source-local transactions. Database sources, for example, are likely to have source-local transactions. We also consider batches of updates that are reported together to be a single, source-local, transaction.

3. *Global transactions.* In this scenario there are global transactions that contain actions performed at multiple sources. We assume that there is a global serialization order of the global transactions. (If there is not, it does not matter how we order the transactions at the warehouse.) The goal is therefore to reflect the global transactions atomically at the warehouse. Depending on how much information the warehouse receives about the transaction, this goal is more or less achievable. For example, unless there are global transaction identifiers, or the entire transaction is reported by a single source, the warehouse cannot tell which source-local transactions together comprise a global transaction.

For each transaction scenario, we make slightly different assumptions about the content of messages.

3.2 Messages

There are two types of messages from the sources to the warehouse: reporting an update and returning the answer to a query. There is only one type of message in the other direction; the warehouse may send queries to the sources.

We assume that each single update transaction and source-local transaction is reported in one message, at the time that the transaction commits. For example, a relational database source might trigger sending a message on transaction commit [15]. However, batching multiple transactions into the same message does not affect the algorithms of Section 5. For global transactions, updates can be delivered in a variety of ways. For example, the site that commits the transaction may collect all of the updates and send them to the warehouse at the commit point. As an alternative, each site may send its own updates, once it knows the global transaction has committed. In Section 5.4 we discuss the implications of the different schemes.

3.3 Event Ordering

Each source action, plus the resulting message sent to the warehouse, is considered one event. For example, evaluating a query at a source and sending the answer back to the warehouse is considered one event. We assume events are atomic, and are ordered by the sequence of the corresponding actions. (In [18] we discuss what to do when this assumption does not hold.) We also assume that any two messages sent from one source to the warehouse are delivered in the same order as they were sent. (This can be enforced by numbering messages.) We place no restrictions on the order in which messages sent from different sources to the warehouse are delivered.

3.4 Discussion

In practice, the update transaction scenario seen at the warehouse depends primarily on the capabilities of the underlying sources. For example, it is currently common practice to report updates from a source periodically. Instead of reporting each change, a monitor might send all of the changes that occurred over the last hour or day to the warehouse, as a single batch transaction. Periodic snapshots may be the only way for the monitor of an unsophisticated legacy source to report changes, or a monitor might choose to report updates lazily when the warehouse does not need to be kept strictly up to date.

In general, smarter monitors (those which help to group or classify updates or those which coordinate global transactions) save the warehouse processing and may enable the warehouse to achieve a higher level of consistency, as we will see in Section 5.4. We believe that today most warehouse transaction environments will support either single-update transactions or source-local transactions (or both), but will not have any communication or coordination between sources. Still, for completeness, we believe it is important to understand the global transaction scenario, which may be more likely in the future.

4 Correctness and consistency

Before describing our algorithms, we first define what it means for an algorithm to be correct in an environment where activity at the sources is decoupled from the view at the warehouse. In particular, we are concerned with what it means for a warehouse view to be consistent with the original source data. Since each source update may involve fetching data from multiple sources in order to update the warehouse view, we first define *states* at the sources and at the warehouse.

4.1 Source and warehouse states

Each warehouse state ws represents the contents of the warehouse. The warehouse state changes whenever the view is updated. Let the warehouse states be $ws_0, ws_1, ws_2, \ldots, ws_f$. (We assume there is a final warehouse state after all activity ceases.) We consider one view V at the warehouse, which is defined over a set of base relations at one or more sources. The view at state ws_j is $V(ws_j)$.

Let there be u sources, where each source has a unique id x ($1 \leq x \leq u$). A source state ss is a vector that contains u elements and represents the (visible) state of each source at a given instant in time. The xth component, $ss[x]$, is the state of source x. Source states represent the contents of source base relations. We assume that source updates are executed is a serializable fashion across all sources, i.e., there is some

serial schedule S that represents execution of the updates. (However, what constitutes a transaction varies according to the scenario.) We assume that ss_q is the final state after S completes. $V(ss)$ is the result of computing the view V over the source state ss. That is, for each relation r at source x that contributes to the view, $V(ss)$ is evaluated over r at the state $ss[x]$.

Each source transaction is guaranteed to bring the sources from one consistent state to another. For any serial schedule R, we use $result(R)$ to refer to the source state vector that results from its execution.

4.2 Levels of consistency

Assume that the view at the warehouse is initially synchronized with the source data, i.e., $V(ss_0) = V(ws_0)$. We define four levels of consistency for warehouse views. Each level subsumes all prior levels. These definitions are a generalization of the ones in [17] for a multi-source warehouse environment.

1. **Convergence:** For all finite executions, $V(ws_f) = V(ss_q)$. That is, after the last update and after all activity has ceased, the view is consistent with the source data.

2. **Weak consistency:** Convergence holds and, for all ws_i, there exists a source state vector ss_j such that $V(ws_i) = V(ss_j)$. Furthermore, for each source x, there exists a serial schedule $R = T_1, \ldots, T_k$ of (a subset of all) transactions such that $result(R)[x] = ss_j[x]$. That is, each warehouse state reflects a valid state at each source, and there is a locally serializable schedule at each source that achieves that state. However, each source may reflect a different serializable schedule and the warehouse may reflect a different set of committed transactions at each source.

3. **Strong consistency:** Convergence holds and there exists a serial schedule R and a mapping m, from warehouse states into source states, with the following properties: (i) Serial schedule R is equivalent to the actual execution of transactions at the sources. It defines a sequence of source states $ss_1, ss_2, \ldots$ where ss_j reflects the first j transactions (i.e., $ss_j = result(R')$ where R' is the R prefix with j transactions). (ii) For all ws_i, $m(ws_i) = ss_j$ for some j and $V[ws_i] = V[ss_j]$. (iii) If $ws_i < ws_k$, then $m(ws_i) < m(ws_k)$. That is, each warehouse state reflects a set of valid source states, reflecting the *same* globally serializable schedule, and the order of the warehouse states matches the order of source actions.

4. **Completeness:** In addition to strong consistency, for every ss_j defined by R, there exists a ws_i such that $m(ws_i) = ss_j$. That is, there is a complete order-preserving mapping between the states of the view and the states of the sources.

Hull and Zhou's definition of consistency for replicated data [10] is similar to our strong consistency, except that they also require global timestamps across sources, which we do not. Also, our strong consistency is less restrictive than theirs in that we do not require any fixed order between two non-conflicting actions. Our definition is compatible with standard serializability theory. In fact, our consistency definition can be rephrased in terms of serializability theory, by treating the warehouse view evaluation as a read only transaction at the sources [18].

Although completeness is a nice property since it states that the view "tracks" the base data exactly, we believe it may be too strong a requirement and unnecessary in most practical warehousing scenarios. In some cases, convergence may be sufficient, i.e., knowing that "eventually" the warehouse will have a valid state, even if it passes through intermediate states that are invalid. In most cases, strong consistency is desirable, i.e., knowing that every warehouse state is valid with respect to a source state. In the next section, we show that an algorithm may achieve different levels of consistency depending on the update transaction scenario to which it is applied.

5 Algorithms

In this section, we present the Strobe family of algorithms. The Strobe algorithms are named after strobe lights, because they periodically "freeze" the constantly changing sources into a consistent view at the warehouse. Each algorithm was designed to achieve a specific level of correctness for one of the three transaction processing scenarios. We discuss the algorithms in increasing level of complexity: the Strobe algorithm, which is the simplest, achieves strong consistency for single update transactions. The Transaction-Strobe algorithm achieves strong consistency for source-local transactions, and the Global-Strobe algorithm achieves strong consistency for global transactions. In Section 6 we present modifications to these algorithms that attain completeness for their respective transaction scenarios.

5.1 Terminology

First, we introduce the terminology that we use to describe the algorithms.

Definition: A view V at the warehouse over n relations is defined by a Project-Select-Join (PSJ) expression $V = \Pi_{proj}(\sigma_{cond}(r_1 \bowtie r_2 \bowtie \ldots \bowtie r_n))$. $\square$

Any two relations may reside at the same or at different sources, and any relational algebra expression constructed with project, select, and join operations can be transformed into an equivalent expression of this form. Moreover, although we describe our algorithms for PSJ views, our ideas can be used to adapt any existing centralized view maintenance algorithm to a warehousing environment.

As we mentioned in the introduction, we assume that the projection list contains the key attributes for each relation. We expect most applications to require keys anyway, and if not, they can be added to the view by the warehouse.

When a view is defined over multiple sources, an update at one source is likely to initiate a multi-source

query Q at the warehouse. Since we cannot assume that the sources will cooperate to answer Q, the warehouse must therefore decide where to send the query first.

Definition: Suppose we are given a query Q that needs to be evaluated. The function $next\_source(Q)$ returns the pair (x, Q^i) where x is the next source to contact, and Q^i is the portion of Q that can be evaluated at x. If Q does not need to be evaluated further, then x is nil. A^i is the answer received at the warehouse in response to subquery Q^i. Query $Q\langle A^i \rangle$ denotes the remaining query after answer A^i has been incorporated into query Q. $\square$

For PSJ queries, $next\_source$ will always choose a source containing a relation that can be joined with the known part of the query, rather than requiring the source to ship the entire base relation to the warehouse (which may not even be possible). As we will see later, queries generated by an algorithm can also be unions of PSJ expressions. For such queries, $next\_source$ simply selects one of the expressions for evaluation. An improvement would be to find common subexpressions.

Example 2: Using $next\_source$

Let relations r_1, r_2, r_3 reside at sources x, y, z, respectively, let $V = r_1 \bowtie r_2 \bowtie r_3$, and let U_2 be an update to relation r_2 received at the warehouse. Therefore, query $Q = (r_1 \bowtie U_2 \bowtie r_3)$, and $next\_source(Q) = (x, Q^1 = r_1 \bowtie U_2)$. When the warehouse receives answer A^1 from x, $Q\langle A^1 \rangle = A^1 \bowtie r_3$. Then $next\_source(A^1 \bowtie r_3) = (z, Q^2 = A^1 \bowtie r_3)$, since there is only one relation left to join in the query. A^2 is the final answer. $\square$

In the above example, the query was sent to source x first. Alternatively, $next\_source(Q) = (z, U_2 \bowtie r_3)$. When there is more than one possible relation to join with the intermediate result, $next\_source$ may use statistics (such as those used by query optimizers) to decide which part of the query to evaluate next.

We are now ready to define the procedure $source\_evaluate$, which loops to compute the next portion of query Q until the final result answer A is received. In the procedure, WQ is the "working query" portion of query Q, i.e., the part of Q that has not yet been evaluated.

Procedure $source\_evaluate(Q)$
    i = 0; $WQ = Q$; $A^0 = Q$;
    $(x, Q^1) \leftarrow next\_source(WQ)$;
    While x is not nil do
        Let i $-$ i+1,
        — Send Q^i to source x;
        — When x returns A^i, let $WQ - WQ\langle A^i \rangle$;
        — Let $(x, Q^{i+1}) \leftarrow next\_source(WQ)$;
    Return(A^i).
End Procedure

The procedure *source_evaluate(Q)* may return an incorrect answer when there are concurrent transactions at the sources that interfere with the query evaluation. For example, in example 1, we saw that a delete that occurs at a source after a subquery has been evaluated there, but before the final answer is computed, may be skipped in the final query result. More subtle problems result when two subqueries of the same query are sent to the same source for evaluation at different times (to join with different relations) and use different source states, or when two subqueries are evaluated at two different sources in states that are inconsistent with each other. The key idea behind the Strobe algorithms is to keep track of the updates that occur during query evaluation, and to later compensate. We introduce the Strobe family with the basic Strobe algorithm.

For simplicity, here we only consider insertions and deletions in our algorithms. Conceptually, modifications of tuples (updates sent to the warehouse) can be treated at the warehouse simply as a deletion of the old tuple followed by an insertion of the new tuple. However, for consistency and performance, the delete and the insert should be handled "at the same time." Our algorithms can be easily extended for this type of processing, but we do not do it here. Further discussion of how to treat a modification as an insert and a delete may be found in [8].

5.2 Strobe

The Strobe algorithm processes updates as they arrive, sending queries to the sources when necessary. However, the updates are not performed immediately on the materialized view MV; instead, we generate a list of actions AL to be performed on the view. We update MV only when we are sure that applying all of the actions in AL (as a single transaction at the warehouse) will bring the view to a consistent state. This occurs when there are no outstanding queries and all received updates have been processed.

When the warehouse receives a deletion, it generates a delete action for the corresponding tuples (with matching key values) in MV. When an insert arrives, the warehouse may need to generate and process a query, using procedure *source_evaluate()*. While a Q query is being answered by the sources, updates may arrive at the warehouse, and the answer obtained may have missed their effects. To compensate, we keep a set $pending(Q)$ of the updates that occur while Q is being processed. After Q's answer is fully compensated, an insert action for MV is generated and placed on the action list AL.

Definition: The unanswered query set UQS is the set of all queries that the warehouse has sent to some source but for which it has not yet received an answer.
□

Definition: The operation $key\_delete(R, U_i)$ deletes from relation R the tuples whose key attributes have the same values as U_i.
□

Definition: $V\langle U \rangle$ denotes the view expression V with the tuple U substituted for U's relation.
□

Algorithm 1:   Strobe algorithm

At each source:

▷ After executing update U_i, send U_i to the warehouse.

▷ Upon receipt of query Q_i, compute the answer A_i over $ss[x]$ (the current source state), and send A_i to the warehouse.

At the warehouse:

▷ Initially, AL is set to empty $\langle\ \rangle$.

▷ Upon receipt of update U_i:

  ○ If U_i is a deletion
  — $\forall Q_j \in UQS$ add U_i to $pending(Q_j)$;
  — Add $key\_delete(MV, U_i)$ to AL.

  ○ If U_i is an insertion
  — Let $Q_i = V\langle U_i \rangle$ and set $pending(Q_i) = \emptyset$;
  — Let $A_i = source\_evaluate(Q_i)$;
  — $\forall U_j \in pending(Q_i)$, apply $key\_delete(A_i, U_j)$;
  — Add $insert(MV, A_i)$ to AL.

▷ When $UQS = \emptyset$, apply AL to MV as a single transaction, without adding duplicate tuples to MV. Reset $AL = \langle\ \rangle$.

End Algorithm 1

The following example applies the Strobe algorithm to the warehouse scenario in Example 1 in the introduction. Specifically, it shows why a deletion needs to be applied to the answer of a previous query, when the previous query's answer arrives at the warehouse later than the deletion.

Example 3:   Strobe avoids deletion anomaly

As in example 1, let view V be defined as $V = r_1 \bowtie r_2 \bowtie r_3$, where r_1, r_2, r_3 are three relations residing on sources x, y and z, respectively. Initially, the relations are

$$r_1 : \frac{\text{A} \quad \text{B}}{1 \quad 2} \qquad r_2 : \frac{\text{B} \quad \text{C}}{- \quad -} \qquad r_3 : \frac{\text{C} \quad \text{D}}{3 \quad 4}$$

The materialized view $MV = \emptyset$. We again consider two source updates: $U_1 = insert(r_2, [2, 3])$ and $U_2 = delete(r_1, [1, 2])$, and apply the Strobe algorithm.

1. $AL = \langle\ \rangle$. The WH receives $U_1 = insert(r_2, [2, 3])$ from source y. It generates query $Q_1 = r_1 \bowtie [2, 3] \bowtie r_3$. To evaluate Q_1, the WH first sends query $Q_1^1 = r_1 \bowtie [2, 3]$ to source x.

2. The WH receives $A_1^1 = [1, 2, 3]$ from source x. Query $Q_1^2 = [1, 2, 3] \bowtie r_3$ is sent to source z for evaluation.

3. The WH receives $U_2 = delete(r_1, [1, 2])$ from source x. It first adds U_2 to $pending(Q_1)$ and then adds $key\_delete(MV, U_2)$ to AL. The resulting $AL = \langle key\_delete(MV, U_2) \rangle$.

4. The WH receives $A_1^2 = [1, 2, 3, 4]$ from source z. Since $pending(Q)$ is not empty, the WH applies

$key\_delete(A_1^2, U_2)$ and the resulting answer $A_2 = \emptyset$. Therefore, nothing is added to AL. There are no pending queries, so the WH updates MV by applying $AL = \langle key\_delete(MV, U_2) \rangle$. The resulting $MV = \emptyset$. The final view is correct and strongly consistent with the source relations. $\square$

This example demonstrates how Strobe avoids the anomaly that caused both ECA-key and conventional view maintenance algorithms to be incorrect: by remembering the delete until the end of the query, Strobe is able to correctly apply it to the query result *before* updating the view MV. If the deletion U_2 were received before Q_1^1 had been sent to source x, then A_1^1 would have been empty and no extra action would have been necessary.

The Strobe algorithm provides strong consistency for all single-update transaction environments. A correctness proof is given in [18]. The intuition is that each time MV is modified, updates have quiesced and the view contents can be obtained by evaluating the view expression at the current source states. Therefore, although not all source states will be reflected in the view, the view always reflects a consistent set of source states.

5.3 Transaction-Strobe

The Transaction-Strobe (T-Strobe) algorithm adapts the Strobe algorithm to provide strong consistency for source-local transactions. T-Strobe collects all of the updates performed by one transaction and processes these updates as a single unit. Batching the updates of a transaction not only makes it easier to enforce consistency, but also reduces the number of query messages that must be sent to and from the sources.

Definition: $UL(T)$ is the *update list* of a transaction T. $UL(T)$ contains the inserts and deletes performed by T, in order. $IL(T) \subseteq UL(T)$ is the *insertion list* of T; it contains all of the insertions performed by T. $\square$

Definition: $key(U_i)$ denotes the key attributes of the inserted or deleted tuple U_i. If $key(U_i) = key(U_j)$ then U_i and U_j denote the same tuple (although other attributes may have been modified). $\square$

The source actions in T-Strobe are the same as in Strobe; we therefore present only the warehouse actions. First, the WH removes all pairs of insertions and deletions such that the same tuple was first inserted and then deleted. This removal is an optimization that avoids sending out a query for the insertion, only to later delete the answer. Next the WH adds all remaining deletions to the action list AL. Finally, the WH generates one query for all of the insertions. As before, deletions which arrive at the WH after the query is generated are subtracted from the query result.

The following example demonstrates that the Strobe algorithm may only achieve convergence, while the T-Strobe algorithm guarantees strong consistency for source-local transactions. Because the Strobe algo-

---

Algorithm 2: Transaction-Strobe algorithm

At the warehouse:

$\triangleright$ Initially, $AL = \langle \ \rangle$.

$\triangleright$ Upon receipt of $UL(T_i)$ for a transaction T_i:
  - For each $U_j, U_k \in UL(T_i)$ such that U_j is an insertion, U_k is a deletion, $U_j < U_k$ and $key(U_j) = key(U_k)$, remove both U_j and U_k from $UL(T_i)$.
  - For every deletion $U \in UL(T_i)$:
    - $\forall Q_j \in UQS$, add U to $pending(Q_j)$.
    - Add $key\_delete(MV, U)$ to AL.
  - Let $Q_i = \bigcup_{U_j \in IL(T)} V\langle U_j \rangle$, and set $pending(Q_i) = \emptyset$;
  - Let $A_i = source\_evaluate(Q_i)$;
  - $\forall U \in pending(Q_i)$, apply $key\_delete(A_i, U)$;
  - Add $insert(MV, A_i)$ to AL.

$\triangleright$ When $UQS = \emptyset$, apply AL to MV, without adding duplicate tuples to MV. Reset $AL = \langle \ \rangle$.

End Algorithm 2

---

rithm does not understand transactions, it may provide a view which corresponds to the "middle" of a transaction at a source state. However, Strobe will eventually provide the correct view, once the transaction commits, and is therefore convergent.

Example 4: T-Strobe provides stronger consistency than Strobe

Consider a simple view over one source defined as $V = r_1$. Assume attribute A is the key of relation r_1. Originally, the relation is: $r_1 = \dfrac{A \quad B}{1 \quad 2}$.

Initially $MV = ([1, 2])$. We consider one source transaction: $T_1 = \langle delete(r_1, [1, 2]), insert(r_1, [3, 4]) \rangle$.

When the Strobe algorithm is applied to this scenario, the warehouse firsts adds the deletion to AL. Since there are no pending updates, AL is applied to MV and MV is updated to $MV = \emptyset$, which is not consistent with r_1 either before or after T_1. Then the warehouse processes the insertion and updates MV again, to the correct view $MV = ([3, 4])$.

The T-Strobe algorithm, on the other hand, only updates MV after both updates in the transaction have been processed. Therefore, MV is updated directly to the correct view, $MV = ([3, 4])$. $\square$

The T-Strobe algorithm is inherently strongly consistent with respect to the source states defined after each source-local transaction.[1] T-Strobe can also pro-

---

[1]Note incidentally that if modifications are treated as a delete-insert pair, then T-Strobe can process the pair within a single transaction, easily avoiding inconsistencies. However, for performance reasons we may still want to modify T-Strobe to handle modifications as a third type of action processed at the

cess batched updates, not necessarily generated by the same transaction, but which were sent to the warehouse at the same time from the same source. In this case, T-Strobe also guarantees strong consistency if we define consistent source states to be those corresponding to the batching points at sources. Since it is common practice today to send updates from the sources periodically in batches, we believe that T-Strobe is probably the most useful algorithm. On single-update transactions, T-Strobe reduces to the Strobe algorithm.

5.4 Global-strobe

While the T-Strobe algorithm is strongly consistent for source-local transactions, it is only weakly consistent if global transactions are present. In [18] we present an example that illustrates this and develop a new algorithm, Global-Strobe (G-Strobe), that guarantees strong consistency for global transactions. G-Strobe is the same as T-Strobe except that it only updates MV (with the actions in AL) when the following three conditions have all been met. (T-Strobe only requires condition 1). Let TT be the set of transaction identifiers that the warehouse has received since it last updated MV.

1. $UQS = \emptyset$;
2. For each transaction T_i in TT that depends (in the concurrency control sense) on another transaction T_j, T_j is also in TT; and
3. All of the updates of the transactions in TT have been received and processed.

Due to space limitations, we do not present G-Strobe here.

6 Completeness and termination of the algorithms

A problem with Strobe, T-Strobe, and G-Strobe is that if there are continuous source updates, the algorithms may not reach a quiescent state where UQS is empty and the materialized view MV can be updated. To address this problem, in this section we present an algorithm, Complete Strobe (C-Strobe) that can update MV after any source update. For example, C-strobe can propagate updates to MV after a particular batch of updates has been received, or after some long period of time has gone by without a natural quiescent point. For simplicity, we will describe C-strobe enforcing an update to MV after each update; in this case, C-strobe achieves completeness. The extension to update MV after an arbitrary number of updates is straightforward and enforces strong consistency.

To force an update to MV after update U_i arrives at the warehouse, we need to compute the resulting view. However, other concurrent updates at the sources complicate the problem. In particular, consider the case where U_i is an insertion. To compute the next MV state, the warehouse sends a query Q_i to the sources. By the time the answer A_i arrives, the

warehouse may have received (but not processed) updates $U_{i+1}...U_k$. Answer A_i may reflect the effects of these later updates, so before it can use A_i to update MV, the warehouse must "subtract out" the effects of later updates from A_i, or else it will not get a consistent state. If one of the later updates, say U_j, is an insert, then it can just remove the corresponding tuples from A_i. However, if U_j is a delete, the warehouse may need to *add* tuples to A_i, but to compute these missing tuples, it must send additional queries to the sources! When the answers to these additional queries arrive at the warehouse, they may also have to be adjusted for updates they saw but which should not be reflected in MV. Fortunately, as we show below, the process does converge, and eventually the warehouse is able to compute the consistent MV state that follows U_i. After it updates MV, the warehouse then processes U_{i+1} in the same fashion.

Before presenting the algorithm, we need a few definitions.

Definition: $Q_{i,-,-}$ denotes the set of queries sent by the warehouse to compute the view after insertion update U_i. $Q_{i,j,-}$ are the queries sent in response to update U_j that occurred while computing the answer for a query in $Q_{i,-,-}$. A unique integer k is used to distinguish each query in $Q_{i,j,-}$ as $Q_{i,j,k}$. $\qquad\Box$

In the scenario above, for insert U_i we first generate $Q_{i,i,0}$. When its answer $A_{i,i,0}$ arrives, a deletion U_j received before $A_{i,i,0}$ requires us to send out another query, identified as Q_{i,j,new_j}. In the algorithm, new_j is used to generate the next unique integer for queries caused by U_j in the context of processing U_i.

When processing each update U_i separately, no action list AL is necessary. In the Strobe and T-strobe algorithms, AL keeps track of multiple updates whose processing overlaps. In the C-strobe algorithm outlined below, each update is compensated for subsequent, "held," updates so that it can be applied directly to the view. If C-strobe is extended (not shown here) to only force updates to MV periodically, after a batch of overlapping updates, then an action list AL is again necessary to remember the actions that should be applied for the entire batch.

Definition: $Q\langle U_i\rangle$ is the resulting query after the updated tuple in U_i replaces its base relation in Q. If the base relation of U_i does not appear in Q, then $Q\langle U_i\rangle = \emptyset$. $\qquad\Box$

Definition: *Delta* is the set of changes that need to be applied to MV for one insertion update. Note that *Delta*, when computed, would correspond to a single *insert*$(MV, Delta)$ action on AL if we kept an action list. (Deletion updates can be applied directly to MV, but insertions must be compensated first. *Delta* collects the compensations.) $\qquad\Box$

We also use a slightly different version of *key_delete*: *key_delete**$(Delta, U_k)$ only deletes from *Delta* those tuples that match with U_k on both key and non-key

---

warehouse. As stated earlier, we do not describe this straightforward extension here.

attributes (not just on key attributes). Finally, when we add tuples to *Delta*, we allow tuples with the same key values but different non-key values to be added. These tuples violate the key condition, but only appear in *Delta* temporarily. However, it is important to keep them in *Delta* for the algorithm to work correctly. (The reason for these changes is that when we "subtract out" the updates seen by $Q_{i,i,0}$, we first compensate for deletes, and then for all inserts. In between, we may have two tuples with the same key, one added from the compensation of a delete, and the other to be deleted when we compensate for inserts.)

In algorithm C-Strobe, the source behavior remains the same as for the Strobe algorithm, so we only describe the actions at the warehouse. C-Strobe is complete because MV is updated once after each update, and the resulting warehouse state corresponds to the source state after the same update. We prove the correctness of C-Strobe in [18].

Algorithm 3: Complete Strobe

At the warehouse:

▷ Initially, $Delta = \emptyset$.

▷ As updates arrive, they are placed in a holding queue.

▷ Process each update U_i in order of arrival:

   o If U_i is a deletion

    — Apply $key\_delete(MV, U_i)$.

   o If U_i is an insertion

    — Let $Q_{i,i,0} = V\langle U_i\rangle$;

    — Let $A_{i,i,0} = source\_evaluate(Q_{i,i,0})$;

    — Repeat for each $A_{i,j,k}$ until $UQS = \emptyset$:

      o Add $A_{i,j,k}$ to *Delta* (without adding duplicate tuples).

      o For all deletions U_p received between U_j and $A_{i,j,k}$:

        — Let $Q_{i,p,new_p} = Q_{i,j,k}\langle U_p\rangle$;

        — Let
$A_{i,p,new_p} = source\_evaluate(Q_{i,p,new_p})$;
When answer arrives, process starting 4 lines above.

    — For all insertions U_k received between U_i and the last answer, if $\neg\exists U_j < U_k$ such that U_j is a deletion and U_j, U_k refer to the same tuple, then apply $key\_delete^*(Delta, U_k)$.

    — Let $MV = MV + Delta$ and $Delta = \emptyset$.

End Algorithm 3

The compensating process (the loop in the algorithm) always terminates because any expression $Q_{i,j,k}\langle U_p\rangle$ always has one fewer base relation than $Q_{i,j,k}$. Let us assume that there are at most K updates that can arrive between the time a query is sent out and its answer is received, and that there are n base relations. When we process insertion U_i we send out query $Q_{i,i,0}$; when we get its answer we may have to send out at most K compensating queries with $n-2$

base relations each. For each of those queries, at most K queries with $n-3$ base relations may be sent, and so on. Thus, the total number of queries sent in the loop is no more than K^{n-2}, and the algorithm eventually finishes processing U_i and updates MV.

The number of compensating queries may be significantly reduced by combining related queries. For example, when we compensate for $Q_{i,i,0}$, the above algorithm sends out up to K queries. However, since there are only n base relations, we can group these queries into $n - 1$ queries, where each combined query groups all of the queries generated by an update to the same base relation. If we continue to group queries by base relation, we see that the total number of compensating queries cannot exceed $(n-1)\times(n-2)\times\ldots\times1 = (n-1)!$. That is, C-Strobe will update MV after at most $(n - 1)!$ queries are evaluated. If the view involves a small number of relations, then this bound will be relatively small. Of course, this maximum number of queries only occurs under extreme conditions where there is a continuous stream of updates.

We now apply the C-Strobe algorithm to the warehouse scenario in Example 1, and show how C-Strobe processes this scenario differently from the Strobe algorithm (shown in Example 3).

Example 5: Complete Strobe

As in examples 1 and 3, let view V be defined as $V = r_1 \bowtie r_2 \bowtie r_3$, where r_1, r_2, r_3 are three relations residing on sources x, y and z, respectively. Initially, the relations are

$$r_1 : \frac{A \quad B}{1 \quad 2} \qquad r_2 : \frac{B \quad C}{- \quad -} \qquad r_3 : \frac{C \quad D}{3 \quad 4}$$

The materialized view $MV = \emptyset$. We again consider two source updates: $U_1 = insert(r_2, [2, 3])$ and $U_2 = delete(r_1, [1, 2])$, and apply the C-Strobe algorithm. There are two possible orderings of events at the warehouse. Here we consider one, and in the next example we discuss the other.

1. $Delta = \emptyset$. The WH receives from source y $U_1 = insert(r_2, [2, 3])$. It generates query $Q_{1,1,0} = r_1 \bowtie [2, 3] \bowtie r_3$. To evaluate $Q_{1,1,0}$, the WH first sends query $Q^1_{1,1,0} = r_1 \bowtie [2, 3]$ to source x.

2. The WH receives $A^1_{1,1,0} = [1, 2, 3]$ from source x. Query $Q^2_{1,1,0} = [1, 2, 3] \bowtie r_3$ is sent to source z for evaluation.

3. The WH receives $U_2 = delete(r_1, [1, 2])$ from source x. It saves this update in a queue.

4. The WH receives $A_{1,1,0} = A^2_{1,1,0} = ([1, 2, 3, 4])$ from source z, which is the final answer to $Q_{1,1,0}$. Since U_2 was received between $Q_{1,1,0}$ and $A_{1,1,0}$ and it is a deletion, the WH generates a query $Q_{1,2,1} = [1, 2] \bowtie [2, 3] \bowtie r_3$ and sends it to source z. Also, it adds $A_{1,1,0}$ to *Delta*, so *Delta* = $([1, 2, 3, 4])$.

5. The WH receives $A_{1,2,1} = ([1, 2, 3, 4])$ and tries to add it to *Delta*. Since it is a duplicate tuple, *Delta* remains the same.

6. $UQS = \emptyset$, so the *WH* updates the view to $MV = MV + Delta = ([1, 2, 3, 4])$.

7. Next the *WH* processes U_2 which is next in the update queue. Since U_2 is a deletion, it applies *key_delete**(MV, U_2) and $MV = \emptyset$. □

In this example, MV is updated twice, in steps 6 and 7. After step 6, MV is equal to the result of evaluating V after U_1 but before U_2 occurs. Similarly, after step 7, MV corresponds to evaluating V after U_2, but before any further updates occur, which is the final source state in this example. In the next example we consider the case where U_2 occurs before the evaluation of the query corresponding to U_1, and we show that compensating queries are necessary.

Example 6: C-Strobe applied again, with different timing of the updates

Let the view definition, initial base relations and source updates be the same as in example 5. We now consider a different set of events at the *WH*.

1. $Delta = \emptyset$. The *WH* receives from source y $U_1 = insert(r_2, [2, 3])$. It generates query $Q_{1,1,0} = r_1 \bowtie [2, 3] \bowtie r_3$. To evaluate $Q_{1,1,0}$, the *WH* first sends query $Q^1_{1,1,0} = r_1 \bowtie [2, 3]$ to source x.

2. The *WH* receives $U_2 = delete(r_1, [1, 2])$ from source x. It saves this update in a queue.

3. The *WH* receives $A^1_{1,1,0} = \emptyset$ from source x. This implies that $A_{1,1,0} = \emptyset$. Since U_2 was received between $Q_{1,1,0}$ and $A_{1,1,0}$, the *WH* generates the compensating query $Q_{1,2,1} = [1, 2] \bowtie [2, 3] \bowtie r_3$ and sends it to source z. Also, it adds $A_{1,1,0}$ to *Delta* and *Delta* is still empty.

4. The *WH* receives $A_{1,2,1} = ([1, 2, 3, 4])$ and adds it to *Delta*. $Delta = ([1, 2, 3, 4])$.

5. Since $UQS = \emptyset$, the *WH* updates the view to $MV = MV + Delta = ([1, 2, 3, 4])$.

6. The *WH* processes U_2. Since U_2 is a deletion, it applies *key_delete**(MV, U_2) and $MV = \emptyset$. □

As mentioned earlier, C-Strobe can be extended to update MV periodically, after processing every k updates. In this case, we periodically stop processing updates (placing them in a holding queue). We then process the answers to all queries that are in UQS as we did in C-Strobe, and then apply the action list AL to the view MV. The T-Strobe algorithm can also be made complete or periodic in a similar way. We call this algorithm C-TStrobe, but do not describe it here further.

7 Conclusions

In this paper, we identified three fundamental transaction processing scenarios for data warehousing and developed the Strobe family of algorithms to consistently maintain the warehouse data. Figure 2 summarizes the algorithms we discussed in this paper and their correctness. In the figure, "Conventional" refers to a conventional centralized view maintenance algorithm, while "ECA" and "ECA-Key" are algorithms from [17].

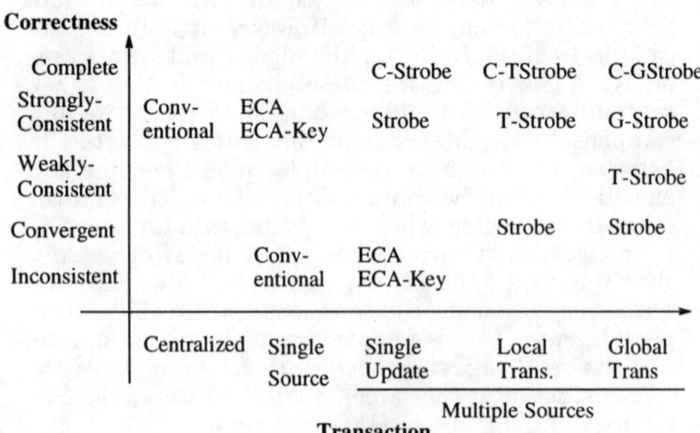

Figure 2: Consistency Spectrum

In Figure 2, an algorithm is shown in a particular scenario S and level of consistency L if it achieves L consistency in scenario S. Furthermore, the algorithm at (S, L) also achieves all lower levels of consistency for S, and achieves L consistency for scenarios that are less restrictive than S (scenarios to the left of S). For example, Strobe is strongly consistent for single update transactions at multiple sources. Therefore, it is weakly consistent and convergent (by definition) in that scenario. Similarly, Strobe is strongly consistent for centralized and single source scenarios.

Regarding the efficiency of the algorithms we have presented, there are four important points to make. First, there are a variety of enhancements that can improve efficiency substantially:

1. We can optimize global query evaluation. For example, in procedure *source_evaluate*(), the warehouse can group all queries for one source into one, or can find an order of sources that minimizes data transfers. It can also use key information to avoid sending some queries to sources.

2. We can find the optimal batch size for processing. By batching together updates, we can reduce the message traffic to and from sources. However, delaying update processing means the warehouse view will not be as up to date, so there is a clear tradeoff that we would like to explore.

3. Although we argued against keeping copies of *all* base relations at the warehouse, it may make sense to copy the most frequently accessed ones (or portions thereof), if they are not too large or expensive to keep up to date. This also increases the number of queries that can be answered locally.

The second point regarding efficiency is that, even if someone determines that none of these algorithms is efficient enough for their application, it is still very important to understand the tradeoffs involved. The Strobe algorithms exemplify the inherent cost of keeping a warehouse consistent. Given these costs, users can now determine what is best for them, given their consistency requirements and their transactional scenario.

Third, when updates arrive infrequently at the warehouse, or only in periodic batches with large gaps in between, the Strobe algorithms are as efficient as conventional algorithms such as [2]. They only introduce extra complexity when updates must be processed while other updates are arriving at the warehouse, which is when conventional algorithms cannot guarantee a consistent view.

Fourth, the Strobe algorithms are relatively inexpensive to implement, and we have incorporated them into the Whips (WareHousing Information Prototype at Stanford) prototype [16]. In our implementation, the Strobe algorithm is only 50 more lines of C++ code than the conventional view maintenance algorithm, and C-strobe is only another 50 lines of code. The core of each of the algorithms is about 400 lines of C++ code (not including evaluating each query). The ability to guarantee correctness (Strobe), the ability to batch transactions, and the ability to update the view consistently, whenever desired and without quiescing updates (C-strobe) cost only approximately 100 lines of code, and one programmer day.

As part of our ongoing warehousing work, we are currently evaluating the performance of the Strobe and T-Strobe algorithms and considering some of the optimizations mentioned above. We are also extending the algorithms to handle more general type of views, for example, views with insufficient key information, and views defined by more complex relational algebra expressions. Our future work includes designing maintenance algorithms that coordinate updates to multiple warehouse views.

Acknowledgments

We would like to thank Jennifer Widom and Jose Blakely for discussions that led to some of the ideas in this paper.

References

[1] E. Baralis, S. Ceri, and S. Paraboschi. Conservative timestamp revised for materialized view maintenance in a data warehouse. In *The Workshop on Materialized Views*, pages 1–9, June 1996.

[2] J. Blakeley, P.-A. Larson, and F. Tompa. Efficiently updating materialized views. In *SIGMOD*, pages 61–71, June 1986.

[3] Y. Breitbart, H. Garcia-Molina, and A. Silberschatz. Overview of multidatabase transaction management. *VLDB Journal*, 1(2):181–239, Oct. 1992.

[4] M. Cochinwala and J. Bradley. A multidatabase system for tracking and retrieval of financial data. In *VLDB*, pages 714–721, 1994.

[5] L. Colby, T. Griffin, L. Libkin, I. Mumick, and H. Trickey. Algorithms for deferred view maintenance. In *SIGMOD*, pages 469–480, June 1996.

[6] R. Gallersdorfer and M. Nicola. Improving performance in replicated databases through relaxed coherency. In *VLDB*, pages 445–456, Sept. 1995.

[7] R. Goldring and B. Hamel, Jan. 1996. Personal correspondence about IBM's data warehouse customer needs.

[8] A. Gupta and I. Mumick. Maintenance of materialized views: Problems, techniques, and applications. *IEEE Data Engineering Bulletin*, 18(2):3–18, June 1995.

[9] A. Gupta, I. Mumick, and V. Subrahmanian. Maintaining views incrementally. In *SIGMOD*, pages 157–166, May 1993.

[10] R. Hull and G. Zhou. A framework for supporting data integration using the materialized and virtual approaches. In *SIGMOD*, pages 481–492, June 1996.

[11] W. Inmon and C. Kelley. *Rdb/VMS: Developing the Data Warehouse*. QED Publishing Group, Boston, Massachusetts, 1993.

[12] B. Lindsay, L. Haas, C. Mohan, H. Pirahesh, and P. Wilms. A snapshot differential refresh algorithm. In *SIGMOD*, May 1986.

[13] D. Lomet and J. Widom, editors. *Special Issue on Materialized Views and Data Warehousing*, IEEE Data Engineering Bulletin 18(2), June 1995.

[14] A. Segev and J. Park. Updating distributed materialized views. *IEEE Transactions on Knowledge and Data Engineering*, 1(2):173–184, June 1989.

[15] Sybase, Inc. *Command Reference Manual*, release 4.9 edition, 1992.

[16] J. Wiener, H. Gupta, W. Labio, Y. Zhuge, H. Garcia-Molina, and J. Widom. A system prototype for warehouse view maintenance. In *The Workshop on Materialized Views*, pages 26–33, June 1996.

[17] Y. Zhuge, H. Garcia-Molina, J. Hammer, and J. Widom. View maintenance in a warehousing environment. In *SIGMOD*, pages 316–327, May 1995.

[18] Y. Zhuge, H. Garcia-Molina, and J. Wiener. The Strobe algorithms for multi-source warehouse consistency. Technical report, Stanford University, Sept. 1996. Available via anonymous ftp from host `db.stanford.edu` as `pub/zhuge/1996/strobe-full.ps`.

Making Views Self-Maintainable for Data Warehousing

Dallan Quass*
Computer Science Dept
Stanford University
Stanford, CA 94305
quass@cs.stanford.edu

Ashish Gupta
IBM Almaden
650 Harry Road
San Jose, CA 95120
agupta@cs.stanford.edu

Inderpal Singh Mumick
AT&T Research
600 Mountain Avenue
Murray Hill, NJ 07974
mumick@research.att.com

Jennifer Widom*
Computer Science Dept
Stanford University
Stanford, CA 94305
widom@cs.stanford.edu

Abstract

A data warehouse stores materialized views over data from one or more sources in order to provide fast access to the integrated data, regardless of the availability of the data sources. Warehouse views need to be maintained in response to changes to the base data in the sources. Except for very simple views, maintaining a warehouse view requires access to data that is not available in the view itself. Hence, to maintain the view, one either has to query the data sources or store auxiliary data in the warehouse. We show that by using key and referential integrity constraints, we often can maintain a select-project-join view without going to the data sources or replicating the base relations in their entirety in the warehouse. We derive a set of auxiliary views such that the warehouse view and the auxiliary views together are self-maintainable—*they can be maintained without going to the data sources or replicating all base data. In addition, our technique can be applied to simplify traditional materialized view maintenance by exploiting key and referential integrity constraints.*

1 Introduction

The problem of *materialized view maintenance* has received increasing attention recently [6, 7, 11], particularly due to its application to *data warehousing* [3, 14]. A view is a derived relation defined in terms of base relations. A view is said to be materialized when it is stored in the database, rather than computed from the base relations in response to queries. The materialized view maintenance problem is the problem of keeping the contents of the stored view consistent with the contents of the base relations as the base relations are modified.

Data warehouses store materialized views in order to provide fast access to information that is integrated from several distributed *data sources* [3]. The data sources may be heterogeneous and/or remote from the warehouse. Consequently, the problem of maintaining a materialized view in a data warehouse differs from the traditional view maintenance problem where the view and base data are stored in the same database. In particular, when changes are reported by one data source it may be necessary to access base data from other data sources in order to maintain the view [9].

For any view involving a join, maintaining the view when base relations change may require accessing base data, even when *incremental view maintenance* techniques are used [5, 8]. For example, for a view $R \bowtie S$, when an insertion to relation R is reported it is usually necessary to query S in order to discover which tuples in S join with the insertion to R. In the warehousing scenario, accessing base data means either querying the data sources or replicating the base relations in the warehouse. The problems associated with querying the data sources are that the sources may periodically be unavailable, may be expensive or time-consuming to query, and inconsistencies can result at the warehouse unless care is taken to avoid them through the use of special maintenance algorithms [14]. The problems associated with replicating base relations at the warehouse are the additional storage and maintenance costs incurred. In this paper we show that for many views, including views with joins, if key and referential integrity constraints are present then it is not necessary to replicate the base relations in their entirety at the warehouse in order to maintain a view. We give an algorithm for determining what extra information, called *auxiliary views*, can be stored at a warehouse in order to maintain a select-project-join view without accessing base data at the sources. The algorithm takes key and referential integrity constraints into account, which are often available in practice, to reduce the sizes of the auxiliary views. When a view together with a set of auxiliary views can be maintained at the warehouse without accessing base data, we say the views are *self-maintainable*.

Maintaining materialized views in this way is especially important for *data marts*—miniature data warehouses that contain a subset of data relevant to a particular domain of analysis or geographic region. As more and more data is collected into a centralized data warehouse it becomes increasingly important to distribute the data into localized data marts in order to reduce query bottlenecks at the central warehouse. When many data marts exist, the cost of replicating entire base relations (and their changes) at each data mart becomes especially prohibitive.

---

*This work was supported by Rome Laboratories under Air Force Contract F30602-94-C-023 and by equipment grants from Digital and IBM Corporations.

158

1.1 Motivating example

We start with an example showing how the amount of extra information needed to maintain a view can be significantly reduced from replicating the base relations in their entirety. Here we present our results without explanation of how they are obtained. We will revisit the example throughout the paper.

Consider a database of sales data for a chain of department stores. The database has the following relations.

```
store(store_id, city, state, manager)
sale(sale_id, store_id, day, month,
     year)
line(line_id, sale_id, item_id,
     sales_price)
item(item_id, item_name, category,
     supplier_name)
```

The first (underlined) attribute of each relation is a key for the relation. The `store` relation contains the location and manager of each store. The `sale` relation has one record for each sale transaction, with the store and date of the sale. A sale may involve several items, one per line on a sales receipt, and these are stored in the `line` relation, with one tuple for every item sold in the transaction. The `item` relation contains information about each item that is stocked. We assume that the following referential integrity constraints hold: (1) from `sale.store_id` to `store.store_id`, (2) from `line.sale_id` to `sale.sale_id`, and (3) from `line.item_id` to `item.item_id`. A referential integrity constraint from $S.B$ to $R.A$ implies that for every tuple $s \in S$ there must be a tuple $r \in R$ such that $s.B = r.A$.

Suppose the manager responsible for toy sales in the state of California is interested in maintaining a view of this year's sales: "all toy items sold in California in 1996 along with the sales price, the month in which the sale was made, and the name of the manager of the store where the sale was made. Include the item id, the sale id, and the line id."

```
CREATE VIEW cal_toy_sales AS
SELECT store.manager, sale.sale_id, sale.month,
       item.item_id, item.item_name, line.line_id,
       line.sales_price
FROM   store, sale, line, item
WHERE  store.store_id = sale.store_id and
       sale.sale_id = line.sale_id and
       line.item_id = item.item_id and
       store.state = "CA" and
       sale.year = 1996 and
       item.category = "toy"
```

The question addressed in this paper is: Given a view such as the one above, what auxiliary views can be materialized at the warehouse so that the view and auxiliary views together are self-maintainable?

Figure 1 shows SQL expressions for a set of three auxiliary views that are sufficient to maintain view `cal_toy_sales` for insertions and deletions to

each of the base relations, and are themselves self-maintainable. In this paper we give an algorithm for deriving such auxiliary views in the general case, along with incremental maintenance expressions for maintaining the original view and auxiliary views. Materializing the auxiliary views in Figure 1 repre-

```
CREATE VIEW aux_store AS
SELECT store_id, manager
FROM    store
WHERE state = "CA"


CREATE VIEW aux_sale AS
SELECT sale_id, store_id, month
FROM    sale
WHERE year = 1996 and
    store_id IN (SELECT store_id FROM aux_store)


CREATE VIEW aux_item AS
SELECT item_id, item_name
FROM    item
WHERE category = "toy"
```

Figure 1: Auxiliary Views for Maintaining the `cal_toy_sales` View

sents a significant savings over materializing the base relations in their entirety, as illustrated in Table 1.

Suppose that each of the four base relations contain the number of tuples listed in the first column of Table 1. Assuming that the selectivity of `store.state="CA"` is .02, the selectivity of `sale.year=1996` is .25, the selectivity of `item.category="toy"` is .05, and that distributions are uniform, the number of tuples passing local selection conditions (selection conditions involving attributes from a single relation) are given in the second column of Table 1. A related proposal by Hull and Zhou [10] achieves self-maintainability for base relation insertions by pushing down projections and local selection conditions on the base relations and storing at the warehouse only those tuples and attributes of the base relations that pass the selections and projections. Thus, their approach would require that the number of tuples appearing in the second column of Table 1 is stored at the warehouse to handle insertions.

We improve upon the approach in [10] by also taking key and referential integrity constraints into account. For example, we don't need to materialize any tuples from `line`, because the key and referential integrity constraints guarantee that existing tuples in `line` cannot join with insertions into the other relations. Likewise we can exclude tuples in `sale` that do not join with existing tuples in `store` whose state is California, because we are guaranteed that existing tuples in `sale` will never join with insertions to `store`. Using our approach can dramatically reduce the number of tuples in the auxiliary views over pushing down selections only. The number of tuples required by our approach to handle base relation insertions in our example appears in the third column of Table 1.

Base Relation	Tuples in Base Relation	Tuples Passing Local Selection Conditions	Tuples in Auxiliary Views of Figure 1
`store`	2,000	40	40
`sale`	80,000,000	20,000,000	400,000
`line`	800,000,000	800,000,000	0
`item`	1,000	50	50
Total	880,003,000	820,000,090	400,090

Table 1: Number of Tuples in Base Relations and Auxiliary Views

We can similarly use key constraints to handle deletions to the base relations without all the base relations being available. We can determine the effects of deletions from `sale`, `line`, and `item` without referencing any base relations because `cal_toy_sales` includes keys for these relations. We simply join the deleted tuples with `cal_toy_sales` on the appropriate key. Even though the view does not include a key for `store`, `store` is joined to `sale` on the key of `sale`, so the effect of deletions from `store` can be determined by joining the deleted tuples with `sale` and joining the result with `cal_toy_sales` on the key of `sale`.

Now consider updates. If all updates were treated as deletions followed by insertions, as is common in view maintenance, then the properties of key and referential integrity constraints that we use to reduce the size of auxiliary views would no longer be guaranteed to hold. Thus, updates are treated separately in our approach. Note that in data warehousing environments it is common for certain base relations not to be updated (e.g., relations `sale` and `line` may be append only). Even when base relations are updateable, it may be that not all attributes are updated (e.g., we don't expect to update the `state` of a `store`). If updates to the base relations in our example cannot change the values of attributes involved in selection conditions in the view, then the auxiliary views of Figure 1 are sufficient (even if attributes appearing in the view may be updated). If, on the other hand, updates to `sale` may change the year (for example), then an additional auxiliary view:

CREATE VIEW aux_line AS
SELECT line_id, sale_id, item_id, sales_price
FROM   line
WHERE item_id IN (SELECT item_id FROM aux_item)

would need to be materialized, which would have 40,000,000 tuples. That is, we would need to store all purchases of items whose category is "toy," in case the year of the corresponding sales record is changed later to 1996. Further, if updates may change the category of an item to "toy", we would need to keep all of the `line` relation in order to maintain the view.

In practice we have found that the attributes appearing in selection conditions in views tend to be attributes that are not updated, as in our example. As illustrated above and formalized later on, when such updates do not occur, much less auxiliary information is required for self-maintenance. Thus, exploiting knowledge of permitted updates is an important feature of our approach.

1.2   Self-Maintenance

Self maintenance is formally defined as follows. Consider a view V defined over a set of base relations $\mathcal{R}$. Changes, $\delta\mathcal{R}$, are made to the relations in $\mathcal{R}$ in response to which view V needs to be maintained. We want to compute δV, the changes to V, using as little extra information as possible. If δV can be computed using only the materialized view V and the set of changes $\delta\mathcal{R}$, then view V alone is self-maintainable. If view V is not self-maintainable, we are interested in finding a set of auxiliary views $\mathcal{A}$ defined on the same relations as V such that the set of views $\{V\}\cup\mathcal{A}$ is self-maintainable. Note that the set of base relations $\mathcal{R}$ forms one such set of auxiliary views. However, we want to find more "economical" auxiliary views that are much smaller than the base relations. The notion of a *minimal* set of auxiliary views sufficient to maintain view V is formalized in Section 3.

A more general problem is to make a set $\mathcal{V} = V_1, \ldots, V_n$ of views self-maintainable, i.e., find auxiliary views $\mathcal{A}$ such that $\mathcal{A}\cup\mathcal{V}$ is self-maintainable. Simply applying our algorithm to each view in $\mathcal{V}$ is not satisfactory, since opportunities to "share" information across original and auxiliary views will not be recognized. That is, the final set $\mathcal{A}\cup\mathcal{V}$ may not be minimal. We intend to investigate sets of views as future work.

1.3   Paper outline

The paper proceeds as follows. Section 2 presents notation, terminology, and some assumptions. Section 3 presents an algorithm for choosing a set of auxiliary views to materialize that are sufficient for maintaining a view and are self-maintainable. Section 4 shows how the view is maintained using the auxiliary views. Section 5 explains that the set of auxiliary views is itself self-maintainable. Related work appears in Section 6.

2   Preliminaries

We consider *select-project-join* (SPJ) views; that is, views consisting of a single projection followed by a single selection followed by a single cross-product over a set of *base relations*. As usual, any combination of selections, projections, and joins can be represented in this form. We assume that all base relations have keys but that a view might contain duplicates due to the projection at the view. In this paper we assume single-attribute keys and conjunctions of selection conditions (no disjunctions) for simplicity, but our results carry over to multi-attribute keys and selection conditions with disjunctions. In Section 3 we will impose certain additional restrictions on the view but we explain how those restrictions can be lifted in the full version of the paper [12]. We say that selection conditions involving attributes from a single relation are *local conditions*; otherwise they are *join conditions*. We say that attributes appearing in the final projection are *preserved* in the view.

In order to keep a materialized view up to date, changes to base relations must be propagated to the view. A *view maintenance expression* calculates the effects on the view of a certain type of change: insertions, deletions, or updates to a base relation. We use a *differential algorithm* as given in [5] to derive view maintenance expressions. For example, if view $V = R \bowtie S$, then the maintenance expression calculating the effect of insertions to R ($\triangle R$) is $\triangle V_R = \triangle R \bowtie S$, where $\triangle V_R$ represents the tuples to insert into V as a result of $\triangle R$.

Since in data warehousing environments updates to certain base relations may not occur, or may not change the values of certain attributes, we define each base relation R as having one of three types of updates, depending on how the updateable attributes are used in the view definition:

- If updates to R may change the values of attributes involved in selection conditions (local or join) in the view, then we say R has *exposed updates*.

- Otherwise, if updates to R will not change the values of attributes involved in selection conditions but may change the values of preserved attributes (attributes included in the final projection), then we say R has *protected updates*.

- Otherwise, if updates to R will not change the values of attributes involved in selection conditions or the values of preserved attributes, then we say R has *ignorable updates*.

Ignorable updates cannot have any affect on the view, so they do not need to be propagated. From now on we consider only exposed and protected updates. Exposed updates could cause new tuples to be inserted into the view or tuples to be deleted from the view, so we propagate them as deletions of tuples with the old values followed by insertions of tuples with the new values. For example, given a view $V = \sigma_{R.A=10} R \bowtie S$, if the value of $R.A$ for a tuple in R is changed from 0 to 10 then new tuples could be inserted into V as a result. Protected updates can only change the attribute values of existing tuples in the view; they cannot result in tuples being inserted into or deleted from the view. We therefore propagate protected updates separately. An alternate treatment of updates is considered in Section 4.1.2.

In addition to the usual select, project, and join symbols, we use $\ltimes$ to represent semijoin, $\uplus$ to represent union with bag semantics, and $\dot{-}$ to represent minus with bag semantics. We further assume that project (π) has bag semantics. The notation $\bowtie_X$ represents an equijoin on attribute X, while $\bowtie_{key(R)}$ represents an equijoin on the key attribute of R, assuming this attribute is in both of the joined relations. Insertions to a relation R are represented as $\triangle R$, deletions are represented as $\triangledown R$, and protected updates are represented as μR. Tuples in μR have two attributes corresponding to each of the attributes of R: one containing the value before update and another containing the value after update. We use π^{old} to project the old attribute values and π^{new} to project the new attribute values.

3 Algorithm for determining auxiliary views

We present an algorithm (Algorithm 3.1 below) that, given a view definition V, derives a set of auxiliary views $\mathcal{A}$ such that view V and the views in $\mathcal{A}$ taken together are self-maintainable; *i.e.*, can be maintained upon changes to the base relations without requiring access to any other data. Each auxiliary view $A_{R_i} \in \mathcal{A}$ is an expression of the form:

$$A_{R_i} = (\pi \sigma R_i) \ltimes A_{R_{j_1}} \ltimes A_{R_{j_2}} \ltimes \ldots \ltimes A_{R_{j_n}}$$

That is, each auxiliary view is a selection and a projection on relation R_i followed by zero or more semijoins with other auxiliary views. It can be seen that the number of tuples in each A_{R_i} is never larger than the number of tuples in R_i and, as we have illustrated in Section 1.1, may be much smaller. Auxiliary views of this form can easily be expressed in SQL, and they can be maintained efficiently as shown in [12].

Intuitively, the first part of the auxiliary view expression, $(\pi \sigma R_i)$, results from pushing down projections and local selection conditions onto R_i. Tuples in R_i that do not pass local selection conditions cannot possibly contribute to tuples in the view; hence they are not needed for view maintenance and therefore need not be stored in A_{R_i} at the warehouse. The semijoins in the second part of the auxiliary view expression further reduce the number of tuples in A_{R_i} by restricting it to contain only those tuples joinable with certain other auxiliary views. In addition, we will show that in some cases the need for A_{R_i} can be eliminated altogether.

We first need to present a few definitions that are used in the algorithm.

> Given a view V, let the *join graph* $G(V)$ of a view be a directed graph $\langle \mathcal{R}, \mathcal{E} \rangle$. $\mathcal{R}$ is the set of relations referenced in V, which form the vertices of the graph. There is a directed edge $e(R_i, R_j) \in \mathcal{E}$ from R_i to R_j if V contains a join condition $R_i.B = R_j.A$ and A is a key of R_j. The edge is annotated with RI if there is a referential integrity constraint from $R_i.B$ to $R_j.A$.

We assume for now that the graph is a forest (a set of trees). That is, each vertex has at most one edge leading into it and there are no cycles. This assumption still allows us to handle a broad class of views that occur in practice. For example, views involving *chain joins* (a sequence of relations $R_1, \ldots, R_n$ where the join conditions are between a foreign key of R_i and a key of $R_{i+1}, 1 <= i < n$) and *star joins* (one relation R_1, usually large, joined to a set of relations $R_2, \ldots, R_n$, usually small, where the join conditions are between foreign keys in R_1 and the keys of $R_2, \ldots, R_n$) have tree graphs. In addition, we assume that there are no self-joins. We explain how each of these assumptions can be removed in [12].

The following definition is used to determine the set of relations upon which a relation R_i depends—that is, the set of relations R_j in which (1) a foreign key in R_i is joined to a key of R_j, (2) there is a referential integrity constraint from R_i to R_j, and (3) R_j has protected updates.

$Dep(R_i, G) = \{R_j \mid \exists e(R_i, R_j)$ in $G(V)$ annotated with RI and R_j does not have exposed updates $\}$

$Dep(R_i, G)$ determines the set of auxiliary views to which R_i is semijoined in the definition of the auxiliary view A_{R_i} for R_i, given above. The reason for the semijoins is as follows. Let R_j be a member of $Dep(R_i, G)$. Due to the referential integrity constraint from R_i to R_j and the fact that the join between R_i and R_j is on a key of R_j, each tuple $t_i \in R_i$ must join with one and only one tuple $t_j \in R_j$. Suppose t_j does not pass the local selection conditions on R_j. Then t_j, and hence t_i, cannot contribute to tuples in the view. Because updates to R_j are protected (by the definition of $Dep(R_i, G)$), t_j, and hence t_i, will never contribute to tuples in the view, so it is not necessary to include t_i in A_{R_i} at the warehouse. It is sufficient to store only those tuples of R_i that pass the local selection conditions on R_i and join with a tuple in R_j that passes the local selection conditions on R_j (*i.e.*, $(\sigma R_i) \bowtie (\sigma R_j)$, where the semijoin condition is the same as the join condition between R_i and R_j in the view). That R_i can be semijoined with A_{R_j}, rather than σR_j, in the definition of A_{R_i} follows from a similar argument applied inductively.

The following definition is used to determine the set of relations upon which relation R_i transitively depends.

$Dep^+(R_i, G)$ is the transitive closure of $Dep(R_i, G)$

$Dep^+(R_i, G)$ is used to help determine whether it is necessary to store A_{R_i} at the warehouse in order to maintain the view or whether A_{R_i} can be eliminated altogether. Intuitively, if $Dep^+(R_i, G)$ includes all relations referenced in view V except R_i, then A_{R_i} is not needed for propagating insertions to any base relation onto V. The reason is that the key and referential integrity constraints guarantee that new insertions into the other base relations can join only with new insertions into R_i, and not with existing tuples in R_i. This behavior is explained further in Section 4.

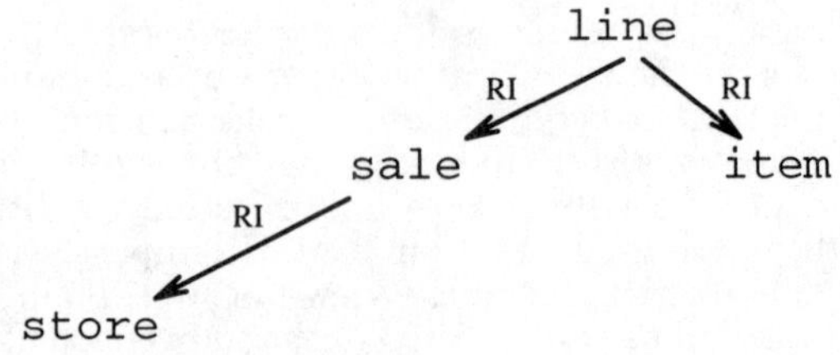

Figure 2: Join Graph $G(\texttt{cal\_toy\_sales})$

The following definition is used to determine the set of relations with which relation R_i needs to join so that the key of one of the joining relations is preserved in the view (where all joins must be from keys to foreign keys). If no such relation exists then $Need(R_i, G)$ includes all other relations in the view.

$$Need(R_i, G) = \begin{cases} \phi & \text{if the key of } R_i \text{ is preserved in } V, \\ \{R_j\} \cup Need(R_j, G) & \text{if the key of } R_i \text{ is not preserved in } V \text{ but there is an } R_j \text{ such that } e(R_j, R_i) \text{ in } G(V), \\ \mathcal{R} - \{R_i\} & \text{otherwise} \end{cases}$$

Note that because we restrict the graph to be a forest, there can be at most one R_j such that $e(R_j, R_i)$ is in $G(V)$.

$Need(R_i, G)$ is also used to help determine whether it is necessary to store auxiliary views. In particular, an auxiliary view A_{R_j} is necessary if R_j appears in the $Need$ set of some R_i. Intuitively, if the key of R_i is preserved in view V, then deletions and protected updates to R_i can be propagated to V by joining them directly with V on the key of R_i. Otherwise, if the key of R_i is not preserved in V but R_i is joined with another relation R_j on the key of R_i and V preserves the key of R_j, then deletions and protected updates to R_i can be propagated onto V by joining them first with R_j, then joining the result with V. In this case R_j is in the $Need$ set of R_i, and hence A_{R_j} is necessary. More generally, if the key of R_i is not present in V but R_i joins with R_j on the key of R_i, then auxiliary views for R_j and each of the relations in $Need(R_j, G)$ are necessary for propagating deletions and protected updates to R_i. Finally, if none of the above conditions hold then auxiliary views for all relations referenced in V other than R_i are necessary.

To illustrate the above definitions we consider again the `cal_toy_sales` view of Section 1.1. Figure 2 shows the graph $G(\texttt{cal\_toy\_sales})$. The Dep, Dep^+, and $Need$ functions for each of the base relations are given in Table 2. Assume for now that each base relation has protected updates.

Algorithm 3.1 appears in Figure 3. We will explain how the algorithm works on our running `cal_toy_sales` example. The auxiliary views generated by the algorithm are exactly those given in Figure 1 of Section 1.1. They are shown in relational algebra form in Table 3.

Algorithm 3.1
Input
   View V.
Output
   Set of auxiliary view definitions $\mathcal{A}$.
Method
   Let $\mathcal{R}$ be the set of relations referenced in V
   Construct graph $G(V)$
   for every relation $R_i \in \mathcal{R}$
      Construct $Dep(R_i, G)$, $Dep^+(R_i, G)$, and $Need(R_i, G)$
   for every relation $R_i \in \mathcal{R}$
   if $Dep^+(R_i, G) = \mathcal{R} - \{R_i\}$ and
      $\nexists R_j \in \mathcal{R}$ such that $R_i \in Need(R_j, G)$,
   then A_{R_i} is not needed
   else $A_{R_i} = (\pi_P \sigma_S R_i) \bowtie_{C_1} A_{R_{k_1}} \bowtie_{C_2} A_{R_{k_2}} \bowtie_{C_3} \ldots \bowtie_{C_m} A_{R_{k_m}}$, where
      P is the set of attributes in R_i that are preserved in V, appear in join conditions, or are
         a key of R_i,
      S is the strictest set of local selection conditions possible on R_i,
      C_l is the join condition $R_i.B = R_{k_l}.A$ with A a key of R_{k_l}, and
      $Dep(R_i, G) = \{R_{k_1}, R_{k_2}, \ldots, R_{k_m}\}$

$\diamond$

Figure 3: Algorithm to Derive Auxiliary Views

$Dep(\mathbf{store}, G)$	$=$	ϕ
$Dep(\mathbf{sale}, G)$	$=$	$\{\mathbf{store}\}$
$Dep(\mathbf{item}, G)$	$=$	ϕ
$Dep(\mathbf{line}, G)$	$=$	$\{\mathbf{sale}, \mathbf{item}\}$
$Dep^+(\mathbf{store}, G)$	$=$	ϕ
$Dep^+(\mathbf{sale}, G)$	$=$	$\{\mathbf{store}\}$
$Dep^+(\mathbf{item}, G)$	$=$	ϕ
$Dep^+(\mathbf{line}, G)$	$=$	$\{\mathbf{sale}, \mathbf{item}, \mathbf{store}\}$
$Need(\mathbf{store}, G)$	$=$	$\{\mathbf{sale}\}$
$Need(\mathbf{sale}, G)$	$=$	ϕ
$Need(\mathbf{item}, G)$	$=$	ϕ
$Need(\mathbf{line}, G)$	$=$	ϕ

Table 2: Dep and $Need$ Functions for Base Relations

A_{store}	$=$	$\pi_{store\_id,\ manager}\ \sigma_{state=CA}\ \mathbf{store}$
A_{sale}	$=$	$(\pi_{sale\_id,\ store\_id,\ month}$
		$\sigma_{year=1996}\ \mathbf{sale}) \bowtie_{store\_id} A_{store}$
A_{item}	$=$	$\pi_{item\_id,\ item\_name}\ \sigma_{category=toy}\ \mathbf{item}$

Table 3: Auxiliary Views for Maintaining the **cal_toy_sales** View

For each relation R_i referenced in the view V, the algorithm checks whether $Dep^+(R_i, G)$ includes every other relation referenced in V and R_i is not in $Need(R_j, G)$ for any relation R_j referenced in V. If so, it is not necessary to store any part of R_i in order to maintain V. Relation **line** is an example where an auxiliary view for the relation is not needed.

Otherwise, two steps are taken to reduce the amount of data stored in the auxiliary view A_{R_i} for R_i. First, it is possible to push down on R_i local selection conditions (explicit or inferred) in the view so that tuples that don't pass the selection conditions don't need to be stored; it is also possible to project away all attributes from R_i except those that are involved in join conditions, preserved in V, or are a key of R_i. Second, if $Dep(R_i, G)$ is not empty, it is possible to further reduce the tuples stored in A_{R_i} to only those tuples of R_i that join with tuples in other auxiliary views A_{R_k} where R_k is in $Dep(R_i, G)$. The auxiliary view for **sale** is an example where both steps have been applied. A_{sale} is restricted by the semijoin with A_{store} to include only tuples that join with tuples passing the local selection conditions on **store**. The auxiliary views for **store** and **item** are examples where only selection and projection can be applied.

Although view definitions are small and running time is not crucial, we observe that the running time of Algorithm 3.1 is polynomial in the number of relations, and therefore is clearly acceptable. We now state a theorem about the correctness and minimality of the auxiliary views derived by Algorithm 3.1.

Theorem 3.1 *Let V be a view with a tree-structured join graph. The set of auxiliary views $\mathcal{A}$ produced by Algorithm 3.1 is the unique minimal set of views*

that can be added to V such that $\{V\} \cup \mathcal{A}$ is self-maintainable. □

The proof of Theorem 3.1 is given in [12]. By *minimal* we mean that no auxiliary view can be removed from $\mathcal{A}$, and it is not possible to add an additional selection condition or semijoin to further reduce the number of tuples in any auxiliary view and still have $\{V\} \cup \mathcal{A}$ be self-maintainable. We show in Section 4 how V can be maintained using $\mathcal{A}$, and we explain in Section 5 that we can maintain $\mathcal{A}$ without referencing base relations.

3.1 Effect of exposed updates

Recall that so far in our example we have considered protected updates only. Suppose `sale` had exposed updates (i.e., updates could change the values of `year`, `sale_id`, or `store_id`). We note that the definition of *Dep* does not include any relation that has exposed updates. Thus, the *Dep* function for `line` will not include `sale`, and we get:

$$Dep(\texttt{line}, G) = \{\texttt{item}\} \qquad Dep^+(\texttt{line}, G) = \{\texttt{item}\}$$

in which case an auxiliary view for `line` would be created as:

$$A_{line} = \texttt{line} \ltimes_{item\_id} A_{item}$$

No selection or projection can be applied on `line` in A_{line} because there are no local selections on `line` in the view and all attributes of line are either preserved in the view or appear in join conditions. Section 4.1 explains why exposed updates have a different effect on the set of auxiliary views needed than protected updates.

4 Maintaining the view using the auxiliary views

Recall that a view maintenance expression calculates the effects on the view of a certain type of change: insertions, deletions, or updates to a base relation. View maintenance expressions are usually written in terms of the changes and the base relations [5, 2]. In this section we show that the set of auxiliary views chosen by Algorithm 3.1 is sufficient to maintain the view by showing how to transform the view maintenance expressions written in terms of the changes and the base relations to equivalent view maintenance expressions written in terms of the changes, the view, and the auxiliary views.

We give view maintenance expressions for each type of change (insertions, deletions, and updates) separately. In addition, for each type of change we apply the changes to each base relation separately by propagating the changes to the base relation onto the view and updating the base relation. The reason we give maintenance expressions of this form, rather than maintenance expressions propagating several types of changes at once, is that maintenance expressions of this form are easier to understand and they are sufficient for our purpose: showing that it is possible to maintain a view using the auxiliary views generated by Algorithm 3.1. View maintenance expressions for insertions are handled in Section 4.1, for deletions are handled in Section 4.2, and for protected updates are handled in Section 4.3. Since exposed updates are handled as deletions followed by insertions, they are treated within Sections 4.1 and 4.2.

4.1 Insertions

In this section we show how the effect on a view of insertions to base relations can be calculated using the auxiliary views chosen by Algorithm 3.1. The view maintenance expression for calculating the effects on an SPJ view V of insertions to a base relation R is obtained by substituting $\triangle R$ (insertions to R) for base relation R in the relational algebra expression for V. For example, the view maintenance expressions calculating the effects on our `cal_toy_sales` view (Section 1.1) of insertions to `store`, `sale`, `line`, and `item` appear in Table 4.

$$
\begin{aligned}
\triangle V_{St} \;=\; &\pi_{Schema(V)} \\
&(\pi_{store\_id,manager}\, \sigma_{state=CA}\, \triangle St \\
&\bowtie_{store\_id}\, \pi_{sale\_id,store\_id,month}\, \sigma_{year=1996}\, Sa \\
&\bowtie_{sale\_id}\, L \\
&\bowtie_{item\_id}\, \pi_{item\_id,item\_name}\, \sigma_{category=toy}\, I)
\end{aligned}
$$

$$
\begin{aligned}
\triangle V_{Sa} \;=\; &\pi_{Schema(V)} \\
&(\pi_{store\_id,manager}\, \sigma_{state=CA}\, St \\
&\bowtie_{store\_id}\, \pi_{sale\_id,store\_id,month}\, \sigma_{year=1996}\, \triangle Sa \\
&\bowtie_{sale\_id}\, L \\
&\bowtie_{item\_id}\, \pi_{item\_id,item\_name}\, \sigma_{category=toy}\, I)
\end{aligned}
$$

$$
\begin{aligned}
\triangle V_{L} \;=\; &\pi_{Schema(V)} \\
&(\pi_{store\_id,manager}\, \sigma_{state=CA}\, St \\
&\bowtie_{store\_id}\, \pi_{sale\_id,store\_id,month}\, \sigma_{year=1996}\, Sa \\
&\bowtie_{sale\_id}\, \triangle L \\
&\bowtie_{item\_id}\, \pi_{item\_id,item\_name}\, \sigma_{category=toy}\, I)
\end{aligned}
$$

$$
\begin{aligned}
\triangle V_{I} \;=\; &\pi_{Schema(V)} \\
&(\pi_{store\_id,manager}\, \sigma_{state=CA}\, St \\
&\bowtie_{store\_id}\, \pi_{sale\_id,store\_id,month}\, \sigma_{year=1996}\, Sa \\
&\bowtie_{sale\_id}\, L \\
&\bowtie_{item\_id}\, \pi_{item\_id,item\_name}\, \sigma_{category=toy}\, \triangle I)
\end{aligned}
$$

Table 4: Maintenance Expressions for Insertions

A few words of explanation about the table are in order.

- For convenience, in the table and hereafter we abbreviate `store`, `sale`, `line`, and `item` as St, Sa, L, and I, respectively.

- We abbreviate view `cal_toy_sales` as V.

- We have applied the general rule of "pushing selections and projections down" to the maintenance expressions.

- We use the notation $\triangle V_R$ to represent the insertions into view V due to insertions into base relation R. For example, $\triangle V_{St}$ represents insertions into V due to insertions into St.

- Each of the maintenance expressions of Table 4 calculates the effect on view V of insertions to one of the base relations. We show in Section 4.1.3 that even if insertions to multiple base relations are propagated at once, the auxiliary views generated by Algorithm 3.1 are still sufficient.

From the expressions of Table 4 it would appear that beyond pushing down selections and projections, nothing can be done to reduce the base relation data required for evaluating the maintenance expressions. If there are no referential integrity constraints, that is indeed the case. However, referential integrity constraints allow certain of the maintenance expressions to be eliminated, requiring less base relation data in the auxiliary views. Maintenance expressions are eliminated due to the following property and corresponding rule.

Property 4.1 (Insertion Property for Foreign Keys) *If there is a referential integrity constraint from $R_j.B$ to $R_i.A$ ($R_j.B$ is the "foreign key"), A is a key of R_i, and R_i does not have exposed updates, then $R_i \bowtie_{\triangle R_i.A=R_j.B} R_j = \phi$. In general, if the above conditions hold then the following is true.*

$$\pi\sigma R_1 \bowtie \ldots \bowtie \pi\sigma \triangle R_i \bowtie_{\triangle R_i.A=R_j.B} \pi\sigma R_j \bowtie \ldots \pi\sigma R_n$$
$$= \phi \qquad \odot$$

Property 4.1 holds because the referential integrity constraint requires that each tuple in R_j join with an existing tuple in R_i, and because it joins on a key of R_i it cannot join with any of the tuples in $\triangle R_i$, so the join of $\triangle R_i$ with R_j must be empty.

Rule 4.1 (Insertion Rule for Foreign Keys) *Let $G(V)$ be the join graph for view V. The maintenance expression calculating the effect on a view V of insertions to a base relation R_i is guaranteed to be empty and thus can be eliminated if there is some relation R_j such that $R_i \in Dep(R_j, G)$.* $\qquad \odot$

Rule 4.1 is used to eliminate the maintenance expression that calculates the effect on a view V of insertions to a base relation R_i if there is another relation R_j in V such that $R_i \in Dep(R_j, G)$ where $G(V)$ is the join graph for V. The rule holds because, by the definition of Dep, R_i is in $Dep(R_j, G)$ when the view equates a foreign key of R_j to the key of R_i, there is a referential integrity constraint from the foreign key in R_j to the key of R_i, and R_i has protected updates (the effect of exposed updates is discussed in Section 4.1.2). Since the maintenance expression that calculates the effect of insertions to R_i includes a join between $\triangle R_i$ and R_j, it must be empty by Property 4.1 and therefore can be eliminated. Joins and referential integrity constraints between keys and foreign keys are common in practice, so the conditions of Rule 4.1 are often met.

Being able to eliminate certain maintenance expressions when calculating the effect on a view V of insertions to base relations can significantly reduce the cost of maintaining V. Although view maintenance expressions themselves are not the main theme of this paper, nevertheless this is an important stand-alone result.

4.1.1 Rewriting the maintenance expressions to use auxiliary relations. Eliminating certain maintenance expressions using Rule 4.1 allows us to use the auxiliary views instead of base relations when propagating insertions. After applying Rule 4.1, the remaining maintenance expressions are rewritten using the auxiliary views generated by Algorithm 3.1 by replacing each $\pi\sigma R_i$ subexpression with the corresponding auxiliary view A_{R_i} for R_i.

For example, assuming for now that the base relations have protected updates, the maintenance expressions for $\triangle V_{St}$, $\triangle V_{Sa}$, and $\triangle V_I$, in Table 4 can be eliminated by Rule 4.1 due to the referential integrity constraints between `sale.store_id` and `store.store_id`, `line.sale_id` and `sale.sale_id`, and `line.item_id` and `item.item_id`, respectively. Only $\triangle V_L$, the expression calculating the effect of insertions to L, is not guaranteed to be empty. The maintenance expression $\triangle V_L$ is rewritten using auxiliary views as follows. Recall that the auxiliary views are shown in Table 3.

$$\triangle V_L = \pi_{Schema(V)} \left(A_{St} \bowtie_{sale\_id} A_{Sa} \bowtie_{store\_id} \triangle L \bowtie_{item\_id} A_I \right)$$

Notice that the base relation L is never referenced in the above maintenance expression, so an auxiliary view for L is not needed. In addition, Sa is joined with St in the maintenance expression, which is why it is acceptable to store only the tuples in Sa that join with existing tuples in St—tuples in Sa that don't join with existing tuples in St won't contribute to the result. A proof that the auxiliary views are sufficient in general to evaluate the (reduced) maintenance expressions for insertions appears in [12].

4.1.2 Effect of exposed updates. Suppose the view contains a join condition $R_j.B = R_i.A$, A is a key of R_i, there is a referential integrity constraint from $R_j.B$ to $R_i.A$, but R_i has exposed, rather than protected, updates. $Dep(R_j, G)$ thus does not contain R_i. Recall that exposed updates can change the values of attributes involved in selection conditions (local or join). We handle exposed updates as deletions of tuples with the old attribute values followed by insertions of tuples with the new attribute values, since exposed updates may result in deletions or insertions in the view. Thus, if R_i has exposed updates then $\triangle R_i$ may include tuples representing the new values of exposed updates. Because these tuples can join with existing tuples in R_j (without violating the referential integrity or key constraints), Property 4.1 does not hold and Rule 4.1 cannot be used to eliminate the maintenance expression propagating insertions to R_i.

For example, suppose updates may occur to the **year** attribute of Sa. Then an auxiliary view for L would be created as $A_L = L \bowtie_{item\_id} A_I$ as shown in Section 3.1. We cannot semijoin L with A_{Sa} in the auxiliary view for L because new values of updated tuples in Sa could join with existing tuples in L, where the old values of the updated tuples didn't pass the local selection conditions on Sa and hence weren't in A_{Sa}. That is, suppose the year of some sale tuple t was changed from 1995 to 1996. Although the old value of t doesn't pass the selection criteria **year=1996** and therefore wouldn't appear in A_{Sa}, the new value of t would, and since it could join with existing tuples in L we cannot restrict A_L to include only those tuples that join with existing tuples in A_{Sa}.

In this paper we assume that it is known in advance whether each relation of a view V has exposed or protected updates. If a relation has exposed updates, we may need to store more information in the auxiliary views in order to maintain V than if the relation had protected updates. For example, we had to create an auxiliary view for L when Sa had exposed updates, where the auxiliary view for L wasn't needed when Sa had protected updates.

An alternate way to consider updates, which doesn't require advance knowledge of protected versus exposed, is to assume that every base relation has protected updates. Then, before propagating updates, the updates to each base relation are divided into two classes: updates that do not modify attributes involved in selection conditions, and those that do. The first class of updates can be propagated as protected updates using the expressions of Section 4.3. Assuming the second class of updates is relatively small, updates in the second class could be propagated by issuing queries back to the data sources.

4.1.3 Propagating insertions to multiple relations at once.

Maintenance expressions of the form used in Table 4 propagate onto the view insertions to one base relation at a time. To propagate insertions to multiple base relations using the formulas in Table 4, when $\triangle V_{R_i}$ is calculated we assume that the insertions to base relations $R_j (j < i)$ have already been applied to the base relations.

In [5, 8], maintenance expressions are given for propagating changes to all base relations at once. We consider the one relation at a time case because the maintenance expressions are easier to explain; the amount of data needed in the auxiliary views is the same whether insertions (or deletions or updates) are propagated one relation at a time or all at once (see [12]).

4.2 Deletions

In this section we show how the effect on a view of deletions to base relations can be calculated using the auxiliary views. The view maintenance expression for calculating the effects on an SPJ view V of deletions to a base relation R is obtained similarly to the expression for calculating the effects of insertions: we substitute ∇R (deletions to R) for base relation R in the relational algebra expression for V. For example, the view maintenance expressions for calculating the effects on our **cal_toy_sales** view of deletions to **store**, **sale**, **line**, and **item** appear respectively as ∇V_{St}, ∇V_{Sa}, ∇V_L, and ∇V_I in Table 5. We use the notation ∇V_R to represent the deletions from view V due to deletions from base relation R.

Often we can simplify maintenance expressions for deletions to use the contents of the view itself if keys

$$
\begin{aligned}
\nabla V_{St} = {} & \pi_{Schema(V)} \\
& (\pi_{store\_id,manager}\, \sigma_{state=CA}\, \nabla St \\
& \bowtie_{store\_id} \pi_{sale\_id,store\_id,month}\, \sigma_{year=1996}\, Sa \\
& \bowtie_{sale\_id} L \\
& \bowtie_{item\_id} \pi_{item\_id,item\_name}\, \sigma_{category=toy}\, I)
\end{aligned}
$$

$$
\begin{aligned}
\nabla V_{Sa} = {} & \pi_{Schema(V)} \\
& (\pi_{store\_id,manager}\, \sigma_{state=CA}\, St \\
& \bowtie_{store\_id} \pi_{sale\_id,store\_id,month}\, \sigma_{year=1996}\, \nabla Sa \\
& \bowtie_{sale\_id} L \\
& \bowtie_{item\_id} \pi_{item\_id,item\_name}\, \sigma_{category=toy}\, I)
\end{aligned}
$$

$$
\begin{aligned}
\nabla V_L = {} & \pi_{Schema(V)} \\
& (\pi_{store\_id,manager}\, \sigma_{state=CA}\, St \\
& \bowtie_{store\_id} \pi_{sale\_id,store\_id,month}\, \sigma_{year=1996}\, Sa \\
& \bowtie_{sale\_id} \nabla L \\
& \bowtie_{item\_id} \pi_{item\_id,item\_name}\, \sigma_{category=toy}\, I)
\end{aligned}
$$

$$
\begin{aligned}
\nabla V_I = {} & \pi_{Schema(V)} \\
& (\pi_{store\_id,manager}\, \sigma_{state=CA}\, St \\
& \bowtie_{store\_id} \pi_{sale\_id,store\_id,month}\, \sigma_{year=1996}\, Sa \\
& \bowtie_{sale\_id} L \\
& \bowtie_{item\_id} \pi_{item\_id,item\_name}\, \sigma_{category=toy}\, \nabla I)
\end{aligned}
$$

Table 5: Maintenance Expressions for Deletions

are preserved in the view. We do this using the following properties and rule for deletions in the presence of keys.

Property 4.2 (Deletion Property for Keys) *Given view* $V = \pi_{Schema(V)}(\pi \sigma R_1 \bowtie \ldots \bowtie \pi \sigma R_n)$, *if the key of a relation* R_i *is preserved in* V *then the following equivalence holds:*

$$
\begin{aligned}
& \pi_{Schema(V)}(\pi \sigma R_1 \bowtie \ldots \bowtie \pi \sigma R_{i-1} \bowtie \pi \sigma \nabla R_i \bowtie \pi \sigma R_{i+1} \\
& \qquad \bowtie \ldots \bowtie \pi \sigma R_n) \\
& \equiv \pi_{Schema(V)}(V \bowtie_{key(R_i)} \nabla R_i) \qquad\qquad \odot
\end{aligned}
$$

Consider the join graph $G(V)$ of view V. Property 4.2 says that if V preserves the key of some relation R_i (i.e., $Need(R_i, G) = \phi$), then we can calculate the effect on V of deletions to R_i by joining V with ∇R_i on the key of R_i. The property holds because each tuple in V with the same value for the key of R_i as a tuple t in ∇R_i must have been derived from t. Conversely, all tuples in V that were derived from tuple t in ∇R_i must have the same value as t for the key of R_i. Therefore, the set of tuples in V that join with t on the key of R_i is exactly the set of tuples in V that should be deleted when t is deleted from R_i. A similar property holds if the key of R_i is not preserved in V, but is equated by a selection condition in V to an attribute C that is preserved in V. In this case the effect of deletions from R_i can be obtained by joining V with ∇R_i using the join condition $V.C = key(R_i)$.

Property 4.2 is used in [4] to determine when a view is self-maintainable with respect to deletions from a base relation. We extend their result with Property 4.3.

Property 4.3 (Deletion Property for Key Joins) *Given a view* $V =$ $\pi_{Schema(V)}(\pi\sigma R_1 \bowtie \ldots \bowtie \pi\sigma R_n)$ *satisfying the following conditions:*

1. *V contains join conditions $R_i.A = R_{i+1}.B$, $R_{i+1}.A = R_{i+2}.B$, ..., $R_{i+k-1}.A = R_{i+k}.B$*

2. *attribute A is a key for $R_{i+j}(0 <= j <= k)$, and*

3. *$R_{i+k}.A$ is preserved in V,*

then the following equivalence holds (even without referential integrity constraints):

$$\pi_{Schema(V)}(\pi\sigma R_1 \bowtie \ldots \bowtie \pi\sigma R_{i-1} \bowtie \pi\sigma\nabla R_i$$
$$\bowtie \pi\sigma R_{i+1} \bowtie \ldots \bowtie \pi\sigma R_n)$$
$$\equiv \pi_{Schema(V)}(V \bowtie_{R_{i+k}.A} \pi\sigma R_{i+k}$$
$$\bowtie_{R_{i+k}.B=R_{i+k-1}.A} \pi\sigma R_{i+k-1} \bowtie \ldots$$
$$\bowtie_{R_{i+1}.B=R_i.A} \nabla R_i) \qquad \odot$$

Let $G(V)$ be the join graph for view V. Property 4.3 generalizes Property 4.2 to say that if V preserves the key of some relation R_{i+k} and R_i joins to R_{i+k} along keys (that is, $Need(R_i, G) = \{R_{i+1}, \ldots, R_{i+k}\}$ and does not include all the base relations of V), then we can calculate the effect on V of deletions to R_i by joining ∇R_i with the sequence of relations up to R_{i+k} and then joining R_{i+k} with V. The property holds because tuples in V with the same value for the key of R_{i+k} as a tuple t in R_{i+k} must have been derived from t as explained in Property 4.2. Furthermore, since the joins between R_{i+k} and R_i are all along keys, each tuple in R_{i+k} can join with at most one tuple t' in R_i, which means that tuples in V that are derived from tuple t in R_{i+k} must also be derived from tuple t' in R_i. Conversely, if a tuple in V is derived from t' in R_i, then it must have the same value for the key of R_{i+k} as some tuple t in R_{i+k} that t' joins with. Therefore, the set of tuples in V that join on the key of R_{i+k} with some tuple t in R_{i+k} that joins along keys with a tuple t' in R_i is exactly the set of tuples in V that should be deleted when t' is deleted from R_i. As before, a similar property also holds if a key of R_{i+k} is not preserved in V but is equated by a selection condition in V to an attribute C that is preserved in V. In this case the effect of deletions from R_i can be obtained by joining V with R_{i+k} using the join condition $V.C = key(R_{i+k})$.

Rule 4.2 (Deletion Rule) *Let V be a view with a tree structured join graph $G(V)$, and let $Need(R_i, G) = \{R_{i+1}, \ldots, R_{i+k}\}$, where $k \geq 0$. The maintenance expression calculating the effect on a view V of deletions to a base relation R_i may be simplified according to Property 4.3 to reference V unless $Need(R_i, G)$ includes all the base relations of V except R_i.* $\qquad \odot$

Rule 4.2 is used to simplify maintenance expressions for deletions to use the contents of the view and fewer base relations. This allows us to rewrite the maintenance expressions for deletions to use the auxiliary views instead of base relations.

4.2.1 Rewriting the maintenance expressions to use auxiliary relations. After simplifying the maintenance expressions according to Rule 4.2, the simplified expressions are rewritten to use the auxiliary views generated by Algorithm 3.1 by replacing each $\pi\sigma R_i$ subexpression in the simplified maintenance expression with the corresponding auxiliary view A_{R_i} for R_i.

The maintenance expressions of Table 5 are simplified using Rule 4.2 as follows.

$$\nabla V_{St} = \pi_{Schema(V)}(V \bowtie_{sale\_id}$$
$$\pi_{sale\_id,store\_id}\sigma_{year=1996}Sa \bowtie_{store\_id} \nabla St)$$
$$\nabla V_{Sa} = \pi_{Schema(V)}(V \bowtie_{sale\_id} \nabla Sa)$$
$$\nabla V_L = \pi_{Schema(V)}(V \bowtie_{line\_id} \nabla L)$$
$$\nabla V_I = \pi_{Schema(V)}(V \bowtie_{item\_id} \nabla I)$$

A proof that the auxiliary views are sufficient in general to evaluate the (simplified) maintenance expressions for deletions appears in [12].

4.3 Protected updates

In this section we show how the effect on a view of protected updates to base relations can be calculated using the auxiliary views. (Recall that exposed updates are treated separately as deletions followed by insertions.) We give two maintenance expressions for calculating the effect on a view V of protected updates to a base relation R: one returning the tuples to delete from the view (denoted as $\triangledown V_R$) and another returning the tuples to insert into the view (denoted as $\triangle V_R$). In practice, these pairs of maintenance expressions usually can be combined into a single SQL update statement.

The view maintenance expression for calculating the tuples to delete from an SPJ view V due to protected updates to a base relation R is obtained by substituting $\pi^{old}\mu R$ (the old attribute values of the updated tuples in R) for base relation R in the relational algebra expression for V. (Recall that μR, π^{old}, and π^{new} were defined in Section 2.) The view maintenance expression for calculating the tuples to insert is obtained similarly by substituting $\pi^{new}\mu R$ (the new attribute values of the updated tuples in R) for base relation R in the relational algebra expression for V. For example, the view maintenance expressions calculating the tuples to delete from our `cal_toy_sales` view due to protected updates to each of the base relations are given in Table 6. Expressions calculating the tuples to insert into the view `cal_toy_sales` are not shown but can be obtained by substituting π^{new} for π^{old} in the expressions of Table 6. Note that the Table 6 expressions are similar to the deletion expressions of Table 5.

We simplify the maintenance expressions for protected updates similarly to the way we simplify the maintenance expressions for deletions, by using the contents of the view itself if keys are preserved in the view. We give the following properties and rule for updates in the presence of preserved keys. In the following let $P(\mu R_i) =$

$$\bigtriangledown V_{St} = \pi_{Schema(V)}$$
$$(\pi^{old}_{store\_id,manager}\,\sigma_{state=CA}\,\mu St$$
$$\bowtie_{store\_id}\pi_{sale\_id,store\_id,month}\,\sigma_{year=1996}\,Sa$$
$$\bowtie_{sale\_id}L$$
$$\bowtie_{item\_id}\pi_{item\_id,item\_name}\,\sigma_{category=toy}\,I)$$

$$\bigtriangledown V_{Sa} = \pi_{Schema(V)}$$
$$(\pi_{store\_id,manager}\,\sigma_{state=CA}\,St$$
$$\bowtie_{store\_id}\pi^{old}_{sale\_id,store\_id,month}\,\sigma_{year=1996}\,\mu Sa$$
$$\bowtie_{sale\_id}L$$
$$\bowtie_{item\_id}\pi_{item\_id,item\_name}\,\sigma_{category=toy}\,I)$$

$$\bigtriangledown V_{L} = \pi_{Schema(V)}$$
$$(\pi_{store\_id,manager}\,\sigma_{state=CA}\,St$$
$$\bowtie_{store\_id}\pi_{sale\_id,store\_id,month}\,\sigma_{year=1996}\,Sa$$
$$\bowtie_{sale\_id}\pi^{old}_{line\_id,sale\_id,item\_id,sales\_price}\,\mu L$$
$$\bowtie_{item\_id}\pi_{item\_id,item\_name}\,\sigma_{category=toy}\,I)$$

$$\bigtriangledown V_{I} = \pi_{Schema(V)}$$
$$(\pi_{store\_id,manager}\,\sigma_{state=CA}\,St$$
$$\bowtie_{store\_id}\pi_{sale\_id,store\_id,month}\,\sigma_{year=1996}\,Sa$$
$$\bowtie_{sale\_id}L$$
$$\bowtie_{item\_id}\pi^{old}_{item\_id,item\_name}\,\sigma_{category=toy}\,\mu I)$$

Table 6: Maintenance Expressions for Removing Old Updates

$(Schema(\mu R_i)\cap Schema(V))\cup Schema(V)$. We use $\pi^{old}_{P(\mu R_i)}$ and $\pi^{new}_{P(\mu R_i)}$ to project the old and new attribute values respectively of preserved attributes in μR_i and the (regular) attribute values for preserved attributes of other relations in V. We use $\bowtie oldkey(R_i)$ to denote joining on the attribute in which the key value before the update is held.

Property 4.4 (Protected Update Property for Keys) *Given a view* $V =$
$\pi_{Schema(V)}(\pi\sigma R_1\bowtie\ldots\bowtie\pi\sigma R_n)$ *where the key of a relation* R_i *is preserved in* V*, then the following equivalences hold:*

$$\pi_{Schema(V)}(\pi\sigma R_1\bowtie\ldots\bowtie\pi\sigma R_{i-1}\bowtie\pi^{old}\sigma\mu R_i$$
$$\bowtie\pi\sigma R_{i+1}\bowtie\ldots\bowtie\pi\sigma R_n)$$
$$\equiv \pi^{old}_{P(\mu R_i)}(V\bowtie_{oldkey(R_i)}\mu R_i)$$

$$\pi_{Schema(V)}(\pi\sigma R_1\bowtie\ldots\bowtie\pi\sigma R_{i-1}\bowtie\pi^{new}\sigma\mu R_i$$
$$\bowtie\pi\sigma R_{i+1}\bowtie\ldots\bowtie\pi\sigma R_n)$$
$$\equiv \pi^{new}_{P(\mu R_i)}(V\bowtie_{oldkey(R_i)}\mu R_i) \qquad \odot$$

Property 4.5 (Protected Update Property for Key Joins) *Given a view* $V =$
$\pi_{Schema(V)}(\pi\sigma R_1\bowtie\ldots\bowtie\pi\sigma R_n)$ *satisfying the following conditions:*

1. *view* V *contains join conditions* $R_i.A = R_{i+1}.B, R_{i+1}.A = R_{i+2}.B,\ldots,R_{i+k-1}.A = R_{i+k}.B$

2. *attribute A is a key for $R_{i+j}(0 <= j <= k)$, and*

3. *$R_{i+k}.A$ is preserved in V,*

then the following equivalences hold (even without referential integrity constraints):

$$\pi_{Schema(V)}(\pi\sigma R_1\bowtie\ldots\bowtie\pi\sigma R_{i-1}$$
$$\bowtie\pi^{old}\sigma\mu R_i\bowtie\pi\sigma R_{i+1}\bowtie\ldots\bowtie\pi\sigma R_n)$$
$$\equiv \pi^{old}_{P(\mu R_i)}(V\bowtie_{R_{i+k}.A}R_{i+k}\bowtie_{R_{i+k}.B=R_{i+k-1}.A}R_{i+k-1}$$
$$\bowtie\ldots\bowtie_{R_{i+1}.B=R_i.A}\mu R_i)$$

$$\pi_{Schema(V)}(\pi\sigma R_1\bowtie\ldots\bowtie\pi\sigma R_{i-1}$$
$$\bowtie\pi^{new}\sigma\mu R_i\bowtie\pi\sigma R_{i+1}\bowtie\ldots\bowtie\pi\sigma R_n)$$
$$\equiv \pi^{new}_{P(\mu R_i)}(V\bowtie_{R_{i+k}.A}R_{i+k}\bowtie_{R_{i+k}.B=R_{i+k-1}.A}R_{i+k-1}$$
$$\bowtie\ldots\bowtie_{R_{i+1}.B=R_i.A}\mu R_i) \qquad \odot$$

Properties 4.4 and 4.5 are similar to the corresponding properties for deletions. Attributes of R_i that are involved in selection conditions are guaranteed not to be updated, so it does not matter whether we test the old or new value in selection conditions. Property 4.4 is used in [4] to determine when a view is self-maintainable for base relation updates.

Consider the join graph $G(V)$ of view V. Property 4.5 generalizes Property 4.4; Property 4.5 says that if V preserves the key of some relation R_{i+k} and R_i joins to R_{i+k} along keys (that is, $Need(R_i, G) = \{R_{i+1},\ldots,R_{i+k}\}$ and does not include all the base relations of V), then we can calculate the effect on V of protected updates to R_i by joining μR_i with the sequence of relations up to R_{i+k} and then joining R_{i+k} with V. As for deletions, a similar property also holds if a key of R_{i+k} is not preserved in V but is equated by a selection condition in V to an attribute C that is preserved in V. In this case the effect of updates to R_i can be obtained by joining V with R_{i+k} using the join condition $V.C = key(R_{i+k})$.

Rule 4.3 (Protected Update Rule) *Let V be a view with a tree structured join graph $G(V)$, and let $Need(R_i, G) = \{R_{i+1},\ldots,R_{i+k}\}$, where $k \geq 0$. The maintenance expressions calculating the effect on a view V of protected updates to a base relation R_i can be simplified according to Property 4.5 to reference V unless $Need(R_i, G)$ includes all the base relations of V except R_i.* $\qquad \odot$

Similar to the rule for deletions, Rule 4.3 is used to simplify the maintenance expressions for $\bigtriangledown V_R$ and $\triangle V_R$ to use the contents of the view and fewer base relations so that the maintenance expressions can be rewritten in terms of the auxiliary views.

4.3.1 Rewriting the maintenance expressions to use auxiliary relations. After simplifying the maintenance expressions according to Rule 4.3, the simplified expressions are rewritten to use the auxiliary views generated by Algorithm 3.1 by replacing each $\pi\sigma R_i$ subexpression in the maintenance expression with the corresponding auxiliary view A_{R_i} for R_i. The rewriting is similar to the rewriting for insertions and deletions. An example and proof that the auxiliary views are sufficient in general to evaluate the maintenance expressions are given in [12].

5 Maintaining auxiliary views

Due to space constraints we give only an intuitive argument, based upon join graphs, for why the set of auxiliary views is itself self-maintainable. Details on maintaining the auxiliary views efficiently and a proof that the set of auxiliary views is self-maintainable appear in the full version of the paper [12].

Recall that the auxiliary views derived by Algorithm 3.1 are of the form:

$$A_R = (\pi_{Schema(A_R)}\sigma_S R) \bowtie_{C_1} A_{R_1} \bowtie_{C_2} \ldots \bowtie_{C_m} A_{R_m}$$

where C_i equijoins a foreign key of R with the corresponding key for relation R_i. Because the joins are along foreign key referential integrity constraints, each semijoin could be replaced by a join. Thus, each auxiliary view is an SPJ view, and its join graph can be constructed as discussed in Section 3. Further, note that the join graph for each auxiliary view is a subgraph of the graph for the original view, because each join in an auxiliary view is also a join in the original view. Thus, the information needed to maintain the original view is also sufficient to maintain each of its auxiliary views.

6 Related work

The problem of view self-maintainability was considered initially in [1, 4]. For each modification type (insertions, deletions, and updates), they identify subclasses of SPJ views that can be maintained using only the view and the modification. [1] states necessary and sufficient conditions on the view definition for the view to be self-maintainable for updates specified using a particular SQL modification statement (*e.g.*, delete all tuples where $R.A > 3$). [4] uses information about key attributes to determine self-maintainability of a view with respect to all modifications of a certain type.

In this paper we consider the problem of making a view self-maintainable by materializing a set of auxiliary views such that the original view and the auxiliary views taken together are self-maintainable. Although the set of base relations over which a view is defined forms one such set of auxiliary views, our approach is to derive auxiliary views that are much smaller than storing the base relations in their entirety. Identifying a set of small auxiliary views to make another view self-maintainable is an important problem in data warehousing, where the base relations may not be readily available.

In [10], views are made self-maintainable by pushing down selections and projections to the base relations and storing the results at the warehouse. Thus, using our terminology, they consider auxiliary views based only on select and project operators. We improve upon their approach by considering auxiliary views based on select, project, and semijoin operators, along with using knowledge about key and referential integrity constraints. We have shown in Section 1.1 that our approach can significantly reduce the sizes of the auxiliary views. We show in [12] that auxiliary views of the form our algorithm produces can be (self-)maintained efficiently.

In [13], inclusion dependencies (similar to referential integrity constraints) are used to determine when it is possible to answer from a view joining several relations, a query over a subset of the relations; *e.g.*, given V is a view joining R and other relations, when $\pi_{Schema(R)}V \equiv R$. We on the other hand, use similar referential integrity constraints to simplify view maintenance expressions.

References

[1] J. Blakeley, N. Coburn, and P. Larson. Updating derived relations: Detecting irrelevant and autonomously computable updates. *ACM Transactions on Database Systems*, 14(3):369–400, September 1989.

[2] L. Colby, T. Griffin, L. Libkin, I. Mumick, and H. Trickey. Algorithms for deferred view maintenance. In SIGMOD 1996.

[3] *IEEE Data Engineering Bulletin, Special Issue on Materialized Views and Data Warehousing*, 18(2), June 1995.

[4] A. Gupta, H. Jagadish, and I. Mumick. Data integration using self-maintainable views. In *EDBT*, 1996.

[5] T. Griffin and L. Libkin. Incremental maintenance of views with duplicates. In SIGMOD 1995.

[6] A. Gupta and I. Mumick. Maintenance of Materialized Views: Problems, Techniques, and Applications. In *IEEE Data Engineering Bulletin, Special Issue on Materialized Views and Data Warehousing* [3], pages 3–19.

[7] A. Gupta and I. Mumick, editors. *Materialized Views*. MIT Press, Cambridge, MA, 1996. To be published.

[8] A. Gupta, I. Mumick, and V. Subrahmanian. Maintaining views incrementally. In *SIGMOD* 1993.

[9] J. Hammer, H. Garcia-Molina, J. Widom, W. Labio, and Y. Zhuge. The Stanford Data Warehousing Project. In *IEEE Data Engineering Bulletin, Special Issue on Materialized Views and Data Warehousing* [3], pages 41–48.

[10] R. Hull and G. Zhou. A framework for supporting data integration using the materialized and virtual approaches. In SIGMOD 1996.

[11] I. Mumick. The Rejuvenation of Materialized Views. In *Proceedings of the Sixth International Conference on Information Systems and Management of Data (CISMOD)*, Bombay, India, November 1995.

[12] D. Quass, A. Gupta, I. Mumick, and J. Widom Making Views Self-Maintainable for Data Warehousing Available by anonymous ftp from `db.stanford.edu` as the file `pub/quass/1996/self-maint.ps`, 1996.

[13] Odysseas G. Tsatalos, Marvin H. Solomon, and Yannis E. Ioannidis. The GMAP: A versatile tool for physical data independence. In Jorge Bocca, Matthias Jarke, and Carlo Zaniolo, editors, *Proceedings of the 20th International Conference on Very Large Databases*, pages 367–378, Santiago, Chile, September 12-15 1994.

[14] Y. Zhuge, H. Garcia-Molina, J. Hammer, and J. Widom. View maintenance in a warehousing environment. In SIGMOD 1995.

Capabilities-Based Query Rewriting in Mediator Systems*

Yannis Papakonstantinou
Stanford Univ.
Computer Science Dpt.
Stanford, CA 94305
yannis@db.stanford.edu

Ashish Gupta
Junglee Corp.
4149B El Camino Way
Palo Alto, CA 94306
ashish@junglee.com

Laura Haas
IBM Almaden Research Center
650 Harry Road
San Jose, CA 95120
laura@almaden.ibm.com

Abstract

Users today are struggling to integrate a broad
range of information sources providing different levels of query capabilities. Currently, data sources with
different and limited capabilities are accessed either by
writing rich functional wrappers for the more primitive sources, or by dealing with all sources at a "lowest
common denominator". This paper explores a third
approach, in which a mediator ensures that sources
receive queries they can handle, while still taking advantage of all of the query power of the source. We
propose an architecture that enables this, and identify
a key component of that architecture, the *Capabilities-
Based Rewriter (CBR)*. The CBR takes as input a description of the capabilities of a data source, and a
query targeted for that data source. From these, the
CBR determines component queries to be sent to the
sources, commensurate with their abilities, and computes a plan for combining their results using joins,
unions, selections, and projections. We provide a language to describe the query capability of data sources
and a plan generation algorithm. Our description language and plan generation algorithm are schema independent and handle SPJ queries.[1]

1 Introduction

Organizations today must integrate multiple heterogeneous information sources, many of which are
not conventional SQL database management systems.
Examples of such information sources include bibliographic databases, object repositories, chemical structure databases, WAIS servers, etc. Some of these systems provide powerful query capabilities, while others are much more limited. A new challenge for the
database community is to allow users to query this
data using a single powerful query language, with location transparency, despite the diverse capabilities of
the underlying systems.

Figure (1.a) shows one commonly proposed integration architecture [1, 2, 3, 4]. Each data source has
a *wrapper*, which provides a view of the data in that
source in a common data model. Each wrapper can
translate queries expressed in the common language
to the language of its underlying information source.
The *mediator* provides an integrated view of the data

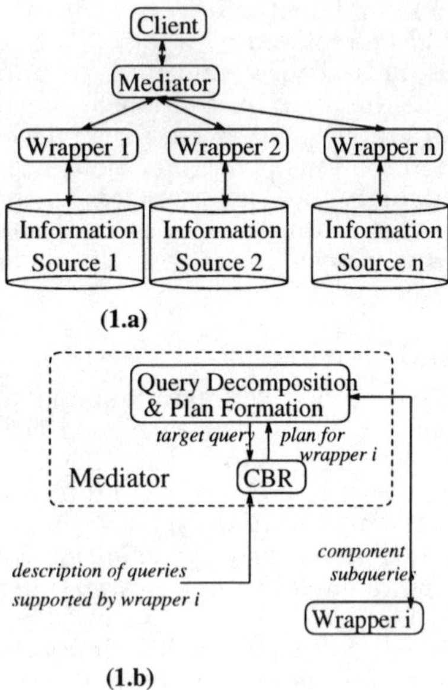

Figure 1: (a) A typical integration architecture. (b)
CBR-mediator interaction.

exported by the wrappers. In particular, when the
mediator receives a query from a client, it determines
what data it needs from each underlying wrapper,
sends the wrappers individual queries to collect the
required data, and combines the responses to produce
the query result.

This scenario works well when all wrappers can support any query over their data. However, in the types
of systems we consider, this assumption is unrealistic. It leads to extremely complex wrappers, needed
to support a powerful query interface against possibly
quite limited data sources. For example, in many systems the relational data model is taken as the common
data model, and all wrappers must provide a full SQL
interface, even if the underlying data source is a file
system, or a hierarchical DBMS. Alternatively, this
assumption may lead to a "lowest common denominator" approach in which only simple queries are sent to
the wrappers. In this case, the search capabilities of
more sophisticated data sources are not exploited, and
hence the mediator is forced to do most of the work, re-

---

[1]Research partially supported by Wright Laboratories,
Wright Patterson AFB, ARPA Contract F33615-93-C-1337.

sulting in unnecessarily poor performance. We would like to have simple wrappers that accurately reflect the search capabilities of the underlying data source. To enable this, the mediator must recognize differences and limitations in capabilities, and ensure that wrappers receive only queries that they can handle.

For Garlic [1], an integrator of heterogeneous multimedia data being developed at IBM's Almaden Research Center, such an understanding is essential. Garlic needs to deal efficiently with the disparate data types and querying capabilities needed by applications as diverse as medical, advertising, pharmaceutical research, and computer-aided design. In our model, a wrapper is capable of handling some set of queries, known as the *supported queries* for that wrapper. When the mediator receives a query from a client, it decomposes it into a set of queries, each of which references data at a single wrapper. We call these individual queries *target queries* for the wrappers. A target query need not be a supported query; it may sometimes be necessary to further decompose it into simpler supported *Component SubQueries (CSQs)* in order to execute it. A *plan* combines the results of the CSQs to produce the answer to the target query.

To obtain this functionality, we are exploring a *Capabilities-Based Rewriter (CBR)* module (Figure 1.b) as part of the Garlic query engine (mediator). The CBR uses a description of each wrapper's ability, expressed in a special purpose *query capabilities description language*, to develop a plan for the wrapper's target query.

The mediator decomposes a user's query into target queries q for each wrapper w without considering whether q is supported by w. It then passes q to the CBR for "inspection." The CBR compares q against the description of the queries supported by wrapper w, and produces a plan p for q, if either (i) q is directly supported by w, or (ii) q is computable by the mediator through a plan that involves selection, projection and join of CSQs that are supported by w. The mediator then combines the individual plans p into a complete plan for the user's query.

The CBR allows a clean separation of wrapper capabilities from mediator internals. Wrappers are "thin" modules that translate queries in the common model into source-specific queries.[2] Hence, wrappers reflect the actual capabilities of the underlying data sources, while the mediator has a general mechanism for interpreting those capabilities and forming execution strategies for queries. This paper focuses on the technology needed to enable the CBR approach. We first present a language for describing wrappers' query capabilities. The descriptions look like context-free grammars, modified to describe queries rather than arbitrary strings. The descriptions may be recursive, thus allowing the description of infinitely large supported queries. In addition, they may be schema-independent. For example, we may describe the capabilities of a relational database wrapper without re-ferring to the schema of a specific relational database. An additional benefit of the grammar-like description language is that it can be appropriately augmented with actions to translate a target query to a query of the underlying information system. This feature has been described in [5] and we will not discuss it further in this paper.

The second contribution of this paper is an architecture for the CBR and an algorithm to build plans for a target query using the CSQs supported by the relevant wrapper. This problem is a generalization of the problem of determining if a query can be answered using a set of materialized queries/views [6, 7]. However, the CBR uses a description of potentially infinite queries as opposed to a finite set of materialized views. The problem of identifying CSQs that compute the target query has many sources of exponentiality even for the restricted case discussed by [6, 7]. The CBR algorithm uses optimizations and heuristics to eliminate sources of exponentiality in many common cases.

In the next section, we present the language used to describe a wrapper's query capabilities. In Section 3 we describe the basic architecture of the CBR, identifying three modules: Component SubQuery Discovery, Plan Construction, and Plan Refinement. These components are detailed in Sections 4, 5 and 6, respectively. Section 7 summarizes the run-time performance of the CBR, while Section 8 compares the CBR with related work. Finally, Section 9 concludes with some directions for future work in this area.

2 The Relational Query Description Language(RQDL)

RQDL is the language we use to describe a wrapper's supported queries. We discuss only Select-Project-Join queries in this paper. In section 2.1 we introduce the basic language features , followed in sections 2.2 and 2.3 by the extensions needed to describe infinite query sets and to support schema-independent descriptions. Section 2.4 introduces a normal form for queries and descriptors that increases the precision of the language. The complete language specification appears in [8].

The description language focuses on conjunctive queries. We have found that it is powerful enough to express the abilities of many wrappers and sources, such as lookup catalogs and object databases. Indeed, we believe that it is more expressive than context-free grammars (we are currently working on the proof).

2.1 Language Basics

An RQDL specification contains a set of *query templates*, each of which is essentially a parameterized query. Where an actual query might have a constant, the query template has a *constant placeholder*, allowing it to represent many queries of the same form. In addition, we allow the values assumed by the constant placeholders to be restricted by specifier-provided *metapredicates*. A query is described by a template (loosely speaking) if (1) each predicate in the query matches one predicate in the template, and vice versa, and (2) any metapredicates on the placeholders of the template evaluate to **true** for the matching

---

[2]In general, there is a one-to-one mapping and no optimization is involved in this translation. All optimization is done at the mediator.

constants in the query. The order of the predicates in query and template need not be the same, and different variable names are of course possible.

For example, consider a "lookup" facility that provides information – such as name, department, office address, and so on – about the employees of a company. The "lookup" facility can either retrieve all employees, or retrieve employees whose last name has a specific prefix, or retrieve employees whose last name and first name have specific prefixes.[3] We integrate "lookup" into our heterogeneous system by creating a wrapper, called `lookup`, that exports a predicate `emp(First-Name, Last-Name, Department, Office, Manager)`. (The `Manager` field may be `'Y'` or `'N'`.) The wrapper also exports a predicate `prefix(Full, Prefix)` that is successful when its second argument is a prefix of its first argument. This second argument must be a string, consisting of letters only. We may write the following Datalog query to retrieve `emp` tuples for persons whose first name starts with `'Rak'` and whose last name starts with `'Aggr'`:

(Q1) `answer(FN,LN,D,O,M) :- emp(FN,LN,D,O,M),`
　　　`prefix(FN,'Rak'), prefix(LN,'Aggr')`

In this paper we use Datalog [9] as our query language because it is well-suited to handling SPJ queries and facilitates the discussion of our algorithms.[4] We use the following Datalog terms in this paper: *Distinguished variables* are the variables that appear in the target query head. A *join variable* is any variable that appears twice or more in the target query tail. In the query (Q1) the distinguished variables are `FN`, `LN`, `D`, `O` and `M` and the join variables are `FN` and `LN`.

Description (D2) is an RQDL specification of `lookup`'s query capabilities. The identifiers starting with `$` (`$FP` and `$LP`) are constant placeholders. `_isalpha()` is a metapredicate that returns `true` if its argument is a string that contains letters only. Metapredicates start with an underscore and a lowercase letter. Intuitively, template (QT2.3) describes query (Q1) because the predicates of the query match those of the template (despite differences in order and in variable names), and the metapredicates evaluate to `true` when `$FP` is mapped to `'Rak'` and `$LP` to `'Aggr'`.

(D2) `answer(F,L,D,O,M) :-`　　　　　　(QT2.1)
　　　`emp(F,L,D,O,M)`
　　　`answer(F,L,D,O,M) :-`　　　　　　(QT2.2)
　　　`emp(F,L,D,O,M),`
　　　`prefix(L, $LP), _isalpha($LP)`
　　　`answer(F,L,D,O,M) :-`　　　　　　(QT2.3)
　　　`emp(F,L,D,O,M),`
　　　`prefix(L, $LP), prefix(F,$FP),`
　　　`_isalpha($LP), _isalpha($FP)`

---

[3] The "lookup" facility is very similar to a Stanford University facility.

[4] We could have used SPJ SQL queries instead of Datalog. Then, we would use a description language that looks like SQL and not Datalog. The same notions, *i.e.*, placeholders, nonterminals, and so on, hold. The CBR algorithm is also the same.

In general, a template describes any query that can be produced by the following steps:

1. *Map* each placeholder to a constant, e.g., map `$LP` to `'Aggr'`.
2. *Map* each template variable to a query variable, e.g., map `F` to `FN`.
3. *Evaluate* the metapredicates and discard any template that contains at least one metapredicate that evaluates to `false`.
4. *Permute* the template's subgoals.

2.2 Descriptions of Large and Infinite Sets of Supported Queries

RQDL can describe arbitrarily large sets of templates (and hence queries) when extended with nonterminals as in context-free grammars. Nonterminals are represented by identifiers that start with an underscore (_) and a capital letter. They have zero or more parameters and they are associated with *nonterminal templates*. A query template t containing nonterminals describes a query q if there is an *expansion* of t that describes q. An expansion of t is obtained by replacing each nonterminal N of t with one of the nonterminal templates that define N until there is no nonterminal in t.

For example, assume that `lookup` allows us to pose one or more substring conditions on one or more fields of `emp`. For example, we may pose query (Q3), which retrieves the data for employees whose office contains the strings `'alma'` and `'B'`.

(Q3) `answer(F,L,D,O,M) :- emp(F,L,D,O,M),`
　　　`substring(O,'alma'), substring(O,'B')`

(D4) uses the nonterminal `_Cond` to describe the supported queries. In this description the query template (QT4.1) is supported by nonterminal templates such as (NT4.1).

(D4)`answer(F,L,D,O,M) :-`　　　　　　(QT4.1)
　　　`emp(F,L,D,O,M), _Cond(F,L,D,O,M)`
　　　`_Cond(F,L,D,O,M) :`　　　　　　(NT4.1)
　　　`substring(F, $FS), _Cond(F,L,D,O,M)`
　　　`_Cond(F,L,D,O,M) :`　　　　　　(NT4.2)
　　　`substring(L, $LS), _Cond(F,L,D,O,M)`
　　　`_Cond(F,L,D,O,M) :`　　　　　　(NT4.3)
　　　`substring(D, $DS), _Cond(F,L,D,O,M)`
　　　`_Cond(F,L,D,O,M) :`　　　　　　(NT4.4)
　　　`substring(O,$OS), _Cond(F,L,D,O,M)`
　　　`_Cond(F,L,D,O,M) :`　　　　　　(NT4.5)
　　　`substring(M, $MS), _Cond(F,L,D,O,M)`
　　　`_Cond(F,L,D,O,M) :`　　　　　　(NT4.6)

To see that description (D4) describes query (Q3), we expand `_Cond(F,L,D,O,M)` in (QT4.1) with the nonterminal template (NT4.4) and then again expand `_Cond` with the same template. The `_Cond` subgoal in the resulting expansion is expanded by the empty template (NT4.6) to obtain expansion (E5).

(E5) `answer(F,L,D,O,M) :- emp(F,L,D,O,M),`
　　　`substring(O,$OS), substring(O,$OS1)`

Before a template is used for expansion, all of its variables are renamed to be unique. Hence, the second occurrence of placeholder $OS of template (NT4.4) is renamed to $OS1 in (E5). (E5) describes query (Q3), *i.e.*, the placeholders and variables of (E5) can be mapped to the constants and variables of (Q3).

2.3 Schema Independent Descriptions of Supported Queries

Description (D4) assumes that the wrapper exports a fixed schema. However, the query capabilities of many sources (and thus wrappers) are independent of the schemas of the data that reside in them. For example, a relational database allows SPJ queries on all of its relations. To support schema independent descriptions RQDL allows the use of placeholders in place of the relation name. Furthermore, to allow tables of arbitrary arity and column names, RQDL provides special variables called *vector variables*, or simply vectors, that match lists of variables that appear in a query. We represent vectors in our examples by identifiers starting with an underscore (_). In addition, we provide two built-in metapredicates to relate vectors and attributes: **_subset** and **_in**. **_subset**($_R$, $_A$) succeeds if each variable in the list that matches $_R$ appears in the list that matches $_A$. **_in**($Position, X, _A$) succeeds if $_A$ matches a variable list, and there is a query variable that matches X and appears at the position number that matches $Position. (For readability we will use *italics* for vectors and **bold** for metapredicates).

For example, consider a wrapper called `file-wrap` that accesses tables residing in plain UNIX files. It may output any subset of any table's fields and may impose one or more substring conditions on any field. Such a wrapper may be easily implemented using the UNIX utility AWK. (D6) uses vectors and the built-in metapredicates to describe the queries supported by `file-wrap`.

```
(D6) (QT6.1) answer(_R) :- $Table(_A),
               _Cond(_A), _subset(_R, _A)
     (NT6.1) _Cond(_A) :-_in($Position,X,_A),
               substring(X,$S), _Cond(_A)
     (NT6.2) _Cond(_A) :
```

In general, to decide whether a query is described by a template containing vectors we must expand the nonterminals, map the variables, placeholders, and vectors, and finally, evaluate any metapredicates. To illustrate this, we show how to verify that query (Q7) is described by (D6).

```
(Q7) answer(L,D) :- emp(F,L,D,O,M),
     substring(O,'alma'), substring(O,'B')
```

First, we expand (QT6.1) by replacing the nonterminal _Cond with (NT6.1) twice, and then with (NT6.2), thus obtaining expansion (E8).

```
(E8) answer(_R) :- $Table(_A),
     _in($Position,X,_A),substring(X,$S),
     _in($Position1,X1,_A),substring(X1,$S1),
     _subset(_R,_A)
```

Expansion (E8) describes query (Q7) because there is a mapping of variables, vectors, and placeholders of (E8) that makes the metapredicates succeed and makes every predicate of the expansion identical to a predicate of the query. Namely, vector $_A$ is mapped to `[F,L,D,O,M]`, vector $_R$ to `[L,D]`, placeholders $Position and $Position1 to 4, $S to 'alma', $S1 to 'B', and the variables X and X1 to O. We must be careful with vector mappings; if the vector $_V$ that maps to $[X_1, \ldots, X_n]$ appears in a metapredicate, we replace $_V$ with $[X_1, \ldots, X_n]$. However, if the vector $_V$ appears in a predicate as $p(_V)$ the mapping results in $p(X_1, \ldots, X_n)$. Finally, the metapredicate **_in**(4, O, `[F,L,D,O,M]`) succeeds because O is the fourth variable of the list, and **_subset**(`[L,D]`, `[F,L,D,O,M]`) succeeds because `[L,D]` is a "subset" of `[F,L,D,O,M]`.

Vectors are useful even when the schema is known as the specification may otherwise be repetitive, as in description (D4). In our running example, even though we know the attributes of **emp**, we save effort by not having to explicitly mention all of the column names to say that a substring condition can be placed on any column.

2.4 Query and Description Normal Form

If we allow templates' variables and vectors to map to arbitrary lists of constants and variables, descriptions may appear to support queries that the underlying wrapper does not support. This is because using the same variable name in different places in the query or description can cause an implicit join or selection that does not explicitly appear in the description. For example, consider query (Q9), which retrieves employees where the manager field is 'Y' and the first and last names are equal, as denoted by the double appearance of FL in **emp**.

```
(Q9) answer(FL,D) :- emp(FL,FL,D,O,'Y')
```

(D6) should not describe query (Q9). Nevertheless, we can construct expansion (E10), which erroneously matches query (Q9) if we map $_A$ to `[FL,FL,D,O,'Y']` and $_R$ to `[FL,D]`:

```
(E10) answer(_R):-$Table(_A), _subset(_R,_A)
```

This section introduces a query and description *normal form* that avoids inadvertently describing joins and selections that were not intended. In the normal form both queries and descriptions have only explicit equalities. A query is normalized by replacing every constant c with a unique variable V and then by introducing the subgoal $V = c$. Furthermore, for every join variable V that appears $n > 1$ times in the query we replace its instances with the unique variables $V_1, \ldots, V_n$ and introduce the subgoals $V_i = V_j, i = 1, \ldots, n, j = 1 \ldots, i - 1$. We replace any appearance of V in the head with V_1. For example, query (Q11) is the normal form of (Q9).

```
(Q11) answer(FL1,D) :- employee(FL1,FL2,D,O,M),
      FL1=FL2, M='Y'
```

Description (D6) does not describe (Q11) because (D6) does not support the equality conditions that

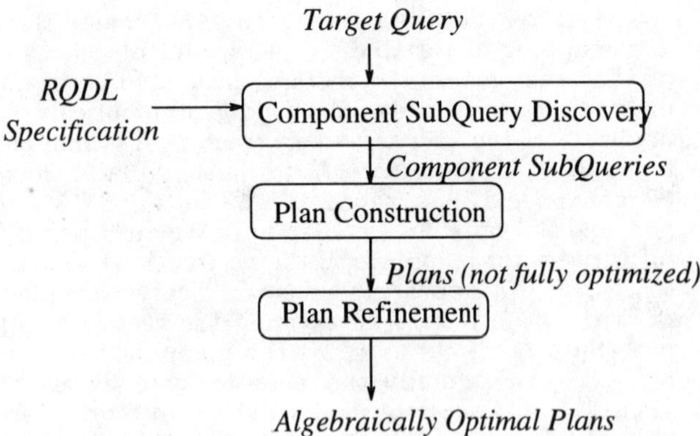

Figure 2: The CBR's components

appear in (Q11). Description (D12) supports equality conditions on any column and equalities between any two columns: (NT12.2) describes equalities with constants and (NT12.3) describes equalities between the columns of our table.

```
(D12) answer(_R) :-                          (QT12.1)
        $Table(_A), _Cond(_A), _subset(_R, _A)
      _Cond(_A) :                            (NT12.1)
       _in($Position,X,_A), substring(X, $S),
       _Cond(_A)
      _Cond(_A) :                            (NT12.2)
       _in($Position1,X,_A), X=$C, _Cond(_A)
      _Cond(_A) :                            (NT12.3)
       _in($Pos1,X,_A), _in($Pos2,Y,_A),
       X=Y, _Cond(_A)
      _Cond(_A) :                            (NT12.4)
```

For presentation purposes we use the more compact unnormalized form of queries and descriptions when there is no danger of introducing inadvertent selections and joins. However, the algorithms rely on the normal form.

3 The Capabilities-Based Rewriter

The Capabilities-Based Rewriter (CBR) determines whether a target query q is directly supported by the appropriate wrapper, $i.e.$, whether it matches the description d of the wrapper's capabilities. If not, the CBR determines whether q can be computed by combining a set of supported queries (using selections, projections and joins). In this case, the CBR will produce a set of plans for evaluating the query. The CBR consists of three modules, which are invoked serially (see Figure 2):

- **Component SubQuery (CSQ) Discovery:** finds supported queries that involve one or more subgoals of q. The CSQs that are returned contain the largest possible number of selections and joins, and do no projection. All other CSQs are pruned. This prevents an exponential explosion in the number of CSQs.

- **plan construction:** produces one or more plans that compute q by combining the CSQs exported by CSQ Discovery. The plan construction algorithm is based on query subsumption and has been tuned to perform efficiently in the cases typically arising in capabilities-based rewriting.

- **plan refinement:** refines the plans constructed by the previous phase by pushing as many projections as possible to the wrapper.

EXAMPLE 3.1 Consider query (Q13), which retrieves the names of all managers that manage departments that have employees with offices in the 'B' wing, and the employees' office numbers. This query is not directly supported by the wrapper described in (D12).

```
(Q13) answer(F0,L0,O1):-emp(F0,L0,D,O0,'Y'),
        emp(F1,L1,D,O1,M1), substring(O1,'B')
```

The CSQ detection module identifies and outputs the following CSQs:

```
(Q14) answer₁₄(F0,L0,D,O0) :-
        emp(F0,L0,D,O0,'Y')
(Q15) answer₁₅(F1,L1,D,O1,M1) :-
        emp(F1,L1,D,O1,M1), substring(O1, 'B')
```

Note, the CSQ discovery module does not output the 2^4 CSQs that have the tail of (Q14) but export a different subset of the variables F0, L0, D, and O0 (likewise for (Q15)). The CSQs that export fewer variables are pruned.

The plan construction module detects that a join on D of **answer₁₄** and **answer₁₅** produces the required **answer** of (Q13). Consequently, it derives the plan (P16).

```
    (P16) answer(F0,L0,O1) :-
            answer₁₄(F0,L0,D,O0),
            answer₁₅(F1,L1,D,O1,M1)
```

Finally, the plan refinement module detects that variables O0, F1, L1, and M1 in **answer₁₄** and **answer₁₅** are unnecessary. Consequently, it generates the more efficient plan (P19).

```
(Q17) answer₁₇(F0,L0,D) :-
        emp(F0,L0,D,O0,'Y')
(Q18) answer₁₈(D,O1) :-
        emp(F1,L1,D,O1,M1), substring(O1, 'B')
(P19) answer(F0,L0,O1) :-
        answer₁₇(F0,L0,D),  answer₁₈(D,O1)
```

$\square$

The CBR's goal is to produce all *algebraically optimal* plans for evaluating the query. An algebraically optimal plan is one in which any selection, projection or join that can be done in the wrapper is done there, and in which there are no unnecessary queries. More formally:

Definition 3.1 (Algebraically Optimal Plan P) A plan P is algebraically optimal if there is no other plan P' such that for every CSQ s of P there is a corresponding CSQ s' of P' such that the set of subgoals of s' is a superset of the set of subgoals of s (*i.e.*, s' has more selections and joins than s) and the set of exported variables of s is a superset of the set of exported variables of s' (*i.e.*, s' has more projections than s.) $\square$

In the next three sections we describe each of the modules of the CBR in turn.

4 CSQ Discovery

The CSQ discovery module takes as input a target query and a description. It operates as a rule production system where the templates of the description are the production rules and the subgoals of the target query are the base facts. The CSQ discovery module uses bottom-up evaluation because it is guaranteed to terminate even for recursive descriptions [10]. However, bottom-up derivation often derives unnecessary facts, unlike top-down. We use a variant of *magic sets rewriting* [10] to "focus" the bottom-up derivation. To further reduce the set of derived CSQs we develop two CSQ pruning techniques as decsribed in Sections 4.2 and 4.3. Reducing the number of derived CSQs makes the CSQ discovery more efficient and also reduces the size of the input to the plan construction module.

The query templates derive **answer** facts that correspond to CSQs. In particular, a derived **answer** fact is the head of a produced CSQ whereas the *underlying* base facts, *i.e.*, the facts that were used for deriving **answer**, are the subgoals of the CSQ. Nonterminal templates derive intermediate facts that may be used by other query or nonterminal templates. We keep track of the sets of facts underlying derived facts for pruning CSQs. The following example illustrates the bottom-up derivation of CSQs and the gains that we realize from the use of the magic-sets rewriting. The next subsection discusses issues pertaining to the derivation of facts containing vectors.

EXAMPLE 4.1 Consider query (Q3) and description (D4) from page 3. The subgoals **emp(F,L,D,O,M)**, **substring(O, 'alma')**, and **substring(O,'B')** are treated by the CSQ discovery module as base facts. To distinguish the variables in target query subgoals from the templates' variables we "freeze" the variables, e.g. **F,L,D,O**, into similarly named constants, e.g. **f,l,d,o**. Actual constants like **'B'** are in single quotes.

In the first round of derivations template (NT4.6) derives fact **_Cond(F,L,D,O,M)** without using any base fact (since the template has an empty body). Hence, the set of facts underlying the derived fact is empty. Variables are allowed in derived facts for nonterminals. The semantics is that the derived fact holds for any assignment of frozen constants to variables of the derived fact.

In the second round many templates can fire. For example, (NT4.4) derives the fact **_Cond(F,L,D,o,M)** using **_Cond(F,L,D,O,M)** and **substring(o,'alma')**, or using **_Cond(F,L,D,o,M)** and **substring(o,'B')**. Thus, we generate two facts that, though identical, they have different underlying sets and hence we must

retain both since they may generate different CSQs. In the second round we may also fire (NT4.6) again and produce **_Cond(F,L,D,O,M)** but we do not retain it since its set of underlying facts is equal to the version of **_Cond(F,L,D,O,M)** that we have already produced.

Eventually, we generate **answer(f,l,d,o,m)** with set of underlying facts **{emp(f,l,d,o,m), substring(o, 'alma'), substring(o,'B')}**. Hence we output the CSQ (Q3), which, incidentally, is the target query.

The above process can produce an exponential number of facts. For example, we could have proved **_Cond(o,L,D,O,M)**, **_Cond(F,o,D,O,M)**, **_Cond(o,o,D,O,M)**, and so on. In general, assuming that **emp** has n columns and we apply m substrings on it we may derive n^m facts. Magic-sets can remove this source of exponentiality by "focusing" the nonterminals. Applying magic-sets rewriting and the simplifications described in Chapter 13.4 of [10] we obtain the following equivalent description. We show only the rewriting of templates (NT4.4) and (NT4.6). The others are rewritten similarly.

```
(D20) answer(F,L,D,O,M) :-              (QT20.1)
         emp(F,L,D,O,M), _Cond(F,L,D,O,M)
      _Cond(F,L,D,Office,M) :            (NT20.4)
         mg_Cond(F,L,D,Office,M),
         substring(Office, $OS),
         _Cond(F,L,D,Office,M)
      _Cond(F,L,D,O,M) :                 (NT20.6)
         mg_Cond(F,L,D,O,M)
      mg_Cond(F,L,D,O,M) :               (MS20.1)
         emp(F,L,D,O,M)
```

Now, only **_Cond(f,l,d,o,m)** facts (with different underlying sets) are produced. Note, the magic-sets rewritten program uses the available information in a way similar to a top-down strategy and thus derives only relevant facts. $\square$

4.1 Derivations Involving Vectors

When the head of a nonterminal template contains a vector variable it may be possible that a derivation using this nonterminal may not be able either to bind the vector to a specific list of frozen variables or to allow the variable as is in the derived fact. The CSQ discovery module can not handle this situation. For most descriptions, magic-sets rewriting solves the problem. We demonstrate how and we formally define the set of non-problematic descriptions.

For example, let us fire template (NT6.1) of (D6) on the base facts produced by query (Q3). Assume also that (NT6.2) already derived **_Cond(_A)**. Then we derive that **_Cond(_A)** holds, with set of underlying facts **{substring(o, 'alma')}**, provided that the constraint "$_A$ contains o" holds. The constraint should follow the fact until $_A$ binds to some list of frozen variables. We avoid the mess of constraints using the following magic-sets rewriting of (D6).

```
(D21) answer(_R) :-                      (QT21.1)
         $Table(_A), _Cond(_A),
         _subset(_R, _A)
```

_Cond(_A) :   (NT21.1)
  mg_Cond(_A), _in($Position,X,_A),
  substring(X,$S), _Cond(_A)
_Cond(_A) : mg_Cond(_A)   (NT21.2)
mg_Cond(_A) : $Table(_A)   (MS21.1)

When rules (NT21.1) and (NT21.2) fire the first subgoal instantiates variable _A to [f,1,d,o,m] and they derive only _Cond([f,1,d,o,m]). Thus, magic-sets caused _A to be bound to the only vector of interest, namely [f,1,d,o,m]. Note a program that derives facts with unbound vectors may not be problematic because no metapredicate may use the unbound vector variable. However we take a conservative approach and consider only those programs that produce facts with only bound vector variables. Magic-sets rewriting does not always ensure that derived facts have bound vectors. In the rest of this section we describe sufficient conditions for guaranteeing the derivation of facts with bound vectors only. First we provide a condition (Theorem 4.1) that guarantees that a program (that may be the result of magic rewriting) does not derive facts with unbound vectors. Then we describe a class of programs that after being magic rewriteen satisfy the condition of Theorem 4.1.

Theorem 4.1 *A program will always produce facts with bound vector variables if in all rules "*__H__*(_V) : −tail"* `tail` *has a non-metapredicate subgoal that refers to _V, or in general _V can be assigned a binding if all non-metapredicate subgoals in* `tail` *are bound.* □

Intuitively, after we magic-rewrite a program it will keep deriving facts with unbound vectors only if a nonterminal of the initial program derives uninstantiated vectors and in the rules that is used it does not share variables with predicates or nonterminals *s* that bind their arguments (otherwise, the magic predicate will force the the rules that produce uninstantiated vectors to focus on bindings of *s*.) For example, specification (MS6) does not derive uninstantiated vectors because the nonterminal _Cond, that may derive uninstantiated variables, shares variables with $Table(_A). [8] provides a formal criterion for deciding whether the bottom-up evaluation derives facts that have vector variables. This criterion is used by the following algorithm that derives CSQs given a target query and a description.

Algorithm 1
Input: Target query Q and Description D
Output: A set of CSQs $s_i, i = 1, \ldots, n$
Method:
    Check if the program derives
          facts with vector variables (see [8])
    Reorder each template R in D such that
      All predicate subgoals occur in
          the front of the rule
      A nonterminal _N appears after _M if _N
          depends on _M for grounding.
      Metapredicates appear at the end of the rule
    Rewrite D using Magic-sets
    Evaluate bottom-up the rewritten description D
          as described in [8]

Note, template R can always be reordered. The proof appears in [8].

4.2 Retaining Only "Representative" CSQs

A large number of unneeded CSQs are generated by templates that use vectors and the _subset metapredicate. For example, template (QT12.1) describes for a particular __A__ all CSQs that have in their head any subset of variables in __A__. It is not necessary to generate all possible CSQs. Instead, for all CSQs that are derived from the same expansion e, of some template t, where e has the form

answer(_V) :- ⟨*predicate and metapredicate list*⟩,
  _subset(_V,_W)

and   _V   does   not   appear in the ⟨*predicate and metapredicate list*⟩ we generate only the *representative* CSQ that is derived by mapping _V to the same variable list as _W.[5] All *represented* CSQs, *i.e.*, CSQs that are derived from e by mapping _V to a proper subset of _W are not generated. For example, the representative CSQ (Q15) and the represented CSQ (Q18) both are derived from the expansion (E22) of template (QT12.1).

(E22) **answer**(_R) :- $Table(_A),
    _in($Position,X,_A), substring(X,'B'),
    _subset(_R,_A)

The CSQ discovery module generates only (Q15) and not (Q18) because (Q15) has fewer attributes than (Q18) and is derived by by mapping the vector _R to the same vector with _A, *i.e.*, to [F1,L1,D,O1,M1]. Representative CSQs often retain unneeded attributes and consequently *Representative plans*, *i.e.*, plans containing representative CSQs, retrieve unneeded attributes. The unneeded attributes are projected out by the plan refinement module.

Theorem 4.2 *Retaining only representative CSQs does not lose any plan, i.e., if there is an algebraically optimal plan p_s that involves a represented query s then p_s will be discovered by the CBR.* □

The intuitive proof of this claim is that for every plan p_s there is a corresponding representative plan p_r derived by replacing all CSQs of p_s with their representatives. Then, given that the plan refinement component considers all plans represented by a representative plan, we can be sure that the CBR algorithm does not lose any plan. The complete proof appears in [8].
Evaluation: Retaining only a representative CSQ of head arity a eliminates $2^a − 1$ represented CSQs thus

---

[5]In general, the ⟨*list of predicates and metapredicates*⟩ may contain metapredicates of the form _in(⟨*position*⟩,⟨*variable$_i$*⟩, _V),$i = 1,\ldots,m$. In this case, the template describes all CSQs that output a subset of _W and a superset of $S = \{⟨variable⟩_1,\ldots,⟨variable⟩_m\}$. The CSQ discovery module outputs, as usual, the representative CSQ and annotates it with the set S that provides the "minimum" set of variables that represented CSQs must export. In this paper we will not describe any further the extensions needed for the handling of this case.

eliminating an exponential factor from the execution time and from the size of the output of the CSQ discovery module. Still, one might ask why the CSQ discovery phase does not remove the variables that can be projected out. The reason is that the "projection" step is better done after plans are formed because at that time information is available about the other CSQs in the plan and the way they interact (see Section 6). Thus, though postponing projection pushes part of the complexity to a later stage, it eliminates some complexity altogether. The eliminated complexity corresponds to those represented CSQs that in the end do not participate in any plan because they retain too few variables.

4.3 Pruning Non-Maximal CSQs

Further efficiency can be gained by eliminating any CSQ Q that has fewer subgoals than some other CSQ Q' because Q checks fewer conditions than Q'. A CSQ is maximal if there is no CSQ with more subgoals and the same set of exported variables, modulo variable renaming. We formalize maximality in terms of subsumption [10]:

Definition 4.1 (Maximal CSQs) A CSQ s_m is a *maximal CSQ* if there is no other CSQ s that is subsumed by s_m. □

Evaluation: In general, the CSQ discovery module generates only *maximal* CSQs and prunes all others. This pruning technique is particularly effective when the CSQs contain a large number of conditions. For example, assume that g conditions are applied to the variables of a predicate. Consequently, there are $2^g - 1$ CSQs where each one of them contains a different proper subset of the conditions. By keeping "maximal CSQs only" we eliminate an exponential factor of 2^g from the output size of the CSQ discovery module.

Theorem 4.3 *Pruning non-maximal CSQs does not lose any algebraically optimal plan.* □

The reason is that for every plan p_s involving a non-maximal CSQ s there is also a plan p_m that involves the corresponding maximal CSQ s_m such that p_m pushes more selections and/or joins to the wrapper than p_s, since s_m by definition involves more selections and/or joins than s.

5 Plan Construction

In this section we present the plan construction module (see Figure 2.) In order to generate a (representative) plan we have to select a subset S of the CSQs that provides all the information needed by the target query, *i.e.*, (i) the CSQs in S check all the subgoals of the target query, (ii) the results in S can be joined correctly, and (iii) each CSQ in S receives the constants necessary for its evaluation. Section 5.1 addresses (i) with the notion of "subgoal consumption." Section 5.2 checks (ii), *i.e.*, checks join variables. Section 5.3 checks (iii) by ensuring bindings are available. Finally, Section 5.4 summarizes the conditions required for constructing a plan and provides an efficient plan construction algorithm.

5.1 Set of Consumed Subgoals

We associate with each CSQ a set of consumed subgoals that describes the CSQs contribution to a plan. Loosely speaking, a component query consumes a subgoal if it extracts all the required information from that subgoal. A CSQ does not necessarily consume all its subgoals. For example, consider a CSQ s_e that semijoins the **emp** relation with the **dept** relation to output each **emp** tuple that is in some department in relation **dept**. Even though this CSQ has a subgoal that refers to the **dept** relation it may not always consume the **dept** subgoal. In particular, consider a target query Q that requires the names of all employees and the location of their departments. CSQ s_e does not output the location attribute of table **dept** and thus does not consume the **dept** subgoal with respect to query Q. We formalize the above intuition by the following definition:

Definition 5.1 (Set of Consumed Subgoals for a CSQ) A set $\mathcal{S}_s$ of subgoals of a CSQ s constitutes a *set of consumed subgoals* of s if and only if

1. s exports every distinguished variable of the target query that appears in $\mathcal{S}_s$, and

2. s exports every join variable that appears in $\mathcal{S}_s$ and also appears in a subgoal of the target query that is not in $\mathcal{S}_s$.

□

Theorem 5.1 *Each CSQ has a unique* maximal *set of consumed subgoals that is a superset of every other set of consumed subgoals.* □

The proof of the uniqueness of the maximal consumed set appears in [8]. Intuitively the maximal set describes the "largest" contribution that a CSQ may have in a plan. The following algorithm states how to compute the set of maximal consumed subgoals of a CSQ. We annotate every CSQ s with its set of maximal consumed subgoals, $\mathcal{C}_s$.

Algorithm 2
  Input: CSQ s and target query Q
  Output: CSQ s with computed annotation $\mathcal{C}_s$
  Method:
      Insert in $\mathcal{C}_s$ all subgoals of s
      Remove from $\mathcal{C}_s$ subgoals that have a
      distinguished attribute of Q not exported by s
      Repeat until size of $\mathcal{C}_s$ is unchanged
         Remove from $\mathcal{C}_s$ subgoals that:
            Join on variable V with subgoal g
            of Q where g is not in $\mathcal{C}_s$, and
            Join variable V is not exported by s
      Discard CSQ s if $\mathcal{C}_s$ is empty.

This algorithm is polynomial in the number of the subgoals and variables of the CSQ. Also, the algorithm discards all CSQs that are not *relevant* to the target query:

Definition 5.2 (Relevant CSQ) A CSQ s is called *relevant* if $\mathcal{C}_s$ is non-empty. □

Intuitively, irrelevant CSQs are pruned out because in most cases they do not contribute to a plan, since they do not consume any subgoal. Note, we decide the relevance of a CSQ "locally," *i.e.*, without considering other CSQs that it may have to join with. By pruning non-relevant CSQs we can build an efficient plan construction algorithm that in most cases (Section 5.2) produces each plan in time polynomial in the number of CSQs produced by the CSQ discovery module. However, there are scenarios (see the extended version [8]) where the relevance criteria may erroneously prune out a CSQ that could be part of a plan. We may avoid the loss of such plans by not pruning irrelevant CSQs and thus sacrificing the polynomiality of the plan construction algorithm. In this paper we will not consider this option.

5.2 Join Variables Condition

It is not always the case that if the union of consumed subgoals of some CSQs is equal to the set of the target query's subgoals then the CSQs together form a plan. In particular, it is possible that the join of the CSQs may not constitute a plan. For example, consider an online employee database that can be queries for the names of all employees in a given division. The database can also be queried for the names of all employees in a given location. Further, the name of an employee is not uniquely determined by their location and division. The employee database cannot be used to find employees in a given division and in a given location by joining the results of two queries - one on division and the other on location. To see this, consider a query that looks for employees in "CS" in "New York". Joining the results of two independent queries on division and location will incorectly return as answer a person named "John Smith" if there is a "John Smith" in "CS" in "San Jose" and a different "John Smith" in "Electrical" in "New York".

Intuitively, the problem arises because the two independent queries do not export the information necessary to correctly join their results. We can avoid this problem by checking that CSQs are combined only if they export the join variables necessary for their correct combination. The theorem of Section 5.4 formally describes the conditions on join variables that guarantee the correct combination of CSQs.

5.3 Passing Required Bindings via Nested Loops Joins

The CBR's plans may emulate joins that could not be pushed to the wrapper, with nested loops joins where one CSQ passes join variable bindings to the other. For example, we may compute (Q13) by the following steps: first we execute (Q23); then we collect the department names (*i.e.*, the D bindings) and for each binding d of D, we replace the $D in (Q24) with d and send the instantiated query to the wrapper. We use the notation /$D in the nested loops plan (P25) to denote that (Q24) receives values for the $D placeholder from D *bindings* of the other CSQs - (Q23) in this example.

(Q23) answer$_{23}$(F0,L0,D,O0):-emp(F0,L0,D,O0,'Y')
(Q24) answer$_{24}$(F1,L1,O1,M1):-emp(F1,L1,$D,O1,M1)

(P25) answer(F0,L0,O1) :- answer$_{23}$(F0,L0,D,O0), answer$_{24}$(F1,L1,O1,M1)/$D

The introduction of nested loops and *binding passing* poses the following requirements on the CSQ discovery:

- **CSQ discovery:** A subgoal of a CSQ s may contain placeholders /$$\langle var \rangle$, such as $D, in place of corresponding join variables (D in our example.) Whenever this is the case, we introduce the structure /$$\langle var \rangle$ next to the **answer**$_s$ that appears in the plan. All the variables of s that appear in such a structure are included in the set $\mathcal{B}_s$, called the *set of bindings needed by* s. For example, $\mathcal{B}_{24} = \{D\}$ and $\mathcal{B}_{23} = \{\}$. CSQ discovery previously did not use bindings information while deriving facts. Thus, the algorithm derives useless CSQs that need bindings not exported by any other CSQ.

  The optimized derivation process uses two sets of attributes and proceeds iteratively. Each iteration derives only those facts that use bindings provided by existing facts. In addition, a fact is derived if it uses at least one binding that was made available only in the very last iteration. Thus, the first iteration derives facts that need no bindings, that is, for which $\mathcal{B}_s$ is empty. The next iteration derives facts that use at least one binding provided by facts derived in iteration one. Thus, the second iteration does not derive any subgoal derived in the first iteration, and so on. The complete algorithm that appears in [8] formalizes this intuition.

The bindings needed by each CSQ of a plan impose order constraints on the plan. For example, the existence of D in $\mathcal{B}_{24}$ requires that a CSQ that exports D is executed before (Q24). It is the responsibility of the plan construction module to ensure that the produced plans satisfy the order constraints.

Evaluation The pruning of CSQs with inappropriate bindings prunes an exponential number of CSQs in the following common scenario: Assume we can put an equality condition on any variable of a subgoal p. Consider a CSQ s that contains p and assume that n variables of p appear in subgoals of the target query that are not contained in s. Then we have to generate all 2^n versions of s that describe different binding patterns. Assuming that no CSQ may provide any of the n variables it is only one (out the 2^n) CSQs useful.

5.4 A Plan Construction Algorithm

In this section we summarize the conditions that are sufficient for construction of a plan. Then, we present an efficient algorithm that finds plans that satisfy the theorem's conditions. Finally, we evaluate the algorithm's performance.

Theorem 5.2 *Given CSQs $s_i, i = 1, \ldots, n$ with corresponding heads* **answer**$_i(V_1^i, \ldots, V_{v_i}^i)$, *sets of maximal consumed subgoals $\mathcal{C}_i$ and sets of needed bindings $\mathcal{B}_i$, the plan*

$$\mathtt{answer}(V_1, \ldots, V_m) : -\mathtt{answer}_1(V_1^1, \ldots, V_{v_1}^1),$$
$$\ldots, \mathtt{answer}_n(V_1^n, \ldots, V_{v_n}^n)$$

is correct if

- **consumed sets condition:** *The union of maximal consumed sets $\cup_{i=1,\ldots,n} C_i$ is equal to the target query's subgoal set.*

- **join variables condition:** *If the set of maximal consumed subgoals of CSQ s_i has a join variable V then every CSQ s_j that contains V in its set of maximal consumed subgoals C_j exports V.*

- **bindings passing condition:** *If $V \in \mathcal{B}_i$ then there must be a CSQ $s_j, j < i$ that exports V.* $\square$

The proof is based on the theory of containment mappings appropriately extended to take into consideration nested loops [8].

The plan construction algorithm in the extended version of the paper [8] is based on Theorem 5.2. The algorithm takes as input a set of CSQs derived by the CSQ discovery process described later, and the target query Q. At each step the algorithm selects a CSQ s that consumes at least one subgoal that has not been consumed by any CSQ s' considered so far and for which all variables of $\mathcal{B}_s$ have been exported by at least one s'. Assuming that the algorithm is given m CSQs (by the CSQ discovery module) it can construct a set that satisfies the consumed sets and the bindings passing conditions in time polynomial in m. Nevertheless, if the join variables condition does not hold the algorithm takes time exponential in m because we may have to create exponentially many sets until we find one that satisfies the join variables condition. However, the join variables condition evaluates to true for most wrappers we find in practice (see following discussion) and thus we usually construct a plan in time polynomial in m.

For every plan p there may be plans p' that are identical to p modulo a permutation of the CSQs of p. In the worst case there are $n_p!$ permutations, where n_p is the number of CSQs in p. Since it is useless to generate permutations of the same plan, The algorithm creates a total order $\prec$ of the input CSQs and generates plans by considering CSQ s_1 before CSQ s_2 only if $s_1 \prec s_2$, *i.e.*, the CSQs are considered in order by $\prec$. Note, a query s_2 must always be considered after a query s_1 if s_1 provides bindings for s_2. Hence, $\prec$ must respect the partial order $\overset{\prec}{b}$ where $s_1 \overset{\prec}{b} s_2$ if s_1 provides bindings to s_2.

The plan construction algorithm first sorts the input CSQs in a total order that respects the PO $\prec$. Then it procedes by picking CSQs and testing the conditions of Theorem 5.2 until it consumes all subgoals of the target query. The algorithm capitalizes on the assumption that in most practical cases every CSQ consumes at least one subgoal and the join variables condition holds. In this case, one plan is developed in time polynomial in the number of input CSQs. The following lemma describes an important case where the join variables condition always holds.

Lemma 5.1 *The join variables condition holds for any set of CSQs such that*

1. *no two CSQs of the set have intersecting sets of maximal consumed subgoals, or*

2. *if two CSQs contain the subgoal $g(V_1, \ldots, V_m)$ in their sets of maximal consumed subgoals then they both export variables $V_1, \ldots, V_m$.* $\square$

Condition (1) of Lemma 5.1 holds for typical wrappers of bibliographic information systems and lookup services (wrappers that have the structure of (D12)), relational databases and object oriented databases – wrapped in a relational model. In such systems it is typical that if two CSQs have common subgoals then they can be combined to form a single CSQ. Thus, we end up with a set of maximal CSQs that have non-intersecting consumed sets. Condition (2) further relaxes the condition (1). Condition (2) holds for all wrappers that can export all variables that appear in a CSQ. The two conditions of Lemma 5.1 cover essentially any wrapper of practical importance.

6 Plan Refinement

The plan refinement module filters and refines constructed plans in two ways. First, it eliminates plans that are not algebraically optimal. The fact that CSQs of the representative plans have the maximum number of selections and joins and that plan refinement pushes the maximum number of projections down is not enough to guarantee that the plans produced are algebraically optimal. For example, assume that CSQs s_1 and s_2 are interchangeable in all plans, and the set of subgoals of s_1 is a superset of the set of subgoals of s_2 and s_1 exports a subset of the variables exported by s_2. The plans in which s_2 participates are algebraically worse than the corresponding plans with s_1. Nevertheless, they are produced by the plan construction module because s_1 and s_2 may both be maximal, and do not represent each other because they are produced by different template expansions. Plan refinement must therefore eliminate plans that include s_2.

Plan refinement must also project out unnecessary variables from representative CSQs. Intuitively, the *necessary* variables of a representative CSQ are those variables that allow the consumed set of the CSQ to "interface" with the consumed sets of other CSQs in the plan. We formalize this notion and its significance by the following definition (note, the definition is not restricted to maximal consumed sets):

Definition 6.1 (Necessary Variables of a Set of Consumed Subgoals:) A variable V is a necessary variable of the consumed subgoals set $\mathcal{S}_s$ of some CSQ s if, by not exporting V, $\mathcal{S}_s$ is no longer a consumed set. $\square$

The set of necessary variables is easily computed: Given a set of consumed subgoals $\mathcal{S}$, a variable V of $\mathcal{S}$ is a necessary variable if it is a distinguished variable, or if it is a join variable that appears in at least one subgoal that is not in $\mathcal{S}$.

Due to space limitations the complete plan refinement algorithm and its evaluation appear in [8]. Its main complication is due to the fact that unecessary variables cannot always be projected out when the maximal consumed sets of the CSQs intersect.

7 Evaluation

The CBR algorithm employs many techniques to eliminate sources of exponentiality that would otherwise arise in many practical cases. The **evaluation** paragraphs of many sections in this paper describe the benefit we derive from using these techniques. Remember that our assumption that every CSQ consumes at least one subgoal led to a plan construction module that develops a plan in time polynomial to the number of CSQs produced by the CSQ detection module, provided that the join variables condition holds. This is an important result because the join variables condition holds for most wrappers in practice, as argued in Subsection 5.4.

The CBR deals only with Select-Project-Join queries and their corresponding descriptions. It produces algebraically optimal plans involving CSQs, *i.e.*, plans that push the maximum number of selections, projections and joins to the source. However, the CBR is not complete because it misses plans that contain irrelevant CSQs (see Definition 5.2 and the discussion of Section 5.1.) On the other hand, the techniques for eliminating exponentiality preserve completeness, in that we do not miss any plan through applying one of these techniques (see justifications in Sections 4.2, 4.3.)

8 Related Work

Significant results have been developed for the resolution of semantic and schematic discrepancies while integrating heterogeneous information sources. However, most of these systems [11, 12, 4, 13] do not address the problem of different and limited query capabilities in the underlying sources because they assume that those sources are full-fledged databases that can answer any query over their schema.[6] The recent interest in the integration of arbitrary information sources, including databases, file systems, the Web, and many legacy systems, invalidates the assumption that all underlying sources can answer any query over the data they export and forces us to resolve the mismatch between the query capabilities provided by these sources. Only a few systems have addressed this problem.

HERMES [11] proposes a rule language for the specification of mediators in which an explicit set of parameterized calls can be made to the sources. At run-time the parameters are instantiated by specific values and the corresponding calls are made. Thus, HERMES guarantees that all queries sent to the wrappers are supported. Unfortunately, this solution reduces the interface between wrappers and mediators to a very simple form (the particular parameterized

calls), and does not fully utilize the sources' query power.

DISCO [14]describes the set of supported queries using context-free grammars. This technique reduces the efficiency of capabilities-based rewriting because it treats queries as "strings."

The Information Manifold [15] develops a query capabilities description that is attached to the schema exported by the wrapper. The description states which and how many conditions may be applied on each attribute. RQDL provides greater expressive power by being able to express schema-independent descriptions and descriptions such as "exactly one condition is allowed."

TSIMMIS suggests an explicit description of the wrapper's query capabilities [5], using the context-free grammar approach of the current paper. (The description is also used for query translation from the common query language to the language of the underlying source.) However, TSIMMIS considers a restricted form of the problem wherein descriptions consider relations of prespecified arities and the mediator can only select or project the results of a single CSQ.

This paper enhances the query capability description language of [5] to describe queries over arbitrary schemas, namely, relations with unspecified arities and names, as well as capabilities such as "selections on the first attribute of any relation." The language also allows specification of required bindings, *e.g.*, a bibliography database that returns "titles of books given author names." We provide algorithms for identifying for a target query Q the algebraically optimal CSQs from the given descriptions. Also, we provide algorithms for generating plans for Q by combining the results of these CSQs using selections, projections, and joins.

The CBR problem is related to the problem of determining how to answer a query using a set of materialized views [16, 6, 7, 17]. However, there are significant differences. These papers consider a specification language that uses SPJ expressions over given relations specifying a finite number of views. They cannot express arbitrary relations, arbitrary arities, binding requirements (with the exception of [7]), or infinitely large queries/views. Also, they do not consider generating plans that require a particular evaluation order due to binding requirements.

[6] shows that rewriting a conjunctive query is in general exponential in the total size of the query and views. [17] shows that if the query is acyclic we can rewrite it in time polynomial to the total size of the query and views. [6, 7] generate necessary and sufficient conditions for when a query can be answered by the available views. By contrast, our algorithms check only sufficient conditions and might miss a plan because of the heuristics used. Our algorithm can be viewed as a generalization of algorithms that decide the subsumption of a datalog query by a datalog program (*i.e.*, the description). Recently [18] proposed Datalog for the description of supported queries. It also suggested an algorithm that essentially finds what we call maximal CSQs.

---

[6] The work in query decomposition in distributed databases has also assumed that all underlying systems are relational and equally able to perform any SQL query.

9 Conclusions and Future Work

In this paper, we presented the Relational Query Description Language, RQDL, which provides powerful features for the description of wrappers' query capabilities. RQDL allows the description of infinite sets of arbitrarily large queries over arbitrary schemas. We also introduced the Capabilities-Based Rewriter, CBR, and presented an algorithm that discovers plans for computing a wrapper's target query using only queries supported by the wrapper. Despite the inherent exponentiality of the problem, the CBR uses optimizations and heuristics to produce plans in reasonable time in most practical situations.

The output of the CBR algorithm, in terms of the number of derived plans, remains a major source of exponentiality. Though the CBR prunes the output plans by deriving a plan only if no other plan pushes more selections, projections or joins to the source, it may still be the case that the number of plans is exponential in the number of subgoals and/or join variables. For example, consider the case where our query involves a chain of n joins and each one of them can be accomplished either by a left-to-right nested loops join, or a right-to-left nested loops join, or a local join. In this case, CBR has to output 3^n plans where each of the plans employs one of the three join methods. Then, the mediator's cost-based optimizer would have to estimate the cost of each one of the plans and choose the most efficient. We could modify the CBR to generate all of these plans or only some of them, depending on the time to be spent on optimization.

Currently, we are looking at implementing a CBR for IBM's Garlic system [1]. We are also investigating tighter couplings between the mediator's cost-based optimizer and the CBR. Finally, we are investigating more powerful rewriting techniques that may replace a target query's subgoals with combinations of semantically equivalent subgoals that are supported by the wrapper.

Acknowledgements

We are grateful to Mike Carey, Hector Garcia-Molina, Anand Rajaraman, Anthony Tomasic, Jeff Ullman, Ed Wimmers, and Jennifer Widom for many fruitful discussions and comments.

References

[1] M.J. Carey et al. Towards heterogeneous multimedia information systems: The Garlic approach. In *Proc. RIDE-DOM Workshop*, pages 124–31, 1995.

[2] Y. Papakonstantinou, H. Garcia-Molina, and J. Widom. Object exchange across heterogeneous information sources. In *Proc. ICDE Conf.*, pages 251–60, 1995.

[3] J.C. Franchitti and R. King. Amalgame: a tool for creating interoperating persistent, heterogeneous components. *Advanced Database Systems*, pages 313–36, 1993.

[4] R. Ahmed et al. The Pegasus heterogeneous multi-database system. *IEEE Computer*, 24:19–27, 1991.

[5] Y. Papakonstantinou, A. Gupta, H. Garcia-Molina, and J. Ullman. A query translation scheme for the rapid implementation of wrappers. In *Proc. DOOD Conf.*, pages 161–86, 1995.

[6] A. Levy, A. Mendelzon, Y. Sagiv, and D. Srivastava. Answering queries using views. In *Proc. PODS Conf.*, pages 95–104, 1995.

[7] A. Rajaraman, Y. Sagiv, and J. Ullman. Answering queries using templates with binding patterns. In *Proc. PODS Conf.*, pages 105–112, 1995.

[8] Y. Papakonstantinou, A. Gupta, and L. Haas. Capabilities-based query rewriting in mediator systems. Available via ftp at `db.stanford.edu` file `/pub/papakonstantinou/1995/cbr-extended.ps`.

[9] J.D. Ullman. *Principles of Database and Knowledge-Base Systems, Vol. I: Classical Database Systems*. Computer Science Press, New York, NY, 1988.

[10] J.D. Ullman. *Principles of Database and Knowledge-Base Systems, Vol. II: The New Technologies*. Computer Science Press, New York, NY, 1989.

[11] V.S. Subrahmanian et al. HERMES: A heterogeneous reasoning and mediator system. http://www.cs.umd.edu/projects/hermes/overview/paper.

[12] J. Hammer and D. McLeod. An approach to resolving semantic heterogeneity in a federation of autonomous, heterogeneous database systems. *Intl Journal of Intelligent and Cooperative information Systems*, 2:51–83, 1993.

[13] A. Gupta. *Integration of Information Systems: Bridging Heterogeneous Databases*. IEEE Press, 1989.

[14] A. Tomasic, L. Raschid, and P. Valduriez. Scaling heterogeneous databases and the design of DISCO. Technical report, INRIA, 1995.

[15] A. Levy, A. Rajaraman, and J. Ordille. Query processing in the information manifold. In *Proc. VLDB*, 1996.

[16] P.A. Larson and H.Z. Yang. Computing queries from derived relations. In *Proc. VLDB Conf.*, pages 259–69, 1985.

[17] Xiaolei Qian. Query folding. In *Proc. ICDE*, pages 48–55, 1996.

[18] A. Levy, A. Rajaraman, and J. Ullman. Answering queries using limited external processors. In *Proc. PODS*, pages 227–37, 1996.

Session 5B

Replication

Repairman Models for Replicated Data Management: A Case Study

Ing-Ray Chen*

Department of Computer & Info. Sciences
University of North Florida
Jacksonville, FL 32224-2645

Ding-Chau Wang

Institute of Inforamtion Engineering
National Cheng Kung University
Tainan, Taiwan

Abstract

Pessimistic control algorithms for replicated data permit only one partition to perform update operations at any time so as to ensure mutual exclusion of the replicated data object. Existing availability modeling and analyses of pessimistic control algorithms are constrained to either site-failure or link-failure only models, but not both, because of the large state space which needs to be considered. Moreover, the assumption of having an independent repairman for each link and each site has been made to reduce the complexity of analysis. In this paper, we remove these restrictions with the help of stochastic Petri nets. In particular, we investigate the effect of repair dependency which occurs when sites and links may have to share the same repairman. Four repairman models are examined in the paper: (a) independent repairman with one repairman assigned to each link and each node; (b) dependent repairman with FIFO servicing discipline; (c) dependent repairman with linear-order servicing discipline; and (d) dependent repairman with best-first servicing discipline. Using dynamic voting as a case study, we compare and contrast the resulting availabilities due to the use of these four different repairman models and give a physical interpretation of the differences.

Index Terms — *Data replication, pessimistic control algorithms, repairman models, availability analysis, dynamic voting, distributed systems, stochastic Petri nets.*

1 Introduction

Pessimistic control algorithms for replicated data permit only one partition to perform update operations at any given time so as to ensure mutual exclusion of the replicated data object. Over the past few years, various pessimistic algorithms based on voting (e.g., [1, 7]) and quorum consensus (e.g., [2, 3, 9, 11]) have been proposed in the literature and many recent works discuss how to distribute replicated data to improve the performance of the system [12, 13]. These past works mainly emphasized the algorithmic aspects and correctness proofs of their approaches with little or inadequate availability modeling and analyses. To

date, the availability analysis of these pessimistic algorithms is constrained to either site or link models, but not both, possibly because of the large state space that needs to be considered. Moreover, an independent repairman associated with each link or site has always been assumed to reduce the complexity of analysis. Ironically, although pessimistic algorithms were designed to deal with network partitioning problems, these past works were content with availability analyses based on site-failure-only system models. The only exception is the work by Jajodia and Mutchler [7] who have considered the site and link models separately, but not altogether in one model.

This paper removes these inadequate modeling restrictions with the help of stochastic Petri nets. In particular, we examine the effect of repair dependency where all sites and/or links may share the same repairman due to repair resource constraints. Using dynamic voting as a case study, we compare and contrast the resulting availabilities under different repairman models. Our objective is to provide a more informative, realistic estimation of the availability metric in the presence of both site/link failures and repair dependencies. Although we have chosen to test the modeling techniques developed in the paper with dynamic voting, it will become clear later that these techniques can be generally applicable to other pessimistic algorithms. We pick dynamic voting as a case study simply because analytical results under site- or link-failures/repairs only models (but not both altogether) are available in [7], against which we can validate our Petri net models at the boundary conditions.

The rest of the paper is organized as follows. Section 2 gives an overview of dynamic voting; states the assumptions and notation used; and develops a stochastic Petri net (SPN) model for dynamic voting that considers both site and link failures/repairs for the case when each site or link has its own independent repairman. Section 3 considers three dependent repairman models in which all sites/links share the same repairman: (a) First In First Out (FIFO) (b) linear-order and (c) best-first. In the linear-order repairman model, we always repair failed sites or links in a prespecified order, whereas in the best-first repairman model, we intelligently select a failed site or link among all whose repair will result in the largest improvement in availability. Section 4 compares the

---

*On leave from National Cheng Kung University, Taiwan.

184

availabilities obtained under various repairman models for a 5-site ring topology and provides a physical interpretation. Section 5 summarizes the paper and outlines some future research areas.

2 System Model and Assumptions

We illustrate the key modeling techniques developed in this paper by an example pessimistic control algorithm called dynamic voting developed by Jajodia and Mutchler [7]. A detailed description of the dynamic voting can be found in [5, 6, 7]. Here, we only give a background overview of the algorithm.

2.1 Background

It is instructive to view voting as a form of quorum consensus which must satisfy the quorum intersection property, i.e., let R and W be the cardinalities of any two read and write quorums on the same data item, respectively, then $R+W$ as well as $2W$ must be greater than the total number of copies to ensure mutual exclusion. Taking this view, dynamic voting is different from static voting in that its quorum set can be adjusted dynamically in reaction to system state changes, as opposed to a fixed quorum set as in the static voting scheme. The principle concept of dynamic voting is that instead of using a static quorum set based on the original set of copies, it uses the current up-to-date copies at any time for deriving its dynamic quorum set. This way, the system can adjust its quorum set dynamically in response to state changes and it results in an increase in availability when compared with static voting because of a higher probability of finding a quorum to serve an operation.

Suppose that a data item (e.g., a file) f is replicated to n copies, stored at sites $S_1, S_2, \ldots, S_n$. The essence of dynamic voting is that it must keep track of the number of up-to-date copies involved in the last update, and also which copies are up-to-date. To achieve this, consider a version of the dynamic voting algorithm where each copy is associated with three variables, VN, SC and DS, such that VN stores the version number of the local copy and can serve as an indicator to tell if the local copy is current; SC records the number of current copies participated in the last update of f; and DS stores the id of the highest linearly-ordered site among all sites that presently store current copies. A copy bearing the highest version number is called a current copy. Let (VN_i, SC_i, DS_i) be the set associated with the copy stored in site S_i. Initially, all copies are current and $VN_i = 0$, $SC_i = n$, $DS_i = n$ for all S_i's, where DS_i is initialized to n because S_n is the highest linearly-ordered site among all initially. When receiving an update operation, a site C (called the coordinator) requests all sites that have a copy of f to send their values of (VN_i, SC_i, DS_i). Let $\mathcal{P}$ denote the set consisting of the coordinator C and all subordinates responded to the request; each site in set $\mathcal{P}$ locks its copy of the data item f during the process. Site C then inspects the largest version number, VN_p, found in set $\mathcal{P}$. Let $\mathcal{I}$ denote the subset consisting of only those sites containing a copy with version number VN_p. Let SC_p and DS_p be the values stored in SC_i and DS_i of any

site in set $\mathcal{I}$, respectively. If one of the following two conditions is true, then site C is in the major partition: (a) the cardinality of $\mathcal{I}$ is larger than one half of SC_p; (b) the cardinality of $\mathcal{I}$ is exactly equal to one half of SC_p and set $\mathcal{I}$ contains site DS_p. If neither condition is true, site C aborts the update, sends ABORT messages to subordinates and releases the lock on its local copy. The update operation can retry at a later time. Otherwise, site C is in the major partition. It thus commits the update locally, sends COMMIT messages to subordinates along with the new update and new value of (VN, SC, DS), and releases the lock on its local copy. The new value of (VN, SC, DS) is set to (VN_p+1, the cardinality of set $\mathcal{P}$, the id of the highest linearly-ordered site found in $\mathcal{P}$). A termination protocol can be used to correctly terminate the execution of the update process if it is interrupted by failures. A possible terminal protocol can be found in [7] and is not described here. To simplify our presentation, this paper only considers update operations, although the SPN models developed in the paper can be easily applied to handle read operations.

2.2 Assumptions and Availability Metric

We first state the system assumptions. We assume that there are n sites connected by a topology to be specified. Each site is assigned a single vote and a unique site id, numbered $1, 2, \ldots, n$ where n is the total number of sites in the system. We use the subscript i to refer to the site id of site i. All sites in the system are linearly ordered in descending order of their site ids. That is, site n is the highest linearly-ordered site. We assume independent failure modes for sites and links, with λ_s and λ_l being the failure rates of sites and links, respectively. A repairman repairs a failed site with rate μ_s and a failed link with rate μ_l. For the case when many failed sites and links shared the same repairman, the repairman can only fix one failed entity at a time. All times between these events are assumed to be exponentially distributed. Other than the *independent repairman model* in which each site or link has its own designated repairman, we consider three *dependent repairman models* in this paper: (a) a shared repairman with FIFO servicing discipline, i.e., all sites and links share the same repairman who repairs failed sites or links in a FIFO order; (b) a shared repairman with a fixed servicing discipline, i.e., the shared repairman repairs failed sites or links in accordance with a fixed linear order; (c) a shared repairman with a best-first servicing discipline, i.e., all sites and links share the same repairman who will pick a failed site or link whose repair afterward will result in the largest availability improvement to the system. We assume frequent updates, i.e., there is an update between two consecutive failure or repair events. This assumption is justified for any data item that is being used frequently enough to justify data replication.

As for the availability evaluation of dynamic algorithms, we consider both the system and site availability metrics. The *site availability* is defined as the probability that an update arriving at an arbitrary site will succeed [7, 11], while The traditional *system availability* metric is defined as the probability that a major partition exists. The site availability metric normally has a smaller value than the system availability metric because for an arriving operation to succeed at a site not only that a major partition must exist but also that the site must be a member in the major partition and is in the state of "up."

2.3 Stochastic Petri Net for the Independent Repairman Model

2.3.1 Site Subnet

Figure 1 shows an SPN subset that describes the behavior of a particular site (site i) upon an update action. Site i may or may not be in the major partition when the update occurs. A site can be in one of 4 states, namely, (up and current), (up and out-of-date), (down and current), or (down and out-of-date). We use 4 places, $upcc_i$, $upoc_i$, $downcc_i$, and $downoc_i$, to represent these 4 states. Since a site can only be in exactly one of these 4 states, we allow only one of these 4 places to contain a non-zero number of tokens, thus identifying the state of site i. Initially, site i is in the state of up and current. However, instead of putting only one token into place $upcc_i$ we deliberately put i tokens into place $upcc_i$ initially so as to easily identify the id of site i. These i tokens will be moved in one unit from one place to another among the 4 places as the state of site i changes in response to update actions. For example, suppose that site i initially is in the state of up and current, i.e., $\#(upcc_i) = i$, $\#(upoc_i) = 0$, $\#(downcc_i) = 0$, and $\#(downoc_i) = 0$. Now suppose an update operation occurs and site i is found not in the major partition (due to network partitioning), then i tokens will flow from place $upcc_i$ to place $upoc_i$, resulting in $\#(upcc_i) = 0$, $\#(upoc_i) = i$, $\#(downcc_i) = 0$, and $\#(downoc_i) = 0$, which means that its new state becomes up and out-of-date since it did not participate in the last update.

Note that in Figure 1 we use the tuple (transition-name, priority-level, enabling function) to label a transition. For example, the transition from place $upcc_i$ to $upoc_i$ is labeled by $(t5_i, 3, \bar{g}_i)$ in which $t5_i$ is the name of the transition, 3 is the priority of transition $t5_i$ relative to other transitions in the net, and $\bar{g}_i()$ is the associated *enabling function* which returns TRUE if site i is found not in the major partition. In our SPN, a transition is enabled when (a) the transition's each input place contains a number of tokens greater than or equal to the *multiplicity* of the associated input arc; and (b) the associated enabling function (if specified) returns TRUE. If multiple transitions are enabled at the same time, the transition with the highest priority level will fire first. Also, when a transition is fired, one or more tokens, depending on the multiplicity of the associated input arc, will be removed from the input place, and one or more tokens, depending on the multiplicity of the associated output arc, will be added to each output place. In Figure 1, only one transition can be enabled at a time and all transitions are of the same priority level. We use the label "$\#i$" to indicate that the multiplicity of some arcs in Figure 1 is i instead of the default value of 1. As an example of these rules, consider the case when place $ready_i$

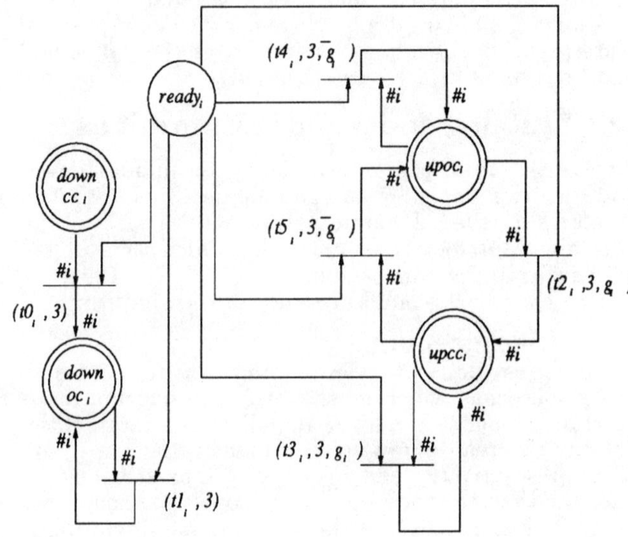

Figure 1. Local Status Update Actions by Site i .

contains one token, place $upcc_i$ contains i tokens, and the enabling function $\bar{g}_i()$ returns TRUE. In this case transition $t5_i$ will be enabled and, after it is fired, the token in place $ready_i$ and the i tokens in place $upcc_i$ will be removed and i tokens will be added to the output place $upoc_i$, signifying that site i is now in the state of up and out-of-date.

Figure 1 is part of a larger net to be explained later. Below, we explain in detail how we construct it.

1. When an update operation arrives and a major partition exists, a token will be put into place $ready_i$ by the "system subnet" (to be described later) so that site i can start a local status update. There are six immediate transitions competing to fire at site i at this moment. However, only one out of the six transitions can fire, which will consume the token in place $ready_i$. These six transitions are $t0_i$, $t1_i$, $t2_i$, $t3_i$, $t4_i$, and $t5_i$, all of which have the same priority level (i.e., 3).

2. Transition $t0_i$ will fire if site i is in a state in which it is down and current. In this case, i tokens will flow from place $downcc_i$ to place $downoc_i$. This means that if an update occurs and site i is in the state of down and current, then the new state of site i will be down and out-of-date since site i is down and will not be able to participate in the update.

3. Transition $t1_i$ will fire if site i is in the state of down and out-of-date. In this case, site i remains in the state of down and out-of-date.

4. Transition $t2_i$ will fire if site i is in the state of up and out-of-date, as well as in the major partition. In this case, i tokens will flow from place

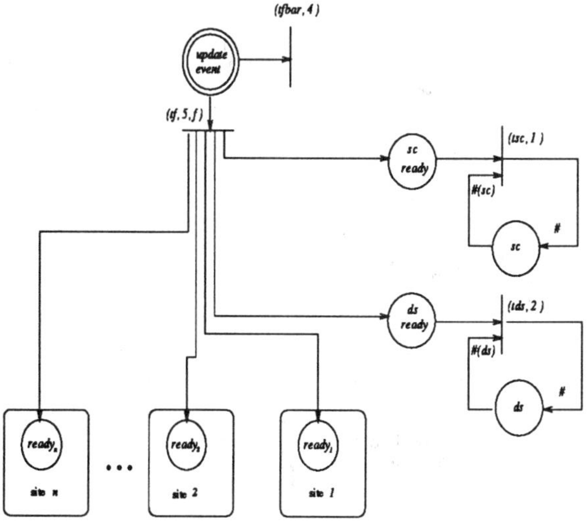

Figure 2. Global Status-Update Actions Triggered by An Update Operation .

$upoc_i$ to $upcc_i$ and the new state of site i will become up and current, since site i will participate in the update. Transition $t2_i$ is associated with an enabling function $g_i()$ which returns TRUE if site i is in the major partition at the moment. See Table 4 later for the meaning of $g_i()$ and its counterpart $\bar{g}_i()$.

5. Transition $t3_i$ will fire if site i is in the state of up and current, as well as in the major partition. In this case, site i will remain in the state of up and current. The enabling function $g_i()$ is associated with transition $t3_i$.

6. Transition $t4_i$ will fire if site i is in the state of up and out-of-date, as well as *not* in the major partition (say, due to network partitioning). In this case, site i will remain in the state of up and out-of-date since site i will not be able to participate in the update. Transition $t4_i$ is associated with an enabling function $\bar{g}_i()$ which returns TRUE if site i is *not* in the major partition at the moment.

7. Transition $t5_i$ will fire if site i is in the state of up and current, as well as *not* in the major partition. In this case, the new state of site i becomes up and out-of-date since it will not be able to participate in the update. The enabling function $\bar{g}_i()$ is associated with transition $t5_i$.

Note that all transitions in Figure 1 are immediate transitions, thus modeling that the state change at a site in response to an update event consumes little time, as opposed to an exponentially distributed time for a site and link failure/repair, or for an update arrival.

2.3.2 System Subnet

Figure 2 shows an SPN subnet that describes the system behavior as it responds to the arrival of an update operation. At the bottom of Figure 2, each of the boxes labeled site i is the SPN subset shown in Figure 1. There are several priority levels shown in Figure 2. The two transitions, tf and $tfbar$, at the top of Figure 2 are given the highest priority levels (i.e., 5 and 4). When an update event arrives, a token will be put in place *update_event* (by "state-affecting subnets" to be described later) to initiate an update action. Transition tf is evaluated prior to transition $tfbar$ since it has the highest priority. If a major partition exists at the moment, the enabling function $f()$ associated with tf shall return TRUE and tf will subsequently fire, resulting in the removal of the token from place *update_event* and the placement of one token each into places sc, ds and $ready_i$ for all i's. If a major partition does not exist at the moment, $tfbar$ will fire instead, thus removing the token in place *update_event*.

The next higher priority level (i.e., 3) is assigned to each of the boxes which are evaluated as described previously in the subsection "Site Subnet." After all the sites have been evaluated and each site's status has been updated, transitions tds and tsc which have lower priority levels (i.e., 2 and 1) will subsequently execute. Here, transition tsc is used to update the site cardinality. The input arc multiplicity from place sc to transition tsc is set to $\#(sc)$, meaning that all the tokens originally stored in place sc will be removed. On the other hand, the output arc multiplicity from transition tsc to place sc is defined by a multiplicity function which returns the number of sites with $mark(upcc) > 0$ in the major partition (see Table 2 later). This way, whenever an update changes the status of the system, the site cardinality can be updated properly and the new value can be simply stored as the number of tokens in place sc. In a similar way, transition tds is used to update the distinguished site. The input arc multiplicity from place ds to transition tds is $\#(ds)$ while the output arc multiplicity from transition tds to place ds is determined by a multiplicity function which returns the maximum $\#(upcc)$ value among all the sites in the major partition at the moment (also see Table 2). This way, the site id of the new distinguished site after the update will be stored as the number of tokens in place ds. Recall that we used i tokens to identify the id of site i (Figure 1). Therefore, by merely looking at the maximum $\#(upcc)$ value among all the sites in the major partition, we can determine the site id of the new distinguished site easily.

2.3.3 Site Failure/Repair Subnets

Figure 3 shows two subsets for describing the effect of site i's failure and repair on the system state, for the independent repairman model. At the top, state transitions are between the following two states: (up and current) and (down and current), while at the bottom, state transitions are between (up and out-of-date) and (down and out-of-date). Again, since site i

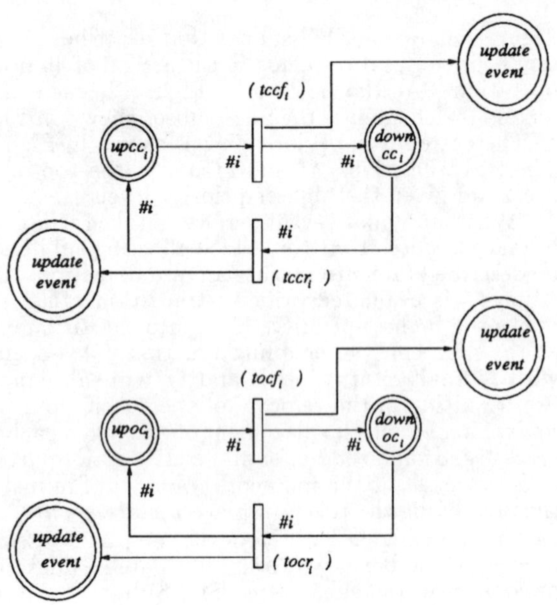

Figure 3. Site Failure/Repair Events .

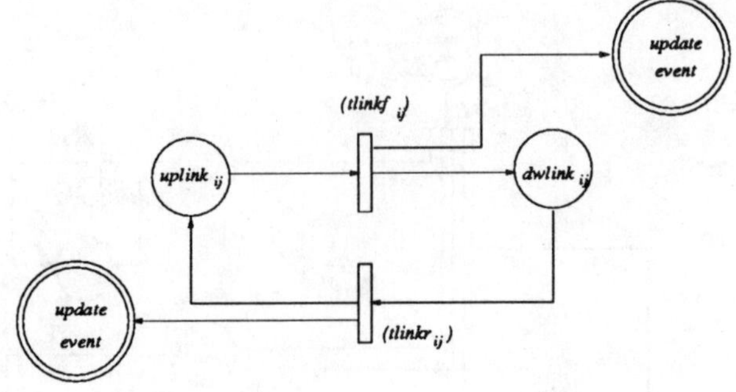

Figure 4. Link Failure/Repair Events .

can only be in one state at a time, only one transition out of these two subnets is possible at a time. For the failure events, if site i is in the state of (up and current) and subsequently fails, then its new state will be (down and current). Similarly, if site i is in the state of (up and out-of-date) and subsequently fails, then its new state will be (down and out-of-date). These are modeled by associating transitions $tccf_i$ and $tocf_i$ each with a rate of λ_s, meaning that the firing time of these transitions is exponentially distributed with rate λ_s. For the repair events, if site i is in the state of (down and current) and is subsequently repaired, then its new state will be (up and current). Similarly, if site i is in the state of (down and out-of-date) and is subsequently repaired, then its new state will be (up and out-of-date). These are similarly modeled by associating transitions $tccr_i$ and $tocr_i$ each with a site repair rate of μ_s. The multiplicity of all the arcs in Figure 3 for site i is i.

Note that since we assume frequent updates, an update will always arrive at the system before the next failure or repair event. This in effect means that an update will immediately follow a site failure or repair event. In Figure 3, we model this situation by also putting a token into place $update\_event$ when site i is failed or repaired. The system thus behaves as if an update operation were received after a failure or repair event. The system subnet described earlier will respond to this update event and properly update the states of all sites, including site i.

Table 1. Meanings of Places.

Place	Meaning
$upcc_i$	$copy_i$ is up and current
$downcc_i$	$copy_i$ is down and current
$upoc_i$	$copy_i$ is up and out of date
$downoc_i$	$copy_i$ is down and out of date
$uplink_{ij}$	$link_{ij}$ is up
$dwlink_{ij}$	$link_{ij}$ is down
$update\_event$	an update is initiated
sc_ready	a SC is initiated
sc	$\#(sc)$ indicates the SC
ds_ready	a DS change is initiated
ds	$\#(ds)$ indicates the id of the DS
$ready_i$	a local update at site i is in process

Table 2. Arc Multiplicity Functions.

Arc	Multiplicity
$sc \rightarrow tsc$	$\#(sc)$
$tsc \rightarrow sc$	# of sites in the major partition with mark($upcc$) > 0
$ds \rightarrow tds$	$\#(ds)$
$tds \rightarrow ds$	max $\#(upcc)$ among all sites in the major partition

2.3.4 Link Failure/Repair Subnets

Figure 4 shows a subset for describing a link's failure and repair, for the independent repairman model. Here we use the subscript ij to refer to the (bidirectional) link between sites i and j. For the ring topology, for example, there will be n such subnets, one for each link. For example, for a 5-site ring topology as in our case study, there will be links 12, 23, 34, 45 and 51. A token in place $uplink_{ij}$ means that the link between sites i and j is in the state of "up", while a token in place $dwlink_{ij}$ means that the link between sites i and j is in the state of "down." Failures and repairs of links occur independently with failure and repair rates of λ_l and μ_l, respectively. Similar to the subnet for site failure/repair, we note that in order to model frequent updates, we also put a token into place *update_event* when a link is failed or repaired.

Combining Figures 1, 2, 3 and 4 together, we obtain a composite SPN for the independent repairman model. In the composite SPN, a common place among all the subnets is labeled with double circles. Tables 1-4 help annotate this composite SPN.

Table 3. Rates of Timed Transitions.

Timed Transition	Rate Value
$tccf_i$	λ_s
$tccr_i$	μ_s
$tocf_i$	λ_s
$tocr_i$	μ_s
$tlinkf_{ij}$	λ_l
$tlinkr_{ij}$	μ_l

Table 4. Enabling Functions.

Tr.	Enabling Function

tf	$f()$
	 {IF $\exists$ a partition $\mathcal{M}$ with sum equal to
	    # of sites in $\mathcal{M}$ with mark($upcc$) > 0;
	    AND IF (sum > #(sc)/2) OR
	      (sum = #(sc)/2 AND
	        mark($upcc_{\#(ds)}$) AND site #(ds) $\in \mathcal{M}$)
	 THEN RETURN 1;
	   ELSE RETURN 0}

$t2_i$	$g_i()$
	 {Look at mark($uplink_{jk}$) $\forall j \forall k$ to
	     determine site i's partition;
	 IF site i's is in the major partition $\mathcal{M}$
	 THEN RETURN 1;
	   ELSE RETURN 0}

$t3_i$	$g_i()$
$t4_i$	$\bar{g}_i()\{1 - g_i()\}$
$t5_i$	$\bar{g}_i()$

3 SPNs for Dependent Repairman Models

In this section, we consider the case in which many sites and links may have to share the same repairman due to repair resource limitations. To illustrate the modeling techniques used in addressing this issue, we focus on the case where all sites and links share a repairman. Three repairman models are considered: (1) FIFO: failed sites and links are repaired in a first in first out order; (2) linear-order: failed sites and links are repaired in a prespecified linear order; and (3) best-first: among all failed sites and links, we choose the one whose repair will yield the largest improvement in availability relative to the current state. Apparently, among the three repair models, best-first may incur the highest overhead in deciding who to repair next; in return, it can provide the best achievable availability under a single repairman constraint. In this paper, we ignore the overhead issue and focus on availability modeling.

Table 5. Rates of Timed Transitions for FIFO Repair.

Time Tr.	Rate Value
$tccf_i$	λ_s
$tccr_i$	$\dfrac{\mu_s}{\sum_{j,k,k\neq j} \#(downcc_j + downoc_j + dwlink_{jk})}$
$tocf_i$	λ_s
$tocr_i$	$\dfrac{\mu_s}{\sum_{j,k,k\neq j} \#(downcc_j + downoc_j + dwlink_{jk})}$
$tlinkf_{ij}$	λ_l
$tlinkr_{ij}$	$\dfrac{\mu_l}{\sum_{j,k,k\neq j} \#(downcc_j + downoc_j + dwlink_{jk})}$

To model the FIFO repairman model, we note that by queueing theory [8] the performance characteristics (e.g., queueing delay) of a client under the FIFO service discipline for a single server would be the same as that under the processor sharing (PS) discipline where the processing power of the server is divided equally among all clients in the queue. Therefore, without having to introduce any extra places in the SPN to keep track of the queueing order of failed sites and links in a state, we simply make use of the SPN for the independent repairman model described earlier and modify the repair rates to account for repair dependencies. Specifically, Table 5 replaces Table 3 with each repair rate now becoming a function of the total number of failed sites and links that depends on the current state of the system. For example, if a particular state has 2 failed sites and one failed link, then instead of using repair rates of μ_s, μ_s and μ_l, respectively, for these three failed entities based on the independent repairman model, we now use repair rates of $\mu_s/3$, $\mu_s/3$ and $\mu_l/3$, respectively, to model the fact that the same repairman is being shared among these three failed entities. In general, if a particular state has M failed sites and links, then the respective repair rates of these failed entities in that state are "deflated" by a factor of M to account for the effect of repair resource sharing.

As for the linear-order repairman model, there is a prespecified order among failed entities. Determining which order to use is a search problem itself and requires availability studies in its own right. Since a linear order already exists in dynamic voting for the purpose of selecting the distinguished site (DS), a natural way is to follow that order for repair as well. The intuition is that it is more likely that a higher linearly-ordered site will become a distinguished site in the event that the number of sites within the major partition is an even number. Therefore, giving a higher repair priority to a higher linearly-ordered site increases the chance of finding the majority partition. An example is a state in which there are only two sites D and E left in the major partition with E being the distinguished site. Suppose sites D and E subsequently fail. Then, repairing D would not result in a major partition being found while repairing E would. It is less clear whether site repairs should take precedence over link repairs or vice versa. However, for the site availability metric considered here, giving the fact that a single site can still provide services if it is the distinguished site regardless of the network status, it seems intuitive to give site repairs a higher priority over link repairs. For the same reason, links that connect higher linearly-ordered sites should be given a higher priority than links that connect lower linearly-ordered sites.

We model the linear-order repairman model by directly modifying the SPN for the independent repairman model. We create a new enabling function associated with the transition of each site or link repair event. All such enabling functions shall execute the same code, with each enabling function knowing the id of the site or link it is designated to. Only one enabling function at any state shall return TRUE based on the prespecified linear order and all others shall return FALSE. For example, suppose that the linear order is (sites 5,4,3,2,1; links 54,51,43,32,21) for a 5-site ring topology and sites 4, 2 and link 51 are down in a particular state. In this case, the enabling functions associated with sites 4, 2 and link 51 will return the boolean values of TRUE, FALSE, and FALSE, respectively, meaning that site 4 will be repaired next over site 2 and link 51. Note that in this state all other enabling functions are not activated since the input places of the corresponding transitions would be empty. This technique prevents concurrent firing of multiple repair transitions. Consequently, in any state at most one repair event can occur with the correct repair rate based on the specified repair order. Table 6 shows a description of the set of additional enabling functions needed for the linear-order repairman model.

Table 6. Enabling Functions for Linear-Order Repair

Transition	Enabling Function

$tccr_i, tocr_i$	$h1_{site}(i)$
	{IF site i failed and the repair rank of
	  site i is higher than those of other
	  failed sites or links in the linear order
	THEN RETURN TRUE;
	ELSE RETURN FALSE}

$tlinkr_{ij}$	$h1_{link}(i,j)$
	{IF link ij failed and the repair rank of
	  link ij is higher than those of other
	  failed sites or links in the linear order
	THEN RETURN TRUE;
	ELSE RETURN FALSE}

While the linear-order repairman model applies a fixed repair order which is not changed at the run time, the best-first repairman model changes the repair order on-the-fly, with the preference always given to the site or link which can most improve the site availability of the system after its repair with respect to the current state. To do so, the best-first repairman model executes the following repair strategies.

1. If there exists a distinct failed site or link whose repair would lead to the existence of a major partition in which the number of current copies is the largest among all possible repair choices in that state, then the distinct failed site or link will be selected to be repaired next.

2. If there exist more than one failed sites or links whose repair would lead to the existence of a major partition in which the number of current copies is the largest among all possible repair choices in that state, then a tie-breaker rule will be applied to select one distinct member of the group to be repaired next. We consider the following tie-breaker rules in this paper, with the reasons explicitly given.

   (a) If the group contains both failed sites and failed links as repair candidates, then the preference is given to the failed sites if $\mu_s/\lambda_s \geq \mu_l/\lambda_l$; otherwise, the preference is given to the failed links. Then, the tie-breaker rule (described next) for just either failed sites or links applies. The reason behind this rule is that the preference is given to the failed entity which can be repaired faster, which means faster recovery given the same availability improvement outcome.

   (b) If the group contains just failed sites, then the preference is given to the highest linearly-ordered site in the group. The reason behind this rule is that a higher linearly-ordered site is more likely to become a distinguished site and thus repairing a higher linearly-ordered site has the effect of moving more available sites toward the current distinguished site. This creates a higher probability of uniting more sites in the major partition in the future. Intuitively, we like to repair sites or links closer to the current distinguished site so that the system will be in a better position to unite more sites at a later time. To see this, consider a particular state of a 5-site ring system[1] in which the major partition contains only the distinguished site, say site 4, while all other sites (sites 1, 2, 3 and 5) and links (links 12, 23, 34, 45 and 51) have failed. This is a scenario in which repairing any of the failed sites or links yields the same availability improvement, i.e., no improvement after therefore the preference is

---

[1] A 5-site ring consists of sites 1, 2, 3, 4 and 5 and links 12, 23, 34, 45 and 51.

given to repairing sites over repairing links. Then, repairing site 5 will put the system in a better position to unite sites 4 and 5 (after a future repair of link 45), while repairing a lower linearly-ordered site, say site 2, has no such benefit. One may argue that another scenario would give a totally different result but the point is that site 4 has a higher probability than site 2 to become the distinguished site.

(c) If the group contains just failed links, then the preference is given to the link that connects the highest linearly-ordered sites among all links in the group. The reason follows that for the tie-breaker rule for sites except that we now like to repair links around the current distinguished site. Consider the same scenario mentioned above except that $\mu_s/\lambda_s \geq \mu_l/\lambda_l$ is false, so that repairing links take precedence over repairing sites. In this case, repairing link 45 would be able to unite sites 4 and 5 after a future repair of site 5, while repairing any other link, say link 12, will not result in a major partition containing more than one site after any subsequent repair. Again, since a higher linearly-ordered site has a higher probability of becoming the distinguished site, repairing a link connecting higher linearly-ordered sites has the effect of putting the system in a better position to unite more sites after some future selective repairs.

Table 7. Enabling Functions for Best-First Repair

Transition	Enabling Function

$tccr_i, tocr_i$	$h1_{site}(i)$
	{IF site i failed and the hypothetical
	    site availability after repairing site i
	    is higher than those of other failed
	    sites or links in the system
	    THEN RETURN TRUE;
	    ELSE RETURN FALSE}

$tlinkr_{ij}$	$h1_{link}(i,j)$
	{IF link ij failed and the hypothetical
	    site availability after repairing link ij
	    is higher than those of other failed
	    sites or links in the system
	    THEN RETURN TRUE;
	    ELSE RETURN FALSE}

For the analysis of the best-first repairman model, we also modify the SPN for the independent repairman model. Similar to the linear order repairman model, we again associate an enabling function with the repair transition of each site or link; let all enabling functions execute the same code, with each enabling function knowing the id of the site or link it is designated to; and let only one enabling function at any state return TRUE while all others return FALSE. The difference is that the encoding of the enabling function ranks all failed sites and links in a particular state based on the hypothetical site availability values (which would result if they were chosen to be repaired next). Only the enabling function designated to the highest-ranked site or link for that particular state returns TRUE and all others return FALSE. Table 7 shows a description of the set of additional enabling functions needed for the best-first repairman model.

4 Evaluation

We test the modeling techniques developed in the paper with a 5-site ring topology. Sites were labeled with 1, 2, 3, 4 and 5 with site 5 being the highest linearly-ordered site among all initially; links were labeled with 12, 23, 34, 45 and 51 (bidirectional). Four different repairman models were examined. For the independent repairman model, sites and links fail and repair independently of each other. The SPN for the independent repairman model consists of Figures 1, 2, 3 and 4 with Tables 1, 2, 3, and 4. The underlying Markov chain contains 8674 states. For the remaining three dependent models, we let all sites and links share the same repairman. In particular, for the linear-order repairman model, we assume that failed sites and links are repaired in the order of site 5, site 4, ..., down to site 1 and then link 54, link 54, ..., down to link 12, so that a higher repair rank is assigned to a higher linearly-ordered site (among sites) and a link connecting higher linearly-ordered sites (among links). The SPN for the dependent repairman model with FIFO consists of Figures 1, 2, 3 and 4 with Tables 1, 2, 4, and 5, with the number of states in the underlying Markov chain being 8774. The SPN for the dependent repairman model with linear-order consists of same four figures with Tables 1, 2, 3, 4, and 6, with the underlying Markov chain containing 5429 states. Finally, the SPN for the dependent repairman model with best-first consists of same four figures with Tables 1, 2, 3, 4 and 7; the number of states in this case is 3821.

The site and system availability metrics considered in the case study were obtained by assigning proper "rewards" with states of the system [4]. The system availability metric, i.e., the steady-state probability that a major partition exists, was obtained by associating a reward rate of 1 with those states in which the enabling function $f()$ returns TRUE and a reward rate of 0 otherwise. The site availability metric was obtained by associating a reward rate of $1 \times k/n$ with those states in which the enabling function $f()$ returns TRUE and a reward rate of 0 otherwise, with k representing the number of "up" sites in the major partition (if it exists) in a particular state and n is the total number of sites (copies) in the system.

4.1 Availability For the Independent Repairman Model

Figure 5 shows the site availability values for the independent repairman model under various combinations of site and link repair-rate/failure-rate ratios. Here, the x-axis is the ratio of the mean time to fail-

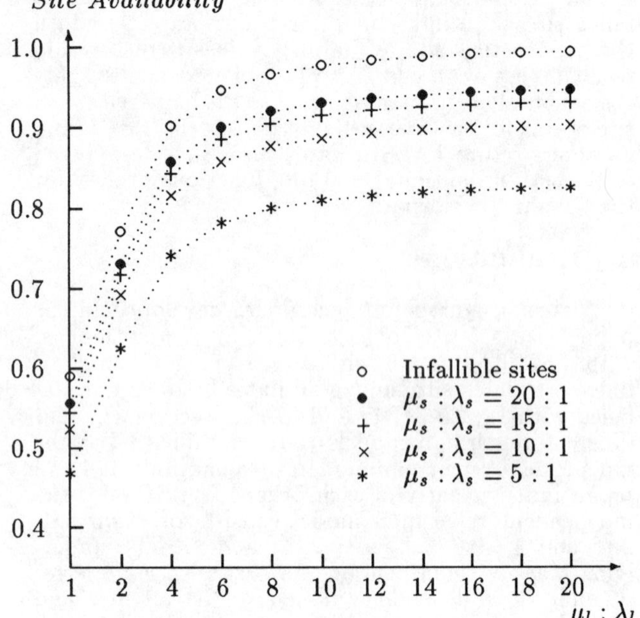

Figure 5. Site Availability of 5-Site Ring Under
Independent Repairman.

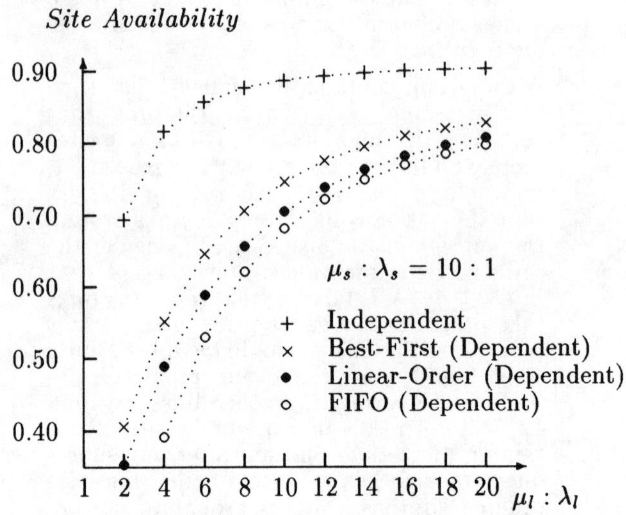

Figure 6. Site Availability of 5-Site Ring under
Various Repairman Models.

ure per link to the mean time to repair per link, or,
equivalently, the ratio of link repair rate to link failure
rate. The asymptotic case where only links are fallible as obtained in previous studies [7] is also shown for
comparison reasons. From the significant difference in
site availability shown in the figure, we conclude that
models which consider either only fallible sites or fallible links, but not both, in previous studies can very
unrealistically overestimate the site availability metric.

4.2 Comparing Availability Metrics Under Various Repairman Models

Figures 6 shows the site availability values obtained
under 4 different repairman models, with the ratio of
the site repair rate to the site failure rate fixed at 10:1.
Figure 7 shows the same data except using the system
availability as the comparison metric. The x-axis is
again the ratio of the mean time to failure per link
to the mean time to repair per link. From the figure,
we observe the effect of repair dependency: the site
availability of dynamic voting with independent repair
is much higher than those with dependent repair. This
is because in the latter cases only one repairman is
available and all failed sites and links must compete
for the same repair resource, while in the former case
every site or link has its own designated repairman.
Only when the ratio of repair rate to failure rate is
very high, i.e., greater than 20, can the availability
of the best-first repairman model approximate that of
the independent repairman model.

Among the three dependent repairman models,
however, the best-first repairman model can always

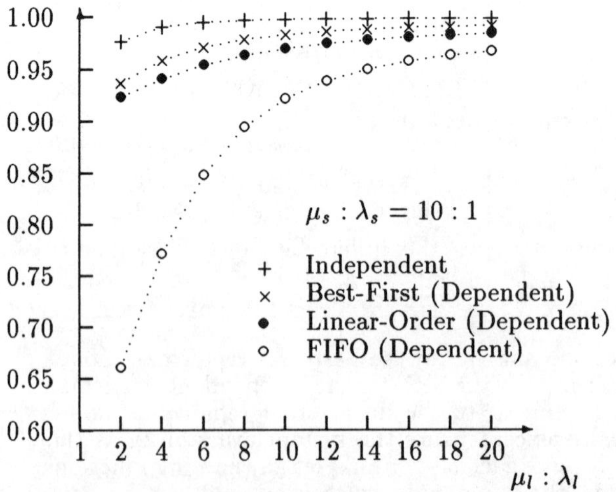

Figure 7. System Availability of 5-Site Ring under
Various Repairman Models.

provide a better site availability value than the other two. These are two reasons by which best-first improves the availability when compared with other dependent repairman models.

1. The best-first repairman model can avoid unfavorable states which other dependent repairman models cannot. These unfavorable states occur when the system contains either (a) one or more up but out-of-date copies, or (b) one up and current copy which is not the distinguished copy, and one or more up but out-of-date copies. These unfavorable states result from ineffective repair activities which occur during a period in which a major partition does not exist. For the FIFO and linear-order repairman models, it is possible that a major partition still could not result even after several repairs. For the best-first repairman model, however, if the system is in such a state (in which a major partition does not exist), it will avoid going into these unfavorable states (in which no major partition exists again after some repairs) by repairing the distinguished site first such that after a selective repair a major partition always results.[2]

2. If the system is in a state in which a major partition exists and some failed sites and links need to be repaired, then best-first will choose a failed site or link to repair next such that the size of the major partition after the repair will become the largest among all possible choices. This eliminates the bad effect of ineffective repairs. As an example, consider a system being partitioned into two parts, with one part containing two up sites and one other part containing two up sites and one down site. An ineffective repair in this case can repair the down site (as could be done by FIFO and linear-order) instead of the failed link which partitions the five sites, thus resulting in a major partition of size 3. Best-first would select the failed link to repair and after the repair the size of the major partition is 4 instead. In addition, in cases repairing any member of a group results in the same availability improvement outcome, it will select the one with the shortest repair time so that the system most of time can stay in those states in which the system has a high availability.

Figure 8 shows the difference in site availability between best-first and linear-order, and also between best-first and FIFO, as a function of the ratio of the repair rate to the failure rate, assuming that the repair rates for sites and links are identical and the failure rates for sites and links are also identical, i.e., $\mu_s = \mu_l = \mu$ and $\lambda_s = \lambda_l = \lambda$. Figure 9 shows the same except using the system availability as the

---

[2] We should mention that these arguments are valid only under the assumption of frequent updates. Without frequent updates, even the best-first repairman model cannot guarantee the existence of a major partition after a repair.

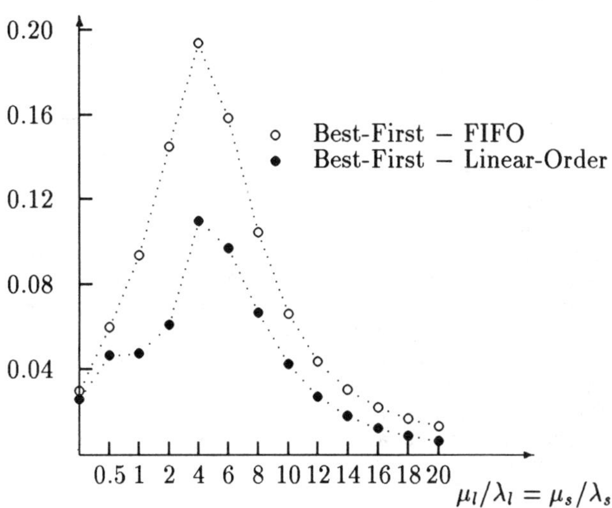

Figure 8. Difference in Site Availability Among Dependent Repairman models.

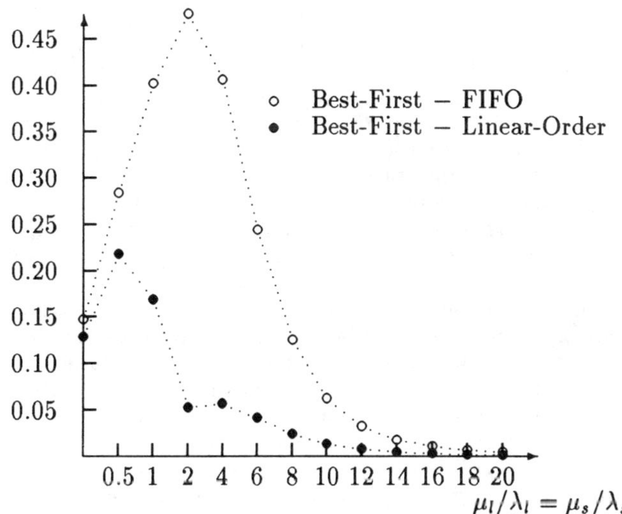

Figure 9. Difference in System Availability Among Dependent Repairman Models.

metric. These two figures show the impact of "effective repairs" employed by the best-first repairman model (and to some extent by the linear-order repairman model). When the ratio of the repair rate over the failure rate (μ/λ) is very high, i.e., greater than 20, the difference among these three dependent repairman models is small since sites/links can be repaired much faster than they can fail, so it matters little which repairman model is being used. However, as the ratio of μ/λ becomes lower (say between 5-15), the impact of effective repairs becomes more manifested (because at any time there can be many failed entities waiting to be repaired) and the difference in availability becomes higher. This also reflects the condition under which the best-first repairman model can benefit the system most when compared with the other two repairman models. Finally, when the ratio becomes very low (i.e., around 1) in which sites/links can fail faster than they can be repaired, the site or system availability metric is so low anyway that the effect of effective repairs becomes less significant. The concave curves shown in Figures 8 and 9 indicate that there exists a data point at which best-first has the largest edge over the other two repairman models.

5 Conclusions

In this paper, we proposed and investigated four repairman models which can exist in replicated data management. Using dynamic voting as a case study, we developed modeling techniques based on Petri nets to analyze the effect of these repairman models on availability. We discovered that (a) an availability model that considers only site or link failures/repairs, but not both, can give a very unrealistic, overestimated value of the availability metric; (b) a significant difference in availability exists between two systems with independent and dependent repairman models, except when the repair rate is much higher than the failure rate (i.e., when μ/λ is greater than 20); (c) when several sites and links have to share the same repairman, the best-first repairman model can always provide a better availability than the FIFO and linear-order repairman models; the difference in availability becomes more pronounced as the site/link failure rate increases relative to the site/link repair rate; and there exists a region in which the difference in availability is significant. From these results, we conclude that ignoring concurrent site/link failure modes or repair dependency can unduly overestimate the availability of replicated data. We urge that tools such as those developed in the paper be used to realistically estimate the resulting availability metric of replicated data, since after all the main reason of using replicated data is to improve the data availability of the system.

Some possible future research areas include (a) extending and applying the modeling techniques to analyzing other pessimistic algorithms such as those based on coteries [10] and (b) developing modeling techniques to study the tradeoff between the reduction in data processing overheads (say due to the use of a more constrained quorum sets based on a hierarchical or tree structure) and the sacrifice in availability (due to the more constrained way of finding a quorum) for database environments where a combined performance/availability design goal must be met.

Acknowledgement

This work was supported in part by the National Science Council, Republic of China, under Grant NSC 86-2745-E006-020.

References

[1] N.R. Adam, "A new dynamic voting algorithm for distributed database systems." *IEEE Trans. Knowledge and Data Engineering,* June 1994, pp. 470-478.

[2] H.K. Chang and S.M. Yuan, "Performance characterization of the tree quorum algorithm," *IEEE Trans. Parallel and Distributed Systems,* June 1995, pp. 658-662.

[3] S.Y. Cheung, M.H. Ammar and M. Ahamad, "The grid protocol: a high performance scheme for maintaining replicated data," *IEEE Trans. Knowledge and Data Engineering,* Vol. 4, No. 6, Dec. 1992, pp. 582-592.

[4] G. Ciardo, J.K. Muppala, and K.S. Trivedi, "SPNP: stochastic Petri net package," *Proc. 3rd Int. Workshop Petri Nets and Performance Models,* Kyoto, Japan, Dec. 1989, pp. 142-151.

[5] S. Jajodia and D. Mutchler, "A pessimistic consistency control algorithm fir replicated files which achieve high availability," *IEEE Trans. Soft. Eng.* Vol. 15, No. 1, Jan. 1989, pp. 39-45.

[6] S. Jajodia and D. Mutchler, "A hybrid replica control algorithm combining static and dynamic voting," *IEEE Trans. Knowledge and Data Engineering,* Vol. 1, No. 4, Dec. 1989, pp. 459-469.

[7] S. Jajodia and D. Mutchler, "Dynamic voting algorithms for maintaining the consistency of replicated database," *ACM Trans. Database Systems,* Vol. 15, No. 2, June 1990, pp. 230-280.

[8] L. Kleinrock, *Queueing Systems, Volume 1: Theory,* John Wiley and Sons, 1975.

[9] A. Kumar, "Hierarchical quorum consensus: A new algorithm for managing replicated data," *IEEE Trans. Computers,* Vol. 40, No. 9, Sept. 1991, pp. 996-1004.

[10] H. Garcia-Molina and D. Barbara, "How to assign votes in a distributed system," *JACM,* Vol. 32, No. 4, June 1985, pp. 841-860.

[11] S. Rangarajan, S. Setia and S.K. Tripathi, "A fault-tolerant algorithm for replicated data management," *IEEE Trans. Parallel and Distributed Systems,* Dec. 1995, pp. 1271-1282.

[12] P. Triantafillou and D.J. Taylor, "The location-based paradigm for replication: Achieving efficiency and availability in distributed systems," *IEEE Trans. Software Engineering*, Vol. 21, No. 1, Jan. 1995, pp. 1-18.

[13] O. Wolfson and S. Jajodia, "An algorithm for dynamic data replication in distributed systems," *Information Processing Letters*, 53, 1995, pp. 113-119.

Reliable Data Distribution Middleware for Large-scale Massive Data Replication

Teruji Shiroshita, Osamu Takahashi, Masahide Yamashita, and Yukihiro Nakamura*

NTT Information and Communication Systems Laboratories
1-2356 Take, Yokosuka, 238-03 Japan
siro@isl.ntt.jp

*Department of Electronics and Communication
Graduate School of Engineering, Kyoto University
Kyoto, 606-01, JAPAN

Abstract

For massive data replication, Infocast, a communication middleware, is proposed. It distributes large data sets to thousands of receivers without any data loss. This paper examines the distributed processing feature of Infocast and also evaluates its performance. Reliability is achieved by an effective receiver-initiated recovery algorithm and server's complete supervision of all receiver states. Infocast provides reliable data distribution with high-performance to most receivers through the advantage of network-provided multicast while also supporting temporarily unavailable or performance impaired receivers by parallel state transitions. Implementation and performance test results including very large data distribution by VLDD scheme are examined through experiments. Scalability of receiver number and data size is discussed for various conditions.

1. Introduction

Large-scale distribution has been expected with the advent of interconnected wide area data networks such as the Internet. Data replication is one of the key factors to realize large scale distributed systems [1]. A large-scale massive data distribution middleware, Infocast, is proposed to support "reliable" data distribution from a server to thousands of receivers over networks. "Reliable" information distribution means complete loss recovery and status negotiation; both of which are indispensable for commercial distribution services.

This paper focuses on weakly-consistent massive-data distribution where data consistency of receivers is not strict; it may depend on receiver availability at the time of distribution. A typical application is on-line publishing and massive data replication for resource discovery [2]. This type of service is very promising and fundamental in the broadband networks that allow high data traffic, and is categorized as Distribution Service in B-ISDN standardization activities [3].

The key concept of Infocast is to provide high-performance to most receivers through the advantage of IP-multicast [4] which is a network routing mechanism with packet replication while still supporting temporarily unavailable or performance-degraded receivers due to causes such as user movement in a wireless network and intervention by other applications.

Infocast adopts a receiver-initiated recovery algorithm in which receiver processes are responsible for detecting data loss or damage and reporting data loss by negative response (NACK) to the server process. An analysis based on a generalized model reports that receiver-initiated algorithms provide substantially higher performance than sender-initiated algorithms [5]. Infocast follows this idea and based on receiver-initiated recovery. The response concentration problem called ACK implosion which is inevitable with end-to-end confirmation can be solved by using the backoff time algorithm [6], [7]. The applicability of the backoff time algorithm is examined for large-scale distribution through the experiments on Infocast.

Reliable solutions have not been created to the common problem of exceptional receiver condition; causes include temporary unavailability and performance degradation. Infocast adopts two exception handling procedures: separate retransmission for temporally unavailable receivers and soliciting by inquiry packets POLL for silent receivers. Separate retransmission is achieved by bifurcating the exceptional receiver's state transitions and allowing parallel state transitions.

Infocast is based on the Reliable Multicast Transport Protocol (RMTP)[*] [8] over an unreliable transport protocol UDP and connectionless best-effort network protocol IP. Responses from receivers are reported to the server as end-to-end transport communications instead of using gateways (inter-mediate node) which gather some responses and respond to the server (root node) or upper gateways. The reason why gateways are not used is that imposing gateway functions on the intermediate hosts or routers creates unwarranted costs when constructing and maintaining a large-scale information delivery system.

RMTP is a connection oriented protocol which explicitly uses connection establishment and release procedures. The aim of this connection oriented approach is to clarify the data delivery success or fail for each receiver.

While RMTP has been developed for distributing megabytes data, the repeated and continuous use of RMTP procedures (VLDD scheme) achieves very massive-data distribution. This paper also examines and confirms such distribution through experiments.

The requirements considered when designing Infocast are summarized below.

(1) Reliability

100% error free digital information distribution: Digital information such as structure encoded documents and computer programs need to be distributed to receivers without a flaw. Receivers must be confirmed before and after data distribution for commercial use. Delivery order and atomic action which are important for transaction applications are not required.

Fault tolerant: The distribution system must tolerate network quality declines and exceptional receiver conditions such as temporary unavailability

Chargeable: Information should be delivered only to registered users and charged after distribution.

(2) Scalability

Number of users (receivers): Thousands of users must be supported within a reasonable period.

Data scalability: Data amounts of several Mbytes must be supported. A 32 page daily paper newspaper amounts to 2 M bytes (text and compressed images). The Internet version of the NYTimesFax (8 A4 pages) occupies about 100 Kbytes, which infers that a 160 page book would compress to 2 Mbytes.

(3) Network applicability: The distribution system should be used with various existing and promising networks that offer multi-point communication, Ethernet and Token ring LAN, Satellite, CATV, and ATM,

at widely differing levels of quality (error rate and transmission delay) .

(4) Performance

Distribution time: Distribution must be completed within an appropriate time limit depending on service requirement. Time constraint is not severe as real-time applications.

Processing load: Distribution load should be kept within the limits that ensure system reliability.

(5) Availability: The middleware must be run in prevailing operating systems and must provide common distribution functions to various applications.

The data distribution procedure of Infocast is explained in terms of state transitions and communication protocols in Section 2. In Section 3, after examining the buffer overflow process, the performance of Infocast in terms of distribution time and server processing load is evaluated in experiments. Furthermore, an extension for very massive data distribution and test results are shown in Section 4. Related works are summarized in Section 5.

2. Data distribution procedures

2.1 Parallel distribution state transition

The proposed data distribution procedure is shown in Figure 1. Data distribution consists three phase; connection establishment, multicast distribution/ retransmission, and separate retransmission.

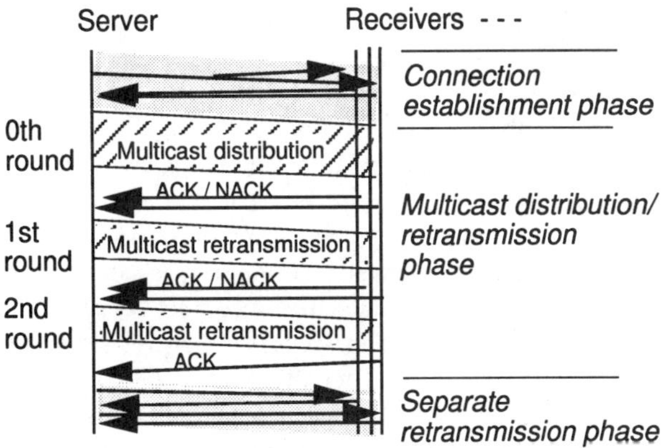

REL and RACK are used after each round of transmission /retransmission.
POLL, BUSY, ReceiveReady are omitted.

Figure 1: Overview of end-to-end procedures

---

[*] RMTP was developed through a collaboration between NTT Laboratories and IBM Tokyo Research Laboratory.

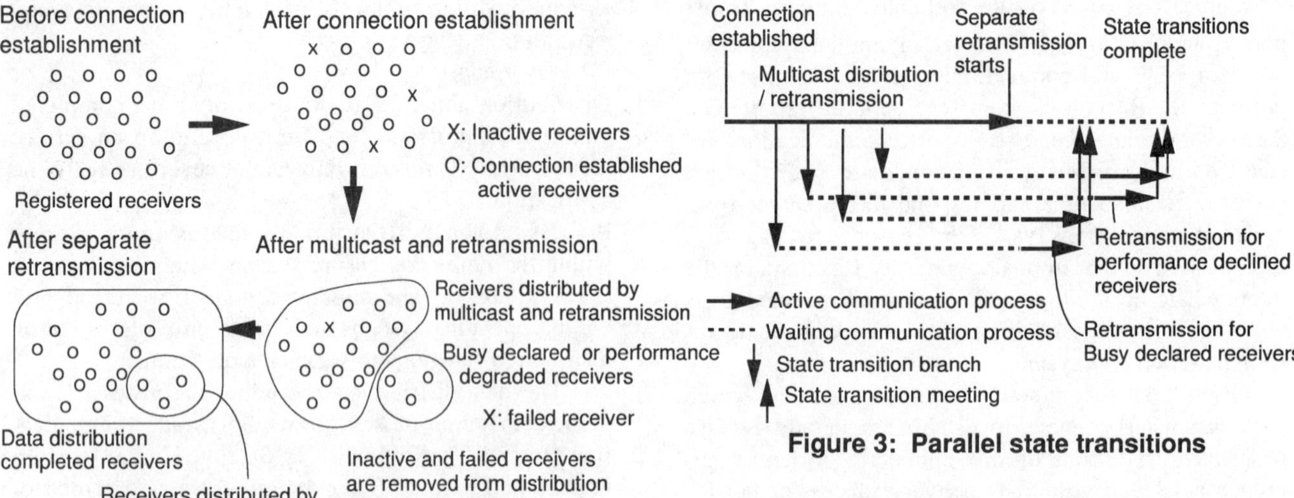

Figure 2: Receiver state transitions

Figure 3: Parallel state transitions

Figure 2 shows data distribution phase transition as determined by receiver condition. Receivers which declare temporal unavailability by BUSY can be handled after distribution to active normal receivers is completed. These receivers are called BUSY declared receivers. Those receivers that become inactive and failed to complete the multicast distribution/ retransmission phase or separate retransmission phases are recorded and notified for later distribution by the server. These receivers are called performance declared receivers. This procedure suits vulnerable environments such as distribution to mobile receivers in a wireless environment. Thus, the proposed procedure prioritize active normal receivers while also supporting temporarily unavailable or performance impaired receivers.

These state transition bifurcation and integration processes in the server are described in Figure 3. State transitions of BUSY declared receivers and performance declined receivers are bifurcated from the main multicast re/transmission state transition and become inactive while the main state transition is active and retransmitting. The states of received packets are kept in both the server and receiver until separate retransmission starts. After the main state transition completes the retransmission cycle and become inactive, the bifurcated state transitions become active and resume retransmission. Upon finishing this retransmission cycle, each bifurcated state transition reports its results to the main state transition and expires. Figure 3 shows the case that retransmission to BUSY declared receivers is prioritized to those for performance declined receivers. The scheduling scheme used to handle separate retransmission receivers depends on the priority policy adopted.

2.2 Core recovery scheme

The core scheme that guarantee reliable multicast data distribution is shown in the multicast distribution/retransmission phase in Figure 1 and is summarized as follows.

(Step 1)The whole data set such as a file, is split into multiple transport packets with sequence numbers.

(Step 2) After the first round of multicasting all packets, packets not received due to error or loss are

reported to the server from receivers.

(Step 3) The server determines the retransmission packets needed from the unreceived packet reports

in NACK; packet duplication is prevented by referring to their sequence numbers.

(Step 4) The server then multicasts the retransmission packets in the second round data distribution.

(Step 5) The server continues retransmission until no packet loss is reported by receivers or until a limit is reached.

Thus, retransmission is based on the selective-repeat scheme which requires fewer retransmission packets than the go-back N scheme.

This multi-round procedure assumes retransmission management tables which are used to record the numbers of successfully transmitted packets both in the server and receivers. The server supervise all packet distribution conditions for each receiver. The size of the whole data set, the total number of data packets, and data packet size are indicated in the connection establishment phase prior to the data distribution phase from the server to the receivers and the information is used for packet retransmission management at both sides.

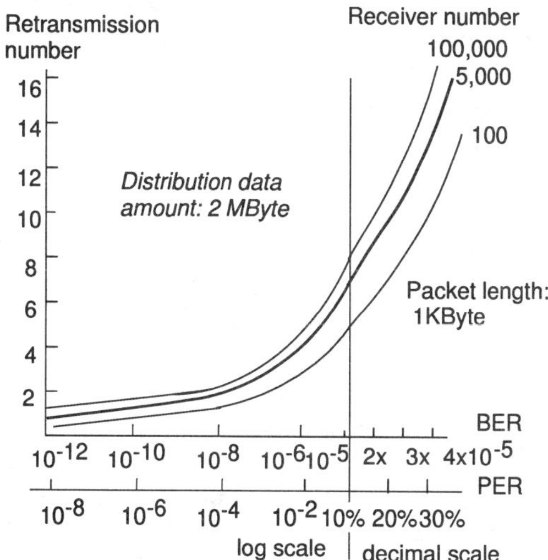

Figure 4: Retransmission number vs error rate

The number of retransmissions as a function of packet error rate was assessed. Packet loss and error are not distinguished in the discussion.

Here, we give attention to the number of packets to be confirmed by the receivers in the kth round of data retransmission, that is, the number of the packets that have not yet received by the receivers just before the kth round transmission. Let the number be Sk. Sk is expressed as $Sk = e^k M N$, where N: Number of receivers, M: Message size (number of packets forming the whole data set), and e: packet error rate (PER) for a packet multicasted through the network and received by each receiver. The number of retransmissions R is obtained as the value of k when Sk becomes smaller than 1 and retransmission completes. That is, $R = [\log_{1/e} MN]$, [ ]: integer value.

Figure 4 shows the number of retransmissions needed to complete multicast retransmission versus the bit error rate (BER) and packet error rate (PER). Distribution amount is 2 Mbytes and the packet error rate is shown for the 1 Kbyte user-data packet size case. Several curves are drawn for differing numbers of receivers up to 100,000 and error rates up to 30% PER.

As an example, for the 5000 receiver case, the graph shows the number of multicast retransmissions needed for 10,000,000 packets (2000 packets x 5000 receivers) to be correctly received. For the PER of 10^{-2} (BER 1.22 x 10^{-6}), four retransmissions are need to complete data distribution. This shows that the recovery procedure of Infocast is feasible since the BER of typical digital networks is less than 10^{-9}. Furthermore, the retransmission procedure is tolerant to even the high error rate of 10% PER which may occur in the Internet.

Figure 4 also shows that receiver number does not strongly affect the retransmission number. The size of the whole data set also has a limited impact on retransmission number. These estimations confirm that the proposed recovery procedure is scalable in terms of receiver number and data size.

2.3 Data recovery procedure in detail

(1) Data recovery in multicast distribution phase

For data recovery in the multicast distribution phase, ACK and NACK are used as follows. The sequence numbers of all data packets not received for each round of data distribution are included in a NACK and reported to the server by unicast. When a receiver receives all packets, the receiver sends ACK to the server by unicast. Some papers propose to multicast responses and receivers do not send the responses which have been received from other receivers before responding [5]. This approach does not guarantee complete data reception because the server cannot distinguish whether the message was received successfully or ACK/NACK was lost. The analysis in [5] assumes the latter case never occurs.

A receiver also uses a timer for data packet receipt and reports NACK when the timer expires. The server also uses a ACK/NACK waiting timer and sends POLL which solicits ACK/NACK when the timer expires. If ACK is not used, server timeout cannot detect whether all packets were received by a receiver or the NACK was lost. POLL is used against the exceptional case that ACK/NACK is lost in the network or the server by overflow.

One-to-one reliable protocol NETBLT [9] also uses ACK/NACK (the names are OK/RESEND) for one round of buffer data distribution and NACK includes all missing packet numbers. In NETBLT, the whole data set is transmitted by using multiple buffers, while in RMTP, only one large buffer is used. In order to reduce ACK/NACK loss, NETBLT makes frequent use of long-lived control packets which include previous ACK/NACK information in addition to new information until the packet is acknowledged by the server. RMTP does not use this method since it uses only one acknowledgment per receiver for one round of data distribution in order to avoid ACK/NACK implosion.

There are two causes of ACK implosion. One is the frequency of ACK/NACK issued from receivers and this can be avoided by restricting ACK/NACK to just once per distribution /retransmission round. This requires large buffers in both the server and receivers.

Recent memory advances have made this possible and the 32 Mbytes of main memory now common in standard workstations is enough to send 10 Mbytes of data and manage a distribution table.

The other cause is receiver number and this offset by using the backoff time algorithm as follows [7]. Each receiver holds its response (ACK/NACK) for some, random, uniformly distributed delay period, called the backoff time, before sending it to the server. The applicability of the algorithm to large scale multicasting is examined in later sections.

If one or more receivers cannot complete multicast data distribution procedures for some reason such as poor receiver performance or human interruption, separate unicast retransmission is conducted after the rounds of multicast retransmission finish.   Such a receiver issues a BUSY packet to declare its condition to the server in the multicast distribution phase. After recovering from its exceptional state, the receiver issues a ReceiveReady packet (RRDY) to show that it is able to receive retransmission packets.   Even if RRDY is received during the multicast retransmission phase, retransmission to these receivers is delayed until after multicast retransmission is completed to prioritize the normal receivers.

Those receivers that became inactive and failed to complete the multicast distribution/ retransmission phase or separate retransmission phases are recorded for later distribution by the server. Notification packets are used from the server to these receivers.

(2) Connection management

An explicit connection establishment procedure is used in order to pass to the receivers the information needed for retransmission control such as total packet number. Furthermore, connection establishment and release procedures are necessary to confirm the availability of registered users prior to data distribution and to charge for successful data distribution.

Membership is decided before the connection establishment phase by some other protocol or manually and is assumed to be constant during the data distribution phase until communication is complete and all connections are released.   This assumption is realistic for massive-data multicasting, while other interactive multicasting services such as whiteboard sharing may require dynamic membership control during the data distribution phase.

The connection management procedures are described as follows.   The server sends connection establishment request (CONN) to all receivers via multicast based on the membership list given by the application. Each receiver sends an acknowledgment (CACK) which includes Yes (ready to communicate) or No (unable to communicate) to the server via "unicast" in the same way as ACK is sent in the multicast retransmission phase. Furthermore, an authentication parameter can be included for the server to authenticate the responding receivers.

The server also uses a timer to wait for CACK responses and retransmit CONN by "unicast".   The timer value depends on receiver number and the limit of CACK (when to give up) depends on the application. The reason why unicast is used for CONN retransmission is based on the assumption that most receivers are ready to communicate and CONN retransmission occurs in only a few case.

The server multicasts a connection release packet (REL) after each round of data distribution or retransmission for the succeeded receivers. NACK or BUSY reported receivers just ignore REL packets. This explicit release procedure is for the purpose of charging or accounting after successful data distribution.

Implosion by CACK/RACK is avoided by using the backoff time algorithm as in the case of ACK.

3. Performance evaluations

3.1 Buffer overflow analysis

Buffer overflow in the server, which is caused by ACK implosion is analyzed in this section. In our experiments as well as other reports [7], overflow was observed at the socket buffer of the operating system, which has a priority lower than that of a network interface buffer.

Packet are processed in the server as follows. The server has a FIFO socket buffer of limited size. The first packet in the socket buffer is processed by the server Infocast process and the remaining packets in the buffer wait by forming a queue. Buffer overflow occurs when a packet arrives at the buffer which is full.

The buffer overflow including transient state toward equilibrium state is examined as follows.
Term definitions
e: packet loss rate of a packet transiting the whole
   network one way.
$P_{n,b}$: buffer overflow probability when the n th packet
   arrives at the server where the buffer size is b.
$V(x)$: mean number of packets overflowing at the
   server buffer as received from x receivers in a re/
   transmission round.

$V(x)$ and $P_{n,b}$ are calculated through queuing system analysis in Appendix A as follows.

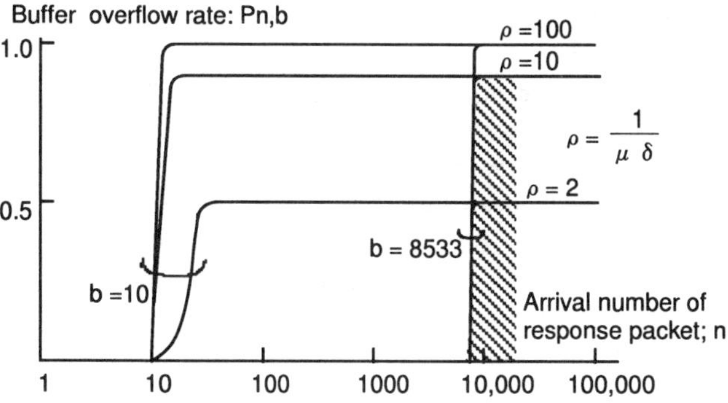

Example : mean number of overflowed packets V(x),
receiver number x=20,000, buffer size b= 8333 packets,
system utilization rate $\rho = 10$

Figure 5: Buffer overflow rate vs arriving packet

$$V(x) = \sum_{n=\,b+1}^{x} P_{n,b},$$

$$\text{where} \quad P_{n,b} = (1 - 1/\rho)^{b} \sum_{m=0}^{n-b-1} {}_{m+b-2}C_{b-2}\; 1/\rho^{m},$$

system utilization rate $\rho = 1/\delta\mu$, μ: service rate at server, δ: mean response production interval at the receiver set according to a uniform random distribution over $[0, \delta x]$ in backoff time algorithm where x is the number of receivers. $1/\delta$ corresponds to packet arriving rate.

Figure 5 shows the buffer overflow probability $P_{n,b}$ for several buffer sizes and receiver numbers. The mean number of overflowed responses V(x) is shown as the shadowed area. $P_{n,b}$ converges to $1-1/\rho$ when enough time has passed. $P_{n,b}$ increases as the response producing interval δ decreases.

In the experimental system, the socket buffer size was 50 Kbytes and ACK and CACK sizes were 5 and 6 Kbyte, respectively. Buffer overflows never occurs with up to 10240 ACKs and 8533 CACKs.
On the other hand, NACK size is variable. The NACK header is 8 bytes and the following NACK information size is (the set of lost packet numbers and/or range symbol) x (lost packet sequence number; 2 bytes). The range symbol is used to express the continuous burst packets in a shorter NACK packet. Packet loss of 1% yields 48 byte NACK   for 2 Mbytes data transfer with 1 Kbyte UDP packets. Thus, NACK is more likely to cause "NACK" implosion when very low quality networks or receivers are used.

3.2 Experimental evaluations on transfer time and processing load

(1) Implementation

We implemented Infocast on Sun workstations SS4/20, SS4/2, etc. with Solaris 2.3 OS. Infocast was implemented as an application process over a UNIX socket interface. It provides a file transfer Application Program Interface (API) to various data distribution applications.
[API list]
Server: send_request, abort_request, and
    status_report_requests
Receiver: busy_request, receive_ready_request, and
    abort_request
[Infocast code features]
Language: C (ANSI)
Program size:
Server: 5.5 Klines, Receiver: 3 Klines

For the performance evaluation, the following tests were executed using the network environment formed by a 10 Mbps Ethernet LAN with three subnetworks connected by a router that supports IP multicast.

(2) Performance tests for large-scale information distribution

Two different emulators were used, Mars and Lares, in order to create a large scale communication environment consisting of hundreds and thousands of receivers.

(a) Full-specification medium-scale emulator (Mars)

Mars produces an environment of hundreds of receivers in high delay and erroneous networks. Mars can produce an artificial packet loss and an artificial delay according to the value specified. Mars consists of a process which produces error and delay, and multiple Infocast receiver processes.   Ten to twenty receiver processes can be installed on the main memory of one workstation, so 5 or 6 workstations were used to realize the full 100 receiver environment.

(b) Limited-specification large-scale emulator (Lares)

Lares produces an environment of thousands of receivers using the backoff time algorithm. Lares is a Infocast receiver process which emulates 1000 receivers and responds positively with CACK, ACK, and RACK every time a response is needed. The ACK arriving process, based on the backoff time algorithm, was reproduced by specifying the inter-packet gap in the responding Lares process.

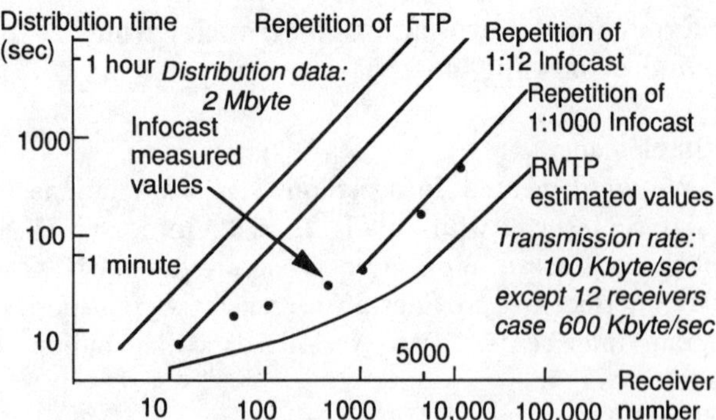

Figure 6: Distribution time vs distribution scale

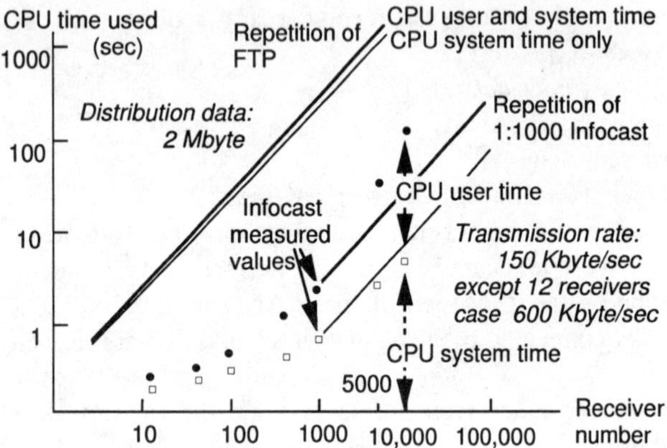

Figure 7: CPU load in the server vs distribution scale

[Experimental results]

By combining Mars and Lares we generated environments of differing receiver scale, packet loss rate, and network delay. The following results are based on the 1 % packet loss of Mars by specifying the loss rate and by choosing the transmission rate to show good transfer performance. The go-and-back delay values (turn around time) were 100 msec (assuming two ATM switches and two routers over 3000 km optical networks) and 600 msec (assuming two satellite links or a public packet-switched network). However, the delay does not strongly impact the transfer time or CPU processing load and are neglected in the performance graph shown below.

UDP socket buffer is 50 Kbytes and UDP packet size is 1 Kbyte. The responses are sent according to a uniform random distribution over $[0, \delta x]$, where x is the number of receivers. The backoff time is used for 1000, 5000, and 10000 receiver cases with choosing response interval, δ, of 2 to 4 msec.

Figure 6 and 7 show the transfer time and processing load as functions of receiver numbers. In the case of about 10 receivers, only real receivers were used. Seven workstations running Mars were used to emulate 100 receivers for the 100 to 5000 receiver

cases. Mars was also used for the 50 receiver case. Two to ten workstations running Lares were used for the 500 to 10000 receiver cases. The data size was always 2 Mbyte.

Tests were done several times for the same case and the graphs in the figure are the mean values. The transfer time obtained by summing up each transmission time and turn around time of the protocol RMTP [8] is depicted as RMTP estimated values in Figure 6. The fact that the surplus time in the timers was set large enough to accept normal responses explains the difference between observed values and RMTP estimated values.

Figure 6 shows that the values are acceptable for practical applications. For example, 2 Mbytes (one newspaper) can be delivered to 5000 users within 3 minutes. For comparison, repeated use of four parallel FTP processes with no artificial packet loss was also tested in the same LAN environment. Furthermore, the values of repeated uses of Infocast for 12 and 1000 receivers are also shown in the graphs. The curve of one time Infocast linearly increases with the number of receivers for over 1000 receivers. That is, the ten repeated uses of Infocast for 1000 receivers achieve the same effect of Infocast delivery for ten thousands receivers at once. This scalability limitation comes from the backoff time algorithm which requires a total response time in proportion to the receiver number.

As for packet processing load at the server, the same characteristics can be observed in Figure 7. In this case, the delivery by Infocast for over one thousand receivers consumes more CPU time than the ten repeated use of Infocast for 1000 receivers.

These observations conclude that Infocast which utilize the backoff time algorithm for ACK implosion is strongly scalable up to about one thousand receivers.

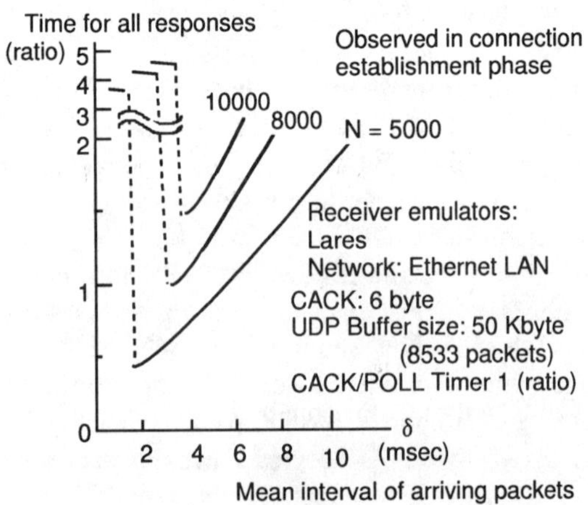

Figure 8: Effect of backoff time

Lastly the impact of backoff time on transfer time is shown in Figure 8. The time for connection establishment in the server is observed for several thousands of receivers using large-scale emulator Lares. The tests were executed for various packet arriving intervals (the backoff time intervals). The curves show that the backoff time needs to be small for large numbers of receivers for transfer time efficiency while too small backoff time yields drastic overhead by lost packet waiting timeout. UDP buffer overflow is also observed in small backoff time in 5000 and 8000 receiver cases even if enough buffer (8533 packets) is used. This may be caused by too much UDP buffer management.

4. Very large-size data distribution (VLDD)

4.1 VLDD scheme

The limitation of fundamental multicast retransmission is mainly determined by the size of the entire data set. One issue is the buffer size of the server and receivers. This may resolved by implementing the buffer on a hard-disk or by swapping memory usage with some i/o processing overhead. Another problem is distribution table management. As data size increases, the overhead of distribution table management also increases.

To avoid these deficiencies, repeated use of Infocast is proposed as a common application function over the Infocast module. The common application function divides a very large data set into several smaller data sets, such as 10 Mbytes, and each block is given a block number. The entire data set is sent by calling the Infocast process several times and managing the block number. Very large massive-data distribution is indicated in the initial connection request packet, and the entire data size and block size are also set in it.

In the proposed procedure, backoff time overhead in the connection establishment phase is not negligible. Therefore, in very massive-data distribution, an Infocast version may be used that eliminates all connection establishment response (CACK) procedures except the first one. The initial connections are inherited by subsequent connections without CACK.

However, connection establishment request CONN is used to inform the receivers of the start of the next round of dividend data distribution. Further, duplicated use of CONN packet is effective to offset the loss of CONN packet in the network.

4.2 Experimental results of VLDD

The performance test results for the distribution of a 650 Mbyte data set (CD-ROM size) by Infocast and the VLDD scheme are as follow. CACKs are eliminated except the initial ones as stated in the connection amendment in VLDD scheme in section 4.1.

Figure 9 and 10 show the distribution time and processing load as functions of receiver numbers. The values of both criteria are increased compared to the 2 Mbyte curves shown in Figure 6 and 7. However, both the distribution time and CPU time (650 Mbyte) are less sensitive to receiver number compared to the 2 Mbyte. Especially, Figure 9 shows that for over one thousand receivers, one time use of Infocast achieves higher transfer time performance than the ten repeated uses of one thousand delivery by Infocast. This is explained by the elimination of CACK in the VLDD scheme.

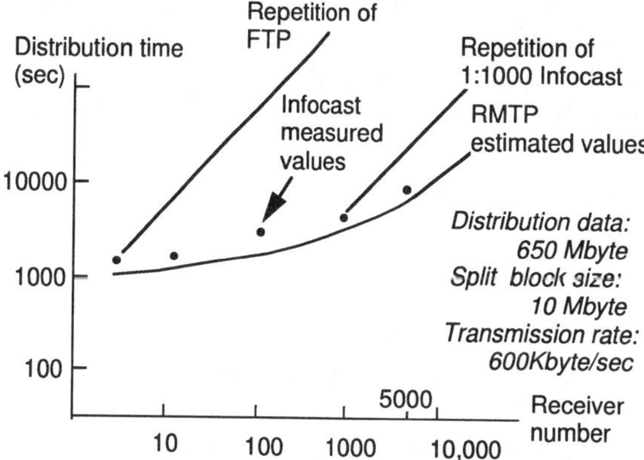

Figure 9: Distribution time vs distribution scale Very large size data case

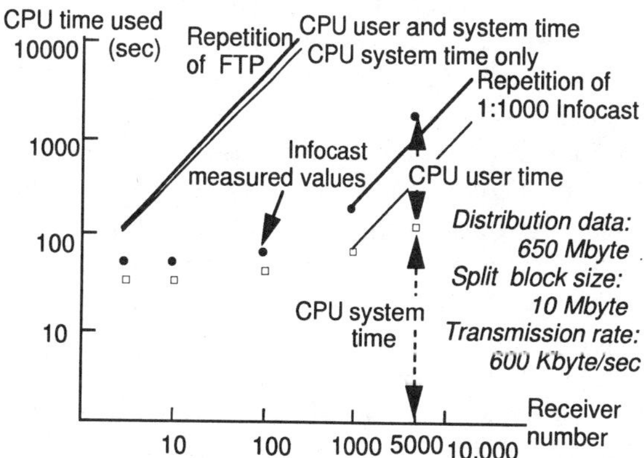

Figure 10: CPU load in the server vs distribution scale Very large size data case

5. Related works on reliable large-scale distribution

Reliable multicast protocols applicable to massive-data distribution are described below and compared against our RMTP [8]. The trends in reliable multicast protocols for massive information delivery and group communication are reported exhaustively in [10] and [11].

Multicast Transport Protocol (MTP) [12] is a general purpose multicast protocol over UDP and IP-multicast. It bases retransmission on receiver-initiated NACK and fixed-size window control which causes heavy retransmission overhead. MTP also adopts dynamic membership control via a group master which is also responsible for retransmission. Due to these heavy control overheads, MTP has not been implemented. MTP's retransmission idea can be found in Reliable Broadcast Protocols(RBP) [13]. RBP was proposed for broadcast LANs and is not scalable beyond LANs.

Reliable Multicast Protocol (RMP) [14] is a successor of RBP. RMP reduces the group master overhead by rotating the role of group master among all members as in RBP. However, its scalability is still questionable and reported tests cover less than 10 receivers. RMP seems to be somewhat dedicated to other communication applications since it also supports multiple remote procedure calls and atomic transactions.

Adaptive File Distribution Protocol (AFDP) [15] is a promising, recently proposed multicast protocol that is realized as middleware. AFDP is also a receiver-initiated massive-data distribution protocol which only uses NACK. For the distribution of megabytes of data , testing of AFDP has been reported up to 20 receivers and no consideration of response implosion was reported for large number of receivers.

Against ACK implosion, a promising solution is the backoff time algorithm which was proposed by [6]. Its behavior with limited socket buffers was analyzed by the queuing model and tested for ten real receivers and rather large response packets [7]. The analysis and tests for Infocast in this paper was conducted for large receiver numbers and short packet size cases.

This paper focused on the massive-data distribution for on-line publication and resource replication. The order of sets of data is not a research issue, since different data sets are not delivered at the same time. As for the ordered data distribution to a group of processes, there are works on ordered multicast which distributes transaction messages and focuses on fault-tolerant distribution [16].

Forward error correction (FEC) can be also used for error recovery of multicast distribution. FEC executes error recovery by adding extra data and does not cause the delay that a retransmission scheme is subjected to [17]. However, the server must add sufficient data to achieve a high quality error recovery. Thus, FEC seems to be suitable for audio-video real-time applications which are delay sensitive but do not require a complete data replication. This paper concentrated on retransmission scheme to achieve a complete data replication. The integration of FEC into retransmission scheme may improve the transfer performance by reducing retransmission.

6. Concluding remarks

The reliable data distribution middleware, Infocast, was proposed to provide the function of distributing massive-data sets to large numbers (thousands of) receivers in a weakly-consistent manner. Performance tests for connection establishment and multicast distributions phases were made. The tests showed that the proposed procedure achieves acceptable time and processing performance for thousands of receivers. The tests also confirmed the feasibility of the backoff time algorithm for response concentration in large-scale delivery. The repeated use of Infocast by VLDD scheme can achieve very large massive-data distribution.

As the user number increases, other administration factors such as user authentication, information charging mechanism, and network administration will also become important issues. Infocast is going to be introduced for corporate data replicating service while overcoming these practical issues.

References

[1] B. C. Neuman, Scale in Distributed Systems, *Readings in Distributed Computing Systems,* IEEE Computer Society Press, 1994.

[2] C. M. Bowman, P. B. Danzig, U. Manber, and M. F. Schwartz, Scalable Internet Resource Discovery: Research Problems and Approaches, *Communications of the ACM* , Vol. 37, No. 8, pp.98-107, Aug. 1994.

[3] B-ISDN SERVICE ASPECTS, ITU-T, *Recommendation I.211* ,1991.

[4] S. E. Deering, "Multicast Routing in Internetworks and Extended LANs," *ACM Transactions on Computer Systems,* No.8, pp.85-110, 1990.

[5] S. Pingali, D. Towsley, and J. F. Kurose, "A Comparison of Sender-Initiated and Receiver Initiated Reliable Multicast Protocols," *ACM SIGMETRIX '94* , Vol.22, No.1, pp.221-230,1994

[6] D. R. Cherington and W. Zwaenepoel, "Distributed Process Groups in the V-Kernel," *ACM Transactions on Computer Systems*, Vol.3 No.2, pp.77-107, May 1985.

[7] P. B. Danzig, "Flow Control for Limited Buffer Multicast," *IEEE Transactions on Software Engineering*, Vol.20, No.1, pp.1-12, Jan. 1994.

[8] T. Shiroshita, O. Takahashi, M. Yamashita, N. Yamanouchi, and T. Kushida, "Reliable Multicast Transport Protocol and its Applicability to Emerging Networks," *Technical Report of IEICE*, IN95-140, Mar.. 1996. (in Japanese)

[9] D.D. Clark, M. L. Lambert, and L. Zhang, "NETBLT: A High Throughput Transport Protocol," *ACM SIGCOMM, CCR* Vol.18, No.5, Aug.1987.

[10] K. Obraczka, "Massively Replicating Services in Wide-area Internetworks," PhD dissertation, Computer Science Department, University of Southern California, Dec. 1994.

[11] W. Dabbous, and C. Diot, "Group Communication; a state of the art," Submitted to *IEEE Journal on Selected Area in Communication*. Special Issue on Group Communication, 1996.

[12] S. Armstrong, A. Freier, and K. Marzullo, "Multicast Transport Protocol," *RFC1301*, IETF, 1992.

[13] J. M. Chang, and N. F. Maxemchuk, "Reliable Broadcast Protocol," *ACM Transactions on Computer Systems*, Vol.2, No.3, pp.251-273, 1984.

[14] B. Whetten, T. Montgomery, and S. Kaplan, "A High Performance Totally Ordered Multicast Protocol,Theory and Practice in Distributed Systems," Springer Verlag, *LCNS* 938.

[15] S. Kotsopoulos and J. R. Cooperstock, "Why Use a Fishing Line When You Have a Net? An Adaptive Multicast Data Distribution Protocol," *Proc.USENIX Technical Conference,* Jan.1996.

[16] L. E. Moser, P. M. Melliarr-Smith, D. A. Agawal, R. K. Budhia, and C. A. Lingley-Papadopoulos, Totem: A Fault-Tolerant Multicast Group Communication System, *Communications of ACM*, Vol. 39, No. 4, pp. 54-63, Apr. 1996.

[17] N. Shacham, P. McKenny: A, Packet recovery in high-speed networks using coding, *Proc. IEEE Infocom'90*, pp. 124-131, Jun. 1990.

[18] L. Kleinrock, *Queuing Systems, Vol. 1*, Wiley-Interscience Publication, 1975.

[19] E. T. Whittaker, and G. N. Watson, *A Course of Modern Analysis,* Fourth edition, Cambridge University Press, 1969.

Appendix A. Buffer overflow analysis

This appendix analyzes the buffer overflow process based on queuing system model and derives $P_{n,b}$: buffer overflow probability when the n th packet arrives at the server where the buffer size is b. This analysis includes transient state at the onset of overflow, which cannot be obtained from an equiblium state analysis of the M/M/1/K model (K= buffer size b); Chapter 3.6 of [18].

[Definitions and assumptions]

i: system length; the number of packets in the server socket buffer including the packet under processing.

μ: service rate at server

δ: packet arriving rate, which is equal to mean response production interval at the receiver set.

$\rho = 1/\delta\mu$: system utilization rate.

b: buffer size (in packets).

V(x): mean number of packets overflowing at the server buffer as received from x receivers in a re/transmission round.

$P_{n,i}$: Probability that the system length is i just before the n th packet arrival.

Service time and arriving interval are assumed to follow exponential distributions. Since buffer overflow never occurs for $\rho \leq 1$, the case $\rho > 1$ is analyzed.

At most one packet is assumed to be processed at the server in a packet arrival interval. This assumption is valid for $\rho = (1/\delta\mu) > 1$.

[Buffer state transition]

State pairs of n th arrival and system length (n, i) obey the following transition equation.

For $2 \leq n \leq b+1$,

$$P_{n,i} = (1-1/\rho) P_{n-1,i-1} + 1/\rho \, P_{n-1,i} \quad (1 \leq i \leq n-1)$$

$$\text{and} \quad P_{1,0} = 1, P_{1,i} = 0 \quad (i > 0). \tag{1}$$

For $n \geq b+2$,

$$P_{n,i} = (1-1/\rho) P_{n-1,i-1} + 1/\rho \, P_{n-1,i} \quad (0 \leq i \leq b-2),$$

$$P_{n,b-1} = (1-1/\rho) P_{n-1,b-2} + 1/\rho \, (P_{n-1,b-1} + 1/\rho \, P_{n-1,b}),$$

$$P_{n,b} = (1-1/\rho) \, (P_{n-1,b-1} + P_{n-1,b}) \tag{2}$$

[Derivation of buffer overflow rate]

For $1 \leq n \leq b+1$,

$$P_{n,i} = {}_{b-1}C_i \, (1-1/\rho)^i \, 1/\rho^{n-i-1} \quad (0 \leq i \leq n-1) \tag{3}$$

For $n \geq b + 2$,

$$P_{n,b} = (1-1/\rho)^b \sum_{m=1}^{n-b-1} {}_{m+b-2}C_{b-2} \, 1/\rho^m . \tag{4}$$

Furthermore, since the term of $\sum$ in (4) is hypergeometric series and converges to $(1-1/\rho)^{1-b}$, under the condition of $\rho > 1$ [19].

$$\lim_{n \to \infty} P_{n,b} = 1-1/\rho. \tag{5}$$

Note that the value of (5) is equal to the block rate value of an equilibrium state by M/M/1/K model; $p_b = (1-\rho)\rho^b/(1-\rho)^{b+1}$; equation (3.43) of [18] if buffer size b $> \infty$.

Session 6A

Query Processing

Scrambling Query Plans to Cope With Unexpected Delays

Laurent Amsaleg[*†]
University of Maryland
amsaleg@cs.umd.edu

Michael J. Franklin[†]
University of Maryland
franklin@cs.umd.edu

Anthony Tomasic
INRIA
Anthony.Tomasic@inria.fr

Tolga Urhan[†]
University of Maryland
urhan@cs.umd.edu

Abstract

Accessing data from numerous widely-distributed sources poses significant new challenges for query optimization and execution. Congestion and failures in the network can introduce highly-variable response times for wide-area data access. This paper is an initial exploration of solutions to this variability. We introduce a class of dynamic, run-time query plan modification techniques that we call query plan scrambling. We present an algorithm that modifies execution plans on-the-fly in response to unexpected delays in obtaining initial requested tuples from remote sources. The algorithm both reschedules operators and introduces new operators into the query plan. We present simulation results that demonstrate how the technique effectively hides delays by performing other useful work while waiting for missing data to arrive.

1 Introduction

Ongoing improvements in networking technology and infrastructure have resulted in a dramatic increase in the demand for accessing and collating data from disparate, remote data sources over wide-area networks such as the Internet and intranets. Query optimization and execution strategies have long been studied in centralized, parallel, and tightly-coupled distributed environments. Data access across widely-distributed sources, however, imposes significant new challenges for query optimization and execution for two reasons: First, there are semantic and performance problems that arise due to the *heterogeneous* nature of the data sources in a loosely-coupled environment. Second, data access over wide-area networks involves a large number of remote data sources, intermediate sites, and communications links, all of which are vulnerable to congestion and failures. From the end user's point of view, congestion or failure in any of the components of the network are manifested as *highly-variable response time* — that is, the time required for obtaining data from remote sources can vary greatly depending on the specific data sources accessed and the current state of the network at the time that such access is attempted.

The query processing problems resulting from heterogeneity have been the subject of much attention in recent years (e.g., [SAD+95, BE96, TRV96]). In contrast, the impact of unpredictable response time on wide-area query processing has received relatively little attention. The work presented here is an initial exploration into addressing problems of response-time variability for wide-area data access.

1.1 Response Time Variability

High variability makes efficient query processing difficult because query execution plans are typically generated statically, based on a set of assumptions about the costs of performing various operations and the costs of obtaining data (i.e., disk and/or network accesses). The causes of high-variability are typically failures and congestion, which are inherently runtime issues; they cannot be reliably predicted at query optimization time or even at query start-up time. As a result, the execution of a statically optimized query plan is likely to be sub-optimal in the presence of unexpected response time problems. In the worst case, a query execution may be blocked for an arbitrarily long time if needed data fail to arrive from remote data sources.

The different types of response time problems that can be experienced in a loosely-coupled, wide-area environment can be categorized as follows:

- **Initial Delay** - There is an unexpected delay in the arrival of the *first* tuple from a particular remote source. This type of delay typically appears when there is difficulty connecting to a remote source, due to a failure or congestion at that source or along the path between the source and the destination.

- **Slow Delivery** - Data is arriving at a regular rate, but this rate is much slower than the

---

*Laurent Amsaleg is supported by a post-doctoral fellowship from INRIA Rocquencourt, France.

†Supported in part by NSF Grant IRI-94-09575, an IBM SUR award, and a grant from Bellcore.

expected rate. This problem can be the result, for example, of network congestion, resource contention at the source, or because a different (slower) communication path is being used (e.g., due to a failure).

- **Bursty Arrival** - Data is arriving at an unpredictable rate, typically with bursts of data followed by long periods of no arrivals. This problem can arise from fluctuating resource demands and the lack of a global scheduling mechanism in the wide-area environment.

Because these problems can arise unpredictably at runtime, they cannot be effectively addressed by static query optimization techniques. As a result, we have been investigating a class of dynamic, runtime query plan modification techniques that we call *query plan scrambling*. In this approach, a query is initially executed according to the original plan and associated schedule generated by the query optimizer. If however, a significant performance problem arises during the execution, then query plan scrambling is invoked to modify the execution *on-the-fly*, so that progress can be made on other parts of the plan. In other words, rather than simply stalling for slowly arriving data, query plan scrambling attempts to *hide* unexpected delays by performing other useful work.

There are three ways that query plan scrambling can be used to help mask response time problems. First, scrambling allows useful work to be done in the hope that the cause of the problem is resolved in the meantime. This approach is useful for all three classes of problems described above. Second, if data are arriving, but at a rate that hampers query processing performance (e.g., in the Slow Delivery or Bursty Arrival cases), then scrambling allows useful work to be performed while the problematic data are obtained in a background fashion. Finally, in cases where data are simply not arriving, or are arriving far too slowly, then scrambling can be used to produce partial results that can then be returned to users and/or used in query processing at a later time [TRV96].

1.2 Tolerating Initial Delays

In this work, we present an initial approach to query plan scrambling that specifically addresses the problem of Initial Delay (i.e., delay in receiving the initial requested tuples from a remote data source). We describe and analyze a query plan scrambling algorithm that follows the first approach outlined above; namely, other useful work is performed in the hope that the problem will eventually be resolved, and the requested data will arrive at or near the expected rate from then on. The algorithm exploits, where possible, decisions made by the static query optimizer and imposes no optimization or execution performance overhead in the absence of unexpected delays.

In order to allow us to clearly define the algorithm and to study its performance, this work assumes an execution environment with several properties:

- The algorithm addresses only response time delays in receiving the initial requested tuples from

remote data sources. Once the initial delay is over, tuples are assumed to arrive at or near the originally expected rate. As stated previously, this type of delay models problems in connecting to remote data sources, as it is often experienced in the Internet.

- We focus on query processing using a data-shipping or hybrid-shipping approach [FJK96], where data is collected from remote sources and integrated at the query source. Only query processing that is performed at the query source is subject to scrambling. This approach is typical of mediated database systems that integrate data from distributed, heterogeneous sources, e.g., [TRV96].

- Query execution is scheduled using an iterator model [Gra93]. In this model every run-time operator supports an *open()* call and a *get-next()* call. Query execution starts by calling open() on the topmost operator of the query execution plan and proceeds by iteratively calling get-next() on the topmost operator. These calls are propagated down the tree; each time an operator needs to consume data, it calls get-next() on its child (or children) operator(s). This model imposes a schedule on the operators in the query plan.

The reminder of the paper is organized as follows. Section 2 describes the algorithm and gives an extended example. Section 3 presents results from a simulation study that demonstrate the properties of the algorithm. Section 4 describes related work. Section 5 concludes with a summary of the results and a discussion of future work.

2 Scrambling Query Plans

This section describes the algorithm for scrambling queries to cope with initial delays in obtaining data from remote data sources. The algorithm consists of two phases: one that *changes the execution order of operations* in order to avoid idling, and one that *synthesizes new operations* to execute in the absence of other work to perform. We first provide a brief overview of the algorithm and then describe the two phases in detail using a running example. The algorithm is then summarized at the end of the section.

2.1 Algorithm Overview

Figure 1 shows an operator tree for a complex query plan. Typically, such a complicated plan would be generated by a static query optimizer according to its cost model, statistics, and objective functions. At the leaves of the tree are base relations stored at remote sites. The nodes of the tree are binary operators (we focus our study on hash-based joins) that are executed at the query source site.[1]

As discussed previously, we describe the scrambling algorithm in the context of an iterator-based execution

---

[1]Unary operators, such as selections, sorting, and partitioning are not shown in the figure.

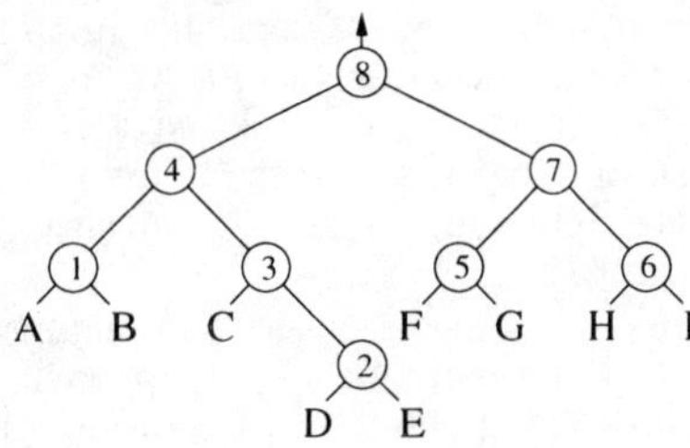

Figure 1: Initial Query Tree

model. This model imposes a schedule on the operators of a query and drives the flow of data between operators. The scheduling of operators is indicated in Figure 1 by the numbers associated to each operator. In the figure, the joins are numbered according to the order in which they would be completed by an iterator-based scheduler. The flow of data between the operators follows the model discussed in [SD90], i.e., the left input of a hash join is always materialized while the right input is consumed in a pipelined fashion.

The schedule implied by the tree in Figure 1 would thus begin by materializing the left subtree of the root node. Assuming that hash joins are used and that there is sufficient memory to hold the hash tables for relations A, C, and D (so no partitioning is necessary for these relations), this materialization would consist of the following steps:

1. Scan relation A and build hash-table H_A using selected tuples;
2. In a pipelined fashion, probe H_A with (selected) tuples of B and build a hash-table containing the result of A⋈B (H_{AB});
3. Scan C and build hash-table H_C;
4. Scan D and build hash-table H_D;
5. In a pipelined fashion, probe H_D, H_C and H_{AB} with tuples of E and build a hash-table containing the result of (A⋈B)⋈(C⋈D⋈E).
6. ...

The execution thus begins by requesting tuples from the remote site where relation A is stored. If there is a delay in accessing that site (say, because this site is temporarily down), then the scan of A (i.e., step 1) is blocked until the site recovers. Under a traditional iterator-based scheduling discipline, this delay of A would result in the entire execution of the query being blocked, pending the recovery of the remote site.

Given that unexpected delays are highly probable in a wide-area environment, such sensitivity to delays is likely to result in unacceptable performance. The scrambling algorithm addresses this problem by attempting to *hide* such delays by making progress on other parts of the query until the problem is resolved. The scrambling algorithm is invoked once a delayed relation is detected (via a timeout mechanism). The algorithm is iterative; during each iteration it selects part of the plan to execute and materializes the corresponding temporary results to be used later in the execution.

The scrambling algorithm executes in one of two phases. During *Phase 1*, each iteration modifies the schedule in order to execute operators that are not dependent on any data that is known to be delayed. For example, in the query of Figure 1, Phase 1 might result in materializing the join of relations C, D and E while waiting for the arrival of A. During *Phase 2*, each iteration synthesizes new operators (joins for example) in order to make further progress. In the example, a Phase 2 iteration might choose to join relation B with the result of (C⋈D⋈E) computed previously.

At the end of each iteration the algorithm checks to see if any delayed sources have begun to respond, and if so, it stops iterating and returns to normal scheduling of operators, possibly re-invoking scrambling if additional delayed relations are later detected. If, however, no delayed data has arrived during an iteration, then the algorithm iterates again. The algorithm moves from Phase 1 to Phase 2 when it fails to find an existing operator that is not dependent on a delayed relation. If, while in Phase 2, the algorithm is unable to create any new operators, then scrambling terminates and the query simply waits for the delayed data to arrive. In the following sections we describe, in detail, the two phases of scrambling and their interactions.

2.2 Phase 1: Materializing Subtrees
2.2.1 Blocked and Runnable Operators

The operators of a query tree have producer-consumer relationships. The immediate ancestor of a given operator consumes the tuples produced by that operator. Conversely, the immediate descendants of a given operator produce the tuples that operator consumes. The producer-consumer relationships create *execution dependencies* between operators, as one operator can not consume tuples before these tuples have been produced. For example, a select operator can not consume tuples of a base relation if that relation is not available. In such a case the select operator is blocked. If the select can not consume any tuples, it can not produce any tuples. Consequently, the consumer of the select is also blocked. By transitivity, all the ancestors of the unavailable relation are blocked.

When the system discovers that a relation is unavailable, query plan scrambling is invoked. Scrambling starts by splitting the operators of the query tree into two disjoint queues: a queue of *blocked operators* and a queue of *runnable operators*. These queues are defined as follows:

Definition 2.1 Queue of Blocked Operators: Given a query tree, the queue of blocked operators contains all the ancestors of each unavailable relation.

Definition 2.2 Queue of Runnable Operators: Given a query tree and a queue of blocked operators, the queue of runnable operators contains all the operators that are not in the queue of blocked operators.

Operators are inserted in the runnable and blocked queues according to the order in which their execution would be initiated by an iterator-based scheduler.

2.2.2 Maximal Runnable Subtree

Each iteration during Phase 1 of query plan scrambling analyzes the runnable queue in order to find a *maximal runnable subtree* to materialize. A maximal runnable subtree is defined as follows:

Definition 2.3 Maximal Runnable Subtree: Given the query tree and the queues of blocked and runnable operators, a runnable subtree is a subtree in which all the operators are runnable. A runnable subtree is maximal if its root is the first runnable descendant of a blocked operator.

None of the operators belonging to a maximal runnable subtree depend on data that is known to be delayed. Each iteration of Phase 1 initiates the materialization of the first maximal runnable subtree found. The notion of maximal used in the definition is important, as materializing the biggest subtrees during each iteration tends to minimize the number of materializations performed, hence reducing the amount of extra I/O caused by scrambling. The materialization of a runnable subtree completes only if no relations used by this subtree are discovered to be unavailable during the execution.[2] When the execution of a runnable subtree is finished and its result materialized, the algorithm removes all the operators belonging to that subtree from the runnable queue. It then checks if missing data have begun to arrive. If the missing data from others, blocked relations are still unavailable, another iteration is begun. The new iteration analyzes (again) the runnable queue to find the next maximal runnable subtree to materialize.

2.2.3 Subtrees and Data Unavailability

It is possible that during the execution of a runnable subtree, one (or more) of the participating base relations is discovered to be unavailable. This is because a maximal runnable subtree is defined with respect to the *current* contents of the blocked and runnable queues. The runnable queue is only a guess about the real availability of relations. When the algorithm inserts operators in the runnable queue, it does not know whether their associated relations are actually available or unavailable. This will be discovered only when the corresponding relations are requested.

In the case where a relation is discovered to be unavailable during the execution of a runnable subtree, the current iteration stops and the algorithm updates the runnable and blocked queues. All the ancestors of the unavailable relation are extracted from the runnable queue and inserted in the blocked queue. Once the queues are updated, the scrambling of the query plan initiates a new Phase 1 iteration in order to materialize another maximal runnable subtree.

---

[2]Note that in the remainder of this paper, we use "maximal runnable subtree" and "runnable subtree" interchangeably, except where explicitly noted.

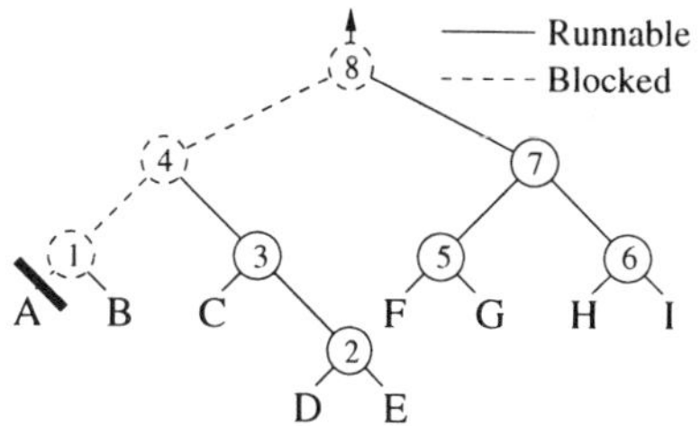

Figure 2: Blocked and Runnable Operators with Relation A Unavailable

2.2.4 Termination of Phase 1

At the end of each iteration, the algorithm checks for data arrival. If it is discovered that an unavailable relation has begun to arrive, the algorithm updates the blocked and runnable queues. The ancestors of the unblocked relation are extracted from the blocked queue and inserted in the runnable queue. Note that any ancestors of the unblocked relation that also depend on other blocked relations are not extracted from the queue. Phase 1 then terminates and the execution of the query returns to normal iterator-based scheduling of operators. If no further relations are blocked, the execution of the query will proceed until the final result is returned to the user. The scrambling algorithm will be re-invoked, however, if the query execution blocks again.

Phase 1 also terminates if the runnable queue is empty. In this case, Phase 1 can not perform any other iteration because all remaining operators are blocked. When this happens, query plan scrambling switches to Phase 2. The purpose of the second phase is to process the available relations when all the operators of the query tree are blocked. We present the second phase of query plan scrambling in Section 2.3. First, however, we present an example that illustrates all the facets of Phase 1 described above.

2.2.5 A Running Example

This example reuses the complex query tree presented at the beginning of Section 2. To discuss cases where data need or do need not to be partitioned before being joined, we assume that tuples of relations A, B, C, D and E do not need to be partitioned. In contrast, we assume that the tuples of relations F, G, H and I have to be partitioned. To illustrate the behavior of Phase 1, we follow the scenario given below:

1. When the execution of the query starts, relation A is discovered to be unavailable.
2. During the third iteration, relation G is discovered to be unavailable.
3. The tuples of A begin to arrive at the query execution site before the end of the fourth iteration.
4. At the time Phase 1 terminates, no tuples of G have been received.

The execution of the example query begins by requesting tuples from the remote site owning relation A. Following the above scenario, we assume relation A is

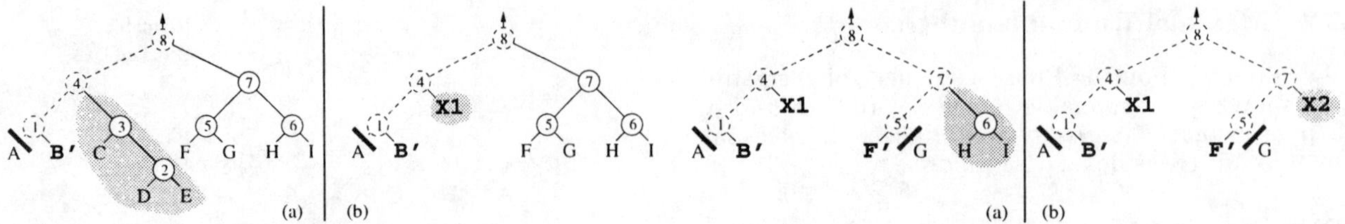

Figure 3: Query Tree During Iterations 1 and 2

Figure 4: G Unavailable; X2 Materialized

unavailable (indicated by the thick solid line in Figure 2). The operators that are blocked by the delay of A are depicted using a dashed line.

The unavailability of A invokes Phase 1 which updates the blocked and runnable queues and initiates its first iteration. This iteration analyses the runnable queue and finds that the first maximal runnable subtree consists of a unary operator that selects tuples from relation B.[3] Once the operator is materialized (i.e., selected tuples of B are on the local disk stored in the relation **B'**), the algorithm checks for the arrival of the tuples of A. Following the above scenario, we assume that the tuples of A are still unavailable, so another iteration is initiated. This second iteration finds the next maximal runnable subtree to be the one rooted at operator 3. Note the subtree rooted at operator 2 is *not* maximal since its consumer (operator 3) is not blocked.

Figure 3 shows the materialization of the runnable subtrees found by the first two iterations of query scrambling. Part (a) of this figure shows the effect of materializing of the first runnable subtree: the local relation **B'** contains the materialized and selected tuples of the remote relation B. It also shows the second runnable subtree (indicated by the shaded grey area). Figure 3(b) shows the query tree after the materialization of this second runnable subtree. The materialized result is called **X1**.

Once **X1** is materialized, another iteration starts since, in this example, relation A is still unavailable. The third iteration finds the next runnable subtree rooted at operator 7 which joins F, G, H and I (as stated above, these relations need to be partitioned before being joined). The execution of this runnable subtree starts by building the left input of operator 5 (partitioning F into **F'**). It then requests relation G in order to partition it before probing the tuples of F. In this scenario, however, G is discovered to be unavailable, triggering the update of the blocked and runnable queues. Figure 4(a) shows that operators 5 and 7 are newly blocked operators (operator 8 was already blocked due to the unavailability of A). Once the queues of operators are updated, another iteration of scrambling is initiated to run the next runnable subtree, i.e., the one rooted at operator 6 (indicated by the shaded grey area in the figure). The result of this execution is called **X2**.

Figure 5 illustrates the next step in the scenario, i.e., it illustrates the case where after **X2** is materialized it is discovered that the tuples of relation A have begun to arrive. In this case, the algorithm updates the runnable and blocked queues. As shown in Figure 5(a), operators 1 and 4 that were previously blocked are now unblocked (operator 8 remains blocked however). Phase 1 then terminates and returns to the normal iterator-based scheduling of operators which materializes the left subtree of the root node (see Figure 5(b)). The resulting relation is called **X3**.

After **X3** is materialized, the query is blocked on G so Phase 1 is re-invoked. Phase 1 computes the new contents of the runnable and blocked queue and discovers that the runnable queue is empty since all remaining operators are ancestors of G. Phase 1 then terminates and the scrambling of the query plan enters Phase 2. We describe Phase 2 of the algorithm in the next section.

2.3 Phase 2: Creating New Joins

Scrambling moves into Phase 2 when the runnable queue is empty but the blocked queue is not. The goal of Phase 2 is to *create* new operators to be executed. Specifically, the second phase creates joins between relations that were not directly joined in the original query tree, but whose consumers are blocked (i.e., in the blocked queue) due to the unavailability of some other data.

In contrast to Phase 1 iterations, which simply adjust scheduling to allow *runnable* operators to execute, iterations during Phase 2 actually *create* new joins. Because the operations that are created during Phase 2 were not chosen by the optimizer when the original query plan was generated, it is possible that these operations may entail a significant amount of additional work. If the joins created and executed by Phase 2 are too expensive, query scrambling could result in a net degradation in performance. Phase 2,

---

[3] As stated earlier, operators are inserted into the queues with respect to their execution order.

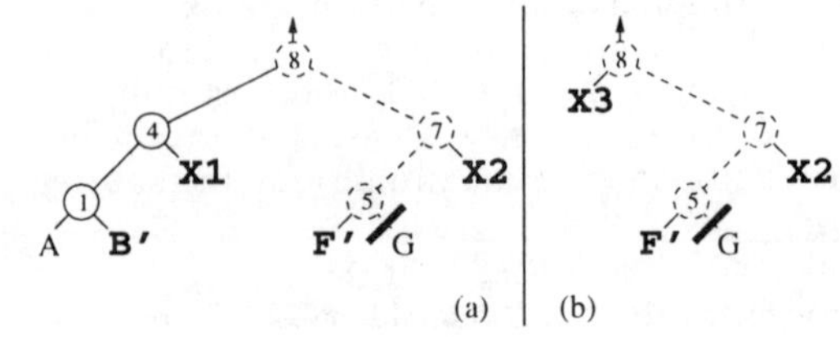

Figure 5: Relation A Available

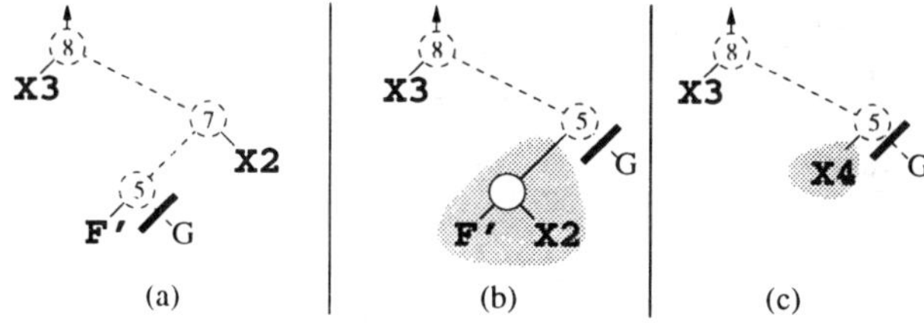

(a)   (b)   (c)

Figure 6: Performing a New Join in Phase 2

therefore, has the potential to negate or even reverse the benefits of scrambling if care is not taken. In this paper we use the simple heuristic of avoiding Cartesian products to prevent the creation of overly expensive joins during Phase 2. In Section 3, we analyze the performance impact of the cost of created joins relative to the cost of the joins in the original query plan. One way to ensure that Phase 2 does not generate overly expensive joins is to involve the query optimizer in the choice of new joins. Involving the optimizer in query scrambling is one aspect of our ongoing work.

2.3.1 Creating New Joins

At the start of Phase 2, the scrambling algorithm constructs a graph G of possible joins. Each node in G corresponds to a relation, and each edge in G indicates that the two connected nodes have common join attributes, and thus can be joined without causing a Cartesian product. Unavailable relations are not placed into G.

Once G is constructed, Phase 2 starts to iteratively create and execute new join operators. Each iteration of Phase 2 performs the following steps.

1. In G, find the two *leftmost* joinable (i.e., connected) relations i and j. The notion of *leftmost* is with respect to the order in the query plan. If there are no joinable relations in G, then terminate scrambling.

2. Create a new join operator $i \bowtie j$.

3. Materialize $i \bowtie j$. Update G by replacing i and j with the materialized result of $i \bowtie j$. Update runnable and blocked queues. Update query tree.

4. Test to see if any unavailable data has arrived. If so, then terminate scrambling, else begin a new iteration.

Figure 6 demonstrates the behavior of Phase 2 by continuing the example of the previous section. The figure is divided into three parts. Part (a) shows the query tree at the end of Phase 1. In this case, G would contain **F'**, **X2**, and **X3**. Assume that, in G, relations **F'** and **X2** are directly connected but relation **X3** is not connected to either (i.e., assume it shares join attributes only with the unavailable relation G). In this example, therefore, **F'** and **X2** are the two leftmost *joinable* relations; **X3** is the leftmost relation, but it is not joinable.

Figure 6(b) shows the creation of the new join of **F'** and **X2**. The creation of this join requires the removal of join number 7 from the blocked queue and its replacement in the ordering of execution by join number

5. Finally, Figure 6(c) shows the materialization of the created operator. The materialized join is called **X4**. At this point, G is modified by removing **F'** and **X2** and inserting **X4**, which is not joinable with **X3**, the only other relation in G.

2.3.2 Termination of Phase 2

After each iteration of Phase 2, the number of relations in G is reduced. Phase 2 terminates if G is reduced to a single relation, or if there are multiple relations but none that are joinable. As shown in the preceding example, this latter situation can arise if the attribute(s) required to join the remaining relations are contained in an unavailable relation (in this case, relation G).

Phase 2 can also terminate due to the arrival of unavailable data. If such data arrive during a Phase 2 iteration, then, at the end of that iteration, the runnable and blocked queues are updated accordingly and the control is returned to the normal iterator-based scheduling of operators. As mentioned for Phase 1, query scrambling may be re-invoked later to cope with other delayed relations.

2.3.3 Physical Properties of Joins

The preceding discussion focused on restructuring *logical* nodes of a query plan. The restructuring of *physical* plans, however, raises additional considerations. First, adding a new join may require the introduction of additional unary operators to process the inputs of this new join so that it can be correctly executed. For example, a merge join operator requires that the tuples it consumes are sorted, and thus may require that sort operators be applied to its inputs. Second, deleting operators, as was done in the preceding example, may also require the addition of unary operators. For example, relations may need to be repartitioned in order to be placed as children of an existing hybrid hash node. Finally, changing the inputs of an existing join operator may also require modifications. If the new inputs are sufficiently different than the original inputs, the physical join operators may have to be modified. For example, an indexed nested loop join might have to be changed to a hash join if the inner relation is replaced by one that is not indexed on the join attribute.

2.4 Summary and Discussion

The query plan scrambling algorithm can be summarized as follows:

- When a query becomes blocked (because relations are unavailable), query plan scrambling is initiated. It first computes a queue of blocked operators and a queue of runnable operators.

- Phase 1 then analyses the queue of runnable operators, picks a maximal runnable subtree and materializes its result. This process is repeated, i.e., it iterates, until the queue of runnable operators is empty. At this point, the system switches to Phase 2.

213

- Phase 2 tries to create a new operator that joins two relations that are available and joinable. This process iterates until no more joinable relations can be found.

- After each iteration of the algorithm, it checks to see if any unavailable data have arrived, and if so, control is returned to normal iterator-based scheduling of operators, otherwise another iteration is performed.

There are two additional issues regarding the algorithm that deserve mention, here. The first issue concerns the knowledge of the actual availability of relations. Instead of discovering, as the algorithm does now, during the execution of the operations performed by each iteration that some sources are unavailable, it is possible to send some or all of the initial data requests to the data sources as soon as the first relation is discovered to be unavailable. Doing so would give the algorithm immediate knowledge of the availability status of all the sources. Fortunately, using the iterator model, opening multiple data sources at once does not force the query execution site to consume all the tuples simultaneously — the iterator model will suspend the flow of tuples until they are consumed by their consumer operators.

The second issue concerns the potential additional work of each phase. As described previously, Phase 1 materializes existing subtrees that have been optimized prior to runtime by the query optimizer. The relative overhead of each materialization may be more or less significant depending on the I/O pattern of the scrambled subtree compared to its unscrambled version. For example, if a subtree consists of a single select on a base relation, its materialization during Phase 1 is pure overhead since the original query plan was selecting tuples as they were received, without involving any I/O. On the other hand, the overhead of materializing an operator that partitions data is comparatively less important. In this case, both the original query plan and the scrambled plan have to perform disk I/Os to write the partitions on disk for later processing. The scrambled plan, however, writes to disk one extra partition that would be kept in memory by the original non-scrambled query plan.

Phase 2, however, can be more costly as it creates new joins from scratch using the simple heuristic of avoiding Cartesian products. The advantage of this approach is its simplicity. The disadvantage, however, is the potential overhead caused by the possibly suboptimal joins. We study the performance impact of varying costs of the created joins in the following section.

The costs of materializations during Phase 1 and of new joins during Phase 2 may, in certain cases, negate the benefits of scrambling. Controlling these costs raises the possibility of integrating scrambling with an existing query optimizer. This would allow us to estimate the costs of iterations in order to skip, for example, costly materializations or expensive joins. Such an integration is one aspect of our ongoing work.

Parameter	Value	Description
NumSites	8	number of sites
Mips	30	CPU speed (10^6 instr/sec)
NumDisks	1	number of disks per site
DskPageSize	4096	size of a disk page (bytes)
NetBw	1	network bandwidth (Mbit/sec)
NetPageSize	8192	size of a network page (bytes)
Compare	4	instr. to apply a predicate
HashInst	25	instr. to hash a tuple
Move	2	instr. to copy 4 bytes

Table 1: Simulation Parameters and Main Settings

3 Performance

In this section, we examine the main performance characteristics of the query scrambling algorithm. The first set of experiments shows the typical performance of any query that is scrambled. The second set of experiments studies the sensitivity of Phase 2 to the selectivity of the new joins it creates. We first describe the simulation environment used to study the algorithm.

3.1 Simulation Environment

To study the performance of the query scrambling algorithm, we extended an existing simulator [FJK96, DFJ+96] that models a heterogeneous, peer-to-peer database system such as SHORE [CDF+94]. The simulator we used provides a detailed model of query processing costs in such a system. Here, we briefly describe the simulator, focusing on the aspects that are pertinent to our experiments.

Table 1 shows the main parameters for configuring the simulator, and the settings used for this study. Every site has a CPU whose speed is specified by the *Mips* parameter, *NumDisks* disks, and a main-memory buffer pool. For the current study, the simulator was configured to model a client-server system consisting of a single client connected to seven servers. Each site, except the query execution site, stores one base relation.

In this study, the disk at the query execution site (i.e., client) is used to store temporary results. The disk model includes costs for random and sequential physical accesses and also charges for software operations implementing I/Os. The unit of disk I/O for the database and the client's disk cache are pages of size *DskPageSize*. The unit of transfer between sites are pages of size *NetPageSize*. The network is modeled simply as a FIFO queue with a specified bandwidth (*NetBw*); the details of a particular technology (Ethernet, ATM) are not modeled. The simulator also charges CPU instructions for networking protocol operations. The CPU is modeled as a FIFO queue and the simulator charges for all the functions performed by query operators like hashing, comparing, and moving tuples in memory.

In this paper, the simulator is used primarily to demonstrate the properties of the scrambling algorithm, rather than for a detailed analysis of the algo-

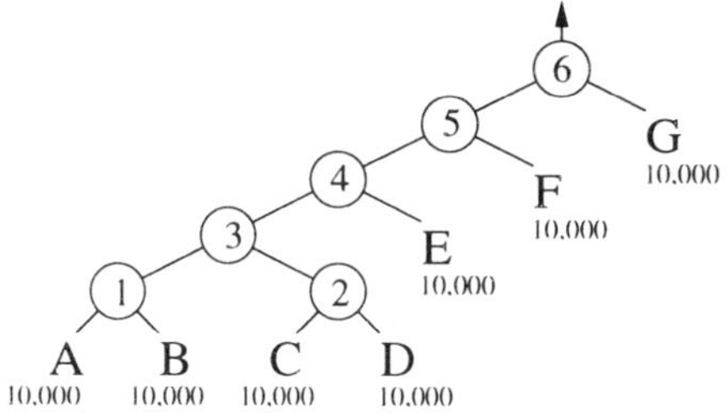

Figure 7: Query Tree Used for the Experiments

rithm. As such, the specific settings used in the simulator are less important than the way in which delay is either hidden or not hidden by the algorithm. In the experiments, the various delays were generated by simply requesting tuples from an "unavailable" source at the end of the various iterations of query plan scrambling. That is, rather than stochastically generating delays, we explicitly imposed a series of delays in order to study the behavior of the algorithm in a controlled manner. For example, to simulate the arrival of blocked tuples during, say, the third iteration of Phase 1, we scrambled the query 3 times, and then initiated the transfer of tuples from the "blocked" relation so that the final result of the query could eventually be computed.

3.2 A Query Tree for the Experiments

For all the experiments described in this section, we use the query tree represented in Figure 7. We use this query tree because it demonstrates all of the features of scrambling and allows us to highlight the impact on performance of the overheads caused by materializations and created joins.

Each base relation has 10,000 tuples of 100 bytes each. We assume that the join graph is fully connected, that is, any relation can be (equi-)joined with any other relation and that all joins use the same join attribute. In the first set of experiments, we study the performance of query plan scrambling in the case where all the joins in the query tree produce the same number of tuples, i.e., 1,000 tuples. In the second set of experiments, however, we study the case where the joins in the query tree have different selectivities and thus produce results of various sizes.

For all the experiments, we study the performance of our approach in the case where a single relation is unavailable. This relation is the *left-most* relation (i.e., relation A) which represents the case where query scrambling is the most beneficial. Examining the cases with others unavailable relations would not change the basic lessons of this study.

For each experiment described below, we evaluate the algorithm in the cases where it executes in the context of a small or a large memory. In the case of large memory, none of the relations used in the query tree (either a base relation or an intermediate result) need to be partitioned before being processed. In the case of small memory, every relation (including intermediate results) must be partitioned. Note, that since all joins in the test query use the same join attribute, no

re-partitioning of relations is required when new joins are created in this case.

3.3 Experiment 1: The Step Phenomenon

Figure 8 shows the response time for the scrambled query plans that are generated as the delay for relation A (the leftmost relation in the plan) is varied. The delay for A is shown along the X-axis, and is also represented as the lower grey line in the figure. The higher grey line shows the performance of the unscrambled query, that is, if the execution of the query is simply delayed until the tuples of relation A begin to arrive. The distance between these two lines therefore is constant, and is equal to the response time for the original (unscrambled) query plan, which is 80.03 seconds in this case. In this experiment, the memory size of the query execution site is small. With this setting, the hash-tables for inner relations for joins can not entirely be built in memory so partitioning is required.

The middle line in Figure 8 shows the response time for the scrambled query plans that are executed for various delays of A. In this case, there are six possible scrambled plans that could be generated. As stated in Sections 2.2 and 2.3, the scrambling algorithm is iterative. At the *end of each iteration* it checks to see if delayed data has begun to arrive, and if so, it stops scrambling and normal query execution is resumed. If, however, at the end of the iteration, the delayed data has still not arrived, another iteration of the scrambling algorithm is initiated. The result of this execution model is the step shape that can be observed in Figure 8.

The *width* of each step is equal to the duration of the operations that are performed by the current iteration of the scrambling algorithm, and the *height* of the step is equal to the response time of the query if normal processing is resumed at the end of that iteration. For example, in this experiment, the first scrambling iteration results in the retrieval and partitioning of relation B. This operation requires 12.23 seconds. If at the end of the iteration, tuples of relation A have begun to arrive then no further scrambling is done and normal query execution resumes. The resulting execution in this case, has a response time of 80.10 seconds. Thus, the first step shown in Figure 8 has a width of 12.23 seconds and a height of 80.10 seconds. Note that in this case, scrambling is effective at hiding the delay of A; the response time of the scrambled query is nearly identical to that of original query with no delay of A.

If no tuples of A have arrived at the end of the first iteration, then another iteration is performed. In this case, the second iteration retrieves, partitions, and joins relations C and D. As shown in Figure 8, this iteration requires an additional 26.38 seconds, and if A begins to arrive during this iteration, then the resulting query plan has a total response time of 80.90 seconds. Thus, in this experiment, scrambling is able to hide delays of up to 38.61 seconds with a penalty of no more than 0.80 seconds (i.e., 1%) of the response

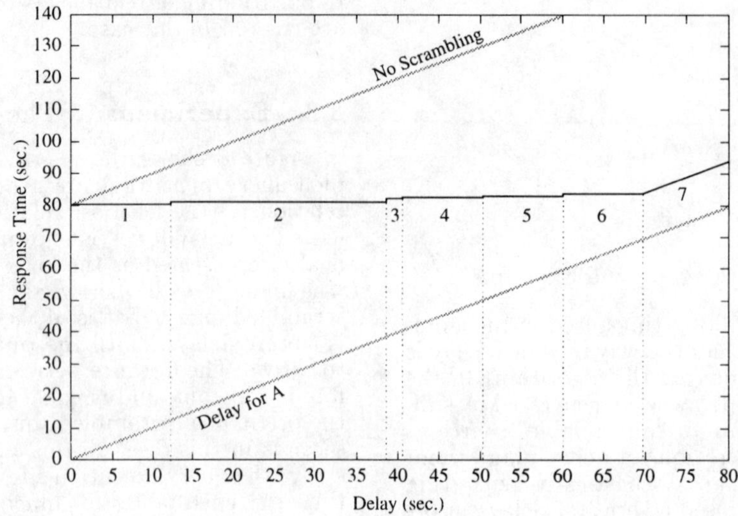

Figure 8: Response Times of Scrambled Query Plans (Small Memory, Varying the Delay of A.)

time of the original query with no delay. This corresponds to a response time improvement of up to 32% compared to not scrambling.

If, at the end of the second iteration, tuples of A have still failed to arrive, then the third iteration is initiated. In this case however, there are no more runnable subtrees, so scrambling switches to Phase 2, which results in the creation of new joins (see Section 2.3). In this third iteration, the result of C⋈D is partitioned and joined with relation B. This iteration has a width of only 2.01 seconds, because both inputs are already present, B is already partitioned, and the result of C⋈D is fairly small. The response time of the resulting plan is 82.22 seconds, which again represents a response time improvement of up to 32% compared to not scrambling.

The remaining query plans exhibit similar behavior. Table 2 shows the additional operations and the overall performance for each of the possible scrambled plans. In this experiment, the largest relative benefit (approximately 44%) over not scrambling is obtained when the delay of A is 69.79 seconds, which is the time required to complete all six iterations. After this point, there is no further work for query scrambling to do, so the scrambled plan must also wait for A to arrive. As can be seen in Figure 8, at the end of iteration six the response time of the scrambled plan increases linearly with the delay of A. The distance between the delay of A and the response time of the scrambled plan is the time that is required to complete the query once A arrives.

Although it is not apparent in Figure 8, the first scrambled query is slightly slower than the unscrambled query plan when A is delayed for a very short amount of time. For a delay below 0.07 seconds, the response time of the scrambled query is 80.10 seconds while it is 80.03 seconds for the non-scrambled query. When joining A and B, as the unscrambled query does, B is partitioned *during* the join, allowing one of the

partitions of B to stay in memory. Partitioning B *before* joining it with A, as the first scrambled query plan does, forces this partition to be written back to disk and to be read later during the join with A. When A is delayed by less than the time needed to perform these additional I/Os, it is cheaper to stay idle waiting for A.

3.4   Experiment 2: Sensitivity of Phase 2

In the previous experiment all the joins produced the same number of tuples, and as a result, all of the operations performed in Phase 2 were beneficial. In this section, we examine the sensitivity of Phase 2 to changes in the selectivities of the joins it creates. Varying selectivities changes the number of tuples produced by these joins which affects the width and the height of each step. Our goal is to show cases where the benefits of scrambling vary greatly, from clear improvements to cases where scrambling performs worse than no-scrambling.

For the test query, the first join created in Phase 2 is the join of relation B with the result of C⋈D (which was materialized during Phase 1). In this set of experiments, we vary the selectivity of this new join to create a result of a variable size. The selectivity of this join is adjusted such that it produces from 1,000 tuples up to several thousand tuples. The other joins that Phase 2 may create behave like functional joins and they simply carry all the tuples created by (B⋈(C⋈D)) through the query tree. At the time these tuples are joined with A, the number of tuples carried along the query tree returns to normality and drops down to 1,000. Varying the selectivity of the first join produced by Phase 2 is sufficient to generate a variable number of tuples that are carried all along the tree by the other joins that Phase 2 may create.

The two next sections present the results of this sensitivity analysis for a small and a large memory case.

Scrambled Plan #	Performed by Iteration	Total Delay	Response Time	Savings
1	Partition B	0–12.23	80.10	up to 13.18%
2	X1←C⋈D	12.23–38.61	80.90	12.31–31.81%
3	X2←B⋈X1	38.61–40.62	82.22	30.69–31.85%
4	X3←X2⋈E	40.62–50.32	82.51	31.61–36.70%
5	X4←X3⋈F	50.32–60.07	83.05	36.28–40.72%
6	X5←X4⋈G	60.07–69.79	83.52	40.38–44.21%

Table 2: Delay Ranges and Response Times of Scrambled Query Plans

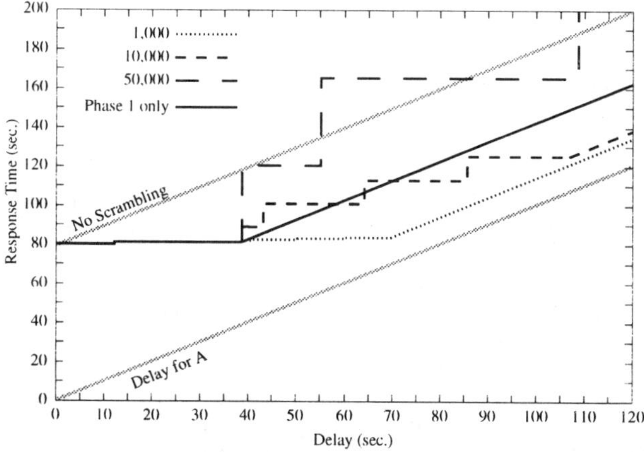

Figure 9: Response Times of Scrambled Query Plans (Small Memory, Varying Selectivity and Delay.)

As stated previously, when the memory is small, relations have to be partitioned before being joined (as in the previous experiment). This partitioning adds to the potential cost of scrambled plans because it results in additional I/O that would not have been present in the unscrambled plan. When the memory is large, however, hash-tables can be built entirely in memory so relations do not need to be partitioned. Thus, with large memory the potential overhead of scrambled plans is lessened.

3.4.1 Small Memory Case

In this experiment, we examine the effectiveness of query scrambling when the selectivity of the first join created by Phase 2 is varied. Figure 9 shows the response time results for 3 different selectivities. As in the previous experiment, the delay for A is shown along the X-axis and is also represented as the lower grey line in the figure. The higher grey line shows the response time of the unscrambled query, which as before, increases linearly with the delay of A. These two lines are exactly the same as the ones presented in the previous experiment.

The solid line in the middle of the figure shows the performance of a scrambled query plan that stops scrambling right at the end of Phase 1 (in this case, two iterations are performed during Phase 1) without initiating any Phase 2 iterations. Note that this line becomes diagonal after the end of Phase 1 since the system simply waits until the tuples of A arrive before computing the final result of the query.

Intuitively, it is not useful to perform a second phase for scrambled queries when the resulting response time would be located above this line. Costly joins that would be created by Phase 2 would consume a lot of resources for little improvement. On the other hand, Phase 2 would be beneficial for scrambled queries whose resulting response time would be below this line since the additional overhead would be small and the gain large.

The dashed and dotted lines in the figure illustrate the tradeoffs. These lines show the response time for the scrambled query plans that are executed for various delays of A and for various selectivities. Note all these scrambled query plans share the same response times for the iterations performed during Phase 1. These two first iterations correspond exactly to the scrambled plans 1 and 2 described in the previous experiment. At the end of the second iteration (38.61 seconds), however, if the tuples of A have still failed to arrive, a third iteration is initiated and the query scrambling enters Phase 2 which creates new joins.

The dotted line shows the performance when the selectivity for the new join is such that it produces a result of 1,000 tuples. This line is identical to the one showed in the previous experiment since all the joins were producing 1,000 tuples.

With the second selectivity, the first join created by the second phase produces 10,000 tuples. If at the end of this iteration, the tuples of A have still not arrived, another iteration is initiated and this iteration has to process and to produce 10,000 tuples. The corresponding line in the figure is the lowest dashed line. In this case, where 10 times more tuples have to be carried along the scrambled query plans, each step is higher (roughly 12 seconds) and wider since more tuples have to be manipulated than in the case where only 1,000 tuples are created. Even with the additional overhead of these 10,000 tuples, however, the response times of the scrambled query plans are far below the response times of the unscrambled query with equivalent delay.

When the new join produces 50,000 tuples (the higher dashed line in the figure), the response time of the scrambled plans are almost equal to or even worse than that of the original unscrambled query *including the delay for A*. In this case, it is more costly to carry the large number of tuples through the query tree than to simply wait for blocked data to arrive.

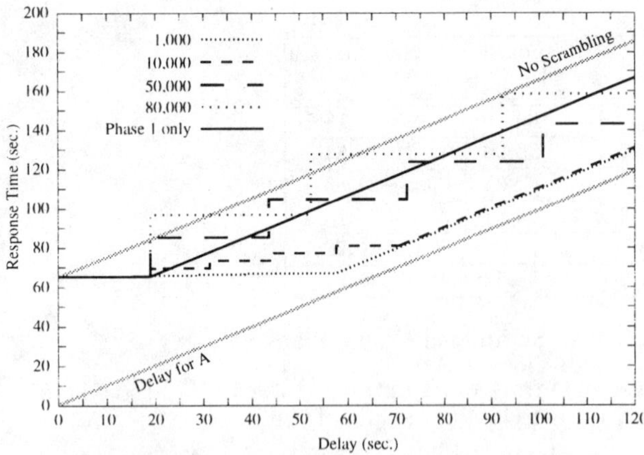

Figure 10: Response Times of Scrambled Query Plans
(Large Memory, Varying Selectivity and Delay.)

3.4.2 Large Memory Case

Figure 10 shows the same experiment in the case where the memory is large enough to allow inner relations for joins to be built entirely in main memory. With large memory, no partitioning of relations needs to be done.

For the large memory case, the lines showing the increasing delay of A and the response time of the unscrambled query when this delay increases are separated by 65.03 seconds and Phase 2 starts when A is delayed by more than 18.95 seconds. Four different selectivities are represented in this figure.

In contrast to the previous experiment where 50 times more tuples negated the benefits of scrambling, in this case up to 80 times more tuples can be carried by the scrambled query plans before the benefits become close to zero. With a large memory, results computed by each iteration need only be materialized and can be consumed as is. In contrast, when the memory is small, materialized results have to be partitioned before being consumed. With respect to a small memory case, not partitioning the relation when the memory is large reduces the number of I/Os and allows the scrambled plans to manipulate more tuples for the same overhead.

3.5 Discussion

The experiments presented in this section have shown that query scrambling can be an effective technique that is able to improve the response time of queries when data are delayed. These improvements come from the fact that each iteration of a scrambled query plan can hide the delay of data. The improvement, however, depends on the overhead due to materializations and created joins.

The improvement that scrambling can bring also depends on the amount of work done in the original query. The bigger (i.e., the longer and the more costly) the original query is, the more improvement our technique can bring since it will be able to hide larger delays by computing costly operations. The improvement also depends on the shape of the query

tree: bushy trees offer more options for scrambling than deep trees.

With respect to the Figures 9 and 10 presented above, when many iterations can be done during Phase 1, the point where Phase 2 starts shifts to the right. This increases the distance between the Phase 1-only diagonal line and the response time of the unscrambled query. In turn, the scrambling algorithm can handle a wider range of bad selectivities for the joins it creates during Phase 2.

4 Related Work

In this section we consider related work with respect to (a) the point in time that optimization decisions are made (i.e., compile time, query start-up time, or query run-time); (b) the variables used for dynamic decisions (i.e. if the response time of a remote source is considered); (c) the nature of the dynamic optimization (i.e. if the entire query can be rewritten); and (d) the basis of the optimization (i.e., cost-based or heuristic based).

The Volcano optimizer [CG94, Gra93] does dynamic optimization for distributed query processing. During optimization, if a cost comparison returns *incomparable*, the choice for that part of the search space is encoded in a *choose-plan* operator. At query start up time, all the incomparable cost comparisons are reevaluated. According to the result of the reevaluation, the choose-plan operator selects a particular query execution plan. All final decisions regarding query execution are thus made at query start-up time. Our work is complimentary to the Volcano optimizer since Volcano does not adapt to changes once the evaluation of the query has started.

Other work in dynamic query optimization either does not consider the distributed case [DMP93, OHMS92] or only optimizes access path selection and cannot reorder joins [HS93]. Thus, direct considerations of problems with response times from remote sources are not accounted for. These articles are, however, a rich source of optimizations which can be carried over into our work.

A novel approach to dynamic query optimization used in Rdb/VMS is described in [Ant93]. In this approach, multiple different executions of the same logical operator occur at the same time. They compete for producing the best execution – when one execution of an operator is determined to be (probably) better, the other execution is terminated.

In [DSD95] the response time of queries is improved by reordering left-deep join trees into bushy join trees. Several reordering algorithms are presented. This work assumes that reordering is done entirely at compile time. This work cannot easily be extended to handle run-time reordering, since the reorderings are restricted to occur at certain locations in the join tree.

[ACPS96] tracks the costs of previous calls to remote sources (in addition to caching the results) and can use this tracking to estimate the cost of new calls. As in Volcano, this system optimizes a query both at query compile and query start-up time, but does not change the query plan during query run-time.

The research prototype Mermaid [CBTY89] and its commercial successor InterViso [THMB95] are heterogeneous distributed databases that perform dynamic query optimization. Mermaid constructs its query plan entirely at run-time, thus each step in query optimization is based on dynamic information such as intermediate join result sizes and network performance. Mermaid neither takes advantage of a statically generated plan nor does it dynamically account for a source which does not respond at run-time.

The Sage system [Kno95] is an AI planning system for query optimization for heterogeneous distributed sources. This system interleaves execution and optimization and responds to unavailable data sources.

5 Conclusion and Future Work

Query plan scrambling is a novel technique that can dynamically adjust to changes in the run-time environment. We presented an algorithm which specifically deals with variability in performance of remote data sources and accounts for *initial* delays in their response times. The algorithm consists of two phases. Phase 1 changes the scheduling of existing operators produced as a result of query optimization. Phase 1 is iteratively applied until no more changes in the scheduling are possible. At this point, the algorithm enters Phase 2 which creates new operators to further process available data. New operators are iteratively created until there is no further work for query plan scrambling to do.

The performance experiments demonstrated how the technique hides delays in receiving the initial requested tuples from remote data sources. We then examined the sensitivity of the performance of scrambled plans to the selectivity of the joins created in Phase 2.

This work represents an initial exploration into the development of flexible systems that dynamically adapt to the changing properties of the environment. Among our ongoing and future research plans, we are developing algorithms that can scramble under different failure models to handle environments where data arrives at a bursty rate or at a steady rate that is significantly slower than expected. We are also studying the use of partial results which approximate the final results. We also plan to study the potential improvement of basing scrambling decisions on cost-based knowledge.

Finally, query plan scrambling is a promising approach to addressing many of the concerns addressed by dynamic query optimization. Adapting the query plan at run-time to account for the actual costs of operations could compensate for the often inaccurate and unreliable estimates used by the query optimizer. Moreover, it could account for remote sources that do not export any cost information, which is especially important when these remote sources run complex subqueries. Thus, we plan to investigate the use of scrambling as a complimentary approach to dynamic query optimization.

Acknowledgments We would like to thank Praveen Seshadri, Björn Jónsson and Jean-Robert Gruser for their helpful comments on this work. We would also like to thank Alon Levy for pointing out related work.

References

[ACPS96] S. Adali, K. Candan, Y. Papakonstantinou, and V. Subrahmanian. Query Caching and Optimization in Distributed Mediator Systems. *ACM SIGMOD Conf.*, Montréal, Canada, 1996.

[Ant93] G. Antoshenkov. Dynamic Query Optimization in Rdb/VMS. *ICDE Conf.*, Vienna, Austria, 1993.

[BE96] O. Bukhres and A. Elmagarmid. *Object-Oriented Multidatabase Systems.* Prentice Hall, 1996.

[CBTY89] A. Chen, D. Brill, M. Templeton, and C. Yu. Distributed Query Processing in a Multiple Database System. *IEEE Journal on Selected Areas in Communications*, 7(3), 1989.

[CDF+94] M. Carey, D. DeWitt, M. Franklin, N. Hall, M. McAuliffe, J. Naughton, D. Schuh, M. Solomon, C. Tan, O. Tsatalos, S. White, and M. Zwilling. Shoring Up Persistent Applications. *ACM SIGMOD Conf.*, Minneapolis, MN, 1994.

[CG94] R. Cole and G. Graefe. Optimization of Dynamic Query Execution Plans. *ACM SIGMOD Conf.*, Minneapolis, MN, 1994.

[DFJ+96] S. Dar, M. Franklin, B. Jónsson, D. Srivastava, and M. Tan. Semantic Data Caching and Replacement. *22nd VLDB Conf.*, Bombay, India, 1996.

[DMP93] M. Derr, S. Morishita, and G. Phipps. Design and Implementation of the Glue-Nail Database System. *ACM SIGMOD Conf.*, Washington, DC, 1993.

[DSD95] W. Du, M. Shan, and U. Dayal. Reducing Multidatabase Query Response Time by Tree Balancing. *ACM SIGMOD Conf.*, San Jose, CA, 1995.

[FJK96] M. Franklin, B. Jónsson, and D. Kossmann. Performance Tradeoffs for Client-Server Query Processing. *ACM SIGMOD Conf.*, Montréal, Canada, 1996.

[Gra93] G. Graefe. Query Evaluation Techniques for Large Databases. *ACM Computing Surveys*, 25(2), 1993.

[HS93] W. Hong and M. Stonebraker. Optimization of Parallel Query Execution Plans in XPRS. *Distributed and Parallel Databases*, 1(1), 1993.

[Kno95] C. Knoblock. Planning, Executing, Sensing, and Replanning for Information Gathering. In *Proc. of the 14th Int. Joint Conf. on Artificial Intelligence*, Montréal, Canada, 1995.

[OHMS92] J. Orenstein, S. Haradhvala, B. Margulies, and D. Sakahara. Query Processing in the ObjectStore Database System. *ACM SIGMOD Conf.*, San Diego, CA, 1992.

[SD90] D. Schneider and D. DeWitt. Tradeoffs in Processing Complex Join Queries via Hashing in Multiprocessor Database Machines. *16th VLDB Conf.*, Brisbane, Australia, 1990.

[SAD+95] M. Shan, R. Ahmen, J. Davis, W. Du, and W. Kent. *Modern Database Systems: The Object Model, Interoperability, and Beyond*, chapter Pegasus: A Heterogeneous Information Management System. ACM Press, 1995.

[THMB95] M. Templeton, H. Henley, E. Maros, and D. Van Buer. InterViso: Dealing with the Complexity of Federated Database Access. *VLDB Journal*, 4(2), 1995.

[TRV96] A. Tomasic, L. Raschid, and P. Valduriez. Scaling Heterogeneous Databases and the Design of DISCO. *ICDCS Conf.*, Hong Kong, 1996.

Building Regression Cost Models for Multidatabase Systems *

Qiang Zhu
Department of Comp. and Inf. Science
University Michigan - Dearborn
Dearborn, MI 48128

Per-Åke Larson [†]
Department of Computer Science
University of Waterloo
Waterloo, Canada N2L 3G1

Abstract

A major challenge for performing global query optimization in a multidatabase system (MDBS) is the lack of cost models for local database systems at the global level. In this paper we present a statistical procedure based on multiple regression analysis for building cost models for local database systems in an MDBS. Explanatory variables that can be included in a regression model are identified and a mixed forward and backward method for selecting significant explanatory variables is presented. Measures for developing useful regression cost models, such as removing outliers, eliminating multicollinearity, validating regression model assumptions, and checking significance of regression models, are discussed. Experimental results demonstrate that the presented statistical procedure can develop useful local cost models in an MDBS.

Keywords: multidatabase system, global query optimization, cost model, cost estimation, multiple regression

1 Introduction

A multidatabase system (MDBS) integrates information from pre-existing local databases managed by heterogeneous database systems (DBS) such as ORACLE, DB2 and EMPRESS. A key feature of an MDBS is the local autonomy that each local database retains to manage its data and serve its existing applications. An MDBS can only interact with a local DBS at its external user interface.

A user can issue a global query on an MDBS to retrieve data from several local databases. The user does not need to know where the data is stored and how the result is obtained. How to efficiently process such a global query is the task of global query optimization.

There are a number of new challenges for query optimization in an MDBS, caused primarily by local autonomy. Among these challenges, a crucial one is that local information needed for global query optimization, such as local cost formulas (models), typically are not available at the global level. To perform global query optimization, methods to derive approximate cost models for an autonomous local DBS are required.

This issue has attracted a number of researchers recently. In [3], Du *et al.* proposed a calibration method to deduce necessary local cost parameters. The idea is to construct a special local synthetic calibrating database and then run a set of special queries against this database. Cost metrics for the queries are used to deduce the coefficients in the cost formulas for the access methods supported by the underlying local database system. In [14], Zhu and Larson presented a query sampling method to tackle this issue. The idea of this method will be reviewed below. In [15, 16], Zhu and Larson proposed a fuzzy optimization method to solve the problem. The idea is to build a fuzzy cost model based on experts' knowledge, experience and guesses about local DBSs and perform query optimization based on the fuzzy cost model. In [6, 13], Lu and Zhu discussed issues for employing dynamic (adaptive) query optimization techniques based on information available at run time in an MDBS.

The idea of the query sampling method that we proposed in [14] is as follows. The first step is to group all possible queries for a local database[1] into more homogeneous classes so that the costs of queries in each class can be estimated by the same formula. This can be done by classifying queries according to their potential access methods. For example, unary queries whose qualifications have at least one conjunctive

---

*Research supported by IBM Toronto Laboratory and Natural Sciences and Engineering Research Council (NSERC) of Canada

[†]Current address: Microsoft Corporation, One Microsoft Way, Redmond, WA 98052–6399, palarson@microsoft.com

[1]We assume that each local DBS has an MDBS agent that provides a uniform relational interface to the MDBS global server. Hence all local DBSs can be viewed as relational ones.

term[2] $R.a = C$, where $R.a$ is an indexed column in table R, can be put in one class because they are usually executed by using an index scan in a local DBS and, therefore, follow the same performance pattern. Several such unary and join query[3] classes can be obtained. The second step of the query sampling method is to draw a sample of queries from each query class. A mixture of judgment sampling and simple random sampling is adopted in this step. The sample queries are then performed against the relevant local database and their costs are recorded. The costs are used to derive a cost formula for the queries in the query class by multiple regression. The coefficients of the cost formulas for the local database system are kept in the multidatabase catalog and retrieved during query optimization. To estimate the cost of a query, the query class to which the query belongs needs to be identified first, and the corresponding cost formula is then used to give an estimate for the cost of the query.

Although a number of sampling techniques have been applied to query optimization in the literature[5, 8, 11], all of them perform data sampling (i.e., sampling data from databases) instead of query sampling (i.e., sampling queries from a query class). The query sampling method overcomes several shortcomings of Du $et\ al.$'s calibration method[14].

However, the statistical procedure for deriving cost estimation formulas in [14] was oversimplified. In this paper, an improved statistical procedure is presented. The formulas are automatically determined based on observed sampling costs. More explanatory variables in a formula are considered. A series of measures for ensuring useful formulas are adopted.

The rest of this paper is organized as follows. Section 2 reviews the general linear regression model and the related terminology. Section 3 identifies potential explanatory variables for a regression cost model. Section 4 discusses how to determine a cost model for a query class. Section 5 discusses the measures used to ensure that the developed cost models are useful. Section 6 presents some experimental results. Section 7 summarizes the conclusions.

---

[2] We assume that the qualification has been converted to conjunctive normal form.

[3] A select that may or may not be followed by a project is called a unary query. A (2-way) join that may or may not be followed by a project is called a join query. Only unary and join queries are considered in this paper since most common queries can be expressed by a sequence of such queries.

2 Multiple Linear Regression Model

Multiple regression allows us to establish a statistical relationship between the costs of queries and the relevant contributing (explanatory) variables. Such a statistical relationship can be used as a cost estimation formula for queries in a query class.

Let X_1, X_2, $\cdots$, X_k be k explanatory variables. They do not have to represent different independent variables. It is allowed, for example, that $X_3 = X_1 * X_2$. The response (dependent) variable Y tends to vary in a systematic way with the explanatory variables X's. If the systematic way is a statistical linear relationship between Y and X's, which we assume is true in our application, a multiple linear regression model is defined as

$$Y_i = B_0 + B_1 X_{i,1} + B_2 X_{i,2} + \cdots + B_k X_{i,k} + \varepsilon_i,$$
$$(i = 1, \cdots, n)$$

where $X_{i,j}$ $(j = 1, 2, \cdots, k)$ denotes the value of the j-th explanatory variable X_j in the i-th trial; Y_i is the i-th dependent random variable corresponding to $X_{i,1}$, $X_{i,2}$, $\cdots$, $X_{i,k}$; ε_i denotes the random error term; B_0, B_1, $\cdots$, B_k are regression coefficients. The following assumptions are usually made in regression analysis:

0. B_0, B_1, $\cdots$, B_k are unknown constants, and $X_{i,1}$, $X_{i,2}$, $\cdots$, $X_{i,k}$ are known values.

1. Any two ε_{i_1} and ε_{i_2} $(i_1 \neq i_2)$ are uncorrelated.

2. The expected value of every ε_i is 0, i.e., $E(\varepsilon_i) = 0$, and the variance of ε_i is a constant σ^2, for all i.

3. Every ε_i is normally distributed.

For n sample observations, we can get the values of Y_i, $X_{i,1}$, $X_{i,2}$, $\cdots$, $X_{i,k}$ $(i = 1, \cdots, n)$. Applying the method of least squares, we can find the values $\widehat{B}_0$, $\widehat{B}_1$, $\cdots$, $\widehat{B}_k$ for B_0, B_1, $\cdots$, B_k that minimize

$$LS = \sum_{i=1}^{n} [Y_i - (B_0 + B_1 X_{i,1} + B_2 X_{i,2}$$
$$+ \cdots + B_k X_{i,k})]^2 = \sum_{i=1}^{n} \varepsilon_i^2.$$

The equation

$$\widehat{Y} = \widehat{B}_0 + \widehat{B}_1 X_1 + \widehat{B}_2 X_2 + \cdots + \widehat{B}_k X_k \qquad (1)$$

is called a fitted regression equation. For a given set of values of X's, (1) gives a fitted value $\widehat{Y}$ for the response variable Y. If we use a fitted regression equation as an estimation formula for Y, a fitted value is an estimated value for Y corresponding to the given X's.

To evaluate the goodness of estimates obtained by using the developed regression model, the variance σ^2 of the error terms is usually estimated. A point estimate of σ^2 is given by the following formula:

$$s^2 = SSE/[n - (k + 1)]$$

where $SSE = \sum_{i=1}^{n}(Y_i - \widehat{Y_i})^2 = \sum_{i=1}^{n} e_i^2$; Y_i is an observed value; $\widehat{Y_i}$ is the corresponding fitted value; and $e_i = Y_i - \widehat{Y_i}$. The square root of s^2, i.e., s, is called the standard error of estimation. It is an indication of the accuracy of estimation. The smaller s is, the better the estimation formula.

Using s, the i-th standardized residual is defined as follows:

$$e_i^* = [e_i - \sum_{i=1}^{n} e_i/n]/s \ .$$

A plot of (standardized) residuals against the fitted values or the values of an explanatory variable is called a residual plot.

In addition to s, another descriptive measure used to judge the goodness of a developed model is the coefficient of multiple determination R^2, which is defined as:

$$R^2 = 1 - SSE/SST$$

where $SST = \sum_{i=1}^{n}[Y_i - (\sum_{j=1}^{n} Y_j)/n]^2$. R^2 ($\in [0, 1]$) is the proportion of variability in the response variable Y explained by the explanatory variables X's. The larger R^2 is, the better the estimation formula.

The standard error of estimation measures the absolute accuracy of estimation, while the coefficient of multiple determination measures the relative strength of the linear relationship between the response variable Y and the explanatory variables X's. A low standard error of estimation s and a high coefficient of multiple determination R^2 are evidence of a good regression model.

3 Explanatory Variables

In our application, the response variable Y represents query cost, while the explanatory variables X's represent the factors that affect query cost. It is not difficult to see that the following types of factors usually affect the cost of a query:

1. *The cardinality of an operand table.* The higher the cardinality of an operand table is, the higher the query (execution) cost. This is because the number of I/O's required to scan the operand table or its index(es) usually increases with the cardinality of the table.

2. *The cardinality of the result table.* A large result table implies that many tuples need to be processed, buffered, stored and transferred during query processing. Hence, the larger the result table is, the higher the corresponding query cost. Note that the cardinality of the result table is determined by the selectivity of the query. This factor can hence be considered as the same as the selectivity of a query.

3. *The size of an intermediate result.* For a join query, if its qualification contains one or more conjunctive terms that refer to only one of its operand tables, called separable conjunctive terms, they can be used to reduce the relevant operand table before further processing is performed. The smaller the size of such an intermediate table is, the more efficient the query processing would be. For a unary query, if it can be executed by an index scan method, the query processing can be viewed as having two stages: the first stage is to retrieve the tuples via an index(es), the second stage is to check the retrieved tuples against the remaining conditions in the qualification. The number of tuples that are retrieved in the first stage can be considered as the size of the intermediate result for such a unary query.

4. *The tuple length of an operand table.* This factor affects data buffering and transferring cost during query processing. However, this factor is usually not as important as the above factors. It becomes important when the tuple lengths of tables in a database vary widely; for example, when multimedia data is stored in the tables.

5. *The tuple length of the result table.* Similar to the above factor, this factor affects data buffering and transferring cost, but it is not as important as the first three types of factors. It may become important when it varies significantly from one query to another, compared with other factors.

6. *The physical sizes (i.e., the numbers of used disk blocks) of operand tables and result tables.* Although factors of this type are obviously controlled by factors of types 1, 2, 4 and 5, they may reflect additional information, such as the percentage of free space assigned to an operand table (or a result table) and a combined effect of the previous factors.

7. *Contention in the system environment.* Factors of this type include contention for CPU, I/O, buffers, data items, and servers, etc. Obviously, these factors affect the performance of a query. However, they are difficult to measure. The number of concurrent processes, the memory resident set sizes (RSS) of processes, and some other information about processes that we could obtain can only reflect part of all contention factors. This is why contention factors are usually omitted from existing cost models.

8. *The characteristics of an index,* such as index clustering ratio, the height and number of leaves of an index tree, the number of distinct values of an indexed column, and so on. If all tuples with the same index key value are physically stored together, the index is called as a clustered index, which has the highest index clustering ratio. For a referenced index, how the tuples with the same index key value are scattered in the physical storage has an obvious effect on the performance of a query. Other properties of an index, such as the height of the index tree and the number of distinct key values, also affect the performance of a query.

The variables representing the above factors are the possible explanatory variables to be included in a cost formula.

4 Regression Cost Models

4.1 Variables Inclusion Principle

In general, not all explanatory variables in the last section are necessary in a cost model. Some variables may not be significant for a particular model, while some other variables may not be available at the global level in an MDBS. Our general principle for including variables in a cost model is to include important variables and omit insignificant or unavailable variables.

Among the factors discussed in Section 3, the first three types of factors are often more important. The variables representing them are usually included in a cost model. Factors of types 4 and 5 are less important since their variances are relatively small. Their representing variables are included in a cost model only if they are significant. Variables representing factors of type 6 are included in a cost model if they are not dominated by other included variables. Variables representing the last two types of factors will be omitted from our cost models because they are usually not available at the global level in an MDBS. In fact, we assume that contention factors in a considered environment are approximately stable. Under this assumption, the contention factors are not very important in a cost model. The variables representing the characteristics of referenced indexes[4] can possibly be included in a cost model if they are available and significant.

How to apply this variable inclusion principle to develop a cost model for a query class will be discussed in more details in the following subsection. Let us first give some notations for the variables.

Let R_U be the operand table for a unary query; R_{J1} and R_{J2} be the two operand tables for a join query; N_U, N_{J1} and N_{J2} be the cardinalities of R_U, R_{J1} and R_{J2}, respectively; L_U, L_{J1} and L_{J2} be the tuple lengths of R_U, R_{J1} and R_{J2}, respectively; RL_U and RL_J be the tuple lengths of the result tables for the unary query and the join query, respectively. Let S_U and S_J be the selectivities of the unary query and the join query, respectively; S_{J1} and S_{J2} be the selectivities of the conjunctions of all separable conjunctive terms for R_{J1} and R_{J2}, respectively; S_{U1} be the selectivity of a conjunctive term that is used to scan the operand table via an index, if applicable, of the unary query.

4.2 Regression Models for Unary Query Classes

Based on the inclusion principle, we divide a regression model for a unary query class into two parts:

$$model \ = \ basic \ model \ + \ secondary \ part \ . \qquad (2)$$

The basic model is the essential part of the regression model, while the secondary part is used to improve the model.

The set V_{UB} of potential explanatory variables to be included in the basic model contains the variables representing factors of types $1 \sim 3$. By the definition of a selectivity, $TN_U = N_U * S_{U1}$ and $RN_U = N_U * S_U$ are the cardinalities of the intermediate table and result table for a unary query, respectively. Therefore, $V_{UB} = \{ N_U, TN_U, RN_U \}$.

If all potential explanatory variables in V_{UB} are chosen, the full basic model is

$$Y \ = \ B_0 + B_1 * N_U + B_2 * TN_U + B_3 * RN_U . \qquad (3)$$

As it will be discussed later, some potential variable(s) may be insignificant for a given query class and, therefore, is not included in the basic model.

---

[4] Only local catalog information, such as the presence of an index for a column, is assumed to be available at the global level. Local implementation information, such as index tree structures and index clustering ratio, is not available.

The basic model captures the major performance behavior of queries in a query class. In fact, the basic model is based on some existing cost models[4, 10] for a DBMS. The parameters B_0, B_1, B_2 and B_3 in (3) can be interpreted as the initialization cost, the cost of retrieving a tuple from the operand table, the cost of an index loo-up and the cost of processing a result tuple, respectively. In a traditional cost model, a parameter may be split up into several parts (e.g., B_1 may consist of I/O cost and CPU cost) and can be determined by analyzing the implementation details of the employed access method. However, in an MDBS, the implementation details of access methods are usually not known to the global query optimizer. The parameters are, therefore, estimated by multiple regression based on sample queries instead of an analytical method.

To further improve the basic model, some secondary explanatory variables may be included into the model. The set V_{US} of potential explanatory variables for the secondary part of a model contains the variables representing factors of types $4 \sim 6$. The real physical sizes of the operand table and result table of a unary query may not be known exactly in an MDBS. However, they can be estimated by $Z_U = N_U * L_U$ and $RZ_U = RN_U * RL_U$, respectively[5]. We call Z_U and RZ_U the operand table length and result table length, respectively. Therefore, $V_{US} = \{ L_U, RL_U, Z_U, RZ_U \}$. Any other variables, if available, could also be included in V_{US}.

If all potential variables in V_{US} are added to (3), the full regression model is

$$Y = B_0 + B_1 * N_U + B_2 * TN_U + B_3 * RN_U$$
$$+B_4 * L_U + B_5 * RL_U + B_6 * Z_U + B_7 * RZ_U.$$

Note that, for some query class, a variable might appear in its regression model in another form. For example, if the access method for a query class sorts the operand table of a query based on a column(s) before further processing, some terms like $N_U * log\, N_U$ and/or $log\, N_U$ could be included in its regression model. Let a new variable represent such a term. This new variable may replace an existing variable in $V_{UB} \cup V_{US}$ or be an additional secondary variable in V_{US}. A regression model can be adjusted according to available information about the relevant access method.

---

[5] The physical size of an operand table can be more accurately estimated by $(N_U + d_1) * L_U * d_2$, where the constants d_1 and d_2 reflect some overhead such as page overhead and free space. Since the constants d_1 and d_2 are applied to all sample data, they can be omitted. Estimating the physical size of a result table is similar.

4.3 Regression Models for Join Query Classes

Similarly, the regression model for a join query class consists of a basic model plus a possible secondary part.

The set V_{JB} of potential explanatory variables for the basic model contains the variables representing factors of types $1 \sim 3$. By definition, $RN_J = N_{J1} * N_{J2} * S_J$ is the cardinality of the result table for a join query; $TN_{Ji} = N_{Ji} * S_{Ji}$ is the size of the intermediate table obtained by performing the conjunction of all separable conjunctive terms on R_{Ji} $(i = 1, 2)$. $TN_{J12} = TN_{J1} * TN_{J2}$ is the size of the Cartesian product of the intermediate tables. Therefore, $V_{JB} = \{ N_{J1}, N_{J2}, TN_{J1}, TN_{J2}, TN_{J12}, RN_J \}$.

If all potential explanatory variables in V_{JB} are selected, the full basic model is

$$Y = B_0 + B_1 * N_{J1} + B_2 * N_{J2} + B_3 * TN_{J1}$$
$$+B_4 * TN_{J2} + B_5 * TN_{J12} + B_6 * RN_J.$$

Similar to a unary query class, the basic model is based on some existing cost models for a DBMS. The parameters B_0, B_1, B_2, B_3, B_4, B_5 and B_6 can be interpreted as the initialization cost, the cost of pre-processing a tuple in the first operand table, the cost of pre-processing a tuple in the second operand table, the cost of retrieving a tuple from the first intermediate table, the cost of retrieving a tuple from the second intermediate table, the cost of processing a tuple in the Cartesian product of the two intermediate tables and the cost of processing a result tuple, respectively.

The basic model may be further improved by including some additional beneficial variables. The set V_{JS} of potential explanatory variables for the secondary part of a model contains the variables representing factors of types $4 \sim 6$. Similar to unary queries, the physical size of a table is estimated by the table length. In other words, the physical sizes of the first operand table, the second operand table and the result table are estimated by the variables: $Z_{J1} = N_{J1} * L_{J1}$, $Z_{J2} = N_{J2} * L_{J2}$, $RZ_J = RN_J * RL_J$, respectively. Therefore, $V_{JS} = \{ L_{J1}, L_{J2}, RL_J, Z_{J1}, Z_{J2}, RZ_J \}$. Any other useful variables, if available, could also be included in V_{JS}.

If all potential explanatory variables in V_{JS} are added to (4), the full regression model is

$$Y = B_0 + B_1 * N_{J1} + B_2 * N_{J2} + B_3 * TN_{J1}$$
$$+B_4 * TN_{J2} + B_5 * TN_{J12} + B_6 * RN_J$$
$$+B_7 * L_{J1} + B_8 * L_{J2} + B_9 * RL_J$$
$$+B_{10} * Z_{J1} + B_{11} * Z_{J2} + B_{12} * RZ_J.$$

Similar to a unary query class, all variables in V_{JB} and V_{JS} may not be necessary for a join query class. A procedure to choose significant variables in a model will be described in the following subsection. In addition, some additional variables may be included, and some variables could be included in another form.

4.4 Selection of Variables for Regression Models

To determine the variables for inclusion in a regression model, one approach is to evaluate all possible subset models and choose the best one(s) among them according to some criterion. However, evaluating all possible models may not be practically feasible when the number of variables is large.

To reduce the amount of computation, two types of selection procedures have been proposed[2]: the forward selection procedure and the backward elimination procedure. The forward selection procedure starts with a model containing no variables, i.e., only a constant term, and introduces explanatory variables into the regression model one at a time. The backward elimination procedure starts with the full model and successively drops one explanatory variable at a time. Both procedures need a criterion for selecting the next explanatory variable to be included in or removed from the model and a condition for stopping the procedure. With k variables, these procedures will involve evaluation of at most $(k + 1)$ models as contrasted with the evaluation of 2^k models necessary for examining all possible models.

To select a suitable regression model for a query class, we use a mixed forward and backward procedure described below (see Figure 1). We start with the full

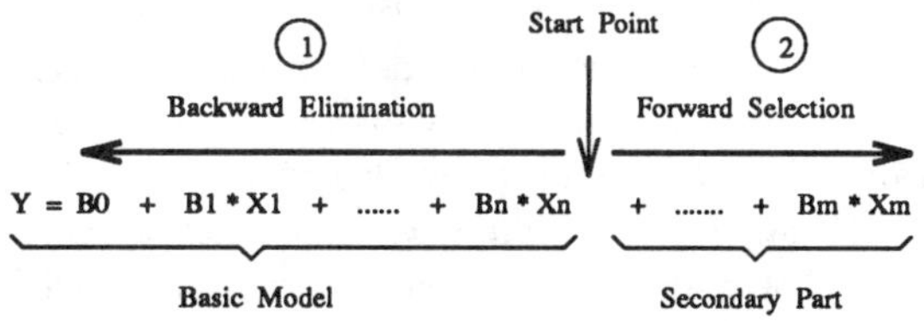

Figure 1: Selection of Variables for Regression Model

basic model (3) or (4) for the query class and apply the backward elimination procedure to drop some insignificant terms (explanatory variables) from the model. We then apply the forward selection procedure to find additional significant explanatory variables from the set (V_{US} or V_{JS}) of secondary explanatory variables for the query class.

The next explanatory variable X to be removed from the basic model during the first backward stage is the one that (1) has the smallest simple correlation coefficient[6] with the response variable Y and (2) makes the reduced model (i.e., the model after X is removed) have a smaller standard error of estimation than the original model or the two standard errors of estimation very close to each other, for instance, within 1% relative error. If the next explanatory variable satisfying (1) does not satisfy (2), or there are no more explanatory variable, the backward elimination procedure stops. Condition (1) chooses the variable which usually contributes the least among other variables in predicting Y. Condition (2) guarantees that removing the chosen variable results in an improved model or affects the model only very little. Removing the variables that affect the model very little can reduce the complexity and maintenance overhead of the model.

The next explanatory variable X to be added into the current model during the second forward stage is the one that (a) is in the set of secondary explanatory variables; (b) has the largest simple correlation coefficient with the response variable Y that has been adjusted for the effect of the current model (i.e., the largest simple correlation coefficient with the residuals of the current model); and (c) makes the augmented model (i.e., the model that includes X) have a smaller standard error of estimation than the current model and the two standard errors of estimation not very close to each other, for instance, greater than 1% relative error. If the next explanatory variable satisfying (a) and (b) does not satisfy (c), or no more explanatory variable exists, the forward selection procedure stops. The reasons for using conditions (a) $\sim$ (c) are similar to the situation for removing a variable. In particular, a variable is not added into the model unless it improves the standard error of estimation significantly in order to reduce the complexity of the model.

A description of the whole mixed forward and backward procedure is given below.

<u>Algorithm</u> 4.1 : Select Explanatory Variables for a Regression Model
Input: the set V_B of basic explanatory variables; the set V_S of secondary explanatory variables; observed data of sample queries for a given query class.
Output: a regression model with selected explanatory variables
Method:
  1. **begin**
  2.   Use observed data to fit the full basic model for the query class;

---

[6]The simple correlation coefficient of two variables indicates the degree of the linear relationship between the two variables.

3.   Calculate the standard error of estimation s;
4.   **for** each variable X in V_B **do**
5.   Calculate the simple correlation coefficient
            between X and the response variable Y
6.   **end**;
7.   backward := 'true';
8.   **while** backward = 'true' **and** $V_B \neq \emptyset$ **do**
9.   Let X' be the explanatory variable in V_B
            with the smallest simple correlation
            coefficient;
10. $V_B := V_B - \{\ X'\ \}$;
11.   Use the observed data to fit the reduced
            model with X' removed;
12.   Calculate the standard error of estimation
            s' for the reduced model;
13.   **if** $s > s'$ **or** $|(s - s')/s|$ very small **then**
14.   **begin**
15.   Set the reduced model as the current
                  model;
16. $s := s'$;
17.   **end**
18.   **else** backward := 'false'
19.   **end**;
20.   forward := 'true';
21.   **while** forward = 'true' **and** $V_s \neq \emptyset$ **do**
22.   **for** each X in V_s **do**
23.   Calculate the simple correlation
                coefficient between X and the
                residuals of the current model
24.   **end**;
25.   Let X' be the variable with the
              largest simple correlation coefficient;
26.   Use the observed data to fit the augmented
              model with X' added;
27.   Calculate the standard error of estimation
              s' for the augmented model;
28.   **if** $s > s'$ **and** $|(s - s')/s|$ not very small
              then
29.   **begin**
30.   Set the augmented model as the
                    current model;
31. $V_s := V_s - \{\ X'\ \}$;
32. $s := s'$
33.   **end**
34.   **else** forward := 'false'
35.   **end**;
36.   Return the current model as the
            regression model
37. **end.**

Since we start with the basic model, which has a high possibility to be the appropriate model for the given query class, the backward elimination and forward selection will most likely stop soon after they are initiated. Therefore, our procedure is likely more efficient than a pure forward or backward procedure. However, in the worst case, the above procedure will still check $(k + 1)$ models for k potential explanatory variables, which is the same as a pure forward or backward procedure.

5   Measures Ensuring Useful Models

To develop a useful regression model, measures need to be taken during the analysis. Furthermore, a developed regression model should be verified before it is used. Improvements may be needed if the model proves not acceptable. In this section, based on the characteristics of the cost models for query optimization, we identify the appropriate statistical methods and apply them to ensure the significance of our developed cost models.

5.1   Outliers

Outliers are extreme observations. In a residual plot, outliers are the points that lie far beyond the scatter of the majority of points. Under the method of least squares, a fitted equation may be pulled disproportionately towards an outlying observation because the sum of the squared deviations is minimized.

There are two possibilities for the existence of outliers. Frequently, an outlier results from a mistake or other extraneous causes. In our application, it may be caused by an abnormal situation in the system during the execution of a sample query. In this case, the outlier should be discarded. Sometimes, however, an outlier may convey significant information. For example, in our application, an outlier may indicate that the underlying DBMS uses a special strategy to process the relevant sample query, which is different from the one used for other queries. Since outliers represent a few extreme cases and our objective is to derive a cost estimation formula that is good for the majority of queries in a query class, we simply discard the outliers and use the remaining observations to derive a cost formula.

In a (standardized) residual plot, an outlier is usually four or more standard deviations from zero[7]. Therefore, an observation whose residual exceeds a certain amount of standard deviations D, such as $D = 4$, can be considered as an outlier and be removed. The residuals of query observations used here are calculated based on the full basic model since such a model usually captures the major behavior of the final model.

5.2   Multicollinearity

When the explanatory variables are highly correlated among themselves, multicollinearity among them is said to exist. The presence of multicollinearity does not, in general, inhibit our ability to obtain a good fit nor does it tend to affect predictions of new observations, provided these predictions are made within the region of observations. However, the estimated regression coefficients tend to have large sampling variability. To make reasonable predictions beyond the region of observations and obtain more precise information about the true regression coefficients, it is better to avoid multicollinearity among explanatory variables.

A method to detect the presence of multicollinearity that is widely used is by means of variance inflation factors. These factors measure how much the variances of the estimated regression coefficients are inflated as compared to when the independent variables are not linearly related. If R_j^2 is the coefficient of total determination that results when the explanatory variable X_j is regressed against all the other explanatory variables, the variance inflation factor for X_j is defined as

$$VIF(X_j) = 1/(1 - R_j^2) \, .$$

It is clear that if X_j has a strong linear relationship with the other explanatory variables, R_j^2 is close to 1 and $VIF(X_j)$ is large.

To avoid multicollinearity, we use the reciprocal of a variance inflation factor to detect instances where an explanatory variable should not be allowed into the fitted regression model because of excessively high interdependence between this variable and other explanatory variables in the model.

More specifically, the set V_B of basic explanatory variables used by Algorithm 4.1 is formed as follows. At the beginning, V_B only contains the basic explanatory variable which has the highest simple correlation coefficient with the response variable Y. Then the variable X_j which has the next highest simple correlation coefficient with Y is entered into V_B if $1/VIF(X_j)$ is not too small. This procedure continues until all possible basic explanatory variables are considered. Similarly, when Algorithm 4.1 selects additional beneficial variables from V_S for the model, any variable X_j whose $1/VIF(X_j)$ is too small is skipped.

5.3 Validation of Model Assumptions

Usually, three assumptions of a regression model (1) need to be checked: *1.* uncorrelation of error terms; *2.* equal variance of error terms; and *3.* normal distribution of error terms.

Note that the dependent random variables Y_i's should satisfy the same assumptions as their error terms since the $X_{i,j}$'s in (1) are known values. In general, regression analysis is not seriously affected by slight to moderate departures from the assumptions.

The assumptions can be ranked in terms of the seriousness of the failure of the assumption to hold from the most serious to the least serious as follows: assumptions *1, 2* and *3*.

For our application, the observed costs of repeated executions of a sample query have no inherent relationship with the observed costs of repeated executions of another sample query under the assumption that the contention factors in the system are approximately stable. Hence the first assumption should be satisfied. This is a good property because the violation of assumption *1* is the most serious to a regression model.

However, the variance of the observed costs of repeated executions of a sample query may increase with the level (magnitude) of query cost. This is because the execution of a sample query with longer time (larger cost) may suffer more disturbances in the system than the execution of a sample query with shorter time. Thus assumption *2* may be violated in our regression models. Furthermore, the observed costs of repeated executions of a sample query may not follow the normal distribution; i.e., assumption *3* may not hold either. The observed costs are usually skewed to the right because the observed costs stay at a stable level for most time and become larger from time to time when disturbances occur in the system.

Since the uncorrelation assumption is rarely violated in our application, it is not checked by our regression analysis program. For the normality assumption, many studies have shown that regression analysis is robust to it[7, 9]; that is, the technique will give usable results even if this assumption is not satisfied. In fact, the normality assumption is not required to obtain the point estimates of $\widehat{B_i}$'s, $\widehat{Y}$ and s. This assumption is required only when constructing confidence intervals and hypothesis-testing decision rules. In our application, we will not construct confidence intervals, and the only hypothesis-test that needs the normality assumption is the F-test which will be discussed later. Like many other statistical applications, if only the normality assumption is violated, we choose to ignore this violation. Thus, the normality assumption is not checked by our regression analysis program either.

When the assumption of equal variances is violated, a correction measure is usually taken to eliminate or reduce the violation. Before a correction measure is given, let us first discuss how to test for the violation of equal variances.

Assuming that a regression model is proper to fit sample observations, the sampled residuals should reflect the assumptions on the error terms. We can, therefore, use the sampled residuals to check the assumptions. There are two ways in which the sampled residuals can be used to check the assumptions[7, 9]: residual plots and statistical tests. The former is subjective, while the latter is objective. Since we try to develop a program to test assumption 2 automatically, we employ the latter.

As mentioned before, if the assumption of equal variances is violated in our application, variances typically increase with the level of the response variable. In this case, the absolute values of the residuals usually have a significant correlation with the fitted values of the response variable. A simple test for the correlation between two random variables u and w when the bivariate distribution is unknown is to use Spearman's rank correlation coefficient[9, 12], which is defined as

$$r_s = 1 - 6 \sum_{i=1}^{n} [r(u_i) - r(w_i)]/[n(n^2 - 1)],$$

where $r(u_i)$ and $r(w_i)$ are the ranks of the values u_i and w_i of u and w, respectively. The null and alternate hypotheses are as follows:

H_0 : The values of u and w are uncorrelated.

H_A : Either there is a tendency for larger values of u to be paired with the larger values of w, or there is a tendency for smaller values of u to be paired with larger values of w.

The decision rule at the significance level α is:

If $\rho_{1-\alpha/2} \leq r_s \leq \rho_{\alpha/2}$, conclude H_0.

If $r_s < \rho_{1-\alpha/2}$ or $r_s > \rho_{\alpha/2}$, conclude H_A.

The critical values $\rho_{\alpha/2} = -\rho_{1-\alpha/2}$ can be found in [9]. If H_A is concluded for the absolute residuals and fitted values, the assumption of equal variances is violated.

If the assumption of equal variances is violated, the estimates given by the corresponding regression model will not have the maximum precision[2]. Since the estimation precision requirement is not high for query optimization, the violation of this assumption can be tolerated to a certain degree. However, if the assumption of equal variances is severely violated, account should be taken of this in fitting the model.

A useful tool to remedy the violation of the equal variances assumption is the method of weighted least squares. The idea is to provide differing weights in (1); that is,

$$LS_w = \sum_{i=1}^{n} w_i * [Y_i - (B_0 + B_1 X_{i,1} + B_2 X_{i,2} + \cdots + B_k X_{i,k})]^2 ,$$

where w_i is the weight for the i-th Y observation. The values for B_j's to minimize LS_w is to be found. Least squares theory states that the weights w_i's are inversely proportional to the variances σ_i^2's of the error terms. Thus an observation Y_i that has a large variance receives less weight than another observation that has a smaller variance. The (weighted) variances of error terms tend to be equalized.

Unfortunately, one rarely has knowledge of the variances σ_i^2's. To estimate the weights, we do the following. The sample data is used to obtain the fitted regression function and residuals by ordinary least squares first. The cases are then placed into a small number of groups according to level of the fitted value. The variance of the residuals is calculated for each group. Every Y observation in a group receives a weight which is the reciprocal of the estimated variance for that group.

Moreover, we use the results of weighted least squares to re-estimate the weights and obtain a new weighted least squares fit. This procedure is continued until no substantial changes in the fitted regression function take place or too many iterations occur. In the latter case, the fitted regression function with the smallest Spearman's rank correlation coefficient is chosen. This procedure is called an iterative weighted least squares procedure.

5.4 Testing Significance of Regression Model

As mentioned previously, to evaluate the goodness of the developed regression model, two descriptive measures are used: the standard error of estimation and the coefficient of multiple determination. A good regression model is evidenced by a small standard error of estimation and a high coefficient of multiple determination.

The significance of the developed model can be further tested by using the F-test[7, 9]. The F-test was derived under the normality assumption. However, there is some evidence that non-normality usually does not distort the conclusions too seriously[12]. In general, the F-test under the normality assumption is asymptotically (i.e., with sufficiently large samples) valid when the error terms are not normally distributed[1]. Therefore, F-test is adopted in our application to test the significance of a regression model although the error terms may not follow the normality assumption.

Class	Characteristics of Queries in the Class	Likely Access Method
G_{u1}	unary queries whose qualifications have at least one conjunct $R_i.a_n = C$ where $R_i.a_n$ is indexed	index scan method with a key value
G_{u2}	unary queries that are not in G_{u1} and whose qualifications have at least one conjunct $R_i.a_n \ \theta \ C$ where $R_i.a_n$ is indexed and $\theta \in \{<, \leq, >, \geq, \}$	index scan method with a range
G_{u3}	unary queries that are not in G_{u1} or G_{u2}	sequential scan method
G_{j1}	join queries whose qualifications have at least one conjunct $R_i.a_n = R_j.a_m$ where either $R_i.a_n$ or $R_j.a_m$ (or both) is indexed	index join method
G_{j2}	join queries that are not in G_{j1} and whose qualifications have at least one index-usable conjunct for one or both operand tables	nested-loop join method with index reduction first
G_{j3}	join queries that are not in G_{j1} or G_{j2}	sort-merge join method

Table 1: Considered Query Classes

6 Experiments

To verify the feasibility of the presented statistical procedure, experiments were conducted within a multidatabase system prototype, called CORDS-MDBS. Three commercial DBMSs, i.e., ORACLE 7.0, EMPRESS 4.6 and DB2/6000 1.1.0, were used as local DBMSs in the experiments. All the local DBMSs were run on IBM RS/6000 model 220 machines. Due to the limitation of the paper length, only the experimental results on ORACLE 7.0 are reported in this paper. The experiments on the other systems demonstrated similar results.

The experiments were conducted in a system environment where the contention factors were approximately stable. For example, they were performed during midnights and weekends when there was no or little interference from other users in the systems. However, occasional interference from other users still existed since the systems were shared resources.

Queries for each local database system were classified according to the query sampling method. The considered query classes[7] are given in table 1. Sample queries are then drawn from each query class and performed on the three local database systems. Their observed costs are used to derive cost models for the relevant query classes by the statistical procedure introduced in the previous sections.

Tables 2 and 3 show the derived cost models and the relevant statistical measures. It can be seen that:

- Most cost models capture over 90% variability in query cost, from observing the coefficients of total determination. The only exception is for G_{u1} when queries can be executed very fast, i.e., small-cost queries, due to their efficient access methods and small result tables.

- The standard errors of estimation for the cost models are acceptable, compared with the magnitudes of the relevant average observed costs of the sample queries.

- The statistical F-tests at the significance level $\alpha = 0.01$ show that all derived cost models are useful for estimating the costs of queries in the relevant query classes.

- The statistical hypothesis tests for the Spearman's rank correlation coefficients at the significance level $\alpha = 0.01$ show that there is no strong evidence indicating the violation of equal variances assumption for all derived cost models after using the method of weighted least squares if needed.

- Derivations of most[8] cost models require the method of weighted least squares, which implies that the error terms of the original regression model (using the regular least squares) violate the assumption of equal variances in most cases.

In summary, the statistical procedure derived useful cost models. Figure 2 shows a typical comparison between the observed costs and our estimated costs for some test queries.

As mentioned, the experimental results show that small-cost queries often have worse estimated costs than large-cost queries. This observation coincides with Du et al.'s observation for their calibration method. The reason for this phenomenon is that (1) a cost model is usually dominated by large costs used to derive it, while the small costs may not follow the same model because different buffering and processing strategies may be used for the small-cost queries; (2) a small cost can be greatly affected by some contention factors, such as available buffer space and the number of current processes; (3) initialization costs, distribution of data over a disk space and some other factors, which may not be important for large-cost queries,

---

[7]Only equijoin queries were considered.

[8]Some unreported cost models for other local database systems in the experiments did not require the method of weighted least squares.

query class	Cost Estimation Formula
G_{u1}	$0.866475e\text{-}1 \ + \ 0.177483e\text{-}2 * TN_U \ + \ 0.926299e\text{-}2 * RN_U \ + \ 0.443237e\text{-}6 * Z_U$
G_{u2}	$0.354301 \ + \ 0.105255e\text{-}2 * TN_U \ + \ 0.32336e\text{-}2 * RN_U \ + \ 0.852187e\text{-}4 * RZ_U$
G_{u3}	$0.16555 \ + \ 0.149208e\text{-}3 * N_U \ + \ 0.307219e\text{-}2 * RN_U \ + \ 0.105712e\text{-}3 * RZ_U$
G_{j1}	$0.192209 \ + \ 0.161011e\text{-}2 * TN_{J2} \ + \ 0.573257e\text{-}7 * TN_{J12} \ + \ 0.426256e\text{-}2 * RN_J$
G_{j2}	$0.176158 \ + \ 0.951479e\text{-}3 * TN_{J12}$
G_{j3}	$-0.236703e\text{-}1 \ + \ 0.143572e\text{-}3 * N_{J2} \ + \ 0.61871e\text{-}3 * TN_{J1} \ + \ 0.680628e\text{-}3 * TN_{J2}$ $+ \ 0.399927e\text{-}6 * TN_{J12} \ + \ 0.316129e\text{-}2 * RN_J$

Table 2: Derived Cost Formulas for Query Classes on ORACLE 7.0

query class	coefficient of multiple determination	standard error of estimation	average cost (sec.)	F-statistic (critical value at $\alpha = 0.01$)	Spearman's rank correlation (critical value at $\alpha = 0.01$)	weighted least square?
G_{u1}	0.65675	0.10578	0.20406	56.76 (> 3.97)	0.54266e-1 (< 0.24292)	yes
G_{u2}	0.96751	0.27357e+1	0.11360e+2	1161.46 (> 4.29)	0.21032 (< 0.21270)	yes
G_{u3}	0.99810	0.87345	0.13595e+2	15397.70 (> 3.97)	0.20930e-1 (< 0.24425)	yes
G_{j1}	0.98992	0.14961e+1	0.60868e+1	3732.28 (> 4.28)	0.61343e-1 (< 0.21541)	yes
G_{j2}	0.92457	0.51609e+3	0.75323e+3	1483.19 (> 7.06)	0.74099e-1 (< 0.21095)	yes
G_{j3}	0.97670	0.15275e+1	0.71334e+1	980.69 (> 3.52)	0.13307 (< 0.21095)	yes

Table 3: Statistical Measures for Cost Formulas on ORACLE 7.0

could have major impact on the costs of small-cost queries.

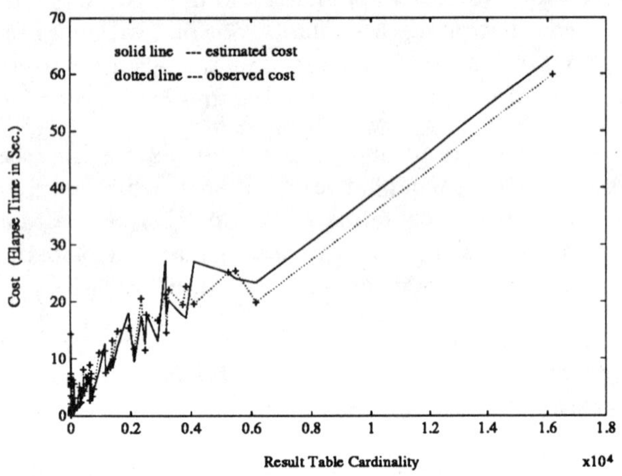

Figure 2: Observed and Estimated Costs for Test Queries in G_{j3} on ORACLE

Since the causes of this problem are usually uncontrollable and related to implementation details of the underlying local database system, it is hard to completely solve this problem at the global level in an MDBS. However, this problem could be mitigated by (a) refining the query classification according to the sizes of result tables; and/or (b) performing a sample query multiple times and using the average of observed costs to derive a cost model; and/or (c) including in the cost model more explanatory variables if available, such as buffer sizes, and distributions of data in a disk space.

Fortunately, estimating the costs of small-cost queries is not as important as estimating the costs of large-cost queries in query optimization because it is more important to identify large-cost queries so that "bad" execution plans could be avoided.

7   Conclusion

Today's organizations have increasing requirements for tools that support global access to information stored in distributed, heterogeneous, autonomous data repositories. A multidatabase system is such a tool that integrates information from multiple pre-existing local databases. To process a global query efficiently in an MDBS, global query optimization is required. A major challenge for performing global query optimization in an MDBS is that some desired local cost information may not be available at the global level. Without knowing how efficiently local queries can be executed, it is difficult for the global query optimizer to choose a good decomposition for the given global query.

To tackle this challenge, a feasible statistical procedure for deriving local cost models for a local database system is presented in this paper. Local queries are grouped into homogeneous classes. A cost model is developed for each query class. The development of cost models are base on multiple regression analysis.

Each cost model is divided into two parts: a basic model and a secondary part. The basic model is based on some existing cost models in DBMSs and used to capture the major performance behavior of queries. The secondary part is used to improve the basic model. Potential explanatory variables that can

be included in each part of a cost model are identified.
A backward procedure is used to eliminate insignificant variables from the basic model for a cost model.
A forward procedure is used to add significant variables to the secondary part of a cost model. Such
a mixed forward and backward procedure can select
proper variables for a cost model efficiently.

During the regression analysis, outliers are removed
from the sample data. Multicollinearity is discovered
by using the variance inflation factor and prevented
by excluding variables with larger variance inflation
factors. Violation of the equal variance assumption is
detected by using Spearman's rank correlation coefficient and remedied by using an iterative weighted least
squares procedure. The significance of a cost model is
checked by the standard error of estimation, the coefficient of multiple determination, and F-test. These
measures ensure that a developed cost model is useful.

The experimental results demonstrated that the
presented statistical procedure can build useful cost
models for local database systems in an MDBS.

The presented procedure introduces a promising
method to estimate local cost parameters in an MDBS
or a distributed information system. We plan to
investigate the feasibility of this method for non-
relational local database systems in an MDBS in the
future.

References

[1] S. F. Arnold. *The Theory of Linear Models and
Multivariate Analysis.* John Wiley & Sons, Inc.,
1981.

[2] S. Chatterjee and B. Price. *Regression Analysis by
Example, 2nd Ed.* John Wiley & Sons, Inc., 1991.

[3] W. Du, R. Krishnamurthy, and M. C. Shan. Query
optimization in heterogeneous DBMS. In *Proc. of
VLDB*, pp 277–91, 1992.

[4] M. Jarke and J. Koch. Query optimization in database systems. *Computing Surveys*, 16(2):111–152,
June 1984.

[5] R. J. Lipton and J. F. Naughton. Practical selectivity estimation through adaptive sampling. In
Proc. of SIGMOD, pp 1–11, 1990.

[6] H. Lu, B.-C. Ooi, and C.-H. Goh. On global multidatabase query optimization. *SIGMOD Record*,
21(4):6–11, Dec. 1992.

[7] J. Neter, W. Wasserman, and M. H. Kutner. *Applied Linear Statistical Models, 3rd Ed.* Richard D.
Irwin, Inc., 1990.

[8] F. Olken and D. Rotem. Simple random sampling
from relational databases. In *Proc. of 12th VLDB*,
pp 160–9, 1986.

[9] R. C. Pfaffenberger and J. H. Patterson. *Statistical
Methods for Business and Economics.* Richard D.
Irwin, Inc., 1987.

[10] P. G. Selinger et al. Access path selection in relational database management systems. In *Proc. of
ACM SIGMOD*, pp 23–34, 1979.

[11] G. P. Shapiro and C. Connel. Accurate estimation
of the number of tuples satisfying a condition. In
Proc. of SIGMOD, pp 256–76, 1984.

[12] G. W. Snedecor and W. G. Cochran. *Statistical
Methods, 6th Ed.* The Iowa State university Press,
1967.

[13] Qiang Zhu. Query optimization in multidatabase
systems. In *Proc. of the 1992 IBM CAS Conf.,
vol.II*, pp 111–27, Toronto, Canada, Nov. 1992.

[14] Qiang Zhu and P.-Å. Larson. A query sampling
method for estimating local cost parameters in a
multidatabase system. In *Proc. of the 10th IEEE
Int'l Conf. on Data Eng.*, pp 144–53, Houston,
Texas, Feb. 1994.

[15] Qiang Zhu and P.-Å. Larson. Establishing a fuzzy
cost model for query optimization in a multidatabase system. In *Proc. of the 27th IEEE/ACM
Hawaii Int'l Conf. on Sys. Sci.*, pp 263-72, Maui,
Hawaii, Jan. 1994.

[16] Qiang Zhu and P.-Å. Larson. Query optimization
using fuzzy set theory for a multidatabase system.
In *Proc. of the 1993 IBM CAS Conf.*, pp 848–59,
Toronto, Canada, Oct. 1993.

Parallel Query Processing Strategies
for Object-oriented Temporal Databases*

Soon J. Hyun[†]
Stanley Y.W. Su
Database Systems Research and Development Center
Department of Computer and Information Science and Engineering
Department of Electrical and Computer Engineering
University of Florida
Gainesville, FL 32611-6125

Abstract

An object-oriented (OO) temporal database management system can better meet the data management requirements of many applications because it not only provides powerful facilities for modeling and processing the structural and behavioral properties of complex objects but also supports the management of temporal data. However, due to the generality and high functionality of an OO system, the append-only nature of temporal databases and the irregular evolutions of object instances, processing efficiency is very difficult to achieve using serial algorithms and conventional computing systems. This paper presents two multi-wavefront parallel query processing strategies, five primitive time-alignment operations and their implementations on a parallel computer nCUBE2. The multi-wavefront algorithms allow asynchronous processing and propagation of temporal object instance identifiers and data in order to identify temporal object instances which satisfy a complex multi-class query. They offer both intraquery parallelism and interquery parallelism in query processing. The time-alignment operations allow data with different evolution time intervals to be aligned to determine the common intervals in which the combined factual information is vaild. Some performance evaluation results are also reported.

1   Introduction

In our information-oriented society, individuals and organizations make decisions daily based on information of the past, present, and the foreseeable future. Although database management systems (DBMSs) have been widely used for data storage and manipulation to aid our decision processes, databases managed by the conventional DBMSs contain only the current information. Updating a database involves the replacement of old data by new data. Temporal data are not stored and maintained. Even though DBMSs allow temporal information to be stored as values of temporal attributes such as Date, Year, etc., the semantics of these temporal attributes are interpreted by the users via their queries and application programs rather than automatically managed by DBMSs. There is a definite need for the development of efficient DBMSs which can support the concepts of time and manage current, historical, and expected data of the future. In recent years, a considerable amount of research has been conducted on temporal databases. The emphasis has been in the development of temporal data models, temporal query languages and their underlying algebras, storage structure models and access methods for the storage and access of temporal databases. Most of the earlier works attempted to extend the relational data model [8, 12, 13, 24, 25, 35] and relational query languages such as Quel and SQL [13, 14, 25, 30] or relational algebra [8, 23, 35] for modeling and processing temporal data. This approach has been taken for a very good reason, i.e., to evolutionally move from nontemporal DBMSs to temporal DBMSs without drastically changing the ways that the users of relational DBMSs manage their databases, thus gaining their acceptance.

Object-oriented (OO) databases, which provide better structural and behavioral abstraction facilities, offer promising alternatives to many advanced application domains and thus have been researched exten-

---

*This work is supported by a grant from the National Science Foundation, CCR-9200756.

[†]Presently at Electronics and Telecommunications Research Institute(ETRI), Taejon, Korea

232

sively. The OO representation of temporal data offers efficiency edges over, say, the relational representation due to the following two main reasons. First, data of complex objects with attributes of different data types, such as set, bag, list, matrix, etc., are stored and accessed together in secondary storage instead of performing many Joins over normalized relations to construct their complex data structures. Second, the use of object identifiers (OIDs) or instance identifiers (IIDs) as pointers to related objects and the use of various "pointer swizzling" techniques allow objects of interest to be located in secondary storage, as well as in main memory, much faster than the relational approach by content matching of attribute values. Following this trend and interest in OO temporal databases, several researchers have undertaken investigations on OO temporal data models and query languages [6, 9, 15, 26, 31, 38], and algebras [4, 10, 27, 33].

Although there has been a considerable amount of research effort in both relational and OO temporal databases and DBMSs, actual implementation experiences are still lacking in this field. Efficiency in processing temporal databases is a very important issue and is very difficult to achieve when DBMSs are implemented on conventional computing systems. Unlike query processing in nontemporal databases, query processing in temporal databases needs the manipulation of temporal information to capture the complex relationship among objects in the time dimension. Thus, the processing overhead is much higher than a nontemporal database processing. Moreover, processing efficiency is very difficult to achieve due to the sheer size of append-only temporal databases and the sequential nature of conventional computing systems. The need for processing large nontemporal databases and performing complex database management functions efficiently has motivated a great deal of work on parallel database computers. Some good examples can be found in [1, 2, 5, 11, 16, 20, 21]. These works have introduced many useful parallel processing techniques and algorithms such as hash-based Join operations, vertical and horizontal data partitions, intraquery parallelism and interquery parallelism, asynchronous dataflow, and pipelining parallelism. A few efforts on parallel temporal database processing have also emerged [19, 22]. They have extended several parallel processing techniques used for processing nontemporal relational databases, such as semi-join and inequality join techniques, and have used them to process temporal relational databases.

In our work, we have adopted several known parallel query processing techniques, such as data-driven query processing [2], asynchronous dataflow [1] and graph-based query processing [3, 5, 32] for processing OO temporal databases. The intended contributions of this paper are (1) the extension of multi-wavefront algorithms introduced in [5, 36] for processing OO temporal databases, (2) the implementation of several temporal alignment operations and multi-wavefront algorithms on a parallel computer nCUBE2, and (3) the report of some performance evaluation results. The rest of this paper is organized as follows. In Section 2 we present the general concept of temporal object associations as a way of representing a temporal database and an association-based query formulation as a way of expressing a user's data retrieval and manipulation need. We also describe a set of time-alignment operations which serve as the basic time processing constructs. In Section 4 we present two parallel temporal query processing strategies. We show the results of a performance evaluation of these implemented strategies in Section 5, and a summary and conclusion are given in Section 6.

2 Overview

2.1 Object-oriented Temporal Data

In an OO world, all things of interest to an application such as physical entities, events, processes or functions can be uniformly defined as objects. Objects having the same structural and behavioral properties are grouped together into an object class which, in addition to serving as the container of objects, defines the common structural and behavioral properties of these objects. The behavioral properties of an object class are defined as operations (or methods) which can be system-defined (e.g., retrieve, update, etc.) and/or user-defined (e.g., hire_an_employee, purchase_a_part, etc.). The structural properties of an object class consist of descriptive data (or attributes) of objects in the class and association data which link the class with other classes. In general, classes are associated with one another through different types of semantic associations, and their objects are interconnected through instances of these association types. The two most commonly recognized association types are *aggregation* and *generalization*. The aggregation association models the a–part–of, a–function–of, or a–property–of relationship, and the generalization association models the is–a or superclass–subclass relationship.

In contrast to nontemporal databases, temporal databases treat database events as *temporal events* and record the effects of these events as the evolutions (or versions) of object instances. There are three typical temporal events which cause object evolutions: *up-*

date, delete and *insert*. For example, "updating John's salary to \$35K," "deleting Mary's record," and "inserting Brown's record" are temporal events in temporal databases. Upon an update event's occurrence, an object instance obtains a new time specification and some new attribute value(s).[1] The old instance, then, becomes a part of the history of the instance. Therefore, the evolutions of an instance are treated as the historical versions of the instance called *temporal instances*.

Different notions of time have been proposed in the literature [24, 29]. Among them, two time notions, *valid time* and *transaction time*, are of general interest. The valid time of a fact is the time when the fact is true in the modeled reality. Valid times are usually supplied by the user. The transaction time of a database fact is the time when the fact is recorded in a database. Data models generally support either valid time or valid time and transaction time; and valid time is the most commonly used time notion. The evolution of an instance is represented by a sequence of temporal instances. The temporal instances are ordered in time; that is, they form *time-lines*[2]. A time-line which records the valid times of an instance is called valid time-line. A time-line which records the transaction times of an instance is called transaction time-line. In this paper, since we employ the valid time only for the description of time-alignment operations, we use "time-lines" to mean vaild time-lines.

2.2 Graphical Representation of OO Temporal Databases

A graphical representation of an OO temporal databases specifies relationships among temporal data objects by explicit association links [26, 31]. Hence, a temporal query can be expressed by a specification of the pattern of associated object classes along with a specification of interested time interval(s). In a graph-based data model, such as OSAM*/T [31], an OO temporal database is represented by two graphs: a *Schema Graph* (SG) and a *Temporal Object Graph* (TOG) which represent the intensional database and the extensional database, respectively.

2.2.1 Schema Graph

Object classes and their association types can be represented by a Schema Graph (SG). In the SG, the database is viewed as a collection of object classes interrelated through various association types. The SG

of an example company database is shown in Figure 1.

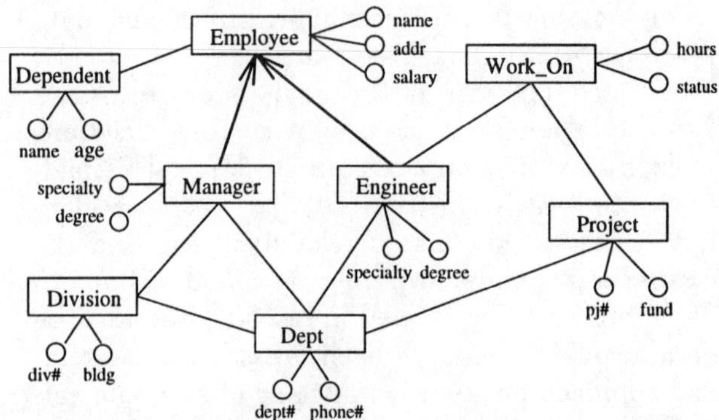

Figure 1: Schema Graph of a Company Database

Rectangles represent entity classes, and circles represent attributes defined over some underlying domain classes. Objects in entity classes are entities of interest in an application domain. Each object is assigned with a system-wide unique OID. The data representation of an object in a class is called an object instance[3] which is uniquely identified by an instance identifier (or IID). An IID is formed by the concatenation of a class identifier and an OID. Objects in a domain class are self-naming (e.g., integer 2, age 5, etc.) and serve as attribute values for defining or describing other entity or domain class objects. Edges in the SG represent associations among object classes. Bold arrows denote *generalization* associations (e.g., class Employee is the superclass of subclasses Manager and Engineer) and plain edges denote *aggregation* associations between object classes.

2.2.2 Temporal Object Graph and Temporal Data Organizations

An extensional database can be represented by the temporal object graph (TOG). In the TOG, vertices represent temporal instances. The associations among temporal instances are represented by interconnection links. The links are typeless because, once the schema of a database is defined, the semantics of the association types become constraints for object manipulations enforced by the OO temporal DBMS, and the user does not have to explicitly specify the association types when formulating queries. Therefore, in the TOG, the database is viewed as a collection of temporal instances interconnected through typeless association links.

---

[1] In the case of a deletion event, all the values of the new instance will become "null" or "not available".

[2] The "time sequence" in [18, 27, 28] is conceptually equivalent to "time-line".

[3] An instance in an OO programming language is the same as an object in this data model.

Similar to the tuple timestamping [25, 30] and the attribute timestamping [7, 13] in the temporal extensions to the relational data model, the evolutions of object instances and their temporal relationships in the OO database can be recorded using two timestamping methods: *instance timestamping* or *attribute timestamping*. In the former method, a temporal event on an attribute of an instance is treated as an event on the entire instance. Therefore, the evolution of an instance on both descriptive data and association references is recoded by a common time-line. In the latter method, a temporal event on an attribute of an instance is treated as an individual event on the attribute and, hence, the evolutions of different attributes are recorded separately. Therefore, the evolution of an instance can be represented by multiple time-lines, i.e., time-lines of descriptive data attributes (e.g., salary, degree, etc.) and those of association reference attributes (e.g., Engineer–Dept, Engineer–Work_On relationships). The temporal data organizations based on two timestamping methods are graphically represented by TOGs and tables in Figure 2. For example, (1) engineer *en*1 joined depart-

method by time-alignment operations (which will be discussed in Section 3. For example, the two time-lines of *en*1 in Figure 2(a) can be merged into the single time-line of *en*1 in Figure 2(b). Also, the individual evolution of an attribute in the instance timestamping method can be "projected out" of a single time-line by a temporal project algebraic operation.

It should be noted that, although the valid times of the data values (or association information) of all the attributes are pre-aligned in the instance timestamping method, time-alignment operations are still needed for relating temporal data of different instances that are associated. For example, in Figure 2(b), time-alignment operations over the valid times of Engineer instances and Dept instances are needed to identify their temporal relationships during the course of query processing. Thus, time-alignment operations in this paper are applicable to processing temporal databases in both timestamping methods. In the remaining part of this paper, we shall use the attribute timestamping method for the presentation of time-alignment operations. Figure 3 shows the TOG of a part of the company database represented in the attribute timestamping method.

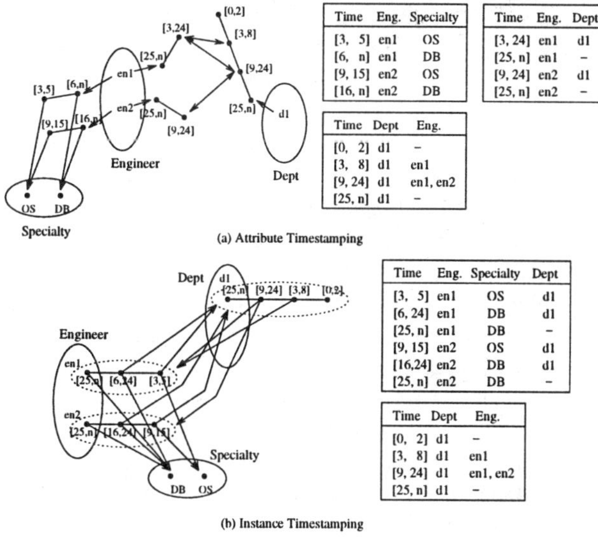

Time	Eng.	Specialty
[3, 5]	en1	OS
[6, n]	en1	DB
[9, 15]	en2	OS
[16, n]	en2	DB

Time	Eng.	Dept
[3, 24]	en1	d1
[25, n]	en1	–
[9, 24]	en2	d1
[25, n]	en2	–

Time	Dept	Eng.
[0, 2]	d1	–
[3, 8]	d1	en1
[9, 24]	d1	en1, en2
[25, n]	d1	–

(a) Attribute Timestamping

Time	Eng.	Specialty	Dept
[3, 5]	en1	OS	d1
[6, 24]	en1	DB	d1
[25, n]	en1	DB	–
[9, 15]	en2	OS	d1
[16, 24]	en2	DB	d1
[25, n]	en2	DB	–

Time	Dept	Eng.
[0, 2]	d1	–
[3, 8]	d1	en1
[9, 24]	d1	en1, en2
[25, n]	d1	–

(b) Instance Timestamping

Figure 2: Temporal Data Organizations

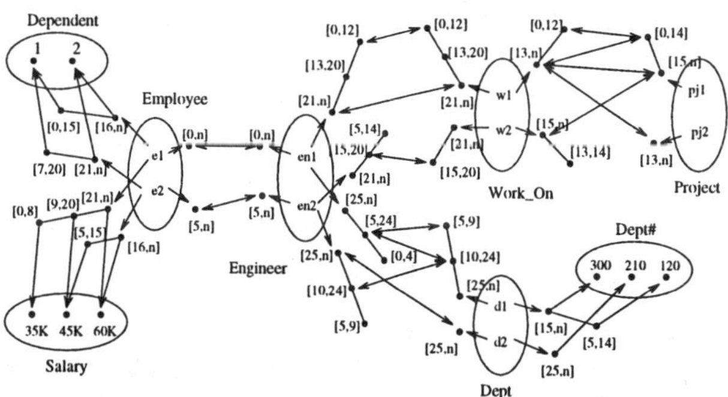

Figure 3: Temporal Object Graph

ment *d*1 at t_3 and changed her specialty to "DB" at t_6, (2) *en*2 joined *d*1 at t_9 and changed his specialty to "DB" at t_{16}, and (3) both engineers left department *d*1 at t_{25} (specified by "–" in the tables). Note that *d*1 evolved at t_9 due to the new participation of *en*2 and, thus, *d*1 had both engineers during [9,24].

The multiple valid time-lines of an instance in the attribute timestamping method can be converted into a single valid time-line in the instance timestamping

A temporal instance in a TOG can be identified by a TIID which is formed by the concatenation of a timestamp and an IID. TIIDs are unique system-wide in a temporal database that uses the instance timestamping method. However, the TIIDs are unique only within a time-line in a temporal database that uses the attribute timestamping method. This is because the evolution of each attribute is stored on its own time-line showing its temporal interconnections with data values of a domain class (or instances of an entity class). Two time-lines associated with the same object instance may have the same valid time-interval, thus forming two identical TIIDs. The existence of a TIID in multiple time-lines does not cause a problem in temporal processing. This is because, when two time-lines of an instance are processed, their time-lines are aligned by a time-alignment operation which combines the two time-lines into one. The two identical TIIDs would become one in the new time-line. For example, in Figure 3, two identical TIIDs of $w1$ appear in two separate time-lines (i.e., [0,12]$w1$): one has an association with $en1$ and the other with $pj1$.

Consistent with the graphical view of an OO temporal database (i.e., SG and TOG), a query can be represented by a *Query Graph* (QG) which is a subgraph of SG and represents the query semantics among the domain/entity classes specified in the query. For example, based on the SG in Figure 1, the following query can be represented by a QG as shown in Figure 4, in which the AND construct specifies the condition that an Engineer instance must be associated with a Project instance and a Dept instance.

$Q1$: Find the degree and the dept# of engineers who participated in some project while belonging to some department during T[15,n].

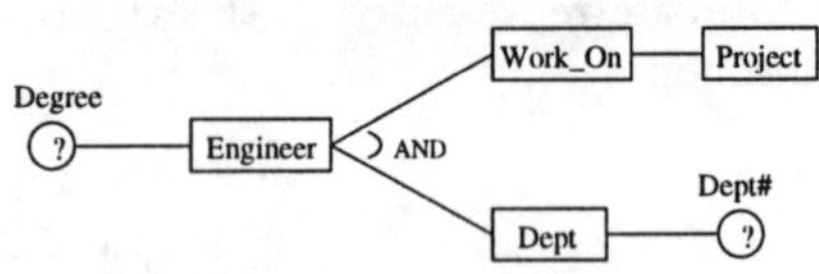

Figure 4: Query Graph of Q1

3 Time-alignment Operations in Temporal Query Processing

The essence of temporal query processing is to identify the relationships among temporal instances that satisfy the time and data conditions specified in the query and to perform system-/user-defined operations on them. In relational query processing, the relationships of tuples of two relations are found by "joining" them. In OO query processing, the relationships of object instances of multiple classes can be identified by "traversing" the association links (or pointers) among them.

The use of time as a part of information element in temporal database management incurs an additional dimension of complexity in query processing and optimization. The complexity mainly stems from the fact that temporal events occur in an irregular and unpredictable fashion so that the evolutions of one instance or attribute can be different from another instance or attribute. Thus, processing the time intervals of associated instances or attributes to identify their temporal relationships is an essential operation

in temporal query processing. For example, employees' salary changes are different from their association changes with departments over time. As a result, different time intervals of the employees need to be maintained for their salary values and their associations with projects (e.g., employee $e2$ made "45K" during interval [5,15] and "60K" during interval [16,n], and worked in department $d1$ during interval [10,24] and $d2$ during [25,n]). During query processing, the traversals of these object instances would require that their intervals be aligned in order to find the common intervals in which the combined factual information are valid or true. For example, the time intervals that record salary change have to be aligned with those that record department change so that the resulting time intervals contain all the distinct pairs of salary and department information (i.e., "45K–$d1$" for [10,15]$e2$, "60K–$d1$" for [16,24]$e2$, and "60K–$d2$" for [25,n]$e2$). This interval alignment operation can produce a large number of temporal instances and their associations if there are many salary and department changes. This operation is necessary only if we are interested in the salary values of employees when they are working in specific departments.

On the other hand, if we are interested only in the salary values of employees when they worked in *any* departments (i.e., we do not care which departments as long as they worked in some departments), then a proper interval alignment operation would be to identify only the valid intervals of salary changes and ignore the detailed evolutions of department change so that fewer intervals and instance associations will be produced (e.g., "45K-any" for [10,15]$e2$ and "60K-any" for [16,n]$e2$). The reduced number of temporal instances would in turn reduce the amount of processing in the next step of object instance traversal. Therefore, efficient temporal query processing is hinged on the use of proper *time-alignment* operations which can produce the correct and the least amount of temporal data. Based on our study and implementation experience, we have found that different query semantics and data properties call for different time-alignment operations. We have identified five primitive time-alignment operations. In this section, we shall briefly describe those query semantics and data properties in Section 3.1 and present a set of primitive time-alignment operations in Section 3.2. Their formal descriptions and applications are given in [17].

3.1 Semantic Information Useful for Defining Time-alignment Operations

(1) *AND, OR* and *NOT*

Temporal queries often specify some logical properties that exist among the object instances of different classes. A logical-AND condition specifies that some data properties or associations have to co-exist. For example, the query "engineers who participated in some projects while working for some departments" has the AND semantics. In this case, the intervals in the time-line for engineer-project associations have to be "intersect-merged" with those of the time-line for engineer-department associations in such a way that the new time-line will contain intervals for the different combinations of these two types of associations. A logical-OR condition specifies that either this data property or the other exists. For example, the query "Engineers who either participated in some projects or worked for some departments." has the OR semantics. In this case, their time-lines should be "union-merged" to produce a time-line that is different from the AND condition. A NOT condition specifies the absence of some data properties or associations. For example, the query "engineers who participated in projects but did not work in some departments" has the NOT semantics. In this case, their time-lines should be "difference-merged" to produce a time-lime which is again different from those produced by AND and OR conditions. The corresponding time-alignment operations are defined as *Intersect-merge* ($\sqcap$), *Union-merge* ($\sqcup$) and *Difference-merge* ($\ominus$), respectively.

(2) *ANY* and *GREATER/LESS-THAN*

A query may express an interest in verifying the existence of a data or association condition but is not interested in the specific data value or associated objects. For example, the query "Find the specialties of engineers when they were working for (any) departments during T[0,n]." possesses this semantics. In this query, the issuer is interested in the specialties of engineers but not in the changes of their departments as long as they worked for some departments. As shown in Figure 3, all the intervals of "en2–dept" {[10,24]en2d1, [25,n]en2d2} satisfy the *ANY* condition. Thus, the adjacent intervals of *en2* can be coalesced into a single interval {[10,n]en2} when they are used for processing against other time-lines. We note here that the coalition of time intervals in a very large temporal databas can result in a tremendous time-saving since much less temporal data can be further processed. Also, data selection conditions such as "greater than" and "less than" in temporal queries can be interpreted in a similar way. The above time-alignment operation is defined as *Coalition with Different Data* (denoted by "⌢").

(3) Data Semantics on Object Association

The semantic properties known as cardinality mapping between object classes (i.e., *One-to-One, One-to-Many, Many-to-One and Many-to-Many*) can also be used to determine the definition of another time-alignment operation called *Coalition with Identical Data* (denoted by "⌢"). The main idea is to use the cardinality mappings captured as constraints in a schema to determine if the adjacent intervals of instances (or their associations with other instances) have identical data. This time-alignment operation applies when an object in a class has associations with more than one object in another class (i.e., One-to-Many association) and multiple objects in a class have association with multiple objects in another class (i.e., Many-to-Many association). For example, "a department can have more than one engineers but an engineer can only belong to a single department", and "more than one project can be associated with more than one work_on status and vise versa". As shown in the TOG of Figure 3, the former constraint causes the adjacent intervals of $d1$ to have identical association data (i.e., [5,9]d1-en1 and [10,24]d1-en1). In the same way, the latter causes the adjacent intervals of $w1$ to have identical association data (i.e., {[0,12]w1-pj1, [13,n]w1-pj1}, and the adjacent intervals of $pj1$ to have identical association data (i.e., {[0,14]pj1-w1, [15,n]pj1-w1}). Therefore, when they are processed, they can be coalesced into {[5,24]d1-en1}, {[0,n]w1-pj1} and {[0,n]pj1-w1}, respectively. The coalesced intervals significantly simplify any further processing.

3.2 Primitive Time-alignment Operations

Figure 5 shows two operand time-lines A and B, and the results of the time-alignment operations. Alphas, betas and gammas represent the valid intervals of time-line A, time-line B and the resulting time-line, respectively. The shaded segments represent the time intervals in which no data is valid or whose data value does not satisfy the search conditions of the query. Also, they can result from the null-intervals of other time-lines during the course of time-alignment operations.

(1) *Intersect-merge* ($\sqcap$), as illustrated in Figure 5(a), identifies the time intervals which are valid in both operand time-lines. Therefore, it implements a temporal logical-AND semantics specified in a temporal query, reflecting the evolution details of both time-lines.

(2) *Union-merge* ($\sqcup$), as illustrated in Figure 5(b), identifies the time intervals which are valid in either one operand time-line or the other, or both. Therefore, this operation implements a temporal logical-OR semantics specified in a temporal query.

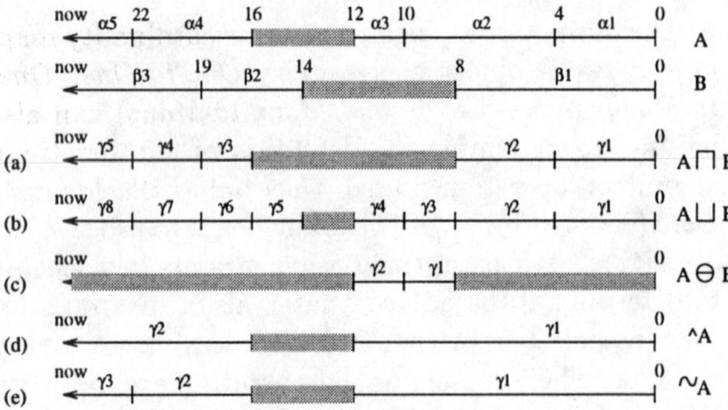

(a)
(b)
(c)
(d)
(e)

Figure 5: Operand Time-lines and Results of Time-alignment Operations

(3) *Difference-merge* ($\ominus$), as shown in Figure 5(c), identifies the valid time intervals of the first operand time-line which are not valid in the second. It implements the semantics of temporal logical-NOT (i.e., the intervals in which object instances are *not* associated).

(4) *Coalition with Different Data* (^) is a unary time-alignment operation which coalesces the adjacent valid intervals on a single time-line during which different data satisfy some selection condition (e.g., "salary greater than 40K"). The coalesced interval(s) can then be further processed against other time-lines. By doing so, the number of valid intervals to be manipulated can be minimized. For example, Figure 5(d) shows coalitions of the adjacent valid intervals on the time-line A supposing all the valid intervals on A satisfy a query condition.

(5) *Coalition with Identical Data* (~) is a unary time-alignment operation which coalesces the adjacent valid intervals on a single time-line whose data (either association data or descriptive data) are identical. By coalescing them, the number of valid intervals to be manipulated in the course of query processing can be significantly reduced. For example in Figure 5(e), α_1, α_2 and α_3 (assuming they have an identical data as noted) are coalesced into a single interval γ_1. In addition, the combined properties of the primitive time-alignment operations, such as $^\wedge A \sqcap {^\wedge}B$, $^\wedge A \sqcup B$, $^\wedge A \sqcap {^\sim}B$, etc., can be used as the underlying constructs for implementing a temporal query processor.

These time-alignment operations implement different query semantics and produce different amounts of temporal instances. A temporal query processor should choose the proper time-alignment operations to minimize the amount of data to be generated and manipulated during the course of temporal query pro-

cessing. Therefore, they are useful for query optimization.

4 Parallel Temporal Query Processing Strategies

We present two different parallel processing strategies: *Temporal Pattern-identification* and *Temporal Pattern-passing*, which are applicable to tree-structured queries. Cyclic queries can be processed by a modified Temporal Pattern-passing Strategy, which is not presented in this paper. The first strategy is a temporal extension of our previous work [32, 36]. The second one is new.

4.1 Architecture and Data Organization

A client-server architecture is used to implement the temporal query processor as shown in Figure 6. The server operates on a master-slave mode. In parallel query processing, a query is translated by a query translator of the master processor into its internal representation which is then given to all the slave processors that store and process the object classes referenced by the query. These processors will carry out one of the parallel algorithms described in the next two subsections to identify the objects which satisfy the query conditions and perform system- or user-defined operations on them. The asynchronous, shared-nothing processors are interconnected through internode communication channels.

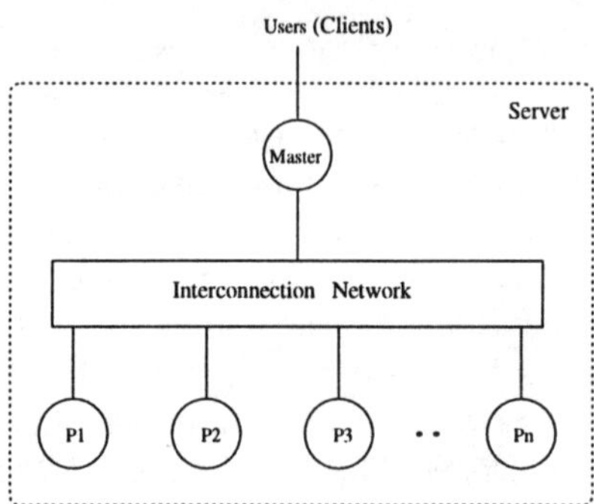

Figure 6: Client-server Model

We use a class-per-node class-to-processor mapping strategy and a vertical data partitioning scheme to distribute data among processor nodes. Instances and methods of a class are stored in one and only one node. More than one class can reside in a node. Instances of a class are vertically partitioned. Each partition stores TIIDs of the temporal instances of the class and their corresponding lists of TIIDs which identify the associated instances of an adjacent class. In each class, there are as many partitions as the number of adjacent classes. Figure 7 illustrates the data structure which bi-directionally interconnects five object classes: Employee, Engineer, Dept, Work_On, and Project, which are stored in the logical nodes E, EN, D, W and Pj, respectively.

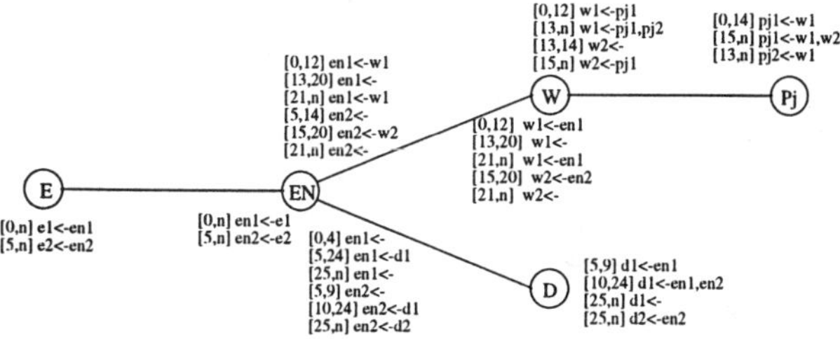

Figure 7: Data Structure of Five Associated Classes

This data structure can be viewed as pre-computed joins or join-indices in relational databases [2, 37]. Data manipulation and the execution of methods (user-defined operations) can be localized in a processing node and bi-directional traversals of temporal instances can be achieved by propagating TIIDs among processing nodes with little communication overhead. Also, the vertical partitioning scheme provides a good data distribution for processing multiple queries issued by different applications in parallel (i.e., interquery parallelism) since these queries may access different classes and different attributes (or instance associations) of a class. However, the class-per-node mapping strategy can create the data skew problem. In a separate study [34], we use a hybrid data partitioning scheme in which instances of a class are horizontally and vertically partitioned and stored in multiple processors.

4.2 Temporal Pattern-identification Strategy

We use the following query example and the data structure shown in Figure 7 to describe this processing strategy.

Q2: Find the employees who, as engineers, participated in some project while belonging to some departments.

As shown in Figure 8, the above query specifies that the Engineer class has an AND branch to classes Project and Dept. Since no time interval is specified in the query, time interval [0,n] is implied. In this parallel processing strategy, query processing starts simultaneously from all the terminal nodes (i.e., E, D and Pj in Figure 7), each of which identifies their object

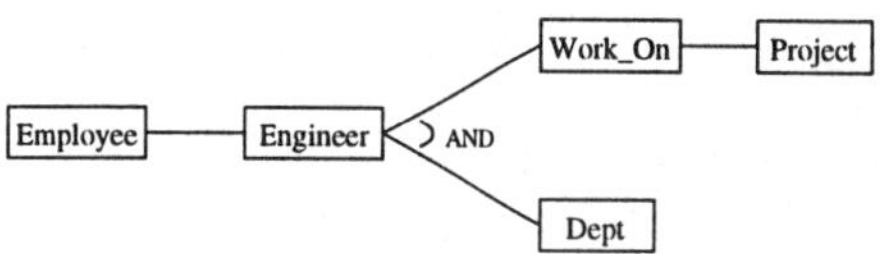

Figure 8: Query Graph of Q2

instances that satisfy their local selection conditions (if given in a query). From its local data structure, each processor finds the instances of its neighboring class that are associated with the selected instances and propagates their TIIDs to its neighbor. Upon receiving the TIIDs, the neighbor does its processing and selects and passes the proper TIIDs to the neighbor's neighbor. Thus, a wavefront of TIIDs would propagate from a terminal node toward all other terminal nodes. Multiple wavefronts initiating from all terminal nodes go across one another asynchronously. The algorithm terminates after all terminal nodes have received and processed all the wavefronts. The above procedure constitutes the first phase (i.e., pattern-search phase) of a two-phase processing strategy. At the end of the first phase, every class (or processing node) has identified a set of local TIIDs that satisfy the temporal association pattern of the query. The results in all the involved processors form a *temporal subdatabase* which is then processed in the second phase (i.e., data-collection or data-operation phase) by the object operation(s) specified in the query. We show the procedure of the first phase by describing the behaviors of terminal and nonterminal classes.

Suppose a class **C** has i edges in the Query Graph and the processing node which contains the temporal instances of class **C** is called P_C.

If **C** is a terminal class;

1. P_C propagates a wavefront of TIIDs to its neighbor;

2. when P_C receives a wavefront from its only neighbor, it will identify the local TIIDs that are connected to the TIIDs of the incoming wavefront by a proper time-alignment operation (e.g., $A \sqcap B$ or $\hat{A} \sqcap \hat{B}$) and, then, terminate.

If **C** is a nonterminal class;

1. if P_C has received less than $(i-1)$ wavefronts from its i neighboring classes, it will wait for more to arrive (this is due to the AND branch assumed [4]);

---

[4] A slightly different procedure in nonterminal classes can be used for queries with OR branches.

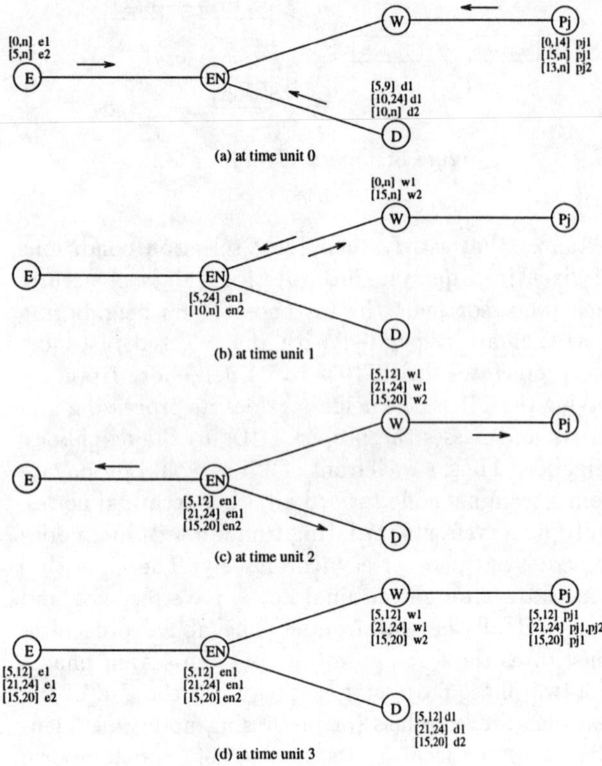

Figure 9: Temporal Pattern-identification Strategy

2. upon the arrival of each incoming wavefront, it will identify the local TIIDs that are connected to the TIIDs of the incoming wavefront by a time-alignment operation (e.g., $A \sqcap B$ or $\hat{A} \sqcap \hat{B}$). The intermediate result will be time-aligned with the previous intermediate result by an appropriate time-alignment operation (according to the temporal semantics specified in the query) to produce a new intermediate result;

3. when P_C receives the $(i-1)$th wavefront, it will repeat the same sequence of operations as above and propagate the $(i-1)$th intermediate result to the only remaining (i.e., i-th) neighboring class;

4. when P_C receives the i-th wavefront, it will repeat the same sequence of operations as above, propagate the final result to all classes except the sender of the i-th wavefront and, then, terminate.

Figure 9 illustrates the above procedure used in processing Q2. Once the temporal instances that satisfy the query have been identified, the second phase starts and the database operations (system-/user-defined operations) are performed on the selected temporal instances using the appropriate methods. Since the temporal instances have been identified locally at each node, if an operation involves only a single class, the operation can be carried out in a straightforward fashion. However, if an operation requires data from multiple classes, such as a multi-class retrieval operation, the second phase would need another class-traversal procedure for reconstructing the temporal association patterns desired by the user. This is because processors only mark the instances but do not retain their relationships in the first phase. We show this second phase by describing the node behaviors of a *result-collecting* processor and *data-passing* processors below.

If P_C is a data-passing processor;

1. if **C** is a terminal class, P_C propagates a wavefront of TIIDs and their requested descriptive data to its neighbor;

2. if **C** is a nonterminal class, P_C will wait for $(i-1)$ wavefront to arrive, perform an *Intersect-merge* alignment operation (i.e., $A \sqcap B$) between the descriptive data of the matching TIIDs, and propagate the final result to the neighboring data-passing processor (if any) toward the result-collecting processor.

If P_C is the result-collecting processor;

1. P_C will wait for i wavefronts from all of its neighbors, perform an *Intersect-merge* alignment operation (i.e., $A \sqcap B$) between the descriptive data of the matching TIIDs, and present the final result to the user.

Although some degree of I/O parallelism can be achieved by the parallel retrieval of the data block(s) from the involved processors, the sequential nature of this pattern reconstruction process can be time-consuming. We present another parallel processing strategy.

4.3 Temporal Pattern-passing Strategy

The main idea of this strategy is to preserve and propagate the temporal association information in the first phase and, hence, avoid the need for reconstructing temporal association patterns in the second phase. We show the procedure by describing the behaviors of terminal and nonterminal nodes below.

If **C** is a terminal class;

1. P_C propagates a wavefront of TIIDs to its neighbor;

2. when P_C receives a wavefront of temporal association patterns each of which is formed by a concatenation of associated TIIDs from its only neighbor, it will concatenate the local TIIDs that are associated with the incoming temporal patterns by an *Intersect-merge* alignment operation (i.e., $A \sqcap B$) and, then, terminate.

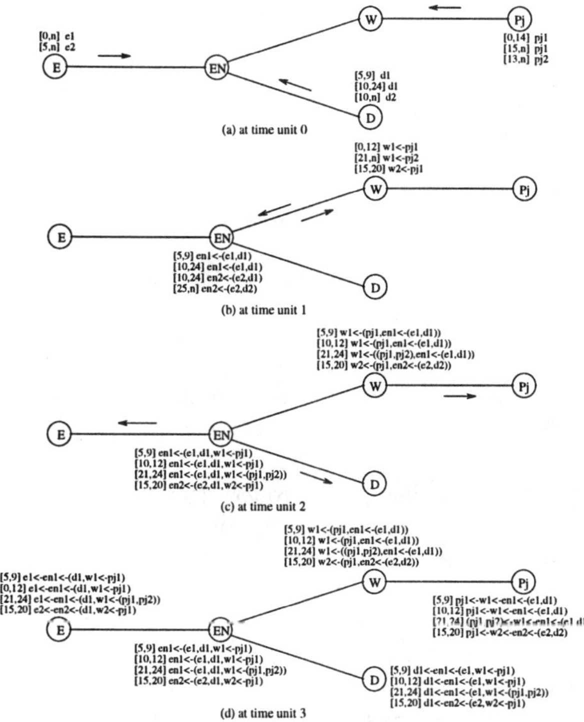

Figure 10: Temporal Pattern-passing Strategy

If **C** is a nonterminal class;

1. if P_C has received less than $(i-1)$ wavefronts from its i neighbors, it will wait for more to arrive;

2. upon the arrival of each incoming wavefront, it will concatenate the local TIIDs with the incoming patterns by an *Intersect-merge* (i.e., $A \sqcap B$) alignment operation. The intermediate result will be time-aligned and concatenated with the previous intermediate result by an *Intersect-merge* alignment operation (i.e., $A \sqcap B$) to produce a new intermediate result;

3. when P_C receives the $(i-1)$th wavefront, it will perform the same sequence of operations as above and propagate the $(i-1)$th intermediate result to the only remaining neighbor from which it has not received a wavefront;

4. when P_C receives the i-th wavefront, it will perform the same sequence of operations as above, propagate the final result to all the neighbor processors except the sender of the i-th wavefront and, then, terminate.

Figure 10 shows the above procedure used in processing Q2. Since every processor has the entire set of temporal association patterns which satisfy the intensional pattern of the query, the second phase becomes very simple. Each class sends its portion of the requested data to the pre-designated result-collecting processor, where the resulting data are assembled. Although message-tokens need to carry more information to propagate the association patterns to the neighboring processors, the processing and transmission overhead is negligible. This is because the temporal association patterns are strings of IIDs (typically, an IID is 8-bytes long). Their sizes are generally very small compared with the size of the message-token. The Temporal Pattern-passing Strategy is efficient for multi-class retrieval queries, since re-traversals of object instances are avoided and only the relevant data are transmitted in the second phase. It is particularly so when the diameter of the query (i.e., the longest path between any two classes in a query graph) is large. A performance evaluation based on this parameter is given in the next section.

5 Performance Evaluation

In this section, we present some results of a performance evaluation of a temporal query processor which we have implemented on an nCUBE2 parallel computer. nCUBE2 is a scalable hypercube-connected multiprocessor system. Each node operates at 2.5 Mflops and runs an independent copy of operating system (called nCX). Its asynchronous, shared-nothing processing nodes communicate by message-passing. A program can be launched onto a subcube of processing nodes (for example, we have used a cube of 8 processors out of 64). The system has a client-server architecture and, further, supports a multiple-server feature. A server contains a copy of our distributed temporal query processor (TQP) and communicates with others by message-passing. The TQP can operate in a mtulti-query mode in which the processor can start processing the next query sent by the client as soon as its role in the processing of the current query is completed. The client takes multi-user queries as the input and submits them in batches. The output is query processing tasks to be sent to the TQP servers in a set of message queues.

We use the 8-class schema shown in Figure 1 as our

test database, in which each class has 100,000 temporal instances (i.e., 10,000 object instances each of which has an average of 10 evolutions). Our evaluation assumes an object selectivity factor of 0.2 and a time-interval selectivity factor of 0.5, so that a temporal database with 10,000 temporal instances per class (i.e., 2,000 object instances each of which has an average of 5 evolutions) is retrieved from the secondary storage into main memory for pattern evaluation. We have evaluated the temporal query procesor over a variety of performace parameters using a set of benchmark queries. In this paper, we present the following evaluation results obtained by varying some selected parallel processing parameters: (1) the performance of intraquery parallelism over different degrees of class distribution, (2) the performance of interquery parallelism (i.e., parallelism in multiple query processing) over different degrees of class-overlap between two queries, and (3) the relative efficiency of the Temporal Pattern-identification Strategy and the Temporal Pattern-passing Strategy using different query diameters in retrieval operations. The total response time measured in this experiment consists of the I/O time, processing time, and communication time.

First, we examine the intraquery parallelism of the system. We use an 8-class benchmark query as shown in Figure 11.

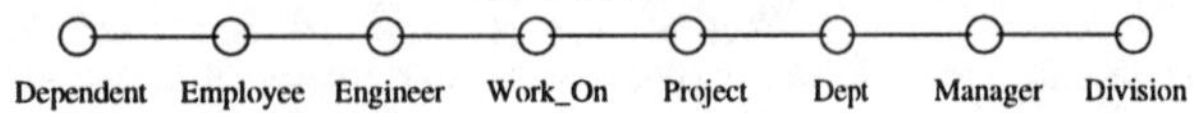

Figure 11: Benchmark Query for Evaluating Intraquery Parallelism

In this experiment, we initially assign all eight classes to a single processing node and, then, we increase the number of processing nodes from 1 to 8 and assign the eight classes to these nodes as evenly as possible, i.e., 4-4, 3-3-2, 2-2-2-2, and so forth. Figure 12 shows the evaluation result. From the curve, it is clear that the change in the response time over the number of processing nodes is not linear. This is because the total response time is determined by the processing node which completes its task last. For example, when the number of processing nodes is increased from 4 to 7, it is seen that there is not much change in the response time. This is because the maximum number of classes held by a processing node remains 2. Thus, it can be concluded that the processing node that has the largest number of classes dictates the response time when the number of classes per processing node is not uniform. The Temporal

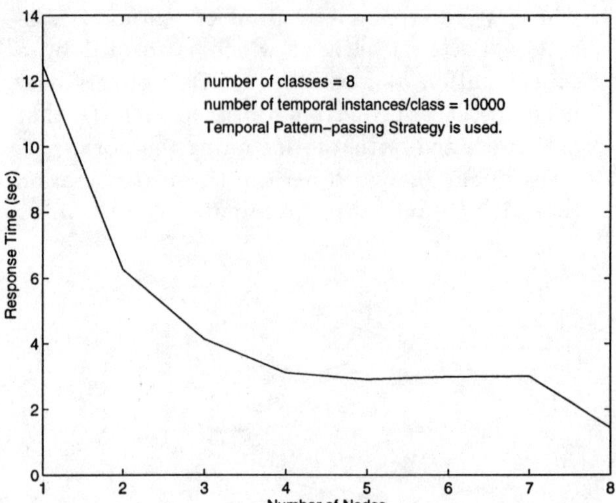

Figure 12: Intraquery Parallelism: Response-time vs. Number-of-node

Pattern-passing Strategy is used in this experiment (the Temporal Pattern-identification Strategy shows a similar result).

Next, we examine the interquery parallelism. In a multi-user database environment, multiple queries can be issued at the same time and contend for accesses to the classes that are common to them. The parallel query processing strategies, the data structure, and the data distribution scheme used in this work allow multiple queries to be processed concurrently. Intuitively, the concurrency between two queries would depend on the number of classes (or processors) that are common to the queries. To study this effect, a performance parameter "degree-of-overlap" has been defined as the ratio of the number of classes common in both queries to the number of classes accessed by both queries. The degree-of-overlap varies between 0 and 1. In this experiment, we have used two benchmark queries each accessing four classes. Figure 13 shows

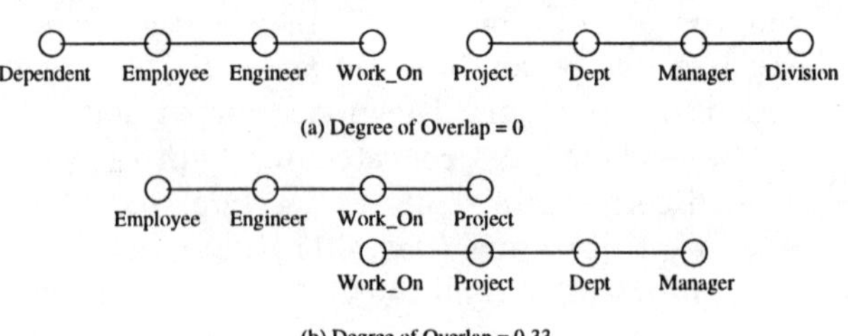

Figure 13: Benchmark Queries for Evaluating Interquery Parallelism

two example sets of benchmark queries with two different values of the degree-of-overlap. In Figure 13(b), for example, the classes common to both queries are {Work_On, Project} and the set of classes accessed by both queries is {Employee, Engineer, Work_On, Project, Dept, Manager}. Thus, the degree-of-overlap is 2/6 or 0.33. Figure 14 shows the result of a performance evaluation on the interquery parallelism.

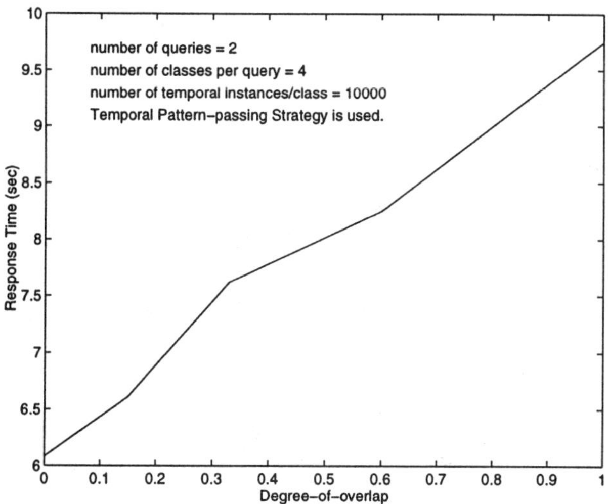

Figure 14: Interquery Parallelism: Response-time vs. Degree-of-overlap

When the degree-of-overlap is 0 (i.e., queries access two totally different sets of classes), the response time is 6.08 seconds. When the degree-of-overlap is 1 (i.e., the same query is issued twice), the response time is 9.75 seconds. This shows a considerable improvement in throughput with interquery parallelism. Since a longer response time indicates a lower degree of concurrency, we can conclude that the concurrency is inversely proportional to the degree-of-overlap.

We note that the above evaluation result also demonstrates a further improvement in the interquery parallelism when multiple queries involve partially or fully overlapping sets of classes. For example, when the degree-of-overlap is 1, the response time (i.e., 9.75 seconds) is less than two times 6.08 seconds (i.e., 12.16 seconds) which is approximately the amount of time for processing a single query. This is because the tasks of all the processors involved in a query are not likely to be completed at the same time and, therefore, the nodes that finish earlier have been assigned to start the processing of the next query to improve the degree of parallelism.

Lastly, we evaluate the performance of the two parallel processing strategies in data retrieval operations. As discussed in Section 4, the advantage of the Temporal Pattern-passing Strategy is the simplified data-collection process in the second phase of the two-phase processing strategy. Intuitively, it can be seen that the advantage will become more pronounced as the retrieval-diameter for a retrieval operation becomes larger. The retrieval-diameter is the distance of two most distant processing nodes which are involved in the retrieval operation. This parameter can be best understood with the graphical representation of a query example.

Q3: List the div#, work-status, and salary of the engineers who worked on the projects of the same division during T[5,25].

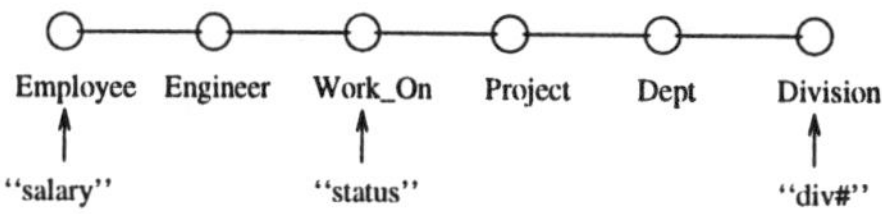

Figure 15: Illustration of the Retrieval-diameter of Q3

This is a linear query with 6 classes. Since the data retrieval operation involves three classes and Employee and Division are farthest apart, the retrieval-diameter of this query is 5. In this experiment, we vary the query diameter from 0 to 5. Figure 16 shows the re-

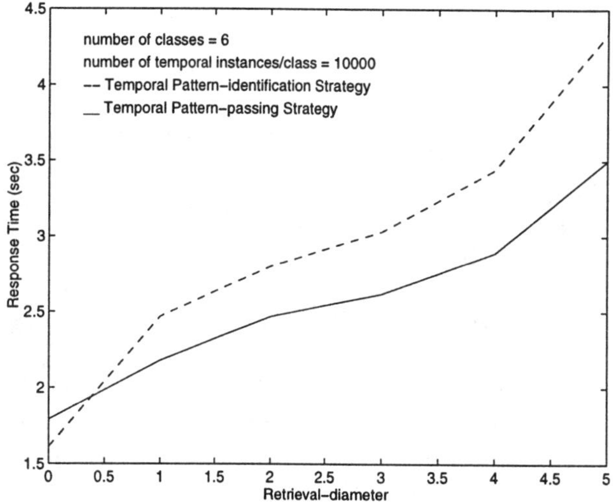

Figure 16: Comparison of Two Strategies: Response-time vs. Retrieval-diameter

sult of a performance comparison between the two processing strategies over different retrieval-diameters. It is seen that when the diameter is 0, the Temporal Pattern-passing Strategy has a longer response time than the Temporal Pattern-identification Strategy.

This is because no internode traversal process is involved in the second phase of both strategies. However, the slightly longer response time of the latter strategy is due to the larger amount of information propagated in the pattern-search operation of the first phase of query processing. As the query diameter increases, the data-collection process of the Temporal Pattern-identification Strategy takes a longer time. The Temporal Pattern-passing Strategy, on the other hand, shows only a slight increase in response time as the retrieval-diameter increases.

6 Conclusion

OO database management systems and their underlying OO models possess many desirable features that are required for modeling and processing complex objects found in a wide range of database applications. However, due to the generality and high functionality of these systems, the performance of large OO temporal databases is often limited by the sequential nature of conventional computer systems. Moreover, the excessive amount of historical data coupled with the irregular and complex evolutions of data objects makes it very difficult to achieve the needed efficiency in processing large temporal databases. With the increasing availability of commercial multiprocessor systems which offer a better price-performance than centralized systems, parallel temporal query processing is a promising alternative.

In this paper, we have discussed two different temporal data organizations (instance and attribute timestamping) and pointed out that both organizations need time-alignment operations during query processing. We then presented a set of time-alignment operations which can serve as the primitive temporal processing constructs for implementing different query semantics. Two parallel temporal query processing strategies were then presented. They aim to maximize the system throughput by minimizing the amount of data to be manipulated by using the proper alignment operations as well as interquery parallelism and intraquery parallelism techniques. A performance evaluation has been carried out on an nCUBE2 parallel computer to study intraquery parallelism, interquery parallelism (in multiple query processing), and relative efficiency of the two multi-wavefront strategies using a set of benchmark queries. The evaluation result shows that the intra-query parallelism can be better achieved when related classes are assigned to adjacent nodes. The interquery parallelism can be further enhanced when multiple queries access data in different processing nodes. Also, it is suggested that the Temporal Pattern-passing Strategy outperforms the Temporal Pattern-identification Strategy for multi-class retrieval operations. However, the Temporal Pattern-identification Strategy performs slightly better for single-class retrieval operations.

References

[1] W. Alexander and G. Copeland, "Process and Dataflow Control in Distributed Data-intensive Systems," *Proc. ACM SIGMOD Int'l Conf. on Management of Data*, Chicago, IL, pp. 90-98, June 1988.

[2] L. Bic and R.L. Hartmann, "AGM: A Dataflow Database Machine," *ACM Trans. on Database Systems*, Vol.14, No.1, March 1989, pp.114-146.

[3] U.S. Chakravarthy and J. Minker, "Multiple Query Processing in Deductive Databases Using Query Graphs," *Proc. Int'l Conf. on VLDB*, Kyoto, Japan, August 1986, pp.384-391.

[4] H.H.M. Chen, "Temporal Knowledge Base Management: Model, Query Language, Algebra and Implementation Techniques," *Ph.D. Dissertation*, Database Systems Research and Development Center, University of Florida, 1993.

[5] Y.H. Chen and S.Y.W. Su, "Identification- and Elimination-based Parallel Query Processing Techniques for Object-oriented Databases," To appear in *IEEE Journal of Parallel and Distributed Computing*, (paper accepted in 1994).

[6] T.S. Cheng and S.K. Gadia, "An Object-oriented model for Temporal Databases," *Proc. Int'l Workshop on an Infrastructure for Temporal Databases*, R. Snodgrass (Ed.), Arlington, Texas, June 1993, pp. N1-19.

[7] J. Clifford and A. Tansel, "On an Algebra for Historical Relational Databases," *Proc. ACM SIGMOD Int'l Conf. on Management of Data*, Austin, Texas, 1985, pp. 247-265.

[8] J. Clifford and A. Croker, "The Historical Relational Data Model (HRDM) and Algebra based on Lifespans," *Proc. IEEE Int'l Conf. on Data Engineering*, Los Angeles, California, 1987, pp. 528-537.

[9] U. Dayal, "Queries and Views in an Object-oriented Data model," *Proc. Int'l Workshop on Database Programming Languages*, 1989.

[10] U. Dayal and G.T.J. Wuu, "A Uniform Approach to processing Temporal Queries," *Proc. Int'l Conf. on VLDB*, British Columbia, Canada, 1992, pp. 407-418.

[11] D.J. DeWitt, S. Ghandeharizadeh, D.A. Schneider, A. Bricker, H.I. Hsiao and R. Rasmussen, "The GAMMA Database Machine Project," *IEEE TKDE*, Vol. 2, No. 1, March 1990, pp. 44-62.

[12] R. Elmasri and G.T.J. Wuu, "A Temporal Model and Query Language for ER Databases," *Proc. IEEE Int'l Conf. on Data Engineering*, Los Angeles, California, February 1990, pp. 76-83.

[13] S.K. Gadia, "A Homogeneous Relational Model and Query Languages for Temporal Databases," *ACM TODS*, Vol. 13, No. 4, 1988, pp. 418-448.

[14] S.K. Gadia and G. Bhargava, "SQL-like Seamless Query of Temporal Data," *Proc. Int'l Workshop on an Infrastructure for Temporal Databases*, R. Snodgrass (Ed.), Arlington, Texas, June 1993, pp. P1-31.

[15] I.A. Goralwalla and M.T. Ozsu, "Temporal extensions to a Uniform behavioral Object Model," *Proc. Int'l Workshop on an Infrastructure for Temporal Databases*, R. Snodgrass (Ed.), Arlington, Texas, June 1993, pp. Z1-10.

[16] G. Graefe, "Encapsulation of Parallelism in the Volcano Query Processing System," *Proc. ACM SIGMOD Int'l Conf. on Management of Data*, Atlantic City, New Jersey, June 1990, pp. 102-111.

[17] S.J. Hyun, "Object-oriented Temporal Database Management: Algebra, Time-alignment Operations and Parallel Query Processing," *Ph.D. Dissertation*, Database Systems Research and Development Center, University of Florida, May 1995.

[18] W. Käfer, "Temporal Selection, Temporal Projection, and Temporal Join Revised," *Proc. Int'l Workshop on an Infrastructure for Temporal Databases*, R. Snodgrass (Ed.), Arlington, Texas, June 1993, pp. U1-20.

[19] S. Karimi, M. Bassiouni and A. Orooji, "Supporting Temporal Capabilities in a Multi-computer Database System," *Proc. Int'l Conf. on Databases, Parallel Architectures, and Their Applications*, Miami Beach, Florida, March 1990, pp. 20-26.

[20] M. Kitsuregawa, H. Tanaka and T. Moto-oka, "Architecture and performance of Relational Algebra Machine GRACE," *Proc. Int'l Conf. on Parallel Processing*, Bellaire, MI, August 1984, pp. 241-250.

[21] H. Lam, C. Lee and S.Y.W. Su, "An Object Flow Computer for Database Applications," *Proc. Int'l Workshop on Database Machines*, Deauville, France, June 1989.

[22] T.Y. Leung and R. Muntz, "Temporal Query Processing and Optimization in Multiprocessor Database Machines," *Proc. Int'l Conf. on VLDB* Vancouver, Canada, 1992, pp. 383-394.

[23] N.A. Lorenitzos and R.G. Johnson, "Extending Relational Algebra to Manipulate Temporal Data. *Information Systems*, Vol.13, 1988, pp. 289-296.

[24] V. Lum, P. Dadam, R. Erbe, J. Guenagur, P. Pistor, G. Walch, H. Werner and J. Woodfill, "Designing DBMS Support for the Temporal Dimension," *Proc. ACM SIGMOD Int'l Conf. on Management of Data*, Boston, Massachusetts, June 1984, pp.115-130.

[25] S. Navathe and R. Ahmed, "A Temporal Relational Model and a Query Language," *Journal of Information Science*, Vol. 48, 1989, pp. 57-73.

[26] E. Rose and A. Segev, "TOODM–A Temporal Object-oriented Data Model with Temporal Constraints," *Proc. Int'l Conf. on the ER Approach*, 1991, pp. 205-229.

[27] E. Rose and A. Segev, "TOOA: A Temporal Object-oriented Algebra," *Proc. European Conf. on OO Programming*, Kaiserslautern, Germany, July 1993, pp. 202-229.

[28] A. Segev and A. Shoshani, "A Temporal Data Model based on Time Sequence," Chap. 11, In *Temporal Databases: Theory, Design, and Implementation*, A. Tansel, J. Clifford, S. Gadia, S. Jajodia, A. Segev and R. Snodgrass (Eds.), Benjamin/Cummings Pub. Co., 1993.

[29] R. Snodgrass and I. Ahn, "A Taxonomy of Time in Database," *Proc. ACM SIGMOD Int'l Conf. on Management of Data*, Austin, Texas, 1985, pp. 236-246.

[30] R. Snodgrass, "The Temporal Query Language TQuel," *ACM TODS*, Vol. 12, No. 2, 1987, pp. 247-297.

[31] S.Y.W. Su and H.H.M. Chen, "A Temporal Knowledge Representation Model OSAM*/T and its Query Language OQL/T," *Proc. Int'l Conf. on VLDB*, Barcelona, Spain, September, 1991, pp.431-442.

[32] S.Y.W. Su, Y.H. Chen and H. Lam, "Multiple Wavefront Algorithms for Pattern-based Processing of Object-oriented databases," *Proc. Int'l Conf. on Parallel and Distributed Information Systems (PDIS)*, Miami, Florida, December 1991.

[33] S.Y.W. Su and H.H.M. Chen, "Modeling and Management of Temporal Data in Object-oriented knowledge Bases," *Proc. Int'l Workshop on an Infrastructure for Temporal Databases*, R. Snodgrass (Ed.), Arlington, Texas, June 1993, pp. HH1-18.

[34] S.Y.W. Su, Y. Huang and N. Akaboshi, "Graph-based Parallel Query Processing and Optimization in Object-oriented databases," *Final Report to Fujitsu Ltd. Co., Japan*, January 1996.

[35] A.U. Tansel, "Adding time dimension to relational Model and Extending Relational Algebra," *Information Systems*, Vol. 11, 1986, pp. 343-355.

[36] A.K. Thakore, S.Y.W. Su, H. Lam and D.G. Shea, "Asynchronous Parallel Processing of Object Bases Using Multiple Wavefronts," *Proc. Int'l Conf. on Parallel Processing*, Chicago, Illinois, August 1990, pp.127-135.

[37] P. Valduriez, "Join Indicies," *ACM TODS*, Vol. 12, June 1987, pp.218-246.

[38] G. Wuu and U. Dayal, "A Uniform Model for Temporal Object-oriented Databases," *Proc. IEEE Int'l Conf. on Data Engineering*, February 1992, pp. 584-593.

Industrial Session 6B

Availability and Replications

OnLine XPS for Highly Available, High-Volume, Complex OLTP
F. Symonds

Parallel Propagation of Updates for Asynchronous Replication
A. Demers

Session 7A

Transactions and Data Consistency

Extending TP–Monitors for Intra-Transaction Parallelism

H. Kaufmann and H.-J. Schek
Swiss Federal Institute of Technology (ETH Zurich)
Institute for Information Systems — Database Research Group
Zurich, Switzerland

Abstract

Inter-transaction parallelism, the concurrent execution of independent client transactions, is currently well supported by database systems. Intra-transaction parallelism, the parallel execution of operations within the same transaction, is generally not supported, even though often necessary especially in non-standard applications. In this paper we show how database operations within the same transaction can be executed concurrently by executing them as independent subtransactions. This is possible because we employ a two-level transaction approach where the lower level is provided by virtually any of today's databases. The higher level is realised by a transaction processing monitor that is extended with an additional transaction manager for the scheduling of application service calls. We present results of a prototype implementation using Tuxedo and a relational database system using a document management application as an example.

1   Introduction

Database systems provide support for *inter*–transaction parallelism, i.e. the concurrent execution of a large number of independent user transactions. Within each transaction, individual operations, e.g. SQL statements, are executed strictly sequentially. From a performance point of view, this is sufficient for most standard applications, where often the parameters of one operation depend on the results of a previous one. However, in non-standard applications such as document management, some or even all operations of a transaction are independent of the others and could therefore be executed in parallel for the benefit of shorter response time. Unfortunately, contemporary database systems provide no or only very limited support for this sort of parallelism, called *intra*–transaction parallelism. Note that the SQL standard so far does not allow asynchronous SQL statements unless the future SQL3 [1] standard is supported.

In this paper we present a novel architecture for a system, which allows the concurrent execution of operations, such as sequences of SQL statements, within a single user–transaction. The specialty of our approach is the fact that we use existing, commercially available technology such as parallel relational databases and an extension of existing transaction processing monitors. The extension consists of a second-level transaction manager added to the transaction processing monitor (in the following abbreviated as TP-Monitor or simply TPM). This transaction manager together with the transactions provided by the underlying database manager form a two-level transaction in the sense of [2, 3]. Therefore, the "trick" is the transformation of *intra*-transaction parallelism at the TP monitor level (i.e. at the user transaction level) into *inter*-transaction parallelism at the database level. The lower level of the system can be provided by any transaction-oriented system, e.g. Oracle, Sybase or ObjectStore. The higher level is realised by enhancing a conventional TPM, e.g. Tuxedo [4] or Encina [5], with the necessary functionality for performing locking and logging on the higher level in order to ensure the integrity of the database. Neither the system used on the lower level nor the one on the higher level must be changed in any way.

The approach we will present can be applied generally whenever user level transactions consist of steps that can be executed in parallel. We show its applicability using document management in (relational) databases as an example. We describe a prototype implementation based on alternatively Oracle and Sybase as database system, and Tuxedo as TP-Monitor. To the best of our knowledge, the idea of applying open-nested transaction management in a TP-Monitor–database environment for the parallelisation of complex transactions has not yet been proposed. Note that Encina provides support for closed-nested, but not open-nested transactions and is therefore not able to transform intra-transaction parallelism to inter-transaction parallelism directly. Work in our own group, e.g. [6, 7, 8, 9], is related: [6] presented the idea of applying multi-level transactions for text management, [7] investigated the use of a multi-level scheduler in a FDBMS environment that is able to exploit the semantics of the user operations. [8] compared the well-known 2PC and 2PL protocols used in most multi-database system to an alternative system using a multi-level transaction scheme with an additional transaction manager on the SQL level. The performance study carried out showed, that performance as well as the execution autonomy of the participating databases can be increased by using multi-level transactions. Finally, [9] investigated the possibility of exploiting intra-transaction parallelism in the process of mapping objects to relations by implementing a two-level transaction manager on top of a commercially available database system. Further related work is e.g. [10], which addressed the issue of intra-query parallelism in relational systems (see as well [11, 12]). Commercial database systems allow the evaluation of a single statement in parallel. For example, Oracle's *Parallel Query Option* decomposes an SQL statement into smaller parts that can be evaluated in parallel. Subsequently, the result sets are merged and returned to the user. Tandem's *NonStop SQL* only allows the internal parallelisation of individual statements, but not the parallel execution of statement sequences as it is possible in our approach. For document insertions parallel to retrieval operations similar directions are being investigated in [13]. Note, that document management only servers as test case to verify our approach.

Our contribution is the following:

- We evaluate the concept of two-level transactions with respect to the transformation of *inter*-transaction parallelism to *intra*-transaction parallelism.

- We show, how the existing technology of TP-Monitors and of databases can be applied for the parallel execution of complex and long-running user transactions.

- We evaluate the concept of two-level transactions with respect to the transformation of *intra*-transaction parallelism to *inter*-transaction parallelism.

- We provide extensive practical performance measurements on large collections of data with our prototype implementation.

This paper is organised as follows: In section 2, we motivate the need for intra-transaction parallelism in textual databases and point out the problems that arise when textual index structures must be maintained by database systems. In section 3, we present *TPM/ONT*, our prototype database system based on a transaction processing monitor and a commercial database system with support for the concurrent execution of operations of a transaction. Section 4 describes the necessary services we have implemented to support the handling of textual documents in TPM/ONT. A number of measurements comparing TPM/ONT with a traditional database system are presented in section 5.

2 Motivation: Dynamic Textual Database

2.1 Document Management on Top of Relational Databases

Over the past few years, the types as well as the amount of documents available in electronic form have changed to a great extent. In order to cope with this data as well as with the users' needs to file and retrieve documents concurrently, information systems capable of handling full text documents must be at hand. However, contemporary database systems (especially relational ones) do not provide any efficient built-in support for textual data. In most cases, they only provide the possibility of storing long segments of text—or any other byte sequence—in so-called BLOBs[1]. BLOBs are chunks of bytes sequences which are not interpreted by the database system. With respect to searching for documents containing certain words or phrases, "not interpreted" means that the user has to fetch every single document, inspect it for the particular words or phrases and decide if the document is a match or not. As there is no access path available, searching results in a sequential scan of one or more document collections stored in e.g. relations. This is possible for small document collections but results in unacceptable response times in cases where thousands or even millions of documents must be searched. Therefore, textual index structures must be provided.

In [14] we investigated the possibility of supporting efficient retrieval of textual documents stored in a relational database system (Oracle) by adding the well-known inverted lists [15] as textual index structures to the database and building a preprocessor on top of SQL. The inverted lists were physically modeled as a binary relation InvList(<u>Word-ID</u>, <u>Document-ID</u>) and stored in the database system. We showed that this simple access structure is powerful enough to answer certain types of boolean queries (small number of selective keywords combined with the logical AND operator) when run against a document collection of some 100'000 textual documents. Surprisingly, even when compared to a commercial database system with textual extensions (Oracle's *SQL*TextRetrieval*) or an information retrieval system *(BASISPlus)* the self-maintained inverted listed along with some simple optimisation strategies showed better results with respect to response time than their commercial counterparts. However, in [14] we only investigated the retrieval of documents. Online insertion, deletion and update of textual documents (as well as the impact of these operations on concurrent retrievers) was not considered.

In this paper, we focus on online updatability of document collections and closely examine the process of inserting documents $\{d\}$ into a database. The documents are modeled as a relation $D(a_1, a_2, \ldots, a_m, t_1, t_2, \ldots t_n)$, where every document (=tuple) d is made up of a set of standard (i.e. non-

---

[1]BLOB=<u>B</u>inary <u>L</u>arge <u>OB</u>jects

textual) attributes a_i ($0 \le i \le m$) as well as textual attributes t_j ($0 \le j \le m$). For each textual attribute t_j an inverted list $InvList_{t_j}(Word, Document\text{-}ID)$ based on the individual words of t_j is maintained[2]. In order to save secondary storage and speed up retrieval, instead of storing the ASCII representation of a word in the inverted lists (attribute *Word*), an integer representing the ASCII string is used. The mapping of the ASCII representation of words to integers is stored in an additional relation *Mapping*(*Word, Word-ID*).

Using the above schema, figure 1 presents the algorithm for inserting and indexing a textual document using pseudo SQL.

```
comment: input document
INSERT INTO D VALUES(a_1, ..., a_m, t_1, ..., t_n)
→ Document-ID
for i = 1 to n do
    set {des} = {}
    extract the individual words of t_i → {des}
    remove common words from {des} → {des}
    reduce {des} to their stems → {des}
    remove duplicates from {des} → {des}
    foreach s in {des} do
        SELECT Word-ID
        FROM Mapping WHERE Word=s
        if NOTFOUND
            generate Word-ID for s
            INSERT INTO Mapping VALUES(s, Word-ID)
        fi
        INSERT INTO InvList_{t_i}(Word-ID, Document-ID)
    od
od
```

Figure 1: Algorithm for the insertion of a document including the maintenance of the textual index structures

The indexing of a document's textual attributes t_j is carried out sequentially even though the inverted lists for different attributes t_i are stored in different relations $InvList_{t_i}$ and could therefore be updated in parallel without interfering with each other.

Further, since many users may want to manage documents in relational databases, we look for ways to provide *document services* which are made available to many clients. For this purpose, among others, transaction processing monitors have been developed.

---

[2]Common words (I, you, he, she, we, they, is, am, ...)—known as *stop words*—are not indexed. All words are reduced to their stems. Duplicates are removed.

2.2 Document Management using a TP-Monitor: Naive Approach

TP-Monitors belong to the category of *middleware products*, i.e. software components located between the clients (users) and the servers (resources like databases) to provide added functionality. In the case of TP-Monitors, this additional functionality is the ability to perform all the processing in a transactional manner, with the TP-Monitor providing tools for logging, locking, recovery, transactional RPC, transactional messaging systems, and so forth. For many, the TP-Monitor is the glue used to tie together heterogeneous data processing applications and, in some cases, it even takes on the role of a transactional operating system [16].

The execution environment of a TPM (see figure 2) comprises a *coordinator process* and a certain number of *server processes* interacting with the *resource managers*. The coordinator performs functions such as locating resources, distributing load, concurrency control, and protocol translation. The server processes act as proxies, within the TPM domain, for the actual data repositories, usually known as resource managers. Each server provides a number of *services* or predefined entry points that can be invoked to interact with the resource managers. These services are known to the coordinator, which will direct calls from the clients to the appropriate server. One of the advantages of this approach is that it is often possible to invoke a service without indicating the actual server that must provide it, allowing the coordinator both to balance the load among servers providing similar services, and to provide a higher resilience to failures.

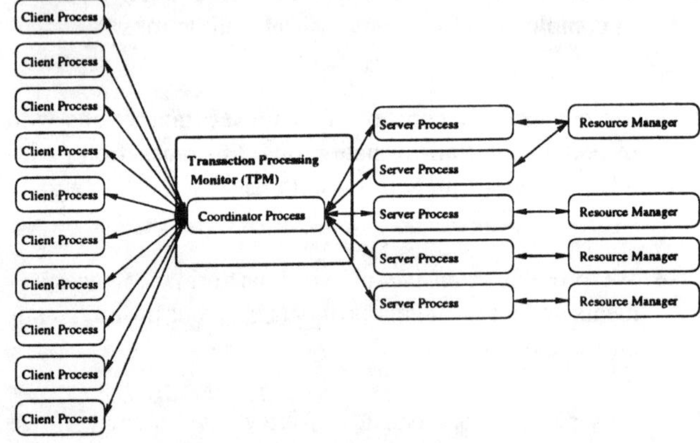

Figure 2: Transaction Processing Monitor: Architecture

For the processing of textual data, the TP monitor must provide the following services (only the services needed for the insertion of documents are listed):

- *InsertDocument:* Inserts a tuple containing textual as well as non-textual attributes into a relation and returns a document identifier.

- *ExatractIndexTerms:* Given a textual attribute, this service extracts the individual words using an attribute-specific extraction algorithms. All words are reduced to their stems and duplicates are removed, and the remaining words are mapped to integers using the *Mapping* relation. Subsequently, we will refer to these integers as the "descriptors" or "features" of a textual attribute.

  The information, which extraction algorithm and stop word list must be used for a specific attribute must be available as meta data.

- *InsertIndexTerms:* This service inserts an attribute's features (obtained using the above service) into the inverted list of this attribute.

Using a TP monitor, the client code to insert a document d is shown in figure 3. Note, that the client is only calling a number of services and is not performing any direct interaction with the database anymore. The actual work (e.g. the execution of SQL statements) is carried out by the server processes which are started at the beginning along with the coordinator process and which are kept constantly up and running.

Unfortunately, using this environment, the textual attributes t_i are still indexed sequentially. Contemporary TP

---

comment: input document
call (InsertDocument, $a_1, \ldots, t_1, \ldots, t_n$) $\rightarrow$ Document-ID
for $i = 1$ **to** n **do**
    call (ExtractIndexTerms, t_i) $\rightarrow$ features
    call (InsertIndexTerms, features, Document-ID)
od

Figure 3: Insertion of a textual document using a transaction processing monitor

---

monitors, like Tuxedo, provide the possibility of calling services asynchronously. Concurrent asynchronous service calls of the same user transaction are executed in parallel, if the servers executing these services are connected to different resource managers. However, if they are connected to the same resource manager, the service calls for this resource manager must be sequentialised and executed one at the time as contemporary databases, such as Oracle or Sybase, cannot execute concurrent services on behalf of the same user transaction.

In the following section we present an extension to TP-Monitors that allows the concurrent execution of services within a single user transaction.

3 TPM/ONT: A Transaction Processing Monitor with Support for Open Nested Transactions

Our approach is based on open nested transactions [3]. The nesting depth is two. The lower level is provided by the already-existing resource managers, e.g. Oracle or Sybase. The higher level is implemented using a conventional TP-Monitor, e.g. Tuxedo, which provides a number of additional services that guarantee the correct execution of the user-transactions as open nested transactions.

Figure 4 shows the overall architecture of a two-level database system called *TPM/ONT*, which stands for Transaction Processsing Monitor with Support for Open Nested Transactions. Externally, the interfaces of TPM/ONT do not differ from a traditional TPM as shown in figure 2.

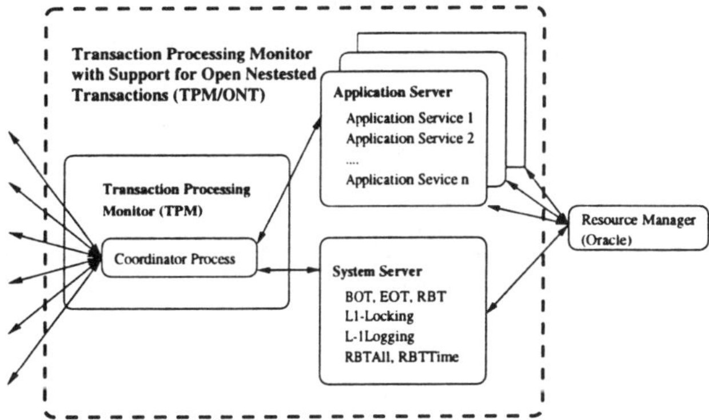

Figure 4: Transaction Processing Monitor with Support for Open Nested Transactions (TPM/ONT)

The main difference between a conventional TPM and TPM/ONT is the way user transactions are executed. In a traditional TPM environment, a user transaction consists of a *begin of transaction* call, the execution of a number of services, followed by an *end of transaction* call. All of these operations are executed using a *single* transaction of the underlying resource manager.

Contrary to this, in TPM/ONT each service called by the user (subsequently called *application service*) is executed as an individual transaction of the underlying resource manager (called *resource manager transaction, RMT*). The advantage of this is that these services can be called asynchronously and executed in parallel. Of course, the unrestricted execution of applications services as independent resource manager transactions would result in the violation of the *atomicity* and *isolation* principles: If a user transaction fails, one or more service calls have already been terminated and are committed on the resource level. Changes cannot be undone anymore. Atomicity is violated from a user transaction point of view. As soon as a resource manager transaction commits (i.e. at the end of a service call), changes made by this service are visible to the outside because all locks help by the resource manager transaction are released. Isolation is violated. In our approach we avoid this undesired behaviour. In order to further guarantee the ACID properties at the service level, additional actions must be taken. In TPM/ONT this is done by providing a number of additional services, so-called *system services*. These services ensure the correct execution of application services as open-nested sub-transactions of a two-level user transaction. Note that local transactions are not permitted in this system and that all users must use these additional services.

The key features of multi-level transactions relevant to TPM/ONT, with its two levels—L_1 at the TPM level and L_0 at the resource manager level—are the following:

- In the general multi-level setting, an operation on level L_i is made up of a sequence of primitive operations on the next lower level $(i - 1)$. These primitive operations are executed as an individual transaction on level $(i - 1)$.

  In TPM/ONT, an operation on level L_1 equals a service call. Operations on L_0 are interactions with the underlying resource manager executed during the execution of a service. Each service call is executed as an individual transaction of the resource manager.

- *Isolation* is guaranteed by maintaining independent locks on objects at each level of the system. Locks on objects of level L_i are acquired during the execution of the operations on that level and released as soon as the L_i transaction commits or aborts.

  In TPM/ONT locks on level L_0 are the locks of the resource manager. On the higher level, a predicate oriented lock manager with user-defined compatibility modes is used. The lock manager is generic in the sense that a compatibility matrix C must be defined. There, the programmer of the application services must set $c_{ij} = +$ if an application service j does not conflict and can therefore be executed without further restrictions even if another application service i has been scheduled before. We set $c_{ij} = \pm$ if an unrestricted execution of service j is not possible. In this case, we must check whether service j accesses objects that are accessed by service i already. We describe these sets of objects by (simple) predicates derived from the parameters of the application services. If the predicates describe disjoint objects sets, we may schedule service j. Otherwise, service j can only be scheduled after the service–i–transaction has committed or aborted and released its predicate locks.

  Due to lack of space, the functionality of the L_1 lock manager is not discussed in further detail.

- *Atomicity:* In case a transaction on level L_i must be rolled back, some transactions on level L_{i-1} might have already been committed. In order to undo the changes applied to the database by these transactions, so-called *compensating transactions* on level L_{i-1}—which undo all changes caused by a transaction—must be executed for each committed L_{i-1} transaction. L_i log records contain information about committed actions and how to construct the compensating action.

In TPM/ONT, each application service is executed as an individual transaction of the underlying resource manager. To compensate changes caused by a service, a so-called *compensating service* must be available for each application service and must be executed by the TPM.

In the current implementation of TPM/ONT, the L_1 log is realised as a relation

L1Log(LSN, Transaction-ID, Subtransaction-ID,
Operation, Parameters)

and stored in the resource manager. *Operation* is the name of the service that has been executed. The name of the compensating operations can then be derived from *Operation*. Any parameter needed for the compensating operation is stored in *Parameters*, an attribute of type BLOB.

The operations for the administration of of L_1 log records could be implemented as a system service. However, L_1 log entries are only written in order to undo the changes of a committed transaction on level L_0. In case the L_0 transaction is aborted by the underlying resource manager, an L_1 log entry will never be needed as changes to the database are undone using the rollback mechanism of the underlying resource manager. For this reason, entries to the L_1 log are written during the execution of the application service (that potentially must be undone) using the same transaction of the underlying resource manager as the service itself. This means, that the entry is actually only written if the transaction of the resource manager commits. Otherwise, the log entry is removed along with all changes made by this transaction using the rollback operation of the resource manager.

Note that the system must guarantee that an L_1-transaction can always be rolled back. Therefore it is necessary to preclaim the locks for the execution of a compensating service together with the lock for the service itself. Hence a lock for the execution of two services s_1 and s_2 can only be granted if s_1 and s_2, s_1 and s_2^{-1}, s_1^{-1} and s_2 as well as s_1^{-1} and s_2^{-1} commute. For more details and weaker conditions see [17].

Finally, in order to coordinate the execution of L_1-transactions, it is necessary to replace the TPM's internal commands for beginning, committing and aborting a user transaction by the following system services:

- *BOT* (Begin Of Transaction) generates and returns a unique transaction identifier to the user. This identifier is subsequently used for locking and logging on level L_1.

- *EOT* (End Of Transaction) writes a *End of L_1–Transaction* entry to the L_1–log, frees all L_1 locks (see below) acquired by the L_1 transaction and invalidates the transaction identifier.

  Alternatively to writing a EOT log entry, all L_1 log entries for this transaction can be removed from the log as transactions committed on level L_1 must never be rolled back.

- *RBT* (RollBack Transaction) rolls back an L_1 transaction. This is done by first aborting all currently running application services (L_0 transactions) that are executed as subtransactions of this transaction. Then, L_1 operations that have already been committed on level L_0 (i.e. all service calls that have already been completed) are compensated by executing their compensating service. The information, which services have been executed successfully, is obtained from the L_1 log.

  If the TPM—like Tuxedo—does not support the immediate termination of a running service, RBT first waits until all currently running application services of this transaction are completed and compensates them along with the already committed services.

Like any transaction-oriented system, TPM/ONT also guarantees the consistency of the data in case either the database system or a client fails. This is realised by providing two additional system services, *Rollback All Aborted L_1 Transactions (RBTAll)* and *Abort Timed Out L_1 Transaction (RBTTime)*:

- *RBTAll* is a system service that is executed as part of the startup routine of the system server before any L_1 user transaction is admitted. RBTAll identifies all L_1 transactions that have not been committed when TPM/ONT was shut down the last time (or failed). RBTAll first searches the L_1 log for transactions without an L_1-EOT entry and then compensates these transactions by calling the compensating service for every application service executed by these transactions.

- *RBTTime* is an operation that continuously records the execution of application services. If a user transaction has not started any service for a certain period of time, *RBTTime* initiates the abort of such a transaction by calling *RBT*.

Using these system services, a new application service can be provided in three steps. First, the application service must be implemented according to the skeleton shown in figure 5. Second, the inverse operation for this application service must be implemented. Third, the compatibility matrix must be defined.

```
application services
begin L₀ transaction
set up the lock predicate and try to acquire the lock
note that the transaction is blocked if the lock cannot
be acquired immediately or a deadlock is detected
if lock is granted
    ┌─────────────────────────────────────┐
    │ application service dependent code   │
    └─────────────────────────────────────┘
else
    comment: risk of deadlock
    abort L₀ transaction
    exit failure
fi
write L₁ log entry
commit L₀ transaction
exit success
```

Figure 5: Skeleton for the implementation of an application service

On the client side, an application program interacting with TPM/ONT basically uses the operations provided by the TP-Monitor. In particular, the native mechanism for calling application services and transferring data from the client process to the server processes and vice versa is used. However, as described before, special services must be called at the beginning and the end of a user transaction. Besides these, the following operations executed on the client side are especially important for TPM/ONT:

- **call**(ServiceName, $Param_1$, $Param_2$, ..., $Param_n$) initiates the synchronously execution of an application service named *ServiceName* with parameters $Param_1$, $Param_2$, ..., $Param_n$.

- **asynccall** takes the same parameters as **call** but initiates the asynchronous execution of the application service and immediately returns an *identifier* for this call. This identifier can subsequently be used to wait for the termination of this application service using the function **wait**(identifier). Alternatively, **wait** can be called with the parameter **ANY**. In this case, **wait** waits for any asynchronously called application service to terminate and returns its identifier. The identifier returned by **wait** can then be used to retrieve the results returned by the terminated application service.

4 TPM/ONT-Test: TPM/ONT for Textual Applications

In this section, we present the services as well as the compatibility matrix C necessary for handling textual documents using TPM/ONT.

TPM/ONT currently offers eight application services for the handling of textual data: InsertDocument, RetrieveDocument, DeleteDocument, ExtractIndexTerms, InsertIndexTerms, RetrieveDocumentIDs, DeleteIndexTerms, and LockDocuments as well as the compensating services InsertDocument^{-1}, InsertIndexTerms^{-1}. Even though all services have been implemented in our prototype system, we limited the description to those actually used to carry out the measurements for this paper:

- *InsertDocument* inserts a document d into the database without maintaining any textual index structures. The ID of the newly inserted document is written to the L_1 log.

  InsertDocument^{-1} first removes all entries made for this document in the inverted lists and then removes the document itself. No L_1 log is written.

- *ExtractIndexTerms* extracts the individual descriptors of an attribute, maps them from their ASCII representation to integers using the *Mapping* relation and returns them to the user.

  If a descriptor is not found in the mapping relation, a new descriptor-ID is generated and inserted into the mapping relation. This entry is not removed in case the transaction subsequently aborts. This is of no disadvantage as the newly inserted descriptor may be used by future calls of *ExtractIndexTerms*. With this, *ExtractIndexTerms*$^{-1}$ is an empty service as the changes to the mapping relation are not undone.

- *InsertIndexTerms* inserts the descriptors of a single attribute obtained from *ExtractIndexTerms* into the database. No L_1 log entry is written, because

  InsertIndexTerms^{-1} is an empty service, i.e. the tuples inserted into an inverted list by *InsertIndexTerms* are not compensated using this service, but are removed when *InsertDocument*$^{-1}$ is executed. This implies that *InsertDocument* must be executed before *InsertIndexTerms*.

- *RetrieveDocument* retrieves all documents matching a query predicate. The query predicate in our case is a conjunction of descriptors. No L_1 log record is written as no changes are applied to the database. *RetrieveDocument*$^{-1}$ is an empty service.

Some services and their compensating services are not symmetric, i.e. the changes made by a service are not undone by its compensating service, but some other service. For example, the inserts into the inverted list done by *InsertIndexTerms* are not undone by *InsertIndexTerms*$^{-1}$ but *InsertDocument*$^{-1}$. This implies, that *InsertDocument*$^{-1}$ must be executed before *InsertIndexTerms*. Otherwise the L_1 log record might not be available. This approach improves performance as it avoids the writing of unnecessary L_1 log records. For example, *InsertDocument*$^{-1}$ deletes the entries from the the in-

verted lists because the information needed for the deletion can be derived from the document that is about to be deleted.

Alternatively, the changes caused by a service can always be undone by its compensating service. However, in that case, L_1 log records must be written for all services as derived information, such as L_1 log records written by a previous subtransaction, cannot be exploited.

If we consider only the main application services needed for the insertion and retrieval of documents, i.e. InsertDocument, InsertDocument^{-1}, InsertIndexTerms, and RetrieveDocument, the compatibility matrix C is defined as

	InsertDocument	InsertDocument^{-1}	ExtractIndexTerms	InsertIndexTerms	RetrieveDocument
InsertDocument	+	+	+	+	±
InsertDocument^{-1}	+	+	+	+	±
ExtractIndexTerms	+	+	+	+	+
InsertIndexTerms	+	+	+	+	+
RetrieveDocument	±	±	+	+	+

No conflict on level L_1 occurs when documents are only inserted. However, if we consider also the service *RetrieveDocument*, which is retrieving all documents containing a set of descriptors $R = \{r_m\}$, this service can be executed parallel to the insertion of a document described by a set of descriptors $I = \{i_k\}$ iff $R \not\subseteq I$. That is to say, the lock can granted if and only if the document to be inserted does not qualify for the search.

It is sometimes claimed, e.g. in [16], that the extraction of lock predicates as well as the conflict test is time-consuming and therefore not beneficial. Where in general this might be true, the extraction of the predicates is straight forward in the case of textual applications. The descriptors of a document or a query are given by the set of the individual words contained in them. Also, predicates can be tested efficiently for overlaps using a signature based approach [18].

Further note that *ExtractIndexTerms* commutes with all other application services as the number assigned to a descriptor is only used internally and hence does not influence the result of a retrieve or insert operation.

Using the above application services, a document $d(a_1, a_2, \ldots, a_m, t_1, t_2, t_n)$ is inserted into a relation D as well as its textual attributes t_i indexed using one of the client programs presented in figures 6 and 7:

- Figure 6 shows an insertion algorithm with a low level of parallelism. After the document is inserted, the features of the individual textual attributes are extracted asynchronously. Subsequently, the inverted lists are updated in parallel using one subtransaction per inverted list.

```
comment: input document
call (InsertDocument, a_1, ..., t_1, ...) → Document-ID
for i = 1 to n
    asynccall (ExtractIndexTerms, t_i) → Call-ID_i
end
invertcalls = n
while (invertcalls > 0) do
    wait(ANY) → terminated
    if (terminated in {Call-ID_i})
      if (terminated call returned features)
        name of the inverted attribute → t
        asynccall (InsertIndexTerms, t, features
        Document-ID) → Call-ID_{n+1}
        invertcalls = invertcalls + 1
      fi
    fi
    invertcalls = invertcalls − 1
od
```

Figure 6: Client code for the insertion and interleaved indexing of a textual document using TPM/ONT

```
comment: input document
call (InsertDocument, a_1, ..., t_1, ...) → Document-ID
for i = 1 to n
    asynccall (ExtractIndexTerms, t_i) → Call-ID_i
end
invertcalls = n
while (invertcalls > 0) do
    wait(ANY) → terminated
    if (terminated in {Call-ID_i})
      if (terminated call returned features)
        NumDes=number of descriptors returned
        name of the inverted attribute → t
        for j = 0 to NumDes step parinsert
          asynccall (InsertIndexTerms, t
          features[i...(i+parinsert)])
          Document-ID) → Call-ID_{invertcalls+1}
          invertcall = invertcalls+1
        end
      fi
    fi
    invertcalls = invertcalls − 1
od
```

Figure 7: Client code for the insertion and interleaved indexing of a textual document using TPM/ONT

- The algorithm presented in figure 7 also exploits parallelism when updating the inverted lists: Instead of using a single subtransaction that inserts all descriptors of a textual attribute, many subtransactions are used. Each of these subtransactions inserts *parinsert* descriptors of an attribute.

  For example, with $parinsert = 50$ and 130 descriptors extracted from an attribute, three subtransactions are used to update the inverted list.

5 Measurements

Below, we are presenting a quantitative analysis of TPM/ONT by comparing the costs for the insertion of textual documents using TPM/ONT to the costs of a traditional approach using a TPM with flat transaction.

5.1 System Environment and Test Data

The experiments are carried out on a SparcCenter 2000 equipped with ten processors and 300 megabytes of main memory running Solaris 2.5. An Oracle database server V7.2.3 as well as the TP-Monitor Tuxedo V5.1 is used. Database pages are sized four kilobytes and the database buffer is set to 2500 pages. For our experiments, twelve equal disks connected to six SCSI controllers are available: One is used for holding the temporary table space, two each for the redo and undo logs, and the remaining seven for storing the actual data. The TP monitor runs twenty servers providing the services presented in section 4. In the experiments where multi-level transactions are employed, the servers also provide the basic system services for TPM/ONT. All experiments are repeated until a confidence level of 90% and a $\pm 10\%$ confidence interval surrounding the mean is reached.

Specifically, we investigate the costs associated with the insertion of articles posted to the Usenet group *talk.politics.libertarian*. The articles are stored in a relation, TP(date article posted, originator's name, originator's organisation, subject of the message, body of the message)[3]. Fast access to the documents is provided by maintaining inverted list based on the individual words for the *subject* (InvList_Subject) and the *body* (InvList_Body) attribute. For every inverted list, an own B-tree is created over the attributes (Term-ID, Document-ID). Additionally, a virtual attribute *combined* consisting of the attributes *sender, organisation, subject* and *body* is created and indexed using an inverted list InvList_Combined. InvList_Combined provides support for queries, where only a number of keywords are specified but not the attributes in which they must be contained. Note, that this virtual attribute is treated like the textual attributes *body* and *subject* with respect to indexing but it is not stored in the document relation TP.

On the average, we find five distinct words in the *subject* and approximately 100 in the *body* attribute. For the insertion and indexing of each document, an own L_1–transaction is

---

[3]For the remainder, the attributes are abbreviated as *date, sender, organisation, subject,* and *body*.

used. All documents are stored on one disk. The inverted lists $InvList_{Subject}$ and $InvList_{Body}$ are striped over three disks, and $InvList_{Combined}$ is striped over another three other disks. The striping granularity is 40 kilobytes (1 track).

As reference measurement we find in a single-user environment using single-level transactions, an average insertion time of 1.5 seconds (i.e. a throughput of 0.62 documents/second). This includes the insertion of the raw document as well as the updates of the textual index structures.

In our experiments, four different indexing methods are investigated:

1. TPM/Flat: The traditional TP monitor approach using flat transactions. The sequential insertion algorithm presented in figure 3 is used.

2. ONT/Seq: TPM/ONT is used to execute the insertion algorithm shown in figure 3. Intra-transaction parallelism is not exploited as the application services of a user transaction are executed synchronously. This means that the execution sequence of the individual services of a user transaction is exactly the same as TPM/Flat.

3. ONT/Par: TPM/ONT is used to execute the parallel indexing algorithm as presented in figure 6. Intra-transaction parallelism is exploited because most of the application services are called asynchronously and therefore are executed in parallel.

4. ONT/Par–*parinsert*: TPM/ONT is used to execute the parallel indexing algorithm as presented in figure 7. Like in ONT/Par, intra-transaction parallelism is exploited by indexing the textual attributes highly in parallel.

Results for an environment with multiple concurrent inserters are presented. Each inserter reads different articles from different files and inserts them continuously without interrupt.

All experiments start with an empty database. The results presented below always exclude the first 2000 documents inserted (startup phase of the database).

5.2 Concurrent Parallel versus Sequential Insertion

Table 1 shows the average insertion time per document as well as the throughput (in documents per second) for an environment with five, ten and twenty concurrent users[4] As to be expected, ONT/Par performs significantly better than TPM/Flat in the environment with 5 and 10 concurrent users. This is because of the parallel extraction of the descriptors for the attributes *subject* and *body* as well as the interleaved, parallel update of $InvList_{Body}$ and $InvList_{Combined}$. The response time benefit of approximately 40% is entirely due to the fact that these inverted lists, which are located on different disks, are

---
[4]No results are available for ONT/Par-50 due to restrictions of Tuxedo (maximum number of concurrent asynchronous calls).

	# inserters		
	5	10	20
TPM/Flat	2.1	3.0	5.4
ONT/Seq	2.1	3.0	5.3
ONT/Par	1.5	2.4	5.1
ONT/Par-50	1.3	2.4	n/a

(a) Average insertion time per document (sec)

	# inserters		
	5	10	20
TPM/Flat	2.1	3.2	3.3
ONT/Seq	2.1	3.1	3.4
ONT/Par	2.8	3.6	3.0
ONT/Par-50	3.1	3.6	n/a

(b) Throughput (document/sec)

Table 1: Insertion time and throughput with 5, 10 and 20 concurrent users

maintained in parallel. Throughput improves also in case of 5 concurrent users by 45%, and in case of 10 by 15%. In case of 20 concurrent users, all algorithms show about the same performance with respect to response time: As only 20 servers are available, each inserter is — on the average — allocated only a single server at a time. Therefore a response time reduction is not possible as the asynchronous calls used by ONT/Par and ONT/Par-50 are sequentialised and executed basically in the same order as in TPM/Flat and ONT/Seq.

In other performance studies that evaluated multi-level transactions, e.g. [19], the response time benefit mostly stemmed from the fact, that subtransactions (in a two-level approach: the L_0 transactions) release their locks as soon as they commit. Hence, the time a user transaction (running on level L_1) is blocked because it is waiting for a lock can be reduced significantly, especially when transactions are long-running. Note, that no such blocking is taking place if concurrent transactions are only performing inserts that do not violate the integrity of the data, e.g. by inserting tuples with the same primary key.

Another notable detail is the fact that ONT/Seq shows results comparable to TPM/Flat. This is surprising, as every service call in ONT/Seq is executed as an independent Oracle transaction which is committed at the end of the service and therefore results into the synchronous writing of log records in order to guarantee atomicity an durability on the RM level. Contrary to this, only a single Oracle transaction is used to insert a document when using TPM/Flat. We would therefore expect TPM/Flat to perform significantly better than

TPM/Flat. The rather unexpected performance of TPM/Flat can only be explained by the overhead associated with the TPM as well as the cost for the XA interface [20] which is used for transaction control.

5.3 Cost of L_0 Durability

An interesting aspect in this context is the question, how much time the database system spends in order to guarantee durability on level L_0, which has been identified as partially redundant in a multi-level environment [21]. Oracle—as single-level system—does normally not allow to turn the redo logging facility off, which is used to guarantee *durability*. However, an undocumented parameter allows to turn off any logging, i.e. redo and undo logging. Of course, this parameter turns off too much for the practical usage, as also the *atomicity* of subtransactions is not guaranteed by the system anymore, which is still necessary on level L_0. As L_0 undo records for an L_0 transaction must only be written before any L_0 object is written, e.g. a database page, the system can write these logs asynchronously beforehand. Therefore, the relative cost for assuring *atomicity* on level L_0 is small.

We have measured the costs for the update of the inverted lists with Oracle's logging facility turned on as well as off using the inserting algorithm presented in figure 7. Measurements for *parinsert*= 50, 25 and 10 were executed in a single user environment. The cost measured is the sum of the elapsed times of all subtransactions executed in order to update the inverted lists divided by the number of tuples inserted.

In case of *parinsert* $= 50$ and *parinsert* $= 25$, the insertion times with logging turned on show no statistically significant difference compared to the times obtained with logging turned off. This is because the time spent for writing logs is relatively small compared to the duration of the transaction used to update the inverted list. What we learn from this first measurement is, that *durability* on level L_0 does not significantly decrease the overall performance of a multi-level database system if a considerable amount of work is carried out by the individual subtransactions. For *parinsert* $= 10$, the measurements carried out with the logging facility turned off, showed an increased performance of roughly 7%. This is due to the fact that the individual L_0 transactions are now rather short and the time spent for the synchronous writing of the L_0 log has become a significant part of the execution time. A further parallelisation has not been investigated as Tuxedo limits the number of concurrently running asynchronous service calls for each client process.

5.4 Influence of Subtransaction Conflicts

In a third set of measurements, we investigate the behaviour of the TMP/ONT versus a traditional TPM with non-compatible locks being acquired by the database system. Conflicts occur e.g., when the insertion algorithm does not only insert

features into the inverted lists, but also does some update on shared data. As an example, we update the term frequencies of the individual descriptors, i.e. for each inverted list InvList_{t_i}(Term, Document-ID) we keep an additional relation $\text{TermFrequency}_{t_i}$(Term, Frequency) in which we record, in how many distinct documents each term occurs. This information is used for the optimisation of retrieval operations as described in [14].

Whenever a new document is inserted and the inverted lists InvList_{t_i} are updated, the corresponding relation *TermFrequency*$_{t_i}$ is updated as well by incrementing the attribute *Frequency* for each feature of the attribute t_i. Clearly, the increment operation executed on behalf of one transaction will block any other concurrently running transaction intending to increment the frequency of the same term.

In table 2 we present the response times and throughputs for the insertion of documents in an environment with 20 concurrent user for ONT/Seq and ONT/Par when term frequencies are maintained. Additionally, we present numbers for ONT/Seq-50 and ONT/Seq-25. These are basically ONT/Seq but they always commit the RM transaction after the execution of 50 (respectively 25) inserts of term into the inverted list. Unfortunately, exact results for TPM/Flat can not be provided: When the experiments for TPM/Flat were run with only ten concurrent users, the average insertion time for a document—measured for the first few hundred documents—was more than 20 seconds. These times are caused by lock contention as neither the CPUs nor the disks were utilised during more than 10% percent. Measurements for the complete test collection were therefore not carried out. However, results for TPM/ONT could be obtained.

From [22] we know, that in textual documents certain words occur in almost any document. We therefore expect concurrent inserts to hinder each other massively when updating the term frequency relation.

	resp. time	throughput
ONT/Seq	16.3	1.16
ONT/Par	12.0	1.14
ONT/Seq-50	11.3	1.70
ONT/Seq-25	8.6	2.15

Table 2: Average insertion times (sec) and throughputs (documents/sec) in an environment with 20 concurrent users when term frequencies are maintained

The figures show that ONT/Seq, executing the subtransactions sequentially, takes significantly longer as ONT/Par. This behaviour is surprising as only 20 servers are available and therefore only a single server is available per inserter. However, the throughput remains the same is both cases, which is as expected.

When ONT/Seq-50 and especially ONT/Seq-25 are used, the response times decrease and the throughputs increase significantly as the locks on the term frequency relations are released early. These results clearly show, that the costs for executing multi-level transactions are insignificant compared to the costs paid for holding locks until the end of a transaction when a single-level system is used.

5.5 Observations using a Database System with Two-Phase-Locking

For the measurements presented so far, on level L_0 the database system Oracle was used, which uses a multi-version transaction manager locking tuples. Therefore, concurrent inserts that do not update statistical information do not hinder each other. Transactions retrieving documents are also not hindered by concurrent inserters if enough versions are kept on the log. If Oracle is replaced by a database system using a strict two phase locking protocol locking pages, a serious lock contention can be expected. This results in an increase of response time and a decrease in throughput in case of multiple concurrent users. By using TPM/ONT, it should be possible to reduce this contention due to the early release of the locks at the end of each L_1 operation.

We have carried out measurements using the database system *Sybase* V10.0.2 configured with 10 server processes. TPM/ONT was run with 10 server processes as well. In the single-user, single-level mode the average insertion time was 3.8 seconds which corresponds to a throughput of 0.24 documents/second. Figure 3 shows the average insertion times as well as the throughputs when 10 users insert documents concurrently. As can be seen, the performance increases significantly when TPM/ONT is used due to the reduction of lock contention. Note, that the insertion time increases by a factor of 10 when the single level approach (TPM/Flat) is used and the throughput remains constant. This result is expected: When one transaction is inserting a document, the others are immediately blocked. Therefore, the average insertion time increases linearly with the number of concurrent inserters. The

	resp. time	throughput
TPM/Flat	35.6	0.24
ONT/Seq	19.2	0.45
ONT/Seq-50	14.0	0.61
ONT/Seq-20	10.6	0.87
ONT/Seq-10	10.0	0.91
ONT/Seq-5	11.0	0.84

Table 3: Average insertion times (sec) and throughputs (documents/sec) in an environment with 10 concurrent users using Sybase

sequential indexing algorithm ONT/Seq (using TPM/ONT) already performs significantly better as the locks on the index structures for a textual attribute t_i are released at the end of the indexing process for this attribute. When ONT/Seq-50, ONT/Seq-20, ONT/Seq-10, or ONT/Seq-5 is used, these locks are not held till the end of the indexing process of a single attribute t_i but are released after 50, 20, 10, or 5 descriptors respectively of the attribute t_i have been inserted into the inverted list. Therefore, lock contention is further reduced. Note that we still benefit from this early release if we release the locks — and therefore commit the RM transaction — after the insertion of only 10 descriptors per attribute. This is surprising becuase the commit of an RM transaction is expensive as changes must be made persistent.

Currently, we are investigating the behaviour of the system with not only concurrent inserters, but also concurrent readers. First results show that response times can be reduced significantly using TPM/ONT in a page-locking, single-version database system like Sybase as readers are hindered substantially by concurrent inserters. Through the early release of locks, this hinderance can be resolved to a great extent. Final results are presented in [23].

6 Conclusions and Future Work

In this study, we described how intra-transaction parallelism in databases can be achieved by transforming it into conventional inter-transaction parallelism. To this end a commercially available transaction processing monitor was extended by a higher level transaction manager. The resulting system architecture, *TPM/ONT*, was described with respect to new system services that help in establishing application-specific services and transaction management at this level. We have applied this framework to a document management application and have implemented a prototype system based on Tuxedo, Oracle, and Sybase.

In the measurements we concentrated on the one hand on the online insertion of large document collections and showed that TPM/ONT can improve the response time of insertions more or less dramatically, depending on the number of concurrent insertions and on the fact whether there are conflicts at the resource manager (Oracle) level or not. On the other hand, we could show that in a database system that uses a strict 2PL protocol (Sybase), performance can be increased as locks are only held for a short period of time. Specifically the following results could be observed:

- Although there are no conflicts between concurrent insertions at the ORACLE level, the parallelisation using TPM/ONT resulted in response time improvements of 30 to 40 percent for a single document insert.

- If we increase the number of concurrent insertions from 1 to 20 users, the response time of a single typical document insert (consisting of the insertion of about 200 descriptors) only increases from 1.5 seconds to 5 seconds with the throughput increasing from 0.6 to more than 3 document insertions per second.

- In case of lower-level conflicts on shared (hot spot) internal data items such as frequency counts we observe significant improvements using TPM/ONT. The parallelisation and decomposition into many small transactions decreases the lock wait times and increases the throughput. We were even able to obtain meaningful results using TPM/ONT in cases where we could not obtain them using a traditional approach due to lock contention.

- When we use a database system with two-phase-locking (e.g. Sybase) instead of one with a multi-version transaction manager (e.g. Oracle), a severe lock contention can be observed when documents are inserted concurrently using native, i.e. flat, transactions. TPM/ONT diminishes this contention and therefore increases the throughput from 0.24 to 0.91 documents per second.

Finally, the performance studies showed another surprising effect: TPM/ONT executing all subtransactions of a transaction sequentially showed comparable—and sometimes even better—response-times than a traditional TP monitor application. This is a hint that the XA protocol used by a transaction processing monitor along with the TPM's internal overhead for maintaining its logs must not be neglected. In addition we will compare the general overhead introduced by the TP-Monitor by comparing with a "direct" use of a database system with stored procedures.

The results obtained will be an important input for our own CONCERT prototype development [24], especially with respect to non-persistent subtransactions.

Acknowledgment The authors would like to thank Gustavo Alonso, Stephen Blott, and Lukas Relly for their helpful comments.

References

[1] "Draft Database Language SQL (SQL3)", ISO-ANSI Working Draft, Feb. 1993.

[2] G. Weikum, "Principles and realization strategies of multi-level transaction management", *ACM Transactions on Database Systems*, vol. 16, no. 1, pp. 132–180, Mar. 1991.

[3] G. Weikum and H.-J. Schek, *Database Transaction Models for Advanced Applications*, chapter Concepts and Applications of Multilevel Transactions and Open Nested Transactions, pp. 515–546, Morgan Kaufmann, 1992.

[4] Novell, Inc., *Tuxedo System: Application Programming*, 1994.

[5] Transarc Corporation, *Toolkit Executive Programmer's Reference*, 1995.

[6] G. Weikum and H.-J. Schek, "Architectural issues of transaction management in layered systems", in *Proceedings International Conference on Very Large Databases*, Singapore, 1984.

[7] A. Deacon, H.-J. Schek, and G. Weikum, "Semantics-based multilevel transaction management in federated systems", in *Proc. of the 10th Int. Conf. on Data Engineering (ICDE'94)*, Houston, Texas, Feb. 1994.

[8] W. Schaad, H.-J. Schek, and G. Weikum, "Implementation and performance of multi-level transaction management in multidatabase environment", in *Proc. of the 5th Int. Workshop on Research Issues on Data Engineering: Distributed Object Management, (RIDE-DOM'95)*, Taipei, Taiwan, Mar. 1995.

[9] M. Rys, M.C. Norrie, and H.-J. Schek, "Intra-transaction parallelism in the mapping of an object model to a relational multiprocessor system", in *Proceedings International Conference on Very Large Databases*, Bombay, India, Sept. 1996.

[10] C. Mohan, H. Pirahesh, W.G. Tang, and Y. Wang, "Parallelism in relational database management systems", *IBM Systems Journal*, vol. 33, no. 2, 1994.

[11] D. DeWitt and J. Gray, "Parallel database systems: The future of high performance database systems", *Communications of the ACM*, vol. 35, no. 6, pp. 85–98, June 1994.

[12] M. Metha and D. DeWitt, "Managing intra-operator parallelism in parallel database systems", in *Proceedings International Conference on Very Large Databases*, Zurich, Switzerland, Sept. 1995, pp. 382–394.

[13] M. Kamath and K. Ramamritham, "Efficient transaction support for dynamic information retrieval systems", in *Proceedings of the International ACM SIGIR Conference on Research and Development in Information Retrieval*, Aug. 1996.

[14] H. Kaufmann and H.-J. Schek, "Text search in database systems revisited—some experiments", in *Proc. of the the 13th Britisch National Conference on Databases*. July 1995, Lecture Notes in Computer Science, pp. 201–225, Springer.

[15] D.E. Knuth, *Sorting and Searching*, The Art of Computer Programming. Addison-Wesley, Reading, 1973.

[16] J. Gray and A. Reuter, *Transaction Processing: Concepts and Techniques*, Morgan Kaufmann, 1993.

[17] R. Vingralek, H. Hasse, Y. Breitbart, and H.-J. Schek, "Unifying concurrency control and recovery of transactions with semantically rich operations", *Journal of Theoretical Computer Science*, 1996.

[18] P. Dadam, P. Pistor, and H.-J. Schek, "A predicate oriented locking approach for integrated information systems", in *Proceedings of the IFIP*, R.E.A. Mason, Ed., 1983.

[19] G. Weikum and C. Hasse, "Multi–level transactions for complex objects: Implementation, performance, parallelism", *The VLDB Journal*, vol. 2, no. 4, 1993.

[20] X/Open Ltd., Reading, England, *Distributed Transaction Processing: The XA Specification*, 1991.

[21] David Lomet, "MLR: A recovery method for multi-level systems", in *Proc. ACM SIGMOD Conf. on Management of Data*, 1992, pp. 183–194.

[22] G.K. Zipf, *Human Behaviour and the Principle of Least Effort*, Addison-Wesley Press, 1949.

[23] H. Kaufmann, *Transaktionsorientierte Verwaltung und Suche von Dokumenten in einer Mehrprozessordatenbankumgebung*, PhD thesis, ETH Zürich, Dept. of Computer Science, 1996.

[24] S. Blott, L. Relly, and H.-J. Schek, "An open abstract-object storage system", in *Proceedings of the 1996 ACM SIGMOD Conference on Management of Data*, Montreal, Canada, June 1996.

Adaptable, Efficient, and Modular Coordination of Distributed Extended Transactions[*]

Tong Zhou
Oregon Graduate Institute[†]

Calton Pu
Oregon Graduate Institute[‡]

Ling Liu
University of Alberta[§]

Abstract

We describe a method for building a variety of coordination protocols as well as distributed extended transaction primitives. The method is called Open Coordination Protocol (OCP), and we apply OCP to construct many variants of Commit_Transaction [15, 13, 22, 12], as well as distributed Split_Transaction [18] and distributed Join_Group [14, 20]. OCP adopts a modular decomposition of popular coordination protocols (e.g., two-phase commit) into microprotocols [17], and then chooses appropriate microprotocols to build new coordination protocols or extended transaction primitives with desired features (e.g., Split_transaction with read-only optimization). We use incremental specialization [6, 19] to improve the efficiency of each implemented protocol.

1 Introduction

In many distributed domains such as software development environments and publication environments, applications require transactional support for long-duration activities, cooperation, and coordination. These requirements naturally call for robust handling of different *extended* transaction management primitives (e.g., `Delegate`, `Split`, `Join`, `Join_group`) [7]. However, extended transaction models either: (1) have not been made distributed, e.g., split/join transactions, or (2) have adopted *ad hoc* distributed transaction coordination, e.g., workflow systems. In order to systematically distribute extended transaction models (ETM), one of the missing building blocks is a flexible coordination facility that fits a variety of ETMs.

Our first contribution is the design of a flexible and powerful distributed coordination protocol as a basic building block of distributed ETMs. We call it *Open Coordination Protocol* (OCP). OCP works with many previously proposed ETMs, and facilitates the integration with future ETMs. Furthermore, the flexibility is combined with low cost in implementation and maintenance, and efficiency in execution. While the space in this paper does not allow for a detailed description of an actual implementation, we focus on the combination of several previously independent techniques to achieve adaptation, efficiency, and modularity in the Open Coordination Protocol.

The second contribution of this paper is our unique methodology in the design and implementation of the Open Coordination Protocol. First, we use the concept of *microprotocols* introduced in the *x*–kernel project [17] to decompose the many flavors of coordination protocols (e.g., 2PC) and then combine microprotocols into the desired coordination protocol variant. Systematic composition of appropriate microprotocols gives us both generality and functionality. Second, we use *specialization* technique being developed in the operating system [19] and programming language communities [6], to improve the performance of OCP's instances. Third, we follow the *open implementation* principles [11] in the design of interfaces and separation of functions in OCP. These principles lead us into the adoption of the *Reflective Transaction Framework* [1] for the practical implementation of ETMs in production TP monitors. Although the aforementioned techniques have been proposed and demonstrated previously, a successful combination to solve a non-trivial problem is novel, to the best of our knowledge.

The remainder of this paper is organized as follows. We first describe the distributed transaction processing architecture we assume in the next section. In section 3, we present the Open Coordination Protocol, its applications in capturing existent protocols and optimizations, and its implementation. We then delineate the specialization process and different quasi-invariants in section 4. We illustrate how the Open Coordination Protocol is used to implement different transaction management primitives in section 5. Related work is reviewed in section 6, and we conclude the paper in section 7.

2 An extensible DTP architecture

To facilitate the presentation of the Open Coordination Protocol, we first describe in this section the architecture we assume for distributed transaction processing (DTP). In general, the architecture conforms to the DTP architecture used by X/Open DTP, OSI-TP, and TP Monitors [2, 9].

[*]The research of the first two authors were supported by the National Science Foundation (NSF) under grant IRI-9510112. The research of the second author was also supported in part by the U.S. Department of Defense Advanced Research Projects Agency (DARPA) under contracts N00014-94-1-0845 and F19528-95-C-0193. The research of the third author was supported in part by NSERC under grants OGP-0172859 and STR-0181014.

[†]Department of Computer Science & Engineering, Portland, OR 97291-1000. E-mail: tzhou@cse.ogi.edu

[‡]Department of Computer Science & Engineering, Portland, OR 97291-1000. E-mail: calton@cse.ogi.edu

[§]Department of Computer Science, Edmonton, Alberta, T6G 2H1 Canada. E-mail: lingliu@cs.ualberta.ca

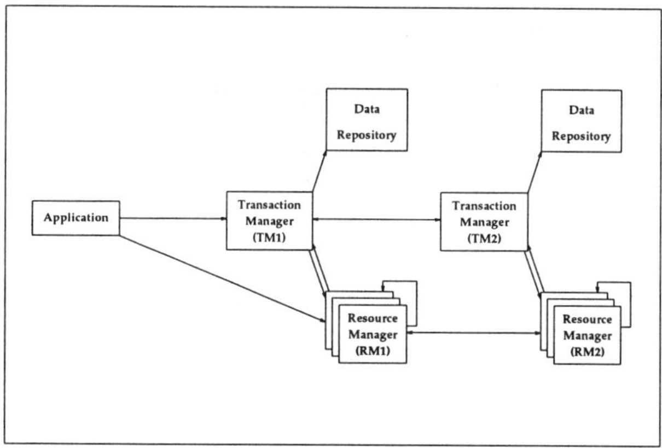

Figure 1: Extensible DTP architecture

However, we assume it contains a richer set of transaction management functions, like `Split_transaction` and `Join_group`, which are introduced by various extended transaction models [7]. The architecture is depicted in Figure 1.

In this architecture, a number of *nodes* are linked together by a reliable communication network. At each node, there is a *transaction manager* (TM), a set of *resource managers* (RMs), and a *data repository* (dictionary). The TM assists application programs in the initiation, execution, and termination of distributed transactions, coordinates transaction participants, and guarantees transactional properties to be met even in presence of failures. Each RM implements a set of persistent data objects, supports transactional operations on them, and coordinates with the TM to ensure their consistency when these objects are involved in transactions. The data repository contains configuration information about the data objects and transaction processing environment at its node.

Both the TM and RM export a collection of interface functions. In this paper, we are particularly interested in interfaces specifically designed for transaction management purpose, which we will uniformly name as *transaction management primitives*, or simply *primitives* when it causes no confusion. For instance, the classic transaction model includes three primitives: `Begin_transaction`, `Commit_transaction`, and `Abort_transaction`; extended transaction models add a variety of new ones, such as `Delegate`, `Split_transaction`, `Join_group`, etc. In comparison, for interface functions like `Update` and `Insert` that operate on an RM's persistent data objects, we will use the term *data operation*, or simply *operation* when the meaning is clear from context.

Participants of a distributed transaction in this architecture are determined dynamically. For example, in Figure 1, `Application` initiates a distributed transaction by calling the `Begin_transaction` function exported by its local TM1,[1] making TM1 the first transaction participant.

---

[1]The application can call `Begin_transaction` via TRPC at another node. But here we assume the more general case.

Then, `Application` calls RM1 and RM2 to operate on their transactional data. The local RM1 becomes a new transaction participant directly. In the remote case, the remote TM2 first joins the transaction by intercepting `Application`'s request to RM2, followed by RM2 joining the transaction.

3 Open coordination protocol (OCP)

In order to systematically distribute extended transaction models, we need a coordination facility to ensure flexible global correctness of the distributed execution of different extended transaction management primitives, even in presence of failures. To achieve such generality in functionality yet efficiency in execution, we combine several system development techniques in our protocol design: first, we decompose many existent coordination protocols, such as two-phase commit, into a set of *microprotocols* [17]; second, we use a set of *quasi-invariants*, guides for *specialization* processes [6, 19], to capture many prevalent protocol optimizations, such as read-only optimization on 2PC; third, we combine these microprotocols and quasi-invariants into our desired coordination facility for distributed ETMs, namely, the Open Coordination Protocol (OCP). OCP's openness stands for its general functionalities: (1) it can be combined with different transaction management primitives, (2) it can be used to ensure different global correctness criteria, and (3) it allows different specialization combinations (see Section 4). OCP's instances can execute efficiently, because the built-in quasi-invariants guide the specialization process during protocol instantiation time to achieve optimal performance.

In this section, we first define some terms and then describe OCP.

3.1 Coordination tree

In most practical situations, the transaction participants can be arranged in a *transaction tree* [9], with the TM initiating the transaction as the root. Due to performance considerations, symmetric coordination protocols such as Byzantine agreement are limited to very special applications. Virtually all of the prevalent TP systems, distributed database systems and applications use asymmetric coordination protocols such as two-phase commit with a central coordinator. In this paper, we concentrate on tree-structured coordination protocols and leave the symmetric protocols for future research.

For each instance of OCP, only a subset of the transaction participants are involved. By applying the "Participant Determination" microprotocol (Section 3.2.1), we reduce the above transaction tree into a subtree, which we call *protocol participant tree*, or *coordination tree*. A *distributed protocol participant* is a transaction participant that also appears in this coordination tree. We distinguish between three different classes of distributed protocol participants: the *coordinator*, *intermediates*, and *leaves*. The coordinator determines the outcomes of different distributed protocol participants to ensure the transaction primitive's correctness. A leaf refers to a distributed protocol participant that is a leaf node in the protocol participant tree. An intermediate is a distributed protocol participant that is neither the coordinator nor a leaf in the coordination tree. Only transaction managers (TMs) can play the role of coordinator or intermediates, while both TMs and resource managers (RMs) can be leaves.

3.2 Protocol structure

OCP has three interfaces: `Coordination`, `Preparation`, and `Action`. `Coordination` is OCP's only external interface and serves as its application programming interface (API). The other two are both OCP's internal interfaces. Every distributed protocol participant exports these three interfaces in order to coordinate with each other.

OCP operates on the coordination tree. Its most generic flow (i.e., without specializations) is abstracted as follows. First, OCP begins with the invocation of the `Coordination` interface of the root (coordinator). Second, the root invokes its own `Preparation` interface from `Coordination`, starting hierarchical invocations of all the distributed protocol participants' `Preparation` interfaces. In specific, each distributed protocol participant's `Preparation` invokes all that participant's children's such interfaces. The results of these hierarchical invocations are returned in a bottom-up fashion in the coordination tree, and eventually reaches the root. Third, the root invokes its own `Action` interface, starting hierarchical invocations of the `Action` interfaces. OCP stops when this round of hierarchical invocations finally returns to the root. In case coordinator migration (see "Coordinator Migration" microprotocol in Section 3.2.1) happens, a sequence of `Coordination` invocations take place along the migration path until the coordinator is determined, followed by above execution flow. Figure 2 illustrates the generic flow within OCP, using entities from Figure 1 as distributed protocol participants. Transaction manager TM1 is the protocol initiator. But because of coordinator migration, it transfers the role of coordinator to TM2, and itself becomes an intermediate. Transaction manager TM2 is the eventual coordinator. Both resource manager RM1 and RM2 are leaves.

Next, we describe the microprotocols contained in each of the three protocol interfaces in turn. Due to space limitation, we focus our description on each microprotocol's functionalities and associated customization mechanisms. A more detailed description of all the microprotocols, including execution flow within each microprotocol, can be found in [25]. In our descriptions, we overload the term *microprotocol* (as in [17]) to refer to a functional step in OCP (instead of the original one that includes explicit marshallings/unmarshallings), and we introduce *selectors* instead of *virtual protocols* to "logically" represent quasi-invariants that guide the specialization process, which we will discuss in Section 4. Note that the word "logically" indicates that our protocol composition graphs are different from flow charts, in that the branching at a "selector" merely illustrates different specialized execution paths, rather than the actual control flow within the protocol. We use rectangles to represent microprotocols, double diamonds to represent selectors, and diamonds to represent ordinary conditional testings.

3.2.1 Coordination

This is OCP's application programming interface (API). It is executed only by the protocol's initiator and each distributed protocol participant on the "coordinator migration path" (as described in the "Coordinator migration" microprotocol). Coordination's structure is shown in Figure 3. We describe the microprotocols in turn.

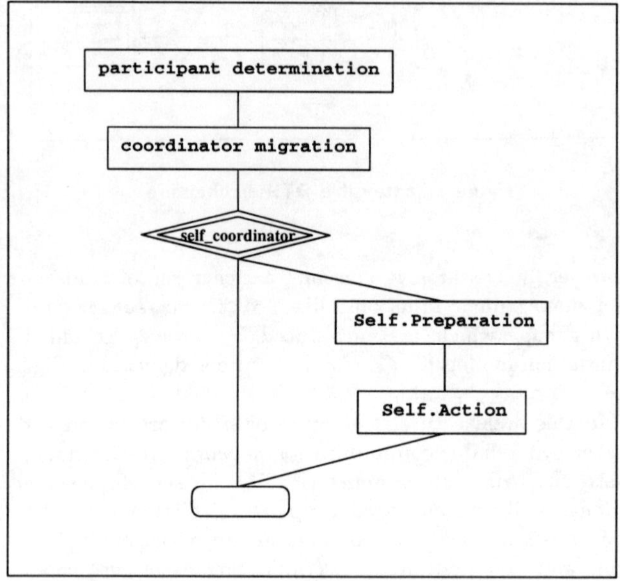

Figure 3: Microprotocols and quasi-invariants in Coordination

Participant determination

For a distributed protocol participant, this microprotocol determines its direct children in the coordination tree, if any. These children might include both intermediates and leaves. The protocol participant executing this microprotocol builds a *protocol participant list*, which holds all of its children participants. Each distributed protocol participant is responsible for determining the outcomes of its children participants, except those who are capable of carrying out autonomous protocol outcomes.

Besides determining members of a protocol participant list, this microprotocol also collects characteristic information about each member, like its availability class (or statistical data about its availability), types of its exported data operations, whether it is able to carry out optimistic outcome, etc. Such information are retrieved either from the data repository at each child participant's node, or through explicitly-supplied microprotocol parameters. They will be used to validate the set of quasi-invariants planted in OCP that are relevant to the specialization process (Section 4), which makes specific protocol instances efficient. An upcall is associated with this microprotocol, allowing customizations on the validation function. Section 5 provides an example for such usage.

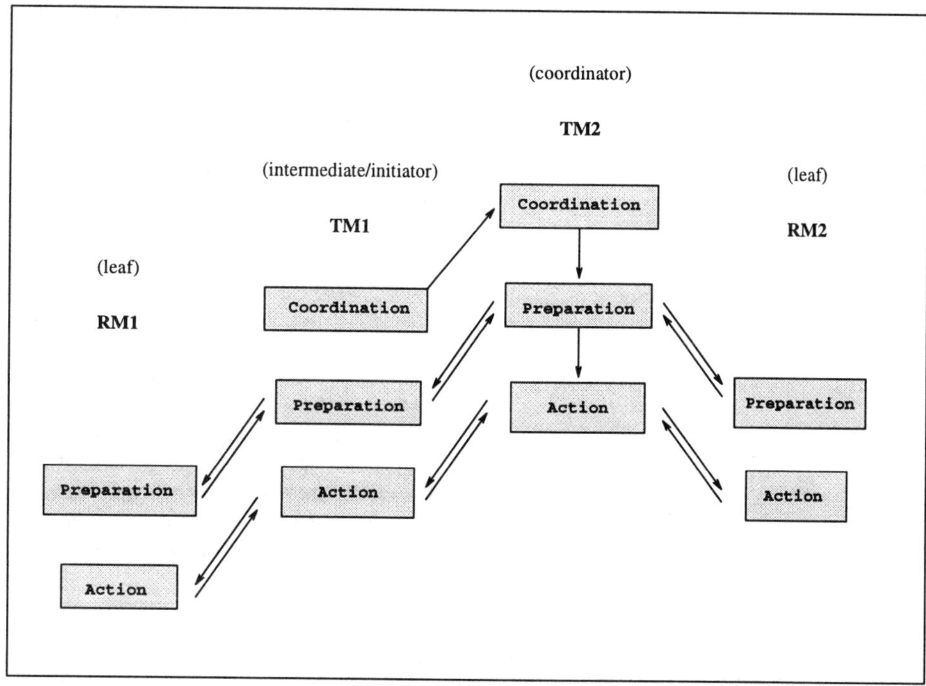

Figure 2: OCP's execution flow

By applying this microprotocol, a "transaction tree" is reduced to a coordination tree, as we mentioned in last subsection (3.1). Note that both the transaction tree and the coordination tree are built dynamically and incrementally from the root to the leaves. As the protocol flows from participant to participant, new participants are "discovered" dynamically and becomes new leaves of the coordination tree.

Coordinator migration

This microprotocol decides in the coordination tree which participant is most suitable to be the coordinator of the entire protocol, and then lets it take that role. Normally, the root of the coordination tree is ok to be the coordinator; however, there are exceptional cases. For example, if the root runs on a PC, it is not highly available and is possible to block the protocol's execution indefinitely. Or, if one of the protocol participant P does not export sufficient coordination interface functions, there is an intrinsic asymmetry among the participants' coordination characteristics that impedes normal protocol flow. It is desirable in both cases to shift the coordinator's role away from the root. A highly-available participant can assume the coordinator's role in the former case, and the special participant P becomes the coordinator in the second case. In general, it is possible for the migration process to go through a path starting from the root to the eventual coordinator. Each protocol participant on this path is selected by its superior as a potential coordinator. We call this path *coordinator migration path*.

Two upcalls are associated with this microprotocol: one for a participant to decide whether itself agrees to take the coordinator's role; another for a participant to customize its coordinator-selection policy.

3.2.2 Preparation

Preparation is not part of the API, since it is only used among protocol participants. Its structure is shown in Figure 4.

Ballot distributing

For a non-leaf protocol participant (i.e., the coordinator or an intermediate) P and P's child participant Q (given as argument), this microprotocol's function is for P to activate Q's Preparation entry, thus signaling Q of the protocol's beginning. P consults the data repository at its node, sending Q the information relevant to Q's voting decision on its preferred outcome. The information might include transaction management primitive name, data operation arguments, characteristic information, etc. In Figure 2, the arrow from TM2's Preparation entry to TM1's Preparation represents this microprotocol's execution by TM2, with TM1 being the child Q.

When OCP is used for different applications, there are cases in which this microprotocol can be bypassed to improve overall performance. For instance, the unilateral commit protocol [10] does not give protocol participants the right to vote. The last-agent optimization on two-phase commit protocol [22] states that if Q is the designated "last-agent", P will first prepare itself and then notify Q, instead

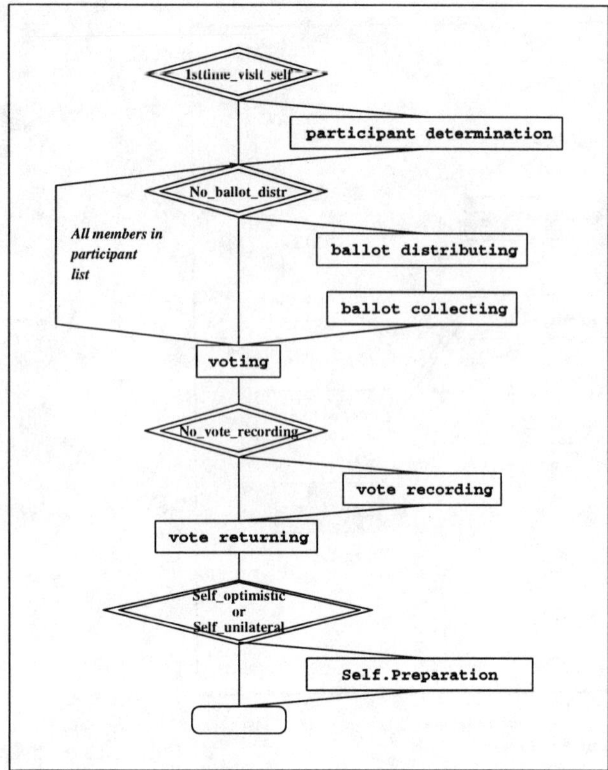

Figure 4: Microprotocols and quasi-invariants in Preparation

of letting Q prepare first. Using OCP to capture such particular protocols or optimizations will render this microprotocol unused.

Ballot collecting

A non-leaf protocol participant P uses this microprotocol to collect the ballot from a child participant Q, which has engaged in the last microprotocol together with P. The collected ballot records Q's vote on its preferred protocol outcome, and possibly some characteristic information about Q. P utilizes a time-out mechanism and consults the data repository at P's node. If P does not receive Q's ballot within the time-out period, P adopts a "presumed" vote for Q. If Q is capable of performing optimistic outcomes, P bookkeeps such information, enabling potential compensation actions in case Q's actual protocol outcome contradicts its voted optimistic outcome.

Voting

For a distributed protocol participant P, this microprotocol combines the votes from P's children participants to derive a vote representing P's own decision about its intended protocol outcome. An upcall is associated with this microprotocol to allow customized vote-combining rules to be introduced to alter the behavior of OCP. Whether built-in or supplied, these vote-combining rules usually reference the characteristic information of P and each of its children participants.

Vote recording

This microprotocol works by making the voting decision of a particular protocol participant durable so that in case of crash recovery, the participant will be identified as "voted" and wait for an outcome resolution from its superior participant or if necessary, the protocol coordinator.

When using OCP to build specific coordination protocol instances, this microprotocol can be bypassed. For example, the optimistic commit protocol [13] allows participants of the distributed Commit transaction primitive to carry out the commit outcome optimistically with the possibility to compensate later. Or, the presumed abort commit protocol [15, 16] allows abort outcome to be carried out unilaterally yet without the need of a forced log record for such voting decision. In both cases, this microprotocol can be bypassed.

3.2.3 Action

Like Preparation, this protocol interface is not part of the API, since it is only used among protocol participants. Its structure is shown in Figure 5.

Deciding

A distributed protocol participant utilizes this microprotocol to decide the final protocol outcomes of its children participants who are not able to perform autonomous outcomes. If the participant making the decision is the protocol coordinator, it will make the decision based on the votes collected from its children participants in Preparation and each child's characteristic information. If the participant executing this microprotocol is not the coordinator of OCP, then it needs to consider both of the above two factors, in addition to its own outcome decision as notified by its parent.

An upcall is associated with this microprotocol to allow customized outcome decision rules to be introduced to alter the behavior of OCP. Like the vote-combining rules in the "Voting" microprotocol, this set of rules also usually reference the characteristic information of the invoking participant and each of its children participants.

Outcome recording

The participant who executes this microprotocol logs the outcomes for all of its children who have not carried out autonomous outcomes. Those who do should have logged such outcomes earlier in Preparation. Logging the outcomes for all its children is spoken from a generic point of view, as different children participants might have different acceptable outcome sets. Practically speaking, since for a large number of applications, the acceptable outcome sets

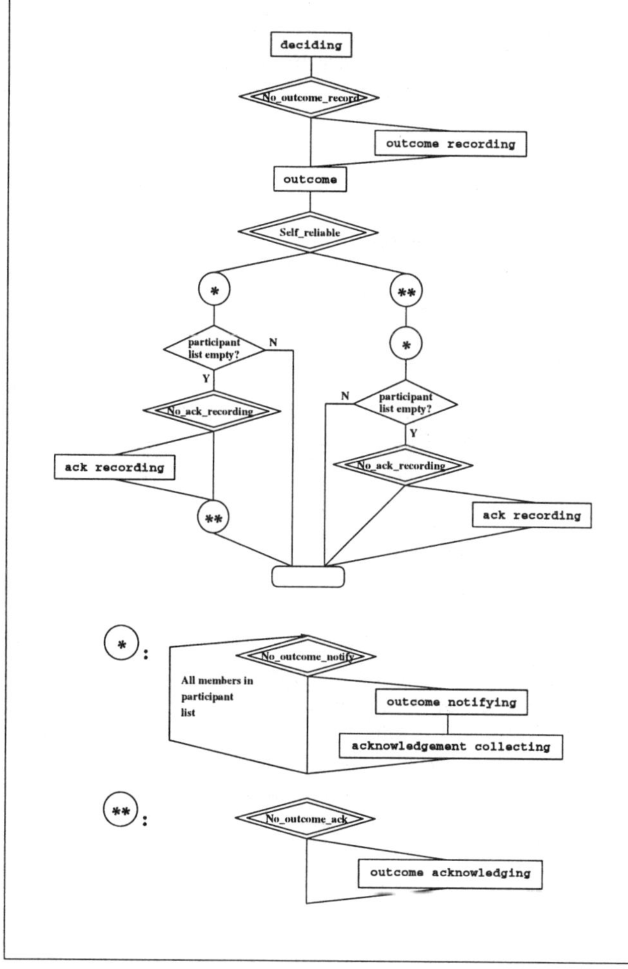

Figure 5: Microprotocols and quasi-invariants in Action

tradicts with its actual protocol outcome, the participant should in addition perform compensating actions in this microprotocol to remedy what it has done optimistically.

Outcome notifying

For a non-leaf protocol participant P and P's child participant Q, this microprotocol's function is for P to activate Q's `Action` entry, notifying Q its actual outcome in the protocol. P sends Q information like transaction management primitive name, data operation arguments, etc., for Q to carry out its own protocol outcome.

Acknowledgement collecting

A non-leaf protocol participant P uses this microprotocol to collect the acknowledgement from a child participant Q, which has engaged in the last microprotocol together with P. The collected acknowledgement indicates that Q has received P's outcome notification. P utilizes a time-out mechanism, as in the "Ballot collecting" microprotocol. If P does not receive Q's acknowledgement within the time-out period, a separate thread is created to make sure Q receive the protocol's decision on its actual outcome. Otherwise, P purges Q from its protocol participant list.

Acknowledgement recording

For a distributed protocol participant P, this microprotocol creates an acknowledgement log record, which indicates that all the protocol participants in the subtree rooted at P have carried out their actual protocol outcomes and have acknowledged their superiors' outcome notifications.

3.3 Existing protocols as OCP instantiations

Many transaction coordination protocols can be implemented as OCP's instances. For example, many prevalent commit protocol variants, like presumed-abort (PA) variant of the two-phase commit protocol [15, 16], open commit protocol [21] that introduced the concept of coordinator migration to commit processing, optimistic commit protocol [13] that allows sites to commit optimistically with the possibility of compensation, unilateral commit [10] that does not give protocol participants the right to vote, etc.

Many optimizations on transaction coordination protocols can also be implemented as OCP's instances. For example, many practical optimizations on two-phase commit protocol described in [22], like read-only, last agent, ok-to-leave-out, voting-reliable, etc.

The following table lists how different microprotocols of OCP can be composed to implement several existent transaction coordination protocols and optimizations. The enabling technology to make such protocol instances efficient, namely, specialization based on a set of quasi-invariants or invariants, will be discussed in next section. The table assumes only two distributed protocol participants, with one being the coordinator and the other being a leaf.

are the same (e.g., {Commit, Abort}), the information being logged could be well-reduced to as little as that for a single protocol participant.

Also note that there exists one outcome within each participant's acceptable outcome set that could be designated as the *presumed outcome* for that participant. If the decided outcome for a child participant happens to be such, it need not be logged by either its superior participant or the child participant. The `Abort` outcome is typically the presumed outcome for all the protocol participants in the two-phase commit protocol, yielding the so-called "presumed abort" commit protocol (PA) [15, 16].

Outcome

For each distributed protocol participant, this microprotocol carries out its final protocol outcome. An upcall is associated with this microprotocol to give each protocol participant the ability to customize its outcome actions. Note that if a protocol participant is capable of performing optimistic outcomes and its voted protocol outcome con-

Microprotocol	optimistic commit (commit case)	presumed abort (abort case)	last agent
participant determination			
coordinator migration			
ballot distributing			X
ballot collecting			
voting			
vote recording	X	X	
vote returning			
deciding			
outcome recording		X	
outcome			
outcome notifying	X	X	
acknowledgement collecting	X	X	X
acknowledgement recording	X	X	
outcome acknowledging	X	X	X

Table 1: Existent protocol and optimizations as OCP's instances

We emphasize on the openness of OCP. The examples listed here are just some particular instances of OCP. They are not the only existent protocols or optimizations that OCP can capture. However, as a first attempt to systematically making extended transaction models distributed, this paper does not try to categorize all the ETMs this protocol can handle but rather leave that as a further research question.

3.4 Implementing OCP

Following the *open implementation* [11] principle, the *Reflective Transaction Framework* (RTF) [1] facilitates the implementation of extended transaction models by exporting both functional and meta transaction interfaces. The latter is achieved by a set of *transaction adapters*, add-on modules on top of existent TP systems to provide extended transaction semantics.

Our design of OCP follows the same principle, allowing us to incorporate OCP into the Reflective Transaction Framework. Such implementation refines both types of interfaces (i.e., functional and meta interfaces) provided by the framework, adding support for distribution handling.

Due to space limitation, we only briefly describe the implementation in this subsection. A detailed implementation can be found in the full version of this paper [25].

As one of the transaction adapters implementing the meta interface of the RTF, the Transaction Management Adapter provides a set of commands: `instantiate`, `reflect`, `exec`, `delegate`, `create_dependency`, ...; it also utilizes two data structures: reflective transaction table and transaction dependency graph. In implementing OCP, the reflective transaction table maintained by the transaction management adapter at a node will be augmented with the following information. For each entry in that table (i.e. an entry corresponding to a specific E-transaction), a field called `primitive_table` is added to record information required for processing specific distributed transaction management primitive (either classical or extended). Each row in `primitive_table` represents a specific transaction management primitive, and each column indicates the sequence number that primitive is invoked (i.e., a primitive like `Split` could be invoked more than once within a specific transaction, thus this field). Each cell in the table records the protocol participants controlled by this transaction manager (i.e., this TM's protocol participant list) for the $\langle primitive, sequence number \rangle$ pair.

Besides, another data structure called primitive upcall list will also be maintained by the transaction management adapter. Each entry in the list corresponds to a list of upcalls relevant to each distributed transaction management primitive's execution. These upcalls are categorized to restrict their usage to specific microprotocols. For example, for upcalls falling into the UPCALL_OUTCOME_TYPE category, they are used only by the "Outcome" microprotocol.

The protocol's functional interface is `Coordination`. Its meta interface is provided through the usage of upcall registration. To build a specific protocol instance, a careful combination of parameterization, upcall registration, and specialization is used. The next section shows how specialization is done to make protocol instances efficient, and Section 5 uses two examples to illustrate in general how protocol instantiation is accomplished.

4 Specializations in OCP implementation

4.1 Specialization

The Open Coordination Protocol (OCP) described in the previous section can be utilized to implement a wide range of distributed transaction management primitives, such as `Commit`, `Split`, `Join_group`, and others. Due to its generality, naive implementations of the protocol would carry high overhead. Consequently, an important question is how to implement the protocol efficiently. The technique we use is *incremental specialization* that has been proven to be beneficial in both operating system [19] and programming language research [5].

An *invariant* is a predicate about the environment that holds true throughout the execution of a module. A *quasi-invariant* is a predicate about the environment that holds true for a period of time and might be falsified at other times. *Specialization* improves software performance by creating and using *specialized versions* of the software that take advantage of invariants and quasi-invariants. Usually, a specialized version is generated for a given set of invariants and quasi-invariants; and this particular version of the software module will be used when all of those invariants and quasi-invariants of the module are true.

Since quasi-invariants do not always hold true, the specialized version associated with them needs to be guarded against potential violations. An important challenge in the use of specialization is the guarding of all the quasi-invariants that must hold true during the specialized code execution. Synthetix [19] is developing tools for both dynamic specialization (using the Tempo specializer [5]) and tools for guarding the quasi-invariants. Consequently, system programmers using the Synthetix specialization toolkit can focus on the appropriate specification of the invariants and quasi-invariants for each specialization.

4.2 Invariants and quasi-invariants in OCP

In this subsection, we describe some representative invariants and quasi-invariants that are relevant to OCP's specialization. They are briefly summarized in Table 4.2. All those listed are for the same distributed protocol participant that exports the protocol API.

There are two main contributing factors in the cost of OCP: network messages and forced logging to disk. The cost of network messages is typically measured by the number of message flows used by the protocol. The cost of logging is typically measured by the number of forced log records to the disk. Many of the quasi-invariants listed aim to reduce either the number of messages or the number of forced log records.

For a distributed protocol participant P and another participant Q directly controlled by P, the NO_BALLOT_DISTR quasi-invariant states that P will not send ballot message to Q, soliciting its vote. It allows the microprotocol "Ballot Distributing" to be bypassed, saving the total number of message flows in the protocol by one. An example scenario in which this quasi-invariant holds is when P is the coordinator and Q is the only other participant of the protocol (e.g., so-called "last agent" in commit processing). In this case, P can first vote itself, then send the vote to Q and let Q assume the role of coordinator for the rest of the protocol, making decisions about both P and Q's final outcomes. Therefore, a ballot message from P to Q is saved.

Similarly, the NO_OUTCOME_NOTIFY quasi-invariant states that P will not send outcome message to Q, letting Q perform corresponding outcome actions. It enables the bypassing of the microprotocol "Outcome Notification", also saving the total number of message flows by one. By way of example, if we are using OCP for distributed **Commit**, and all of Q's operations inside this transaction are read-only, P does not need to send Q an outcome message, as whether Q commits or aborts does not affect the consistency of data

handled by Q[2].

Another benefit of the protocol is that it enables us to use quasi-invariants to capture participant's coordination characteristics like autonomy and optimisticness, so that some participants could perform outcome actions unilaterally without unnecessary waitings. Quasi-invariants SELF_IS_UNILATERAL and SELF_IS_OPTIMISTIC are two representatives of such that enables protocol to be specialized to reflect autonomous outcomes. For a distributed protocol participant P, SELF_IS_OPTIMISTIC states that P could carry out outcome actions optimistically, i.e., P optimistically assumes that its final protocol outcome will be the same as its voted outcome, and thus carries out that outcome right after it votes. This makes P execute its **Action** entry much earlier than otherwise. However, P must be equipped with compensating actions for that particular outcome in order to make that quasi-invariant hold.

All the listed quasi-invariants are validated in microprotocol "Participant Determination", before specialization happens. Alternatively, code templates could be used [5] to amortize the cost of dynamic code generation.

4.3 Guarding the quasi-invariants

Because quasi-invariants may not hold true through the entire execution, specialized code need to guard the quasi-invariants. Protocol correctness is preserved by guarding every place where quasi-invariants might become false. A *guard* is a test placed at a location in the system where a quasi-invariant might be invalidated. If execution at that point invalidates the quasi-invariant, the guard *replugs* all the specialized modules that depend on the quasi-invariant with less specialized modules that do not depend on the falsified quasi-invariant.

We distinguish between two types of quasi-invariants for this particular protocol. Firstly, for a distributed protocol participant P, some quasi-invariants are affected only by P's own characteristics, like: P only exports read-only interfaces to other participants; or, P does not have the capability of making heuristic decisions in case the protocol is blocked. NO_VOTE_RECORDING and NO_ACK_RECORDING are two examples. For a particular participant, like P, these quasi-invariants can be almost like invariants. In the above read-only case, both of these two quasi-invariants will be true all the time. Secondly, still using P as example, some quasi-invariants are affected by the characteristics of those remote participants that are controlled by P. NO_BALLOT_DISTR and NO_OUTCOME_NOTIFY are two such examples. For a remote participant that is capable of carrying out unilateral outcomes, like abort, when its vote in microprotocol **Preparation** happens to be an unilateral outcome, NO_OUTCOME_NOTIFY will be true for P.

For the second category of quasi-invariants in this paper, the microprotocols "Ballot collecting" and "Participant determination" include their guards. And upcalls are associated with these microprotocols allowing customized valida-

---

[2]Here, we assume there are no other applications at Q's node that use the information of whether Q commits or aborts in this particular transaction.

(Quasi-)Invariant	Description	Specialization
NO_BALLOT_DISTR	No ballot messages will be sent.	Bypass microprotocol "Ballot Distributing".
NO_BALLOT_COLLECT	No ballot messages will be collected.	Bypass microprotocol "Ballot Collecting".
NO_VOTE_RECORDING	No vote recording will be performed.	Bypass microprotocol "Vote Recording".
NO_OUTCOME_RECORDING	No outcome recording will be performed.	Bypass microprotocol "Outcome Recording".
NO_OUTCOME_NOTIFY	No outcome notification messages will be sent.	Bypass microprotocol "Outcome Notification".
NO_OUTCOME_ACK	No outcome acknowledgement messages will be collected.	Bypass microprotocol "Acknowledgement Collecting".
NO_ACK_RECORDING	No acknowledgement recording will be performed.	Bypass microprotocol "Acknowledgement Recording"
SELF_OPTIMISTIC	The participant executing the protocol is capable of performing optimistic outcomes.	Replace microprotocol "Vote Recording" with the participant's own "Action".
SELF_UNILATERAL	The participant executing the protocol is capable of performing unilateral outcomes.	Replace microprotocol "Vote Recording" with the participant's own "Action".

Table 2: Invariants and quasi-invariants for protocol specialization

tion functions. For instance, microprotocol "Ballot collecting" utilizes a customized upcall to test if a child participant is able to carry out autonomous outcomes. For children participants without such capability, quasi-invariant NO_OUTCOME_NOTIFY will be invalidated and the unspecialized version of OCP is replugged.

5 Coordination of distributed extended transactions

In this section, we illustrate how the Open Coordination Protocol (OCP) can be used to implement distributed extended transaction management primitives. We use two examples as demonstrations: distributed `Split` with read-only optimization, and distributed `Join_group` with optimistic outcomes.

5.1 Distributed Split with read-only optimization

The split transaction model [18] introduces an extended transaction management primitive `Split` as a means to dynamically restructure a transaction. In specific, when executed within transaction T, `Split` first creates a new transaction T' and then delegates all the uncommitted operations on a given set of data objects (specified by the user) from T to T'. T and T' will proceed independently of each other, yet preserving serializability. "Delegate" means that T' takes over from T the responsibility of either committing or aborting those particular operations at its own decision.

OCP can be instantiated and specialized to work for distributed `Split`. This is achieved via parameterization, upcall registration, and specializations (as described in last section). Parameterization is done

by supplying a set of parameters to OCP's functional interface (i.e., `Coordination`); upcall registration is done by first customly building a set of functions that use other system-supplied low-level primitives (like `create_dependency`, `set_no_conflict`, etc.), and then invoking the `register_upcall` function with a set of appropriate parameters, which we will describe later. Each of these functions serves as an instance of a particular upcall that is associated with a certain microprotocol (e.g., an upcall in the "Voting" microprotocol that enables customized vote-combining rules). The `register_upcall` function is part of OCP's meta-interface, and upcall registration is only necessary when microprotocols' default behavior do not meet an application's need.

For a protocol participant in the distributed `Split` that does not perform any updates, it does not need to participate in the outcome phase of the coordination protocol, i.e., its `Action` entry need not be activated. This is termed read-only optimization, and was originally implemented for two-phase commit protocols [15, 16].

To implement the read-only optimization using OCP, a set of invariants and quasi-invariants are first chosen to reflect the nature of the optimization — in this case: NO_OUTCOME_NOTIFY, NO_OUTCOME_ACK, and NO_OUTCOME_RECORDING. And then, we build a validation function that associates the characteristics of a distributed protocol participant with these quasi-invariants (recall that the characteristics of a distributed protocol participant can be either specified explicitly as protocol parameters or recorded in the data repository at the participant's node). Finally, this function is registered as the upcall that is associated with the "Participant determination" microprotocol to enable customized specialization decisions.

The following is the pseudo-C code for `Split`:

```
...
void split(T, new_T, obj_list)
  IN tran_tid_t T;
  IN tran_tid_t new_T;
  IN object_t *obj_list;
{
  delegate(T, new_T, obj_list);
}


...
void Split(T, obj_list)
  IN tran_tid_t T;
  IN object_t *obj_list;
{
  tran_tid_t new_T;
  new_T = Begin_tran();

  register_upcall("Split", VALIDATION_UPCALL_TYPE,
                    "", is_read_only);
  register_upcall("Split", VOTE_UPCALL_TYPE,
                    "", vote_for_split);
  register_upcall("Split", OUTCOME_UPCALL_TYPE,
                    "split", split);
  register_upcall("Split", OUTCOME_UPCALL_TYPE,
                    "nosplit", nosplit);

  Coordination(T, new_T, "Split", obj_list, ...);
}
```

The `split` function represents the actual outcome action of a protocol participant in the distributed `Split`. The `register_upcall` function plants into the system a supplied function as a customized upcall, which is associated with a particular microprotocol. It takes four arguments. The first is the transaction management primitive's name. The second is the type of the upcall, like `VOTE_UPCALL_TYPE`, `OUTCOME_UPCALL_TYPE`, etc. The third argument represents a protocol outcome's name. And the final argument is the supplied function. The pair of the second and the third argument serves as an index (hash key) into the "primitive upcall list" data structure maintained by the transaction manager. For instance, if the upcall's type is `VOTE_UPCALL_TYPE`, the upcall registered will correspond to the one in the "Voting" microprotocol in `Preparation`; if the type is `OUTCOME_UPCALL_TYPE` and the outcome's name is "commit", the upcall registered will be one of those associated with the "Outcome" microprotocol in `Action`.

The function `is_read_only` is the customized validation function for those quasi-invariants associated with the read-only optimization. The function `vote_for_split` is a customized voting upcall for a particular protocol participant, if necessary.

5.2 Distributed Join_group with optimistic outcomes

The cooperative group transaction model [14, 20] introduces an extended transaction management primitive `Join_group` that allows individual transactions to join a transaction group, which facilitates cooperative accesses to a set of shared data objects. A cooperative group is created by a *group transaction*, and a transaction joining a cooperative group is called a *member transaction*. A member transaction is both Abort- and Commit-dependent on the group transaction creating the transaction group to which the member transaction belong, i.e., a member transaction has to abort if the group transaction aborts, and a member transaction can only commit if the group transaction commits.

OCP can be also instantiated and specialized to work for distributed `Join_group`. It is done similarly to distributed `Split`, with different actual parameters, customized upcalls, and set of associated quasi-invariants. In addition, compensating actions are taken into consideration. Again, in building the customized upcalls, other system primitives like `create_dependency` and `set_no_conflict` are utilized, to add the Abort- and Commit- dependency information, as well as conflict-resolution strategy for concurrent access to shared data objects, into the system.

Like a participant in distributed `Commit` being able to carry out the commit outcome optimistically [13], a protocol participant in the distributed `Join_group` can as well perform optimistic outcomes. For example, the participant can carry out the joining actions optimistically. To qualify as being optimistic, a participant must be equipped with compensating actions for each protocol outcome it can carry out optimistically.

The set of quasi-invariants relevant to the optimistical distributed `Join_group` include SELF_OPTIMISTIC, NO_OUTCOME_NOTIFY, and NO_OUTCOME_ACK. The latter two quasi-invariants might not hold all the time, as they depend on whether the protocol-decided outcome for that particular participant contradicts with its previously performed optimistic outcome. Like in the read-only optimization, a customized validation function is built to guard the truth of these quasi-invariants.

The following is the pseudo-C code for `Join_group`. We assume that only the outcome in which the participant successfully joins a transaction group is possibly carried out optimistically, and we designate `split` as the compensating action.

```
...
void join_group(T, group_T)
  IN tran_tid_t T;
  IN tran_tid_t group_T;
{
  tran_table[T].gid = group_T;
  create_dependency("Commit", T, group_T);
  create_dependency("Abort", group_T, T);
  set_no_conflict(T, group_T);
}


...
void Join_group(T, group_T)
  IN tran_tid_t T, group_T;
{
  register_upcall("Join_group", VALIDATION_UPCALL_TYPE,
                    "", is_optimistic);
  register_upcall("Join_group", VOTE_UPCALL_TYPE,
                    "", vote_for_jgroup);
  register_upcall("Join_group", OUTCOME_UPCALL_TYPE,
```

```
          "jgroup", join_group);
  register_upcall("Join_group", OUTCOME_UPCALL_TYPE,
          "nojgroup", nojoin_group);
  register_upcall("Join_group", COMPENSATE_UPCALL_TYPE,
          "jgroup", split);

  Coordination(T, group_T, "Join_group",
          DEFAULT_OBJECT_LIST, ...);
}
```

6   Related work

Past research and productization in distributed transaction processing yielded many variations of the two-phase commit (2PC) protocol [15, 21, 12, 22]. Instead of describing each optimization separately, we use the microprotocols to compose a wide range of optimizations and extended transaction primitives. The advantage of our approach is a built-in extensibility for many extended transaction primitives.

Much of the work in distributed extended transaction models focused on transaction structures, e.g., multilevel transactions [24], polytransactions [23], etc. Protocols were designed for model–specific transaction management primitives — most prevalently, `Commit` and `Abort` of transactions and subtransactions. By applying the Open Coordination Protocol, our work makes the first attempt to address the implementation of a wider range of distributed extended transaction management primitives in a systematic way.

Apart from those model-specific efforts on extended transaction management, there are a few attempts made to use model-independent building blocks to implement different extended models. The ASSET work at AT&T [3] embeds low-level ACTA-based primitives in the host language of an OODBMS to allow programmers construct extended transactions by composing these primitives. The TSME work at GTE [8] provides a specialized environment containing a set of built-in low-level primitives and a specification language to make the programmer's specification met by a system built-in configuration of these primitives. Our work differs from [3, 8] in that we address the distributed coordination at transaction primitive level with a flexible set of correctness criteria. Our design also extends existing TP monitors.

Our research complements the Reflective Transaction Framework, proposed in [1] to implement different extended transaction models on a commercial TP system. Following the *Open Implementation* approach [11], the framework provides a meta-interface to allow extended transaction semantics (i.e., either new transaction management primitives or new semantics for existing primitives) to be *reflected* into the system. Its novel approach in adapting an existent TP system to handle extended transactions and its careful separation between functional and meta-interface distinguishes the work from other integrated attempts like above two.

Specialization was proposed by the Synthetix project [19], and is closely related with partial evaluation [6] in programming language research. Currently, in the context of the Synthetix project, we are building

tools to facilitate the specialization of C code. This specialization toolkit includes the replugger, the guard checkers (both compile-time and run-time), and the Tempo-C compiler for partial evaluation.

Last but certainly not the least, we continue to follow the OI approach [11] as in [1], yet making one step further in adding power of control over the meta-interfaces provided by the framework.

7   Conclusion

Extended transaction models [7] hold promise for many advanced applications such as long duration activities and collaboration. Many of these applications involve distributed extended transactions. In this paper, we described the Open Coordination Protocol (OCP) that is adaptable, efficient, and modular. The protocol is designed as a set of microprotocols that can be modularly composed to implement a number of extended transaction primitives such as split/join and cooperative groups.

We designed OCP in two steps. First, we decomposed prevalent coordination protocols into *microprotocols* [17], modular building blocks with specific functions. Second, we use *specialization* [6, 19] to guide the composition process to build full-function protocol components for specific situations, e.g., distributed split transaction with read-only optimization and distributed join-group with optimistic outcomes.

OCP is adaptable and flexible because the microprotocol components are designed in a way that they can be combined to implement many extended transaction models (e.g., delegation) and take advantage of known optimization opportunities (e.g., read-only, optimistic outcomes). OCP is efficient because the specialization process can eliminate unnecessary code at both compile-time and run-time (and save message exchanges at run-time), using the invariants and quasi-invariants for each situation. Specialization also addresses the correctness of a variety of extended transaction management primitives in a uniform manner, including the traditional variants of two-phase commit [22].

This research is part of a concerted effort to implement extended transaction models on production softwares. Barga and Pu [1] have proposed the Reflective Transaction Framework to implement extended transaction models on production TP monitors such as the Transarc Encina. This paper extends their results to support the flexible coordination of distributed extended transactions. OCP is also complementary to the ongoing work on supporting recovery of extended transaction models by Chen [4]. We are currently evaluating the performance of OCP in specific distributed transaction management primitives and optimizations, as well as the benefit and overhead brought about by the incremental specialization process. We are also building an Open Coordination Protocol mini-framework, which facilitates the implementation of protocols like OCP (or its instances) in regards of microprotocol incorporation and flexible microprotocol composition.

References

[1] R. S. Barga and C. Pu. A practical and modular method to implement extended transaction models. In *Proceedings of the 21st International Conference on Very Large Data Bases*, Zurich, Switzerland, September 1995.

[2] P. A. Bernstein. Transaction processing monitors. *Communications of the ACM*, 33(11):75–86, 1990.

[3] A. Biliris, S. Dar, N. Gehani, H. Jagadish, and K. Ramamritham. ASSET: A system for supporting extended transactions. In *Proceedings of 1994 ACM SIGMOD*, pages 44–53, May 1994.

[4] S. Chen. *A Recovery Implementation Method for Extended Transaction Models*. PhD thesis, Department of Computer Science, Columbia University, To be determined 1996.

[5] C. Consel and F. Noel. A general approach for run-time specialization and its application to C. In *Proceedings of the 23rd Symposium on Principles of Programming Languages*, Florida, 1996.

[6] C. Consel, C. Pu, and J. Walpole. Incremental specialization: The key to high performance, modularity and portability in operating systems. In *Proceedings of ACM Symposium on Partial Evaluation and Semantics-Based Program Manipulation*, Copenhagen, June 1993.

[7] A. K. Elmagarmid, editor. *Database Transaction Models for Advanced Applications*. Morgan Kaufmann, 1993.

[8] D. Georgakopoulos, M. Hornick, P. Krychniak, and F. Manola. Specification and management of extended transactions in a programmable transaction environment. In *Proceedings of the 1994 IEEE Conference on Data Engineering*, pages 462–473, February 1994.

[9] J. Gray and A. Reuter. *Transaction Processing: Concepts and Techniques*. Morgan Kaufmann, 1993.

[10] M. Hsu and A. Silberschatz. Unilateral commit: A new paradigm for reliable distributed transaction processing. In *Proceedings of the 1991 IEEE Conference on Data Engineering*, February 1991.

[11] G. Kiczales. Towards a new model of abstraction in software engineering. In *Proceedings of the IMSA'92 Workshop on Reflection and Meta-level Architectures*, 1992. See http://www.xerox.com/PARC/spl/eca/oi.html for updates.

[12] B. Lampson and D. Lomet. A new presumed commit optimization for two phase commit. In *Proceedings of the 19th International Conference on Very Large Data Bases*, 1993.

[13] E. Levy, H. F. Korth, and A. Silberschatz. An optimistic commit protocol for distributed transaction management. In *Proceedings of 1991 ACM SIGMOD*, pages 88–97, Denver, Colorado, May 1991.

[14] B. Martin and C. Pederson. Long-lived concurrent activities. In A. Gupta, editor, *Distributed Object Management*, pages 188–206. Morgan Kaufmann, 1992.

[15] C. Mohan and B. Lindsay. Efficient commit protocols for the tree of processes model of distributed transactions. In *Proceedings of 2nd ACM SIGACT/SIGOPS Symposium on PODC*, Montreal, Canada, August 1983.

[16] C. Mohan, B. Lindsay, and R. Obermark. Transaction management in the R* distributed database management system. *ACM Transactions on Database Systems*, 11(4):378–396, 1986.

[17] S. W. O'Malley and L. L. Peterson. A dynamic network architecture. *ACM Transactions on Computer Systems*, 10(2):110–143, May 1992.

[18] C. Pu, G. E. Kaiser, and N. Hutchinson. Split-transactions for open-ended activities. In *Proceedings of the 14th International Conference on Very Large Data Bases*, 26-37, August 1988.

[19] C. Pu, T. Autrey, A. Black et al. Optimistic incremental specialization: Streamlining a commercial operating system. In *Proceedings of the Fifteenth Symposium on Operating Systems Principles*, Colorado, December 1995.

[20] K. Ramamritham and P. Chrysanthis. In search of acceptability criteria: Database consistency requirements and transaction correctness properties. In A. Gupta, editor, *Distributed Object Management*, pages 212–230. Morgan Kaufmann, 1992.

[21] K. Rothermel and S. Pappe. Open commit protocols for the tree of processes model. In *Proceedings of the 10th International Conference on Distributed Computing Systems*, pages 236–244, 1990.

[22] G. Samaras, K. Britton, A. Citron, and C. Mohan. Two-phase commit optimizations and tradeoffs in the commercial environment. In *Proceedings of the 1993 IEEE Conference on Data Engineering*, Vienna, Austria, February 1993.

[23] A. Sheth, M. Rusinkiewicz, and G. Karabatis. Using polytransactions to manage interdependent data. In A. Elmagarmid, editor, *Database Transaction Models for Advanced Applications*. Morgan Kaufmann, 1993.

[24] G. Weikum and H.-J. Schek. Concepts and applications of multilevel transactions and open nested transactions. In A. Elmagarmid, editor, *Database Transaction Models for Advanced Applications*. Morgan Kaufmann, 1993.

[25] T. Zhou and C. Pu. Adaptable, efficient, and modular coordination of distributed extended transactions. Technical report, Department of Computer Science and Engineering, Oregon Graduate Institute, April 1996.

Transient Versioning for Consistency and Concurrency in Client-Server Systems

Sreenivas Gukal*   Edward Omiecinski
Umakishore Ramachandran
College of Computing, Georgia Institute of Technology
Atlanta, GA 30332

Abstract

Synchronization and cache consistency limit the performance of data-shipping client-server systems. Both the problems arise because existing methods treat cached data as replicated data. This paper proposes a new method using transient versioning concepts to reduce the effect of these problems. Copies of data in different client caches are treated as different versions of the data. Multiple versions reduce cache consistency overhead since updating a data page creates a new version and does not require invalidating copies of that page in other caches. The transient versions also increase concurrency by allowing multiple readers and one writer to simultaneously access the same page. Simulation experiments show that this method performs better than the existing methods in different environments and is easily adaptable to mixed and/or changing workloads.

1   Introduction

The advent of fast and inexpensive desktop computers and the standardization of high-bandwidth networks have enabled client-server architectures to become an efficient way of organizing databases. Client-server database systems have a powerful shared server that provides database services to multiple clients. Two types of architectures, *query-shipping* and *data-shipping*, are possible based on the type of interaction between the clients and the server. In query-shipping systems, clients send requests to the server. The server executes the requests on behalf of the clients and sends the results back. Clients are more sophisticated in data-shipping systems. The clients request data from the server and the processing is done at the clients. This architecture makes use of the processing power and the memory of the clients to provide higher performance. Enhancing the throughput of data shipping client-server systems is the focus of this paper.

Cache consistency and synchronization are two important issues in a data-shipping environment. When copies of data are cached at different clients, all copies should be maintained consistent. Synchronization

deals with how transactions executing on different clients are allowed to access shared data in a consistent manner. Several methods for providing cache consistency and synchronization have been proposed, implemented and evaluated (e.g., [Care 91], [WaRo 91], [WiNe 90], [FrCa 92], [LLOW 91]). All these methods assume that the copies of data in different client caches are all copies of a single version of data. With this view, cache consistency becomes costly since if one copy of a data item is modified, to maintain consistency the changes have to be reflected in all other copies of the data item. Single version data also requires global synchronization and reduces concurrency as read and write locks on the same data are incompatible.

Transient-versioning algorithms have been proposed for centralized databases as an elegant way to support queries. These algorithms maintain prior versions of updated data items. Queries can read the prior versions, while transactions use the current versions. The prior versions are transient; they are removed when queries no longer need them. This paper extends transient versioning concepts to a data-shipping client-server architecture. A new consistency method called *Slice Consistency (SC)* is proposed and evaluated. Slice consistency considers copies of data in different client caches as different versions of the data. Transient versioning is used not only to support queries by reducing data contention, but also to simplify cache consistency. Simulation experiments show that slice consistency performs better than existing methods for different environments and is easily adaptable to mixed and/or changing workloads.

The related work is covered in Section 2. Section 3 explains the slice consistency method and describes possible variations. Section 4 presents the simulation experiments and the results. Section 5 discusses the results and the last section presents our conclusions.

2   Related Work

2.1   Client-Server Systems

Existing client cache consistency algorithms are variations of the consistency methods for replicated

---

*Currently with Informix Software, Inc.

databases. A detailed taxonomy of the consistency protocols is presented by Franklin [Fran 93]. The cache consistency algorithms can be divided into two classes: *detection-based* and *avoidance-based*. Detection-based algorithms allow stale data to exist in client caches. A transaction has to check the validity of the data it has accessed before it can commit. On the other hand, avoidance-based algorithms are based on read-one/write-all approach to replica management. Committed updates are immediately propagated to all necessary client caches, thereby avoiding access to stale data. Pessimistic and optimistic variations are possible in both classes of consistency protocols.

Several detection-based algorithms have been proposed in the literature ([Care 91], [WaRo 91], [WiNe 90]). Detection of stale pages can be either pessimistic (on initial access [Care 91], [WaRo 91]) or optimistic (deferred until commit [WiNe 90]). Avoidance-based methods ([WaRo 91], [FrCa 92], [LLOW 91], [Care 91], [WiNe 90]) are more complex as the server has to keep track of the contents of all client caches. The pessimistic variations ([WaRo 91], [FrCa 92], [LLOW 91]) invalidate the copies in other caches immediately on a write fault, while the optimistic methods ([Care 91], [WiNe 90]) wait until the commit time and either invalidate or update the copies in the other caches.

We briefly discuss two algorithms to give a flavor of the design space. The first algorithm is a pessimistic detection-based method called "Caching Two-Phase Locking (C2PL)" ([Care 91], [WaRo 91]). C2PL is a variation of the primary copy locking algorithm. Transactions set read (or write) locks on the data pages they read (or modify). All lock requests are sent to the server which serves as the primary copy site. If the page is currently cached at the requesting client, then the lock request for the page also includes the locally known timestamp of that page. On the reply message, the server piggybacks the updated copy of the page if one exists. All locks are held until the transaction either commits or aborts.

Optimistic avoidance-based algorithms (O2PL) are presented in ([Care 91]). In contrast to C2PL, clients set read and write locks locally without contacting the server. When a needed page is not in the cache, the client sends a request to the server. The server acquires a read lock only to obtain a transaction consistent copy of the page. The read lock is released before the page is forwarded to the requesting client. The server keeps track of the contents of all clients' caches. A transaction performs updates locally and at commit time sends all updated copies to the server. The server then acquires write locks on the updated pages on behalf of the client and sends a prepare-to-commit message to all other clients with cached copies of any of the updated pages. The clients invalidate the cached

copies. The server commits the transaction after all the caching clients have responded.

These two algorithms are compared to other existing methods [Fran 93]. C2PL has better performance than other methods when the data contention is high and O2PL performs best when there is little or no data contention and a high locality of access. We use these two methods as benchmarks to evaluate the slice consistency method.

2.2 Transient Versioning

One of the important concurrency control problems is to prevent the execution of queries from affecting concurrent update transactions. Data versioning helps to avoid data contention between queries and other transactions. Multiversion concurrency control algorithms were first introduced by Reed [Reed 78]. Reed's thesis describes a distributed timestamp ordering scheme, which is a multiversion extension of basic timestamp ordering. Bernstein et al. [BeHG 87] also describe two-version and multiversion two-phase locking methods. Other algorithms ([ABGS 87], [AgSe 89], [Chan 82]) use multiple versions only to support queries with concurrent transactions.

Transient versioning is a multiversioning technique, where the prior versions are maintained temporarily to increase concurrency. The transient versions reduce the storage overhead while providing the same benefits as multiversioning algorithms. Transient versioning was first proposed by Bayer et al. [BaHR 80]. The algorithm is based on the observation that in a shadowing environment an update to a data page makes a copy of the data page and modifies the copy. Since the prior copies of the pages are maintained for recovery purposes, this algorithm proposes that the readers be allowed to read the "before" values. A similar method that uses time-stamp based deadlock prevention has been developed for distributed databases by Stearns and Rosenkrantz [StRo 81]. Recently, transient versioning algorithms based on two-phase locking have been proposed ([MoPL 92], [Chan 82], [BoCa 92], [GuOR 95]). In all these methods, prior versions are deleted when the queries do not need them. All the above methods apply to centralized databases, while [BoCa 92] and [MoPL 92] also extend transient versioning to distributed databases.

3 Slice Consistency

Serializability is the underlying concern for executing transactions. Slice consistency, by using transient-versioning and the notion of slices, enables transactions executing on different clients to be serializable. In this method a data page[1] may have multiple versions. The last version of any page is the write copy and the earlier versions are read-only copies. A slice

---

[1] For ease of explanation, we consider the page as the unit of concurrency control and shipping.

is a part of a transaction-consistent version of the database. A slice consists of a set of versions of different pages. Slices are ordered based on the versions contained in the slices. A slice containing an earlier version of a page is ordered before (i.e., a predecessor of) all slices with a later version of the same page. The relationships among slices are captured in a directed dependence graph. The slices are formed such that the slice dependence graph is *acyclic*.

Figure 1 explains the idea of slices using a simple example. Consider five data pages, A, B, C, D and E. The superscripts denote the versions of the pages. $Slice_1$ contains page versions A^1 and B^2, $Slice_2$ contains page versions B^1 and C^1 and $Slice_3$ contains page E^1. Since $Slice_2$ contains an earlier version and $Slice_1$ a later version of page B, the slice dependence graph contains an edge from $Slice_2$ to $Slice_1$.

Transactions execute completely within a slice. If $Slice_A$ occurs before $Slice_B$, then the global serialization order contains all the transactions executing in $Slice_A$ before all the transactions executing in $Slice_B$. For example, in Figure 1, suppose transactions T_1, T_2 and T_3 execute in $Slice_1$ and transactions T_4 and T_5 execute in $Slice_2$. In the serialization order the set of transactions $\{T_4, T_5\}$ occurs before the set $\{T_1, T_2, T_3\}$.

Each slice is assigned to a single client. However a client may have multiple slices. The server keeps track of all the slices, their assigned clients, the versions of the data pages in the slices and the slice dependence graph. A client knows only about the slices available locally. Each client initially has no slices. As the transactions execute, slices start forming at the clients. A client starts a new transaction in the most recent local slice. If no local slices exist, a new slice is initialized. If a transaction executing in a slice requests for data pages not already in that slice, the client forwards the request to the server. The server extends the slice by adding the appropriate versions of the data pages. If the slice cannot be extended with the requested data pages, the server notifies the client to abort the transaction and start it in a new slice.

A slice consists of both data and the associated locks. In Figure 1, $Slice_1$ contains the write copies and the exclusive locks of the pages A and B. Requests for shared or exclusive locks on pages A and B by transactions executing in $Slice_1$ can be granted locally without notifying the server, yet still maintaining global transaction consistency.

3.1 Supporting Transactions

We first discuss how the write requests are handled and then deal with the read requests. Suppose a transaction executing in a slice S needs to update a data page. If the "write" version of the page belonging to the slice S is available at that client the write lock is granted immediately. Otherwise, the client sends a request for the write copy of the page for slice S to the server. The server extends the slice S, if possible, to include the last version of the page, updates the slice dependence graph and gets that version forwarded to the requesting client. The client then grants the lock request.

The actions of the clients and the server for requests in different scenarios are illustrated using the example in Figure 1. In this example, version 0 of the pages (not shown in the Figure) denotes the initial disk versions of the pages. Suppose $Slice_1$, $Slice_2$ and $Slice_3$ are at processors Pr_1, Pr_2 and Pr_3 respectively. When a transaction executing in $Slice_2$ requests for a write lock for a record in page C, Pr_2 can grant the lock since $Slice_2$ has the write-copy of page C. If a transaction requests for a write lock for a record on page D, the client, in turn, sends a request to the server for the write-copy of page D for $Slice_2$. The server finds that page D is free and extends $Slice_2$ to include the write-copy of D. The server sends a "grant" message to the requesting client at Pr_2. If the page D^1 is available with the server, the page is sent along with the grant message. Otherwise, the server sends a message to the processor where D^1 resides to forward the page to Pr_2. The resulting state is given in Figure 2.

Suppose a transaction in $Slice_2$ requests for a write lock for a record in page E. As before, the local client sends a request to the server for a write-copy of E for $Slice_2$. The server finds that $Slice_3$ currently has the write-copy of E and that $Slice_2$ can be extended without creating a cycle in the dependence graph. The server sends a grant message to the requesting client and a request to Pr_3 to forward the write-copy of E to Pr_2. Pr_3 waits for all transactions in $Slice_3$ having write-locks on records in page E to end, forwards the write-copy to Pr_2 and converts the copy of E in $Slice_3$ to a read-only version. Figure 3 shows the state after $Slice_2$ is extended.

The last case is when a request by a transaction violates the slice consistency rules. Suppose a transaction in $Slice_2$ requests for a write lock for a record in page A. If $Slice_2$ is extended to include the write-copy of A, a cycle will form between $Slice_1$ and $Slice_2$ in the slice dependence graph. The server notifies the client that the request cannot be granted. The transaction that made the request is aborted. The transaction will be restarted in a new slice at Pr_2.

In slice consistency method, read-only versions of data pages can be obtained without aborting the requesting transaction and usually without blocking. The procedure for requesting a read-only version of a data page is the same as that for requesting a write-copy. However, there are two possibilities for the server to satisfy a request for a read-version. The slice can be extended using a read-only version of the page from another slice or the server may have to obtain the write-copy to satisfy the read request. Consider

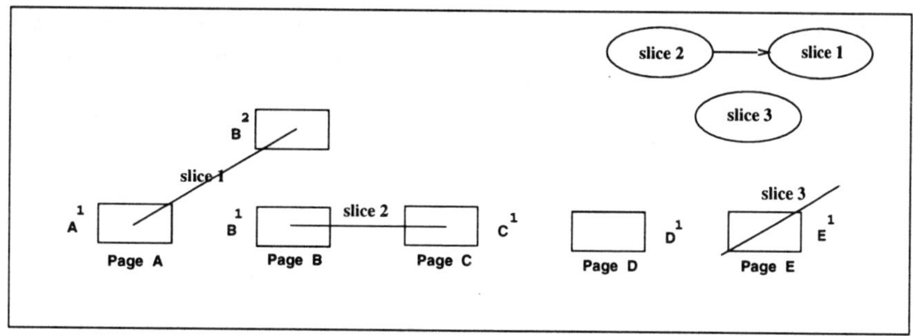

Figure 1: Slices and slice dependency graph

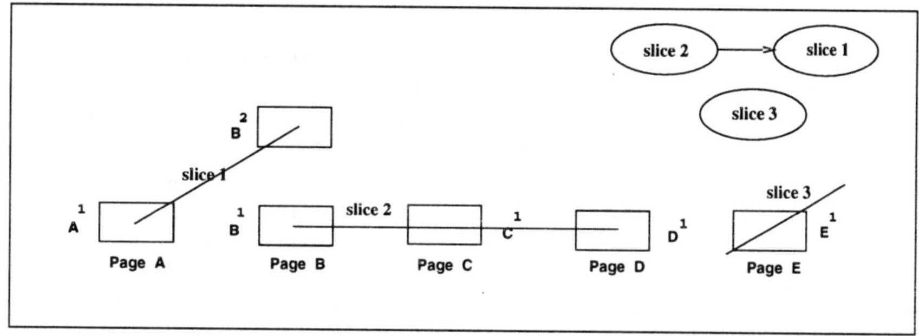

Figure 2: Extending slices - no contention

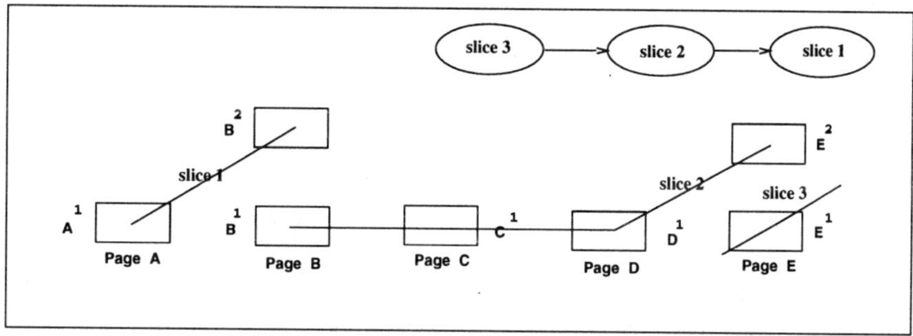

Figure 3: Extending slices - resolvable contention

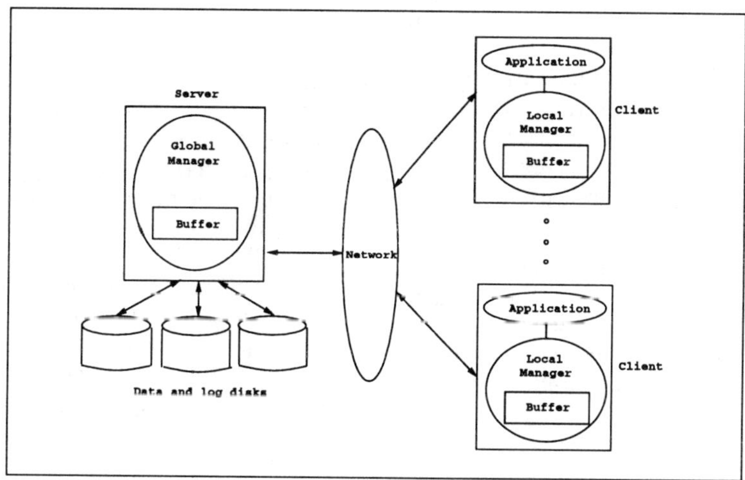

Figure 4: Client-server model

Figure 3 again. If a transaction in $Slice_3$ requests for a read-lock for a record in page B, the disk version of the page B (i.e., version B^0) can be used to extend $Slice_3$. However, if a transaction in $Slice_1$ requests for a read lock for a record in page C, the only way to extend $Slice_1$ to include a version of C without violating the existing order is to get the write-copy of C. The server sends a message to the processor Pr_2 to convert the version C^1 in $Slice_2$ to a read-only version and send the write-copy to the processor Pr_1. In both the cases the slice dependence graph is appropriately modified.

3.2 Supporting Queries

The most important advantage of the slice consistency method is that queries can be executed efficiently. Queries are never blocked, never rolled back and do not affect concurrent transactions.

One way to support queries is to violate serializability for queries. The problem becomes interesting if the queries wish to see a transaction consistent database. Queries execute the same way as transactions. Queries are executed in slices separate from transactions. For ease of reference, slices supporting transactions are called *transaction slices* and those supporting queries are referred to as *query slices*. A query slice never has a write-copy of any page since all the page requests of queries are for read-only versions. Interactions between queries and transactions can be eliminated by making all query slices predecessors of all active transaction slices in the slice dependence graph. As explained in the previous section, the only place where extending a slice is delayed or the transaction aborted is when the slices are involved in a cycle of read-write and write-read dependencies. This cycle is prevented here by making all query slices go before all active transaction slices, thereby avoiding write-read dependencies. The server treats the query slices the same way as transaction slices in maintaining the slice dependence graph.

3.3 Variations of Slice Consistency

Pessimistic concurrency control algorithms perform better in a high data contention environment while optimistic methods are suitable for low contention workloads. To suit different workloads several variations of slice consistency are possible with either pessimistic or optimistic characteristics. The variations depend on and are characterized by how new slices are formed at the clients.

Lazy (SC-L) New slices initially do not contain any pages. Pages are added to a slice only when a transaction in the slice requests for them. This method is comparable to earlier pessimistic methods since the pages are acquired only when needed.

Aggressive (SC-A) The new slice inherits all the hot pages from the earlier slices at the same client.

The idea here is comparable to that in optimistic methods. Two variations are possible depending on when new slices are formed.

Detection-Based A new slice is formed only when a transaction executing in an earlier slice aborts.

Avoidance-Based New slices are periodically formed to purge unnecessary cold pages from earlier slices.

Dynamic This method tries to follow the behavior of the best method in the absence of any prior knowledge of the workloads. Several options for switching among the methods are possible.

A significant drawback of the existing algorithms is that changing from one cache consistency protocol to another is difficult. For example, detection-based methods are different from avoidance-based methods and the protocols for pessimistic and optimistic variations cannot be easily switched. In contrast, the different variations of slice consistency only differ in how the new slices are formed. A simple flag is sufficient for switching between the different variations. It is also possible for each client to follow a different policy based on its workload. Hence, slice consistency will have better performance in an environment of changing or mixed workloads.

3.4 Implementation Issues
Client-Server Architecture

We briefly describe the architecture required to support slices. The server runs a process called *Global Manager (GM)* which ensures consistency and synchronization across all clients. The GM handles client page and lock requests. The GM maintains the slice dependence graph (directed and acyclic) to ensure global transaction consistency. The graph contains one node for each slice and one edge for each dependency among slices. Besides global consistency, the acyclic graph also helps in deadlock avoidance. To provide cache consistency, the GM tracks all cached pages. For each page cached in some client cache, the GM maintains information about the page versions, slices they belong to and where they are cached. The complexity of the GM design compares to that of the existing detection-based methods.

Each client processor runs a *Local Manager (LM)* which manages the cache and synchronization at that client. The LM provides concurrency control within each slice using two-phase locking. Cache maintenance is explained in detail in the next section. The LM may keep track of the data contention (using number of aborts) and hot pages (with reference counts) and use them to change the SC variation followed locally. In the SC-A variation, the LM also includes the hot pages in the current slice while requesting the GM for a new slice.

Managing Versions

Multiple versions may reduce efficient cache utilization without proper garbage collection and version management. A slice contains read-only pages and pages that are updated in that slice. Note from the discussion in the previous sections, a copy of each read-only page in a slice also exists either in another transaction slice (from where it was copied) or in the database (base version).

A slice becomes inactive when all the transactions executing in it terminate. The client keeps only the pages that were updated in the inactive slice. The server is notified that the slice has become inactive. When the server finds an inactive slice with no predecessors in the slice dependence graph, the server asks the client to ship the modified pages of the inactive slice to the server and to remove the slice from the client's cache. The modified pages now become the base versions of the corresponding pages at the server. The server also removes the node for the deleted slice and all its incident edges from the dependence graph. In this method the transient versions exist only in the clients' caches. In contrast to the existing transient versioning algorithms, there is no disk overhead for the transient versions.

Clients may cache multiple slices. If the same read-only version of a page belongs to multiple slices at a client, only a single copy is maintained. The page replacement algorithm at a client first considers pages belonging to deleted slices and then the read-only pages of active slices for replacement. In the worst case when the client's cache is filled with modified pages which cannot be overwritten, the current transaction is aborted and the current slice is flagged as inactive. When space becomes available, the transaction is restarted in a new slice.

4 Simulation Experiments and Results

The performance of the cache consistency methods depends on the type of workload considered. We use the workload model described in ([Care 91], [Fran 93]) for client-server architectures.

HotCold Each client has its own hot region where the majority of its accesses are directed. The remaining accesses refer to the rest of the database. This models a situation where different clients favor disjoint regions of the database, but where some read/write overlap exists.

Private Clients update their own private regions in the database. However, all clients also access a common read-only region.

Feed In this workload, a few clients produce data that all the other clients consume.

Uniform All the clients uniformly access the entire database. This models a situation where there is

Table 1: Common database & transaction parameters

Transaction Parameters	
Lock Acquisition (Release) Time	500 μs
Latch Acquisition (Release) Time	50 μs
Update Time	500 μs
Operation Time	5ms
Database Parameters	
Database Size (pages)	10,000

Table 2: Resource parameters

Resource Parameters	
Data Disks	2
Log Disks	1
Disk Access Time	30ms
No. of Client Processors	10 to 50
Server/Client Speed Ratio	5, 10
Server Memory	30% of DB
Client Memory	15% of DB
Network Bandwidth	1, 10 MB/sec
Msg Processing Cost:	
Small Msg	1ms
Large Msg	1.5ms

no locality of access and hence caching does not provide much performance benefit.

SharedHot Here the hot and cold regions of all the clients are the same. This workload models high data contention and is similar to the workloads used to study shared-disk transaction processing systems.

The above workloads cover the range of sharing possible in client-server databases and emphasize different application characteristics. The main variables here are the level of data sharing among the clients and the locality of access. Some of the workloads model application domains while others are purely synthetic. For example, the feed workload captures the environment (e.g., a hospital) where the data collection sites (e.g., clinical labs) are distinct from where the data is used (e.g., a physician's office). Uniform and shared-hot are synthetic workloads designed to evaluate the performance in extreme conditions.

The simulation experiments evaluate the performance of the slice consistency method relative to the C2PL and O2PL algorithms described in Section 2. The simulation experiments are designed to,

- determine the slice consistency variation most suitable for each workload (consisting of only transactions) and compare its performance to the best existing algorithm,

- evaluate slice consistency in environments of mixed and changing workloads, and

- evaluate the performance of slice consistency in the presence of queries.

The simulation model and the parameters are presented first. The later three subsections contain the results of the simulations.

4.1   Simulation Model & Parameters

The client-server model is shown in Figure 4. The hardware environment consists of a server processor and a set of client processors where each processor can communicate with any of the other processors. The server manages the data disks and the log disk while the clients are diskless.

Transactions execute at the clients. A transaction does not span multiple clients. Transactions request the LM for locks and data records. The LM, in turn, interacts with the GM for concurrency control and cache maintenance. We consider a simple model where transactions execute one at a time at each client. The extension to concurrent transactions at each client is straightforward.

The database is modeled as having a number of data pages. Transactions contain a series of references, each reference made up of a page number, the type of access and the amount of operation time the transaction spends in the CPU after accessing the record. The operation time models the time for accessing the data item, performing any computations using the fetched value and determining the new value for the data item in case of updates. The lock and data requests are handled by the GM and the LMs based on the algorithm being simulated. When a transaction commits, all the log records written by it are sent to the server. Table 1 lists the common database and transaction parameters. The times for lock and latch operations are constant for all requests. The record update time and the operation time are exponentially distributed.

Modeling the resources is more involved here than in centralized databases. Each client is modeled as a single processor executing one transaction at a time. The server is faster than the client processors. We consider two server speeds: 5 and 10 times faster than the client processors. All processing overheads at the server are smaller by this factor compared to the same overheads at the clients. The lower server speed is used to highlight the resource contention in algorithms that require more processing at the server. A very simple network is modeled as a FIFO resource. Two bandwidths, 1MB/sec and 10MB/sec are considered. The lower bandwidth is used to study the effect on algorithms which send more messages than others. The cost of sending a message is modeled as having two

components, the time required to transmit the message and the processing required at the sender and the receiver for handling the message. The resource parameters common to all the experiments are listed in Table 2.

As in [Fran 93], a small database size is used to make the detailed simulations of the complex client-server system computationally feasible. The server and client caches are chosen to hold 30% and 15% of the database respectively. The transaction accesses are such that the relative sizes of the database and the caches simulate needed data contention and cache consistency effects.

Each simulation run uses a set of 1000 transactions. The same sets of transactions are used for all methods. For each set of input parameters, the system is simulated on a number of transaction sets until the 90% confidence interval for the transaction throughput is within a few percent. The simulator is written in CSIM [Schw 90], a process-oriented simulation package.

4.2   Supporting Transactions

Four different workloads are used in the first set of experiments designed to evaluate slice consistency in a transactions-only environment. Table 3 lists the parameters used for the different workloads.

Figure 5 shows the performance of different methods in a high data contention and low resource contention (ratio of server:client speeds is 10 and network bandwidth is 10 MB/sec) environment. All the clients have the same 1000 pages as hot area and the remaining 9000 pages as cold area. O2PL has low performance here due to a high number of aborts. C2PL has less than 10% of the aborts as O2PL and hence performs better than O2PL. However, as the number of clients increases blocking due to data contention becomes severe in C2PL. At 50 clients, each transaction in C2PL spends nearly 70% of its time waiting for locks. The lazy variation of slice consistency (SC-L) performs the best here. This method has lesser number of aborts compared to O2PL (about 60% less) and avoids blocking due to read-write contention. Figure 6 shows the performance results when the resource contention is high. The network bandwidth is reduced to 1MB/sec and the server speed to 5 times the clients' speed. C2PL performs better than the other two methods since it has lower number of aborts. Avoiding blocking due to data contention does not help SC-L as transactions wait for resources instead of waiting for data.

Figure 7 shows the results for the hot-cold workload with low resource contention. Each client has a separate hot area of 200 pages to which 80% of the references are directed. The remaining 20% of the references are uniformly distributed over the rest of the database. This provides an environment where there is a little read-write sharing among the clients. The

Table 3: Workload parameters

Parameter	SharedHot	HotCold	Private	Uniform
References	10	10	10	10
Hot Area	1000 pages all	200 pages each	100 pages each	–
Cold Area	rest of DB	rest of DB	5000 pages	all DB
Hot Access Prob.	0.8	0.8	0.6	–
Cold Access Prob.	0.2	0.2	0.4	1.0
Hot Write Prob.	0.5	0.5	1.0	0.0
Cold Write Prob.	0.5	0.5	0.0	1.0

hot region of each client is small enough to be cached locally. O2PL performs better than C2PL since messages are avoided for the cached hot regions. The aborts are also lower for O2PL in this case compared to the high data contention workload. The avoidance-based slice consistency method has the best performance for this workload. To reduce the overlap among slices at different clients, new slices are periodically formed and only the hot pages from the earlier slices are inherited. SC-A performs better than O2PL by reducing both the number of messages and aborts. The high resource contention case shows a similar pattern. However, all the three methods reach their maximum throughput at about 30 clients beyond which the network becomes the bottleneck.

The results for the private workload are shown in Figure 8. Each client has a private hot area of 100 pages to which 80% of the references (and all the updates) are directed. The workload contains a shared read-only region of 5000 pages, which is uniformly accessed by 20% of the references of the transactions on all the clients. Since there is only read sharing among the clients, even the optimistic methods do not have any aborts. O2PL and SC-A both have identical performance as both have the same message overheads. C2PL has the overhead of acquiring and releasing locks for every access and hence has lower throughput. The uniform workload case is shown in Figure 9. All transactions uniformly access the entire database. In contrast to the private workload, O2PL incurs more messages than C2PL for this workload since the probability of satisfying a reference locally is quite small due to the lack of locality. Further at commit time, O2PL has to send messages to all the clients that have accessed the data pages involved in the commit. SC-L has the same throughput as C2PL. Aggressive variant of slice consistency is not useful for this workload since it relies on locality of access for performance.

The first set of experiments show that for each of the four workloads containing only transactions, either SC-L or SC-A has as good, if not better, performance as the best existing algorithm. SC-L is suitable for high data contention workloads and/or when there

is little locality of access, both of which are extreme cases. SC-A performs the best when there is locality of access and low data contention, which is usually the case in client-server systems.

4.3 Mix of Workloads

The second set of experiments are designed to evaluate slice consistency in an environment of mixed workloads of transactions. In the first experiment, 50% of the clients have the hot-cold workload and the rest use the shared-hot workload. The parameters for the two workloads are the same as before (Table 3). For slice consistency, the clients running the hot-cold workload use the aggressive variation, while the clients with shared-hot workload use the lazy variation. Figures 10 and 11 show the throughputs of the clients running the hot-cold and the shared-hot workloads respectively. The results are consistent with those in the first set of experiments. O2PL has higher throughput than C2PL for clients running the hot-cold workload, while C2PL has higher throughput for clients with the shared-hot workload. Slice consistency has better performance than both C2PL and O2PL for all the clients.

The first set of experiments show that the lazy variation of slice consistency is suitable for a high data contention environment while the aggressive variation is ideal when the data contention is low. When the workloads change, slice consistency method can shift from one variation to another to provide the optimal performance. A simple heuristic such as the number of aborts to detect the level of data contention may be used to select the slice consistency variation. The next experiment considers an environment of changing workloads. The number of clients is fixed at 30. All the clients initially run a hot-cold workload and then shift to a shared-hot workload. In slice consistency, all clients start with the aggressive version. Each client maintains a running average of the number of aborts. When the number of aborts in any period increases to four times the average, the client shifts to lazy slice consistency. This simple experiment demonstrates the feasibility of slice consistency when the workloads change. Figure 12 shows how the throughput changes with time. Slice consistency has better throughput than C2PL and O2PL for both workloads.

4.4 Supporting Queries

The next set of experiments evaluates slice consistency in the presence of both long and short queries. The first experiment considers the "feed" workload. In this workload, five clients are producers generating data and the remaining clients are consumers reading this data. The parameters are listed in Table 4. The hot area for each producer consists of 200 pages and is not shared with the other producers. The total hot area for all five producers (1000 pages) forms the common hot area for all the consumers. Figures 13 and 14 show the throughput curves for the producers and the consumers respectively. The advantages of using transient versioning are evident from the two figures. By removing the interactions between the queries and the transactions, slice consistency shows better performance than both C2PL and O2PL in running a mix of transactions and queries.

The next two experiments evaluate the effect of longer queries on throughput for two different workloads. Figures 15 and 16 show the throughput when 10% of the transactions are queries with 100 references each in the hot-cold and the uniform workloads, respectively. The remaining parameters are the same as in Table 3. Here again, avoiding contention between queries and transactions results in 25% to 50% higher throughput for slice consistency for both the workloads.

5 Discussion

The optimistic methods perform well when the data contention is low and the hot region fits in the local cache. Both SC-A and O2PL satisfy most of the lock and data requests locally, thereby reducing the load on the network and the server. However, SC-A guarantees that all accesses are transaction consistent (by virtue of slices) while O2PL detects conflicts only at commit time. When there is no data contention (private workload) both SC-A and O2PL have the same performance. When there is even a little data contention (hot-cold workload) O2PL results in far more aborts than SC-A and hence has lower performance.

Table 4: Feed workload

Parameter	Transactions	Queries
References	10	10
Hot Area	200 pages each	1000 pages all
Cold Area	rest of DB	rest of DB
Hot Access Prob.	0.8	0.8
Cold Access Prob.	0.2	0.2
Hot Write Prob.	1.0	0.0
Cold Write Prob.	0.0	0.0

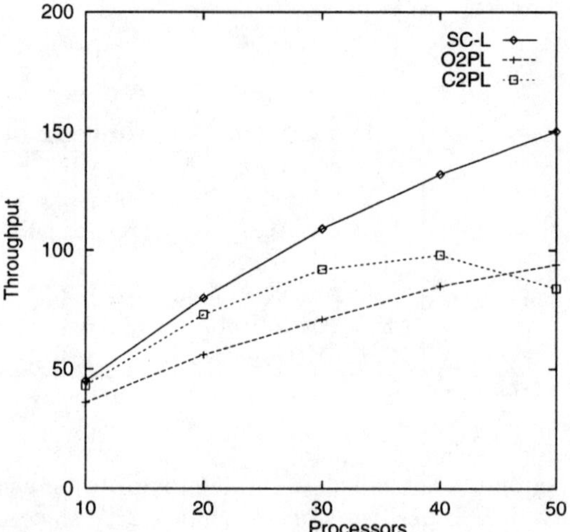

Figure 5: SharedHot, low resource contention

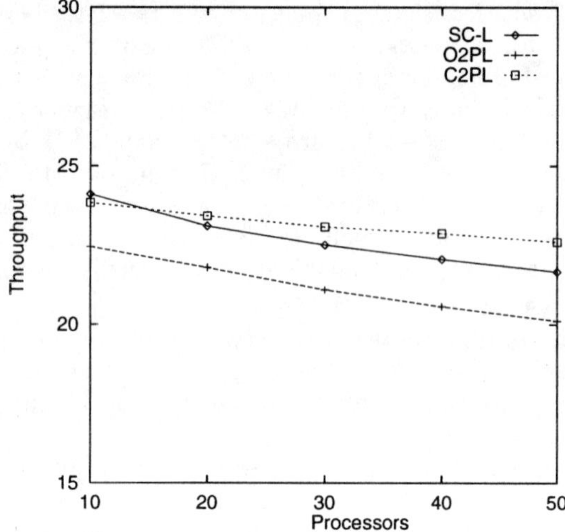

Figure 6: SharedHot, high resource contention

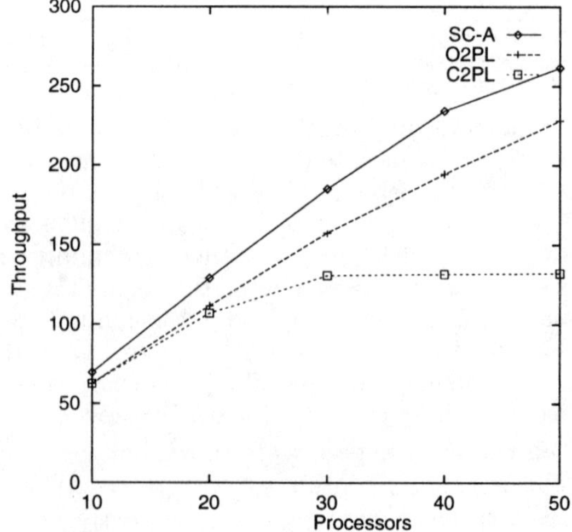

Figure 7: HotCold, low resource contention

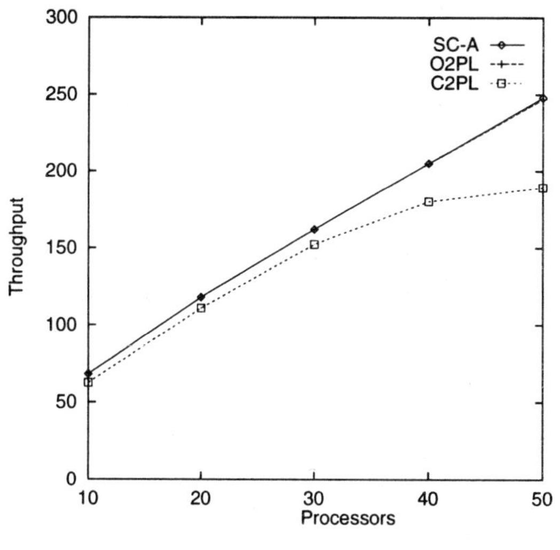

Figure 8: Private

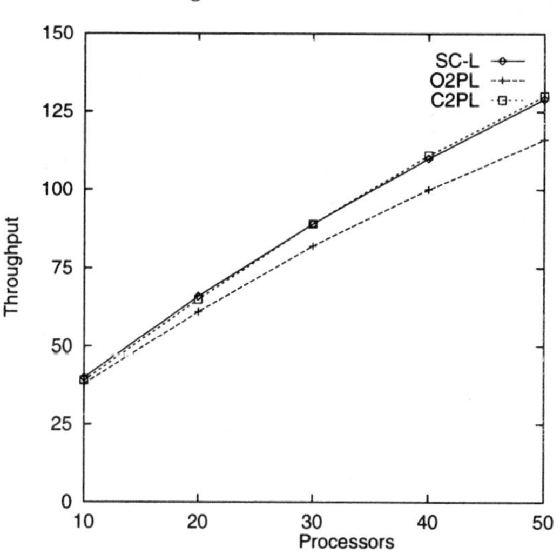

Figure 9: Uniform

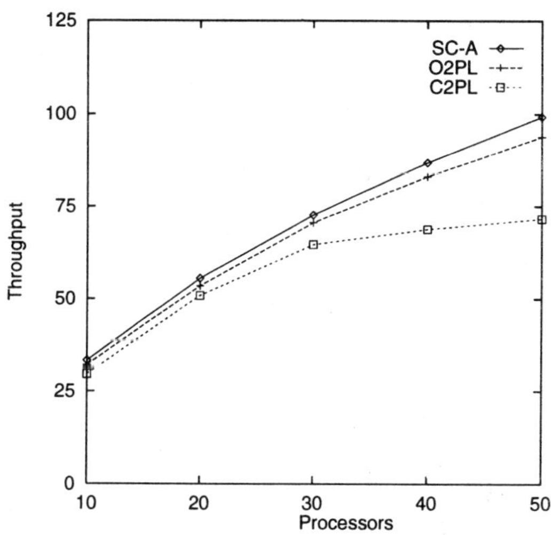

Figure 10: Workload mix, HotCold part

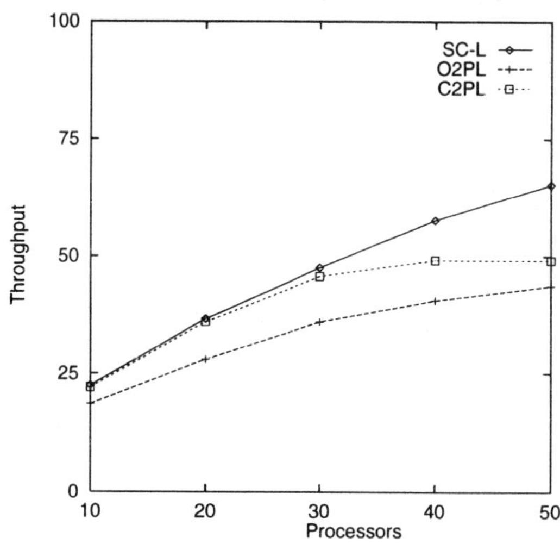

Figure 11: Workload mix, SharedHot part

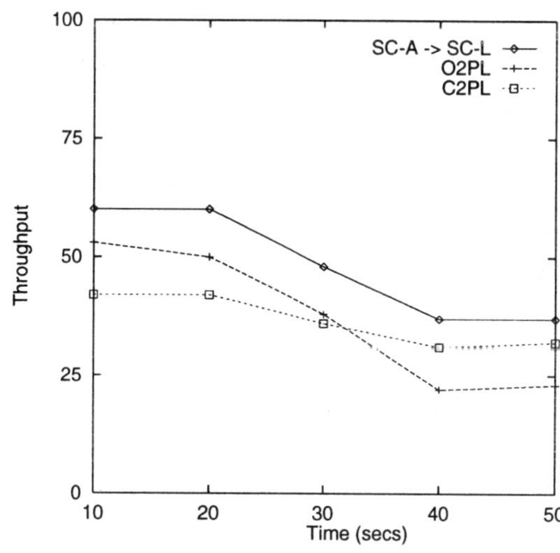

Figure 12: Changing workloads

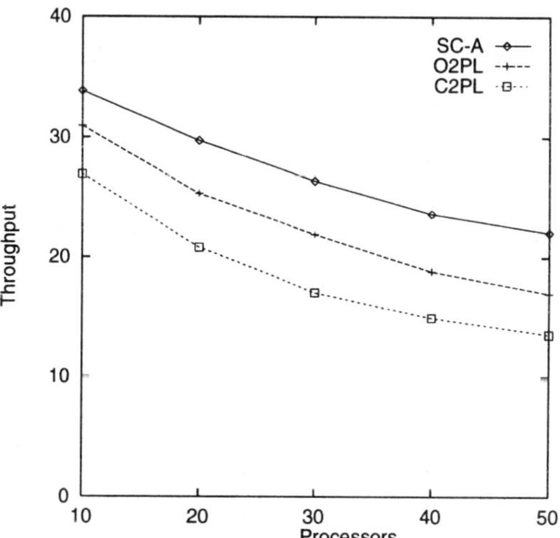

Figure 13: Feed - producers

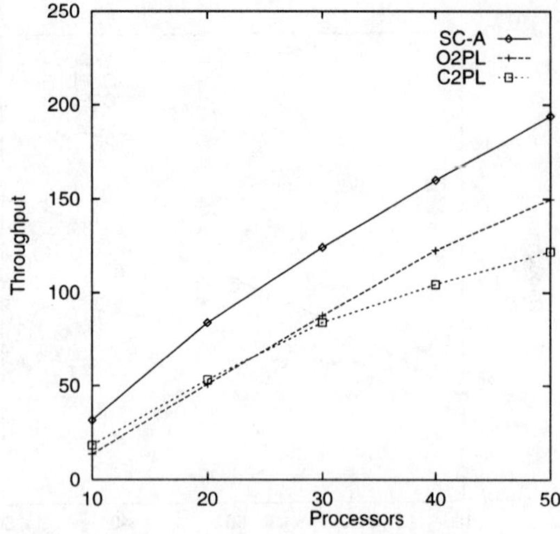

Figure 14: Feed - consumers

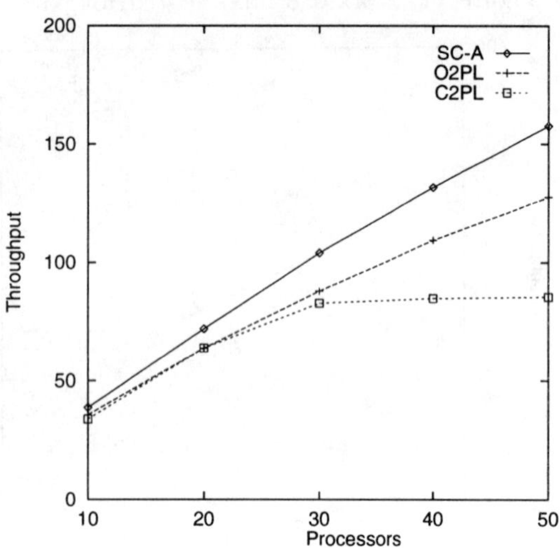

Figure 15: HotCold, supporting queries

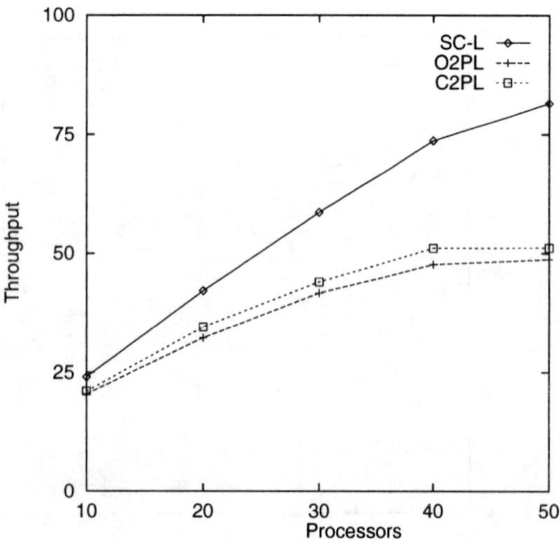

Figure 16: Uniform, supporting queries

The pessimistic methods are suitable when the data contention is high (shared-hot workload) as they reduce the concurrency (by blocking the transactions) and hence the data contention. Both SC-L and C2PL show better performance than the optimistic methods. SC-L allows more concurrency than C2PL and has better performance when the resource contention is low. Note that SC-L can mimic C2PL by running each transaction in a separate slice.

A key advantage of slice consistency is in supporting transactions in mixed or changing workloads. The different variations of slice consistency are still the same concurrency control protocol with minor differences in the way slices are initialized. The two factors that differentiate the workloads are the level of data sharing and the locality of access. Measures such as the number of aborts (to detect the data contention) and access patterns (to identify locality) may be used as triggers for switching. The simulation experiments evaluate a simple case where the number of aborts is used to detect the change and switch from one variation to another. Using the optimal method for each workload predictably results in higher throughput.

Slice consistency is based on transient versioning ideas and hence provides efficient support for queries. However, problems arise when a client runs only queries. Since queries do not abort, a single slice is sufficient to run all the queries at such a client. This has two drawbacks. The single slice grows larger with time and blocks later inactive slices from being garbage collected. The other drawback is that an old slice tends to contain an old version of the database. Queries running in such a slice do not see the later updates. This problem is avoided by periodically forcing the client to start a new slice.

One of the factors affecting performance is the cache overhead for the slices. The number of the slices in the system depends on the data contention. When the contention is low (private, hot-cold, queries) the number of slices is observed to be roughly equal to the number of clients (one slice per client). Lower number of slices reduces the number of versions. In high contention environments (shared-hot), the slices get frequently invalidated. If a client's cache is not sufficient to hold the invalidated slices until garbage collection, cache overflows and transaction rollbacks may reduce the performance. The effect of smaller client cache sizes is less on the existing single-version methods as the clients can ship the modified pages to the server to be stored on the disk. An interesting area for further research is to study the usage of clients' local disks to buffer the transient versions when the cache is small.

6   Summary

The key idea in this paper is to treat copies of data pages in different client caches as different versions of the data pages. This reduces cache consistency overhead and increases concurrency by allowing multiple readers and one writer to simultaneously access the same page. Slices are used to provide transaction-consistent versions of the database to the clients. Several variations of slice consistency, suitable for different workloads, are presented. A detailed client-server model is simulated to evaluate slice consistency. The simulation results show that

- For the different workloads considered, the lazy slice consistency variant performs better than the pessimistic C2PL and the aggressive slice consistency variant performs better than optimistic O2PL.

- Changing workloads or a workload mix can be supported better using slice consistency since the variations of slice consistency differ only in how a new slice is formed.

- None of the other methods provide support for queries. Queries can be efficiently supported in all variations of slice consistency without affecting concurrent transactions.

References

[ABGS 87] Agrawal, D., Bernstein, A., Gupta, P., Sengupta, S. *Distributed Optimistic Concurrency Control with Reduced Rollback*, Journal of Distributed Computing, January 1987.

[AgSe 89] Agrawal, D., Sengupta, S. *Modular Synchronization in Multiversion Databases: Version Control and Concurrency Control*, ACM SIGMOD International Conference on Management of Data, May 1989.

[BaHR 80] Bayer, R., Heller, H., Reiser, A. *Parallelism and Recovery in Database Systems*, ACM Transactions on Database Systems, June 1980.

[BeHG 87] Bernstein, P.A., Hadzilacos, V., Goodman, N. *Concurrency Control and Recovery in Database Systems*, Addison-Wesley Pub. Co., 1987.

[BoCa 92] Bober, P., Carey, M. *Multiversion query locking*, Proc. 18th International Conference on Very Large Data Bases, August 1992.

[Care 91] Carey. M., et. al. *Data Caching Tradeoffs in Client-Server DBMS Architectures*, ACM SIGMOD International Conference on Management of Data, June 1991.

[Chan 82] Chan, A., et al, *The Implementation of an Integrated Concurrency Control and Recovery Scheme*, ACM SIGMOD International Conference on Management of Data, June 1982.

[FrCa 92] Franklin, M., Carey, M. *Client-Server Caching Revisited*, Proc. International Workshop on Distributed Object Management, August 1992.

[Fran 93] Franklin, M.J. *Caching and Memory Management in Client-Server Database Systems*, Ph.D. Thesis, Computer Sciences, University of Wisconsin-Madison, 1993.

[GaWi 82] Garcia-Molina, H., Wiederhold, G. *Read-Only Transactions in a Distributed Database*, ACM Transactions on Database Systems, June 1982.

[GuOR 95] Gukal, S., Omiecinski, E., Ramachandran, U. *An Efficient Transient Versioning Method*, 13th British National Conference on Databases, July 1995.

[LLOW 91] Lamb, C., Landis, G., Orenstein, J., Weinred, D. *The ObjectStore Database System*, Communications of the ACM, October 1991.

[MoPL 92] Mohan, C., Pirahesh, H., Lorie, R. *Efficient and Flexible Methods for Transient Versioning of Records to Avoid Locking by Read-Only Transactions*, ACM SIGMOD Int. Conf. on Mgmt. of Data, June 1992.

[Reed 78] Reed, D. Naming and Synchronization in a Decentralized Computer System, PhD Thesis, Technical Report MIT/LCS/TR-205, MIT, September 1978.

[Schw 90] Schwetman, H. CSIM Users Guide, March 1990.

[StRo 81] Stearns, R.E., Rosenkrantz, D.J. *Distributed Database Concurrency Controls Using Before-Values*, ACM SIGMOD International Conference on Management of Data, April 1981.

[WaRo 91] Wang, Y., Rowe, L. *Cache Consistency and Concurrency Control in a Client/Server DBMS Architecture*, ACM SIGMOD International Conference on Management of Data, June 1991.

[WiNe 90] Wilkinson, W., Neimat, M. *Maintaining Consistency of Client Cached Data*, Proc. 16th International Conference on Very Large Data Bases, August 1990.

Industrial Session 7B

Query Evaluation Technology

Data Warehousing Features in Informix OnLine XPS
P. Sundaresan

The Query Execution Engine in Tandem's New ServerWare SQL Product
P. Celis and H. Zeller

Data Warehousing Features in Informix OnLine XPS

Prakash Sundaresan
Informix Software Inc.
prakash@informix.com

Abstract

*The Data Warehousing application domain is an important area of focus for Informix's OnLine XPS massively parallel server. Fast query processing is a central requirement in this domain. Use of indexes has traditionally been an important query processing technique, helping to reduce response times and increase throughput. The data warehousing environment, characterized by its load-query-refresh mode of operation, offers even greater scope for use of indexes. This talk will describe three new indexing related features in OnLine XPS which together provide significant performance benefits in a wide variety of situations. **Bitmap indexes,** along with multi-index scans, provide orders-of-magnitude improvement for queries typified by the Set Query Benchmark. **Pushdown Semi-Joins** combine the benefits of multi-index scans with the scalability of hash joins to efficiently process star-joins. Finally, **Generalized-key indexes** expand the notion of what can be an index key and provide the ability to store various pre-computed results in an index. Optimizer extensions allow these features to be used in a mix-n-match fashion, thus maximizing the benefits of these features while minimizing the need for user level directives.*

The Query Execution Engine in Tandem's new ServerWare SQL Product

Pedro Celis, Hans Zeller
Tandem Computers (celis_pedro@tandem.com, zeller_hansjorg@tandem.com)

Abstract

Tandem has re-written its SQL compiler and its query execution engine into a new product that will be available on multiple operating systems. The new product uses a novel query execution engine and we will highlight the unique aspects of the new engine.

ServerWare SQL uses a data flow and scheduler driven task model to execute queries. Tasks communicate either via in-memory queues or via interprocess communication. Partitioned, pipelined, or independent operations are executed in parallel. By adding new task types the model can be easily extended. Parallelism in a distributed memory environment is implemented as a special "Exchange" task type, as in the Volcano research prototype [1]. Scheduling and load balancing are performed by separate scheduler tasks.

1. Introduction

ServerWare SQL is an extensible, scalable, and portable relational DBMS.

Its predecessor, NonStop SQL/MP, was the first truly distributed relational DBMS. In its first generation (1986) SQL/MP was mainly developed for OLTP and in its second and third generations (1990 and 1994) for both OLTP and DSS [2]. ServerWare SQL provides a new architecture that supports new levels of scalability, functionality and parallelism and into new hardware architectures. The new architecture will also provide ISO/ANSI compatibility and richer language constructs, like table expressions.

In the remainder of this text we will briefly describe the main aspects of the ServerWare SQL execution engine. The task model described in the next section is the basic feature providing extensibility and scalability.

The section on parallelism describes three basic ways to parallelize work. It is followed by a brief section describing how a combination of those parallelization techniques can lead to a scalable query execution engine.

The last section describes how parallel and sequential query execution algorithms can adapt themselves to dynamic load at run-time.

2. Task Model

Typical query executors use an iterator model [3], where each relational operator (join, scan, union, etc.) provides "get first" and "get next" methods. The query is executed by recursively calling these methods in an operator tree. Parallelism can be implemented using a bracket model like Gamma [4] or an operator model, as suggested by Graefe [1].

ServerWare SQL uses operators like most other systems, but its operators are independent tasks and data flows between operators through in-memory queues (Fig. 1). There are no iterators on operators.

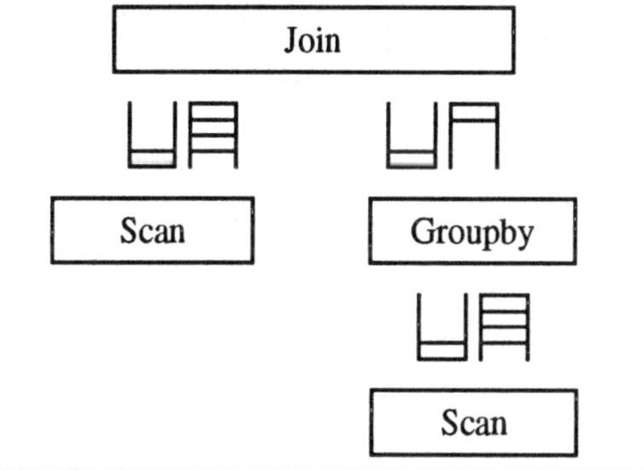

Fig. 1: Tasks and Queues

A scheduler coordinates execution of the tasks. Multiple schedulers can be used in SMP environments.

In cases where multiple processes are involved it uses the "Exchange" operator model [1]. Fig. 2 shows an example query tree where data are read by 3 processes, repartitioned into 4 partitions and from that point on processed in 4 parallel streams.

3. Parallelism

NonStop SQL/MP [2,5,6,7,8] has multiple parallel execution strategies based on partitioned parallelism and pipelining, much like the parallel execution plans in Gamma.

ServerWare SQL extends those strategies in several ways. Queues between tasks allow operators to exchange multiple request or result rows at a time, thus cutting down on procedure calls, messages, and context switches.

The task model also makes it easy to perform all internal operations asynchronously, so that a single server thread can have multiple I/Os outstanding. This allows independent and partitioned parallelism wherever possible. Examples of independent parallelism are the operands of a union operator and join operators in a bushy join tree.

The task model also allows parallelism for both shared memory and distributed memory architectures. In-memory queues can be used to communicate in SMPs, Exchange operators are used for distributed memory.

Operations such as scan or group by can be partitioned based on physical disk partitioning schemes or based on logical partition boundaries, depending on their type (physical for I/O intensive, logical for memory intensive operations). Both types can be combined and should allow us to process very large queries.

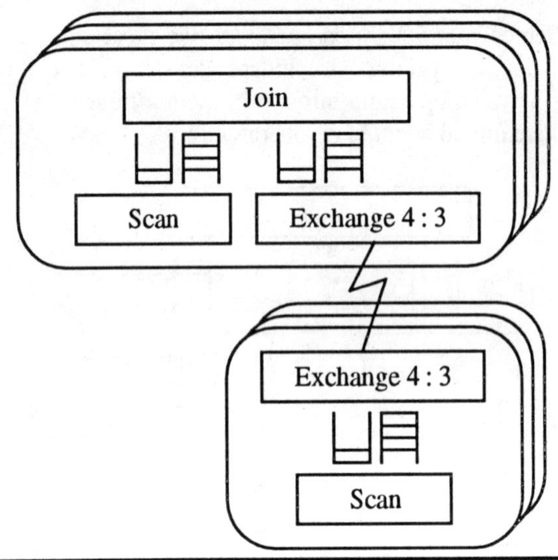

Fig. 2: Exchange Operator

4. Scalability

In order to scale up to large degrees of parallelism, ServerWare SQL utilizes multiple strategies for parallel execution at the same time. For example, a grouping operation on a table with many disk partitions could utilize two operators that provide parallelism, one on a logical level to distribute the CPU load of building hash tables for groups, another on a physical level to read data from all partitions in parallel (Fig. 3).

Data can be repartitioned into multiple schemes, including replication, hash- and range partitioning. With repartitioning it is possible to adjust the degree of parallelism to a meaningful level.

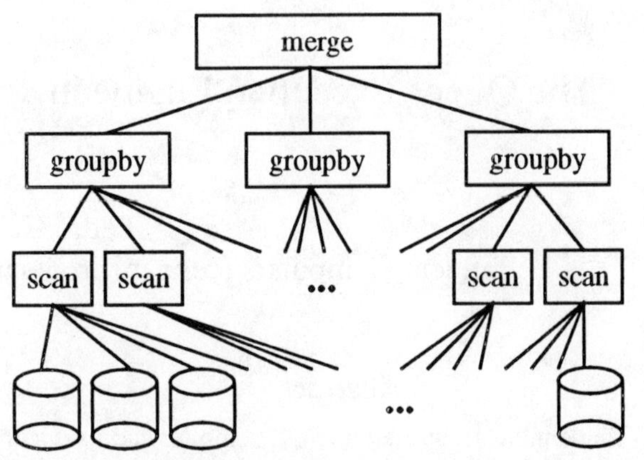

Fig. 3: Scaling up by Parallelizing on Different Levels

5. Load Balancing

SQL/MP uses hash-repartitioning for load balancing of memory intensive tasks such as joins and groupbys. ServerWare SQL uses a superset of the execution plans offerend by SQL/MP, including range-repartitioning if an existing range-partitioned table provides a good means of balancing load.

Several decisions in a query tree are taken dynamically, while its execution is in progress. Temporary disk drives can be allocated dynamically to parallel operators. Join, groupby, and sort operators adapt themselves dynamically to changed availability of memory and to variations in partition size which may be caused by skewed data.

A central load monitor can dynamically assign load to partitioned tasks if those tasks can be scheduled sequentially as well as in parallel. This is typically the case for operators that are not inputs for repartitioning or sort/merge steps.

A user exit is provided to implement user-defined policies for disk space allocation and resource governing. Together with adaptive algorithms this user exit can provide additional help in balancing loads in a multiuser environment.

6. Conclusion

ServerWare SQL is a new, extensible software architecture based on and enhancing the scalability and performance features of NonStop SQL/MP. The main benefits of ServerWare SQL are expected to come from its task model and its consequent design for parallelism and avoidance of design limits. Besides better performance and portability to multiple platforms we expect compliance with the ISO/ANSI SQL92 standard from the new query execution engine.

7. References

[1] G. Graefe
Encapsulation of Parallelism and Architecture-Independence in Extensible Database Query Processing
IEEE Transactions on Software Engineering 19,8 (1993), p. 749 ff

[2] A. Chen, Y. Kao, M. Pong, D. Shak, S. Sharma, J. Vaishnav, H. Zeller
Query Processing in NonStop SQL
IEEE Data Engineering Bulletin 16, 4 (1993), pp. 29-41

[3] G. Graefe
Iterators, Schedulers, and Distributed-memory Parallelism
Software - Practice and Experience 26, 4 (1996), pp. 427-452

[4] D. DeWitt, R. Gerber, G. Graefe, M. Heytens, K. Kumar, M. Muralikrishna
GAMMA - A High Performance Dataflow Database Machine
Proc. VLDB 1986, pp. 228-237

[5] H. Zeller
Parallel Query Execution in NonStop SQL
Proc. IEEE COMPCON 1990, pp. 484-487

[6] H. Zeller
Intra-query parallelism in the NonStop SQL/MP database system
Proc. Supercomputing Symposium '94, Toronto, pp. 423-429

[7] Susanne Englert, Ray Glasstone, Waqar Hasan
Parallelism and its Price: A Case Study of NonStop SQL/ MP
SIGMOD Record 24,4 (1995), pp 61-71

[8] H. Leslie, R.Jain, D. Birdsall, H. Yaghmai
Multi Dimensional Access Method: An Efficient Search Method for Multidimensional B-Trees
Proc. 21. VLDB Conference, 1995, pp. 710-719

[9] H Pirahesh, C. Mohan, J. Cheng, T. Liu, P. Selinger
Parallelism in Relational Data Base Systems: Architectural Issues and Design Approaches
Proc. DPDS, Dublin, 1990, pp. 4-29

Session 8

Panel Discussion

World Wide What?

Moderator:
Marek Rusinkiewicz, MCC

Author Index

Notes

Notes

Notes

Notes

IEEE Computer Society Press Publications

The world-renowned Computer Society Press publishes, promotes, and distributes a wide variety of authoritative computer science and engineering texts. These books are available in two formats: 100 percent original material by authors preeminent in their field who focus on relevant topics and cutting-edge research, and reprint collections consisting of carefully selected groups of previously published papers with accompanying original introductory and explanatory text.

Submission of proposals: For guidelines and information on CS Press books, send e-mail to cs.books@computer.org or write to the Acquisitions Editor, IEEE Computer Society Press, P.O. Box 3014, 10662 Los Vaqueros Circle, Los Alamitos, CA 90720-1314. Telephone +1 714-821-8380. FAX +1 714-761-1784.

IEEE Computer Society Press Proceedings

The Computer Society Press also produces and actively promotes the proceedings of more than 130 acclaimed international conferences each year in multimedia formats that include hard and softcover books, CD-ROMs, videos, and on-line publications.

For information on CS Press proceedings, send e-mail to cs.books@computer.org or write to Proceedings, IEEE Computer Society Press, P.O. Box 3014, 10662 Los Vaqueros Circle, Los Alamitos, CA 90720-1314. Telephone +1 714-821-8380. FAX +1 714-761-1784.

Additional information regarding the Computer Society, conferences and proceedings, CD-ROMs, videos, and books can also be accessed from our web site at www.computer.org.